LAND REFORM AND POLITICS

THE WORLD

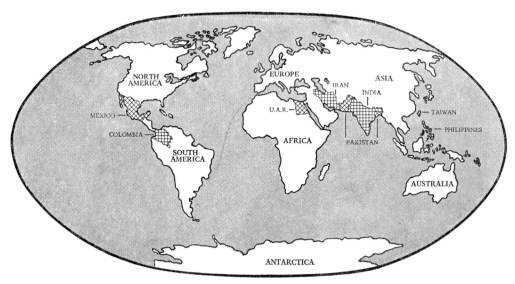

Shaded areas represent the countries under study.

LAND REFORM AND POLITICS:
A Comparative Analysis

HUNG-CHAO TAI

UNIVERSITY OF CALIFORNIA PRESS

Berkeley, Los Angeles, London

University of California Press
Berkeley and Los Angeles, California
University of California Press, Ltd.
London, England
Copyright © 1974, by
The Regents of the University of California
ISBN: 0-520-02337-4
Library of Congress Catalog Card Number: 72-89792
Printed in the United States of America

(C

To my Mother

CONTENTS

AUTHOR'S PREFACE

In the developing world the land reform movement is of universal appeal and long duration. Many countries in Asia, Africa, and Latin America have been striving for decades to effectuate publicly sponsored changes in the traditional land-tenure system, but a very few can be said to have achieved significant results. The relative success of a few developing countries in land reform and the failure of many others, I believe, can be explained primarily by political factors. It was with this thought in mind that I undertook a political analysis of eight developing countries—Colombia, India, Iran, Mexico, Pakistan, the Philippines, Taiwan, and the United Arab Republic.

This study began in 1966 at the Center of International Affairs, Harvard University, and did not reach substantial completion until five years later. Two reasons account for this rather lengthy process of preparation. First, the subject matter was much more extensive and complex than I had originally anticipated. Land reform is a multidimensional change, involving political, economic, and social aspects. Though focusing on the political aspect of land reform, this study requires some appreciation of the latter two aspects as well. Facing the necessity of assembling and analyzing data on these three aspects of land reform for all the eight countries studied, I found myself in effect working on eight volumes of land reform and trying to combine them into one. This was a difficult and at times frustrating task. The problem of obtaining reliable, adequate, and comparable information on the eight countries was formidable. Then there was the time-consuming process of devising conceptual schemes to organize the collected information. The validity of formulated ideas, concepts, and hypotheses had to be tested on the reform experiences of all eight countries. Many of these passed the test and were utilized; others failed and were abandoned. This process went on throughout the several revisions of the manuscript. The second reason for the delay in this work has to do with the intervention of a different but related research. In 1968 and 1969, I undertook a survey of Rural Political Participation in Taiwan and the Philippines. Though this survey yielded valuable information pertinent to the present study, it consumed at least a year and half's time in field work and processing of data.

The extended period of preparation of the present volume necessitated constant updating of the text. In this period, governments were changed, new reform laws enacted, and old programs revised. Most of these changes were incorporated in the final manuscript. Three exceptions should be noted. In September 1971, Egypt dropped its formal name, The United Arab Republic, after it had formed with Libya and Syria a Federation of Arab Republics. Later in the same year, the East Wing of Pakistan rose in revolt and became an independent Bangladesh. In October 1972, President Ferdinand E. Marcos of the Philippines, following the proclamation of martial law for the country, decreed a sweeping new land-reform program and declared the whole country a reform area. Since the final preparation of the present volume had been substantially completed before these changes, the terms U.A.R. and East Pakistan were retained in the text to refer to their traditional meanings, and the new Philippine reform program was not included in the following discussions.

Many institutions have been helpful in this study. I wish to express my gratitude to Harvard's Center for International Affairs for the several grants and excellent research resources it provided me; to the Ford Foundation and the Social Science Research Council for their financial support of my rural survey in Taiwan and the Philippines; to the University of Detroit for the research leaves it granted me and for its assistance in processing some of my survey data; to the Taiwan Provincial Government and the National Land Reform Council of the Philippines for their arrangement of tours in the land-reform areas of the two countries; to the Center of Public Administration, National Chengchi University, Taiwan, for its assistance in the conduct of the rural survey in Tainan *hsien*, Taiwan; to the University of California Press for its permission to cite, in a case study below, many passages from Frances Starner's *Magsaysay and the Philippine Peasantry*; and to the United States Agency for International Development, the Colombia Institute of Land Reform, the Land Tenure Center of the University of Wisconsin, the Land Reform Organization of Iran, the Land Authority of the Philippines, the Chinese-American Joint Commission on Rural Reconstruction, the Planning Commission of India, the Inter-American Committee for Agricultural Development and the Embassy of the United Arab Republic, Washington, D. C., for the voluminous materials on land reform they supplied me.

I wish to extend my thanks to many helpful friends and colleagues. A special intellectual debt is due Professor Samuel P. Huntington of Harvard who read several versions of the draft and whose encouragement, counsel, and challenging questions were most valuable. I am indebted to Professors Raymond Vernon of Harvard, Edwin H. Rutkowski of the State University of New York at Binghamton, Donald Anderson of the University of Michigan, Dearborn Campus, for their critical reading of the first draft which helped refine a number of concepts, and John W. Smith for his patient reading of the entire manuscript, very valuable suggestions, and preparation of the index; to Christopher H. Russell, Executive Director of the Center for Rural Development, for his permission to utilize portions of the data from the Center-sponsored *Organizing Colombia Peasants, A Research Report* by John D. Powell; to Professor Henry A. Landsberger for his permission to cite two mimeographed studies on Mexico which he and Cynthia H. Hewitt had undertaken; to Professor Thomas Payne for his encouragement and assistance in the study of land reform.

I would like to thank many officials and friends in Taiwan and the Philippines who helped me in the conduct of surveys in the two countries. Among these the following should be specially mentioned. In Taiwan— William Peng, formerly adviser to the Governor of the Taiwan Provincial Government; Pao-Wen Lui, Magistrate, Tainan *hsien*; Li-Chung Chang, Chien Hwa Chang, Professor Chien-han Chang of the National Taiwan University, Professor Fei-lung Lui of the National Chengchi University; Shu-shên Lui, Hui-ming Hu, and Wan-lai Lee. In the Philippines—Conrado F. Estrella, Governor of Land Authority, Jose C. Medina of the National Land Reform Council, Manuel P. Manahan, President of the Philippine Rural Reconstruction Movement, Eduardo A. Bigornia of the Presidential Arm on Community Development, Professors Raul P. de Guzman, Santiago Simpas and Manuel T. Corpus, all of the Local Government Center, College of Public Administration of the University of the Philippines.

Mrs. Susan V. Welling whose meticulous editing of this volume (for the University of California Press) much improved the clarity of the work, deserves special thanks. I wish to acknowledge the valuable assistance of Mr. Michael Brehmer, who helped partially with proofreading and index preparation. Several ladies have patiently and faithfully typed the various versions of this work. Barbara Biondo, Terry Grybaite and Bernice Peters

deserve special thanks. To conclude this list, I want to register my gratitude to my wife, Julia, who, a full-time academician herself and a mother
of three, has managed to render invaluable assistance in processing data *as
well as* clarifying the text. I alone, of course, am responsible for what I have
written.

H. C. T.

TABLES

FIGURE 1

MAPS

ABBREVIATIONS

A. I. C. C.	All-India Congress Committee, the top organ of the Indian Congress Party
ASU	Arab Socialist Union, the United Arab Republic
Caja Agraria	*Caja de Crédito Agrario, Industrial y Minero* (the Bank of Agricultural, Industrial, and Mining Credit, Colombia)
CCG	*Confederación Colombiana de Ganaderos* (The Colombian Cattlemen's Confederation)
CCI	*Central Campesina Independiente* (Independent Peasant Central, Mexico)
CIDA	*Comité Interamericao de Desarrollo Agrícola* (Inter-American Committee for Agricultural Development)
CNC	*Confederación Nacional Campesina* (The National Confederation of Peasants, Mexico)
CNPPA	*Confederación Nacional de la Pequeña Propiedad Agrícola* (National Confederation of Small Agricultural Proprietors, Mexico)
CPI	The Communist Party of India
CPM	The Communist Party of India, Marxist
CPML	The Communist Party of India, Marxist, Leninist
CROM	*Confederación Regional Obrera Mexicana* (Regional Confederation of Mexican Workers)
CTM	*Confederación de Trabajadores de Mexico* (Confederation of Workers of Mexico)
EDCOR	The Economic Development Corps of the Armed Forces of the Philippines
ELN	*Ejercito de Liberación Nacional* (The Army of National Liberation, Colombia)
FA	Farmers' Association, Taiwan

FAO	United Nations Food and Agriculture Organization
FARC	*Fuerzas Armadas Revolucionarias de Colombia* (The Colombian Revolutionary Armed Forces)
FUP	*Frente Unido del Pueblo* (The People's United Front, Colombia)
GDP	Gross domestic product
GNP	Gross national product
INCORA	*Institute Colombiano de la Reforma Agraria* (Colombian Institute of Land Reform)
JCRR	Chinese-American Joint Commission on Rural Reconstruction
KMT	The Kuomintang, the Nationalist Party of the Republic of China
LA	Land Authority, the Philippines
LASEDECO	The Land Settlement and Development Corporation, the Philippines
LNC	*Liga Nacional Campesina* (National Peasant League, Mexico)
LTA	Land Tenure Administration, the Philippines
MLA	Members of Legislative Assembly of a state in India
MNR	*Movimiento Nacional Revolucionario* (National Revolutionary Movement, Bolivia)
MP	Members of Parliament (India)
MRL	*Movimiento Revolucionario Liberal* (the Liberal Revolutionary Movement, Colombia)
NAFTAFA	National Federation of Tenants and Farmers Associations, the Philippines
NARRA	The National Resettlement and Rehabilitation Administration, the Philippines
NLRC	National Land Reform Council, the Philippines
NLSA	The National Land Settlement Administration, the Philippines
NRPA	National Rice Producers Association, the Philippines
PCC	*Partido Comunista de Colombia* (The Communist Party of Colombia)
PML	Pakistan Muslim League
PNA	*Partido Nacional Agrarista* (National Agrarian Party, Mexico)

PNR   *Partido Nacional Revolucionario* (The Revolutionary Party, Mexico)

PRI   *Partido Revolucionario Institucional* (Institutional Revolutionary Party, Mexico)

PRM   *Partido Revolucionario Mexicano* or *Partido de la Revolucion Mexicana* (Mexican Revolutionary Party)

RCC   The Revolutionary Command Council (Egypt)

SAC   *Sociedad de Agricultores Colombianos* (The Society of Colombian Agriculturalists)

U. A. R.   The United Arab Republic or Egypt

UGOCM   *Unión General de Obreros y Campesinos de Mexico* (General Union of Workers and Peasants of Mexico)

CONVERSION TABLE OF LAND UNITS

1 hectare	=	2.47109 acres
1 acre	=	0.40468 hectare
1 *chia* (Taiwan)	=	0.96992 hectare = 2.39680 acres
1 *feddan* (Egypt)	=	0.4201 hectare = 1.038 acres

SYMBOLS

ha.	hectare(s)
M/T	metric ton
Kg.	kilograms
₱	peso
NT$	New Taiwan dollar
£E	Egyptian pound (currency unit)
Rs.	Rupee

In Tables

. . .	data not available
- - -	magnitude less than ½ of the unit employed, or nil
—	not applicable

I

INTRODUCTION

The Need for Political Research

Historically, land and politics have maintained a close, interdependent relationship. The type of land tenure constituted a significant determinant of the pattern of political power, and a specific power pattern perpetuated a particular type of tenure. This mutually dependent relationship clearly manifested itself in the communal society, the feudal society, and the agricultural society of family farms. In modern times, it is only in the developing countries that this close relationship of land and politics persists. Unlike the developed countries, where the drastic decline of the importance of agriculture in the national economy has sharply reduced the political significance of landholding, the developing countries find that land remains the principal source of their national income and that landholders still exercise a commanding political influence. But, in contrast to their historical experience, in which politics simply kept perpetuating the existing pattern of land tenure, many developing countries face today a situation in which there is a constant demand in the realm of politics for reform of the tenure structure. Frequently preceded by a serious disturbance in the existing power pattern, such a reform often leads to further changes in that pattern. Land reform in the developing countries thus constitutes an issue with profound political implications.

As land reform has long occupied the attention of scholars, one would assume that its political implications have been given extensive analysis. Yet current research efforts on land reform seem to concentrate predominantly on its economic implications and consequences. Many published works on the subject are almost exclusively concerned with the clarification of the relationship of the changes in land tenure to agricultural development and industrialization.[1] Some of these works, it is true, contain numer-

---

[1] To illustrate, the following are standard works: Walter Froehlich (ed.), *Land Tenure, Industrialization and Social Stability: Experience and Prospects in Asia* (Mil-

ous references to the causal relationships between land reform and such political values as stability, democracy, and equality. However, they almost invariably stop short of an attempt at theorizing such relationships on the basis of broad empirical evidence. One recent publication appears to stand as an exception. In *Twenty-Six Centuries of Agrarian Reform, a Comparative Analysis*, Elias H. Tuma presents a balanced approach to the land reform programs of eight countries by studying their economic, social, and political objectives and effects.[2] On the basis of this study, Tuma offers an analytic scheme by which the implications of contemporary reform programs may be assessed. Tuma's work may well be the first book attempting to offer a theory of land reform with equal emphasis on its economic, social, and political aspects. However, the extremely broad coverage of the book has clearly made it impossible to render an adequate account of each of these aspects of all the programs analyzed. (With slightly more than three hundred pages, the book deals with at least twelve specific programs covering a period from the sixth century B.C. to the 1960s A.D.) Aside from Tuma's book, there are only a few works treating the political

---

waukee: The Marquette University Press, 1961); Kenneth H. Parsons, Raymond J. Penn, and Philip M. Raup (eds.), *Land Tenure* (Madison, Wis.: The University of Wisconsin Press, 1956); Erich H. Jacoby, *Interrelationsip Between Agrarian Reform and Agricultural Development* (Rome: FAO, 1953); Ignacy Sachs, *Agriculture, Land Reforms and Economic Development* (Warsaw: Polish Scientific Publishers, 1964); U.N., *Land Reform, Defects in Agrarian Structure as Obstacles to Economic Development* (New York, 1951); and *Progress in Land Reform, First-Fourth Reports* (New York, 1954, 1956, 1962, 1966); U.S. Department of Agriculture, *Agrarian Reform & Economic Growth in Developing Countries* (Washington, D.C., 1962); Doreen Warriner, *Land Reform and Economic Development* (Cairo: National Bank of Egypt, 1955); and *Land Reform in Principle and Practice* (Oxford: Clarendon Press, 1969).

Periodical literature on land reform similarly reflects the predominance of economic analysis. Three articles, among many, may be noted: Alexander Eckstein, "Land Reform and Economic Development," *World Politics*, VII (July 1955), 650–662; Philip M. Raup, "The Contribution of Land Reforms to Agricultural Development: An Analytical Framework," *Economic Development and Cultural Change*, XII (October 1963), 1–21; and Richard P. Schaedel, "Land Reform Studies," *Latin American Research Review*, I (Fall 1965), 75–122.

This concentration of economic analysis can also be seen in the titles appearing in the following bibliographical works: The University of Wisconsin, Land Tenure Center (LTC), *Agrarian Reform and Tenure: A List of Source Materials* (Madison, 1965); and Thomas F. Carroll, *Land Tenure and Land Reform in Latin America: A Selective Annotated Bibliography* (2nd rev. version; Washington, D.C.: Inter-American Development Bank, 1965).

[2] (Berkeley: University of California Press, 1965). The eight countries are Greece, Rome, England, France, Russia, Mexico, Japan, and Egypt.

aspects of land reform, and generally these few are either descriptive or narrowly concerned with a specific political condition or with a particular country.[3] No work has yet examined comprehensively and comparatively the politics of land reform in different countries.

The lag in political research on land reform may be due to three factors. The first relates to the belated preoccupation of the political science profession with the formulation of concepts useful in the study of the developing countries. Falling behind economists and sociologists, and borrowing heavily from them in conceptual formulations, political scientists today still persist in debating the connotation of such a key concept as political development. Summarizing the divergent views on the subject, Lucian W. Pye noted that political development has come to mean "the political prerequisite of economic development," "politics typical of industrial societies," "political modernization," "the operation of a nation-state," "administrative and legal development," "mass mobilization and participation," "the building of democracy," "stability and orderly change," "mobilization and power," and "one aspect of multi-dimensional process of social change."[4] And this is not an exhaustive list! The absence of a comprehensive political analysis of land reform may thus be justified on

[3] The following works may be cited: Frank Tannenbaum, *The Mexican Agrarian Revolution* (New York: The Macmillan Co., 1929); Clarence Senior, *Land Reform and Democracy* (Gainesville: The University of Florida Press, 1958); Frances L. Starner, *Magsaysay and the Philippine Peasantry: The Agrarian Impact on Philippine Politics, 1953–1956* (Berkeley: University of California Press, 1961); Albert O. Hirschman, *Journeys Toward Progress, Studies of Economic Policy-Making in Latin America* (New York: Twentieth Century Fund, 1963), dealing with, among other things, Colombia's reform; Thomas F. Carroll, "Land Reform as an Explosive Force in Latin America," in John J. Tepaske and Sidney Nettleton Fisher (eds.), *Explosive Forces in Latin America* (Columbus: The Ohio State University Press, 1964), pp. 81–125; Robert R. Kaufman, *The Chilean Political Right and Agrarian Reform: Resistance and Moderation* (Washington, D.C.: Institute for the Comparative Study of Political Systems, 1967); Constantine Manges, *Chile's Landowners Association and Agrarian Reform Politics* and *Politics and Agrarian Reform Bureaucracies in Chile: 1962–1964* (Santa Monica, Calif.: The RAND Corp., 1968); Terry Luther McCoy, "Agrarian Reform in Chile, 1962–1968; a Study of Politics and the Development Process" (Unpublished Ph.D. dissertation, the University of Wisconsin, 1969); John D. Powell, "The Politics of Agrarian Reform in Venezuela: History, System and Process" (Unpublished Ph.D. dissertation, the University of Wisconsin, 1966); Edward J. Mitchell, "Inequality and Insurgency, a Statistical Study of South Vietnam," *World Politics*, XX (April 1968), 421–438; Bruce M. Russett, "Inequality and Instability; the Relation of Land Tenure to Politics," *World Politics*, XVI (April 1964), 442–454.

[4] Lucian W. Pye, *Aspects of Political Development* (Boston: Little, Brown, & Co., 1966).

the ground that the clarification of the concept of political development has to take precedence over the assessment of the relationship of land reform to this concept.

Secondly, in analyzing political conditions of the developing countries, political scientists have been primarily concerned with those problems that are urgent and widespread. One such set of problems is related to political instability. A pervasive and seemingly simple phenomenon, political instability is derived from extremely complex and volatile conditions. In the study of this phenomenon, political scientists have focused attention on such factors as elite behavior, the military, party systems, bureaucracy, social cleavages, competing ideologies, and international power conflicts. These factors are regarded as central to political changes, requiring immediate attention. Land reform, or the lack of it, is recognized as a political issue, but compared to these factors it is of secondary importance, hence a matter occupying a relatively low priority for analysis.

Finally, the lack of political research on land reform may be due to a methodological difficulty in political science. As modern political analysis has an empirical bent, there are problems in selecting appropriate criteria and in devising precise measurements by which relevant political data may be collected and analyzed. The economic effects of land reform can be assessed by such concrete measurements as land and labor productivity; agricultural contribution to the gross national product; interflow of capital, goods, and labor between agricultural and non-agricultural sectors of the economy. Comparable tools for measuring the political effects of land reform are still poorly developed.[5] This methodological deficiency of political science in great part explains why the study of land reform has so far been weighted toward economic analysis, even though land reform is as conspicuously a political program as it is an economic one.

These three factors retarding political research on land reform are still present, one may say, but their inhibiting effect appears to have lessened in recent years. The formulation of concepts relevant to political development has made considerable progress; political survey techniques have greatly improved; some empirical information on political effects of land reform has gradually become available. And it should be especially pointed out that both scholars and policy makers have now gained a fuller appreciation of the problem of political instability. Both recognize that

[5] For a discussion of the difficulties in measuring political development and some suggested remedies, see J. Roland Pennock, "Political Development, Political Systems, and Political Goods," *World Politics*, XVIII (April 1966), 415–434.

instability not only reflects the institutional defects of the political system, but also results from the economic failures of the system. In countries where the political leadership fails over a long period to make economic gains, rising expectations may degenerate into massive frustrations leading to violent political changes. Economic performance has become a crucial test of political legitimacy.[6]

In the sobering search for an effective economic policy, many developing countries have recognized their neglect of agriculture. "The traditional sector," a leading specialist of the developing economies has observed, "has lagged badly—at times even with declining output per man. This has detracted from progress in the modern sector. . . . The major need, therefore, is now increasingly being identified in the lagging traditional components of the economy, including what is usually its largest part, agriculture."[7] As they now pay greater attention to agricultural development than they used to, many developing countries become genuinely conscious of the need for land reform. Thus the United Nations reported in 1962: "Recognition of the importance of land reform in agricultural development has been more marked in the period since the presentation of the last report [in 1956] than at any previous stage. A vastly increased number of countries . . . have given prominence to land reform measures in their development effort."[8]

Having long been exposed to the economic arguments for land reform,

[6] See Samuel P. Huntington, *Political Order in Changing Societies* (New Haven and London: Yale University Press, 1968), pp. 39–56; Seymour M. Lipset, "Some Social Requisites of Democracy: Economic Development and Political Legitimacy," *American Political Science Review*, LIII (March 1959), 69–105, especially 91ff; and James S. Coleman, "The Political Systems of the Developing Areas," in Gabriel A. Almond and James S. Coleman (eds.), *The Politics of the Developing Areas* (Princeton, N.J.: Princeton University Press, 1960), pp. 532–576.

[7] Wilfred Malenbaum, "Government, Entrepreneurship, and Economic Growth in Poor Lands," *World Politics*, XIX (October 1966), 59. The FAO has also commented on this phenomenon in the developing countries: "The comparatively junior position which agriculture occupies . . . tends to be reflected in the low priority given within [member] governments to agricultural matters. Even when very large sums are being allocated to economic development schemes, the emphasis may be largely on the industrial side, and although the idea of achieving balanced development may be present in the minds of the planners, agriculture may in the end have insufficient funds for this to be achieved." *Millions Still Go Hungry* (Rome: FAO, 1957), p. 6. For a cogent analysis of the interdependence of agricultural and non-agricultural sectors in the economy of the developing countries, see Bruce F. Johnson and Soren T. Nielsen, "Agricultural and Structural Transformation in a Developing Economy," *Economic Development and Cultural Change*, XIV (April 1966), 279–301.

[8] U.N., *Progress in Land Reform, Third Report* (New York, 1962), p. 1.

the developing countries now appreciate the primacy of politics. Evidently, merely giving prominence to land-reform measures is no guarantee that these measures are either meaningfully formulated or effectively implemented. Referring to Latin America, one observer has said: "Land reform has become . . . a prized party issue across the political spectrum. Every party, every major candidate, nowadays, must have a land-reform platform." [9] But how many Latin American parties have carried out their pledge? Speaking in similar terms, *Pakistan Observer* commented in 1959: "Virtually every party that came to the helm of [the Pakistani] government was wedded to the policy of agrarian reform. Some of the parties even set up agrarian reform committees. . . ." But the fact was, the paper continued, "their recommendations were consigned to the shelves, for white ants to feed on." [10]

Why is there always this gap between promise and reality? One can perhaps raise more intriguing questions concerning the reform experiences of some other developing countries. Since the 1940s both Taiwan and the Philippines have adopted a number of basically similar reform measures to deal with the same types of land-tenure problems. Why were these measures substantially implemented in Taiwan but repeatedly stalled in the Philippines? Despite their common cultural heritage, geographical proximity, and roughly identical problem of extreme land concentration, why do Mexico and Colombia differ drastically in the scope of their reform? How does one explain that the Shah of Iran, a large landowner himself, vigorously pushed for reform in the 1960s, but not earlier? In 1952 when the "Free Officers" of Egypt overthrew the Farouk regime, they had no conception of instituting any agrarian program. Why did they immediately embrace land reform once they were in power? Why is land reform in India repeatedly urged by the federal government, frequently sabotaged by the states, and often evaded in the villages?

All these questions relate to *political environment, leadership, conflict,* and *commitment.* The search for answers requires an examination of the political processes of land reform of different countries.

Beyond the questions relating to the political processes of reform, it is also time for analysts to inquire into the political effects of reform. The developing countries have introduced many different reform programs, which have varied greatly in the extent of implementation. Do these dif-

---

[9] Carroll, *op. cit.,* p. 105.

[10] Quoted in Pakistan, Planning Commission, Agriculture Section, *Land Reforms in Pakistan* (1959), p. 58.

ferences in reform experiences have different degrees of impact on rural voting behavior and on peasant political consciousness? Can reform help increase the capacity of rural organizations to articulate and promote the interests of their membership? Does land reform always contribute to political stability, as is often assumed? When does reform deter agrarian revolution? And when does it facilitate rural radicalism? These are the types of questions one can perhaps set out to examine systematically on a cross-national basis.

Objectives and Methods of Study

This study represents an effort to analyze comparatively the political *processes* and *effects* of land-reform programs of the developing countries. In dealing with the *political processes* of reform, the study will attempt to identify and explain the political factors crucially affecting the initiation, formulation, and implementation of programs. Three hypotheses will be advanced: (1) the initiation of land reform depends upon the perceived need of the elite for political legitimacy; (2) the process of formulation of a reform program is determined by the relationship between the elite and the landed class; (3) the extent of implementation of reform varies with the degree of political commitment. In assessing the *political effects* of reform, the study focuses attention on five subjects: (1) rural political participation, (2) national integration of the peasantry, (3) rural institutionalization, (4) political stability, and (5) the relationship between reform and Communism.

These hypotheses and subjects (which will be elaborated in due course) will be examined in the context of eight non-Communist developing countries: Taiwan, the Philippines, India, Pakistan, Iran, the United Arab Republic (the U.A.R., a name used interchangeably with Egypt), Colombia, and Mexico. Geographically these countries are evenly distributed in the developing world, with two from each of the following regions: Southeast Asia, South Asia, the Middle East, and Latin America.[11]

[11] In Sub-Saharan Africa, where a unique communal tenure system prevails, the existing land problems as well as their required solutions are radically different from those of other developing regions. Besides, very few, if any, land reform programs have been initiated. For these reasons, Sub-Saharan Africa is excluded from this study. For a general description of the African land system and agricultural development, see Sir Gerard Clauson, *Communal Land Tenure* (Rome: FAO, 1953), René Dumont, *African Agricultural Development: Reflections on the Major Lines of Advance and the Barriers to Progress* (New York: U.N., 1966); FAO, *FAO Africa Survey: Report on the Possi-*

Politically they have adopted different types of government, including democratic-oriented systems, a monarchy, one-party authoritarian systems, and military regimes.[12] In terms of reform experiences, they show significant similarities and diversities. Facing a number of common tenure problems, all these countries have stressed the necessity of land reform in the solution of these problems and have made a greater effort in implementation of programs than most other developing countries. On the other hand, they introduced reform under quite divergent circumstances: peace, coup, civil war, and actual or threatened revolution. They have been concerned with reform for different lengths of time, ranging from a prolonged involvement since the 1910s to a short duration since the 1960s, and they have achieved widely different results in reform.

This sample of countries is fairly representative of the developing countries as a whole and sufficiently large to facilitate the formulation of some broadly relevant generalizations. Nevertheless, in certain specific instances in which data on these countries are inadequate for analysis, pertinent information on other countries will be utilized.

Dealing with so many countries, which display so many diversities in reform background and experience, this study will best accomplish its objectives by following a strictly analytic and comparative approach. A series of schemes will be adopted to identify, interpret, and evaluate the political aspects of the reform of the sample countries. In order to keep the book reasonably concise, no attempt will be made to describe comprehensively the reform programs of the sample countries on a program-to-program basis. For purpose of reference, a digest of the operative reform laws will be provided in an Appendix.

In discussing the politics of land reform, one can discern three principal forces: landlords, the elite, and peasants. Landlords—referring to noncultivating landowners—everywhere predictably assume a negative attitude toward reform, and their political strength declines with the progres-

bilities of African Rural Development in Relation to Economic and Social Growth (New York, 1962); International African Seminar, Lovanium University, Leopoldville, *African Agrarian System: Studies Presented and Discussed,* edited by Daniel Biebuyck (London: Oxford University Press, 1963); and U.N., *Progress in Land Reform, Fourth Report* (New York, 1966; hereafter cited as *Land Reform, Fourth Report*), pp. 40–53.

[12] The reform programs initiated by Communist regimes constitute a separate category, different from those of the non-Communist developing countries in purpose, method, and content. These programs will not be represented in the present study. Reference to these programs and to Communism will nevertheless be made when they specifically relate to the present study.

sive implementation of programs. The attitudes and political influence of the other two forces, however, are variable: they may differ from country to country and may change over time. For this reason, the respective roles of the elite and peasants will be given primary attention. In the analysis of the *political process* of reform, the role of the elite—i.e. the policy makers —deserves special emphasis.[13] In the developing countries, in the absence of well-organized associations effectively representing the interests of the peasantry, land reform is a change of the agrarian structure brought about primarily from the top. With some exceptions, the elite plays almost an exclusive role in reform, from its inception to its fruition. Peasantry like that of Mexico may actually put forward reform proposals, and farmers like those in Mexico and Taiwan may play some role in the implementation of programs. But the cardinal fact is that the initiation of reform, the decision on the shape of a program, and the extent of its enforcement lie basically in the hands of the elite.

In the words of Wolf I. Ladejinsky, a man with prolonged experience in reform:

> Politicians, and only politicians, make good or poor reforms or do not make them at all. They control the political climate, which determines the will or lack of will to proceed with the task; the specific measures with which the reform is or is not endowed; the care or lack of care with which the enabling legislation is formulated; the preparation or lack of preparation of the pertinent and administrative services; . . . and, most important, the drive or lack of drive behind the enforcement of the provisions of the law.[14]

In the assessment of the *political effects* of land reform, the role of peasants must occupy the center of attention. Peasants—i.e. small cultivating farmers—are the intended beneficiaries of reform and they constitute

[13] Used here to refer to primarily government policy makers, the term, *elite*, excludes informal leaders. As such it differs from the familiar Lasswellian concept, which includes both formal and informal leaders. See Harold D. Lasswell, *et al.*, *The Comparative Study of Elites: An Introduction and Bibliography* (Stanford: Stanford University Press, 1952), p. 2ff. The elite may be dominated by one man or composed of a small group of officials; it may be concentrated in the executive branch of the government or separated into executive and legislative components.

[14] Wolf I. Ladejinsky, "Land Reform," in David Hapgood (ed.), *Policies for Promoting Agricultural Development: Report of a Conference on Productivity and Innovation in Agriculture in the Underdeveloped Countries* (Cambridge: Massachusetts Institute of Technology, Center for International Studies, 1965), p. 310.

the most numerous group in the society. From their perspective and from their reaction one can properly assess the political impact of reform.

To conclude these introductory remarks, a few points concerning the mechanical aspects of this study should be noted. First, the source materials of this volume were gathered primarily from government publications, field surveys by the author in Taiwan and the Philippines in 1968 and 1969, research results of specialists, and journalistic reporting. These materials appeared mostly in English, with a minor portion in Chinese and Spanish. Generally they cover up to the late 1960s and, in a very few cases, to early 1971. Second, the statistical information derived from these materials must be used with caution. Standards of measurement by which data are collected are widely different. Certain important data may be completely absent, or lacking in continuity, or incomparable for two or more countries. Statistics on the same subject but coming from different sources may be conflicting. And there is always the problem of reliability. While care has been taken to achieve accuracy and comparability of data, the results of certain statistical exercises in this book are necessarily approximations. A final point concerns the use of terms. In order to achieve uniformity and consistency in usage, and to avoid too many inserted interpretive notes, some frequently used terms will be listed and defined in the Glossary in Appendix IV.

II

CONCEPT OF LAND REFORM

A Definition

The term, *land reform*, has been subject to different interpretations. Some have defined it narrowly as a means to provide land to the landless, while others have conceived it broadly as a comprehensive program for the transformation of the entire agricultural economy.[1] For this study, the term refers to public programs that seek to restructure equitably and rationally a defective land-tenure system by compulsory, drastic, and rapid means. The objectives of reform are to attain just relationships among the agricultural population and to improve the utilization of land. The means by which these objectives are attained are government sponsored tenurial changes.[2] These changes encompass both redistributive programs (land

[1] Doreen Warriner, for instance, prefers the narrow definition in her extensive study on land reform. To her, "land reform means the redistribution of property or rights in land for the benefit of small farmers and agricultural labourers. . . . This is what land reform has meant in practice, past and present." *Land Reform in Principle and Practice* (Oxford, 1969), p. xiv. The United Nations, on the other hand, often employs the broad definition. It conceives land reform as "an integrated programme of measures designed to eliminate obstacles to economic and social development arising out of defects in the agrarian structure." Such a program involves changes of land tenure as well as improvement of agricultural service institutions. See U.N., *Progress in Land Reform, Third Report*, p. vi.

A number of analysts use "land reform" to refer to the narrowly defined meaning, and "agrarian reform" the broad concept. See, for example, Kenneth H. Parsons, "Agrarian Reform Policy as a Field of Research," in U.S. Department of Agriculture, *Agrarian Reform & Economic Growth in Developing Countries*, p. 17. Tuma, also adopting this distinction, divides agrarian reform into two aspects: land-tenure reform and land-operation reform. Elias H. Tuma, *Twenty-six Centuries of Agrarian Reform, a Comparative Analysis* (Berkeley, 1965), pp. 8–14.

[2] Cf. Alfredo M. Saco, "Land Reform as an Instrument of Change, with Special Reference to Latin America," *Monthly Bulletin of Agricultural Economics and Statistics*, XIII (December 1964), 1. The United Nations, in its *Land Reform, Fourth Report*, seems to have slightly shifted toward a narrower concept of land reform. The report

redistribution and tenancy reform) and developmental programs (cooperative farming and publicly instituted land settlement). The former programs seek to reallocate equitably the sources of agricultural income, while the latter aim at improvement of farming efficiency and at expansion of farming areas.

Of all reform programs, land redistribution is the most important. For in the developing countries today the most common, conspicuous, and serious land-tenure problem is inequality of landownership. As a direct response to that problem, land redistribution has practically become a universal feature of all the programs adopted in these countries. None of the other three programs can make such a claim. Because of this, land redistribution is frequently regarded as synonymous with land reform. In reality, land redistribution may be more appropriately considered a basic agrarian change to which all other reform measures bear a more or less dependent relationship. "If this [i.e. land redistribution] is absent," Wolf Ladejinsky has stressed, "all else may prove ephemeral, including security of tenure and rent reduction—measures extremely difficult to enforce." [3] In countries where tenancy improvement measures are adopted (for instance, Taiwan, India, Iran), these measures are frequently conceived to be something complementary to land redistribution. In countries where cooperative farm and land settlement programs are instituted (for instance, Mexico and the U.A.R.), appropriate provisions of land redistribution laws are made applicable to these programs. Moreover, the importance of land redistribution is reflected in the significant consequences that may flow from the programs. Once it is raised as an issue, land redistribution will generate more controversy than any other type of reform program; when implemented, it is likely to effect a more profound alteration of the tenure structure than any other reform measure. Indeed, in any given country, the progress in this program alone may well provide the surest indication of the country's total reform effort. For these reasons, land redistribution will be given considerable emphasis in subsequent analysis.

As used in this book, the term, *land reform*, excludes, by and large, measures that seek to improve and strengthen such services as agricultural

---

defined land reform as "changes in land tenure systems and the accompanying changes in other institutions that are necessary to achieve the objectives for which the changes in land tenure are sought. . . . The reform of land tenure remains a constant point of reference" (pp. 2–3).

[3] Wolf I. Ladejinsky, "Land Reform," in David Hapgood (ed.), *Policies for Promoting Agricultural Development* (Cambridge, Mass., 1965), p. 298.

research, extension, credit, and marketing. These measures, it is true, maintain intimate relationships with tenurial reform. The success of tenurial reform often depends upon the adoption of some or all of these measures. An agricultural policy seeking merely to give land to the landless without providing the new owners with essential agricultural services may result in the fall of crop output, hence defeating one major objective of tenurial changes. This is clearly what happened to Bolivia when it introduced a crash land redistribution program in the early 1950s.[4] Moreover, as will be discussed later, tenure reform frequently leads to significant changes in agricultural service institutions; and an extensively implemented reform program often necessitates the formation of large rural organizations. But since agricultural service institutions are obviously not an integral part of the tenure structure, changes of these institutions are analytically separable from the measures seeking to correct tenure defects.[5]

The Role of Government

In the entire process of land reform—from initiation to completion— the government plays a decisive role. In the words of Kenneth H. Parsons, "In a very deep sense, land tenure problems are power problems, problems of disparity in economic, social, and political power." [6] Hence "land reform

[4] Following the revolution in 1952, the *Movimiento Nacional Revolucionario* (MNR) government of Bolivia immediately started a process of dividing up large estates to provide land to the Indian *campesinos*. Without providing the indigent peasants with the necessary credit, and without helping them to gain the skills to manage their farms, the Bolivian government merely replaced the traditional *latifundia* with the new *minifundia*. This led to a drastic decline in food production, from which the country did not recover until the late 1950s. See FAO, *Report of the FAO Regional Land Reform Team for Latin America* (Rome, 1961), pp. 19, 34; William H. MacLeish (ed.), *Land and Liberty, Agrarian Reform in Americas: A Vision Report* (New York: Vision, Inc., 1962), p. 8; and David G. Green, "Revolution and Rationalization in Bolivia," *Inter-American Economic Affairs*, XIX (Winter 1965), 9–15.

[5] Measures to improve agricultural service institutions, Thomas F. Carroll has observed, "represent the focus not of land reform but of agricultural development, and . . . they are most effective where a healthy land tenure situation exists." "The Land Reform Issue in Latin America," in Albert O. Hirschman (ed.), *Latin American Issues* (New York: The Twentieth Century Fund, 1961), p. 196. Speaking in a similar tone, Edmundo Flores has emphasized that "efforts to increase [agricultural] efficiency must be applied *after* land reform takes place, *not instead of it.*" *Land Reform and the Alliance for Progress* (Princeton, N.J.: Princeton University, Center of International Studies, 1963), p. 8 (emphasis in original).

[6] "Land Reform and Agricultural Development," in Parsons, *et al.* (eds.), *Land Tenure* (Madison, Wis., 1956), p. 9.

programs are distinctly 'public' programs . . . undertaken by public or
governmental agencies." [7] In a sense these programs "are attempts to
modify the economic basis of politics." [8] Therefore, a basic and broad alteration of the tenure structure cannot be brought about under private auspices.
In a number of countries, humanitarian movements that attempt to seek
land redistribution through moral persuasion have failed to create any
significant impact on the existing agrarian structure. For example, in India, Acharya Vinoba Bhave, a faithful disciple of Mahatma Gandhi, organized in 1951 the *Bhoodan Yagna* (land gift movement). Traveling
through many villages, "India's Walking Saint," as Bhave is popularly
known, appealed to landowners to donate one-sixth of their land holdings.
Rejecting the idea of acquiring land by compulsion and threats, he exhorted his followers: "We should approach the landowners with love." [9]
In a decade's time, he was able to collect over four million acres of land.
This extraordinary achievement was possible, it should be stressed, partly
because the movement persistently invoked the image of Gandhi, which
was favorably received in the countryside, and partly because the religious
content of its appeal—i.e. to enrich their spiritual life men should share
their worldly possessions—found a ready response in the religiously oriented
rural Indians. In any event, the real benefits of the *Bhoodan Yagna* were
less impressive than they at first appeared to be to the public. According to
the Indian government, as of April 1961, the movement had obtained
4,352,866 acres of land. Some of these were even donated by poor farmers
themselves, and only 833,466 acres had been actually distributed, amounting to about 0.27 percent of India's 320 million acres of cultivated land.[10]
Much of the undistributed portion was waste land unsuitable for agricultural use.

Similar movements elsewhere may also be noted. In a number of Latin
American countries, the Catholic Church has taken some interest in sponsoring land reform as a means of alleviating rural poverty. In Chile, for

[7] "The Place of Land Reform in a Developmental Agricultural Policy," in University of Illinois, Land Economics Institute, *Modern Land Policy* (Urbana: University of
Illinois Press, 1960), pp. 300–301.

[8] Parsons, "Agrarian Reform Policy as a Field of Research," 20.

[9] For a detailed exposition of the objectives, principles, and methods of the movement, see Acharya Vinoba Bhave, *From Bhoodan to Gramdan* (rev. ed.; Tanjore, India:
Sarvodaya Prachuralaya, 1957). Quotations appear on p. 59. For a summary of the
activities of the movement, see "The Land Gift Movement in India, Vinoba Bhave and
His Achievement," *World Today*, XIV (November 1958), 487–495.

[10] India, Planning Commission, *Progress of Land Reform* (Delhi: Government of
India Press, 1963), p. 21.

instance, the Church has created the *Instituto de Promoción Agraria* (The Institute for Promotion of Agriculture) to carry out land redistribution and agricultural cooperative projects. But, with considerable zeal and expenditure, the institute could settle only two hundred families on five farms of about 3,000 hectares of land. The projects were considered "too slow and costly." [11] In Colombia, to dramatize the Church's interest in reform, the Most Reverend Giulio Franco Arango went on television in July 1967 to declare: "The encyclical 'Populorum Progressio [On the Development of Peoples]' states that 'private property is not an absolute and unconditional right for anyone when others are in need.' " He continued, "Social justice demands that everyone, but especially the Church, use their possessions for the good of all men." On behalf of the Church, he donated 800 acres of land to the government for redistribution.[12] This donation, which was intended to induce the wealthy landowners to follow suit rather than to initiate an extensive program by the Church,[13] amounted to a tiny fraction of the country's 67.7 million acres of crop and pasture land.

Obviously, as these cases show, private efforts to change the agrarian structure are largely inconsequential insofar as the total farm area is concerned. Land reform by moral persuasion is no substitute for land reform by public edict.

The Need for Compulsion

To be efficacious, a land-reform program not only requires government sponsorship, but also government compulsion. In the early 1960s, a number of Latin American countries—for example, the Dominican Republic, Honduras, Paraguay, and Nicaragua—passed in a flurry many land-reform laws and created land-reform institutes to administer them. These laws specified that redistribution of land should be done through "amicable arrangements," "voluntary transfer," or "negotiated sale." [14] Practically speaking, with such laws these countries could not really expect to effect any meaningful tenurial changes, and the newly created land-

[11] Peter Dorner and Juan Carlos Collarte, "Land Reform in Chile: Proposal for an Institutional Innovation," *Inter-American Economic Affairs*, XIX (Summer 1965), 11–12.

[12] *The New York Times*, July 17, 1967, p. 13.

[13] See the comment on this subject by Msgr. Luigi G. Ligutti, Vatican's representative to the United Nations Food and Agriculture Organization, in *ibid.*

[14] For a summary of these laws, see U.N., *Land Reform, Fourth Report*, pp. 7–8 and 12–13.

reform institutes were understandably doomed to inactivity from the beginning.

Land reform requires the kind of tenurial changes that may appear arbitrary to individual landowners but are consonant with the broad interests of the society as a whole. This is so for two reasons. First, a defective land-tenure system, particularly one marked by pronounced unequal distribution of landownership, tends to freeze capital on land and to retard progressive agricultural development. This is so because large landowners are more interested in continuous purchase of land than in constant land improvement. They amass wealth without making productive use of it. Only compulsory tenurial changes can effectively unfreeze the capital of the unproductive large landowners and provide it to enterprising small peasants for increasing production. Voluntary action just cannot lead to this result. As Edmundo Flores has observed, transfer of land through negotiated sale "represents not land reform but merely a real estate transaction," [15] a transaction most peasants are financially incapable of entering into. Second, large owners and small peasants are unequal parties. The former are wealthy, powerful, and domineering; whereas the latter are poor, inarticulate, and submissive. Transfer of wealth—in the form of land or reduced rent—from the former to the latter by amicable arrangement is an act of charity, not an enforceable public policy. It can happen in isolated instances through the generosity of the very few, but it cannot be accepted as a broad-scale, systematic program by all landowners.[16] To be effective, land reform must rely upon the willingness and readiness of the public authority to apply sanctions against the disaffected. Actually, once the serious intention of the government to put land reform into effect is known, physical coercion may not be necessary for its implementation. The reform experiences of Japan and Taiwan are cases in point.

The Drastic Character of Reform

While land reform is a public, compulsory program, it also entails drastic changes. In an agricultural society where land is at once the prin-

[15] Flores, op. cit., p. 9.

[16] This is particularly true when one considers that in many developing countries where the demand for agricultural land is strong, and where the supply of agricultural land is either fixed or only slowly expansible, the value of land has been constantly on the rise. It is not conceivable that landowners would voluntarily divest themselves of what becomes increasingly valuable to them.

cipal source of wealth, the foundation of political power, and the symbol of social prestige, the system of land tenure is nothing less than a vital institution that determines and allocates the values of the society. If a tenure system is seriously defective, corrective action can be meaningful only when it fundamentally alters the entire system. Tinkering with its minor problems or symbolic remedial action cannot produce any lasting result. As is frequently said, land reform is major surgery, not a palliative. It must be a change of "the rules of the game" in rural life, not merely a program of "unfreezing the factors of production." [17] It is in this sense that John K. Galbraith has expressed the view, "In fact, a land reform is a revolutionary step; it passes power, property and status from one group in the community to another. If the government is dominated or strongly influenced by the landholding group . . . no one should expect effective land legislation as an act of grace." [18]

A Rapid Process of Change

Finally, land reform requires that agrarian changes be effected within a short span of time. Where land reform is necessary, evolutionary change is often impracticable or impossible. With centuries-old traditions, the tenure systems of the developing countries have been constantly reinforced in their rigidity through the people's habitual acceptance of stagnant economies as unchangeable and through the devotion of the governments to the preservation of the status quo. To break such rigidity requires a frontal attack on the system, not gradual adjustments. In contrast, the tenurial changes in many Western countries often took place through the working of economic forces.[19] For instance, in England the Enclosures effected two basic alterations of the manorial land-tenure system. Simultaneously they created a concentration of landownership and a contractual tenancy system, which greatly stimulated agricultural production. While scholars still argue about the cause of the Enclosures, the expansion of industries in the cities appears to be the dominant factor. This is particularly evident in the large-scale Enclosures of the eighteenth century when the

[17] Carroll, "Land Reform as an Explosive Force in Latin America," in Tepaske and Fisher (eds.), *Explosive Forces in Latin America* (Columbus, Ohio, 1964), p. 83.

[18] John K. Galbraith, "Conditions of Economic Change in Under-Developed Countries," *Journal of Farm Economics*, XLIII (November 1951), 695. Cf. U.N., *Land Reform, Fourth Report*, p. 4.

[19] French agrarian reform through the French Revolution may be an exception to this statement.

Industrial Revolution had unleashed forces of demand for more food, capital, and particularly labor from the rural areas.[20] In another Western country, the United States, land tenure never appeared to be a serious problem. The American family-farm system developed within a context of abundance of land and of generally adequate non-farm employment opportunities. The Pre-emption Law of 1841 and the Homestead Act of 1862 established the legal basis for the extension of the system into the western frontier. Since the closing of the frontier in the latter part of the last century, a landless farmer can still advance in an agricultural career without being hindered by the tenure system. According to the agricultural ladder theory, he can move up in his career in four steps: from farm laborer to tenant to indebted landowner to solvent landowner.

The English and American experiences are apparently of little value to most of the developing countries. The Enclosures took several centuries to complete, and in the developing countries today the climbing of the agricultural ladder from bottom to top, if possible at all, may take the lifetime of the most industrious farmer.[21] With their revolution of rising expectations, and given their small scale of industrialization, these countries can scarcely afford drawn-out changes worked out entirely by economic forces.[22]

Insofar as land reform is an involuntary, publicly sponsored agrarian program, prompt execution is very essential to its success. Dispatch will avoid the uncertainty shared by all people whose rights and expectations are differentially affected under a prolonged program. Such uncertainty often results in a falling-off of agricultural production as well as in the

[20] For a concise description of the English Enclosures, see Tuma, *op. cit.* (n. 1 above), pp. 37–53.
[21] In fact, the agricultural ladder theory may not be applicable at all in many developing countries. The theory is based on two assumptions: farmer's ability to accumulate savings and a reasonable land price. Commenting on this theory, and with reference to China prior to the Communist rule, Pê-yü Chang and Yin-püan Wang observed that the hard-working Chinese landless farmers could not buy land because they lived at a subsistence level and because land price was very much inflated. *Chung-kuo Nung-tien Wên-t'i (Problems of Chinese Tenancy)* (Shanghai, China: the Commercial Press, 1943), pp. 134–135. These observations certainly apply to the landless of today's developing countries.
[22] "The crucial point is, of course," Ernest Feder has stressed, "that a rational land reform . . . implies that rapid social and economic progress . . . is not possible through the conventional, economic tools such as price or income incentives, statistical production goals, credit on a rationed basis, tax policies and the like." "The Rational Implementation of Land Reform in Colombia and Its Significance for the Alliance for Progress," *América Latina*, VI (January-March 1963), 83.

creation of opportunities for evasion of reform laws. Prompt execution is also necessary to maintain the spirit of reform, which tends to dissipate or fluctuate with the passage of time.

To summarize, a public program of land reform that seeks compulsory, drastic, and rapid tenurial changes is one of substance and meaning. A public program that aims at voluntary, moderate, and gradual tenurial adjustments is bound to be perfunctory and ineffectual.

III

TENURE PROBLEMS, CONSEQUENCES, AND REFORM

The Weight of Agriculture

One basic distinction between developing and developed countries lies in the relationship that agriculture bears to the national economy. Typically, in the developing countries the agricultural sector of the national economy is larger and more important than the non-agricultural sectors; in the developed countries an opposite relationship exists. As the economy of a country develops, its agricultural sector becomes smaller and less important. A comparison of the weight of agriculture in the eight developing countries under study, two rapidly developing countries (Israel and Japan), and one highly developed country (the United States) will show these relationships. The weight of agriculture—i.e. the relative size and degree of importance of the agricultural sector—in the economy of a country can be measured by three indicators: agricultural share of the *population, gross domestic product,* and *export.*

As seen in Table 1, in terms of all the three indicators, and for the periods of time specified, agriculture occupied a much heavier weight in the first eight countries than in the remaining three; and generally the agricultural weight in the first group of countries declined at a slower pace. These data suggest that in the eight countries under study agriculture is of commanding importance and will remain so for some time to come. Consequently land tenure in these countries assumes unusual significance: it directly affects the well-being of half of the population and indirectly bears upon the entire national economy. If a land-tenure system exhibits serious problems, these problems will have nation-wide impact and profound consequences.

TABLE 1

THE WEIGHT OF AGRICULTURE IN THE NATIONAL
ECONOMIES OF ELEVEN COUNTRIES

	Agricultural share of					
	Population[a]		Gross Domestic Product[b]		Export[c]	
Country	Year	Percent	Year	Percent	Year	Percent
Colombia	1951	53[d]	1953	37.87	1964	79.47
	1960	46[d]	1963	30.88	1968	75[e]
India	1951	70[f]	1953	50.67[g]	1964	51.41
	1961	70[h,i]	1963	46.85[g]	1966	50[j]
Iran	1956	55[h,i]	1959	29.82	1960s	8–10[k]
	1960	60[f,l]	1963	23.79	1964	7.76
Mexico	1910	71.9[h,m]	1910	27.40[n]	1962	62.53
	1930	67.7[h,m]	1953	20.65	1964	61.82
	1960	54.2[h,m]	1963	18.04		
Pakistan	1951	92[i]	1953	53.42	mid-1950s	95[o]
	. . .		1963	49.11	1964	73.13
Philippines	1948	69[f]	1953	42.89[g]	1962	82.98
	1960	46.8[p]	1963	34.82[g]	1964	73.53
Taiwan	1953	51.9[q]	1953	39.45	1952	95.2[r]
	1963	47.2[q]	1963	26.78	1964	59.18
U.A.R.	1950s	60.7[s,t]	1957	34.98	1952	95.80[u]
	1960	57[h,i]	1961	24.87	1964	73.02
Israel	1950	18[f]	1953	11.58	1962	30.73
	1961	18[i]	1963	10.34	1964	26.36
Japan	1950	46[d]	1953	22.12[g]	1962	10.03
	1960	37[d]	1963	13.19[g]	1964	3.57
United States	1951	15[d]	1953	5.37	1962	26.92
	1960	8[d]	1963	3.70	1964	28.14

[a] Unless otherwise indicated, agricultural share of the population refers to the proportion of the population dependent upon agriculture for a living (farmers and their families), as a percentage of the total population.

[b] Unless otherwise indicated, the source is U.N., *Yearbook of National Accounts Statistics, 1965* (New York: U.N., 1966).

[c] Unless otherwise noted, agricultural share of export consists of food, live animals, woods, fibers, and crude materials produced on farms. The primary source is U.N., *Yearbook of International Trade Statistics, 1965* (New York: U.N., 1967).

[d] FAO, *The State of Food and Agriculture, 1965* (Rome: FAO, 1965), p. 57.

[e] Colombia Information Service, *Colombia Today* (New York), May 1969.

[f] FAO, *Production Yearbook, 1964* (Rome: FAO, 1965).

[g] Net domestic product.

[h] Percentage of population economically active in agriculture.

[i] U.S., Department of Agriculture, *Changes in Agriculture in 26 Developing Nations, 1948 to 1963* (Washington, D.C., 1965), p. 66.

TABLE 1 (*Continued*)

[j] "India: Today and Tomorrow," *The New York Times*, March 20, 1966, Section 12, p. 10.

[k] Donald C. Taylor, *Research on Agricultural Development in Selected Middle Eastern Countries* (New York: The Agricultural Development Council, Inc., 1968), p. 3.

[l] Percentage of people living on farms.

[m] James W. Wilkie, *The Mexican Revolution: Federal Expenditure and Social Change Since 1910* (Berkeley: University of California Press, 1967), p. 193.

[n] *Ibid.*, p. 202.

[o] Pakistan, National Planning Board, *The First Five Year Plan, 1955–60*, cited in West Pakistan, Land Reforms Commission, *Report of the Land Reforms Commission for West Pakistan* (Lahore, Pakistan: Superintendent of Government Printing, 1959), p. 10.

[p] The Philippines, Department of Commerce and Industry, Bureau of the Census and Statistics, *Census of the Philippines 1960: Agriculture*, Vol. II, *Summary Report* (Manila, 1965), p. 206.

[q] China, Executive Yuan, Council for International Economic Cooperation and Development, *Taiwan Statistical Data Book 1965* (Taipei, Taiwan, 1965), p. 19.

[r] *Ibid.*, p. 117.

[s] The United Arab Republic, National Bank of Egypt, "The Egyptian Economy during the Fifties IV: Agriculture," *Economic Bulletin*, XV (1962), 13.

[t] Employed labor force in agriculture as a percentage of the total employed labor force.

[u] Mohammed A. W. Khalil, "The Present Status and Future of Agriculture in the Egyptian National Economy," *L'Egypte Contemporaine*, No. 311 (Janvier 1963), 29.

Major Tenure Problems

Land tenure refers to the institutional arrangements governing the ownership and utilization of agricultural land. As such, it is an extremely complex system, reflecting the multiplicity of relationships between men and land. The rights and obligations of the parties to a tenure arrangement differ according to the status of the parties, which can be differentiated into numerous categories: landlords, owner-farmers, part-owners and part-tenants, tenants, sharecroppers, lessees, farm laborers, farm managers, intermediaries (rent collectors), and so on. Moreover, the rights and obligations of these different tenure groups vary in content from country to country, or even from locality to locality. Despite its complexity and variations, land tenure in the developing countries tends to show two common types of problems: maldistribution of land and tenancy problems.

MALDISTRIBUTION OF LAND

Maldistribution of land refers to the possession of a large amount of agricultural land by a few people, on the one hand, and the sharing of a small, fragmented farm area by a large number of peasants, on the other.

TABLE 2

Distribution of Farm Holdings, Eight Countries

		Distribution of Total Number of Farm Holdings — Size Groups (Hectares), Percent							Distribution of Total Area of Farm Holdings — Size Groups (Hectares), Percent						
Country	Year	Under 1	1–5	5–20	20–50	50–100	100–200	Over 200	Under 1	1–5	5–20	20–50	50–100	100–200	Over 200
Colombia	1954	18	37	27	9	4	2	3	3		9	9	9	12	58
India	1954	39	45	14		2			5	35	43		17		
Iran[a]	1960	27	39	30		4			2	16	48	20	5	9	
Mexico	1930	29	39	14	8	3	2	5	1	1	1	2	1	2	93
Pakistan[b]	1960	43	45[c]			12[d]			7.4	39.4[c]			53.2[d]		
Philippines	1948	19	65	14		2			3	39	33	11	3	3	8
Taiwan[e]	1952	70.62	27.30[f]	1.86[g]	0.18	0.03	0.01		24.97	50.59[f]	15.77[g]	4.62	1.96	2.09	
U.A.R.	1950	53	39	7		1			9	30	21	12	9	7	12

[a] United States, Department of Agriculture, *Changes in Agriculture in 26 Developing Nations, 1948 to 1963* (Washington, D.C., 1965), pp. 43–44.

[b] FAO, "Preliminary Results of the 1960 World Census of Agriculture, 23rd Issue, Pakistan," Supplement to *Monthly Bulletin of Agricultural Economics and Statistics*, XIII (1964). "Holdings without land" of the original data are eliminated. Percentage in this table is interpolated accordingly.

[c] Of the 1 to 5.6 hectares group.

[d] Of the size group with 5.6 hectares or more.

[e] China, Chinese-American Joint Commission on Rural Reconstruction (JCRR), *Abstract of Land Statistics, Taiwan Province* (Taipei, Taiwan, 1953), pp. 23 and 27. Original data are expressed in terms of Taiwan's land unit, *chia* (1 *chia* = 0.96992 hectare).

[f] Of the 4 to 6 *chia* group.

[g] Of the 6 to 20 *chia* group.

Sources: FAO, *World Agricultural Structure, Study No. 1: General Introduction and Size of Holdings* (Rome, 1961) and other sources as noted. Data on the eight countries were collected either in the early period of land reform (India, Mexico, and West Pakistan) or before the passage of the latest land redistribution laws.

In a number of *developed countries*, such as Australia, the United Kingdom, and the United States, the degree of concentration of agricultural land is rather high.[1] But in these countries the weight of the agricultural sector in the national economy is small; non-agricultural employment opportunities are abundant; concentration of land is not accompanied by fragmentation of farms. Hence unequal distribution of land does not pose serious problems. In the developing countries, where the population pressure on land is generally high and where the capacity of industries to absorb surplus rural population is limited, land concentration and fragmentation of farms are inseparable phenomena. Together they raise grave consequences.

Table 2 presents data on the distribution of farm holdings in the eight countries under study. All these countries showed both excessive concentration and fragmentation of farms, with Mexico and Taiwan representing the two extremes. Five percent of the Mexican farm holdings altogether possessed 93 percent of the land in 1930; over 70 percent of Taiwanese farm holdings each owned less than one hectare of land in 1952. It should be noted that in this table the data on all but two countries related to land distribution by *operation*, not by *ownership*. Only data on Mexico and Taiwan related to the distribution of landownership. Since operators included a sizable number of farmers who did not own land, the maldistribution of land by ownership was more pronounced than that by operation. Data on landownership distribution of most of the studied countries are fragmentary and not comparable. However, a few examples will illustrate the degree of concentration of ownership as well as the actual size of very large estates in some of these countries.

High concentration of landownership. In India, the National Sample Survey of 1953 to 1954 revealed that 7.59 percent of the total farm households owned 50.84 percent of the nation's land; a sample survey of 1951 to 1952 of the *zamindari* holdings in one Indian state, Uttar Pradesh, indicated that 3.34 percent of the *zamindars* (landlords) owned 53.69 percent of the surveyed land in the state; in another state, Kerala, the size of the largest *zamindar* estates in the early 1950s ranged from 1,161 to 63,130 hectares.[2] In Iran in the early 1960s—before the implementation of land

---

[1] For data on the distribution of agricultural land in these three, and forty-seven other, countries, see Bruce M. Russett, *et al.*, *World Handbook of Political and Social Indicators* (New Haven and London: Yale University Press, 1964), pp. 239–240.

[2] India, Planning Commission, *Progress of Land Reform* (Delhi, 1963), pp. 170–

reform—1 percent of the rural population possessed 6,000,000 hectares, or about 60 percent of the arable land; less than 5 percent of the nation's population owned 90 percent of the land.[3] In West Pakistan in the mid–1950s, 6,061 families owned a total of 3,031,539 hectares, or about 500 hectares per family; about 15 percent of the land of the whole province was possessed by 0.11 percent of the total owners, and another 15 percent of the land was shared, in contrast, by 65 percent of the owners.[4] In the Philippines in the 1950s about 3 percent of the landowners owned 42 percent of the land; in 1959, a total of 500 estates in Central Luzon, each ranging from 150 to 12,000 hectares, possessed an aggregate area of 220,000 hectares, or more than one-third of the total land in the region.[5] In Egypt, the 1950 agricultural census showed that 2,119 owners, or 0.07 percent of the total owners, possessed 1,236,300 *feddans* (519,246 hectares), or 20.69 percent of all farm areas; whereas 1,901,518 owners, or 70.24 percent of the total number of owners, had only 653,016 *feddans* (274,267 hectares), or 10.93 percent of all farm areas.[6]

In Colombia, the Land Reform Institute (*Instituto Colombiano de la Reforma Agraria*, INCORA) indicated in 1963 that the 874 largest landholdings (or 0.07 percent of the total landholdings) owned 30 percent of the country's 27 million hectares of farm land; as late as 1967, the size

171: Baljit Singh and Misra Shridhar, A *Study of Land Reforms in Uttar Pradesh* (Honolulu: East-West Center Press, 1965), p. 28; and India, Planning Commission, *Implementation of Land Reforms: A Review* (New Delhi, 1966; mimeo.), p. 114.

[3] Echo of Iran, *Iran Almanac and Book of Facts*, 1963 (3rd ed.: Tehran, n.d.), p. 387; and John A. Hobbs, "Land Reform in Iran: a 'Revolution From Above,'" *Orbis*, VII (Fall 1963), 619. Because of lack of complete, accurate land survey techniques, Iran still follows the ancient way of calculating the size of land by "villages." As a basic unit of land, a "village" consists of 6 *dang*, each of which is divided into 20 *babbe*. In certain areas a *babbe* refers to an area of land that is normally irrigated with a certain amount of water. In other areas, a *babbe* is as large a piece of land as is sufficient to support one family. Hence its size varies. In Isfahan, for instance, a *babbe* is about a hectare. In many areas, the area of land is also counted in *juft* (or *joft*). A *juft* is an area normally plowed by a pair of oxen, varying from 5 to 8 hectares.

[4] West Pakistan, Land Reforms Commission, *Report of the Land Reforms Commission for West Pakistan* (Lahore, Pakistan: The Superintendent of Government Printing, 1959), Appendix I.

[5] Hugh L. Cook, "Land Reform and Development in the Philippines," in Walter Froehlich (ed.), *Land Tenure, Industrialization and Social Stability* (Milwaukee, 1961), p. 169; and Isidro S. Macaspac, "Land Reform Aspects of the Agricultural Development Program," *Economic Research Journal* (Manila), VIII (December 1961), 149.

[6] Donald C. Mead, *Growth and Structural Change in the Egyptian Economy* (Homewood, Ill.: Richard D. Irwin, Inc., 1967), Table III–C–2, p. 325.

of the largest landholdings ranged from 101,000 to nearly 850,000 hectares.[7] In Mexico, in 1910 when the revolution occurred, landownership was more concentrated than it was in 1930, as shown in Table 2. In the earlier year, 1 percent of the population owned 97 percent of the land, whereas 96 percent of the population owned only 1 percent of the land. Among the 30 Mexican states, the number of landowners as a proportion of the population ranged from 0.2 percent in Oaxaca to 11.8 percent in Baja California. In 10 major Mexican states, 2,200 owners possessed land ranging in size from 1,000 to 10,000 hectares; 403 owners, from 10,000 to 100,000; and 14 owners, from 100,000 to more than 400,000. In some states, *haciendas* of the size of Florida could be found; and even as late as 1923, some *haciendas* were so large that they comprised from 15.3 to 93.6 percent of some Mexican states.[8]

The extraordinary concentration of land in Mexico in the early twentieth century, which probably ranked as the highest in the world at the time, deserves an explanatory note on its origin and development. The tendency toward accumulation of private holdings began during Spanish rule and accelerated in the nineteenth century. In the mid–1850s, Mexican liberal politicians and intellectuals favored two policies which were to alter greatly the agrarian system. Believing in the sanctity of private property and individual landholdings, the liberals were intent upon distribution of the Indian communal farms (*ejidos*);[9] at the same time, seeking to reduce the influence of the Catholic Church, they sought to dispossess its enormous landholdings.[10] These policies led to the adoption of the *Leyes de Desamortización* (Law of Expropriation) of June 1856. Subsequently re-

---

[7] Colombia, INCORA, *Informe de Actividades en 1963: Segundo Año de Reforma Agraria* (Bogotá: Imprenta Nacional, 1964), pp. 78–79; and *The New York Times*, July 17, 1967, p. 13.

[8] Rodolfo Stavenhagen, "Social Aspects of Agrarian Structure in Mexico," *Social Research*, XXXIII (Autumn 1966), 465; George M. McBride, *The Land Systems of Mexico* (New York: American Geographical Society, 1923), pp. 79 and 154; Ramon Fernandez y Fernandez, "Land Tenure in Mexico," *Journal of Farm Economics*, XXV (February 1943), 221; and Frank Tannenbaum, *The Mexican Agrarian Revolution* (New York, 1929), p. 97.

[9] See Charles A. Hale, *Mexican Liberalism in the Age of Mora, 1821–1853* (New Haven and London: Yale University Press, 1968), pp. 224–234. For a discussion of the *ejido* system, see Chapter VIII, below.

[10] During the Spanish colonial period, church landholdings in Mexico were variously estimated to cover from one half to three-fourths of the total area of the country. Tannenbaum, *op. cit.*, p. 6. As late as 1850, according to one author, the Church still owned over half of the country's territory. Gonzalo Blanco, *Agriculture in Mexico* (Washington, D.C.: Pan American Union, 1950), p. 9.

vised and incorporated into the Constitution of 1857, the law prohibited "ecclesiastical and civic corporations" from possessing farm land. This so-called Liberal Reform resulted in the liquidation of the vast church landholdings, but, as various Indian communities (*ejidos, comunidades, pueblos*) were classified as civic corporate bodies, they also had to break their communal farms into individual holdings. Unaccustomed to individual landownership, many Indian farmers sold or just lost their possessions. Eventually, much of the Indian land was "absorbed into the great haciendas or gobbled up by unscrupulous speculators." [11] Late in the last century a new development took place, greatly intensifying the concentration of land and the dispossession of Indian farms. In an effort to encourage colonization in public land, President Porfirio Díaz issued a decree in 1883 granting "survey companies" one third of the land they were to develop and authorizing these companies to take possession of titleless small private holdings lying within the colonization areas. According to Helen Phipps, a total of "134,547,885 acres [54,451,530 hectares] or twenty-seven percent of the total area of Mexico, passed to the ownership of a few individuals and companies during the Díaz regime"; the dispossessed Indian land amounted to 919,782 hectares.[12] There were other measures leading to what Eyler N. Simpson called "the rape of the pueblos"; "alienation through manipulation of water rights," "punishments through rebellion," and "losses through denunciation" (i.e. many Indians, who used to possess their land as a matter of customary right without formal title, lost their land because they could not legally prove their ownership).[13] In 1854, there were about 5,000 Indian villages with communal landownership, covering 45,000 square miles. By the end of the Díaz regime in 1910, "90 percent of the villages and towns on the central plateau had no communal lands of any kind." [14]

Absenteeism. A concomitant of high concentration of land is absentee landownership. Many owners maintain residence far away from their farms, leaving the managerial or rent-collecting responsibilities to appointed managers or intermediaries. The *zamindari* system of India and Pakistan provides a notable example. Introduced by the British through

[11] Eyler N. Simpson, *The Ejido, Mexico's Way Out* (Chapel Hill: The University of North Carolina Press, 1937), p. 25.

[12] Helen Phipps, *Some Aspects of the Agrarian Question in Mexico, A Historical Study,* University of Texas Bulletin No. 2515 (Austin: The University of Texas Press, 1925), pp. 110–111 and 115.

[13] Simpson, *op. cit.,* pp. 29–31.

[14] *Ibid.,* p. 31; and McBride, *op. cit.,* pp. 131–133.

the Permanent Settlement Act of 1793, the system covered nearly half of India's land at the time of independence. *Zamindars* were originally land-revenue collectors for the British administration, and for compensation of their services they were allowed to retain one-tenth of what they collected. In time, they became landlords themselves, collecting rent through designated intermediaries, and these middlemen frequently delegated the rent collection responsibility to still someone else. As a rule, *zamindars* and the middlemen neither did any agricultural work nor lived on their farms. Absenteeism also existed in many other countries. In Iran, as Ann K.S. Lambton has observed, traditionally, large landowners ran their farms through "a bailiff who often practices extortion on the peasants."[15] In Colombia "the prevalence of absentee landownership" can be seen in "*the 1959–60 Census of Agriculture* [which] showed that over one-third of Colombia's land in farms was operated through a farm manager."[16] In Central Luzon, the Philippines, "a special 1948 census tabulation shows that 85 percent of the farmland in units of 24 hectares and over . . . was owned by" absentee landlords.[17] In Egypt, "almost all the very large landowners resided or settled in the towns (especially Cairo and Alexandria) . . ." prior to land reform in 1952.[18]

Fragmentation. In sharp contrast to the concentration of landownership is the diminution of most farming units. Table 2 reveals that in the eight countries studied a little less than one-fifth to over two-thirds of all holdings operated on farms of one hectare or less. These small holdings were further divided into tiny, widely scattered parcels. The following instances are illustrative. In Boyaca, Colombia, some small holdings consisted of as many as 29 parcels each; in one instance, a farmer with 27 parcels of land had one parcel 10 meters away from the homestead and another 14 kilometers (14,000 meters); a second farmer with 22 parcels of land needed 5 minutes to reach one parcel and 2 hours to reach another.[19] In some

[15] Ann K.S. Lambton, *Landlord and Peasant in Persia, A Study of Land Tenure and Land Revenue Administration* (London: Oxford University Press, 1953), p. 271.

[16] Dale W. Adams, "Colombia's Land Tenure System: Antecedents and Problems," *Land Economics,* XLII (February 1966), 50.

[17] Generosa F. Rivera and Robert T. McMillan, *An Economic and Social Survey of Rural Households in Central Luzon* (Manila: Philippine Council for the United States Aid and the United States Operations Mission, 1954), p. iv.

[18] Gabriel Baer, *A History of Landownership in Modern Egypt, 1800–1950* (London: Oxford University Press, 1962), p. 138.

[19] Orlando Fals-Borda, "Fragmentation of Holdings in Boyaca, Colombia," *Rural Sociology,* XXI (June 1956), 160.

fragmented areas of Iran, such as, for example, Joushaqan and Mur-
chenkhwart, the size of farm plots ranged from 0.08 to 0.61 hectares.[20]
The 1960 Census of Agriculture of the Philippines indicated that about
44 percent of the nation's farm holdings had from 2 to more than 10 parcels of land each.[21] In Taiwan, a 1962 survey of 16 townships by the Chinese-American Joint Commission on Rural Reconstruction (JCRR)
indicated that the average size for owner-operated farms was 1.1 hectares,
each divided into 14 parcels, and that the average size for tenant-operated
farms was a little less than 1 hectare, each divided into 9 parcels. Another
JCRR survey found that "in one typical area, plot size averaged 0.07 hectares, or 700 square meters, with a number under 100 square meters." [22] In
Egypt in 1950, about 1,050,000 hectares of land, or about 40 percent of the
total cultivated area, was divided into 2 million plots.[23]

Diminution of plots is not merely a condition of small holdings. In a
number of countries, holdings of large landlords are rented out in tiny
pieces to tenants. This is generally true of India;[24] and in the former Northwest Frontier Province of West Pakistan, the mean size of landlord holdings was 13 hectares, which was divided on the average into 5.2 plots, with
a mean plot size of 2.5 hectares.[25] In the early 1950s, in three Egyptian land
reform districts—Demera, Zafaran, and Maania—5 large estates owned 37
farms with a total of 25,733 *feddans* (10,807 hectares). Most of the land on
these farms was leased to farmers in plots of from 1 to 10 feddans (0.42 to
4.2 hectares).[26]

In recent years, largely because of the continual increase in rural population, fragmentation of the farms has intensified. For example, in Colombia from 1954 to 1960 there was an increase of 32 percent in the number of
farm holdings and a decrease of 25 percent in the average size of holdings.

[20] Lambton, *op. cit.*, pp. 277–278.
[21] The Philippines, Department of Commerce and Industry, Bureau of the Census
and Statistics, *Census of the Philippines 1960: Agriculture*, Vol. II, *Summary Report*
(Manila, 1965), p. 205.
[22] Arthur F. Raper, *Rural Taiwan—Problem and Promise* (Taipei, Taiwan: JCRR,
1953), p. 147; and JCRR, *This Land Is Ours, Land Reform in Taiwan* (Taipei, Taiwan,
n.d.), p. 11.
[23] Saad M. Gadalla, *Land Reform in Relation to Social Development, Egypt* (Columbia: The University of Missouri Press, 1962), p. 14.
[24] See P. S. Sharma, "Pattern of Land Concentration," *The Economic Weekly*,
XVII (December 11, 1965), 1827.
[25] Christopher Beringer, "Welfare and Production Efficiency: Two Objectives of
Land Reform in Pakistan," *Pakistan Development Review*, II (Summer 1962), 186.
[26] Gadalla, *op. cit.*, pp. 47–49.

During the same period the number of farm holdings with one hectare or less of land rose from 18 percent of all holdings to 33.3 percent.[27] Similarly, in India from 1954 to 1960/61, while the number of farm holdings increased by 10 percent, the average size of holdings decreased by 10 percent; and in the same period the number of holdings with less than one acre (0.4 hectares) of land rose by 8.59 percent while the number of holdings with 50 acres (20.23 hectares) or more of land declined by 23.54 percent.[28] In Taiwan, from 1952 to 1964, the number of farm families rose by 23 percent, while the average farm size declined from 1.29 to 1.06 hectares.[29] In Egypt, private and religious landholdings with a size below 5 feddans (2.10 hectares) operated on 25 percent of the nonpublic land in 1910, and they covered 35.3 percent in 1950.[30]

This massive evidence on the maldistribution of land reveals the seriousness, and even the intensification, of the tenure problem. It underlines the urgency of tenure reform.

INEQUITABLE TENANCY ARRANGEMENTS

Practiced in both developed and developing countries, tenancy is not necessarily a defective form of land tenure. Only when the prevailing tenancy arrangements of a country impose an excessive and unreasonable burden on a vast number of cultivators, will they raise serious problems. As Walter Froehlich has observed: "Tenancy in itself is socially admissible if the rentals are not exorbitant and if the tenant has a reasonable degree of security and stability, especially if the form of tenancy does not preclude final acquisition of land." [31] However, in most of the eight countries under study, large proportions of farmers work under precisely what Froehlich would consider socially inadmissible and economically undesirable tenancy conditions. The incidence of tenancy is widespread and geographically uneven; tenants are obliged to pay a major share of their income as rent

[27] See Table 2 above; FAO, *The State of Food and Agriculture, 1965* (Rome, 1965), p. 64; and CIDA, *Inventory of Information Basic to the Planning of Agricultural Development in Latin America, Regional Report* (Washington, D.C.: Pan American Union, 1963), p. 127.

[28] FAO, *The State of Food and Agriculture, 1965*, p. 64; and B. R. Kalra, "Regional Variations in Policy Regarding Size of Agricultural Holding," *Indian Journal of Agricultural Economics*, XX (April-June 1965), 38.

[29] China, Executive Yuan, Council for International Economic Cooperation and Development, *Taiwan Statistical Data Book 1965* (Taipei, Taiwan, 1965), p. 20.

[30] Baer, *op. cit.* (n. 19 above), p. 78.

[31] Walter Froehlich, "Economic Development, Land Tenure, and Social Stability: Some Preliminary Remarks," in Froehlich, *op. cit.* (n. 6 above), p. 9.

and to provide free labor; they enjoy little freedom and protection with respect to their agricultural activities; and they are precluded from acquiring ownership of land.

Incidence of tenancy. Table 3 provides information on the incidence of tenancy in these countries. From one-third to two-thirds of the farm holdings of these countries were operated by owner-farmers, with the rest by pure-tenants or part-tenants.

It should be pointed out that, though in this table the number of tenant holdings in most of the countries studied appears fairly large, the actual number is even larger. This is because the definition of tenure status used in some countries is frequently ambiguous. For example, prior to its abolition, the Indian *zamindari* system covered some 40 percent of the agricultural area of the country.[32] After the abolition of the system, official estimates of the area of tenanted land in India varied from only 12.53 percent to 22.41 percent of the agricultural area.[33] Certain of these estimates were based on the assumption that the tenants who used to work under the *zamindari* system became full owners after abolition. The fact is that the overwhelming majority of them can still be considered as tenants. Having never obtained the ownership of the land they worked on, they still paid rent—only now to the government instead of the *zamindars*. Basically for this reason, as an official Indian document has conceded, even the highest of the estimates "may not . . . reflect correctly the existing picture regarding the extent of leasing [i.e. tenancy]." [34] Moreover, the term, *owner-farmer*, as used in the Indian agricultural census frequently is meant to include part-tenant and part-owner farmers.[35] Much of what is said of India applies to Pakistan, particularly its East Wing. Similarly, definitional and statistical deficiencies appear to contribute to an under-

[32] M. L. Dantwala, "Financial Implications of Land Reforms: Zamindari Abolition," *Indian Journal of Agricultural Economics*, XVII (October-December 1962), 1.

[33] The lower estimate, for the years 1960–1961, is from India, Ministry of Food, Agriculture, Community Development and Cooperation, Directorate of Economics & Statistics, *Indian Agriculture in Brief* (7th ed., New Delhi, 1965), p. 65. The higher estimate, dated 1961, is from Table 3, p. 32. For unofficial estimates, which generally held the tenanted land to be about one-fifth to one-fourth of the agricultural area, see Raj Krishna, "Some Aspects of Land Reform and Economic Development in India," in Froehlich, *op. cit.* (n. 6 above), p. 228; and John W. Mellor, *et al.*, *Developing Rural India, Plan and Practice* (Ithaca, N.Y.: Cornell University Press, 1968), p. 53.

[34] India, *Progress of Land Reform*, p. 6.

[35] For a detailed comment on this definitional problem, see Daniel Thorner, "India's Agrarian Revolution by Census Redefinition," *Indian Economic Review* (August 1956), 1–21.

TABLE 3

FARM HOLDINGS AND LAND TENURE, EIGHT COUNTRIES

| | Farm Holdings[a] | | | | Land Tenure (percent) | | | | | | |
| | | | Total Area[b] | Average Area Per Holding | | Owner | | Tenant | | Mixed[c] | |
Country	Year	Total Number	Hectares	Hectares	Year	No. of Holdings	Area	No. of Holdings	Area	No. of Holdings	Area
Colombia[d]	1960	1,209,669	27,399,772	22.65	1960	62.7	75.2	23.3	8.1	14[e]	16.7[e]
India[f]	1954	44,354,000	135,160,287	3.05	1961	76.34	77.59	23.16	22.41	...	...
Iran[g]	1960	1,877,299	11,356,254	6.05	1960	33.25	26.20	55.90	66.22	10.84	11.58
Mexico[h]	1950	1,383,212	145,516,943	105.20	1950	68	...	3	...	29	29
Pakistan[i]	1960	10,999,463	28,592,831	2.60	1960	54	47	17	24	29	29
Philippines[j]	1960	2,166,216	7,772,485	3.59	1948	52.56	61.46	37.35	27.13	10.09	11.41
					1960	44.67	53.18	39.91	25.73	15.42	21.09
Taiwan[k]	1960	808,267	880,000	1.09	1949	35.06	55.47[l]	38.73	44.53	26.21	29.11
					1960	64.47	60.69	14.07	10.20	21.46	...
U.A.R.[m]	1956	1,254,400	2,509,040	2.00	1950	66	61	20	20	14	19
					1956	58	59	28	22	14	19

[a] "Farm holdings" refer to farm units by operation, including owner-operated and non-owner-operated farm units.

[b] Includes all lands that belong to the farm holdings, whether under crops or not.

[c] Part-owner and part-tenant holdings. In Iran, Pakistan, the Philippines, Taiwan, and the U.A.R. the area of holdings under the mixed-tenure group contained land operated by part-tenant and part-owner farmers. Information concerning the precise proportions of tenanted land and owned land of this tenure group in these countries is unavailable. But the amount of tenanted land was substantial in most cases. Therefore, in comparing the incidence of tenancy of these countries, one has to take into account the data on the mixed tenure group. In Colombia and Mexico, the mixed holdings do not include tenanted land.

^d Information on land tenure is from CIDA, *Tenancia de la Tierra y Desarrollo Socio-Economico del Sector Agrícola: Colombia* (Washington, D.C.: Unión Panamericana, 1966), p. 68.

^e Squatter and miscellaneous holdings.

^f Data on Indian farm holdings are from FAO, *World Agricultural Structure, Study No. 1* (Rome, 1961), p. 50; tenure data of 1961 from P. S. Sharma, "A Study of the Structural and Tenurial Aspects of Rural Economy in the Light of 1961 Census," *Indian Journal of Agricultural Economics* (October-December 1965), 49. Original data were grouped into two categories: "rural areas" and "urban areas." Data cited in table consist of only the former.

^g Data on both farm holdings and land tenure are from FAO, *Report on the 1960 World Census of Agriculture: Census Results by Countries*, Vol. 1, Part A (Rome: FAO, 1966), p. 91.

^h Farm holdings and tenure data include *ejido* (communal) holdings and areas. An *ejido* is counted collectively as one holding. Data on farm holdings are from FAO, *World Agricultural Structure, Study No. 1*, p. 49, and tenure data from U.S., Department of Agriculture, *Changes in Agriculture in 26 Developing Nations, 1948 to 1963* (Washington, D.C., 1965), pp. 36–37.

ⁱ Tenure data are from *ibid.*

^j Data on farm holdings and 1960 tenure data are from the Philippines, *Census of the Philippines 1960: Agriculture*, Vol. II (Manila, 1965), p. 12; and 1948 tenure data from the Philippines, Bureau of Census and Statistics, *Summary Report on the 1948 Census of Agriculture under ECA Counterpart Project No. 5* (Manila, 1952), pp. 136 and 150.

^k Total area of farm holdings excludes public land. Tenure data of 1949 and 1960 are from, respectively, Taiwan, Provincial Government, Department of Agriculture and Forestry, *Taiwan Agricultural Yearbook, 1951* (Taipei, Taiwan, 1951), pp. 20–21; and Taiwan, Provincial Government, Committee on Census of Agriculture, *General Report on the 1961 Census of Agriculture, Taiwan, Republic of China* (Taichung, Taiwan: Taiwan Provincial Government Printing Press, 1963), pp. 13 and 54.

^l Includes area of land owned by farmers in the mixed-tenure group.

^m Data on agricultural holdings are from Donald C. Mead, *Growth and Structural Change in the Egyptian Economy* (Homewood, Ill.: Richard D. Irwin, Inc., 1967), Table III-3-C; and tenure data from Gabriel S. Saab, *The Egyptian Agrarian Reform, 1952–1962* (London: Oxford University Press, 1967), p. 14.

SOURCE: Unless otherwise noted, the source is FAO, *Production Yearbook 1964* (Rome, FAO, 1965).

estimate of the tenancy rates in Egypt. An official publication revealed that, in 1949, the *tenanted land* in Egypt covered 60.7 percent of the total agricultural area;[36] yet the tenure data of 1950 (collected by the government two years before land reform), as shown in Table 3, above, indicated that the *owner-operated* land accounted for 61 percent of the total agricultural area. Thus there was a 21.7 percent increase in the owner-operated area within a single year—an extremely unlikely event. The discrepancy in the tenure data of 1949 and 1950, two specialists have explained, is apparently due to faulty calculations in the 1950 statistics.[37]

Uneven geographical distribution. While in most of the countries studied the incidence of tenancy is high, the geographical distribution of tenancy rates is very uneven. For instance, in India in 1961, one source indicated, the tenanted area in West Bengal was 20 percent of the state's cultivated area, in Punjab 25 percent, in Gujarat 46 to 59 percent, and in certain districts of the former State of Bombay 63 percent.[38] In West Pakistan the tenanted land was once reported to cover 50 percent of the agricultural area, but regional variations of the high-tenancy area ranged from 56 percent in the former Punjab province to over 80 percent in the former Sind province.[39] In the Philippines, the 1948 agricultural census indicated that the tenancy rate for the whole nation was 35.5 percent, but that among the 51 provinces of the country the rates varied from 0.4 percent in Batanes to 88.2 percent in Pampanga.[40]

Heavy burden of tenancy. A comparison of the data on the area of owner holdings and tenant holdings in Table 3 will provide some indica-

[36] Egypt, Ministry of Agriculture, *Monthly Agricultural Bulletin*, No. 6 (October 1949), 16.

[37] With reference to the owner-operated area in Egypt, as shown in Table 3, Gabriel S. Saab commented: "Big farm operators who generally reserved for themselves the cotton crop (and sometimes the wheat crop), often leased large areas of clover, maize, or rice, divided into small plots, to tenants or agricultural labourers on a seasonal basis. These seasonal tenancy arrangements were not taken into account at the time of the [1950] farm census. Moreover, even in the case of sharecropping arrangements, holdings were frequently classed as owner-operated." Gabriel S. Saab, *The Egyptian Agrarian Reform, 1952–1962* (London: Oxford University Press, 1967), p. 14. Cf. Baer, *op. cit.* (n. 19 above), pp. 71ff. The inclusion in Table 3 of the 1950 land-tenure data rather than the 1949 data is based on the consideration that the latter data are incomplete, revealing only tenure statistics on area distribution but not on distribution of holdings.

[38] Krishna, *op. cit.*, p. 228.

[39] West Pakistan, *Report of the Land Reforms Commission for West Pakistan*, p. 7.

[40] See Robert E. Huke, *Shadows on the Land: An Economic Geography of the Philippines* (Manila: The Bookmark, Inc., 1963), p. 198.

tion of the heavy burden placed on tenants. In most cases, owner-farmers have a larger share of the land than tenants. Hence, with a smaller area of land—and often with poorer quality land—tenants have the exclusive responsibility for providing rent. Invariably, rent takes up a major portion of the tenants' income.

To understand this last point, it is necessary to describe briefly how rent is determined. In a comparative study of the subsistence agriculture of a number of countries, authors Colin Clark and Margaret Haswell indicated that three factors—one primary and two secondary—affect rent.[41] The primary factor is the marginal productivity of land. This can be explained as follows. According to the classical theory of rent as formulated by David Ricardo, rent is a consequence of the differences in the costs of production on farms with different qualities of land. Theoretically, the farm with the lowest quality land entails the greatest production cost. That is, the production cost on such a farm takes up the total harvest. When leased out, such a farm can yield no rent because the tenant tilling it cannot have a higher income than is necessary to sustain the life of his family and himself. Then, the farm with the second lowest quality land entails the second greatest production cost. On such a farm, the production cost is slightly smaller than the harvest in value, and hence there is a surplus from which comes the rent. Finally, the farm with the highest quality land will yield the largest surplus, thus the largest rent. One of the secondary factors affecting rent is the net population pressure on agricultural land (i.e. the total population of an area minus the people in non-agricultural occupations). In an area with a high concentration of agricultural population, rental rates are high, and vice versa. Clark and Haswell cited data from Egypt, Malaya, the Philippines, France, and Italy to substantiate this statement. The other secondary factor affecting rent is the non-monetary value of landownership. If landownership is highly valued by people as a means of personal security and as a source of social prestige, rental rates are high; and vice versa. The authors cited data from China, Egypt, India, Japan, Belgium, Denmark, and England to demonstrate this point.

It becomes apparent that rent in the developing countries can become excessively high because both the net population pressure on agricultural land and the non-monetary value of agricultural land are known to be very high. Under this condition, Clark and Haswell calculated, rental rates

[41] Colin Clark and Margaret Haswell, *The Economics of Subsistence Agriculture* (New York: St. Martins Press, 1964), Chap. vi., "Rents and Prices of Agricultural Land," pp. 95–110.

vary around 50 percent of the production of the land. In general, this appears to be the case with the countries under study, though in certain countries rental rates could go up to 70 percent.[42]

This level of rent is unreasonable. On the one hand, it reduces a substantial proportion of the farming population—tenants—to subsistence farmers, hence contributing to agricultural stagnation. On the other hand, in making land available to tenants as a factor of production, landlords earn an income in the form of a rent larger than their due. That is to say, high rental rates arising from the social conditions prevalent in traditional agriculture benefit landlords at the expense of tenants and the society at large. Moreover, as population pressure and the high non-monetary value of land drive up rental rates, land price will rise, making it difficult for tenants to purchase land and to become owner-farmers. At the same time, high rentals induce large landowners to rent rather than to farm their land, thus leading to rising tenancy. Data from Egypt, the Philippines, and India confirm this trend.[43]

[42] Before the adoption of land reforms, the rental rates in India were about 50 to 60 percent of gross output, in Egypt 50 percent of gross output or 75 percent of net output, in Taiwan 50 to 70 percent of gross output, and in the high-tenancy area of Central Luzon in the Philippines about 50 percent. See Konrad Bekker, "Land Reform Legislation in India," *The Middle East Journal*, V (Summer 1951), 321; Doreen Warriner, *Land Reform and Development in the Middle East: A Study of Egypt, Syria, and Iraq* (2nd rev. ed.; London: Oxford University Press, 1962), pp. 27 and 29; Chen Cheng, *Land Reform in Taiwan* (Taipei, Taiwan: China Publishing Company, 1961), p. 9; and Rivera and McMillan, *op. cit.* (n. 18 above), p. vii.

The rental rates in Iran in the pre-reform period were determined according to local custom. On the whole, the harvest was divided into five portions, with each portion assigned to one of the following elements of production: land, water, draught animals, seed, and labor. The landlord frequently supplied both land and water and sometimes draught animals, hence receiving two or three portions. Though the normal rent (or return) for each element of production was one-fifth of the harvest, in certain dry areas the rent for water could be higher. In certain extreme cases, the landlords, by supplying more than one element of production, could claim as much as four-fifths of the output. See Lambton, *op. cit.* (n. 16 above), pp. 306, 322–323; Monsoor Atai, "Economic Report on Agriculture in the Isfahan and Yazd Areas," *Tahqiqat é eqtesadi*, III (August 1965), 117–120; and Gideon Hadary, "The Agrarian Reform Problem in Iran," *The Middle East Journal*, V (Spring 1951), 187–188.

[43] One study showed that from 1946 to 1948 an Egyptian landowner would have received a net income of £E16.19 per *feddan* (0.4201 hectare) of land if he operated it by himself, but £E22 to 23 if he rented it. Between 1939 and 1949, land under tenancy rose from 17 to 60 percent of the total farm area. Saab, *op. cit.*, pp. 11–12; and Warriner, *op. cit.*, pp. 25–26. A survey in Central Luzon, the Philippines reported in 1954: "The average net return to landlords was equivalent to . . . twice the total amount of their [share of] farm operating expenses, and to more than tenants and their households

In addition to delivering regular rent, the tenants have to perform certain free services for the landlords and to pay extra dues and cesses.[44] Though shouldering the heavy burden of tenancy, the tenants enjoy no security as to their working rights because they are seldom provided with a written contract of fixed term. Lacking freedom in farm operations, they are frequently required to grow certain specified crops and sometimes prohibited from raising others.[45] Instances of subleasing are common, leading to a feudalistic system of hierarchical exploitation.[46]

---

earned in wages from farming operations." It is not surprising to find that "the proportion of all farms in the Central [Luzon] Plains operated by tenants increased from 38 percent in 1903 to 60 percent in 1948. For the Philippines generally, the corresponding percentages were 18 in 1903 and 37 in 1948." Rivera and McMillan, *op. cit.* (n. 18 above), pp. iii and ix. In India, from 1921 to 1936, the number of non-cultivating landlords increased by 11 percent; owner cultivators decreased by 12 percent; and agricultural workers (sharecroppers) increased by 54 percent. Even long after India started land reform, a study of the rural conditions in the village Senapur, Uttar Pradesh (one of the country's most important agricultural states), found that "the amount of land in sharecropping has probably increased by 50 percent in the ten year period from 1954 to 1964." Sheldon R. Simon, "The Village of Senapur," in Mellor, *et al., op. cit.,* p. 317.

[44] For a description of the extra rents, dues, and *begar* (forced labor) under the Indian *zamindari* system, see Radhakamal Mukerjee, *Land Problems of India* (London: Longmans Green & Co., 1933), p. 141. For a narration of the services and dues that Iranian tenants used to provide to their landlords, see Lambton, *op. cit.* (n. 16 above), pp. 330–334ff. In Taiwan, there were such practices as "iron-clad rent"—a minimum rent payable under any circumstances, natural or man-made disasters notwithstanding—security deposits, guarantee money, and advance payment of rent. In addition, tenants had to deliver to landlords 50 percent of certain by-products of farming, and to raise livestock and to grow fruit trees, bamboo, or lumber for the landlords—all without compensation. Hui-sun Tang, *Land Reform in Free China* (Taipei, Taiwan: JCRR, 1954), pp. 27–28.

[45] In Egypt before land reform, cotton and wheat were the preferred crops of landowners. They took practically all the cotton output and half or more of the wheat output, leaving such other crops as maize and berseem to tenants. Warriner, *op. cit.,* p. 26. In Iran, tenants were not allowed to grow trees and own gardens, lest they become prosperous and independent. Lambton, *op. cit.* (n. 16 above), p. 391. In Colombia small farmers were once prohibited from growing coffee.

[46] Before its abolition, the *zamindari* system in India and Pakistan provided certain extreme examples of multiple exploitation of tenants. In one case in India, a *zamindar* with 2,000 acres of land cultivated by 320 tenants had to deal with, in hierarchical order, four groups of 264 intermediaries. Against 200 rupees assessed for government revenue, the *zamindar* and the intermediaries collected from the tenants 4,800 rupees. Mukerjee, *op. cit.,* p. 111. In East Pakistan, an official report noted in 1961 that in extreme cases "as many as 50 or more intermediary interests had been created between the *zamindar* at the top and the actual cultivator at the bottom." See Pakistan, Planning Commission, *Survey of Land Reform in Pakistan, June 1961* (Karachi: Government of Pakistan Press, 1962), p. 1.

Under these tenancy conditions, the tenants have to exert extraordinary efforts to maintain a subsistence living and to yield a large surplus for rental payments. In contrast, the landowners enjoy, with little effort, a guaranteed income. The basic problem today is that, if left alone, these inequitable tenancy arrangements will not only continue to exist but, because of the rise in the rural population, will increasingly worsen and affect a larger and larger number of farmers.

Consequences of Tenure Problems

ECONOMIC CONSEQUENCES

Overconcentration of landownership tends to freeze the level of agricultural production. Large landowners, particularly absentee landlords, often indulge in conspicuous consumption in cities or abroad, thus drawing away capital from rural areas.[47] "Much of their income went into luxurious mansions, jewelry, works of art, and many other nonproductive uses characteristic of wealthy leisure classes. A considerable part of their land income may have been invested in domestic and foreign industries and contributed to capital formation there."[48] When they do come to

---

In Iran, two-level tenancy was practiced in certain regions. An intermediary known as the *gavband*, literally the ox owner, leased land from an owner for a fixed share of crop, and then rented the land together with oxen—and sometimes seeds as well—to the cultivator. The *gavband* collected several shares of rent from the tenant, delivering one to the owner. U.N., *Land Reform, Fourth Report*, p. 22. See also Lambton, *op. cit.* (n. 16 above), p. 272. Subleasing was also practiced in Taiwan and Egypt. See Tang, *op. cit.*, p. 28; and Warriner, *op. cit.*, p. 27.

[47] A study estimated that "if the richest 5 per cent of Latin Americans were to reduce their *per capita* consumption from its present level of 15 times the average *per capita* consumption of the poorer half of the population to a level only 9 times higher, the increase in investment made possible thereby could raise the annual growth rate for the continent [Latin America] as a whole from 1 per cent to 4 per cent. The fact that wealthy and unproductive landowners make up a good portion of that upper 5 per cent makes this a powerful argument for land redistribution in Latin America." Raúl Prebisch, "Hacia una Dinámica del Desarrollo Latino Americano," *Suplemento de Comercio Exterior, Mexico, Banco Nacional de Comercio Exterior, S.A.* (April 1963), pp. 5–6. Cited in U.N., *Land Reform, Fourth Report*, p. 158.

[48] "Land Reform and Agricultural Production, Report of the Working Party," in Kenneth H. Parsons, *et al.* (eds.), *Land Tenure* (Madison, Wis., 1956), p. 581. In India, one author has noted, "the upper classes in the villages have a strong 'hoarding propensity,' . . . The Reserve Bank of India estimated at 105 million ounces the stock of gold, and at 4,235 million ounces the stock of silver in private hands in the country . . . , with a market value in India of about 5,000 crores of rupees, or the equivalent of about one fourth of the reproducible tangible wealth of India. . . ." Ignacy

invest in rural areas, the investment is more frequently in the form of additional land purchases than of farm improvements.[49] Extensive holding is both profitable—because it yields a sufficiently large income—and prudent—because it enhances the social prestige of the landowner and because it protects him from the ill effects of inflation. This strong demand for land, coupled with the low land tax that prevails in most developing countries, drives land prices to an unreasonably high level and "adds to the general inflationary trend."[50]

Fragmentation of landholdings also raises problems. Because of dispersion of farm plots, agricultural operations require an unnecessarily large amount of labor and capital resources. For instance, the Board of Economic Enquiry in Punjab, Pakistan, estimated that the expenditure of cultivation there would increase "by 5.3% for every 500 meters of distance (between plots) for ploughing, 20 [to] 25% for the transport of manure and from 15 to 32% for the transport of crops."[51] Where farmers do not have sufficient manpower and other resources to farm adequately their dispersed parcels, the parcels lying in the far distance are understandably neglected. This is what happened, for instance, in Boyaca, Colombia;[52] and in Egypt "losses in production due to fragmentation have been estimated at 30 percent of gross production."[53] Fragmentation obviously also creates such problems as wastage of land for purposes of demarcation and access roads, and disputes over water use.

Tenancy, particularly when it is associated with maldistribution of land, contributes to the underutilization of land. With a greater interest in landownership than in the management of farms, large landowners in many developing countries often underutilize their land; and *haciendas* in Latin America frequently include a sizable portion of land not cultivated at all. This point will be elaborated in Chapter V. At present, for illustration, two references to the land utilization pattern in Colombia may be cited. In its study of the economy of Colombia, the International Bank for

---

Sachs, *Patterns of Public Sector in Underdeveloped Economics* (Bombay: Asis Publishing House [1964]), p. 40 (1 crore = 10,000,000).

[49] For instance, in Egypt about £E500 million was frozen in land purchase in the period from 1913 to 1952. Saab, *op. cit.* (n. 38 above), p. 12. This was roughly equivalent to US $100 million according to the exchange rate before 1933.

[50] U.N., *Land Reform, Fourth Report*, p. 159.

[51] West Pakistan, *Report of the Land Reforms Commission for West Pakistan*, p. 16.

[52] See Fals-Borda, *op. cit.* (n. 20 above), pp. 160–162.

[53] Saab, *op. cit.* (n. 38 above), p. 10.

Reconstruction and Development reported in 1950, "land use [in this country] follows an unusual pattern. As a rule the fertile level valleys are used mostly for grazing, while the steep mountainside slopes are cultivated. . . . The cattle fatten on the plains while the people often have to struggle for a bare existence in the hills." [54] Ironically, this pattern of land use is due in part to a land-reform program of 1936, which stipulated that if land was unused for ten consecutive years, it would be subject to expropriation. To circumvent the law, large landowners in the Cauca Valley raised cattle on their fertile land. And cattle raising has proved to be a more profitable undertaking than growing crops. Though efforts have been made in recent years to revert from grazing to cropping, not much progress has occurred.[55] Another reference to land use in Colombia is provided by the Land Reform Institute of Colombia. In its annual report for 1963, INCORA noted that among the 6,021,219 hectares of land possessed by 810 large estates, only 2,986,353 hectares, or a little under 50 percent, were cultivated.[56]

Under the traditional land-tenure system, while many large landowners tend to underutilize their land, small farmers can hardly improve their agricultural production. To improve production, these farmers must have the necessary capital, a feeling of security of ownership or of working rights, a profit incentive, and an innovating attitude. As a rule, they do not meet all these conditions. Frequently heavily indebted, they cannot accumulate savings to be used for new investment. Nor can they be expected to exert greater physical effort and provide greater ingenuity than they already do to improve labor productivity. To many small farmers and tenants, "the margins for subsistence are so slight that they can afford little risk; any innovation in production practice that goes wrong may lead to near starvation for the family; . . ." [57]

As a result, agriculture in the developing countries suffers from low

[54] International Bank for Reconstruction and Development, *The Basis of a Development Program for Colombia* (Washington, D.C., 1950), pp. 62–63. Cf. Albert O. Hirschman, *Journeys Toward Progress* (New York, 1963), pp. 111–114; and Pat M. Holt, *Colombia Today—and Tomorrow* (New York: Frederick A. Praeger, Publishers, 1964), p. 99.

[55] See Antonio J. Posada and Jeanne de Posada, *The CVC: Challenge to Underdevelopment and Traditionalism* (Bogatá: Ediciones Tercer Mumdo, 1966), p. 44; and Cole Blasier, "Power and Social Change in Colombia: The Cauca Valley," *Journal of Inter-American Studies*, III (July 1966), 388–389.

[56] INCORA, *Informe de Actividades en 1963*, p. 81.

[57] Parsons, "Land Reform and Agricultural Development," in Parsons, *et al.*, *op. cit.*, pp. 21–22.

labor productivity (output per unit of labor) and, excepting for countries with fertile soil, low land productivity (output per unit of land). This can be seen in an agricultural survey of fifty-two countries conducted by the FAO.[58] Covering 1956 to 1960, the survey showed that most developing countries had both lower land productivity and lower labor productivity than the developed countries. With respect to the eight countries under study, in terms of output per hectare of land the U.A.R. ranked the highest among the 52 surveyed countries, Taiwan the 3rd, the Philippines the 21st, Pakistan the 24th, India the 33rd, Iran the 36th, Colombia the 37th, and Mexico 47th. Only in the U.A.R. and Taiwan was land productivity high. But data on both countries were of the post-land reform era, and the soil of both countries is very fertile. In terms of output per adult farmer, data on only 36 countries are available. Of these 36 countries, Colombia ranked the 24th highest, Taiwan the 25th, Iran the 30th, the Philippines the 32nd, and India, next to the lowest, the 35th.

In the developing countries, the combination of low land productivity and low labor productivity, together with the rapid rise in population, has contributed to agricultural stagnation. As reported by the FAO in 1966, in the two decades after World War II, per capita agricultural output showed a continuous rise in the developed regions of the world, but experienced, on the whole, no increase in the developing regions, and a decline in the Far East and Latin America.[59]

Agricultural stagnation or decline means that the expansion of agricultural export for the increase of foreign exchange earnings, the provision of sufficient food for a growing urban population, the augmentation of capital outflow from agriculture to industries, and the enlargement of rural demand for non-agricultural goods and services—all these are conditions essential to a developing country's incipient industrial development—will hardly materialize. Unless it possesses readily exploitable, rich extractive resources, a developing country will thus find industrialization only a distant hope.

SOCIAL CONSEQUENCES

While the traditional land system of the developing countries directly impedes economic progress, it indirectly creates certain undesirable social consequences. Located at the bottom of the social strata, farmers are con-

[58] FAO, *The State of Food and Agriculture 1963* (Rome: FAO, 1963), pp. 110 and 116.

[59] FAO, *The State of Food and Agriculture 1966* (Rome, 1966), p. 17.

stantly subject to the exactions of landlords, money-lenders, and businessmen. Their painstaking pursuits in land enable them to maintain only a
meager living for themselves and to meet their direct and indirect obligations toward others. As a consequence, they can hardly expect to move
upward in the social ladder or sideways to other economic occupations.

Under the circumstances, small owners, tenants, and farm laborers
frequently develop an ambivalent attitude toward large landowners and
landlords—an outward appearance of subservience and deference combined with an innate feeling of suspicion and resentment.[60] On the other
hand, as Ann K.S. Lambton has observed, in reference to the landlord-
tenant relationships in Iran, "the landowner regards the peasant virtually
as a drudge, whose sole function is to provide him with his profits and
who will, if treated with anything but severity, cheat him of his due." [61]
The subservient-dominant relationship between the landlord and the tenant
is sometimes sanctioned by religion and reinforced by social practices. In
Mexico, for instance, before and during the initial period of land reform,
certain priests exhorted the *campesinos* to pay deference to their masters.
One priest pronounced to the peasants:

> . . . everyone should go forth to farm the land, to harvest the crops,
> to deliver the fruits of the earth to their [*sic*] legitimate landlord,
> a Christian landlord who pays for the obligations of his privilege by
> promptly delivering a tent to Holy Mother Church. God punishes
> disobedience.
> —And justice, father?
> —Final justice is imparted up there, son. Do not look for it in
> this vale of tears.[62]

Another prelate of Mexico would say:

[60] In Sind, West Pakistan, peasant's ambivalent feelings (submissiveness combined with resentment) toward the landlord was vividly illustrated in the following
report. Prior to the land reform of 1958, there was a saying in this region "that it is
dangerous for a peasant to have a beautiful wife," *The New York Times* reported in
1966. But "he can hardly avoid this, as Sind women in general are rather pretty. A
Martial Law in 1958 saw the eruption of 1,700 complaints from peasant-tenants whose
wives had been abducted. This resulted in the landlords' returning about 800 women
to their husbands within a week. Several of these women brought with them children,
deeds of land, ornaments and cash—an apparent attempt by the landlords to pacify the
angry husbands." *The New York Times*, December 19, 1966, p. 4.
[61] Lambton, *op. cit.* (n. 16 above), p. 263.
[62] Originally appeared in Carlos Fuentes, *La Muerte de Artemio Cruz* (México,
Fondo de Cultura Económica, 1962), p. 46. Quoted in Kenneth F. Johnson, "Ideological Correlates of Right Wing Political Alienation in Mexico," *American Political Science
Review*, LIX (September 1965), 663.

As all authority is derived from God, the Christian workman should sanctify and make sublime his obedience by serving God in the person of his bosses. . . . Poor, love your humble state and your work; turn your gaze towards heaven; there is the true wealth.[63]

In Egypt, while the indifferent and submissive attitude of the *fellah* (peasant) was much shaped by his agricultural experiences, the society stressed the values that helped perpetuate this attitude. The *fellah* "is mild and peaceful because he is patient, and patient because he is subject to men and events, and . . . he has become like the Nile, indifferent rather than idle," Henry Habib Ayrout has observed. Yet such a frame of mind was constantly reinforced by the repetition of "the following fellah sayings . . . : 'Patience demolishes mountains,' 'Patience is beautiful,' 'Greed is humiliation, but satisfaction with one's lot is a full' " virtue.[64]

It is only natural for the peasant to adopt a pessimistic view toward life and society. The rigidity of the social order frequently generates a sense of the fixity of the natural order. And inability to alter the natural environment reinforces the unchangeableness of the social order. This is the circle from which the peasant in a traditional society is unable to free himself. As he looks back to the life of his ancestors, he cannot but assume a fatalistic attitude, accepting the idea that his miserable life and low social status are something pre-ordained and unchangeable. Alienation and fatalism, in short, are often the by-products of a social structure shaped by a defective land tenure system.

POLITICAL CONSEQUENCES

The undesirable consequences of tenure problems cannot be over-stressed. By concentrating "both institutional and arbitrary power in the hands of those who control land," Andrew Pearse has pointed out, the traditional land system results in excluding "from political participation and representation the class of primary producers in such a form that public services and institutions serve private or sectional interests, rather than the society as a whole." [65] The mass peasantry may have been given the fran-

[63] Pastoral letter by Archbishop Francisco Orózco y Jiménez of Guadalajara, Mexico. Quoted in Clarence Senior, *Land Reform and Democracy* (Gainesville, Fla., 1958), p. 19. For a description of "an intense propaganda against agrarianism" by a number of Mexican clergymen in the midst of land reform in Mexico, see *ibid.*, pp. 59–61.

[64] Henry Habib Ayrout, *The Egyptian Peasant*, trans. from the French by John Alden Williams (Boston: Beacon Press, 1963), pp. 143 and 145.

[65] Andrew Pearse, "Land Tenure, Social Structure and 'Development' in Latin America," *América Latina*, VI (July-September 1963), 78.

chise; but, as in pre-reform Egypt, "bribe or [sic] lash were the two methods usually used to secure the fellah's vote . . . ;" or as in pre-reform West Pakistan, "the peasant may have had a vote, but his landlord told him what to do with it." [66] Peasants constitute the most numerous element of traditional society. Yet, inarticulate as to their interests, dispersed in their voting strength, incapable of uniting themselves into a nation-wide organization, they remain apolitical, leaving the formation of public policies and the operation of the government to landlords and other social forces.

The traditional land system also fosters regionalism, rivaling national authority. Prior to 1952, the "feudal estate" was one dominant Egyptian rural institution. "It means that the landowner keeps a private army to defend his house and his person; and that armed men stand guard over the crops." [67] In Latin America, the *hacienda* system, Frank Tannenbaum has observed, is something more than a landed estate. It "is a society, under private auspices." It helped perpetuate *caciquismo* (regional power centers based on big landholdings). "The rule that developed, and was logically required by the situation, was that each region followed its own leader— if necessary, against the national one." [68] For instance, prior to 1910, the Mexican *hacienda* was more or less economically self-sufficient and politically autonomous. As Nathan Whetten has described,[69] it encompassed a wide variety of natural resources including farms, grazing lands, woodlands, and streams. It maintained "a store, a church, a post office, a burying ground, a jail, and occasionally a school." Frequently with several villages located within its boundaries, and sometimes formally recognized as a local government unit (the *municipio*), the *hacienda* had from a hundred to several thousand inhabitants. It exercised government-like authority through a full complement of administrative and other personnel: one administrator, several bosses known as *mayordomos*, a number of foremen, a few clerks, a storekeeper, and, on larger *haciendas*, a priest, a police force, and a teacher. Paid with low wages, and sometimes in tokens usable only

---

[66] Ayrout, *op. cit.*, p. 14, and Keith B. Callard, *Political Forces in Pakistan, 1947–1959* (New York: Institute of Pacific Relations, 1959), p. 12.

[67] Quoted in Warriner, *op. cit.* (n. 43 above), p. 13.

[68] Frank Tannenbaum, "The Hacienda," in John D. Martz (ed.), *The Dynamics of Change in Latin American Politics* (Englewood Cliffs, N.J.: Prentice-Hall, 1965), pp. 28–29 and 32.

[69] The following description of the traditional Mexican *hacienda* is based on Nathan Whetten, *Rural Mexico* (Chicago: University of Chicago Press, 1948), Chap. v, "The Hacienda (Prior 1910)."

for purchase of goods in the *hacienda* operated store (*tienda de raya*), the peasant workers were made permanently dependent on their master. Once in debt, they had to pay back in the form of labor. As they were perpetually in debt, they were bound to the *hacienda* for life. Lacking the most elementary civil rights, they could appeal for their grievances to no higher authority than their patron, for all local government was dominated by him.

The bulk of the Mexican population found itself in this state of affairs at the time of the revolution. The 1910 census indicated that there were 834 *hacendados* in Mexico, and that 3,103,402 peons were held in service for debt. "The latter, with their families, conservatively estimated, would number 9,000,000 to 10,000,000, or from three-fifths to two-thirds of the population." [70] Evidently in pre-revolution Mexico, it was the few *hacendados* rather than Mexico City that governed the countryside.

The implications of a defective tenure system for political instability are also fairly evident. History abounds in instances of wars and social upheavals that originated from rural unrest. In ordinary times, farmers might be content with their poor lives. But in times of distress, such as war or prolonged periods of natural disasters, their latent unhappy feelings were easily inflamed by men seeking political power. Thus, in the past, dissatisfied farmers took up arms against established regimes in the belief that by violence they could permanently improve their lot. In reality, their sacrifice in life and property during a revolt resulted only in creating a new regime that again sanctioned the old land system. Today, farmers' demands for greater economic and political power, in general, and for equitable ownership of land, in particular, may be sharpened by the spread of rural education or whetted by a political elite that makes broad promises of improving rural life. If this stimulated demand is not satisfied, the farmers are less likely than before to fall back on their old way of life. The situation is complicated by the ever-present Communists' efforts to identify themselves with the land-reform issue. Communists are trying by words and actions to persuade farmers of the developing countries that Communist revolution is the only way to improve their plight and that the Communist farm system is the most productive. Thus, if peaceful and equitable land reform is not instituted, farmers who do not always have

[70] Phipps, *op. cit.* (n. 13 above), p. 127. For other estimates of the peon population around 1910, see Simpson, *op. cit.* (n. 12 above), pp. 32–37; and Senior, *op. cit.*, p. 217.

sufficient knowledge of the human sufferings attending the Communist farm system and of the system's failures in agriculture may grow more receptive to Communist propaganda.

Justifications and Limitations of Land Reform

Since the most obvious consequence of defects in a traditional land-tenure system is agricultural stagnation, a basic alteration of the system constitutes a precondition to agricultural progress. Provided with ownership of land, security of holding, and an equitable share of agricultural products, small owner-farmers and tenants will be disposed to exert a greater effort and to make a greater investment, and will have a greater incentive to increase production. Only then can they favorably respond to and effectively utilize added material inputs and improved services. Thus, the removal of institutional defects in land tenure is a step toward shaping a progressive peasant mentality as well as a measure leading to a rationalized pattern of land use. In this sense, land reform is as much a change of the land as a change of the man who tills it.

However, at the risk of repetition, it should be emphasized that the contribution of land reform to agricultural production is limited. It is a necessary, but not a sufficient, condition for increasing crop yields. More material inputs and improved rural services are the other necessary conditions complementing land reform in a broad policy for agricultural development. In a developing country with serious tenure problems, modernization of agriculture without land reform is not likely to succeed; nor will land reform by itself lead to agricultural modernization. Moreover, a significant augmentation of food supply and a really meaningful improvement of rural welfare depend on the relief of the generally high, and still rising, population pressure on land in rural areas. As will be discussed later, though some developing countries have experienced significant advances in industrial expansion, in almost no developing country have industries been so expanded as to absorb sufficient surplus rural labor. Thus, land reform operates in an unfavorable economic environment, accepting high population as a concomitant.

If the role of land reform in agricultural development is absolutely essential but necessarily limited, the impact of land reform on social and political development may be significant but also restricted. Land reform may remove or lessen social and economic exploitation, but the creation of an independent, prosperous peasantry and the attainment of equality between the peasantry and other members of the society depend upon full agricultural development, and such other measures as community development and education. Land reform may break the monopoly of power of the big landed gentry, but the establishment of an open, competitive, free political system in rural areas is also heavily contingent upon, among other things, the commitment and orientation of the national elite and the building of effective rural political institutions.

The justifications and limitations of land reform are so obvious that to state them seems unnecessary. But, evidently, in the debates over the issue of land reform, advocates and opponents are prone to use sweeping terms to justify their stands, creating semantic confusion as well as policy complications. Land reform is defended as a program which can, by itself, achieve rural prosperity and justice. It is, on the other hand, criticized by some as unwarranted interference in the productive process, causing the decline of production and the spread of rural poverty.[71] What is needed is to make the justifications for land reform clearly recognizable and its limitations properly understood. Only then can various approaches to land reform be discussed and reform programs evaluated with reasonableness and realism.

[71] Debates along these lines can be found later. For the moment, consider the work by Elias H. Tuma as cited in Chapter I. In *Twenty-Six Centuries of Agrarian Reform*, the author, after a comparative analysis of the reform programs of eight countries, reached the conclusion that non-socialist reforms have failed to meet the objective economic and social needs of rural populations and have failed to reach the goals the reformers have proclaimed for themselves (see chapters xii–xiv). In rendering this sweeping judgment on most of the programs analyzed, Tuma sets up standards of evaluation probably no reform program can reach. Tuma expected land reform alone to create rural prosperity, social justice, democracy, and stability. The problem with the author's analysis is that he fails to draw a distinction between the full achievement of these goals and their partial realization. The full achievement of these goals depends on many variables, of which land reform is only one. Tuma's effort to evaluate a reform program on the basis of the proclaimed goals of the reformers only brings to focus the point that policy makers, often using exhortatory, idealistic terms to describe their policies in order to gain maximum public support, have more reason than others to deemphasize the limited utility of land reform.

PART ONE
The Political Processes of Land Reform

Introduction

In the following six chapters, the political processes of land reform will be discussed. Chapte. IV will analyze the conditions and circumstances affecting the initiation of reform. Chapter V will deal with the various approaches employed by elites to formulate programs. Chapter VI will offer a case study to illustrate how a specific reform program was formulated. Chapters VII and VIII will provide a detailed comparison of the major provisions of two principal types of reform programs: Redistributive and Developmental. Finally, Chapter IX will present an assessment of the effort of elites to implement programs and an evaluation of the results achieved.

IV

INITIATION OF REFORM AND POLITICAL LEGITIMACY

In the face of their tenure problems, all eight countries under study have, in time, come to recognize the need for land reform. Though these countries introduced reform programs under widely divergent circumstances, their experiences do indicate the existence of certain common and recurrent conditions likely to lead to reform.

Conditions Likely to Lead to Reform

Revolution. As a process of forceful change of the existing political system and its economic and social foundations, revolution shares with land reform a number of characteristics. Both revolution and land reform are movements possessing such idealistic aspirations as the promotion of social justice and popular welfare. Both prefer compulsory to voluntary means of change. Both seek not just innovation in policies but also alteration of institutions. And, most important of all, both aim at the removal, or at least substantial reduction, of the political power of the landed class. Revolution frequently leads to land reform.

Rural unrest. Often desultory in occurrence, rural unrest can frequently be attributed to the discontent of the peasants with existing tenure conditions. With or without the intention to seek a basic alteration of these conditions, peasants may take direct, forceful actions against them, including banditry and terrorism against landlords (as in Colombia and India), land invasions (as in Colombia, Mexico, and East Pakistan), rebellion (as in the Philippines), and participation in large-scale civil war (as in Bolivia and Mexico). All these actions are violent manifestations of the pressure for change; to a certain extent, they signify the incapacity of the government to preserve the rural status quo. In themselves, these actions can become a persuasive argument for tenurial changes; land reform of a sort is then thought necessary to alleviate rural tensions.

Deterrence to Communism. In many developing countries, the vigorous effort by Communists to develop rural power and to enlist peasant support has caused widespread interest in reform. The radical collectivization of farming in mainland China and Cuba and the abortive Communist-supported reform in Guatemala under the Jacob Arbenz Guzmán regime have compelled non-Communist governments to think of alternatives. In countries such as Egypt, Iran, and Pakistan, which face no serious internal Communist threat, policy makers have frequently stressed the preventive value of reform.[1] In countries like Colombia, the Philippines, and Taiwan, where Communist insurgents have posed at one time or another an active challenge to the existing political order, political elites have viewed land reform as a major instrument to combat the insurgents. In both cases, reform is perceived as a means to deter rural Communism.

Ideological commitment. In a number of cases, ideology of various persuasions has provided an impetus for the initiation of reform. In India, the agrarianism championed by Mahatma Gandhi and the socialism advocated by Jawaharlal Nehru influenced, to a certain extent, the Congress Party's attitude toward the rural issue. In Taiwan, Sun Yat-sen's *Three Principles of the People*, the ideology of the Kuomintang (the Nationalist Party, KMT), provided the intellectual basis, as well as the legislative content, for the land-to-the-tiller program. In Colombia, the advocates of reform frequently cited the theory of social function of property as a justification for land redistribution measures. In certain countries, nationalism also appears to be a motivating factor for reform. One can identify, for instance, a strong nationalistic undercurrent in Mexico's seizure of enormous foreign holdings and in India's and Pakistan's abolition of the *zamindari* system.

---

[1] In 1952, when Egypt, following a series of minor rural disturbances, introduced land reform, an observer noted, "a number of intellectuals and army officers felt the necessity to do something to forestall a deeper upheaval or a Communist revolution." In Iran, a government publication commented: "In order to halt the menace of Communism, . . . the . . . Government took the timely initiative to promulgate a far-reaching six-point programme, the most important part of which was . . . land reform." Explaining, in 1960, the background of his reform programs in West Pakistan, General Mohammad Ayub Khan emphasized the idea of making "ourselves immune from Communism." See respectively Gabriel Baer, *A History of Landownership in Modern Egypt, 1800–1950* (London, 1962), p. 211; Iran, Land Reform Organization, *Land Reform in Iran* [Tehran, 1967], p. 6; and Mohammad Ayub Khan, *Speeches and Statements*, Vol. II, *July 1959–June 1960* (Karachi, n.d.), pp. 108–109.

International climate. For a number of years the repeated endorsements of land reform by the United Nations, its specialized agencies (particularly, the Food and Agriculture Organization), world-land-reform conferences, and, lately, the Vatican, have generated such an international atmosphere that it is virtually unfashionable for a developing country to refrain from adopting some measure of reform.[2] In Latin America, with the advent of the Alliance for Progress, many years' advocacy of reform was finally transformed into a continent-wide policy. The Charter of Punta del Este declared in 1961 that the signatory nations agreed to

> . . . encourage . . . programs of the comprehensive agrarian reform . . . with a view to replacing *latifundia* [large estates] and dwarf holdings with an equitable system of land tenure so that . . . the land will become for the man who works it the basis of his economic stability, the foundation of his freedom and dignity.[3]

The meaning of this joint undertaking is twofold. On the one hand, in spite of the fact that the big landed interests were perhaps more politically powerful in Latin America than in any other region of the world, the nations on this continent now came to make a common pledge to restructure their tenure systems. On the other hand, the United States openly and unequivocally signified its intention to exert pressure on these nations to make good their pledges. Through Teodoro Moscoso, the former administrator for the Alliance, the United States declared: "We are insisting on reforms as a condition of our material support to Latin America. We would rather withhold our assistance than to participate in the maintenance of a status quo characterized by social injustice." [4] Aside from

---

[2] The United Nations first expressed its support for land reform in 1950 when the General Assembly adopted a resolution [GA 401 (V)] recommending an immediate study of the impact of defective agrarian structure on economic development. For summaries of the subsequent activities of the United Nations and other international agencies, see U.N., *Land Reform, Third Report*, pp. 91–104; and *Land Reform, Fourth Report*, pp. 167–178. One of the latest manifestations of the Vatican's interest in land reform is seen in a statement by Pope Paul VI. While attending, in August 1968, the 39th International Eucharistic Congress in Colombia, the Pope took the opportunity to address an assembly of 35,000 peasants. He denounced "unjust economic inequalities between rich and poor" and exhorted "the governments of Latin America and also those of other continents" to sustain necessary land and fiscal reforms. *The New York Times,* August 24, 1968, p. 2.

[3] Quoted in William H. MacLeish (ed.), *Land and Liberty* (New York, 1962), p. 1.

[4] Quoted in Thomas F. Carroll, "Land Reform as an Explosive Force in Latin America," in John J. Tepaske and Sidney Nettleton Fisher (eds.), *Explosive Forces in Latin America* (Columbus, Ohio, 1964), p. 112.

these multilateral efforts, the United States has unilaterally facilitated
tenurial changes by providing advice, technical assistance, and material
aid to a number of countries—notably Japan, the Philippines, South Vietnam, and Taiwan—in the formulation and execution of their programs.

Population pressure. In the developing countries, the rapid growth of
population is one compelling reason for rationalizing the pattern of land
use. In many of these countries the increase of food supply has not kept
pace with population growth, and the total demand for food has risen
even faster than the growth of population, reflecting what economists have
called high income elasticity of demand for food.[5] This imbalanced demand and supply of food often necessitates large agricultural imports, thus
consuming a sizable amount of foreign exchange earnings which might
otherwise be used to finance industrialization. In 1966, for instance, food
imports from the United States, Canada, Western Europe, and other
surplus areas to the developing countries amounted to US $4.5 billion, or
more than 40 percent of the latter's export earnings from agricultural products.[6] This situation has prompted public planning agencies and some
non-landowning, industrial and commercial interests in the developing
countries to stress, with varying degrees of enthusiasm, the economic
necessity of land reform.

The recent technological advances in agriculture, it must be especially
noted, do not appear to reduce the need for tenurial reform. In the late
1960s, the adoption by a number of countries of high-yielding seed varieties
—the most widely known of which are the Mexican dwarf wheat and the
IR–8 rice seed developed by the International Rice Research Institute in
the Philippines—together with an expanded supply of chemical fertilizers
and an increase in irrigation areas have contributed to a "miraculous" increase of food grains. Heralded as a "Green Revolution," the technological

---

[5] That is, of their increasing income the people in the developing countries tend
to spend disproportionately more on food. An FAO study estimated that the income
elasticity of demand for food of most of the developing countries ranges from 3 to 5.5
times greater than that of the countries in North America and Western Europe excluding
the European Economic Community countries. See FAO, *Agricultural Commodity Projections for 1970* (Rome: FAO, 1962), Table 12.

[6] *The New York Times*, October 12, 1967, p. 14. In certain developing countries,
to grow high priced exportable crops and to exchange them for relatively cheap foreign
food may be a sound economic policy. But for most of the developing countries, the
dependence on industrialized nations for a food supply is a patently unsound situation.
In countries where food import actually contributes to a large trade deficit, lagging
agricultural production is totally unjustifiable.

breakthrough has made it possible to double or even triple crop output in a number of Asian countries. As a consequence, some of these countries have visualized the possibility of a victory in the "War on Hunger." In 1968, the Philippines already claimed to have achieved self-sufficiency in rice, considerably reducing the need for food imports. India, Pakistan, Indonesia, and Malaysia have spoken of food self-sufficiency in the next few years.

Some believe, however, that the spread of the Green Revolution in the future may not be as fast as has been hoped. To be successful, this revolution requires a greater allocation of public funds for agriculture than is envisaged in the national economic plans, the development and strengthening of agricultural institutions, the improvement of rural services, a dramatic increase of supply of modern farm inputs, and a change from traditional to modern farming practices. It is very difficult to achieve all these adjustments within a short span of time. Consequently it is over-optimistic to expect an early solution of the food problem. In any case, the prospect of a fast-moving Green Revolution has not diminished the urgency of the need for land reform. On the contrary, it underscores the urgency of the need for changes in the traditional land tenure systems that have hindered the adoption of new agricultural technology. As an eminent agricultural specialist has observed: "The very slow spread of Mexico's success with new varieties of wheat and corn to its neighbors to the South" has been largely due to the lack of agrarian reforms in Latin American countries. "Land reform must be conducted quickly," another specialist has commented; "otherwise the uncertainties associated with any long-term investment in agriculture will discourage the new land owners from making the needed investments or even from occupying the new land." [7]

Political Elite and Political Legitimacy

In the eight countries under study, the people playing a role in the initiation of land reform possess various backgrounds. They include politicians in most of these countries; intellectuals in India; generals and colonels

[7] See Clifton R. Wharton, Jr., "The Green Revolution: Cornucopia or Pandora's Box?" *Foreign Affairs*, XLVII (April 1969), 467; and Lester R. Brown, *Seeds of Change: The Green Revolution and Development in the 1970's* (New York: Praeger Publishers, 1970), p. 113. For a similar comment on this subject by the FAO, see *The New York Times*, October 12, 1967, p. 14.

in Mexico, Pakistan, Taiwan, and Egypt; the monarch of Iran; and peasants in Mexico. As advocates of tenurial change, peasants differ from all other reform proponents in two aspects. Peasants are committed to a single issue —the acquisition of land—and regard reform as an end in itself. But, being incapable of assuming the role of the political elite, they are unable by themselves either to formulate a comprehensive, practicable program or to carry one out. In contrast, all other reform proponents have broad political goals and consider reform to be of instrumental value. Since only these proponents can assume the role of the political elite, they will determine— in accordance with their goals and interests—the timing of initiation and the content of the program to be initiated.

It is submitted, as the first hypothesis of this book, that *in initiating land reform a political elite is decisively influenced by the perceived need to gain political legitimacy, i.e. to strengthen popular support for a new political order or to safeguard an existing regime against threatened political changes. When the political elite perceives the need to gain legitimacy, the conditions likely to lead to reform will become relevant and important; when it fails to perceive such a need, the mere presence of these conditions may not lead to reform.*

From the point of view of the elite, land reform has political utilities as well as political liabilities. The political utilities are primarily two. First, the elite is well aware of the fact that the peasants, like itself, can play a variable political role. They can be participants in a revolution seeking to destroy the extant political order or a conservative force upholding the existing regime.[8] When seeking power, the elite can use land reform to radicalize the peasantry; when controlling power, the elite can use reform to heighten the conservatism of the peasantry. By such uses of reform, the elite will be able not only to establish a broad rural base but also to make the peasants an important ally if it confronts political challenges from nonpeasant forces. Second, when the elite initiates a program for the benefit of the largest group of society—the peasants—it strikes a stance in favor of the masses. Hence it may win the sympathy of the peasants as well as of all other less-endowed groups. Land reform, therefore, is both a program for economic and social change and an instrument for building up the popular image of the elite.

The political liabilities of reform emanate from the fact that it engenders the certainty of opposition from the influential landed class. In

[8] For some lucid discussions on this subject, see Samuel P. Huntington, *Political Order in Changing Societies* (New Haven, 1968), pp. 72–78 and 291–300.

countries in which the elite includes a sizable number of landlords, reform will generate dissension within the elite which may weaken its overall power position. In addition, reform may reduce the effectiveness of the landed class as a stabilizing force in the countryside, burdening the government with the necessity of dealing directly with all major and minor rural disturbances. In countries where the elite has excluded the landed class from its membership, disaffected landlords may become a rural center of opposition, fighting against the elite. In all these countries, the elites are sensitive to the danger that in initiating reform they may immediately encounter the opposition of the landed class but only slowly gain the support of the peasants. Conceivably, they may lose the loyalty of the landed class before obtaining that of the peasants.

To the elite, weighing the political utilities and liabilities of reform and arriving at a decision as to whether or when to initiate reform are delicate and difficult tasks. But it must perform these tasks. In doing so, its dominant concern is how its stand on reform will best serve its own interest, i.e. the right to continue to rule. If, from this point of view, the elite perceives the balance of utilities and liabilities to be in favor of reform, it will initiate reform, emphasizing to the public its devotion to the peasant welfare as a major motivating factor. If, on the other hand, the elite perceives the balance to be against reform, it will not bring about a program, all justifications for reform and even its professed sympathy with the peasants notwithstanding.

To Strengthen New Political Orders

It appears that in introducing their respective reforms, the elites of Mexico, Egypt, India, and Pakistan aimed at eliciting peasant support for new political orders.

MEXICO: REVOLUTION, MILITARY NECESSITY, AND 1915 DECREE

The Mexican revolution of 1910 broke out against a background of a thirty-year authoritarian rule by President Porfirio Díaz and of an accelerating process of land accumulation. A protracted and violent upheaval, this revolution included various groups of participants: politicians, intellectuals, generals, and—for the first time in the chronicle of contemporary revolutions—peasants. Initially the revolution was "largely a blind, blundering, haphazard spontaneous outbreak" without a political philosophy or a social program.[9] Francisco I. Madero, a scion of a wealthy family in northern Mexico, sparked the upheaval with the publication of his book, *The Presidential Succession of 1910*. To launch an "Effective Suffrage, No Re-election" campaign against Díaz, "the Apostle of the Revolution," as Madero was known, sought primarily to replace the old authoritarian regime with a liberal one of his own. In his major pronouncement *Plan de San Luis Potosí* of October 5, 1910, he made only a bland observation on the land issue. He declared:

> Through abuse of the law regarding the public domain, numerous small proprietors, principally Indians, have been deprived of their lands, either by acts of the Minister of *Fomento* or decisions of the courts. Since justice demands the restitution to their owners of lands thus arbitrarily taken, such acts and decisions are hereby declared subject to revision; and those who acquired property in so immoral a manner, or their heirs, will be required to restore the same to its previous owners, whom they will also indemnify for the injury suffered.[10]

Madero's advocacy of the resolution of the land problem incited the peasants and unleashed a violent force that immediately set the country in flame. Emiliano Zapata rose in rebellion in the southern State of Morelos, and Pancho Villa in the northern State of Chihuahua. The former insisted on the restitution of the usurped Indian lands, while the latter demanded the breaking-up of large estates. Both supported Madero and fought to bring down the Díaz regime. But when Madero became President in 1911, he was hesitant to proceed with the promised land reform. Apparently misreading the sentiment of the day, Madero believed that "the people do not demand bread; they demand liberty." [11] His failure to act on the land issue prompted Zapata to revolt against him. Adopting a "Land and Liberty" slogan, and proposing in 1911 a reform program in his own *Plan de Ayala*, the peasant leader declared to the nation:

> Let Señor Madero—and with him all the world—know that we shall not lay down our arms until the *ejidos* of our villages are restored

[9] Eyler N. Simpson, *The Ejido, Mexico's Way Out* (Chapel Hill, N.C., 1937), p. 46.

[10] Quoted in Helen Phipps, *Some Aspects of the Agrarian Question in Mexico* (Austin, Texas, 1925), p. 133.

[11] Quoted in Simpson, *op. cit.*, p. 48.

to us, until we are given back the lands which the *hacendados* stole from us during the dictatorship of Porfirio Díaz, when justice was subjected to his caprice. We shall not lay down our arms until we cease to be unhappy tributaries of the despotic magnates and land-holders of Morelos.[12]

He urged immediate return of the usurped lands and expropriation of one-third of large estates for redistribution among small farmers.[13]

Ironically it was not Madero, who was in fact sympathetic with the peasant cause, but Venustiano Carranza—who had less interest in the land issue—who proclaimed the first land-reform decree. As a factional leader fighting for power,[14] Carranza had first hoped to gain legitimacy for his cause by raising the issue of *constitucionismo* when General Victoriano Huerta forced Madero out of the presidency in 1913. In the *Plan de Guadalupe* of March 26, 1913, Carranza declared his revolt against Huerta, demanding the restoration of constitutional government. His declaration contained not a single reference to the economic and social issues of the day. Absorbed in the fighting, he had first ignored the idea of land re-distribution, recommended by Pancho Villa and General Alvaro Obregón, both of whom were then supporting the constitutionalist cause.[15] In fact Carranza once emphatically disapproved the measures of land redistribu-tion in the Villa-controlled area. He told Villa's representative in 1913: "Not only am I in disagreement with the distribution of land to the people, but tell General Villa he must return to the owners lands which had been distributed. . . ."[16] But when subsequently confronted with serious military challenges of the Zapata and Villa forces, and when ac-tually forced out of Mexico City after he had first taken over the govern-ment, he issued the January 6, 1915 decree laying down the foundation for

[12] Quoted in Phipps, *op. cit.*, p. 137.

[13] For the full text of *Plan de Ayala*, see John Womack, Jr., *Zapata and the Mexican Revolution* (New York: Alfred A. Knopf, 1969), pp. 400–404.

[14] Carranza was Governor of Coahuila in 1910 and a former Senator in the Díaz regime.

[15] In a joint statement dated September 21, 1913, Villa and Obregón expressed the belief that as the *Plan de Guadalupe* failed to "specify what reforms shall be taken up, there is [a] danger that the agrarian question, which may be called the soul of the revo-lution, may be relegated to a secondary position, . . ." It was necessary now, they sug-gested, to give priority to "the passing of measures which shall forthwith result in the division of lands. . . ." Quoted in Frank Tannenbaum, *The Mexican Agrarian Revolu-tion* (New York, 1929), pp. 166–167.

[16] Quoted in William Weber Johnson, *Heroic Mexico, the Violent Emergence of a Modern Nation* (New York: Doubleday & Co., 1968), p. 173.

future land reform.[17] He took this action to steal the issue of agrarianism from his opponents; at the same time General Obregón negotiated an agreement with the labor unions to obtain the workers' support.[18] In 1917, after defeating Villa and subduing Zapata, Carranza became President of the Republic.

The 1915 decree provided for the restitution of land usurped by *hacendados* and land-survey companies, and expropriation of other large holdings for redistribution. Two years later, the decree was written into Article 27 of the Constitution, committing future political leaders to its implementation. In retrospect, the historical significance of the decree was twofold. It "was more nearly than anything else *the* crucial commitment on which the new political leadership rose to power." [19] And it provided social content to what had until then been only a political movement.

EGYPT: REVOLUTION, POLITICAL ISOLATION, AND 1952 DECREE

Like its Mexican counterpart, the Egyptian revolution in the beginning was innocent of either political ideology or doctrinal guidance. The coup of July 23, 1952, was a violent expression by the "Free Officers" of the cumulative dissatisfaction with the existing state of affairs: prolonged foreign domination; military defeat in the Arab-Israeli war of 1948 to 1949; and political instability, corruption, and incompetence. In the face of these conditions, these young officers sought primarily a change of regime without long-range economic and social programs.

After deposing the Farouk regime, the Free Officers found themselves politically isolated and uncertain of their own future role. They constituted then a very thin group with neither an established image nor any significant share of power within the military hierarchy. The Revolutionary Command Council (RCC) that presided over the national upheaval contained eleven members, with an average age of thirty-three.[20]

[17] Thus wrote Eyler N. Simpson: "Carranza, with Villa attacking from the north and Zapata from the south, was in dire straits. His only hope was to find some way to crystallize revolutionary sentiment in his own behalf. Out of this necessity was born the decree of 1915." *Op. cit.*, p. 61. Cf. Tannenbaum, *op. cit.*

[18] For the text of the agreement Obregón negotiated with labor union leaders, see Tannenbaum, *ibid.*, pp. 168–170.

[19] James G. Maddox, "Mexican Land Reform," *American Universities Field Staff, Reports Service*, Vol. 4, No. 5 (July 3, 1957), 10.

[20] Georgiana G. Stevens, *Egypt, Yesterday and Today* (New York: Holt, Rinehart & Winston, 1963), p. 112.

The only man in the council with some national reputation was General Mohammed Naguib, and primarily for that reason he was chosen to head the RCC. On the political scene the RCC could not immediately identify with any major political group or social force. The traditional Wafd Party was discredited and inert, and was formally dissolved in January 1953. The Muslim Brotherhood, a religious fanatic group, which preferred an exclusive hold of power to sharing it with the military, stayed out of the political arena. The Communists went underground; the left-leaning intellectuals were impotent and unable to agree on any action or program among themselves. The masses were ignorant and unconcerned.[21] The political vacuum was complete. Unsure of their political competence, the Free Officers had originally expected to play the role of, in Gamal Abdel Nasser's words, "commando vanguard" to storm "the walls of the fort of tyranny."[22] They were in favor of a civilian reformist government to carry out the responsibility for post-revolution national reconstruction. Thus they installed civilian Ali Maher as prime minister and left the traditional bureaucracy largely intact. But as the Maher administration failed to proceed promptly with political and social reforms and eradicate foreign dominance, the Free Officers were soon confronted with two alternatives: either to return the government completely to the civilians, thereby facing the prospect of dissipating the momentum of the revolution, or to assume full rule of the nation and effectuate a total military regime.

When the RCC finally decided in September 1952 to move into the ministries, the issue of land reform assumed critical importance. As General Naguib recalled afterwards, among all issues the RCC then confronted, "the most important of all, by far, are the agrarian reforms on which the success or failure of the Egyptian Revolution will depend."[23] Signifying the importance it attached to land reform, the military regime proclaimed on September 9, 1952, in its very first decree, the redistribution of land. The issuance of this decree was clearly intended to break the isolation in which the regime found itself and to consolidate its power. "Agrarian reform," one author has commented, "was a potent psychological measure. It gave

---

[21] For an account of the shock and dismay with which the Free Officers reacted toward the public apathy and idleness in the period immediately following the revolution, see Gamal Abdel Nasser, *The Philosophy of the Revolution* (Buffalo, N.Y.: Smith, Keynes, & Marshall, Publishers, 1959), pp. 32–34.

[22] *Ibid.*, p. 32.

[23] Mohammed Naguib and Leigh White, *Egypt's Destiny* (New York: Doubleday & Co., 1955), p. 157. Cf. Doreen Warriner, *Land Reform and Development in the Middle East* (London, 1962), p. 12.

the Free Officers their first political link with the peasant masses." [24]
Concurred another, "This first decree by the junta set the tone of its
regime and raised the hopes of Egypt's people for a new and better life.
No other measure would have had the same general appeal." [25]

When the RCC adopted the 1952 decree, it should be noted, the
army regime did not face a peasant demand for tenurial changes. Sporadic
rural violence before the revolution had been known: for example, in
1951 a number of isolated instances of tenant revolts on private estates and
squatter uprisings in the public domain did take place. But the scale
and intensity of rural violence were limited.[26] After the Egyptian revolution occurred, the *fellahin* (peasants) neither joined the movement nor
staged spontaneous uprisings to push land redistribution, as Mexican
campesinos had done forty years earlier. It should also be noted that
though the traditional tenure system was defective, the Egyptian farms
were endowed with exceptionally fertile soil and a well-managed irrigation system, hence were highly productive. To change the tenure system to
increase output was an argument inapplicable to the Egyptian case. The
absence of serious peasant pressure for reform and the existence of productive farms make it evident that the Free Officers introduced reform mainly
out of their own needs. They took this initiative because, after appraising
the political conditions of the times, they regarded reform an act ad-
vantageous to the young army regime. With predominantly middle-class
backgrounds, these officers felt no internal restraints in acting against the
landed gentry; at the same time they could design a program which
sacrificed no interests of their own but was bound to be popular with the
masses and even with certain latent political groupings.[27] Thus, whereas
in Mexico, Carranza issued the 1915 decree out of a military necessity, in
Egypt, the Free Officers promulgated the 1952 decree as an act of political
prudence. The circumstances under which the two decrees were issued

[24] Panayiotis J. Vatikiotis, *The Egyptian Army in Politics: Pattern for New Nations?*
(Bloomington: Indiana University Press, 1961), p. 75.

[25] Stevens, *op. cit.*, p. 110.

[26] See Warriner, *op. cit.*; and Gabriel Baer, "Egyptian Attitudes toward Land Reform, 1922–1955," in Walter Z. Laquer (ed.), *The Middle East in Transition: Studies
in Contemporary History* (New York: Frederick A. Praeger, Publishers, 1958), p. 84–
85 and 97–98.

[27] The Muslim Brotherhood, Misr al-Fatāt (at the time a nationalistic group), and
the Communists, all of whom were out of the political scene, were known to favor some
measures of land reform. Baer, *op. cit.*, pp. 92–94.

were markedly different, but the purpose was identical, to legitimize the new government.

After the issuance of 1952 decree, the Egyptian army regime took a step to sanctify the reform, a step identical to that which the Carranza government had taken several decades earlier. The regime reaffirmed the 1952 decree in the 1956 Egyptian constitution. To provide ideological coloration to the events of 1952, Nasser was to expound several years later the idea that the Free Officers had conceived the revolution of 1952 as a two-front movement, a political one to topple the monarchy and a social one to promote justice for all. Symbolic of the union of the two fronts was a reform program that was initially aimed at the enormous land-holdings of the royal family. Nasser declared: "The day we marched along the path of political revolution and dethroned Farouk we took a similar step along the path of social revolution by limiting the ownership of agricultural land." [28]

INDIA: INDEPENDENCE MOVEMENT AND THE CONGRESS REFORMS

If in Mexico and Egypt revolution furnished the principal impetus for land reform, in India the independence movement was the driving force behind a long struggle for tenurial changes. In leading the independence movement, the Indian National Congress had first ignored the land issue, but it gradually found the union of the large landed class with the British administration a compelling reason for its identification with the *kisans* (peasants). Out of this polarization of political forces, the Indian National Congress's orientation to reform was born.

The union of the landlords with the British was a matter of long duration, stemming from the administrative and political necessities of the colonial government. The introduction of the *zamindari* system under the Permanent Settlement Act of 1793 assured the British administration of the regular collection of land revenue while dispensing with the need for maintaining a large complement of revenue officials. At the same time in playing their dual role as revenue collectors and landlords, the *zamindars* were kept permanently tied to the administration. This identification of interests was reinforced subsequently, as India experienced sporadic rural unrest. In the nineteenth century, particularly after the 1857 Mutiny in which many *kisans* participated, the British began to feel the need for

[28] Nasser, *op. cit.*, pp. 36ff. Quotation appears on pp. 38 and 40. Cf. Warriner, *op. cit.*, p. 14.

strengthening their control of the countryside through their landed allies.[29] A few years after the First World War, a number of mishaps, including famine, epidemic, and falling agricultural production, together with war-wrought economic dislocation, greatly disturbed the countryside. Now, with the rural situation almost assuming "the appearance of a revolutionary upsurge . . . the government turned to the landed aristocracy . . . to provide the basis for an anti-revolutionary front." [30]

In the meantime, the Indian National Congress gradually discovered that the *kisans* possessed a revolutionary propensity highly valuable to its independence drive. Created in 1885, the Congress Party (as the Indian National Congress was subsequently known) was originally composed of a small group of intellectuals who initially took no defined position on the agrarian issue. Not until the 1920s when the party sought to convert itself into a massive independence movement did it take an interest in the *kisans*. As Jawaharlal Nehru told his colleagues in 1928, the Congress Party consisted then of "largely the intelligentsia of this country only. We represent, directly at any rate, the two or three or five percent [of the country's population]." [31] The party soon became aware that it would be utopian to think of overthrowing the British raj "if the peasantry, which represented the overwhelming majority of the population of the country, had not been won over by the national movement and taken active part in it." [32]

The principal instrument that sealed the union of the party and the *kisans* was the *satyagraha* (non-violent civil disobedience) movement. In the late 1910s and early 1920s, the agitated *kisans*, long dissatisfied with their plight, began to organize themselves in various parts of the country into *kisan sabhas* (peasant leagues) in preparation for a struggle against the landed interests. Seizing the opportunity, the Congress immediately sought to unite this social struggle with the political movement it was leading. In 1918, *kisan* delegates were invited for the first time to attend the party's annual session in Delhi; in 1920, the Oudh *kisan sabha* in the United Provinces became the first peasant organization endorsing the Congress's civil disobedience movement.[33] Hailing the *kisans* as the

---

[29] See Thomas R. Metcalf, "The Struggle over Land Tenure in India, 1860–1868," *The Journal of Asian Studies*, XXI (May 1962), 295–307.

[30] Peter Reeves, "The Politics of Order, 'Anti-Non-Cooperation' in the United Provinces, 1921," *The Journal of Asian Studies*, XXV (February 1966), 261.

[31] Quoted in H. D. Malaviya, *Land Reforms in India* (New Delhi: All India Congress Committee, 1954), p. 18.

[32] *Ibid.*, p. 22.

[33] *Ibid.*, p. 4; and Reeves, *op. cit.*, p. 263.

"bulwark of the nationalist movement," [34] the Congress began to propose a series of reform programs. Mild in content initially, these programs became progressively more radical as Congress increasingly felt the necessity for broadening rural support for its independence drive. The party first merely suggested a reduction of rent; in 1930 it launched a no-rent campaign in the United Provinces; and then in 1935 it mounted a frontal assault on the most powerful, the longest established rural institution: the *zamindari* system. In that year it adopted a resolution at the *Kisan* Conference in Allahabad urging the abolition of the system that "was introduced with the advent of the British Government and [that] has led to the absolute destruction of village life." [35] Unrelenting in its effort to enlist *kisan* support, the Congress adopted in 1936 an "Agrarian Programme" at Faizpur, which included, among other things, reduction of rent, fixity of tenure, and collective farming. This was a program that set forth the basic principles of Congress's agrarian policy for the post-independence period.[36] Through these promises, the party was able to bring the *kisans* into its expanded organizational network and to strengthen the *satyagraha* movement. In turn, the massive identification by the peasantry with the nationalist movement obliged the party to carry out its promises on reform when the first opportunity arrived. As the *zamindars* were allied with the British administration, it was only natural for Congress to proceed immediately with a program for the abolition of the *zamindari* system when independence came. Following the adoption of this program, the Congress then began to initiate other reform programs.

PAKISTAN: NATION-BUILDING AND REFORMS OF 1950 AND 1959

In a sense, the elites of India and East Pakistan had a similar motivation for reform. In both cases, it was to uphold the nationalist sentiment that agrarian changes were made; and it was the *zamindari* system that became the foremost target of attack. The Indian leaders abolished the system because it was a British-sponsored institution. The East Pakistani

---

[34] Reeves, *ibid.*

[35] Malaviya, *op. cit.*, p. 59. Attacking the landed interests, Nehru said: "The *taluqdars* [landlords] and big *zamindars* . . . had been the spoilt child of the British Government. . . . [They] aligned themselves completely with the [British] Government, preferring their class interest to national freedom." Quoted in *ibid.*, pp. 6 and 55.

[36] The Allahabad Resolution and the Faizpur Agrarian Programme of 1936 were subsequently reaffirmed by the Congress Party in various public announcements and documents, including the Congress Election Manifestos of 1936 and 1946. See *ibid.*, pp. 65–88.

leaders had more reasons to reject the system: it was a British-sponsored institution, as well as one dominated by an alien minority, the Hindus. Besides, during British rule the system had its worst effects in heavily populated Bengal, a substantial portion of which went to East Pakistan after the partition. In 1940, even the British-controlled Bengal Land Revenue Commission conceded that one of the "most serious defects" of the system was the growth of a "fantastic proportion" (or number) of intermediaries between the government revenue office and the farmers. The commission recommended the elimination of the intermediary in- terests, "bringing the actual cultivators into the position of tenants hold- ing land directly under Government." [37] As independence came, the presence of the Hindu-dominated *zamindari* system in a Muslim nation became all the more intolerable for the East Pakistanis. Thus, following the 1947 partition of India and Pakistan, in the midst of chaos, killings, and massive forced exchanges of Hindus and Muslims, the peasants in East Pakistan seized farms from the fleeing Hindu landowners and de- stroyed the records of land titles.[38] As the Pakistani Planning Commission has put it, in a deliberately mild tone: "Most of the Hindu Zamindars who generally held . . . lands in large quantities left Pakistan after Independ- ence." [39] It is against this background of forceful land transfers that the new East Pakistani government enacted a reform law: the East Bengal State Land Acquisition and Tenancy Act of 1950. This act, in essence, was more of a law to sanction an established reality rather than a program seeking a planned change. The law "provided the opportunity for the Muslim majority to free itself from the economic control of the Hindu

[37] Report of the Bengal Land Revenue Commission, headed by Sir Francis Flood. Cited in Elliot Tepper, "Changing Patterns of Administration in Rural East Pakistan" (East Lansing: Michigan State University, Asian Studies Center, Occasional Paper, No. 5, 1966), pp. 8–9.

[38] "The million of refugees [from Pakistan and India] who crossed the border of the new states left behind land and buildings and commercial and industrial property. Often a whole village or section of a town was abandoned and left unprotected. . . . In many instances the original owners died and documentary titles as well as records of loans and mortgages were incomplete or missing." Keith B. Callard, *Pakistan: A Political Study* (London: Allen & Unwin, 1957), p. 17. Cf. Herbert Feldman, *Pakistan: An Introduction* (Karachi: Oxford University Press, 1960), p. 8; and Hugh Tinker, *India and Pakistan: A Political Analysis* (New York: Frederick A. Praeger, Publishers, 1962), p. 69.

[39] Pakistan, Planning Commission, *Papers Pertaining to Preparation of Second Five Year Plan in the Agricultural Sector*, Vol. III, *Land Reform and Colonization* (Karachi: Government of Pakistan Press, 1962), p. 63.

minority";[40] as such, it helped strengthen the identity of a freshly born and geographically separated nation and bolster the confidence of the masses in the newly established government.[41]

The conditions under which reform was brought about in West Pakistan were different. Here the reform program was largely derived from the idea of one man, Field Marshal Mohammad Ayub Khan; and the program was not to legalize an accomplished fact but to initiate changes. However, the purpose of reform was quite similar: to broaden the base of the government and to consolidate the nation. In 1954, in a statement entitled "A Short Appreciation of Present and Future Problems of Pakistan," the then Defense Minister Ayub Khan stated his belief in reform:

> Nothing much will be gained unless we carry out land reform in a scientific fashion. Possession of vast areas of land by a few is no longer defensible nor is acquisition of land without compensation. The Egyptian example is a very good one; they allowed the owner a certain limit of holding, buying the rest for distribution among peasants, who will pay the cost in seventy [sic] yearly instalments.[42]

The principal cause for the military to intervene in politics was, of course, not related to the land issue. Like the colonels of Egypt in 1952, General Ayub Khan of Pakistan launched a coup in October 1958 mainly because of his disillusionment with the political conditions of the country. In the eleven years following its independence in 1947, Pakistan was plagued with excessive government instability, political assassinations, corruption, and serious partisan disputes. "To save the country from disintegration and total ruination," Ayub Khan seized power, abrogated the constitution, dissolved the legislative assemblies, and declared martial law throughout the country.[43]

[40] William Bredo, "Land Reform and Development in Pakistan," in Walter Froehlich (ed.), *Land Tenure, Industrialization and Social Stability* (Milwaukee, 1961), p. 263.

[41] Referring to this point, Callard has commented: "The idea that a country has a foreign 'enemy' is easy for the mass of the people to understand, and it also provides a powerful stimulus to national unity. For Pakistan, India has filled this role." *Op. cit.*, p. 17.

[42] The text of the entire statement appears in Karl von Vorys, *Political Development in Pakistan* (Princeton, N.J.: Princeton University Press, 1965), pp. 299–306. Quotation appears on p. 304.

[43] See Mushtaq Ahmad, *Government and Politics in Pakistan* (2nd ed.; Karachi: Pakistan Publishing House, 1963), pp. 190–191.

The assumption of power by the Pakistani army posed problems quite similar to those which the Egyptian Free Officers had faced. Without the training, experience, and skill necessary for operating the government, how could the army expect to operate the administrative machinery at a level of efficiency that would justify its abrogation of civilian authority? Then there was the problem of image. Though Ayub Khan was a much better known personality in Pakistan in 1958 than the Free Officers were in Egypt in 1952, he and his military colleagues still needed to replace their image as experienced professional soldiers with a new identity as dedicated political leaders. The Pakistani and Egyptian responses to these problems were again alike. Ayub Khan assumed the supreme authority of the government, purged the traditional politicians, and left the civil servants largely undisturbed. To the junior military officers, the retention of authority—though curtailed—by the bureaucracy under the army regime was an unsatisfactory arrangement. As Ayub Khan recalled afterwards, in the first months after the coup "there was a feeling in the army that things were not moving fast enough; that civilians were not reacting as quickly as they should and people were beginning to feel frustrated." [44] Aware of the disaffection in the army and of the need to retain the confidence of the public, Ayub Khan commented: "My first anxiety [then] was to introduce land reforms and to settle the refugee problem." [45] Thus, in October 1958 he established a Land Reforms Commission as his first reform agency, and in January 1959 he proclaimed, through a martial-law decree, a land-reform program which was to be the first major political act of the new government. Together with other reform measures—mainly in education, administration, and finance—this decree proved useful in enlisting popular support for the army regime. "The first years of the revolution were," Ayub wrote in 1967, "in many ways, the most rewarding years. The régime enjoyed widespread public support. . . . Every measure we took evoked immediate response. I took full advantage of the situation and introduced my full programme of reforms without losing time." [46]

To Safeguard the Existing Regimes

If the elites discussed thus far sought through land reform to strengthen a new political order, the elites in Colombia, Iran, the Philip-

---

[44] Mohammad Ayub Khan, *Friends Not Masters, a Political Autobiography* (London: Oxford University Press, 1967), p. 78.

[45] *Ibid.*, p. 79.

[46] *Ibid.*, p. 81.

pines, and Taiwan initiated reform primarily to safeguard the existing regimes against threatened political changes.

COLOMBIA: RURAL VIOLENCE, CIVIL STRIFE, AND REFORM

A country with a prolonged background of rural violence, Colombia has since its independence repeatedly experienced serious crises of political legitimacy.[47] The first most devastating civil strife occurred in 1899 to 1902, when the War of the Thousand Days claimed 100,000 lives.[48] This war, one of a series of deadly conflicts between the Conservative and Liberal Parties, was not fought over social issues, much less over tenure problems. But it did involve the rural populace in the fighting, setting a precedent of massive peasant participation in political conflicts. Understandably, when in the 1920s and 1930s rural unrest recurred in Colombia, the ruling Liberal government viewed the matter with the utmost concern.

The recurrent unrest stemmed from a convergence of two problems: the disputes between *colons* (squatters) with landowners over land titles, and the discontent of sharecroppers with their relation to *hacendados*. The title problem was of long standing. Originally the Spanish Crown and subsequently the Colombian government "granted indeterminant and often overlapping titles to huge holdings of land."[49] The lack of a cadastral survey, the inadequacy of land records, and the absence of demarcation between the public domain and certain private properties all compounded the problem. Under the circumstances, landless *colons* frequently moved into idle land in both public and private domains, developed it into an agricultural area, and sought permanent occupation of it.[50] Abetted by the economic depression of the 1930s, this practice of

---

[47] "On a scale of political deaths per generation, Colombia has one of the highest levels of conflict in the world. In nearly 150 years since independence the country has been racked by ten national civil wars: 1830–31, 1839–41, 1851, 1854, 1860–61, 1876, 1885, 1899–1902, and the covert guerrilla war of 1949–53." James L. Payne, *Patterns of Conflict in Colombia* (New Haven: Yale University Press, 1968), p. 4. To these wars one can add *la Violencia* of 1948–1958.

[48] Robert H. Dix, *Colombia: The Political Dimensions of Change* (New Haven: Yale University Press, 1967), pp. 77ff; and Pat M. Holt, *Colombia Today—and Tomorrow* (New York, 1964), p. 30.

[49] For a brief description of the causes and evolution of the title problem, see Joseph R. Thome, "Title Problems in Rural Areas of Colombia: a Colonization Example," *Inter-American Economic Affairs*, XIX (Winter 1965), 82–84. Quotation appears on pp. 83–84.

[50] There were instances in which landowners knowingly let *colons* occupy their uncultivated land without protest or warning, but when the latter, believing that the land belonged to the public, had fully developed it, the owners presented their claim in court

land invasion was so prevalent that it became known as Colombia's *problema social.* While *colons* invaded land, many sharecroppers challenged their *hacendados'* ownership of land and refused to pay rent. Other small *campesinos* also demanded that they be allowed to grow coffee, a crop hitherto monopolized by large planters.

These "mutinous" practices in the countryside brought strong reactions from the big landowners. They enlisted police help or organized private bands of *fieles* (faithfuls) to eject *colons* and to punish recalcitrant *campesinos* who refused rent payment or attempted to grow coffee. Some *campesinos* yielded to this pressure; others engaged in isolated physical clashes with the *hacendados;* still others banded themselves together to fight for their rights.[51] Taking advantage of the situation, the *Partido Comunista de Colombia* (PCC, the Communist Party of Colombia) immediately launched a drive to organize the disaffected *campesinos.* Concentrating their activities mainly in the Andes mountains along the southern part of the *cordillera oriental* (the eastern range), the Communists soon established their rural bases in the departments of Cundinamarca, Tolima, Huila, Caquetá, and Meta. They helped form "peasant leagues" (*ligas de campesinos*) and "self-defense" organizations to fight off the *hacendados.* In the Viotá area, they set up "the Republic of Tequendama," allegedly with their "own system of justice, . . . own militia, and . . . own tax-collection procedures." [52]

The increasingly anarchical conditions in the countryside troubled not just the large landowners but the government as well.[53] With a tradition of massive violence, and now with the Communist threat, Colombia's failure to act on the land issue could conceivably result in an intensification of violence, endangering the precarious political stability that had been maintained since the last civil war. Reacting to this situation, Liberal

---

or directly forced out the *colons.* See T. Lynn Smith, *Colombia: Social Structure and the Process of Development* (Gainesville: University of Florida Press, 1967), pp. 84–85.

[51] For a concise description of the rural discontent of the time, see Albert O. Hirschman, *Journeys Toward Progress* (New York, 1963), pp. 101–107.

[52] Dix, *op. cit.,* p. 274.

[53] In 1929, a circular letter of the Minister of Labor contained the following passage: "The idea is prevalent among the hacienda owners that the Government must give them police protection for the solution of the [land] problem. It is clear that above all the danger of revolt must be avoided. . . . But it is also necessary that the landowners become convinced that this is not the solution of the problem, for, as we believe to have shown, the communist propaganda is not the only cause of the malaise whose existence nobody can any longer deny." Quoted in Hirschman, *op. cit.,* p. 106.

President Alfonso López Pumarejo put forward a reform proposal to defuse the explosive rural situation and to identify the masses with his government. To justify his reform, López first advocated in a message to Congress in 1935 his concept of the social function of property.

> The security of the hired laborer should be of no less concern to the State than security for private property, because both are social functions which cannot be left with excessive liberty, without the risk that they be caught up in anarchical movements, . . . My Government serves notice that . . . [it would not forcefully eject] the *colono* who in good faith has invaded uncultivated lands in the belief that they were *baldíos* [in the public domain]. . . . Property should be safeguarded in its use—not in its abuse—so that it will fulfill its social and economic function.[54]

In the following year López secured the passage of an amendment to the Colombian Constitution to incorporate this theory. "Property is a social function that implies obligations," Article 30 of the amended Constitution declared. The Article authorized the government to expropriate and, if necessary, to confiscate private land. Having thus laid down the legal foundation of his reform, he introduced the Land Law of 1936 (Law 200) which provided for, among other things, a presumption of landownership on the basis of actual economic utilization, restrictions on eviction of squatters, and reversion of private land to the public domain after the owners failed to use it for ten consecutive years.[55]

Never effectively implemented, Law 200 reduced peasant discontent to a certain extent but did not basically resolve the tenure problems. In 1948, with the potential of rural violence remaining high, Colombia entered a decade of dreadful civil conflict in which 200,000 lives were conservatively estimated to have been lost.[56] Ignited by the assassination of the Liberal Party leader Jorge Eliecer Gaitán in Bogotá on April 9 of that year, the explosive conflict between the Conservatives and Liberals—

---

[54] Alfonso López, "*Latifundismo* and the Need for Agrarian Reform in Colombia," in T. Lynn Smith (ed.), *Agrarian Reform in Latin America* (New York: Alfred A. Knopf, 1965), 86–87.

[55] For a digest of the law, see Appendix I.

[56] A government source estimated in 1958 that some 280,000 people had died "in the past dozen years." *The New York Times*, August 21, 1958, p. 3. Another source listed the monthly death toll as 367.5 in 1958 and 177.2 in 1959. See John D. Martz, *Colombia, a Contemporary Political Survey* (Chapel Hill: The University of North Carolina Press, 1962), p. 320.

known as *la Violencia*—soon engulfed the whole nation. Acts of rampage and wanton killing permeated the countryside. Not until the late 1950s did this national carnage gradually subside. The occurrence of this most destructive Colombian civil war once again signified a profound lack of confidence by the Conservatives and Liberals in their own political system and demonstrated to the Colombian people at large the dismal and repeated failure of the government to provide a peaceful alternative to massive violence as a means of political change.

In the face of such a crisis of legitimacy, the Conservatives and Liberals sought strenuously to re-establish the shattered political order. Through a series of negotiations and agreements they created the National Front which assured the two parties of a monopolization of political power and an equal sharing of governmental positions.[57] With these arrangements, they hoped to perpetuate the biparty system without encountering either a recurrence of interparty warfare or a serious challenge from radical forces. This was a difficult task, for conditions in the countryside were still unsettling.

> In mid–1960, renewed concern over possible peasant movements arose. . . . There were scattered reports about land invasions. In March the widely read weekly *Semana* had carried a special report on "El incendio agrario" (the agrarian blaze) with detailed data about the numerous rural conflicts.[58]

Added to this renewed concern over peasant unrest was again a fear of the Communist threat. With the "independent republics" still operating in the Andes, Communists running on the ticket of the *Movimiento Revolucionario Liberal* (MRL, the Liberal Revolutionary Movement), a left-wing faction of the Liberal Party, "achieved the election of a few of its members to office in 1958. . . ."[59] Then in 1959, the Cuban revolution occurred which demonstrated to Latin American Communists the

---

[57] The Pact of Benidorm of 1956 and the Sitges Agreement of 1957, negotiated by the leaders of the two parties and subsequently approved by a national plebiscite in 1957, established for a fixed period of time, 1958–1974 (originally ending in 1970), the *Frente de Transformación Nacional* or the National Front. Two principles guide the operation of the Front: *alteración* and *paridad*. According to the *alteración* principle, the two parties rotate in nominating presidential candidates to be supported in election by both parties. According to the *paridad* principle, the two parties are allocated equal shares of seats in all legislatures, national and departmental. Candidates contending for public offices must be identified with either of the two parties.

[58] Hirschman, *op. cit.*, p. 142.

[59] Dix, *op. cit.*, p. 273.

possibility of acquiring political power through a rural guerrilla movement, a possibility that enchanted some leftists in Colombia and aroused the fear of the National Front.

These developments soon convinced the National Front leadership of the urgent need to pacify the countryside. In 1959, Alberto Lleras Camargo, the first Liberal president under the National Front system, proposed a land-reform bill. In the following year, after Congress twice rejected the Lleras proposal, Conservative Senator Diego Tovar Concha declared: "I do not wish to be a prophet of doom: but if the next Congress fails to produce an Agrarian Reform, revolution will be inevitable." [60] Eugenio Colorado, a Catholic trade union leader, concurred: "The Agrarian Reform must take place anyway, for the people have been realizing the need to break up the present structure of land property and if this need is not satisfied by legal means, a revolutionary movement is likely to do so." [61] Agreeing with these assessments, and undaunted by the earlier legislative defeats, President Lleras appointed on August 31, 1960, a National Agrarian Committee to propose a new reform law. Representing a broad spectrum of interests, and headed by the then Liberal Party leader Carlos Lleras Restrepo, the committee worked out a reform proposal in 1961 which, under the effective legislative leadership of Lleras Restrepo, eventually became the Social Agrarian Reform Law of 1961 (Law 135).

The enactment of this law, it is pertinent to point out, was not due exclusively to the need to pacify the countryside. Two other considerations were relevant. First, some members of the elite and certain influential social groups stressed the economic necessity for reform. As Hirschman has put it:

> Economic policymakers facing inflationary pressures and balance-of-payment deficits cannot help noticing that low agricultural production and productivity share in the blame for both these recurrent difficulties. At the same time, . . . industrialists and even the progressive farm owners and operators cannot always be counted on to stand up in public for their backward, semi-feudal brethren, . . .[62]

Second, in adopting Law 135, the elite of Colombia was in a way influenced by foreign pressure in favor of reform. During *la Violencia*, for instance, two survey missions of the International Bank for Recon-

---

[60] Quoted in Hirschman, *op. cit.*
[61] Quoted in *ibid.*, p. 143.
[62] *Ibid.*, pp. 155–156.

struction and Development recommended a basic change in the pattern of land use.[63] The first mission, headed by Lauchlin Currie, urged in its report of 1950 the adoption of a regressive land tax system to penalize underutilization of land. The aim was to "let the peasants laboring on the slopes take over the fertile lands of the valleys and [to] drive the cattle to graze in the hills." [64] The second mission in 1956 suggested a slightly different approach. In order to stimulate cultivation of idle lands, the mission proposed that a tax assessment of land be made on the basis of the "optimal potential use which the quality and location of the land warrants, not on the land's current use." [65] Because of the lack of an adequate cadastral survey and of the enormous administrative and technical difficulties involved in the implementation of these two proposals, Colombia adopted neither of them.

Though not accepted by Colombia, the World Bank proposals helped stimulate debate and discussion within the country on alternative approaches. And a number of other international agencies, for instance, the United Nations Economic Commission for Latin America, an *ad hoc* committee of the Organization of American States, and the FAO all provided advice and assistance to Colombia in the formulation of agrarian policy. In addition to these international organizations, the United States exercised some parallel influence. In September 1960, it signed with Latin American nations the Act of Bogotá recommending "the initiation or acceleration of appropriate programs to modernize and improve the existing legal and institutional framework to ensure better conditions of land tenure. . . ." [66] In August 1961, it reiterated this recommendation in the Charter of Punta del Este and tied its willingness to provide aid to the commitment of the recipient countries to implement tenurial changes. Finally, the following November, at the last stage of consideration of the reform bill by the Colombian Congress, Senator Hubert Humphrey of the United States, then visiting Colombia, provided timely assistance to the forces supporting the bill when he declared: "The United States does not want to contribute to the wealthy few through industrialization loans

[63] For discussions on the World Bank missions and their recommendations, see *ibid.*, pp. 117–135; and Ernest A. Duff, *Agrarian Reform in Colombia* (New York: Frederick A. Praeger, Publishers, 1968), pp. 150–154.

[64] Hirschman, *op. cit.*, p. 118.

[65] International Bank for Reconstruction and Development, *The Agricultural Development of Colombia* (Washington, D.C., 1956), pp. 66–67.

[66] Quoted in Duff, *op. cit.*, p. 34.

if there is no agrarian reform to permit the domestic power of consumption to increase." [67]

The initiation of Law 135, it must be noted, owes much less to the economic merit of reform and to international influence than to the elite's effort to preserve rural stability and to demonstrate the viability of the National Front. Differentiating the political and economic motives in the introduction of the law, Robert H. Dix has observed:

> The agrarian reform enacted as Law 135 of 1961 . . . has been at once the most important and most controversial undertaking of the National Front in the area of social reform and economic development. . . . The immediate motivation for the law's passage was neither economic nor social, however, but political. A number of the leaders of both parties . . . realized that for the National Front ever to attain real popular appeal it must offer a comprehensive, attractive program that would prove its interest in the Colombian masses. Moreover, it was hoped that the initiation of an agrarian reform would help to prevent an agrarian revolution, or a recrudescence of violence on the pre–1958 scale. [68]

As to the international influence on the passage of Law 135, such influence appears indirect and peripheral. International organizations merely helped in identifying the tenure problems and in advancing certain technical solutions. The United States limited its support to generalized exhortations, refraining from any direct involvement in program formulation. The elite of Colombia had rejected the tax proposals by the World Bank; conceivably it could have spurned the advice of the United States by not enacting Law 135 had it not recognized the political consequences of inaction. In any case, from its inception to its enactment, Law 135 was exclusively the making of the Colombians themselves. It is the Colombian elite's own response to the country's tenure problems.

IRAN: THREATENED MONARCHY AND 1962 DECREE

In terms of the political background of reform, Colombia and Iran offer interesting contrasts. A century-old republic ruled by a biparty system,

---

[67] Quoted in *ibid.*, p. 59.

[68] Dix, *op. cit.* (n. 49 above), p. 154. Cf. Charles W. Anderson, "Land Reform in Colombia: Some Ideas," *Land Reform and Social Change in Colombia* (Madison: University of Wisconsin, Land Tenure Center, Discussion Paper, 1963), p. 6, and Duff, *op. cit.*, pp. 186–187.

Colombia repeatedly experienced intrasystem warfare and rural violence. Law 135 of 1961 was introduced primarily to restore the confidence of the Conservatives and Liberals in their reshaped system and to tame rural violence. Iran, an ancient empire under the reign of a monarch, witnessed periodic conflicts between the king and the urban middle class but enjoyed stability in the villages. Mohammad Reza Shah Pahlavi, the king, adopted a reform decree in 1962 basically in order to safeguard the monarchy; he hoped to enlist rural support to counteract opposition in the cities.

The principal forces challenging the Shah were grouped behind the banner of the National Front. Founded in 1949 by Muhammad Mossadeq, the National Front was a conglomeration of a number of political groupings: the Iran Party, the National Resistance Movement, the Pan–Iran Party, the Third Force, and the People of Iran Party.[69] Disagreeing among themselves with respect to political ideology and program, these forces were loosely united in their opposition to the Shah's authoritarian, Western-leaning regime. In the early 1950s, the Front gradually gained political strength as the issue of nationalization of oil came to the fore. In 1951, at the height of the anti-British movement, Mossadeq became premier. But his assumption of power did not alleviate the tension between the Front and the Shah. Instead, the conflict intensified, culminating in the crisis of August 1953. In that month the Mossadeq forces confronted the Shah with a demand for a substantial reduction of his authority, particularly with respect to his control of the army; and to back up the demand they staged massive demonstrations in the cities. Unsuccessful in his initial attempt to remove Mossadeq as premier, the Shah hastily left the country; but within the month through a counter mass demonstration organized by his followers, the Shah wrested the power back from Mossadeq.[70]

Though considerably weakened after the 1953 crisis, in the following few years the National Front continued to pose a threat to the Shah's regime. Then a series of new crises arose. In 1960, the government held two elections to choose members for the Majlis (lower house of parliament). Both were patently rigged: the results of the first election

[69] See Donald N. Wilber, *Contemporary Iran* (New York: Frederick A. Praeger, Publishers, 1963), pp. 148–153.

[70] For a concise description of the events of August 1953, known in Iran as "Twenty-Eight Mordad," see Richard W. Cottam, *Nationalism in Iran* (Pittsburgh: University of Pittsburgh Press, 1964), pp. 223–230. For the Shah's own account of his encounters with Mossadeq, see Mohammad Reza Shah Pahlavi, *Mission For My Country* (New York: McGraw-Hill, 1961), Chap. V, "Tumultuous Years."

had to be annulled, and candidates elected on the second balloting sat in the Majlis only until May 1961, when the lower house was abruptly dissolved. In 1961, boycotting the second election, the National Front staged protest demonstrations; in retaliation, the government arrested almost all of the Front's leaders. In the same year, as a teachers' strike brought down the government of Premier Sharif-Imami, student demonstrations resulted in the occupation by the police of Tehran University. In the meantime, the problems of inflation and balance-of-payment deficits compelled the government to impose an austerity program which proved to be highly unpopular with urban residents. "The economic crisis of 1961," Hossein Mahdavy has remarked, "shook the confidence of the régime and increased the doubts of those who were already in opposition or indifferent to it. Unemployment and the higher cost of living were causing discontent in urban centers." [71]

Facing these problems, the Shah became all the more apprehensive about the future of his reign and of the monarchy when he himself was subject to several assassination attempts and when he pondered the seemingly contagious revolutionary movements going on in the neighboring countries. The fall of the throne in Egypt in 1952 and in Iraq in 1958, the precarious existence of the kingdoms of Jordan and Saudi Arabia, and the coup d'état in Turkey in 1960—all highly unsettling developments in the Middle East—sharply heightened the Shah's sensitivity over the revolutionary prospect in his own country. To diminish such a prospect, the Shah launched his own "White Revolution," the most vital part of which was the land-reform decree of 1962.[72] The issuance of the decree was a highly risky political gamble. Facing the combined opposition of the

[71] Hossein Mahdavy, "The Coming Crisis in Iran," *Foreign Affairs*, XLIV (Oct. 1965), 136.
[72] This "White Revolution" consists of six reform programs: land reform, nationalization of forests, sale of publicly owned factories to finance land reform, sharing by workers in the profits of industries, revision of electoral laws, and creation of a Literacy Corps. Two facts underscored the political significance that the Shah attached to land reform. Though its agriculture was underdeveloped, Iran—unlike many other developing countries—enjoyed near self-sufficiency in agricultural products, requiring little food import. See Iran, Plan Organization, Division of Economic Affairs, Agriculture Sector, *Third Plan Frame: Agriculture, Third Draft* (Tehran, 1961), p. 59; and J. Price Gittinger, *Planning for Agricultural Development: the Iranian Experience* (Washington, D.C.: National Planning Association, 1965), p. 101. Moreover, in spite of its feudalistic land tenure, Iran experienced no overt rural unrest and peasant discontent. As was true in the case of Egypt, there was thus in Iran neither a compelling economic justification nor a strong peasant pressure for the initiation of reform. The principal motivation for reform was starkly political: to preserve the monarchy.

urban middle class and the Muslim clergy,[73] but retaining the support of the army and the bureaucracy, the Shah's regime "came to view the current opposition of the landlords as less of a risk than the future opposition of the peasantry."[74] What the Shah undertook to do with to reconstitute a coalition of social forces supporting the throne; land reform was the instrument for substituting the expected allegiance of the mass peasantry for the loyalty of the landed aristocracy.

THE PHILIPPINES: RURAL VIOLENCE, THE HUKS, AND REFORM

If, as seen above, Iran and Colombia show marked differences in the backgrounds of land reform, the Philippines and Colombia have had quite similar experiences in their reform efforts. Both the Philippines and Colombia have faced chronic peasant unrest and a Communist threat in certain geographically confined areas (the Luzon plains in the Philippines and the south central mountain districts in Colombia). In response to the rural challenges, both countries initiated and rewrote laws in roughly the same time periods.[75] And the elites of both countries perceived land reform to be a major instrument to preserve a threatened biparty system of government.

In the Philippines, Central Luzon—a densely populated and major rice-producing region—has been for decades a center of peasant unrest and radical movements.[76] In the late 1920s, the *Tangulans*, a rural secret organization with "40,000 members mostly laborers and tenants" developed its strength in this region, culminating in an uprising in Tayug in the Province of Pangasinan in 1931.[77] The rebels briefly took over the town, disarmed the local unit of the Constabulary, hacked the officers to

[73] The Moslem mullahs became disenchanted with the Shah partly because they would lose their land holdings under land reform and partly because they were disturbed by the secularizing tendency of the Shah's other reform measures.

[74] Huntington, *op. cit.* (n. 9 above), p. 165.

[75] Both countries started their reform effort in the 1930s, adopting their first major land redistribution laws in 1936: Commonwealth Act 20 of the Philippines and Law 200 of Colombia. Both countries enacted new and comprehensive reform laws in the 1960s: the Agricultural Land Reform Code of 1961 in the Philippines and the Social Agrarian Reform Law of 1961 in Colombia.

[76] For the geographical location of Central Luzon and the provinces within the region, see Region III on Map 1, below.

[77] Antonio J. Ledesma, "The Agrarian Problem and the 'Unrepresented Minorities' during the Commonwealth," *Philippine Journal of Public Administration*, XI (July 1967), 221.

pieces, burned the barracks and the post office, and destroyed the land records on file. Though the movement was nationalistic in orientation and fanatical in its religious belief, "the poor peasants who rose against constituted authority at Tayug were rebelling chiefly against 'caciquism,' agrarian oppression, and Constabulary abuses." [78]

A few years later, a more powerful radical organization, the Sakdalista Party, emerged in Central Luzon. Capitalizing on rural grievances, the party made considerable political gains in the 1934 election, winning from this region three seats "in the House of Representatives, one governorship, and numerous municipal presidents, vice-presidents and councilors." [79] Not pacified by its electoral success, the party launched on May 2, 1935, bloody uprisings, in at least fifteen towns surrounding Manila and in the neighboring provinces. One account of the event indicated that in four specific towns 2,250 Sakdalista followers participated in the uprisings "with 59 dead and 38 wounded," and that "the Constabulary suffered 4 dead and 11 wounded." [80] Another account suggested that a total of 5,000 to 7,000 of the party's members were involved in the entire incident.[81] Like the Tayug revolt, the Sakdalista uprising manifested deep-seated peasant discontent in Luzon and a popular yearning for national independence. As Acting Governor-General Joseph Ralston Hayden commented: "The Sakdal uprising was a blow against *caciquism* as well as for independence." [82] Stressing the gravity of the rural situation in Luzon, Commonwealth President Manuel Quezon told the National Assembly: the Sakdal rebellion involved "the problem in the relationship between tenants and landowners . . . [which] transcends in importance all other social problems of the Philippines." [83] In the 1930s and 1940s, Socialists under Pedro Abad Santos and Communists under Crisanto Evangelista also sought to develop their political strength in Central Luzon. This was

[78] Joseph Ralston Hayden, *The Philippines: A Study in National Development* (New York: The Macmillan Co., 1942), p. 380.

[79] *Ibid.*, p. 363. For a map depicting the distribution of voting strength of the party in the central and southern Luzon provinces, see Carl H. Landé, *Leaders, Factions, and Parties: The Structure of Philippine Politics* (New Haven: Yale University, Southeast Asia Studies, Monograph Series, No. 6, 1965), p. 94.

[80] Teofilo Sison, "Report on the Sakdalista Uprisings," June 5, 1935. Cited in Ledesma, *op. cit.*, p. 222.

[81] Erich H. Jacoby, *Agrarian Unrest in Southeast Asia* (New York: Columbia University Press, 1949), p. 193.

[82] Hayden, *op. cit.*, p. 400.

[83] Quoted in Ledesma, *op. cit.*, p. 223.

followed by the emergence during the Second World War of the Huk movement (*Hukbo ng Bayan Laban sa Hapon*, or People's Army against the Japanese, which was subsequently renamed *Hukbong Magpalayang Bayan*, or People's Liberation Army), which launched a guerrilla movement against the government immediately after the war.

The fact that rural violence, radical parties, and guerrilla movements have continuously concentrated in Luzon can be explained primarily by the tenure conditions of the locality. The 1948 agricultural census showed that while the number of tenant farms constituted 37.3 percent of all farms in the whole country, the corresponding figure for Central and Southern Luzon was 60.2 percent; "nine of the 11 provinces in the Philippines with more than one-half of the farms operated by tenants" were found in these regions.[84] While the incidence of tenancy here was much higher than in other parts of the country, it was here also that the social contact between the landowners and tenants—because of the prevalence of absentee ownership—was at a minimum.

> At the same time, the large size of estates in this region means that the proportion of the tenants of an estate who are tied by kinship to its owner is considerably smaller than elsewhere in the Philippines. . . . This helps explain why violent agrarian revolts and political movements representing a rejection of the political leadership of the land owning gentry have been confined almost entirely to the provinces of this region.[85]

Observations of the Huk insurgency by a number of specialists clearly affirm the validity of these explanations. For instance, in 1954 in *An Economic and Social Survey of Rural Households in Central Luzon* Generoso F. Rivera and Robert T. McMillan reported: "In the Central [Luzon] Plain provinces, . . . the intensity of the Huk menace seems to be correlated with the degree of tenancy."[86] Fourteen years later, in 1968, Conrado F. Estrella, the head of the land-reform agency said essentially the same thing: "There wasn't any doubt that the condition of the share tenants was the worst in the areas where the Huks were most powerful, [that is] in Central Luzon."[87] A study conducted in the same year by Edward J. Mitchell on the causal relationship of economic and social vari-

---

[84] Generosa F. Rivera and Robert T. McMillan, *An Economic and Social Survey of Rural Households in Central Luzon* (Manila, 1954), p. 7.

[85] Landé, *op. cit.*, p. 97.

[86] Rivera and McMillan, *op. cit.*, p. 7.

[87] *The New York Times*, April 12, 1968, p. 14.

ables and the Huk-controlled barrios in Central Luzon concluded: "Huk control will be greater where most men are farmers and most farmers are tenants." [88]

The persistent challenges by agrarian radical movements to the Philippine government required continuous political responses. To the elite, land-reform legislation appeared to be one perennial weapon to meet these challenges. Whenever there was a period of rural violence, there was going to be a series of new reform laws; and as rural violence became larger in scale, the proposed laws became more drastic in content. The Tayug and Sakdalista uprisings of the 1930s produced the first Philippine reform laws, which sought to create new farms through government purchase and resale of land and to provide some protection to tenants.[89] When the Socialists and Communists began to develop their strength in Central Luzon in the latter half of the 1930s, President Manuel Quezon declared: "I am one of those who believe that no man has the right to own more land than he can work. . . . The purpose of the government should be to have as many people owning their land as possible. No better weapon can be placed in the hands of a country against communism than the ownership of land in the hands of the small man." [90] In line with his concept of "Social Justice," he proposed new laws, strengthening the early reform programs.

After the Second World War, as none of the earlier reform laws had been implemented, and as the Huks rose in rebellion, land reform once again became a political issue. But the elite was not yet ready to act upon the issue. When the United States advised in a number of special studies that the Philippines institute basic tenurial changes, some elite members rejected the advice as interference in domestic affairs, while others simply ignored it.[91] Only when the Huk rebellion became a serious threat to the survival of the young republic, did the government discern the urgent need for reform. It was Defense Minister Ramon Magsaysay who took the initiative in breaking the link between the Huk movement and the

---

[88] Edward J. Mitchell, "Some Econometrics of the Huk Rebellion," *The American Political Science Review*, LXIII (December 1969), 1165.

[89] For a brief description of the reform laws adopted in the 1930s through 1940s, see Chapter VI, below.

[90] Quoted in Raul S. Manglapus, "Land, Industry and Power," *Larawan* (issued by the Philippine Embassy to the United States), Series IX, No. 10 (September 19, 1963), 3.

[91] For the United States views on the rural conditions of the Philippines and recommendations for tenurial changes, see Chapter VI, below.

land issue. Through an army-supported Economic Development Corporation, he tried to pacify the insurgents by resettling them on public land. After winning the presidential election in 1953, Magsaysay persuaded a reluctant Congress to adopt a number of new reform laws, the most important of which was the Philippine Land Reform Act of 1955, the country's first program for compulsory expropriation of large private holdings. Again, as these laws were not effectively enforced, and as the Huks revived their strength in the early 1960s, the initiation of the Agricultural Land Reform Code of 1963 was in order.[92] The code, the country's current reform law, has considerably broadened the scope of the 1955 program and strengthened the earlier tenancy improvement measures.

TAIWAN: COMMUNIST THREAT AND THE KMT REFORM

If the elite of the Philippines initiated reform laws primarily because of the long existence of rural violence, the Kuomintang began its reform effort in Taiwan in 1949 basically because of an acute apprehension of the occurrence of agrarian radicalism in the future.

An understanding of the KMT's motivation in initiating reform in Taiwan requires a discussion of the land issue in the context of Chinese history. For centuries the dynastic changes of the country were governed by a cyclical pattern of violence and stability, which was, in turn, intimately affected by the land problem. As Chen Cheng, the principal sponsor of Taiwan's reform programs, has noted:

A study of Chinese history for the last 2,000 years shows recurring patterns of war and peace. Many causes may be listed, but the

[92] Secondary in importance to the political motivation for the initiation of the 1963 law was a consideration of using the reform as a means to improve the economic condition of the country. The Philippines has suffered until recently a constant large shortage of food. For example, in 1963 to 1964, one-tenth of the country's food supply, or about 1,130,000 tons of agricultural products, had to come from abroad. See Bernardo G. Bantegui and Juan O. Sumogui, "The Food Supply Situation in the Philippines 1963–64," *The Statistical Reporter* (January-March 1966), 23. To the extent that land reform might increase agricultural productivity, the proponents of the 1963 law argued, it could help reduce foreign exchange expenditure on food imports. In addition, as President Diosdado Macapagal and Senator Raul Manglapus, the two principal sponsors of the law have suggested, reform could stimulate industrial expansion as it would "release large capital resources tied up in absentee landlordism to business and industry" and would increase rural demand for manufactured goods. See Jean Grossholtz, *Politics in the Philippines* (Boston: Little, Brown and Company, 1964), p. 71; and Manglapus, *op. cit.*, p. 4. These economic arguments for reform were persuasive only to a limited few reform supporters but not decisive for the passage of the 1963 law. Discussions in Chapters V and VI, below, will make this evident.

most important is inability to maintain a proper balance between land and population for any length of time. Whenever population increased to a point where land was insufficient, violent uprisings broke out and civil wars ensued. But with resulting reduction of population and restoration of the land-population equilibrium, another period of social and political stability would begin. Lasting peace and stability are not possible until this vicious cycle has been ended.[93]

To resolve the land problem, China has experimented with numerous reform ideas. As early as over twenty centuries ago a proposal for land redistribution was made by Tung Chung-shu. Tung, an official of the Han Dynasty and a contemporary of Emperor Wu (140–86 B.C.), suggested, "Let us set a limit to the amount of land an individual may own, give the excess land to those who really need it, and put a stop to the concentration of landownership in the hands of a few." [94] Subsequently, every two or three hundred years a major proposal was made. While varying in details, all reform proposals tried to achieve some form of equalization of land ownership.[95] A number of these proposals were implemented; others gave rise to lengthy discussion in the imperial court. But, despite this constant effort at reform, the cycle of violence and stability remained unbroken.

In modern times, when Dr. Sun Yat-sen began the anti-Manchu movement at the turn of this century, he renewed the effort to resolve the land problem. Upon founding in 1905 the *Tung Min Hui* (an early revolutionary organization), Dr. Sun emphasized "Equalization of Land Rights" as one of the four fundamental objectives of his movement.[96] After the revolution of 1911, which replaced the Manchu Dynasty with the Republic of China, Dr. Sun elaborated a number of times his idea of reform. In 1924, in what subsequently became the embodiment of the KMT ideology, *The Three Principles of the People*,[97] he diagnosed the cardinal

[93] Chen Cheng, *Land Reform in Taiwan* (Taipei, Taiwan, 1961), p. ix.

[94] Quoted in Hui-sun Tang, *Land Reform in Free China* (Taipei, Taiwan, 1954), "Foreword."

[95] For a brief enumeration of these reform proposals and programs, see *ibid.*

[96] The other three fundamental objectives were "Termination of the Manchu Dynasty," "Restoration of Chinese Rule," and "Establishment of a Republic." Hsiao Tseng, *The Theory and Practice of Land Reform in China* (Taipei, Taiwan: The Chinese Research Institute of Land Economics, 1953), p. 40.

[97] The book contains the serialized speeches delivered by Dr. Sun in 1924. The three principles refer to "the principle of nationalism," "the principle of democracy," and "the principle of people's livelihood."

land problem of China as one of tenancy, and expounded the land-to-the-tiller principle:

> Although the system of large-holding is not developed in China, nine-tenths of her farmers are nevertheless tenants. What they cultivate is someone else's land, and those who own land do not as a rule cultivate it. It is only just that the farmers should have their own land and own what they produce. . . . According to one of our latest rural surveys, sixty per cent of the annual yield from the land goes to the landlord and only forty per cent goes to the farmer. . . . If this state of affairs is allowed to go on, the farmers, as they become better educated, will not be willing to work hard for nothing, and they will desert the farms, leaving the land waste[d] and unproductive. Conversely if the farmers own their land and have complete possession of their produce, all of them will be happy to produce as much as possible.
>
> Thus the only sound method of increasing our food production is legislative protection of peasant interests. . . . The ultimate solution of the peasant problem . . . will be for every farmer to own his land. Not until this is realized can the problem of the people's livelihood be solved.[98]

In his address to the Government Institute for the Training of Workers for the Peasant Movement in Canton in 1924, Dr. Sun stressed the importance of farmers to the KMT movement.

> In a democracy the ultimate sovereign power is with the people; and one of the aims of the Nationalist Revolution is to establish a democratic government in China. Since farmers constitute the great majority of the Chinese population, they must participate in this Revolution if it is to succeed.[99]

In the same year, Dr. Sun's reform idea was first incorporated into a KMT document, "The Outline of National Reconstruction," and then reaffirmed by the First National Congress of the party. The Congress pledged that "the state shall provide farm land to tenants who do not have sufficient land to cultivate."[100] In 1926, the Second National Con-

---

[98] *Sun Yat-sen: His Political and Social Ideals: a Source Book* compiled, translated and annotated by Leonard Shihlien Hsü (Los Angeles: University of Southern California Press, 1933), pp. 448–449.

[99] *Ibid.*, p. 23.

[100] Quoted in Wen-yi Têng, *Taiwan Shih Shih Kêng Che Yu Chi Tien Chi Shih* (A *Factual Report on the Enforcement of the Land-to-Tiller Program*) (Taipei, Taiwan: Chung Yang Wen Wu Kung Ying Shê, 1955), p. 27. Translation by the author.

gress adopted a platform in favor of a nation-wide, 25 percent reduction of rent.[101] Subsequently, the KMT repeated in many resolutions, platforms, and declarations its intention to carry out its agrarian commitment.[102] But in contrast to its avowed intention, the KMT took little action during its mainland rule.[103] In 1930, the national government adopted the Land Law, which established 37.5 percent of the annual yield of the main crop as the standard amount of rent, but "most of the law remained a dead letter." [104] Only in certain districts of Hupeh, Chekiang, Szechwan, Kwangsi, Kweichow, and Kwangtung provinces was rent reduction given sporadic implementation, and land redistribution was attempted on a very meager scale for a limited period of time in Fukien province.[105] Except for the rent-reduction measure in Hupeh, none of these attempts at reform achieved any appreciable results.

It is pertinent in this connection to compare the Kuomintang revolution of 1911 with its Mexican counterpart of 1910. Both revolutions were initially aimed only at a change of the existing political system, and, after toppling the *ancien régime*, both faced a prolonged period of conflict among warlords. However, the roles of the peasants in the two revolutions were significantly different. In Mexico, as participants in the revolution from the beginning, the *campesinos* became a vital political force whose demand on the land issue could not be ignored by any of the politicians and generals vying for power. It was to alleviate the military pressure of Zapata and Villa and to gain *campesino* allegiance that Carranza issued the decree of 1915. In China, the peasants, remaining persistently as by-standers in the KMT-led revolution, made no demand upon, and posed no threat to, either the KMT or the warlords. Conceivably, in the aftermath of Dr. Sun's death in 1925 the KMT leadership could have taken

[101] Pan Lien-fang, *Taiwan T'u Ti Kai Keh Chih Hui Ku Yü Chan Wang* (A Review and an Outlook of Land Reform in Taiwan) (Tapei, Taiwan: Lien Ho Ch'u Pan Chung Hsin, 1965), p. 8.

[102] For a summary of the KMT decisions on land reform during the mainland period, including the declarations of the First through the Sixth Congresses of the party, see Têng, *op. cit.*, pp. 27–29.

[103] As late as 1948, one year before the defeat of the KMT on the mainland, several reform bills were still pending in the national legislature. None was enacted. Pan, *op. cit.*, p. 6.

[104] Hsiao, *op. cit.*, p. 49.

[105] For a narration of the KMT's reform experiences during the mainland period, see China, JCRR, Farmers' Service Division, *JCRR Annual Reports on Land Reform in the Republic of China, from October 1948 to June 1964* (Taipei, Taiwan: JCRR, 1965; mimeo.), pp. 1–7, and 13–19; and Pan, *op. cit.*, pp. 7–11.

the initiative to resolve the land issue even without being actually confronted with a peasant demand for reform. But, absorbed in the successive campaigns against the warlords, the Communists, and the Japanese, the KMT concentrated its energy on the military front, without taking any serious action to resolve the land issue. Unlike the Mexican revolution which evolved from a state of violent upheaval to a massive movement in favor of the promotion of general welfare, the KMT revolution on the mainland remained a political-military movement, never entering a social phase. While the KMT failed to identify with the peasants, the Communists seized the land issue, skillfully projecting their image, both domestically and internationally, as land reformers.[106] Having gradually gained control of the vast peasantry, the Communists were able to build up a massive rural base from which they drew strength in the contest with the KMT. In retrospect, one may say, the failure of the KMT to resolve the land issue weighed as heavily as any other factor in the defeat of the KMT on the mainland.

This lengthy review of events on the mainland serves to emphasize the political motivation of the KMT reform in Taiwan. When the KMT retreated to Taiwan, conditions in the cities were perhaps unsettling, but there was no visible evidence of any peasant discontent or violence. Moreover, though the land productivity of pre-reform Taiwan was low compared to today's standard, it was much higher than that of many other Asian countries.[107] Consequently, rural violence and low agricultural productivity were not factors as important in the initiation of reform in Taiwan as they were in the case of many other countries. Having lost the

---

[106] Commenting on this point, Secretary of State Dean Acheson noted in 1949 in the United States White Paper on China: "The population of China during the eighteenth and nineteenth centuries doubled, thereby creating an unbearable pressure upon the land. The first problem which every Chinese Government has had to face is that of feeding this population. So far none has succeeded. The Kuomintang attempted to solve it by putting many land-reform laws on the statute books. Some of these laws have failed; others have been ignored. In no small measure, the predicament in which the National Government finds itself today is due to its failure to provide China with enough to eat. A large part of the Chinese Communists' propaganda consists of promises that they will solve the land problem." U.S., Department of State, *United States Relations with China, with Special Reference to the Period 1944–1949* (Washington, D.C., 1949), pp. iv–v.

[107] See U.N., Economic Commission for Asia and the Far East, *Economic Survey of Asia and the Far East, 1965* (Bangkok, 1966), Table 10, "Area and Production of Selected Agricultural Commodities," pp. 274–277.

peasantry to the Communists on the mainland, the dominant concern of the KMT leadership was to avoid the mistake of again alienating the peasantry on the island. That the Rent Reduction program was introduced in 1949, the very year in which the civil war came to a close, attests to the immediate political significance of the program. As Chen Cheng, then Governor of Taiwan, explained, the traditional tenancy system created "irreconcilable opposition" between the landlord and the tenant. In the past, "this provided the Communist agitators with an opportunity to infiltrate into the villages." He continued:

> It was one of the main reasons why the Chinese mainland fell into Communist hands. On the eve of rent reduction in Taiwan, the situation on the Chinese mainland was becoming critical and the villages on this island were showing signs of unrest and instability. It was feared that the Communists might take advantage of the rapidly deteriorating condition to fish in troubled waters. But with the implementation of rent reduction, the livelihood of the broad masses of the farming population was immediately improved. The Chinese Communists were effectively deprived of propagandistic weapons by a new social order that had arisen in the rural areas.[108]

Clearly the Kuomintang viewed rent reduction as a primary move to ward off Communist efforts to penetrate the rural areas. It was with this

---

[108] Chen, *op. cit.*, pp. 47–48. Similarly, Wen-yi Têng, a former Chairman of the Taiwan Provincial Committee of the KMT, has written: "The Kuomintang and the National Government have since the founding of the Republic upheld the 'land-to-the-tiller' idea as a basic policy. . . . Because of our failure to implement this revolutionary policy, . . . the Communists have been able to utilize the land-reform slogan to deceive and manipulate the farmers. . . . Consequently our National Revolution has lost the support of the vast peasantry, suffering a serious defeat on the mainland. This, indeed, is a painful experience and a profound lesson. . . . Learning from this lesson, the government has now started to implement in Taiwan the land-to-the-tiller policy. . . ." Têng, *op. cit.*, p. 692. Translation by the author.

There is also some evidence indicating that the KMT deemed its failure in reform on the mainland as having at least partially contributed to an international misunderstanding as to the nature of the Chinese Communist movement. A party document commented in 1954: "During the Second World War the United States Embassy in China mistook the Communists as land reformers," and the White Paper issued in 1949 still showed some trace of this misunderstanding. Reform in Taiwan was essential to the correction of this misunderstanding. The Kuomintang, *Chung-Kuo Kuomintang Tú Ti Cheng Tsê Yü Taiwan Sheng Shih Shih Kêng Che Yu Chi Tien* (*The Land Policy of the Kuomintang and the Implementation of the Land-to-Tiller Program in Taiwan*) (Taipei, Taiwan, 1954), p. 16. Translation by the author.

same motivation that the party launched successively the public land sale program in 1951 and the land-to-the-tiller program in 1953.[109]

A Brief Appraisal

The reform experiences of the eight countries discussed above appear to confirm the validity of the hypothesis that political elites initiate reform primarily to gain political legitimacy. In the light of this discussion, a brief appraisal of the significance of the conditions likely to lead to reform can now be made. Revolution resulted in reform in Mexico and Egypt, but not in KMT China. Rural unrest was a factor figuring prominently in the initiation of agrarian laws in Colombia, India, Mexico, and the Philippines; but not in the other four countries. The KMT adopted reforms in Taiwan in 1949 to 1953 to forestall a Communist threat and to

[109] Because of the ineptitude and corruption of General Chi Yi, the first KMT Governor of Taiwan after World War II, a revolt by native Taiwanese against Chen's administration took place on February 28, 1947. In view of this incident, some Western observers conjectured that the KMT initiated reform for the purpose of removing the landed gentry as a potential source of opposition. Thus John Israel surmised that in Taiwan "the landlords, well-endowed and deeply entrenched, were a likely rallying point for opposition. For the Nationalists enlightened self-interest called for sweeping reform." "Politics on Formosa," in Mark Mancall (ed.), *Formosa Today* (New York: Frederick A. Praeger, Publishers, 1964), p. 59. Similarly George H. Kerr has suspected that land reform in Taiwan "was designed as much to destroy the base of the emergent middle class (the class which produced the leaders of 1947) as it was to aid the landless peasant." *Formosa Betrayed* (Boston: Houghton Mifflin Company, 1965), p. 420.

It seems plausible to suggest that the KMT initiated reform partly because it wished to compensate for the misrule of Chen Yi. But the speculative statements cited above are hardly tenable. The fact is that because of its very desire to retain the loyalty of the landlord, the KMT failed to initiate any meaningful reform on the mainland. Had the KMT refrained from introducing land reform in Taiwan, the landlord would have become an ally of the party rather than a potential opponent. Indeed, during the 1947 incident, violence occurred largely in urban areas without any conspicuous participation by the landed gentry. Moreover, as Kerr himself noted, "Few Formosans— very few—had great landholdings before 1945, . . ." (*ibid.*) As seen in Table 2, above, pre-reform land tenure in Taiwan was characterized more by fragmentation than by high concentration of ownership. In 1952, just before the implementation of the land-to-the-tiller program, only *sixty-six* landowners (including both landlords and cultivating farmers) on the entire island, or 0.01 percent of all landowners, had farms with a size of more than 100 *chia* (about 97 hectares) of land; these large owners possessed an aggregate area of 14,225 *chia* (13,797 hectares), or 2.09 percent of the entire private farm area. See Taiwan Provincial Land Bureau, *Statistics on Landownership Classification in Taiwan* (Taipei, Taiwan, 1952). In view of the small number of large owners, and of the meager area of their possessions, it is difficult to imagine how they could have become a "rallying point for opposition."

fulfill an ideological commitment, but it had not initiated reform earlier on the mainland in the face of an existing Communist challenge and of numerous pledges to carry out the land policy of *The Three Principles of the People.* In proposing reform laws, a number of countries may have been open to international influence, but Colombia and the Philippines have at one time or another rejected specific foreign recommendations for reform. A number of countries have experienced severe population pressure on the land, but such pressure does not appear to be a factor critically affecting the elites' attitude toward reform. While in many countries the presence of conditions likely to lead to reform did not always result in reform, countries like Iran and, to a lesser extent, Pakistan and Egypt initiated reform in the absence of many or all of these conditions. One may conclude: in a country with tenure problems, without the elite's recognition of the need for legitimacy, none of the conditions mentioned here appears to be *sufficient* for reform; with such a recognition, none of these conditions appears *necessary.*

V

PROCESS OF PROGRAM FORMULATION

In the process of formulating a reform program the political elite must resolve differences among three principal groups of protagonists—the landed class, the peasantry, and the elite itself. As the opponent of reform, the landed class will insist on minimizing its material loss; as the intended beneficiary, the peasantry will wish to maximize its gains; as the sponsor of reform, the elite—after appraising these conflicting demands and after assessing the relationship of reform to its other political programs—will present a proposal most conducive to the perpetuation of its rule. Since the landed class is generally much more politically articulate and influential than the peasantry, and since the peasantry is seldom capable of formulating detailed reform proposals of its own, it is submitted, as a second hypothesis of this book, that *the manner in which the elite formulates a program and the content of the program it finally adopts are determined primarily by the relations between the elite and the landed class.* This hypothesis will be discussed extensively in several chapters. The present chapter will concern itself with the classification of elites and with the identification and analysis of issues and conflicts in the process of program formulation. A case study of the evolution of a reform law and a comparative study of the contents of different reform programs adopted by the eight sample countries will constitute the subjects of subsequent chapters.

Classification of Elites

In the context of the present study, elites sponsoring land reform can be divided into two primary categories. One consists of elites that are *separated* from the landed class; the other comprises those *cooperative* with that class. Separated elites include a *non-indigenous* type (Taiwan) and a *revolutionary* type (Mexico, the U.A.R.); cooperative elites consist

TABLE 4

TYPES OF POLITICAL ELITE, EIGHT COUNTRIES

Elites Separated from Landed Class		Elites Cooperative with Landed Class	
Non-Indigenous	Revolutionary	Dominant	Conciliatory
Taiwan	Mexico U.A.R.	India Iran Pakistan	Colombia Philippines

of a *dominant* type (India, Iran, Pakistan) and a *conciliatory* type (Colombia and the Philippines). These different types of elites are summarized in Table 4.

SEPARATED ELITES: NON-INDIGENOUS AND REVOLUTIONARY

Separated elites exclude the landed class from their membership, and the latter plays no role in the formulation of programs.[1] The exclusion of the landed class results possibly from the assumption of power by an elite that is not indigenous to the community that it rules. This exclusion may also result from a rejection of the landed class by an elite that comes to power through revolution. In Taiwan, political power has been concentrated in the hands of the KMT since the end of the Second World War. Coming from mainland China, the KMT leadership included no representatives of the local landed gentry.[2] In Mexico, the landed aristocracy was the very class that the revolutionaries destroyed. As Mexican historian Daniel Cosío Villegas said of the revolution: "It totally swept away not only the political régime of Porfirio Díaz but all of the Porfirian society, that is, the social classes. . . . Landowners, urban, and especially agricultural, were almost entirely replaced by new ones. . . . Official bureaucracy

---

[1] Separated elites initiating land reform are few in number, but the cases listed here are not exhaustive. One can, for example, classify the American occupational authority in Japan after the Second World War as a non-indigenous elite and the MNR leadership in Bolivia as revolutionary.

[2] Cf. Hung-chao Tai, "The Kuomintang and Modernization in Taiwan," in Samuel P. Huntington and Clement H. Moore (eds.), *Authoritarian Politics in Modern Society: The Dynamics of Established One-Party Systems* (New York: Basic Books, Inc., 1970), pp. 424–425, 429–430.

—federal, state, and municipal—was wholly reformed." [3] In Egypt, the Free Officers were of middle-class origin, having no ties to the large land-owners.[4] When they came to power, they completely dispossessed and supplanted the old elite. In these three cases, the separation between the elites and the landed class is too evident to require further elaboration.

COOPERATIVE ELITES: DOMINANT AND CONCILIATORY

Cooperative elites—both dominant and conciliatory types—are those elites whose membership includes a substantial number of representatives of the landed interests. In the pursuance of reform, these elites must seek some collaboration from the landed interests. The two types of coopera-tive elites differ, however, in the amount of power that the landed interests possess. Within the dominant elite, a non-land-based group or individual assumes a commanding position, possessing a much greater share of power than the landed interests. With due respect to these interests, this group or individual dominates in the formulation of the reform program. Within the conciliatory elite, in contrast, the power is more or less evenly dis-tributed among the landed and all other, non-landed groups. The adoption of a specific reform program depends on a full reconciliation of views of all groups—landed and non-landed—within the elite.

It must be mentioned that for several reasons the influence com-manded by the landed interests within a cooperative elite over the issue of land reform is difficult to assess. In the first place it is not easy to meas-ure accurately the size of political representation of these interests within the elite. Objective, reliable information on the land possessions of elite members may be either non-existent or unavailable to the public. Published information concerning the occupational background of the elite has only limited utility. Some of this information may identify those in agriculture but it invariably fails to distinguish large landowners from small ones, who obviously have different views on land reform. Moreover, as

[3] Quoted in Frances M. Foland, "Agrarian Reform in Latin America," *Foreign Affairs*, XLVIII (October 1969), 107. For a perceptive analysis of the composition of the Mexican elite since the revolution see Frank Ralph Brandenburg, *The Making of Modern Mexico* (Englewood Cliffs, N.J.: Prentice-Hall, Inc., 1964), Chap. i, "The Revolutionary Family and the Mexican Proposition," esp. pp. 1–7.

[4] See Doreen Warriner, *Land Reform and Development in the Middle East* (London, 1962), p. 10; Panayiotis J. Vatikiotis, *The Egyptian Army in Politics* (Bloomington, Ind., 1961), pp. 47–48, 54–55; and Leonard Binder, "Egypt: the Integrative Revo-lution," in Lucian W. Pye and Sidney Verba (eds.), *Political Culture and Political Development* (Princeton, N.J.: Princeton University Press, 1965), pp. 388–389 and 405.

will be evident shortly, elite members with non-agricultural occupations may possess directly or indirectly quite extensive acreages of land. These members' views on reform are conceivably more akin to those of large landowners, even though they have ostensibly no agricultural connections. In the second place, representatives of the landed interests frequently do not speak publicly against land reform but rather conceal and disguise their opposition. Consequently, within a cooperative elite the people supporting the cause of the landed interests are more numerous than those explicitly identified with these interests, and actual resistance to reform is greater than it appears to be on the surface. For these reasons, an analysis of the influence of the landed interests within a cooperative elite requires the use of both statistical evidence and the considered opinion of experienced observers.

Dominant Elites

In India, Iran, and Pakistan, non-landed interests have achieved a dominant position in the political elites. They have all severed ties to the large landlords but have remained cooperative with the lesser ones.

India.   Under certain circumstances, consideration of political legitimacy may significantly alter the relationship between the elite and the landed interests. This is what has occurred in India and Iran. In pre-independence India, the leadership of the Indian National Congress was composed primarily of people without land. From 1919 to 1923, when the party transformed itself from a narrowly based group into a massive organization, the All-India Congress Committee (A.I.C.C.), the party's then highest directing organ, consisted mainly of intellectuals and professionals —lawyers, journalists, teachers, physicians, and an insignificant number of landowners.[5] These Congress leaders were predominantly high-caste Hindus. Drawn from a narrow social stratum, they came to represent the entire population mainly because of their dedication to the nationalist cause and their willingness to renounce their privileges. When independence arrived, these non-landed professionals—on the basis of their past contribution to the nationalist movement and their personal sacrifices— had almost exclusive control of the Congress Party and also, of course, the new government. However, with independence achieved, the strategic importance of the peasantry declined, and there has since been a persistent

[5] See Gopal Krishna, "The Development of Indian National Congress as a Mass Organization, 1918–1923," *The Journal of Asian Studies*, XXV (May 1966), 424.

trend toward increasing representation of the landed interests in both the Congress Party and the national, state, and local governments. Consisting mainly of medium-sized landlords and large owner-farmers, these interests also appear increasingly more influential at the lower levels of the Congress and government hierarchies. In contrast, the professionals have gradually lost some of their strength, as exemplified by the decline in the representation of lawyers. In the pre-independence period and the early years of the new nation, the law, among all professions, supplied the largest number of elite members; gradually agriculture (here referring to a profession consisting mainly of landowners rather than small cultivators) became the most dominant group. To illustrate this trend of change, Table 5 presents data on the representation of lawyers and agriculturalists within the leadership groups of the Congress Party (national: A.I.C.C. and members of parliament; state: members of Legislative Assembly of Uttar Pradesh) as well as within the Lok Sabha (House of the People, Lower House of Parliament).

This table indicates that the political representation of the agriculturalists has registered consistent, significant increases at the national and state levels; other evidence suggests that agriculturalists may have gained an even greater influence than their representation appears to command. This is because many who identified themselves as members of non-agricultural occupations have a vital stake in land. A survey of 224 of Congress's 375 members of the Second Lok Sabha (MPs) conducted in 1960 by Stanley A. Kochanek illustrates this point. If these 224 MPs were classified according to occupational background, 54 (or 24.1 percent) were identified as agriculturalists; if classified according to landownership, 157 (or about 70 percent) were landowners; and if classified according to "main source of income," 95 (or 42.4 percent) identified land as their main source of income. The pertinent survey results are summarized in Table 6. One may safely assume that many non-agriculturalist MPs who owned land or depended on land as the main source of income would side with the agriculturalist MPs on matters relating to the land issue.

While the landowning interests have maintained a large representation in the national legislature, they have obtained an even larger representation in state and local governments. "The vast majority of the members of state legislatures," Duncan B. Forrester has written, "were born and brought up in their constituencies, . . . As India is a land of villages, this means that the legislators are now rural, not urban in back-

TABLE 5

PROPORTION OF LAWYERS AND AGRICULTURALISTS IN THE
CONGRESS PARTY AND IN THE LOK SABHA, INDIA

Leadership Groups	Year[a]	Occupational Groups					
		Lawyers		Agriculturalists		All Occupations	
		No.	Percent	No.	Percent	No.	Percent
Congress Party							
A.I.C.C.[b]	1919	104	64.6	7	4.4	160	100
	1921	83	50.9	4	2.5	163	100
	1923	72	21.3	5	1.5	338	100
	1956	108	16.9	71	11.1	639	100
MPs[c]	1952	130	38.3	62	18.3	339[d]	100
	1957	52	23.3	54	24.2	224[d]	100
	1962	90	26.4	93	27.2	357[d]	100
	1967		22.2		36.8		
Uttar Pradesh	1952	86	22.1	151	38.7	390	100
MLA[e]	1957	49	17.1	108	37.8	286	100
	1962	39	15.7	105	42.2	249	100
Lok Sabha[f]	1950	100	32.0	20	6.4	313	100
(All parties)	1952		35.6		22.4		
	1957		30.3		29.1		
	1962		24.5		27.4		
	1967		17.5		31.1		

[a] Refers to the year in which election took place.

[b] All-India Congress Committee. Data for 1919 to 1923 are from Gopal Krishna, "The Development of the Indian National Congress as a Mass Organization, 1918–1923," *The Journal of Asian Studies*, XXV (May 1966), 424. Data for 1956 are from Stanley A. Kochanek, *The Congress Party of India, the Dynamics of One-Party Democracy* (Princeton, N.J.: Princeton University Press, 1968), p. 358.

[c] Members of Parliament (i.e., members of Lok Sabha, the House of the People). Data for 1952 to 1962 are from Kochanek, *ibid.*, p. 380; and data for 1967 from Ratna Dutta, "The Party Representative in Fourth Lok Sabha," *Economic and Political Weekly*, IV (January 1969), 179.

[d] Total number of Congress MPs giving information on occupational background.

[e] Members of Legislative Assembly, Uttar Pradesh. Data are from Kochanek, *op. cit.*, p. 374.

[f] Data for 1950—referring to MPs of the Provisional Lok Sabha, including those elected in 1946—are from W. H. Morris-Jones, *Parliament in India* (Philadelphia: University of Pennsylvania Press, 1957), p. 120. Data for 1952 and 1957 are from India, Parliament, Lok Sabha, *Second Lok Sabha, Activities and Achievements 1957-62* (New Delhi [1962]), p. 9; and data for 1962 and 1967 from Dutta, *op. cit.*

TABLE 6

CONGRESS PARTY REPRESENTATION IN THE LOK SABHA, 1960

N = 224

Occupation	Congress Party MPs		Main Source of Income						
	No.	Per-cent	Owned Land	Land	Parlia-ment	Busi-ness	Profes-sion	Other	Un-known
Agriculture	54	24.1	53	48	3	1	—	2	—
Business	25	11.2	17	4	—	18	—	3	—
Law	52	23.2	36	14	12	2	20	4	—
Profession	16	7.1	10	1	7	2	6	—	—
Public work	63	28.1	35[a]	25	26	4	2	2	4
Other	13	5.8	6	3	6	—	2	2	—
Unknown	1	0.4	0	—	—	—	—	—	1
Total	224	100	157[a] (70.1%)	95 (42.4%)	54 (24.1%)	27 (12.1%)	30 (13.4%)	13 (5.8%)	5 (2.2%)

[a] Not including two who did not answer the question as to whether they owned any land.

SOURCE: Stanley A. Kochanek, "The Relation between Social Background and Attitudes of Indian Legislators," *Journal of Commonwealth Political Studies*, VI (March 1968), 40–41.

ground."[6] They were, Myron Weiner agreed, men of "means whose families were part of the local rural agricultural gentry."[7] Congress Party's representation in the state legislature of Uttar Pradesh, for instance, provides some statistical evidence to this effect. As seen in Table 5, over 40 percent

[6] Duncan B. Forrester, "Changing Patterns of Political Leadership in India," *The Review of Politics*, XXVIII (July 1966), 315.

[7] Myron Weiner, "Traditional Role Performance and the Development of Modern Political Parties: the Indian Case," *The Journal of Politics*, XXVI (November 1964), 836. The rising influence of the landed interest also appears in the Congress Party's local organizations. In Belgaum, Mysore, for instance, "inamdars, watandars, kulkarnis, gaudas, patels or their descendants—to use the local terminology to refer to landlords and to village officers—abound in local Congress party. . . . The proportion of agriculturalists who are active party members (most of whom are landowners) has actually increased from 56.6% in 1952 to 64.2% in 1959, . . . In matters of crucial importance to the established party leadership—control over land—these men exercise overwhelming influence on local officials." *Ibid.*, 836 and 847. See also Donald B. Rosenthal, "De-urbanization, Elite Displacement, and Political Change in India," *Comparative Politics*, II (January 1970), 182.

of Congress members in the Legislative Assembly in the said state were classified as agriculturalists. At the bottom layer of the government, the village *panchayats* (councils), the landed interests constitute more than just a majority; they dominate the political scene, as will be elaborated later.

These data on the changing composition of the Indian elite indicate that the landed interests gained a greater prominence at the lower level of the elite hierarchy and that the increase of their representation became more pronounced with the passage of time. The non-landed interests, it must be emphasized, still commanded a dominant position in the national elite, particularly in the first decade of post-independence India. Significantly, it was in that decade, when the national elite was clearly free from the pressure of the large landed interests, that India abolished the *zamindari* system. At the same time, as the national elite gradually felt the rising influence of the lesser landed interests, it was content to lay down only broad principles with regard to reform programs affecting these lesser interests, leaving the local elite to work out the details.

Iran. The change in the relationship between the elite and the landed interests in Iran is partially similar to and slightly more complicated than the Indian case. When the present Shah ascended to the throne in 1941, the royal family was the largest landholder in Iran; and private landlords of large properties comprised a major share of the One Thousand Families that ruled the country. In fact the political influence of landlords received legal recognition. When the First Majlis was inaugurated in 1906, landlords and five other privileged groups were given guaranteed representation in the national legislature.[8] For decades thereafter, landlords maintained their political preeminence, and, together with the army and Muslim mullahs, they constituted the vital pillars on which the Peacock Throne of Iran rested.[9]

---

[8] The five other groups were "aristocrats, dignitaries, religious leaders, traders, [and] guilds." *Iran Almanac 1966 and Book of Facts* (5th ed.; Tehran, Echo of Iran, n.d.), p. 126.

[9] Estimates of landlords' political strength in pre-reform Iran vary. Gideon Hadary wrote in 1951 that about two-thirds of the Majlis's members were landlords. "The Agrarian Reform Problem in Iran," *The Middle East Journal,* V (Spring 1951), 187. Donald N. Wilber intimated in the early 1960s that some 150 families—many of whom possessed great landholdings—wielded enormous political power. "Members of these families and their relatives constitute more than a third of the members of the Majlis and the Senate and two-thirds of the total membership of successive cabinets." *Contemporary Iran* (New York, 1963), p. 46.

In the early 1960s, the collaborative relationship between the Shah and the landed gentry underwent a radical change. In 1962, when the Shah considered it imperative to obtain peasant support for the survival of the threatened monarchy, he cut off his ties to the big landlords. He suspended the Majlis and promulgated land reform. However, his action was not intended to disturb his relationship with the lesser landed interests, whose loyalty he still wished to retain. The Shah made a distinction between the big and small landlords:

> Much of the worst managed land in Iran is in the hands of the big-gest landlords. Typically they are absentees who give little thought to improvement . . . [of] the welfare of the peasants, . . . As a class the big private landlords are parasites. . . . Quite different are many of the smaller landlords, who may own one or a few villages and not infrequently live in close association with their tenants. While some of them are selfish and self-centered, many take a lively interest in the welfare of the families who live on their land.[10]

Accordingly, the Shah framed a policy to take away the privileges of the big landlords but to preserve the rights of the small ones. He declared: "Our aims are not to destroy small landlords. What we are doing is a means of making it possible [for more people] to become small landlords [sic]. Those who became owners of land today, we hope, will become small landlords in the future."[11]

Though not necessarily pleased by this policy, the small landlords have gradually reached a *modus vivendi* with the Shah. For, as Richard W. Cottam has put it: "Theirs is no choice at all. The alternatives to the Shah or another rightist dictatorship are at best the nationalists and at worst the Communists and under either the destruction of the rural social base of the landowning system would proceed apace."[12] Hence the Shah and the small landlords remain mutually dependent: the Shah desires the latter's cooperation to maintain a broad political base, while the small landlords accept the former's political hegemony in order to preserve their remaining privileges

Pakistan. In Pakistan, political leadership was dominated at the time

---

[10] Mohammad Reza Shah Pahlavi, *Mission for My Country* (New York, 1961), p. 200.

[11] Quoted in U.N., *Land Reform, Fourth Report*, p. 24.

[12] Richard W. Cottam, *Nationalism in Iran* (Pittsburgh, 1964), pp. 49–50. Cf. Hossein Mahdavy, "The Coming Crisis in Iran," *Foreign Affairs*, XLIV (October 1965), 141–142.

of partition by Muslim politicians. In the East Wing, with the Hindu *zamindars* fleeing the country, the leadership could enact in 1950 the East Bengal State Acquisition and Tenancy Act without encountering any difficulty. As Henry Frank Goodnow has observed: "The fact that most of the large landowners were Hindus who had relatively little political influence after partition greatly facilitated the passage of land reform legislation in 1950. When present laws have been fully executed, there will be no large landowners." [13] In reality, however, medium-size landlords and large owner-farmers remain numerous to this day; their political support was relied upon by the Ayub Khan regime.

Unlike the Hindu *zamindars* in the East Wing who vanished after the partition, the big landlords in the West Wing were Muslims whose power was never challenged in the first decade of Pakistan's existence. They exercised a preponderant influence at all levels of government, controlling a sizable share of seats in the National Assembly and the provincial legislature.[14] In the provincial administration they occupied key positions. For instance, in the former Punjab Province the first three Chief Ministers were successively "prominent landlords." [15] In the countryside their influence rested on their close contact with civil servants who ran the local administration.

> The landlord was normally on good terms with the district officer in his area (usually a [civil servant] . . .). The latter was responsible for law enforcement, the preservation of the public peace, and revenue collection—all subjects of great interest to the landlord. . . . [The landlord] understood the system of government well and had immediate access to the nearest ranking government official. . . . His lines of communication extended also to village leaders and subordinate officials.[16]

Following his seizure of power, Ayub Khan soon undertook to reduce, but not remove, the political power of the big landlords. As a professional

[13] Henry Frank Goodnow, *The Civil Service in Pakistan, Bureaucracy in a New Nation* (New Haven: Yale University Press, 1964), pp. 84–85.

[14] Herbert Feldman estimated that before the 1958 coup, out of the eighty seats in the National Assembly no less than twenty-eight were occupied by West Pakistan's landlords or their representatives. *Revolution in Pakistan: A Study of the Martial Law Administration* (London: Oxford University Press, 1967), p. 61. Comparable figures for the West Pakistan Provincial Assembly are not available, but the big landlords' share of representation was substantial. See Goodnow, *op. cit.*, pp. 82–83; and Keith B. Callard, *Political Forces in Pakistan, 1947–1959* (New York, 1959), p. 12.

[15] Goodnow, *op. cit.*, p. 83.

[16] *Ibid.*, p. 81.

military man with the strong backing of the army, Ayub Khan enjoyed a measure of political independence that was denied his predecessors. In a radio broadcast in January 1959 he stated: "In view of the special prestige which ownership of land enjoys over large areas political power is concentrated in the hands of a privileged few. . . . Such concentration of power hampers the free exercise of political rights and stifles the growth of free political institutions." [17] Considering land reform part of his nation-building effort, he expressed determination to bring about a proper program. If the big landed interests tried to hamper his program, he was quite ready to subdue them. However, from the beginning of his regime, Ayub Khan apparently had no intention of antagonizing any but the largest landlords. With respect to all other landlords, it soon became evident, he merely wished to establish political ascendancy over them, without removing their political and economic privileges. "The power of landlords could be curtailed," Ayub Khan explained. But it was also important to build up "a strong middle class. . . . My anxiety was not to destroy the existing system but to improve upon it so that it should provide opportunities for enterprise and produce leadership capable of influencing rural life." [18]

The Land Reforms Commission for West Pakistan, which Ayub Khan created to frame a program, was particularly explicit in acknowledging the mild intent of the proposed reform:

> In recent years agrarian reforms have been undertaken in a number of countries with the object of breaking up of the power of the "old ruling oligarchy with its roots in big estates." Such a consequence may follow in some measure if our recommendations in this report are implemented, *but this is not one of the specific objectives for the achievement of which we have been asked to propose measures.*[19]

Ayub Khan's intention to spare the medium-sized landowners from his reform in West Pakistan was understandable. As one author has noted, it was from these landowners that "most of the army officers had been drawn. . . . Having antagonized the big landowners by introducing land reforms, which no previous government had the courage to undertake, Gen-

[17] Mohammad Ayub Khan, *Speeches and Statements*, Vol. I (Karachi: Pakistan Publications, n.d.), pp. 48–49.

[18] Ayub Khan, *Friends Not Masters* (London, 1967), pp. 88 and 90.

[19] *Report of the Land Reforms Commission for West Pakistan* (Lahore, 1959), p. 19 (italics mine).

eral Ayub could not afford to alienate his own army officers as well." [20]
If Ayub Khan's compromise with the lesser landowners in West Pakistan
was a matter of political necessity, his policy of favoring the middle-class
farming interests in East Pakistan was a deliberate action. In 1959 the
Land Revenue Commission of East Pakistan, created the previous year,
went to some length to criticize the State Acquisition Act of 1950. The act,
the commission noted,

> has already hit hard the middle class families living in the rural
> areas, whose main sources of income were rents from their tenants
> and the proceeds of their *khas* [self-cultivated] lands. This is the class
> who form the intelligentsia of the country and from whom come
> most of our lawyers, doctors, engineers, public servants, teachers, etc.
> When all their surplus lands are actually acquired and taken posses-
> sion of by the Government, this class will be reduced to compara-
> tive poverty and will not have the means to give their children proper
> education, which cannot but have a disastrous effect on the social
> and economic life of the country. . . . It is to be realised also that
> even if all the available lands are acquired by Government and are
> settled with landless cultivators . . . Government will not be able
> to provide land for more than 5 percent of such people.[21]

Considering that the original reform would ruin the middle class and yet
would not solve appreciably the problems of the landless, the commission
recommended a fourfold increase in the ceiling of private holdings. Ayub
Khan fully agreed. "In East Pakistan," he has written, "the politicians . . .
divided the country into bits and pieces, and by adopting punitive and
extreme types of so-called reforms destroyed the entire middle class. . . .
A Land Revenue Commission set up for East Pakistan in 1958 led to an
amendment of the East Bengal State Acquisition and Tenancy Act [of]
1950 by which I was able to raise the ceiling of *khas* (self-cultivated) land
from 33 acres to about 120 acres or so." [22]

It is evident, then, that while enjoying a political hegemony none of
his predecessors had remotely approached, Ayub Khan only subdued the
power of the landlord class but still tried to retain the class's loyalty.

[20] Khalid B. Sayeed, *The Political Systems of Pakistan* (Boston: Houghton Mifflin
Company, 1967), p. 96.

[21] East Pakistan, Revenue Department, *Report of the Land Revenue Commission,
East Pakistan, 1959* (Dacca, East Pakistan, 1959), pp. 50–51.

[22] Ayub Khan, *Friends Not Masters*, p. 91.

Conciliatory Elites

In Colombia and the Philippines, conciliatory elites hold the reins of government. Unlike all the countries discussed previously, Colombia and the Philippines have never since independence experienced a decisive shift in power within the elites. While the non-landed elements in the elites may have enlarged their numbers, the political strength of the landed interests does not appear to have declined appreciably. Today, the landed class and all other non-land-based groups within the elites can be considered genuinely co-equals; a successful attempt to modify the vested interests of any of these groups rests on a consensus among them all.

Colombia. In Colombia, the landed gentry constitutes a principal component of the *sistema* (the Establishment) from which the elite draws its strength, and whose interests it must respect. Both the Liberal and Conservative Parties, commented John D. Martz, "continue the tradition of drawing upon members of the small ruling group to perpetuate their rule. . . . And it has become generally accepted . . . that [this group] includes large landowners, major businessmen and merchants, and the expanding ranks of industrial producers." [23] Similarly, in analyzing the "social class and politics" of Colombia, Robert H. Dix pointed out that "most forms of social power, along with control of the political system, have primarily rested in the hands of the upper class, . . . The supremacy of such a class [is] founded, . . . in the first instance, on ownership of large tracts of land." Dix noted specifically:

> Members of both party hierarchies have been officers of the powerful, semiofficial National Federation of Coffee Growers, which tends to be dominated by the large growers and exporters. Former Conservative President Mariano Ospina Pérez . . . was for four years its manager. Carlos Lleras Restrepo, elected president in 1966, has been a member of the Federation's national committee. . . . A perusal of Colombia's *Quién es Quién* (*Who's Who*) confirms the large degree of fusion among the elites of property, social standing, education, and political power.

In recent years, the fusion of the landed and the industrial interests is particularly evident. Dix continued:

> . . . a large percentage of Colombian capitalists of both industry and agriculture have their origins in families of the traditional [landed]

---

[23] John D. Martz, "Political Parties in Colombia and Venezuela: Contrasts in Substance and Style," *The Western Political Quarterly*, XVIII (June 1965), 322.

elite. . . . Very often elite families have shiften to urban commercial or industrial pursuits while maintaining strong rural ties. . . . A reverse process is also at work. Some of the younger sons of families that visited their haciendas only occasionally, living in the city as absentee landowners, are beginning to take a real interest in their properties and in their increased productivity. Often, also, those not of the traditional elite who have made their money and their name in industry are investing in land for prestige and other reasons; . . .[24]

While meaningful statistical analysis of the political representation and influence of the Colombian landed class is not available,[25] one can, in

[24] Robert H. Dix, *Colombia: The Political Dimensions of Change* (New Haven, 1967), pp. 43–45 and 49–50.

[25] In *Patterns of Conflict* James L. Payne cited evidence to the effect that the landed interests in Colombia have for a considerable length of time maintained only a meager share of representation in the government. A survey by the Colombian National Statistical Office of the occupations of officeholders in 1936 revealed, for instance, the following information: 1 (2 percent) of 57 senators, 3 (3 percent) of 115 members of the House, 18 (7 percent) of 267 members of department assemblies, 902 (17 percent) of 5,308 members of town councils identified their occupation as that of *hacendados*; in addition, 6 (11 percent) of the 57 senators and 5 (4 percent) of the 115 members of the House were identified as *agricultores* (small farmers). In most instances, law, business, and other professions constituted the dominant occupational groups (p. 39). In 1965 Payne conducted a survey of the social backgrounds of 130 members of Colombia's "upper leadership group" which consisted of incumbent or aspiring officeholders of the national, department, and of municipal governments. The survey indicated that of these 130 leaders only 4 (3 percent) fall into the "cattle-raiser, farmer" occupational category. Again, lawyers (N:58, 45%) businessmen (N:17, 13%), and professionals (N:18, 14%) constituted the overwhelming majority (N:93, 72%) (pp. 323–324). On the basis of these data and also of his interviews with some Conservative politicians (who, he said, showed no bias against reform), Payne came to the conclusion: "The agrarian reform conflict . . . had little to do with the subject matter. It reflected the strategic relationships prevailing between factions." Payne argued, in essence, that whether or not a political faction voted for the reform bill of 1961 depended on how it perceived the vote to affect its immediate political fortune (pp. 262–263). He believed that the political strength of the landed interests was not sufficient to create any major impact on reform legislation. Payne's evidence and conclusion raise a number of doubtful points that considerably impair their utility for the present study. First, both the 1936 and 1965 surveys fail to take into account the fusion of the landed and non-landed interests in political representations, as Robert H. Dix has particularly noted. Many landed interests who invest in commerce and industry may identify their occupation as that of the latter. Many lawyers and other professionals may own a considerable amount of land and receive from it a good portion of their income. (In the case of India, Stanley A. Kochanek's survey on the Congress MPs in the Lok Sabha showed precisely this point [see Table 6].) A mere occupational analysis of officeholders in a developing country like Colombia would obviously leave out a large hidden representation of the landed interests. Second, in view of the popularity of the issue of land reform, opponents in Colombia and, indeed, in most of the countries where reform is an issue, seldom espouse

view of the observations cited above, safely say that this class possesses at least a veto power within the National Front Government on matters touching its vital interests. In proffering a reform program in 1961, the liberal elements of the National Front did not act out of conviction in seeking a fundamental alteration of the agrarian structure. Rather, they used land reform as a symbolic gesture to relieve rural tensions—tensions that threatened the very interests they tried to protect.

The Philippines. In recent decades, the Philippine elite has enlarged its membership and diversified its social composition, but the landed interests within it have retained their political strength. As Jose V. Abueva has observed, historically, Philippine political leadership always rested on landownership. Since the beginning of American rule, and particularly since the Second World War, the elite has admitted to its membership a large number of professionals, prominent bureaucrats, and businessmen, but "national political leadership remained, by and large, in the hands of wealthy landowners, some of whom had branched out into urban real estate, logging, commerce and manufacturing." [26] Today "the Philippine elite," Carl H. Landé has similarly observed, "is drawn largely from those who can afford to be patrons, i.e. from landowners who have tenants, from employers, and from professional men whose occupations permit them to do favors for large numbers of ordinary voters. Members of this elite, ranging themselves under the banners of two national parties, compete with each other for elective offices." [27]

Among the members of the Philippine elite, it should be mentioned, those explicitly identifying themselves as agriculturalists (a synonym for landowners) were numerous only at the lower level of the government,

---

a stance of direct, uncompromising resistance to agrarian changes. They can effectively present their case in a closed caucus rather than in an open forum or in interviews with foreigners. Third, while partisan considerations undoubtedly affected how a Colombian political faction voted on the 1961 bill, it is difficult to substantiate the argument that these considerations were the sole determinant of a faction's voting pattern. It is also hardly tenable that in a country like Colombia, where agricultural interests weigh very heavily in the national economy (see Table 1), and where landownership is much concentrated, these interests do not have a large number of faithful legislative spokesmen of their own and do not exert a strong influence on Congressmen and their votes on bills critically affecting their power and wealth.

[26] Jose V. Abueva, "Bridging the Gap between the Elite and the People in the Philippines," *Philippine Journal of Public Administration*, VIII (October 1964), 326.

[27] Carl H. Landé, *Leaders, Factions, and Parties* (New Haven, 1965), pp. 1–2. Cf. Onofre D. Corpuz, *The Philippines* (Englewood Cliffs, N.J.: Prentice-Hall, Inc., 1965), pp. 103–104.

TABLE 7

DISTRIBUTION OF OCCUPATIONAL GROUPS AMONG CHIEF EXECUTIVE OFFICERS
OF LOCAL GOVERNMENT, THE PHILIPPINES, 1959–1967

| Officeholders | Year Elected | Total | | Occupational Groups | | | | | |
| | | | | Lawyers | | Businessmen[a] | | Agriculturalists[b] | |
		No.	Per-cent	No.	Per-cent	No.	Per-cent	No.	Per-cent
Provincial	1959	54	100	30	55.55	8	14.85	5	9.25
Governors	1963	56	100	21	37.49	8	14.28	6	10.72
	1967	65	100	25	38.45	7	10.77	8	12.31
City	1959	28	100	12	42.86	4	14.29	4	14.29
Mayors	1963	39	100	18	46.14	3	7.69	5	12.82
	1967	48	100	18	37.53	7	14.58	8	6.66
Municipal	1959	1,199	100	181	15.07	138	11.49	312	25.98
Mayors	1963	1,326	100	163	12.29	196	14.77	394	29.71
	1967	1,373	100	180	13.11	248	18.05	389	28.34

[a] Including also merchants and contractors.

[b] Including landlords, ranchers, farmers, poultrymen, and hog raisers.

SOURCES: The Philippines, Commission on Elections, *Reports of Commission on Elections to President of the Philippines and the Congress* . . . *1959, 1965, 1969* (Manila: Bureau of Printing, 1960, 1965, 1969).

gradually tapering off at the higher levels. This can be seen in tables 7 and 8. Table 7 presents data on the distribution of three principal occupational groups—lawyers, businessmen, and agriculturalists—among the chief executive officers of the provincial, city, and municipal governments.[28] Only at the municipal level did agriculturalists constitute the largest group. At the provincial and city levels they ranked behind lawyers and businessmen.

At the national level, direct representation by agriculturalists was even smaller, and appears to have declined. In a study of the social and economic backgrounds of members of the Philippine Congress for 1923 to 1962, Robert B. Stauffer found that in both the Senate and the House of Representatives lawyers were by far the largest occupational group and that businessmen and agriculturalists, respectively, experienced a rise and a decline in their size of representation. Table 8 provides the pertinent data.

[28] Administratively, the Philippines is divided into provinces and cities (both have equal administrative status); provinces are broken into municipalities; and municipalities into barrios.

TABLE 8

PROPORTION OF REPRESENTATION OF OCCUPATIONAL GROUPS
IN THE CONGRESS, THE PHILIPPINES, 1921–1962

In percentages[a]

	Senate					House of Representatives				
Occupation	1921–1923	1932	1946	1954	1962	1921–1923	1932	1946	1954	1962
Lawyers	87.5	78.2	79.1	78.2	62.5	68.8	68.7	63.9	71.2	75.9
Businessmen	—	13.0	8.3	13.0	25.0	8.6	11.4	9.2	6.9	18.2
Agriculturalists	20.8	21.7	8.3	4.3	16.6	32.2	30.2	15.4	13.8	6.7

[a] Totals exceed 100% because of multiple occupations.
SOURCE: Robert B. Stauffer, "Philippine Legislators and Their Changing Universe,"
The Journal of Politics, XXVIII (August 1966), 580.

It is significant to point out that from 1921 to 1962, while the proportion of *legislators identified as agriculturalists* declined in both chambers of
Congress, the proportion of *legislators representing agricultural interests*
increased in the House and remained fairly large in the Senate. Stauffer
observed in 1966: "Through the past thirty years the number of Representatives who can be identified as either defending or promoting crops
used . . . [for domestic consumption] has steadily and persistently increased; and . . . the number 'representing' export crops has, with the
exception of the 1946 Senate, remained at the 20–30% level in both
houses." [29]

As in the case of Colombia, this discrepancy between representation
of the *agricultural occupation* and *agricultural interest* in the Philippine
Congress can be explained by reference to the fusion of interests among
agricultural, professional, and business occupations.[30] Philippine lawyers

[29] Robert B. Stauffer, "Philippine Legislators and Their Changing Universe," *The
Journal of Politics*, XXVIII (August 1966), 587. Stauffer did not mention how he
ascertained the number of legislators representing agricultural interests, and he only
graphically demonstrated the increase of this number in 1921 to 1962 (*ibid.*, p. 586).
No detailed data were provided.

[30] To a certain extent, this explanation is confirmed by a survey of social backgrounds of 175 national leaders (19 Senators, 29 Representatives and 127 top administrators) of the Philippines by Jose V. Abueva. See Abueva, "Social Backgrounds and
Recruitment of Legislators and Administrators in the Philippines," *Philippine Journal
of Public Administration*, IX (January 1965), 10–29, particularly his data on the socio-
economic class of legislators and of their fathers (*ibid.*, 17 and 22).

frequently come from families owning considerable land; businessmen managing agriculture-related industries (sugar, tobacco, lumber) and crop-export firms—which constitute the bulk of business interests in the country—have direct or indirect investment in land. This group of lawyers and businessmen are not identified as agriculturalists in terms of occupational background, but they certainly defend the latter's interests. In the Philippines, it is this group, whose economic preeminence extends to both the countryside and the city, that lies at the very center of the power structure.

Primary Objective of Reform: Productivity v. Equity

In the formulation of a reform program, a matter of central importance to the political elite is the selection of increasing productivity or social justice as the primary objective of reform. For reasons to be mentioned later, a division of opinion frequently occurs among both policy makers and experts as to which of these two objectives should be emphasized in reform.[31] This matter deserves close inquiry, for the choice made by the elite deeply affects the nature and content of the program presented. As an objective of land reform, increasing productivity means the rise of agricultural output both per unit of land and per unit of labor; social justice signifies equity, i.e. equalization of agricultural income, rights, and opportunities.

PRODUCTIVITY AS THE PRIMARY OBJECTIVE

Certain specialists believe that reform must first seek to raise production. "Land reform which does not increase production merely equalizes poverty," Chiang Mon-lin, the late JCRR chairman of Taiwan has remarked.[32] "The fundamental problem of poverty," Pedro C. M. Teichert has noted in reference to the Mexican reform, "could . . . not be solved

---

[31] For a brief but useful discussion of these two objectives of land reform from a historical, worldwide perspective, see Vernon W. Ruttan, "Equity and Productivity Objectives in Agrarian Reform Legislation: Perspectives on the New Philippine Land Reform Code," *Indian Journal of Agricultural Economics*, XIX (July–December 1964), 114–119. For a treatment on the same subject in the light of Latin American experiences, see Thomas F. Carroll, "Land Reform as an Explosive Force in Latin America" (Columbus, Ohio, 1964), pp. 85–100.

[32] Quoted in Clarence Senior, *Land Reform and Democracy* (Gainesville, Fla., 1958), p. 189.

by the 'right distribution of land.' . . . ." [33] Many who agree with these
opinions concede that the traditional land-tenure system contains a disincentive for production. But they consider scarcity or underutilization
of agricultural resources as a problem deserving more attention. In a
country with limited per capita arable land, equalization of landownership would only reduce farm holdings to an uneconomical scale, hampering the prospect of introduction of farm mechanization and other
modern agricultural practices. Such a measure would also freeze a large
number of people on farms, thus making it difficult to improve the per
capita income of farmers.

Max F. Millikan has made the familiar observation: "The basic hope
of improvement in the lot of the less fortunate lies in increasing the size
of the pie rather than the way it is cut." Consequently when equity is "in
conflict with increasing productivity, the increase in productivity must
take precedence." [34] According to this view, a rational reform program
should include some moderate redistributive measures but concentrate on
ways to assist and encourage large and medium landholders to make more
productive use of their land. Upholding this view, Raul Branco concluded
in his study of Latin American reform:

> A bold program of land reform should be enforced in those instances
> of unutilized or grossly underutilized landholdings. In the case of
> land already under cultivation some subdivision of landholding should
> be encouraged. But a crash program as in Mexico, Bolivia and Cuba
> should be avoided. Primary consideration should be given to the use
> of indirect measures such as the establishment of maximum legal
> size for agricultural holdings, . . . Outright expropriation of land-
> holdings should be reserved only for those specific cases warranted
> by socio-political considerations, . . .[35]

In analyzing the Indian experiences of agricultural and economic development, N. A. Khan shares this view.

[33] Pedro C. M. Teichert, *Economic Policy, Revolution and Industrialization in
Latin America* (University of Mississippi, Bureau of Business Research, 1959), quoted
in Howard F. Cline, *Mexico, Revolution to Evolution* (London: Oxford University
Press, 1962), p. 221.
    [34] Max F. Millikan, "Equity Versus Productivity in Economic Development," in
Myron Weiner (ed.), *Modernization: The Dynamics of Growth* (New York: Basic
Books, Inc., 1966), p. 311.
    [35] Raul Branco, "Land Reform: The Answer to Latin American Agricultural De-
velopment?" *Journal of Inter-American Studies*, IX (April 1967), 235.

Parity for agriculture cannot be bought at the cost of stagnation or slow progress which scarcity of agricultural commodities would necessarily imply. The inegalitarian trend can be checked . . . but it cannot be altogether terminated. For, paradoxical though it may seem, the most effective cure of gross inequalities is inequality itself, which, by stepping up capital formation and the rate of development, increases employment and income for all sections of the society.[36]

In essence, all people emphasizing productivity as the primary objective of reform share the belief that meaningful improvement in the well-being of small farmers can only be achieved in a growing and prosperous agricultural economy, with accelerating industrialization. Best representing an attempt to incorporate this thinking into a nation's development policy is what is known as the Currie Plan for Colombia. Lauchlin Currie, who first led the 1949 World Bank mission to Colombia and subsequently became an economic adviser to the country, advanced the thesis that the fundamental rural problem in Colombia was one of low income caused by underemployment. Too many people worked on too little land. To raise income required the removal of the disincentive inherent in the existing land-tenure system and the reduction of the rural population. This could best be accomplished by expanding agricultural exports and by developing industrial employment opportunities to absorb surplus rural labor. Economic development priority should, therefore, be given to investment in export crops and in industrialization. Land-reform measures merely emphasizing redistribution without relieving rural underemployment are seen as essentially a wrong approach to the problem of rural poverty.[37]

EQUITY AS THE PRIMARY OBJECTIVE

There are people who differ with this line of thinking. Raúl Prebisch believes that to suggest economic development must precede social reforms is *"a profound error. There will be no acceleration in the rate of economic development without a transformation of the social structure."* [38] It can be argued that economic stagnation in a traditional society is in part caused by the inequality of distribution of wealth. Those who are affluent do not

[36] N. A. Khan, "Resource Mobilization from Agriculture and Economic Development in India," *Economic Development and Cultural Change*, XII (October 1963), 54.
[37] See Lauchlin Currie, "Reflections on Colombian Agricultural Policy" (Bogatá: Foundation for the Progress of Colombia, 1962; mimeo.). Cf. Currie, *Obstacles to Development* (East Lansing, Mich.: Michigan State University Press, 1967), pp. 11–17.
[38] Quoted in Carroll, *op. cit.*, p. 98 (original italics).

make productive use of their wealth. An extensive study of the income distribution data of many developing and developed countries found that national income was more unequally distributed—in both the agricultural and non-agricultural sectors of the economy—in the developing countries than in the developed. The study concluded that unequal income distribution would hamper economic growth if higher incomes "are used to strengthen monopolistic positions or wasted on frivolous consumer luxuries" —the very conditions often associated with heavy concentration of land-ownership.[39]

To many who regard the political and social inequality implicit in the traditional land-tenure system as the major rural problem, equity must be the primary objective of land reform. They would advocate, as far as practicable, equal sharing among the farming population of landownership and agricultural income. Their hope for increasing agricultural output rests on the following considerations. First, a considerable amount of evidence has indicated that in countries with pronounced land concentration, the size of farm holdings correlates negatively with productivity. In other words, large estates produce less per unit of land than small farms. Studies of land productivity in Argentina, Brazil, Chile, Colombia, Ecuador, Guatemala, India, Iran, and Mexico uniformly demonstrated this tendency.[40] As an illustration, the pertinent data for five of these countries are presented in Table 9.

[39] Simon Kuznets, "Quantitative Aspects of the Economic Growth of Nations: VIII, Distribution of Income by Size," Economic Development and Cultural Change, XI (January 1963), Part II, 12ff. Quotations appear on p. 69. Cf. Gunnar Myrdal, "Land Reform in its Broader Economic and Social Setting," in the U.N., Report of the World Land Reform Conference, 1966 (New York: U.N., 1968), p. 64.

[40] For the first seven countries, see CIDA, Land Tenure Conditions and Socio-Economic Development of the Agricultural Sector in Seven Latin American Countries (Washington, D.C.: Unión Panamericana, 1966), Table 3; for India, Erven J. Long, "The Economic Basis of Land Reform in Underdeveloped Economies," Land Economics XXXVII (May 1961), 113–123; N. S. Randhawa, "Returns to Scale and Cooperative Farming," Indian Journal of Agricultural Economics, XV (1960), 22–33; and Hanumantha Rao, Agricultural Production Functions, Costs and Returns in India (London: Asia Publishing House, 1965), pp. 6–62; for Iran, U.S., Department of Agriculture, Changes in Agriculture in 26 Developing Nations, 1948–1963 (Washington, D.C., 1965), p. 42; for Mexico, Folke Dovring, Land Reform and Productivity: the Mexican Case, a Preliminary Analysis (Urbana: University of Illinois, Department of Agricultural Economics, Agricultural Experiment Station, 1966). For additional studies on these countries, see Don Kanel, "Size of Farm and Economic Development" (Madison: University of Wisconsin, Land Tenure Center, LTC No. 17, 1966); and Peter Dorner, Marion Brown, and Don Kanel, "Land Reform: Issues in Latin American Development," Land Tenure Center Newsletter, No. 29 (March–August 1969), 1–10.

TABLE 9

RELATIVE LAND PRODUCTIVITY OF FARMS: OUTPUT PER UNIT OF LAND
OF DIFFERENT SIZE GROUPS AS PERCENTAGE OF OUTPUT
OF THE SMALLEST SIZE, FIVE COUNTRIES

Country and Year of Data	Size Groups[a]	Relative Land Productivity[b] Percent
Brazil, 1950	Sub-family farm	100
	Family farm	59
	Medium farm	24
	Large farm	11
Colombia, 1960	Sub-family farm	100
	Family farm	47
	Medium farm	19
	Large farm	7
Ecuador, 1954	Sub-family farm	100
	Family farm	130
	Medium farm	87
	Large farm	35
India, 1950s	Smallest farm	100
	Second smallest farm	86
	Second largest farm	78
	Largest farm	73
Mexico, 1960	Small private farm	100
	Large private farm	97
	Ejido	95

[a] The size groups of farms for Brazil, Colombia, and Ecuador are defined as follows: sub-family farm—farm large enough to provide employment for less than 2 people; family farm—for 2 to 3.9 people; medium farm—for 4 to 12 people; large farm—for more than 12 people. The size groups for Mexico are: small private farm—5 hectares or less; large private farms—over 5 hectares; *ejido* farms are averaged at 7 hectares for each *ejidatario*. It must be noted the *average* size of an *ejido* farm is several times smaller than that of private large farms. Consequently the relative productivity of these two size groups stands as an exception to the rule that smaller farms are more productive. More on this point will be discussed in Chapter IX.

[b] The term "land" refers to agricultural land for the first three countries, and to crop land for the latter two countries. Percentages for large private farms and *ejido* farms in Mexico have been rounded.

SOURCES: Data on Brazil, Colombia, and Ecuador are from CIDA, *Land Tenure Conditions and Socio-Economic Development of the Agricultural Sector in Seven Latin American Countries* (Washington, D.C.: Unión Panamericana, 1966), Table 3; data on India, covering areas in seven states, from Erven J. Long, "The Economic Basis of Land Reform in Underdeveloped Economies," *Land Economics*, XXXVII (May 1961), 113–123; and data on Mexico from the 1960 census quoted in Folke Dovring, *Land Reform and Productivity: the Mexican Case, a Preliminary Analysis* (Urbana: University of Illinois, Department of Agricultural Economics, Agricultural Experiment Station, 1966), Table 4.

This negative correlation between size of farms and productivity is mainly due to the fact that small farms are more labor intensive and frequently more capitalized than large ones.[41] A study of land tenure in India has found: "Relatively higher pressure of workers in small sized holdings enable them to use their land and other associated resources more intensively and thus perhaps get higher per acre gross production." [42] Another study on the agriculture of India—relative to only Telengana, Andhra Pradesh—showed that both land output and labor and capital input varied negatively with the size of farms.[43] Similarly, a 1956 survey of Philippine agriculture indicated that "the net capital [formation] . . . and the stock of capital per hectare [in the farm] decreased as the size of the farm increased." [44] These findings demonstrate that, under the prevailing conditions in most developing countries, existence of large farms is economically unjustifiable, and that a redistribution of farms may open up the prospect for further capital investment and labor intensive farming, hence, increased production. Hanumantha Rao's comment on Indian agriculture is of broad relevance: "The 'smallness' of size has not proved a particular deterrent to capital construction through the application of surplus labor. Nor has it prevented the cultivators from realizing higher net income per acre." Consequently, Rao continued, "under the system of family-farming and labour-intensive techniques, productivity of land and total output can be increased if the structure of landownership is altered and a more even distribution is ensured as this would, among other things, make for a greater identity between the factors of ownership, management and labour." [45]

[41] See U.N., *Land Reform, Fourth Report*, pp. 144–145. An FAO survey of the agricultural productivity of 52 countries for 1956 to 1960 has provided pertinent information on this point. The survey divided the 52 countries into 4 groups according to land productivity and labor intensity (number of persons employed per unit of land). The survey indicated that the group with the highest land productivity is also the group with the greatest labor intensity. FAO, *The State of Food and Agriculture, 1963*, Table III–7. Collating this information with the FAO survey on the world agrarian structure in 1961 (FAO, *World Agricultural Structure, Study No. 1: General Introduction and Size of Holdings*, Table 1), one can find that the most productive group of countries is also the group with the smallest average size of holdings.

[42] P. S. Sharma, "Pattern of Land Concentration," *The Economic Weekly*, XVII (December 11, 1965), 1827.

[43] Rao, *op. cit.*, pp. 9–11.

[44] Levy A. Trinidad, "Private Capital Formation in Philippine Agriculture," *The Philippine Economic Journal*, III (Second Semester, 1964), 143.

[45] Rao, *op. cit.*, pp. 62–63. Herein lies the inappropriateness of the analogy between land redistribution and cutting a pie. Land is a factor of production, not a consumable commodity, as pie is. Whether a piece of land is actually productive depends on, among other things, its availability to the tiller and his incentive to make good use of it. A land

This is conclusively demonstrated in the post-reform experiences of Taiwan and Japan, where farms are very small, but highly labor and capital intensive as well as productive.[46]

To raise agricultural production, those suggesting equity as the main reform objective entertain a second consideration. They believe that to raise agricultural production through farm mechanization and through industrial absorption of surplus rural labor is an attractive idea but not realizable in most developing countries in the immediate future. After examining the population changes in sixteen fully industrialized nations, Folke Dovring found that in most of these nations the size of "agricultural population remained relatively stable over a long time and has shown decline in absolute numbers only recently, long after the countries were definitely industrialized." He concluded, "in most of the less developed countries today, there is no reason to expect reduction of absolute numbers in the agricultural population within the near future." [47] In fact, as a recent FAO survey of the "changes in the occupational distribution of the population" in forty-five countries has indicated, in the developing countries—with very few exceptions—"the absolute size of the agricultural population and labor force has continued to increase." [48] The implication

---

redistribution program providing landownership to the tiller can stimulate him to apply maximal labor and capital inputs to farm for increasing production. It is clearly conceivable to divide land while making it more productive, but it is impossible to cut a pie while making it bigger.

[46] In terms of land productivity Taiwan ranked third and Japan fourth among fifty-two nations for 1956–1960 as surveyed by the FAO. See FAO, *The State of Food and Agriculture, 1963*, p. 110. For the increase of labor and capital inputs in post-reform Taiwanese farms, see S. C. Hsieh and T. H. Lee, "The Effect of Population Pressure and Seasonal Labor Surplus on the Pattern and Intensity of Agriculture in Taiwan," *Industry of Free China*, XXIII (January 1965), 2–19; and Young-chi Tsui, "A Preliminary Assessment of the Impact of Agrarian Reform on Taiwan's Agricultural Economy," *Industry of Free China*, XXIII (February 1965), 28–37. In 1960, the average size of a farm holding in Taiwan (see Table 3, this book) was 1.09 hectares, the smallest among the eight countries under study. In the same year, according to FAO's *Production Yearbook 1964*, Japan's average size of farm holdings was quite close to Taiwan's: 1:18 hectares.

[47] Folke Dovring, "The Share of Agriculture in a Growing Population," *Monthly Bulletin of Agricultural Economics and Statistics*, VIII (August-September 1959), 8 and 11. Similarly, a CIDA study on land tenure of seven Latin American countries concluded: "The arithmetic of development argues against the possibility of solving the agrarian problem simply by moving the rural poor into urban areas. In the study countries, total population could not be absorbed much more rapidly than at present, even if there were rapid forced-draft industrialization." CIDA, *Land Tenure Conditions . . .* , p. 39.

[48] FAO, *The State of Food and Agriculture, 1965*, p. 57.

of these findings is evident. For some time to come the best hope for increasing agricultural output in the developing countries is to raise land productivity by adopting labor-intensive rather than labor-displacement techniques. The best way to encourage farmers to resort to labor-intensive farming is to provide them with ownership of land and an equitable share of agricultural income.

A final consideration for increasing agricultural production may be cited. In the high tenancy areas of Asia and the Middle East, as noted before, concentration of landownership does not mean concentration of farm operations. Land of large estates is already fragmented. Transfer of landownership from the absentee landlord to the incumbent tenant or substantial reduction of rent will not adversely affect farm operations. Only the physical division of well-managed commercial farms may lead to a decline of production. This can be avoided by exempting them from land reform or by placing them under joint management.

It is apparent, then, that productivity and equity are competitive objectives of land reform. They may be pursued simultaneously but not at the same pace. A program emphasizing improvement of productivity and allowing limited redistributive measures may make some contribution to equity, but it will make much less contribution than a program of substantive land redistribution and rent reduction. Conversely, a program stressing equity as the major objective may result in some increase in agricultural production, but not as much as the increase resulting from a program concentrating on the improvement of agricultural techniques, services, and supplies.

PREFERENCE OF ELITES

In the developing countries today, because the persistence of low national income and the prevalence of rural social discontent and political instability constitute equally pressing problems, political elites often claim that their reform programs aim at achieving productivity and equity simultaneously. "My object in setting up the Land Reforms Commission," Ayub Khan announced in 1959, would be to devise a program "which will satisfy, on the one hand, the social need for greater equality of opportunity and social status and, on the other hand, the economic need for increasing agricultural production and improving the standard of rural living. . . ."[49] The framers of the Colombian Social Agrarian Reform Law of 1961 de-

[49] Ayub Khan, *Speeches and Statements*, I, p. 48.

clared that the purpose of the law was, among other things, to "reform the social land structure of the country, eliminating the inequitable concentration of rural holdings" and to "increase overall agricultural and livestock production alongside the development of the other sectors of the economy." (Article 1) The Philippine Congress proclaimed in the Agricultural Land Reform Code of 1963: "It is the policy of the State . . . to achieve a dignified existence for the small farmers free from pernicious institutional restraints and practices; [and] to create a truly viable social and economic structure in agriculture conducive to greater productivity and higher farm incomes." (Section 2)

In reality, in view of the competitiveness of productivity and equity, political elites must give priority to one or the other. Experience reveals that *separated elites* (those separated from the landed class) tend to emphasize equity, whereas *cooperative elites* (those collaborating with the landed class) generally stress productivity. With the landed class becoming powerless in the policy process or destroyed in revolution, separated elites can first satisfy the primary wish of the peasantry—the desire for landownership and a greater share of crops—and later seek to increase production. Hoping to maintain the loyalty of both the landed class and the peasantry, cooperative elites frequently offer the prospect of increased production to the former to compensate for its loss and provide limited benefits to the latter to win its allegiance. Since the wishes of peasants are assumed to be easier to satisfy than the desires of powerful landlords, the programs adopted by cooperative elites will emphasize productivity as the main objective.

Separated Elites

Subsequent chapters will attempt to make a comparison of the specific provisions of the reform programs of the eight countries under study to substantiate these observations. It is now appropriate to analyze briefly the basic preferences of the elites of these countries. Heavily motivated by political and ideological considerations, and facing no opposition from the local landed gentry, the Kuomintang adopted reforms in Taiwan mainly for the purpose of gaining the political loyalty of the peasants. Economic gains were thought of as a natural consequence of the reform, but initially they were not given any prominent mention in official pronouncements or in writings of policy makers. In 1949 to 1953 when the main reform measures—rent reduction, public land sales, and land-to-the-tiller programs—were implemented, there were scarcely any public programs designed to improve land use and to increase production. The primary concern was how to provide expeditiously the bulk of the peasantry with an enlarged share of the land and its products. Well after the completion of the land-to-the-tiller measure of 1953 the government began to stress the development of water resources, consolidation of holdings, increasing production of fertilizers, and improvement of farming practices.

The Mexican reform experience reveals a similar pattern of development. With the *hacendados* eliminated as a class, the thrust of Mexican land reform in the first three decades after revolution was to give land to the landless and to set up *ejidos*. To the *campesinos*, "emancipation came first, production second." To the revolutionary leaders, "what mattered under the circumstances was the creation of a *fait accompli* and the rest had to take care of itself later." [50] It was only after 1940, when the revolutionary elite was firmly entrenched in power and when the *ejidatarios* had been awarded a very large share of the nation's land, that the elite devoted its efforts to agricultural growth. The massive colonization development projects in the country's northwest and the vast expansion of irrigation facilities occurred in the last three decades, not in the first three, of the post-revolution period.

Likewise in Egypt, as already emphasized in the last chapter, when the Free Officers adopted reform, increase of production was not the major consideration. Their primary concern was to provide what the *fellahin* wanted the most—land. Again, after the land was substantially redistributed the army regime adopted measures for improving agricultural production—they strengthened cooperative farming projects, developed new lands, and expanded the water supply.

Cooperative Elites

Indian land reform experience in this regard is slightly more complicated. Congress's hostility toward the *zamindari* system and cooperation with the lesser landed interests led the party to adopt different programs, with a different emphasis on productivity and equity. One sees in Congress's program for abolition of the *zamindari* system a primary effort to provide substantive benefits to the incumbent *kisans* without any serious concern for the improvement of their productive capacity. In subsequent programs, while the egalitarian principle still remained evident, the dominant concern was to augment the over-all supply of food. Land redistribu-

---

[50] Henrik F. Infield and Koka Freier, *People in Ejidos, A Visit to the Cooperative Farms of Mexico* (New York: Frederick A. Praeger, Publishers, 1954), pp. 94 and 130.

tion and rent reduction laws were haphazardly formulated and implemented, but such measures as "package districts," experimentation with
new seeds, increased supply of chemical fertilizers, and irrigation water
were given official attention and provided with most of the funds earmarked for rural development.

In the remaining four countries, the elites have never emphasized
equity as their main objective. In Iran, as the United Nations reported,
"it is, indeed, the explicit intention of the reform not to establish equality,
but to create an extended tenure ladder. . . . [The hope is] that these
new landlords [created by the reform], being close to the productive
process, are in fact more concerned with raising productivity than were
the original absentee landlords, . . ." [51] In Pakistan, though Ayub Khan
emphasized his preference for both social equality and increasing production as reform objectives, he also acknowledged that "the requirements of
social justice and the interests of economic development are not always
identical." [52] While he was content to let some 6,000 landlords in West
Pakistan lose a fraction of their holdings, he was convinced that the "no-
tion that everybody must own land just does not make sense. We do not
have enough land to give everybody. You can broaden the base of ownership but you must have a class of people interested in investing in land
and working on it on a sound economic and progressive basis." [53] Thus
Ayub Khan stressed from the inception of his reform program measures
designed to benefit this class of farming interests. In Colombia, two recent
presidents have given strong indications that reform was aimed at production. In October 1964, Conservative President León Valencia declared,
"We are carrying through a land reform whose primary objective is not
so much to change the number of land-owners as to increase the national
production . . . through a more intensive, more scientific and more diversified exploitation of land." [54] This declaration of intent was supported
by his Liberal successor, President Carlos Lleras Restrepo, who espoused
the belief: "The strategy of economic development is intricately linked up
with the strategy of social development because only a growth in productivity and in total income can produce a substantial change in the level of
living of the masses, . . ." [55] As subsequent analysis will make evident, in

[51] U.N., *Land Reform, Fourth Report*, p. 24.
[52] Ayub Khan, *Friends Not Masters*, p. 88.
[53] *Ibid.*, p. 92.
[54] Quoted in U.N., *Land Reform, Fourth Report*, p. 21.
[55] Colombia Information Service, *Colombia Today*, Vol. 4, No. 5 (May 1969).

executing the 1961 law, the Lleras administration, 1966–1970, concerned itself primarily with measures for raising the productive capacity of the *campesinos*. Finally, an inquiry into the content of the Philippine reform law of 1963 would reveal that it was "drafted to imply a solution of the social reform versus productivity dilemma so as to give clear first priority to productivity. Change is to be introduced gradually and avoided altogether if it entails the risk of a fall in production." [56]

Processes of Conflict Resolution

In formulating a program, the elite confronts two different but interrelated sets of problems. The first is political. How does an elite overcome the almost unanimous opposition of the entrenched landed class? How can it effectively fight for the cause of the peasantry, which is politically inarticulate, disorganized, and lacking competent leadership, hence unable to provide concerted and sustained support in a prolonged struggle? How does it frame a program that can help strengthen its rule but avoid the threat posed either by antagonized landlords or disillusioned peasants? A second set of problems relates to complex policy questions. The establishment of criteria according to which land rights are to be altered; the option between redistributive and developmental schemes; the determination of a financing formula; the selection of beneficiaries; the choice of gradual and selective versus immediate and comprehensive processes of program implementation—all these policy questions give rise to different and often conflicting views not only between proponents and opponents of reform but among the proponents as well.

Basically, political elites approach the two sets of problems through either a unilateral decision in more or less arbitrary manner or a bargaining process to achieve a consensus. Separated elites typically follow the first approach; conciliatory elites generally prefer the second; and dominant elites may change from one approach to another over time, with most of them favoring the first.

SEPARATED ELITES: UNILATERAL DECISION

Separated elites as a rule exclude the landed interests from the process of program formulation; they tend to resolve policy problems primarily with a view to satisfying the interests of the peasants. They try to adopt

[56] U.N., *Land Reform, Fourth Report*, p. 28.

measures that can easily be enforced without imposing on themselves excessive financial and administrative burdens. They often act speedily and without careful deliberation, preferring executive decrees to legislative enactments as the forms of their programs.

In Taiwan, all three principal programs—the Rent Reduction Act of 1949, the Regulations for the Sale of Public Land of 1951, and the Land-to-the-Tiller Act of 1953—were framed by the Kuomintang, the Executive Yuan (cabinet), and the Provincial Council (executive branch of the Provincial Government), with only limited participation by the national and provincial legislatures. Of all these organs, only the Provincial Assembly had some representation from the landed interests. But the Assembly was the least influential, possessing only advisory or consultative functions. In fact, the 1949 rent-reduction program was implemented under the authority of executive "regulations." The origin of this program can be traced back to the experiences of the Kuomintang on the mainland. The Chinese Land Law of 1930 had first provided that rent be limited to 37.5 percent of the annual yield of the main crop.[57] In the late 1930s, General Chen Cheng, then Governor of Hupeh Province, implemented this provision of the law in that province. Upon becoming Governor of Taiwan in 1949, Chen determined to bring about a similar reform. After a three-month deliberation, the Taiwan Provincial Council promulgated on April 14, 1949, the "Regulations Governing the Lease of Private Farm Lands in Taiwan Province" and put the measure immediately in force. In November 1950, these regulations formed the basis of a bill to be enacted as a national statute. In May 1951, two years after rental reform had been implemented, the Legislative Yuan (the national legislature) passed the "Farm Rent Reduction to 37.5% Act." Like the rent-reduction program, the program for selling public land was introduced and promptly formulated by the executive authority. The Taiwan Provincial Council first adopted in 1948 a set of regulations to sell a limited amount of public land, but

[57] This provision of the Land Law was in turn based on a provision of the platform of the KMT of 1926, which recommended a 25 percent reduction from the prevailing rental rate. Since the existing rental rate in China was generally 50 percent of the main crop, the rate after reduction would be 37.5 $[(50 - 50 \times 25/100)]$ percent. In 1946 the Land Law was revised limiting maximum rental rate to 8 percent of the land value. Because of the absence of a statutory formula for appraising land value, the Executive Yuan issued a decree in 1947 again setting the maximum rental rate at 37.5 percent of the main crop. Ying-jui Liu, "Tsu Yu Chung Kuo T'u Ti Li Fa Tsung Shu" ("A Summary of Land Legislation in Free China"), Land Reform Monthly (in Chinese), V (June 1955), 9–10.

suspended the program in 1949 because of the intervening rental reform. In 1951, the council drew up a new set of "Regulations Governing the Implementation of the Sale of Public Land to Help Establish Owner-Farmers in Taiwan Province." After consulting the Taiwan Provincial Assembly, the council submitted the drafted regulations to the Executive Yuan, which approved them on June 4, 1951. They were enforced forthwith.

The only reform program in Taiwan that took the form of a legislative act before it was implemented was the land-to-the-tiller program. Even in this program, the KMT and the executive authorities dominated the process of formulation, with the national and provincial legislatures playing no decisive roles. In 1952, the Land Bureau of the Taiwan Provincial Government submitted a draft of the program, which remained substantively unchanged when enacted by the Legislative Yuan in 1953.[58] In the interval, the Taiwan Provincial Government, the Executive Yuan, the JCRR, as well as the Legislative Yuan and the Provincial Assembly did enter into substantive debate of the proposed law, but no important changes were entertained. When the Provincial Assembly, where landlords had some voice, tried to weaken the program by introducing a number of amendments, "President Chiang Kai-shek immediately called on July 24 [1952] the 371st session of the Central Reform Committee of [the] Kuomintang. The Committee resolved: (1) the Land-to-the-Tiller program must be inaugurated in January 1953 and (2) all party members in both executive and legislative branches of the Government must comply with the party's determination in this undertaking." [59] The assembly, whose concurrence was not required, dropped its amendments.[60] Subsequently, after some consideration and minor changes by the Executive Yuan, the bill was referred on November 12, 1952, to the Legislative Yuan, which passed it practically intact on January 20, 1953. The Land-to-the-Tiller Act became effective on January 26, 1953, when it was signed by President Chiang Kai-shek.

In Mexico, the 1915 reform decree, which served as the foundation of the agrarian program of the last half century, was hastily issued by

[58] For a summary of the original draft of the bill by the Land Bureau, see JCRR, *JCRR Annual Reports on Land Reform in the Republic of China*, pp. 58–59.
[59] *Ibid.*, p. 60.
[60] The Assembly submitted four amendments designed to allow landlords to retain more land and receive a greater compensation than they would under the Land Bureau's draft bill. For a description of these amendments, see *ibid.*

Carranza under the pressure of civil war and heavily influenced by Zapata's demand for the restoration of usurped Indian land. As Eyler N. Simpson has put it, "the decree had only one string to its bow—land to village. . . . [It] was primarily a 'negative' program, a procedure for righting past wrongs, and not a 'positive' attempt to face the land problem as a whole." [61] When Carranza held the constitutional convention in 1916 to 1917 to revise the Constitution of 1857, the convention—dominated by revolutionary generals, intellectuals, and labor and peasant leaders—incorporated, with some amplifications, the 1915 decree into Article 27 of the new constitution. Subsequently, as the *hacendados* had disappeared as a class, the national legislature enacted numerous agrarian codes and statutes to provide details to the reform outline that had been sketched out in 1915 and 1917.

In Egypt, the 1952 reform decree was likewise hastily formulated. In July, when the coup occurred, most of the Free Officers had no reform program of their own; they had first thought of letting the interim civilian government under Ali Maher frame a program. But as the Maher government demonstrated its lukewarm attitude to the matter, Wing Commander Gamal Salim of the Free Officer group promptly set to work on a new proposal.[62] "Under Salim's supervision two left wing economists, Ahmed Fuad, a former Deputy Judge and an old friend of Nasser, and Professor Rashid Barawi . . . drew up a scheme which, after six weeks of brief but feverish composition," became the basis of the 1952 decree.[63] On September 9, two days after the replacement of the Maher government with the military regime, the decree was formally promulgated.

In Taiwan, Mexico, and Egypt the elites excluded the landed class from the policy process and promptly framed reform programs. As will be evident in later chapters, all these elites adopted comprehensive programs that emphasized immediate application; substantive redistribution of land with low compensation; inclusion of a large number of the incumbent cultivating farmers as beneficiaries; and, with respect to Taiwan and Egypt, substantial rent reduction.

[61] *The Ejido, Mexico's Way Out* (Chapel Hill, N.C., 1937), p. 58.

[62] See Keith Wheelock, *Nasser's New Egypt, A Critical Analysis* (New York: Frederick A. Praeger, Publishers, 1960), pp. 75–77.

[63] Jean Lacouture and Simonne Lacouture, *Egypt in Transition* (London: Methuen & Co., 1958), p. 166.

COOPERATIVE ELITES: THE CONTEXTS OF BARGAINING

For cooperative elites, the task of conflict resolution is understandably far more arduous. The elites have to bargain with representatives of the landed class within the legislative arena to work out a program that may entail immediate sacrifice to the powerful few but yield no sufficiently meaningful benefits to the masses. Thus, these elites become scrupulous in dealing with policy questions. They endorse both redistributive and developmental measures, but neither is provided with effective enforcement provisions. They generally adopt a financial formula so generous to the owners that the government is fiscally incapable of implementing it on any large scale. They tend to formulate detailed programs that can be enforced only gradually, benefiting a limited number of farmers at a time.

The reform sponsors often have to argue their case in unfavorable constitutional and political contexts. In advocating a law that entails compulsory changes of the tenure structure, they have to meet the test of constitutionality with regard to private property rights. Two issues are involved: the right of the nation to alter the property rights of one individual in favor of another and the question of compensation for those whose property rights are adversely affected. The first issue necessitates a reinterpretation of the doctrine of "eminent domain." Having long been accepted as the right of a nation to expropriate private property for public use, the doctrine has to be broadened to mean that the state has the authority to transfer private property from one individual to another (on the ground that a *public purpose* is served) as well as to acquire such property for its own use. This broadened meaning of eminent domain is predicated on the proposition that property rights are not absolute and cannot be so exercised as to be detrimental to the public interest. The second constitutional issue concerns whether the government must, in expropriation proceedings, pay full, prompt indemnification to landowners, and whether the legislature or the court has the right to determine the adequacy of compensation. Both constitutional issues occurred in the battles over land reform in Colombia, India, and the Philippines.

In 1936, President Alfonso López of Colombia had to amend the constitution to incorporate the theory of social function of property before he could proceed with reform. Perhaps inspired by the Mexican agrarian reformers who had first applied this theory of the Mexican constitution,[64] Alfonso López helped write Article 30 into the Colombian constitution: "For reasons of public utility or social interest, as defined by the legislature, property may be expropriated by judicial order with prior indemnification. Nevertheless, the legislature, for reasons of equity, may deny idemnification by means of an absolute majority vote of the members of both houses." Only after the passage of this amendment was the Land Law of 1936 enacted.

In India, before the state governments enacted reform laws, the Constituent Assembly wrote Article 31 into the Indian Constitution of 1949, allowing compulsory requisition of property with compensation. When the Supreme Court decided in 1953 in the Bela Banerjee case (in connection with the land reform law of West Bengal) that compensation to landowners had to be "a just equivalent of" the expropriated land and that "full indemnity" was necessary, a constitutional amendment had to be adopted, in 1955, to remove from the court's jurisdiction the question of compensation, leaving it for state governments to decide.[65]

The Philippine Constitution has not been amended to facilitate land reform, but opponents of tenurial change have repeatedly invoked the constitution in the courts to challenge the legality of reform statutes. For instance, Commonwealth Act. No. 539 of 1940, which authorized the President to redistribute private lands, was attacked as illegal because such redistribution was not intended to benefit the general public, but rather specific individuals. In *Guido v. Rural Progress Administration*, the Supreme Court laid down the famous ruling: expropriation of property of small holders for the benefit of a limited number of people was constitutionally untenable, but "expropriation of large estates, trusts in perpetuity and land that embraces a whole town, or a large section of a town or city, bears direct relation to the public welfare," hence, constitutes a legitimate exercise of government power.[66] In *Urban Estates, Inc. v. Hon. Agustin P. Montesa* the court reaffirmed this point: "In brief, the Constitution contemplates large scale purchases or condemnation of lands

---

[64] See Eyler N. Simpson's comment on this subject in *op. cit.*, pp. 72–74.

[65] H. D. Malaviya, *Land Reforms in India* (New Delhi, 1954), pp. 436–438; and Susanne H. Rudolph, "Some Aspects of Congress Land Policy" (Cambridge: Massachusetts Institute of Technology, Center for International Studies, 1957; mimeo.), pp. 30–31.

[66] U.S., Mutual Security Agency, Special Technical and Economic Mission, *Philippine Land Tenure Reform, Analysis and Recommendations* (Prepared by Robert S. Hardie, cited hereafter as *Hardie Report*; Manila, 1952), Appendix G.

with a view to agrarian reforms. . . . Condemnation of private lands in a makeshift or piecemeal fashion, random taking of a small lot here and a small lot there to accommodate a few tenants or squatters is a different thing." [67] Thus the Philippine Supreme Court has sustained in principle the legality of land redistribution legislation. The lower courts have also generally sustained the constitutionality of tenancy reform laws in a number of cases.[68]

It appears that in all three countries where the constitutionality of reform laws has been challenged, the courts or the legislatures have upheld the case of the reformers. But it is not to be concluded that they have easily and completely won their cases. Constitutional battles have frequently lasted over a period of years, and sometimes minor legal controversies and suits have persisted after the major constitutional issues have been settled. For instance, Article 62 of the Colombian Social Agrarian Reform Law of 1961, which provides for payment of compensation for expropriated land in the form of bond, was challenged in 1962 as unconstitutional. It took the Supreme Court two years to reach a decision upholding this provision. With reference to this same law, a supplementary regulatory decree (No. 1904), which set the price of expropriated land at 130 percent of the cadastral value of the land, was challenged by the *Sociedad de Agricultores Colombianos* (SAC, the Society of Colombian Agriculturalists) as a violation of the law. After the Council of State sustained the decree in March 1963, the SAC persisted in its campaign against the decree, eventually convincing the National Agrarian Council of the need to abandon the pricing formula. In November of the same year, Decree 1904 was replaced by Decree 2895, which allowed landowners to declare the value of their land by themselves.[69] In East Pakistan, although the East Bengal State Acquisition and Tenancy Act was promulgated in 1950, a legal challenge to the compensation provision of the law held up its enforcement until 1957, when the Supreme Court in

[67] *Ibid.*
[68] See, for instance, *Primero v. Court of Industrial Relations*, 54 O.G. 5506; *Sibulo v. Altar*, 46 O.G. 5502 (No. L–1916, 1949); *Jacinto v. Catacutan, et al.* (CIR No. 179, 1941). For a detailed legal analysis of the key provisions of the Agricultural Land Reform Code of 1963 in the light of previous judicial decisions, see Don M. Ferry, "The Constitutional and Social Aspects of Land Reform," in Gerardo P. Sicat (ed.), *The Philippine Economy in the 1960's* (Quezon City: University of the Philippines, Institute of Economic Development and Research, 1964), pp. 120–162.
[69] See Ernest A. Duff, *Agrarian Reform in Colombia* (New York, 1968), pp. 115–117 and 196–197.

Dacca upheld its legality.[70] In the Philippines, a legal battle over the issue of "just compensation" for expropriated land under a 1955 reform law lasted nearly a decade, with the landowners winning the case in the end.[71]

All these legal cases caused uncertainty and confusion over the validity of reform laws, often resulting in the delay of enforcement.

In addition to having to resolve the constitutional difficulty, cooperative elites face the problem of political isolation. In parliament, they encounter the determined opposition of the rightists and the apathy or enmity of the leftists, who prefer more extreme or revolutionary changes. In Colombia, during congressional consideration of the reform bill in 1961, the National Front government found itself in precisely such a predicament. The *Laureanista* Conservatives, on the right, and the MRL, on the left, mounted a common, if uncoordinated, attack on the bill, compelling the Liberal Party leader Lleras Restrepo, the sponsor of the measure, to fight a two-front battle. This joint opposition lasted well after the law was enacted.[72] Similarly, in India, when the Congress Party sponsored reforms in the years immediately following independence, the conservative elements of the party, though not openly resisting these measures, tried to subvert them by formulating provisions difficult to enforce. At the same time, in parliament and some of the state legislatures, the Communists followed a militant approach to the agrarian problem, rendering no assistance to Congress's reform effort. Only after the failure of their rural agitational activities did the Communists begin to endorse Congress's stand.

Cooperative elites also face political isolation outside parliament. They enjoy no determined, consistent support from either a vital interest group or the broad masses. The intellectuals, the press, the labor unions, and the business community maintain different attitudes toward the issue of land reform, ranging from artificial endorsement, to political neutrality, to total apathy. The landed and the peasant classes, the groups of people most directly affected by reform, have completely different patterns of behavior. With its members already represented in the legislature, the landed class can apply added pressure through a vigorous propaganda

[70] Pakistan, *Land Reforms in Pakistan*, p. 13.

[71] For a brief reference to this legal dispute, see Chapter VII, below.

[72] See Duff, *op. cit.*, chap. iii, "The Law of Agrarian Reform: Law 135 of 1961;" and Ernest A. Duff, "Agrarian Reform in Colombia: Problems and Social Reform," *Journal of Inter-American Studies*, VIII (January 1966), 75–76.

campaign and effective lobbying, behaving in a way no different from a typical interest group in the Western democracies. For example, *the Sociedad de Agricultures Colombianos* and the *Federacíon Nacional de Cafeteros* (National Federation of Coffee Growers) in Colombia; and the National Rice Producers Association, the National Sugarcane Planters Association, and the Chamber of Agriculture in the Philippines are organized groups actively defending the landed interests. Aside from extending their influence through their own representatives in the legislatures, these groups have sought vigorously to present their opinions in legislative hearings, have directly approached congressmen to solicit support, and have launched publicity campaigns through press releases and through commentaries by news media sympathetic to their views.[73] In contrast, the peasants, with a low level of political consciousness and ineffective organization, often show little awareness of a reform bill under debate, much less any enthusiasm to lend it support by staging demonstrations or by voting discriminately in elections. This appears to be the case in all countries ruled by cooperative elites. Ernest A. Duff's description of the Colombian peasants' indifference to the reform bill of 1961 may well apply to many other cases. "During the entire Senate debate, not one *campesino* group spoke in favor of this measure, which was designed to benefit them. There had been no demonstrations in the streets in favor of agrarian reform." [74] Without a concerned clientele, cooperative elites savor the taste of legislative victory or defeat all by themselves.

In fighting alone for agrarian changes, cooperative elites also face in the legislative arena a group of opponents skillful in parliamentary procedures and adept in employing a variety of arguments—some convincing, some specious and contradictory—calculated to its best advantage. These opponents can resort to various maneuvers to prevent, delay, and sabotage a meaningful proposal. In certain instances, by their own strength or through an alliance with other groups, the landed interests can defeat outright a bill they oppose. In other instances, the opponents may offer weakened alternatives to the proposed law, engage in protracted debate over technical details, demand inordinate concessions, and introduce crippling amendments to the original proposal. In taking these courses of action, the central purpose of the opponents is to enact a law with weak implementation provisions, thereby giving the appearance of supporting

---

[73] For descriptions of these activities of Colombian landed interests, see Duff, *Agrarian Reform in Colombia, passim*; for the case of the Philippines see next chapter.

[74] Duff, *ibid.*, p. 55.

the welfare of the rural masses but, in reality, slowing down the momentum of genuine agrarian changes.

The arguments of the opponents are familiar. First, they contend that a law emphasizing tenurial changes benefits neither the peasants nor the national economy. Given new land, peasants who lack managerial experience and a sense of independence may not be able to operate the farms entirely on their own. With reduced rental payments, tenants may consume their increased income immediately without investing it in improvements on their land. Lacking financial and administrative resources, the government cannot provide any large number of beneficiaries with the necessary assistance to enable them to become productive farmers. In the end, reform may lead to a situation in which, while a majority of the beneficiaries cannot improve their lot because of the unavailability of public assistance, a minority of farmers receiving assistance may become permanently dependent upon it. As a result, no significant economic benefits can be expected. In certain instances, overall agricultural production may actually decline. Such a development is doubly unfortunate: public money is spent to increase rural poverty.

Second, in opposition to specific land redistribution programs, the opponents stress one point. A developing country typically experiences heavy population pressure on existing cultivated areas; hence it just does not have enough land to go around. Even in Iran, where cultivated land is relatively abundant, the Shah once indicated, "if all the agricultural land in the country were divided among the farmers, each farmer would receive only two acres while he requires twelve acres to support his family." [75] Precisely for this reason, Mossadeq, while Prime Minister of the country, rejected land redistribution; instead he offered, in 1953, the Farmer's Share Law to effect a 20 percent reduction in rents.[76] In such countries as Colombia and the Philippines, where large areas of undeveloped land exist, the opponents frequently urge colonization as a substitute for land redistribution. Also, they often refer to industrialization as the only sound and long-range remedy for rural population pressure. The argument behind the Currie Plan of Colombia, cited earlier, is often echoed in the debates on reform in many other countries.

Finally, reform opponents may play up the issue of Communism to weaken the position of the proponents. The opponents sometimes charge that the proponents, though claiming to use land reform to combat Com-

[75] Wilber, *op. cit.* (n. 9 above), p. 187.
[76] *Ibid.*, p. 182.

munism, may end up adopting Communist practices in violation of the institution of private property. In Colombia, during congressional debate on the 1961 reform bill, conservative forces frequently made this charge. For instance, Senator Arango Londoño asserted that the sponsors of the bill were "inspired solely by fear of communism"; his colleague, Senator Alfonso Uribe Misas, declared his opposition to the measure

> because this reform is a derivation or development of the Constitution of 1936 that, with communist criterion, beheaded the natural right of property by considering it solely as a "social function" and by authorizing expropriation without indemnification. . . . [And] because this Reform is not a remedy against the communism that menances this country, but on the contrary is the road that opens the way for this devastating sect to perturb our traditional juridical order and do away with the natural right of property.[77]

In both Iran and the Philippines, some opponents made the strange charge that land reform was imposed by the United States to strengthen Communism.[78]

CONCILIATORY ELITES: A GRADUALISTIC APPROACH

Confronted with these tactics and arguments, how do cooperative elites bring about reform? For *conciliatory* elites, the only sensible way to proceed is gradually. Conciliatory elites, as initiators of reform, are generally more committed to passing some kind of law than to fighting for its effective implementation. The landed interests, as opponents of reform, have gradually come to accept the necessity of agrarian change. They recognize that, with the accelerating, multifaceted social, economic, and political changes taking place in the developing world it is impossible for any society, however traditional, to maintain the status quo. They consider it more prudent to enact some measure of reform than to adopt none at all. Thus the central bargaining point is not the enactment of a law but the content of the law to be enacted. Hence, conciliatory elites can persist in the legislative battle. First obtaining a bill with whatever provisions are agreeable to the opposition, they seek to improve the measure whenever possible, positing a hope of still greater improvement in the future. Initially, conciliatory elites are willing to accept a law which is perfunctory, ineffective, and pregnant with rigidities. For a perfunctory law, once adopted, will have the effect of denying some measure of legiti-

---

[77] Quoted in Duff, *Agrarian Reform in Colombia*, pp. 45 and 125–126.

[78] For reference to this charge made in Iran, see *Iran Almanac and Book of Facts*, 1963, p. 398; and in the Philippines, see next chapter.

macy to the privileges of the landed class. In the long run, pressures for more effective laws will accumulate; when circumstances become more propitious, effective laws may be adopted without strong opposition. Occasionally, Albert O. Hirschman has argued, this gradualistic, pragmatic approach may actually bring forth a revolutionary program without a violent battle—a "revolution by stealth." [79]

The legislative history of the present reform laws of Colombia and the Philippines reveals the utility of this approach. Though by no means as drastic and effective as the laws of, say, Mexico and Taiwan, the Colombian Social Agrarian Reform Law of 1961 and the Philippine Agricultural Land Reform Code of 1963 do provide for compulsory redistribution of large private estates with low retention limits. That these provisions are included in both laws is a result of prolonged legislative battles that began in both countries, coincidentally, in the 1930s. In obtaining these enactments, the elites of the two countries appear to have adopted similar tactics and arguments. They tried to break their political isolation in Congress by enlisting the support of the public. They conducted publicity campaigns in cities while making electoral appeals in the countryside so as to make it politically hazardous for representatives of the landed interests to oppose openly measures in favor of the rural masses. In Colombia, the 1961 bill was drafted on the recommendation of a National Agrarian Committee that included representatives of all sectors of the public.[80] Appointed by President Alberto Lleras Camargo, and headed by Senator Carlos Lleras Restrepo, the committee commanded much social respect, and its members regularly aired their views in "the daily press and weekly periodicals. Consequently, with the exception of the Laureanista *El Siglo* and some provincial Conservative newspapers, the press carried numerous articles favoring Lleras' concept of agrarian reform. The articles . . . [were highly effective as] they were written by distinguished citizens not readily identifiable with the Liberal-Conservative polemics—above politics, as it were." [81] During congressional consideration of the bill, Lleras Restrepo made it a practice of "defending the bill in Bogotá during the week and

[79] *Journeys Toward Progress* (New York, 1963), pp. 155–156.

[80] The Committee consisted of Senator Carlos Lleras Restrepo as Chairman, the Archbishop of Bogotá, two cabinet ministers, several members of the Senate and the House from the Conservative and Liberal parties, one general representing the armed forces, an official of *Caja Agraria* (Agrarian Bank), President of the *Sociedad de Agricultores Colombianos*, two labor union officials, and one official of a cooperative movement. *Laureanista* and MRL members of the committee boycotted its proceedings. See Duff, *Agrarian Reform in Colombia*, pp. 42 and 62.

[81] *Ibid.*, p. 43.

then both defending the bill and attacking his critics during his weekend political trips" in rural areas.[82] With the presidential and congressional elections coming in 1962, Lleras Restrepo's trips to "explain agrarian reform to the people" helped brighten the electoral prospect of the Liberal Party, which he headed, as well as muster public support for the bill. He projected his party's image as one for reform and for the *campesinos*, leaving the *Laureanista* conservatives much infuriated but helpless in opposing him on the issue.[83]

In the Philippines, the publicity generated in the prolonged debates over land reform led the entire press to endorse the cause of agrarian changes. Newspapers and magazines incessantly carried articles, editorials, and news on reform, reaching a crescendo whenever a major bill was to be enacted in Congress. In 1963, when President Diosdado Macapagal pushed for new reform legislation, he created a Land Reform Committee to study the measure and specifically put on the committee Teodoro M. Locsin as a representative of the public. The editor of a very influential weekly *Philippines Free Press*, Locsin had long advocated agrarian changes and had publicized many reform measures in his widely read periodical.

On the political front, efforts to enlist rural support for reform may be said to have begun as early as the 1953 presidential election, when Ramon Magsaysay criss-crosssed the countryside to emphasize his concern for rural welfare. During his brief presidential term, in which several reform measures were submitted to Congress for enactment, he traveled far and wide in the island nation; at times he was away in the villages, trying to identify the peasants with his programs, more often than he was in the capital. In his presidential campaign in 1961, Macapagal followed this populist approach with even greater vigor, reaching many peasants in remote villages where no presidential candidate had ever traveled. These activities of the sponsors of reform placed the opponents of reform entirely on the defensive. When the 1963 draft reform bill was submitted to Congress, Locsin could write: "How could anyone oppose it? Who would vote for poverty . . . ? Those who did would reveal themselves as unworthy to represent the people, as hopelessly stupid at best, as conscious tools of privilege at worst, the main stumbling blocks to progress, to a better life

[82] *Ibid.,* p. 46.

[83] This should not be interpreted to mean that the *campesinos* were then capable of effectively utilizing their electoral power to support reform. Rather, to bring the issue of reform directly to them, Lleras Restrepo introduced into the legislative battle an invisible political force which the opponents did not wish to antagonize. They had to remain silent in public and conceal and disguise their objections.

for all." [84] Locsin and other supporters of the bill were, of course, aware that many congressmen and senators opposed the measure. But the land reform issue had been publicized so much that the opposition could not prudently take an uncompromising stand on the issue. The best policy was to weaken the bill but not to defeat it.

In both Colombia and the Philippines, once they had secured the tacit agreement of the opposition on the necessity for enacting a reform law, the conciliatory elites could consider their legislative battle more than half won. How many concessions they could obtain from the landed interests depended primarily on their bargaining skill. On the whole, the reform sponsors of both countries disposed of the arguments of the opposition without undue difficulty. They effectively refuted the contention that small peasants were not ready for reform. It was *hypothetical* to assume, the sponsors pointed out, that the beneficiaries could not be transformed into productive farmers. The fact was that large landlords under the traditional tenure system had long been *proved* unproductive. Reform experience of countries such as Japan and Taiwan definitely demonstrated that small farmers under a reformed tenure system had significantly increased agricultural output; however, no country with a defective tenure system had ever been able to achieve agricultural success. As to the suggestion that colonization and industrialization be substituted for land redistribution, reform sponsors simply cited the actual experiences in both countries as a basis for rejection. The colonization projects undertaken in the past had proved more costly for the public and less beneficial for the settlers than a redistribution of cultivated areas. There was never a diversion of such large sums of public money to agricultural development as to hamper industrial development; yet industrialization neither lessened the problem of rural underemployment nor provided a strong stimulus for agricultural production. Finally, the charge that reform was Communist-inspired provided the reform sponsors with a most effective counter-argument. No one in either Colombia or the Philippines could refute the claim that repeated peasant discontent and violence were directed toward the existing tenure system and were the main source of strength of Communist guerrillas. Pointing to the unsettling rural conditions, reform sponsors constantly conveyed to their opponents the message: "Give some of your land and privileges and retain the rest through peaceful reform. Or lose everything in violent revolution." Such words often proved more persuasive to the landed interests than any other argument.

[84] *Philippines Free Press*, March 23, 1963.

DOMINANT ELITES: THE MIXED APPROACH

To resolve conflicts in the process of program formulation, the *dominant* elites tend to shift from one approach to another. A dominant elite may unilaterally frame one program and then negotiate with the landed interests for other programs. It may also first engage in a lengthy process of bargaining with the landed interests in parliament but subsequently refuse to deal with them and formulate a program by executive action. In either case, the dominant elite follows a mixed approach, following the course of action of separated elites at one time and that of conciliatory elites at another.

In India, the decision to abolish the *zamindari* system was made by the Congress Party at the Allahabad Conference of 1935 and was subsequently reiterated in numerous party documents and pronouncements.[85] After independence, without any significant number of *zamindars* in its midst, the Congress leadership was able to adopt promptly a program for the abolition of intermediary tenure. In 1947, the party appointed a committee to formulate some general principles of land reform; within two years, in 1949, the *Report of the Congress Agrarian Reforms Committee* was issued. It recommended, among other things, the elimination of all intermediary interests in land, the payment of compensation to *zamindars,* and the assumption by incumbent cultivators of occupancy rights to the land. As the Indian Constitution assigns to state governments the responsibility for enacting reform laws, the Congress Party's top directing organ, the Working Committee, immediately urged "the State governments to proceed expeditiously with the legislation and delegated authority to Congress President Rajendra Prasad to oversee the legislation." [86] Prasad discharged his duty with considerable vigor; brushing aside the objections of the *zamindars,* he lent an unsympathetic ear to their complaints.[87]

---

[85] These include the Agrarian Programme adopted at Faizpur in 1936, the Congress Election Manifesto of 1946, the Report of the Economic Programme Committee of 1948, the Report of the Congress Agrarian Reforms Committee of 1949, and the Congress Election Manifesto of 1951. See Malaviya, *op. cit., passim.*

[86] Stanley A. Kochanek, *The Congress Party of India, the Dynamics of One-Party Democracy* (Princeton, N.J.: Princeton University Press, 1968), p. 191.

[87] For instance, Prasad personally urged his colleagues to speed up the legislative work when its pace slowed down. He accepted complaints from the disaffected interests but stood by Congress's determination to proceed with the program. He called a special session of the Working Committee on April 30, 1948, to hear a delegation of *zamindars* from Bihar concerning their demands on compensation, but told them that "Congress policy could not be changed." And from then on he refused to accept any further complaints. *Ibid.,* pp. 191–194.

Soon, in April 1950, the Conference of Chief Ministers of States and Presidents of State Congress Committees adopted a resolution on "Agriculture and Agrarian Reform" to support the program for abolishing intermediaries. In the next few years, the legislative phase of the program was completed without encountering serious difficulties. The Congress leadership accomplished this task by adopting, in essence, the unilateral approach. Its decision to abolish the intermediary interests, which had been made long before India became a sovereign nation, was never open to argument; the subsequent legislative process provided an opportunity for implementation of a decision already made, but not for bargaining between the leadership and *zamindars*.

The legislative process of the post-abolition reform programs is, however, entirely different. The *Report of the Congress Agrarian Reforms Committee*, in recapitulating the party's reform proposals since the Faizpur Agrarian Programme of 1936, recommended the adoption in the post-abolition period of three measures: the imposition of ceilings on private holdings and redistribution of excess land, tenancy improvement, and cooperative farming. In seeking to enact these measures, Congress leadership could no longer act unilaterally or complete the legislative process with dispatch. It had to reckon with the rising political influence of the *non-zamindari* landed interests and to formulate bills acceptable to them. The ceilings measure constituted the main issue. "The central leadership and particularly the Prime Minister were strongly committed to the imposition of ceilings. They attempted to use the Working Committee as a means of committing the Congress to the principle of ceilings. . . ." But the committee, facing "the strong resistance to ceilings on the part of some state leaders," was not able to arrive at a consensus until January 1953, when it passed its first resolution endorsing the measure.[88] Later, in 1953 and 1954, the committee adopted a number of resolutions reiterating this point; one of these resolutions, approved by the All-India Congress Committee, recommended that "the state Governments should take immediate steps in regard to the collection of the requisite land data and the fixation of ceilings on land holdings, with a view to redistribution, as far as possible, among landless workers." [89] The national leadership's concern for immediate action was not shared by state governments, where

---

[88] *Ibid.*, pp. 196–197.

[89] India, All-India Congress Committee, *Resolutions on Economic Policy and Programme, 1924–1954* (New Delhi: A.I.C.C., 1954), p. 81. Quoted in Kochanek, *op. cit.*, pp. 197–198.

Congress's reform sponsors had to engage in a lengthy process of negotiation. The opponents, however, were not trying to defeat the legislative effort, for Congress's identification with reform was of such long duration that it could hardly be repudiated. Instead, their strategy was to accept ceilings legislation eventually but to draft deliberately a defective law to hamper its implementation. Thus "pressure from the Working Committee or from the Prime Minister himself may force a state parliament to prepare some kind of legislation to satisfy the popular demand. . . . The state party can then say with assurance to the Working Committee, 'We have produced an Act.'" The state party then defended the act as that best suited to local conditions and claimed a stronger bill would be impracticable, leaving the Working Committee and the central government with no alternative but to accept the weak law.[90] "Although in principle Congress politicians favor land reform," Walter C. Neale has correctly observed, "in fact they are often landlords, related to landlords, or members of the same caste or social groups as the landed. As a result, means of evasion are written into the tenure laws—vaguely formulated criteria of 'self-cultivation' or 'efficiencies of large scale' exempt many owners from the reforms. . . ."[91]

The experiences of the Indian elite in the shaping of reform programs indicate a change from a unilateral approach to a bargaining one. When the elite maintained no tie with the *zamindars* it could decide upon a program for the abolition of their interests. When later the other landed interests gradually gained representation and influence in the Congress Party, the elite had to follow a bargaining, gradualistic approach in formu-

---

[90] Thomas J. Shea, Jr., "Implementing Land Reform in India," *Far Eastern Survey*, XXV (January 1956), 3.

[91] Walter C. Neale, *India: The Search for Unity, Democracy and Progress* (Princeton, N.J.: D. Van Nostrand, 1965), p. 73. The ambiguities purposely incorporated in reform legislation can be seen, for example, in the West Bengal Land Reforms Act of 1955. (For the text of the act, see Appendix I, below.) It imposes a ceiling on private holdings held by individuals, but not by families. Consequently a family could retain an area of land many times larger than the size of land allowed for individuals. Also, since there was no statutory definition of family, many families were enlarged during reform in order to claim extra exemptions. In many instances, family members included such individuals as stepmother of the family head, employees, the "fourth relative of the [family] head." S. K. Basu and S. K. Bhattacharyya, *Land Reforms in West Bengal, A Study of Implementation* (New Delhi: Oxford Book Company, 1963), pp. 85–87. The law allows a landowner to resume land from sharecroppers (*bargadars*) for his "personal cultivation." One of the several definitions of "personal cultivation" adopted by the law reads as follows: "Cultivation by servants or labourers on wages payable in cash or in kind or both."

lating other programs. A completely opposite pattern of change occurred in the reform history of Iran and West Pakistan. The elites of both countries first attempted to follow the bargaining, gradualistic approach. But having been unsuccessful in this attempt, the reform proponents ceased to negotiate with the landed interests, arrogating to themselves the authority to formulate programs. This switch of strategy resulted largely from the emergence of dynamic political leaders in both countries who combined a commitment to reform with authoritarian rule. In Iran, the Shah started the reform movement at the very beginning of his reign. On September 21, 1941, immediately after succeeding his father as the new king, Mohammad Reza Shah issued a decree to hand over his vast land possessions to the government. In 1951, he issued another decree ordering an immediate distribution of these lands at a discount price to the peasants. In 1955, he signed a parliament-passed law to distribute among peasants the state land. By these actions, the Shah demonstrated that he was a king with a social conscience and a reform spirit. His programs of distribution of the royal and state lands, though at times facing delays and resistance, proceeded at a reasonable pace. But it was over the redistribution of private holdings, which occupied roughly 75 percent of Iran's agricultural land, that he had to enter into protracted negotiations with the landed interests. Not until 1960 was the government able to obtain from the Majlis the first major land redistribution measure, the Law on the Limitation and Reform of Landed Property, a much weakened version of a bill which the government had submitted in 1959.[92] Weak as it was, the law was never implemented.

In 1961, as the Shah faced cumulative economic, political, constitutional, and personal crises, he became aware that comprehensive, drastic land reform was essential to his realignment of political loyalties. He decided to switch to the unilateral approach to bring about a program. The decision appears to be a sudden one. In early 1961, when the Plan Organization drafted Iran's Third Plan for economic development, it had emphasized the *desirability* of land reform but specifically ruled out its *possibility*.[93] Yet, in November 1961, the Shah instructed the Prime Minister

[92] The law set the maximum limit of a holding at 400 hectares for irrigated land and 600 hectares for dry land. Excess land was to be purchased by the government at its appraised value, with fifteen annual payments at a 3 percent interest, and could be purchased by farmers at the same price payable in fifteen annual installments at 4 percent interest.

[93] See J. Price Gittinger, *Planning for Agricultural Development* (Washington, D.C., 1965), pp. 87–88; and Iran, *Third Plan Frame*, pp. 18 and 205.

to draft a reform program immediately. Completed in December, the draft took "a bold and practical new approach to the land reform needs of Iran." [94] With the Majlis dissolved the previous May, the Shah proclaimed reform on January 15, 1962, through a decree, which he subsequently submitted directly to the people for approval. With heavy reliance on the military and the *Savak* (the security police), the Shah resolutely deprived the landed gentry of any means of effective expression on the issue.

In West Pakistan, efforts at reform began long before Ayub Khan's regime. In April 1949, the then ruling party, the Muslim League, appointed an Agrarian Reforms Committee to examine needed tenurial changes. In June, the committee issued a report recommending, among other things, the imposition of a set of ceilings on private holdings—150 acres for irrigated land, 300 acres for semi-irrigated land, and 450 acres for land wholly dependent on rainfall—and the redistribution of excess lands. Subsequently this report received much attention and became the basis of a number of bills. The government, however, was never able to persuade the landlord-dominated provincial legislature to accept the committee's recommendations, and only some very mild measures were adopted in Sind, Punjab, and the North-West Frontier Provinces.[95] In 1957, the National Planning Board (the predecessor of the Planning Commission), upon issuing the First Five Year Plan (1955–1960), gave its endorsement to the ceiling proposal of the Muslim League, but again nothing came of it. By October 1958, when the coup occurred, the effort to bring about a meaningful reform law had been completely unsuccessful. Speaking of the failure of the civilian regime to bring about reform, Ayub Khan commented:

> Ever since Independence, politicians had been tinkering with the problem but nothing effective had been done. The main purpose of the so-called reforms introduced in West Pakistan before the Revolution was to preserve the privileges of the *zamindars* and not to secure the rights of the tenants. The landlords subverted all attempts at a more rational distribution of land through the influence they exercised over the political parties. Even the very mild land reforms

[94] Kenneth B. Platt, "Land Reform in Iran," U.S., Agency for International Development, *Spring Review*, Country Paper (June 1970), p. 39.
[95] See Pakistan, *Land Reforms in Pakistan*, p. 10.

enacted in the Punjab in 1952 were annulled by Malik Firoz Khan Noon, the Republican Chief Minister, in 1953.[96]

Upon assuming power, Ayub Khan espoused a firm, if inchoate, determination to bring strength, stability, and modernization to the then politically weakening and economically faltering Pakistan. Conceiving land reform as a significant part of his nation-building effort, he created a Land Reforms Commission on October 31, 1958—the first of the two dozen or so reform agencies he created during his rule—to draft a program. He made the basic decision to reduce the power and wealth of the largest landlords of West Pakistan, and let the commission work out the details.

Recounting the circumstances in which he reached the decision to launch land reform at the beginning of his administration, Ayub Khan wrote in the early 1960s:

> I made out a list of reforms and asked my colleagues which one, according to them, would be the hardest to implement. The unanimous view was land reforms. "Well, then, let us have the land reforms first!" I decided. A Land Reforms Commission was set up on 31 October 1958. Seven to eight thousand powerful families were involved and, knowing how attached our people were to land, I had no illusions about the extent of resistance I should have to face. I knew if I could get this through, other reforms would have comparatively smooth passages.[97]

After some deliberation, the commission drafted a report on January 20, 1959, which was approved by the Cabinet within four days. On February 7, 1959, Martial Law Decree No. 64 was issued proclaiming reform throughout West Pakistan. Thus, exactly four months after the coup, the military regime presented West Pakistan with a reform program that its civilian predecessors had not been able to bring about during their eleven-year tenure. The promptness with which the military regime accomplished this task was, of course, due to the fact that, with the country under the tight control of the military, and with the National and Provincial Assemblies abrogated, the landlords could in no way challenge the program Ayub Khan chose to endorse. The landlords also muted their opposition because they did have some representation on the Land Reforms Commission. Of the seven appointed members of the commission "three . . .

---

[96] Ayub Khan, *Friends Not Masters*, p. 87.
[97] *Ibid.*, p. 86.

represented landed interests . . . ; indeed, two of these three were them-selves big landowners." [98] And there was ample evidence showing the bias of the majority of the commission in favor of the landed interests. During its deliberations on the proposed reform, the commission first noted with-out comment a little considered suggestion that the ceiling of private holdings be set at 1,000 acres, with the excess amount expropriated on a graduated scale for redistribution. It also reviewed the Muslim League's triple-ceiling proposal and took notice of the endorsement of the pro-posal by the National Planning Board. However, without giving a reason, the majority of the commission rejected the League's proposal and adopted a ceiling formula of its own. The ceilings were to be 500 acres for irrigated land and 1,000 acres for dry land, with the landlords permitted to retain additional land up to an amount equalling 36,000 produce index units, which would be established on a regional basis. Two members of the com-mission dissented. Considering the formula too generous to the landlords, Ghulam Ishaque Khan argued that, in view of the low land-man ratio in West Pakistan, high ceilings would have a number of undesirable con-sequences. They would perpetuate a society of "inferior and superior strata of 'haves' and 'have-nots' "; hamper free access by peasants to economic opportunities, and lead to agricultural stagnation. He suggested that a modified version of the Muslim League formula be adopted. G. S. Kehar was opposed specifically to the use of produce index units as a basis for calculation of the amount of land to be retained by owners. He believed that this formula would lead to wide anomalies and extensive evasions. Brushing aside these arguments, the majority insisted on its own formula:

> We are anxious that the transition from unlimited ownership to ceil-ing on individual holdings . . . should not involve for *the landlord too abrupt a break with the past making it difficult for him to adjust to the new way of life.* . . . We are also anxious that farming as a profession *should remain sufficiently lucrative to attract and engage suitable talent on a wholesome basis.* . . . We recognise that looked at from the point of view of social justice alone an upper limit of 500 acres of irrigated land will appear large. But in determining the extent

[98] Sayeed, *op. cit.*, p. 96. The seven members of the commission were Akhter Hu-sain, Governor of West Pakistan as Chairman; Said Hasan, Deputy Chairman of the Planning Commission; Ahsanuddin, official of the Ministry of Food and Agriculture; G. S. Kehar, member of the Planning Commission; I. U. Khan, member of the Board of Revenue of West Pakistan; Ghulam Ishaque Khan, member of Water and Power Development Authority of West Pakistan; and M. Shafi Niaz, Chief of Agriculture Sec-tion of the Planning Commission

of the ceiling, social justice has not been the only criterion before us. Even if we were to recommend a much lower ceiling than what we have suggested, the surplus land which would have been available for redistribution among landless tenants would have been too small to secure for each of them a subsistence farm unit.[99]

It appears, then, that though the reform program of West Pakistan was adopted through the unilateral action of the executive, a commission heavily influenced by the views of the landed interests actually drafted its main provisions. As a result it was not basically dissimilar to that which the conciliatory elites of Colombia and the Philippines obtained through a lengthy bargaining process. The primary difference between the programs of West Pakistan, on the one hand, and those of Colombia and the Philippines, on the other, relates to how fast they were obtained, not to what they contained.

The Military and the Urban Middle Class

Implicit but recurrent in the preceding discussions on the process of program formulation are references to the roles played by the military and by what may be loosely called the urban middle class. It is of some interest to compare how these two groups play their roles and how effective they respectively are.

In countries where the military and the urban middle class are politically active, they tend to agree on the reasons for land reform. They generally share one political aspiration: to unseat the traditional oligarchy. Viewing the landed gentry as a vital part of the oligarchy, they consider land reform useful to the realization of their aspirations. In addition, both groups consider land reform instrumental to modernization of the nation. However, the two groups have basically different perceptions of politics and of the process of modernization. To the military, modernization must be preceded by political stability, and political stability requires the imposition of strong discipline on all social forces. Since frequently the city is the center of instability, and since the urban middle class is one of the most vocal and most politicized social forces in the city, the military's demand for stability means restraint on that class. To cope with actual or threatened opposition from that class and to guard against the revival

---

[99] West Pakistan, *Report of the Land Reforms Commission for West Pakistan*, p. 30 (italics mine).

of the traditional oligarchy, the military must rely on the support of the countryside. Their commitment to land reform must hold good in order to win this support. On this point Samuel P. Huntington has written: In a modernizing country

> the social precondition for the establishment of stability is the reappearance in politics of the social forces dominant in the countryside. . . . The ability of the military to develop stable political institutions depends . . . upon [among other things] their ability to identify their rule with the masses of the peasantry and to mobilize the peasantry into politics on their side. . . . In Egypt, Iraq, Turkey, Korea, Pakistan, governments born of military coups pushed land reform measures.[100]

To the urban middle class, economic progress is the central and most dynamic aspect of modernization. Only sustained economic growth will lead to modernization of the entire society. Thus, economic progress must be given priority. To achieve this goal, the urban middle class considers it imperative that the productive forces be freed from the restraints of political authoritarianism as well as of antiquated, rigid economic institutions. Consequently, while preferring liberal democracy to authoritarian rule, this class views land reform as a precondition for raising agricultural production, which in turn stimulates urban industrial growth. In Colombia, for instance, the 1936 land reform program first ushered in a period in which "urban populism allied itself with a peasantry in the process of politicization and threatened the traditional order. . . ."[101] Subsequently this alliance was reinforced, as urban industrial and commercial interests supported various reform proposals, including the 1961 reform law, as necessary cures for the chronic economic ills of the country: inflation and trade deficit. In Iran, one writer noted in 1951, "the strongest advocates of agrarian reform are those merchants and professionals who themselves own no land. The Chamber of Commerce, for example, has on several occasions urged that the government revise the tenure system."[102] In the Philippines, there were advocates of reform "whose interest is not improvement of rural life as such, but the release of capital and government resources from the agrarian sector. This is the pressure for industrialization

[100] Samuel P. Huntington, *Political Order in Changing Societies* (New Haven, 1968), pp. 240–242.

[101] Andrew Pearse, "Agrarian Change Trends in Latin America," *Latin American Research Review*, I (Summer 1966), 58.

[102] Hadary, *op. cit.* (n. 9 above), p. 189.

led by entrepreneurs but enjoying broad support among intellectuals, students, civil servants and the growing middle class." [103] Summing up the interest of the urban middle class in land reform, Manfred Halpern, on the basis of his study of the Middle East, has written:

> In the exploitation of land, urban leaders see a major source of capital for new investments by the state. The leaders of the new urban middle class are confronted by the political fact that their rule remains insecure as long as the landowners retain the economic basis of their traditional political predominance. Hence they have a direct interest in the kind of thorough land reforms that not only redistributes the land, but also increases output, makes production more efficient, and offers security of tenure and income.[104]

In certain cases, because of their obviously different conceptions of politics, the urban middle class and the military may come into serious conflict. In 1969, an amalgam of disparate forces in the cities in both East and West Pakistan brought Ayub Khan's rule to an abrupt end. In Iran, though the urban middle class and the military were not involved in a direct clash, they had different political loyalties: the former was against the throne; the latter was the monarch's principal supporter. In certain other cases, the urban middle class may be persuaded or intimidated to accept the political hegemony of the military. This is apparently the case of Egypt. As Nasser once said of the revolutionary movement he was leading: "This is a middle-class revolution against capitalism and against communism. . . . I have to exclude all the old politicians and prevent the capitalists and landlords from muscling in. The new Party must be composed of exclusively middle-class people—doctors, lawyers, teachers— with a sense of public service." [105] In fact, of course, with the Free Officers assuming a commanding role in the government, the urban middle class elements of Nasser's regime were made politically subordinate to the military. In Mexico, liberal politicians like Madero sparked a revolution that soon led to the creation of a succession of middle-class governments strongly dominated by the military. It was not until several decades after

[103] Jean Grossholtz, *Politics in the Philippines* (Boston, 1964), pp. 48–49.

[104] Manfred Halpern, *The Politics of Social Change in the Middle East and North Africa* (Princeton, N.J.: Princeton University Press, 1963), p. 98.

[105] *New Statesman*, January 22, 1955. Quoted in Georgiana G. Stevens, *Egypt, Yesterday and Today* (New York, 1963, pp. 117–118. Cf. Vatikiotis, *op. cit.* (n. 3 above), pp. 47–48 and 54–55

the outbreak of the revolution that the military relinquished power to urban middle-class politicians.

Whether in collaboration or in opposition, the military and the urban middle class exercise quite different impacts on the formulation of reform programs. The influence of the military is decisive. Generals Carranza and Obregón of Mexico, General Chen Cheng of Taiwan, the Free Officers of Egypt, and General Ayub Khan of Pakistan were the principal sponsors or formulators of reform programs in these countries. In the early 1950s, the army of the Philippines under Secretary of Defense Ramon Magsaysay launched a reform program that to a certain extent induced future presidents to initiate a series of comprehensive laws. In Iran, the army was perhaps the key force the Shah could rely on in his confrontation with the landlords. In most of these countries, without the positive support of the military, it was inconceivable that the programs actually implemented could have been adopted in the first place. Only in Colombia and India did the military play no conspicuous role in land reform. In contrast, the impact of the urban middle class on land reform is somewhat ambiguous. Though in all eight countries studied, this class furnished the legal talents for drafting legislation, nowhere did it fight a determined parliamentary battle against the landed gentry; though some of its members were highly vocal in propagating the cause of small farmers, they never effectively mobilized the peasantry to sustain their legislative effort.

The uneven impact of the military and the urban middle class is due to the differences in the organizational character of the two groups and to their different approaches to program formulation. Because of uniform recruitment standards and rigid organizational principles, the military is a much more cohesive group than the urban middle class. In countries where the military intervenes on behalf of reform, it generally intervenes as a united force, its leaders' views being accepted as the views of the entire establishment. In formulating a program, the military never enters into lengthy bargaining with the landed interests. It prefers speedy action, relies on its own opinions in the drafting of a law, and imposes its view on the landed interests. Confronted with the united might of the army, the landed class generally has to accept what it is offered.

In contrast, the urban middle class consists of people with different occupations and different sources of income who maintain a common identity only in terms of locality of residence and range of income. With respect to the issue of reform, the class may display a public stance in favor of it, but in reality maintain no class view at all. For in a developing society, this class typically includes a significant proportion of members whose principal source of income is land. Data on Congress members in the Indian Lok Sabha in Table 7, clearly illustrate this point. Evidently these people cannot be expected to give enthusiastic support to legislation adversely affecting their interests. In fact, some of them may actually oppose it. Thus the net impact of the entire class on reform may be minimal.

In securing a program, reform advocates of the urban middle class prefer negotiation with the landed interests. Not facing a choice of either submission or defeat, as when dealing with the military, the landed interests can use all the delaying tactics they can muster to stall legislation. In the meantime, reform advocates find their principal argument—the beneficial impact of tenurial changes on industrial development—unappealing to the peasantry. Such an argument may even be unconvincing to the city dwellers, for reform requires the allocation to the countryside of a large sum of public money which may, at least initially, hamper urban economic development. During the debates over reform bills in the legislatures of Colombia and the Philippines, middle-class representatives were eloquent in presenting their economic arguments, but they failed to stir the barrios; they were generous in granting compensation to landowners but quite stringent in making necessary appropriations. The advocates' case is, therefore, a weak one, and their arguments cannot be convincingly presented. The landlords, on the other hand, fight a battle that really threatens their vested interests. They try at all times to defend their case with great vigor and determination. Under such circumstances, one can expect that after protracted negotiation reform advocates bring about only a weak bill.

Perhaps one can speculate that the weight that the urban middle class exercises on reform will grow with the increase of the size of the class. A growing urban middle class in all probability means the reduction of the proportion of landowning interests within the class and the progressive development of industrialization. Hence the class will be able to play a more positive role in reform, and the nation will have a greater financial capacity to support tenurial changes. But then the question is: can a developing country with a problematical tenure system afford the time necessary for the evolution of a strong middle class to solve its land problems?

VI

THE ENACTMENT OF THE PHILIPPINE LAND REFORM ACT OF 1955: A CASE STUDY

In the last chapter, the process of program formulation was analyzed from a broad comparative perspective. To provide some depth to this analysis, the present chapter will focus attention on the evolution of a specific reform law. Since to frame a reform law is a more difficult and complicated task for an elite employing the bargaining approach than for an elite resorting to unilateral decision, it will be useful to examine a law brought about by an elite through the bargaining approach.

The legislative history of the Philippine Land Reform Act of 1955 appears a fitting topic for this case study. The law was a product of lengthy negotiations between a conciliatory elite and the landed interests. It came as a breakthrough for the principle of nation-wide compulsory redistribution of private land, a principle the landed interests had successfully resisted for over two decades. The subsequent 1963 Agricultural Land Reform Code merely followed this principle and incorporated, with modifications and amplifications, the 1955 law. But the major provisions of this legislation reflected compromises between a president strongly committed to rural welfare, and the entrenched landed interests that dominated in the Congress, especially the House of Representatives. In a sense, the Philippine elite was split over the land issue, with the chief executive and a substantial portion of the national legislators taking opposite sides on the issue.

In the following analysis, for want of time to conduct a thorough research myself on the legislative process of the 1955 law, I will rely primarily on a well-documented study of the subject, *Magsaysay and the Philippine Peasantry* by Frances Starner.

Earlier Reform Efforts

A discussion of the background of the 1955 law may properly begin with the reform efforts of the 1930s and 1940s, when the Philippine government enacted numerous bills to deal with the increasingly serious land problems. These laws included two principal categories: one seeking to create new owner-farmers, and the other to improve tenancy conditions.[1] In the first category were Commonwealth Act (CA) 20 of 1936, CA 260 and CA 378 of 1938, CA 420 of 1939, and CA 539 of 1940. These acts generally authorized the President to "acquire portions of large estates" through expropriation, negotiated purchase, or lease and to make them available at cost to small farmers. In the second category were CA 4113 and CA 4054 of 1933, CA 178 of 1936, CA 608 of 1940, and Republic Act (RA) 34 and RA 44 of 1946. These laws sought to protect rights of tenants and to establish fixed rental payments. Republic Act 34 (the Philippine Rice Share Tenancy Act)—the most important of these laws—stipulated that on a rice-producing tenanted farm the gross output after deduction of harvest cost be divided into five shares with each share going to one factor of production according to the following fixed formula: land, 30 percent; labor, 30 percent; work animals, 5 percent; farm implements, 5 percent; and other costs involved in planting and cultivating, 30 percent. Because of inadequacy of enforcement provisions, all the laws enacted in the 1930s and 1940s were totally ineffective, and did not curb the tendency toward increasing land concentration and worsening tenancy conditions.

By the early 1950s, on account of two developments, the land issue suddenly seized national attention. One related, of course, to the Huk rebellion. Concentrated in the high tenancy area of Central Luzon, and capitalizing on the intermittent rural unrest, the Huks had, by 1950, reached the height of their rebellious activities. In March of that year the Communist guerrillas marked their "8th anniversary by staging a widespread attack in several towns and barrios in Rizal, Laguna, Batangas, Pampanga, and Nueva Ecija [Provinces]. . . . The Huks made violent and bloody assaults in August, 1950, in 11 different places scattered in Isabela, Laguna, [and] Quezon [Provinces]. It was an orgy of murder, pillage, and burning." [2] While terrorizing the countryside, the Huks vigorously exploited the land issue. Recruiting a large number of discontented

---

[1] For a summary of these reform laws, see *Hardie Report*, Appendix G.

[2] Jorge R. Coquia, *The Philippine Presidential Election of 1953* (Manila: University Publishing Co., 1955), p. 173.

farmers as followers, they condemned landlordism and stressed their stand for "land for the landless" and "equal justice for all."

A second development calling attention to the land issue had to do with a series of reports bearing on the Philippine land-tenure system by United States foreign aid officials. The Bell Mission, which President Harry S. Truman dispatched to the Philippines to examine the economic conditions of the newly independent republic, noted in 1950:

> The strained relationship between the landlords and their tenants and the low economic condition generally of the tillers of the soil compose one of the main factors retarding the recovery of agricultural production. While some laws have been passed to relieve the tenant's plight, they have not worked out as expected. The land problem remains the same or worse than four years ago and the dissident trouble is spread to wider areas.[3]

In 1952, the United States Mutual Security Agency in the Philippines published a report prepared by Robert S. Hardie, an expert who had previously worked on the American-sponsored land reform in Japan. Commenting on the problems of land concentration and inequitable tenancy arrangements, the Hardie Report said:

> Chronic economic instability and political unrest among farm tenants has culminated in open and violent rebellion. The rebellion derives directly from the pernicious land tenure system; . . . In championing the cause of tenants, communism wins their sympathies—just as governments, . . . careless of causes—whose actions are limited to the suppression of symptoms and maintenance of the status quo— are bound to win their enmity. . . . Because of these defects, the land tenure system stands as an obstacle, wasting all efforts of the United States to foster the development of a stable democratic economy.[4]

The document stressed the need for the abolition of tenancy and the creation of family farms. To achieve these objectives, it recommended the expropriation of all land of absentee owners for redistribution, the retention of 3 to 8 hectares of land by other owners, the replacement of tenancy with a leasehold system, and the creation of a system of land commissions

---

[3] U.S., Economic Survey Mission to the Philippines, *Report to the President of the United States* (Mission headed by Daniel W. Bell; Washington, D.C., 1950), p. 55.

[4] See *Hardie Report*, p. 7.

—composed of landlords, owner-farmers, and tenants—to help enforce tenurial reform.[5]

Later in 1952, the Philippines Council for United States Aid and the Mutual Security Agency issued still another report, which contained findings of a rural survey of 26 barrios in 13 provinces. The survey, conducted by Generoso F. Rivera and Robert T. McMillan, revealed that Philippine "farm tenure and related problems . . . are characterized by widespread landlessness, concentration of landownership, fragmentation of fields, small operating units, inequitable crop-sharing arrangements, unscrupulous money-lending practices, emphasis upon single-crop farming, and the resulting poverty." [6] The report endorsed the idea of a basic, comprehensive alteration of the tenure system.

Presidential Election and Partisan Politics

Upon their release, the Hardie and Rivera-McMillan reports immediately became subjects of controversy. Some Philippine officials considered the criticisms of the tenure system too severe; others regarded the recommendations in the Hardie Report inappropriate. The fact that these reports were released on the eve of the presidential election of 1953 also created political repercussions. The Liberal Party, then in control of the government, took these reports as implicit criticism of the administration, denouncing specifically the Hardie Report "as gross misrepresentation of actual conditions" and as "Communist inspired." [7] Liberal House Speaker Eugenio Perez severely criticized the Hardie Report, considering it laden "with radical ideas which can be considered as leftist in inclinations . . . derived from unreliable sources with communist tendencies. . . . It is grossly malicious and another attempt to incite the Filipino people against their government." [8] The Liberals also assailed the Rivera-McMillan report as an erroneous portrayal of the rural Philippines, and Perez emphatically pointed to the failure of the report to mention the positive achievements of the various rural programs sponsored by the administration. A

[5] *Ibid.*, pp. vii–x.

[6] Generoso F. Rivera and Robert T. McMillan, *The Rural Philippines* (Manila: The Philippine Council for United States Aid and the United States Mutual Security Agency, 1952), p. 118.

[7] Quoted in Coquia, *op. cit.*, p. 168.

[8] Quoted in *ibid.*

number of Liberals branded both reports as an American "intervention plan in local politics" in favor of the Nacionalista Party.[9]

On the other hand, a number of congressional members came to the defense of these documents. Nacionalista Congressman Numeriano Babao, for instance, said that in preparing these reports, the "American experts . . . [had] no other intention than to assist our country in the multifarious economic and social problems," and even a Liberal senator, Quintin Paredes, found it unjustifiable "to insinuate that these American public officials are moved by Communist tendencies, or that the United States Government, a friendly power, is lax in sending us experts."[10]

"Whether or not these reports had been released to help [the Nacionalista presidential candidate Ramon] Magsaysay's cause," as Jorge R. Coquia has commented, "was not the concern of the people, for they saw that these reports represented the true picture of . . . [the rural] areas."[11] It is of interest to point out that Magsaysay did not have a peasant background; nor was he a land-reform advocate in his early political career as a congressman. It was only during the anti-Huk military campaign and in the execution of the rural pacification program that he became familiar with the problems of the peasantry. He considered the land issue a root cause of the Huk rebellion, which had to be dealt with through a broad rural development program. Disagreeing with President Elpidio Quirino's emphasis on a military approach to the Communist insurgency, he resigned on February 28, 1953, as Secretary of National Defense in the Liberal administration. In a letter to President Quirino, he said:

> Under your concept of my duties as Secretary of National Defense, my job is just to go on killing Huks. But you must realize that we cannot solve the problem of dissidence simply by military measures. It would be futile to go on killing Huks, while the administration continues to breed dissidence by neglecting the problems of our masses. . . . Some eight months ago, I informed you that the military situation was under control, and I offered to leave the Department of National Defense in order to speed up the land settlement program of the government. My purpose was to shift our attack on

[9] Quoted in *ibid.*, pp. 169–71. It was widely believed that the United States was sympathetic toward the Nacionalista Party in the presidential campaign, particularly after Ramon Magsaysay became the party's candidate.

[10] Quoted in *ibid.*, pp. 168–169.

[11] *Ibid.*, p. 172.

Communism to one of its basic causes in our country: land hunger. In this, as in many other matters, the administration has met the people's need with inaction.[12]

Later when he became presidential candidate of the Nacionalista Party, Magsaysay anchored his electoral strategy on his appeal to the rural masses, and the land-reform issue inevitably became a matter of major importance in the campaign. In their platforms, the Liberal, the Nacionalista, and the newly formed Democratic parties all emphasized the need for the resolution of the tenure problems.[13] The Nacionalistas announced:

> As the best means to combat and eradicate communism, [we shall] effect land reforms through legislative and executive action, to bring into realization the principle declared in the Constitution that the State should concern itself with insuring the well-being and economic security of all the people so that every Filipino shall have a home and a farm which he can call his own.

In the "Bill of Economic Rights" section of their platform, the Nacionalistas further declared that they would try to provide the Philippine farmer a "right to own as much land as he can till; and to count upon government assistance in securing implements, tools, animals, seeds, and scientific advice which he may need." And finally they pledged:

> We will execute a more liberal and expeditious plan for the disposition of our public agricultural lands, and make lots of convient sizes available to discharged members of our armed forces, to government employees, and to the laboring class. We will embark on a large-scale campaign to purchase, sub-divide and distribute large landed estates to their tenants at cost.

The Liberal platform emphasized the accomplishments of the administration's rural programs and affirmed the party's intention to carry forward effectively these programs. The Liberals stated:

> We have substantially complied with our pledge in the original plank of our party to provide our tenant population with a just and fair share of their crops with the passage of the 70–30 and 55–45 Rice Share Tenancy Law. Big landed estates in Manila and nearby prov-

---

[12] Quoted in Carlos Quirino, *Magsaysay of the Philippines* (Manila: Alemar's, 1958), p. 108.

[13] The following excerpts of the platforms of the three political parties are from Coquia, *op. cit.*, Appendixes A, B, and C, pp. 343–368.

inces and in Central Luzon have been acquired for sub-division and resale to tenants at cost. . . . We are giving high priority to the needs of the small farmer by improving his methods of cultivation and increasing the yields of his labor, and the rapid distribution of public lands to the landless, by accelerating the construction of roads through virgin lands and the simultaneous survey and subdivision of said lands into small lots for immediate occupation by qualified settlers.

The Democratic platform stressed the belief that "the land is under God the property and the source of life of our people. . . . No society can thrive, no people can be happy or even moderately secure, unless there is an equitable distribution of the national patrimony of the land. . . . This nation needs far-reaching reforms in the maldistribution of this national patrimony." The Democrats offered a number of solutions to the land problem.

To the farm hand, the tenant, and the small farmer we propose to extend such state assistance as may be constitutionally lawful, to enable him by his own industry to mount the ladder from hired hand to tenant, and from tenant to owner, . . . We propose to make immediate and effective implementation of the acquisition and distribution of large private landed estates. . . . We propose . . . to re-examine our land laws with a view to expediting the issuance of land title to the landless. . . .

It was something new in Philippine politics that in a presidential election all political parties attached considerable importance to the land issue and pledged to effect large-scale reforms. But the positions of all three parties remained mild and vague. They all sought to provide material assistance to the tenants and small farmers but failed to mention how the necessary public funds were to be obtained. They promised to "purchase, sub-divide and distribute large landed estates," but at the same time they declared that this should be done "as public funds would permit," or done within the limits of the constitution, which were not specified. They committed themselves to expand existing reform programs or to adopt some new measures, but they did not enunciate how the expanded programs and new measures could be enforced more effectively than the many existing ones. It is significant, therefore, to note that Magsaysay showed a greater sense of urgency toward the land issue and a greater commitment to the peasantry than did the three parties, including his own Nacionalista. As Frances L. Starner has observed:

Although the platforms of all three parties cautiously avoided any mention of the word "expropriation," Magsaysay himself explicitly called for expropriation of lands in some of his speeches. Moreover, the relative emphasis which he would give this rural program when he assumed the presidency was already apparent from a number of his statements during the campaign—that his "obsession" was the problem of the landless and that he considered himself duty-bound to see to it that the landless acquired their own lands . . . and, finally, that he would devote 90 percent of his time to the improvement of the barrios.[14]

Moreover, Magsaysay's barrio-to-barrio presidential campaign helped activate rural interest in electoral participation, enabled him to win the election, and influenced the course of his future reform programs. In the seven-month campaign, Magsaysay traveled to "about three-fourths of the country's municipalities and more than half of the 17,403 barrios and sitios [small neighborhood units]. He shook more hands than both presidential candidates [Elpidio] Quirino [of the Liberal Party] and Carlos Romulo [of the Democratic Party] combined." [15] Reaching out to many remote areas where politicians never traveled before and where communications media did not exist, Magsaysay obtained many rural votes without competition, capturing forty-eight of the fifty-two provinces of the country. Out of a total of 4,227,719 votes cast for all presidential candidates, Magsaysay received 2,912,992, or 68.90 percent, over twice the votes of his principal opponent Quirino, who received 1,313,991, or 31.08 percent.[16] Magsaysay's votes were overwhelmingly rural, with over four-fifths of the total coming from the provinces.[17] Since Quirino's votes in the 1953 election were not extraordinarily smaller than what he had received in the 1949 election,[18] and since there was a sharp increase in voters between the two elections, broadened rural electoral participation accounted for Magsaysay's impressive victory.[19] This fact caused politi-

[14] Frances L. Starner, *Magsaysay and the Philippine Peasantry* (Berkeley, 1961), p. 39.

[15] Coquia, *op. cit.*, p. 220.

[16] *Ibid.*, p. 377. Romulo withdrew from the election before the voting. A third presidential candidate Gaudencio Bueno received 736 votes.

[17] Of the 2,912,992 votes cast for Magsaysay, 2,437,257, or 83.67 percent, came from the provinces, and 475,735, or 16.33 percent, from the cities. *Ibid.*, pp. 376–377.

[18] Quirino received 1,803,808 votes in 1949.

[19] Excluding from consideration the 1955 voting statistics of two provinces in which the 1949 voter registration lists were known to be fraudulent, Starner estimated

cians to reevaluate the role of the electorate. No longer could they regard the electorate as completely docile and indifferent to political issues.
In decisively rejecting the incumbent President Quirino, the voters showed
an independence of judgment in making electoral choices and a ready
response to the appeals of a man who convinced them of his dedication
to their well-being. Since the electorate was predominantly rural, and since
Magsaysay directed much of his appeal to the peasantry, politicians began
to take cognizance of the importance of the rural votes. From Magsaysay's
point of view, the massive rural support he received reinforced his commitment to the resolution of the land issue, and his ability to mobilize a large
rural vote became a potentially influential factor in future legislative battles
over his agrarian programs.

The Legislative Background

The Philippine Congress, shaped in accordance with American constitutional experience, resembles its United States counterpart not only
with respect to structure and powers but also in the different orientations
of the two houses. The members of the Philippine House of Representatives, chosen from single-member districts, are amenable to the pressures
of local politics, where landed interests are influential. They tend to be
conservative with regard to economic and social policies and often show
strong opposition to land-reform legislation. The senators, elected by the
entire national electorate, usually take a relatively moderate to liberal
stand on major domestic policies. Though some senators who come from
families with large land possessions may strongly oppose reform measures,
the Senate as a whole tends to show less reluctance than the House to
support these measures. The center of the battlefield for the 1955 law was,
therefore, in the House. However, in view of the popularity of the reform
issue, the favored tactics of the reform opponents in the House were to
delay and weaken legislation rather than to oppose it outright.

As Philippine political parties display no substantial differences in
ideology and social background of their membership, land reform was
not a partisan issue. As the head of the Nacionalista Party, Magsaysay
could not depend on the support of his own party to enact his programs.
In fact, over the agrarian issue he was sometimes vigorously opposed by

that there was an overall increase of voters by 30 percent between 1949 and 1953. *Op.
cit.*, pp. 61–62.

Nacionalista congressional members and supported by the Liberals and Democrats.

The legislative battle of the 1955 reform gradually took shape after Congress had approved a number of Magsaysay's minor reform measures. These included bills to replace the Land Settlement and Development Corporation with the National Resettlement and Rehabilitation Administration, to create a new Land Registration Commission, to expand the revolving fund of the Agricultural Credit and Cooperative Financing Administration, to liberalize the Rural Banks Act, and to authorize the President to issue bonds to finance public works projects.

Two other administration agrarian measures, however, encountered some difficulty. One dealt with tenancy reform. In 1954, Magsaysay called for the enactment of a "single, concise and easily understood farm tenancy code" in place of what he referred to as "too many laws on too many books."[20] Congressional debates on the tenancy measure centered on two items. One related to the idea of substitution of leasehold for tenancy. The leasehold idea was first advanced in the Hardie Report, but by the time that Congress considered the tenancy legislation, American aid officials had abandoned efforts to obtain basic tenure reform. This changed American stand materially affected the administration's position on the issue. The land-tenure committee appointed by Magsaysay to study reform measures recommended only that tenants be allowed *to elect* the leasehold system. As a consequence, the idea of establishing a mandatory leasehold system secured little congressional support. The other item concerned the extension of the share tenancy arrangements for rice farms—as specified in the Rice Share Tenancy Act of 1946 (RA 34)—to sugar land. The House, under pressure of the sugar interests, resisted the proposal. The final version of the tenancy law as enacted in 1954, known as the Agricultural Tenancy Act of the Philippines, amounted to merely a clarification and some strengthening of the 1946 legislation. It accepted the leasehold idea but without mentioning how a lease arrangement could be entered. Thus, as Senator Justiniano Montano said of the 1954 law: it made "the kasamá [tenancy] still the ruling system."[21] The coverage of the 1954 law was practically still restricted to the rice crop, though the law made the meaningless stipulation: "The landholder and the tenant on lands which produce crops other than rice shall be free to enter into any contract

---

[20] Quoted in *ibid.*, p. 134.
[21] Quoted in *ibid.*, p. 139.

stipulating the ratio of crop division." [22] The other measure encountering congressional resistance was an administration proposal to abolish the jurisdiction of the Court of Industrial Relations over tenancy matters and to create a Court of Agrarian Relations to handle all cases relating to land-tenure matters. In 1954, the Senate endorsed the measure, but the landed interests in the House sabotaged it by enacting a bill merely to expand and reorganize the Court of Industrial Relations. In 1955, after considerable pressure from Magsaysay, a bill to create the Court of Agrarian Relations was finally accepted by the House and became Republic Act 1267.

The measures enacted in Congress in the first days of the Magsaysay administration were by and large not controversial. Most of these dealt with public assistance to farmers and entailed minor revisions of the existing laws. They broke no new ground and contained no provisions seriously reducing the interests of the landed class. The land-tenure bill proposed by Magsaysay, which eventually became the 1955 Land Reform Act, was radically different from these earlier measures. This bill precipitated a lengthy legislative battle that lasted through three congressional sessions, and its fate remained persistently uncertain during this period—even to the last moment when the measure was finally voted upon.

Efforts by the administration to bring about a comprehensive reform program began in 1954, the first year of Magsaysay's presidential term, when he announced he would initiate land redistribution through purchase or expropriation of large estates. He created a number of committees to study tenure conditions and to make appropriate recommendations. On the basis of the study of these committees, the administration drafted a bill which was introduced in 1954 as House Bill 2468 and Senate Bill 90. Basically, the measure provided for land redistribution through expropriation of large estates. The debates over the bill related to two broad categories of issues. One concerned the necessity and desirability of the bill, and the other the bill's specific provisions. These issues were repeatedly raised throughout three congressional sessions.

THE NECESSITY AND DESIRABILITY OF THE BILL

In proposing the bill the administration and its congressional supporters contended that since much of the Huk insurgency could be at-

[22] For the text of the Agricultural Tenancy Act of 1954 (RA 1199), see *ibid.*, pp. 211–224.

tributed to the prevailing tenure problems, a solution of the problems would significantly contribute to the national safety and welfare. Land reform was, therefore, a matter vitally affecting the public interest, requiring prompt, forceful governmental action. Moreover, while it was objectively ascertainable that tenancy conditions in the country as a whole and in Central Luzon in particular had continued to worsen, existing reform laws were beyond doubt inadequate. Extremely weak in enforcement provisions, the tenancy laws were practically ignored by the rural community and the government. Land redistribution laws adopted thus far did not incorporate the feature of compulsory expropriation of private farms; they were also patently unspecific as to the process of implementation. They failed to define the priority of the types of land subject to government acquisition, the maximum area the landowners were allowed to retain, and the methods of land evaluation and compensation. To resolve the land problems, the proponents of the bill argued, a comprehensive, compulsory redistribution program was indispensable. It must provide the government with mandatory authority to obtain land, and clearly set forth the enforcement provisions.

The arguments of the opponents were varied, but all were forcefully presented. The National Rice Producers Association (NRPA), the organization representing the interests of the *haciendas* of Central Luzon, led the attack from outside Congress. In the summer of 1955, the NRPA President Manuel V. Gallego, a man who had fought against land reform since the 1930s, launched "in a series of public addresses, debates, and press releases" a barrage of attacks on the proposed bill. He first revived the charge that land redistribution was a Communist-inspired idea:

> The present land tenure bill of equal redistribution on a family or household size farms [*sic*] follows the communist program in China, in its fifth stage of land reform beginning October 1947. It seems logical that if we have to adopt a communist program, we should turn communist first, and institute a communist government. Otherwise this will constitute a confession of failure of democracy for failing to evolve a formula that is not patterned after communist plan.[23]

In a paper entitled "Communism Under the Guise of Democracy," Gallego alleged that the "history of land reform in the Philippines has all the earmarks of the CHINESE COMMUNIST LAND REFORM SYSTEM UNDER

[23] "Answer to Dean Bocobo," *The Manila Times*, June 3, 1955. Quoted in Starner, *op. cit.*, p. 163.

THE GUISE OF DEMOCRACY, and apparently, under the sponsorship of the United States Technical Advisers as promoters and Philippine tutors of democratic way of life." [24] Though most of the opponents of the bill would not attack it in Gallego's terms, his charge did echo in congressional debates. For example, Liberal Congressman Eugenio Perez, who had first denounced the Hardie Report as having "communist tendencies," said that the adoption of the bill would reflect the substitution of the "free enterprise philosophy" by a philosophy of socialism, and that socialism was "one step advanced toward Communism." [25]

Gallego further assailed the measure as unconstitutional. Calling compulsory land expropriation "legalized robbery," he argued,

> . . . the Constitution provides that no man may be deprived of his life, liberty or property without due process of law, nor may his property be expropriated without just compensation—nor may Congress expropriate [sic] money except for a public purpose. The process by which Congress intends to expropriate property that belongs to Juan with the idea of giving it to Pedro is intended primarily for Pedro's private gain, and does not make the purpose public, to a degree that makes the use of public money permissible. It makes little difference how many Pedros you benefit—that will not make private gain co-extensive with public interest, and this view is in accordance with the doctrine laid down by our Supreme Court in a series of cases. . . .[26]

Belittling the seriousness of the rebellion in Central Luzon, Gallego, in a debate with Judge Jorge Bocobo, Chairman of the Philippine Code Commission, asked:

> Is not the unrest more imagined than real and actually . . . caused by agitators and communist propagandists who are present not only in the Philippines but even in such democratic countries as the United States . . . regardless of form of government, and where there is not

---

[24] Quoted in *ibid.*, p. 273 (original emphasis).

[25] Quoted in *ibid.*, p. 178. Also, right after Congressman Emilio Cortez delivered his sponsoring speech for the bill, Lamberto L. Macias, a Nacionalista Congressman from Negros Occidental province, denounced the bill as "Communistic" and ridiculed Cortez for sponsoring it. *Ibid.*, p. 270.

[26] *Ibid.*, pp. 162–163. Obviously Gallego was twisting the Supreme Court's position on this issue. As noted earlier, in the *Guido v. Rural Progress Administration* and *Urban Estates, Inc. v. The Hon. Austin P. Montesa* cases, the Supreme Court held that a "makeshift" transfer of small pieces of land from one to another was not constitutionally allowable and that expropriation of large estates for purpose of reform "clothes the expropriation with public interest and public use," hence, constitutionally justified.

even a land tenure problem? Don't we take pride in the fact that our countrymen, who are generally poor, can point with pride to foreigners that we have also a little of "the landed gentry" who live . . . better, . . . and that we are not a nation of peasants as you would like to have [us]? [27]

To many advocates of land reform, Gallego's arguments were so patently untenable that they were hardly worthy of being refuted. As a Manila columnist commented, Gallego's line of reasoning was out of date; "no one outside of the Philippines and a few other countries" had spoken in that tone for many decades.[28]

In Congress, few of those representing the landed interests thought it wise and efficacious to take an uncompromising position on the issue, and many congressmen who, for various reasons, opposed the bill were reluctant to be openly hostile to a measure intended to benefit the rural masses. Instead, congressional opponents tried to defeat the bill by questioning if land redistribution was the correct approach to the economic ills of the nation, and by proposing alternative approaches. For instance, Senator Claro M. Recto, a powerful Nacionalista leader who initially supported his party's "invitation" to Magsaysay to become its presidential candidate and who broke with the President after the election, first asserted that the land-tenure bill was sponsored by the United States to make the Philippines follow an agriculturally oriented economic policy, thus keeping the country subservient to the American economy. He said: "It was bad enough that they [American advisers] hatched this idea of making our economy subserve theirs but they wanted to add insult to injury by brazenly attempting to press us into legislating it as our declared national policy to make it appear our own doing." Then, insisting that he was not opposed to land reform, but that the nation should orient its economic policy to industrialization, Recto asserted:

Not only am I not opposed to the land tenure reform but I believe the adoption of such reform and of any other social and economic reforms imperative. I advocate those measures not only as measures of social justice but—and this is more important—as economic measures to help increase the national output through industrialization. We are today one of the poorest nations in the world. . . . The need for

[27] Starner, *ibid.*, p. 163.
[28] Carmen Nakpil, "My Humble Opinion," *Manila Chronicle*, June 3, 1955. Quoted in Starner, *op. cit.*, p. 164.

increasing the national produce is even more pressing than the need for making a more just distribution of the same, which is what is meant by social justice. But a real concern for social justice should not blind us to our main objective, that of increased production, which can only be attained if industrialization is given top priority in our economic planning.[29]

Recto's allegation about the intention of American economic advisers seemed hardly more credible than the charge that the land-tenure bill was Communist inspired. But the nationalistic undertone of Recto's statement found much sympathy among a group of small but vocal intellectuals, and Recto's stress on the need for industrialization was also favorably received by many businessmen who regarded Magsaysay's commitment to a policy of agrarian development as a possible deterrent to industrial development.

Many supporters of land reform were not convinced that the nation should give priority to industrialization. The Philippine economy, they contended, was predominantly agricultural in character; to emphasize industrialization while agriculture was highly unproductive would be to reverse the natural order. As Teodoro M. Locsin wrote in the *Philippines Free Press*:

> The Philippines should certainly industrialize. . . . But everybody has been calling for industrialization these many years—Recto may be among the last to advocate it. But where is the capital coming from for the new industries? The bulk of Filipino capital is frozen in real estate; it is invested in the tenantry system. That capital could only be unfrozen, could only be diverted to industry—by abolishing tenancy. Recto does not want foreign capital; he knows where local capital is hiding.[30]

As to whether redistribution constituted a desirable form of agrarian change, the opponents followed a familiar line of argument: a division of large estates would result in the fall of production, thus benefiting neither farmers nor the national economy. Nacionalista Congressman Joaquin Roces, publisher of *The Manila Times*, questioned the bill on this ground. In an article titled "Restudy the Land Tenure Bill," *The Times* declared:

> Our objections to the bill, which we have presented from the very beginning, are based chiefly on the fact that whatever benefits

[29] Quoted in *ibid.*, pp. 168–170.
[30] Quoted in *ibid.*, p. 170.

are derivable from the bill will in a short time prove self-cancelling. Breaking up estates of 200, or 500 hectares . . . into two or five-hectare farms won't boost production in any sense, solve any social or economic grievance, or create a middle-class. A *further reduction of individual farm units to two-hectare sizes would perhaps be an effective political stunt that would pay off handsomely from the purely political standpoint*, but it will backfire over the long haul, creating a new set of agrarian problems.[31]

To Roces and *The Times*, "commercialization" of farming, rather than land redistribution, represented the correct approach to the land problem. Seemingly aligned with this argument, congressional opponents also urged the exploitation and distribution of underdeveloped land to solve the tenure problem. House Majority Leader Arturo Tolentino was reported to hold the view that the principal objection of many congressmen to the bill lay in the redistribution idea it contained, and "that it would have been more practical if the government would encourage the exploitation of virgin lands than expropriate already cultivated lands." [32]

From the point of view of the administration and its supporters, rural unrest was the matter of utmost concern. While commercialization of farming did not offer the prospect of reducing the number of landless farmers, the record on land resettlement thus far hardly gave any hope for alleviation of the tenancy problem. But unless the farmers' demands for land were reasonable satisfied, there would not be rural peace, which was a prerequisite of economic progress. Subdivision of large estates, they asserted, would not necessarily lead to a decline of agricultural output, because ownership of land would provide farmers with an incentive to increase production.

THE KEY PROVISIONS OF THE BILL

In the 1954 session of Congress, opponents of the land-tenure bill successfully stalled the measure; the session ended without a final vote on it. In 1955, the administration's reform proposal was reintroduced as House Bill 2557 by Emilio Cortez, Chairman of the House Committee on Agrarian and Social Welfare, and as Senate Bill 332 by Senator Justiniano Montano. These two bills were basically similar but not identical. As the forces of opposition to land reform were concentrated in the

---

[31] *Ibid.*, p. 174 (original italics).
[32] *Manila Chronicle*, May 17, 1955. Quoted in Starner, *op. cit.*, p. 160.

House, the House bill was subject to most intensive debate and to numerous crippling amendments. Before it was enacted, no less than seven different substitutes were proposed. The key provisions that caused most controversy concerned the type and amount of land subject to expropriation, the methods of financing, the compensation payments, and the sizes of new farms to be created.

Type of land subject to expropriation. In their original versions, both House Bill 2557 and Senate Bill 332 would require expropriation of lands that were "suitable for subdivision," and lands whose redistribution would serve the "public interest," i.e. to restore peace in insurgency areas. The House bill imposed an additional, stringent limitation: the landowner had to be proved guilty of violating the Agricultural Tenancy Act of 1954 five times in three months before expropriation proceedings against him could be initiated. Among the substitute versions of this bill, one would have required expropriation of only "private agricultural lands owned by a single person . . . when the public welfare so requires." A second version would have required the expropriation of lands of absentee landlords first, and then lands of resident landlords. In addition, lands of those owners who were found guilty of violation of tenancy laws three times could be expropriated on court recommendation. A third version would have placed uncultivated lands, abandoned lands, and lands owned by persons not residing in the Philippines ahead of the lands listed in the order of priority mentioned above.

Areas subject to expropriation. The administration's measure provided that holdings in excess of 144 hectares were to be subject to expropriation. All except one of the proposed amendments considerably increased the maximum areas of exemption. The size of holdings that these amendments would have exempted from expropriation ranged from 150 hectares to 2,000 hectares. A number of amendments also prescribed different exemption areas according to the type of landownership (individual or corporation), the kinds of crops produced, and the presence or absence of rural unrest. One amendment, which made no reference to the area of exemption, proposed to create a commission to "survey" farm holdings with at least 50 tenants and, presumably, to recommend areas to be expropriated.

The method of payment. The administration's measure provided outright cash payment for lands acquired by expropriation and a combination of negotiable land certificates for land acquired through purchase. Amendments to this provision offered different formulas for compensation payment. Generally, they favored a more generous compensation, with cash and negotiable land certificates as the preferred forms of payment. In addition, since the government owned urban real property, industrial enterprises, and extensive lands in Mindanao, several amendments—supported by a number of planters' organizations, including the National Rice Producers Association and the Philippine Chamber of Agriculture—provided for an exchange of government properties for expropriated land.

Authorization of funds. The requirement for payment in cash and negotiable land certificates for certain lands necessitated the authorization of a large amount of public funds. The administration's measure proposed to authorize the issuance of up to ₱600,000,000 worth of land certificates, an annual appropriation of ₱1,000,000 for a sinking fund, and ₱500,000 for administration. All amendments on this provision sought to reduce the proposed amount of authorization. One amendment which came closest to the original provision would have authorized ₱100,000,000 for negotiable certificates, and ₱100,000 for administration, plus ₱50,000,000 worth of bonds to be issued under the authority of another law (Republic Act 1000). The amendment which proposed the smallest amount of appropriation would have authorized only ₱500,000 for administration and ₱1,000,000 for a sinking fund.

The size of new farms. In proposing the land-tenure bill, the administration intended to create a system of family farms. But what constituted a minimum area for a family farm? This question unexpectedly raised a great deal of controversy. The basic problem was that, given the area of land liable to expropriation and purchase, there was simply not enough to provide each of the nation's tenants with a farm of moderate size. If the administration insisted on creation of new family farms, many tenants not only would be unable to obtain land but also would lose the opportunity to continue to work on existing farms, which would have to be transferred to new owners. Was it desirable to displace a number of tenants so that other tenants might become owners? What would one do with the dispossessed tenants? If the administration did not seek to establish a minimum size for the new farms, then the problem of small, fragmented holdings would remain unresolved. It was in the midst of the debate over this issue that the idea of exploitation of new land rather than dividing existing holdings found its strongest appeal. The original version of House Bill 2557 incorporated the family idea but made no mention of the size of the new farms. Senate Bill 332 would have divided land into farms of 6 to 12 hectares, selected the owners by lot, and resettled displaced families on new land. All of the proposed amendments preferred retaining the family farm idea but disagreed on the propriety of establishing a minimum size for new farms, and those favoring a minimum size differed with respect to the disposition of the displaced tenants.

THE CONGRESSIONAL SESSIONS

In the 1954 session of Congress, partly because of the delaying tactics of the opposition legislators, and partly because of the preoccupation of the administration with the enactment of tenancy legislation, there was little congressional action on the land-tenure bill. When House Bill 2557 and Senate Bill 332 were introduced in the 1955 session, the administration promptly endorsed them. But for some unexplainable reason, President Magsaysay remained silent on these bills until very late in the session. "On May 8, only eleven days before the adjournment of Congress, Magsaysay certified to the urgency of thirty-three bills as administration measures, and among these was the land tenure bill." [33] Four days later, on May 12, House Bill 2557 was brought to the House floor. There, with only a week's time remaining, the bill encountered serious objections. Despite another intervention by Magsaysay, who called upon congressional leaders on May 14 to give immediate attention to the bill, the measure made no appreciable progress. Two days later, when it became clear that House Bill 2557 would stand no chance of passage in its original form, a group of congressmen headed by Jose Roy, a Democrat from Tarlac, hastily drafted a substitute. The next day, May 17, Cortez accepted the Roy measure as an amendment by substitution for his bill. The substitute bill (still titled House Bill 2557) seriously weakened the expropriation provisions of the original version, but it fared no better in the House. The press reported that the measure was a far cry from the administration bill, which had been "mutilated" or "emasculated" by congressmen. In the final evening of the session, on May 19, resistant congressmen employed a series of delaying tactics, successfully preventing the House from acting upon the Roy bill. Meanwhile the Senate, just a few hours before its adjournment, approved Senate Bill 332. But as the House failed to vote upon its own measure, the session ended without enacting the land-tenure bill.

Thirty minutes after Congress adjourned *sine die*, Malacañang (the Presidential Mansion) announced that the President would shortly call

[33] *Ibid.*, pp. 144–145.

a special session to consider a number of measures, including the land-tenure bill. Between then and July 7, when the special session of Congress convened, the bill was subject to extensive debate in the press, and the administration sought vigorously to mobilize congressional support through a newly appointed executive-legislative committee. A joint congressional committee, composed of members of both houses, was also created to effect some general agreement on the content of the bill to be enacted.

When the special session convened, Senate Bill 332 was adopted without difficulty, but House Bill 2557 once more became the center of attention; it again encountered serious obstructions, being subject to one amendment after another. The bill that the House finally managed to pass, by an overwhelming vote of 52 to 2, was so different from the original that a critical congressman, Manuel Cases from La Union, sarcastically called the measure "An Act Defining a Landlord Tenure Policy . . . dedicated to the preservation and perpetuation of the feudal system." [34]

The conference committee created to reconcile the House and Senate versions of the bill undertook an extensive redrafting of the measure. The report that finally emerged from the committee resembled the Senate bill more than the House bill. The Senate immediately adopted the compromise measure, but the House balked. In the meantime, Congressman Justino Z. Benito suddenly questioned the constitutionality of the conference report, insisting that this report, which included an authorization of funds for the future Land Tenure Administration, was essentially an appropriation bill; and under the constitution it should have been originated in the House. On August 2, one week before the mandatory expiration of the thirty-day special session, the House accepted Benito's argument and rejected the report.

Facing a prospect that the special session might again fail to adopt a land redistribution measure, Magsaysay applied further pressure on Congress. He was reportedly thinking of carrying the fight directly to the barrios; he threatened to reconvene Congress immediately in a new session if the special session closed without a bill. In the face of the impending senatorial and local elections, which were to be held within a few months, many congressmen were reluctant to stay in the capital;[35] confronted with

---

[34] Quoted in *ibid.*, p. 178.

[35] House members were not facing an election in 1955, but they were very much

a President who had popular backing, congressmen were also uneasy at taking a public stand against the wishes of the chief executive. Under the circumstances, many opponents began to change their minds. In the meantime, the Senate conferees, in order to meet the House's objection to the constitutional issue, agreed to modify the report so as to make it conform to House Bill 2557 in format, but retained the substance of the report. In the House the opposition leaders continued to stall the measure, but they finally gave in and adopted the bill "in the last few minutes of the session." [36]

The Non-Congressional Contestants

Among the non-congressional forces opposing the law, the most active was the National Rice Producers Association. In addition to launching an extensive publicity campaign against the bill, the NRPA also energetically sought to influence Congress through its lobbying activities. Starner has noted:

> The top officials of the NRPA not only were able to bombard individual congressmen with letters, mimeographed statements, and proposed amendments without limitation, but they could also attempt to influence legislative votes through a variety of personal contacts, and could even exert pressure while a measure was under discussion on the floor. Indeed, during the final week of the regular session, while the Roy bill was under discussion, members of the NRPA appeared personally in the gallery of the House to invite congressmen to a social function for an Association official. In addition, officials of the Rice Producers took prominent positions in the gallery whenever the bill was about to be called upon for discussion; when critical action on the measure was under way, they frequently summoned congressmen from their seats, or intercepted them as they entered the session hall, to confer on the bill's status and to influence, if possible, the action on the bill. . . . In a Congress that included a large number of landholders and, indeed, even some members of the NRPA, the informal and social contacts which the Association promoted there attracted little comment from the outside.[37]

concerned with the politics of their constituencies which became active as the senatorial and local election approached.

[36] *Ibid.*, p. 180.

[37] *Ibid.*, pp. 164–165. In reference to the NRPA social function that congressmen

Other organizations of the landed interests also played important roles in the legislative process, but they tended to exert their influence less obtrusively. For example, the National Sugarcane Planters Association preferred to channel its influence through its own members who "were well represented at top levels in both the executive and the legislative branches of government. . . ."[38] Moreover, the proposed tenure bill posed a less serious threat to sugar interests than to rice producers. As the operation on sugar lands was largely commercialized and mechanized, these lands were generally exempted from expropriation proceedings. The sugar planters' primary concern lay in the provisions of the bill on exchange of governmental property for private land, and on the maximum area to be exempted from expropriation. The planters sent representatives to committee hearings to present their views and maintained a watchful eye on the proceedings of Congress, but they issued no press releases, held no public meetings, and exerted no open pressure on Congress. The Philippine Chamber of Agriculture, which included the Philippine Federation of Palay and Corn Planters and the National Sugarcane Planters Association as its affiliates, was also present during congressional deliberations. Like the sugarcane organization, the Chamber maintained a representation in Congress; its board of directors included one senator and three congressmen.[39] Working directly through congressional members, it was confident that its views were well respected in Congress.

Aside from these groups from the landed class, there were many unorganized absentee landowners who expressed strong opposition to the proposed bill. "It was extremely commonplace, in private conversations, for professional people to register emphatic disapproval of land redistribution; these included doctors, lawyers, engineers, dentists, college professors, and even minor public officials who resided" in cities but drew a steady income from the countryside.[40] They lacked an organization to coordinate their views, but because they were more numerous than the

---

were invited to attend, Starner observed: "A number of congressmen reported that they had attended this lavish function, held in the Jai Alai Skyroom on May 17. Congressman Roy himself told the writer that he had been there. Furthermore, he said that he was at that time, and had been for some years, an honorary member of the NRPA, though he owned no argicultural lands. Significantly, a member of the Association's board not only held extensive palay lands in Roy's district in Tarlac, but owned also an entire town there." *Ibid.*, p. 274.

[38] *Ibid.*, p. 165.
[39] *Ibid.*, p. 274.
[40] *Ibid.*, p. 167.

big planters, and because they could individually reach members of Congress, their influence was very pervasive.

While the landed interests launched, through their organizations as well as through individual contacts with congressmen, an animated, broad-front attack on the land-tenure bill, the measure's intended beneficiaries—the peasants—remained silent. Many of them had actively responded to Magsaysay's appeal by participating in the 1953 election, but on the whole they failed to lend any sustained assistance to him during congressional consideration of the bill. Some two thousand peasants did meet in Bulacan in June 1955 to demonstrate their support, but the bulk of the farmers were not even aware of the existence of the measure.[41] The farmers' organizations were no more helpful. One of the larger organizations, the National Federation of Tenants and Farmers Associations (NAFTAFA) dispatched its officials to Congress to follow the legislative action and communicated with the legislators regarding its position on the measure, and on one occasion the NAFTAFA even sponsored a demonstration in favor of the bill. But the pressure was not effectively or consistently maintained. Most of the other organizations, like the peasantry itself, remained inactive during the entire congressional proceedings. When the House Committee on Agrarian and Social Welfare held hearings on the bill, "none of the agrarian tenant unions were represented [there] . . . even though public notice was given well in advance. Under these circumstances, hearings amounted to little more than verbal exchanges between members of the large planter associations, who opposed land reform of any sort . . . and Chairman Emilio Cortez, who frequently felt obliged to engage in spirited defense of the land redistribution principle." [42]

As the peasantry and its organizations were unable to bring their influence to bear on Congress, the major non-congressional source of support was found only in the administration. A group of the President's advisers on land reform played an important role in organizing congressional support for the bill and in defending it before the public. Judge Jorge Bocobo, Chairman of the Code Commission, Fernando A. Santiago of the Agricultural Tenancy Commission, and Secretary of Agriculture Salvador Araneta, all participated extensively in public debates rallying popular endorsement for land reform.

The most vital force supporting the land-tenure bill was provided by President Magsaysay himself, but while Magsaysay's strong commitment

[41] *Ibid.*, p. 175.
[42] *Ibid.*, p. 146.

to reform and popularity in rural areas were the crucial factors inducing many resistant congressmen finally to vote for the measure, the President's role in the entire legislative process was subject to a number of limitations. In the first place, he never firmly established his leadership position in the Nacionalista Party. Senators Jose P. Laurel and Claro Recto, the party's powerful old guard, initiated the move to endorse Magsaysay as the Nacionalista presidential candidate because they thought Magsaysay's prestige and success in the anti-Huk campaign could enable the party to win both the Presidency and a congressional majority. They were not particularly in sympathy with Magsaysay's political views; much less were they willing to relinquish party control to him. In fact both Senators broke with the President in the first year of Magsaysay's term, and Recto became a principal opponent of the land-tenure bill. Second, despite the fact that Magsaysay had served in both Congress and the administration before becoming President, he appeared to lack the kind of political expertise necessary for effective national leadership. As a man of action, he often traveled in the country's remote areas leaving no one in the capital to attend to presidential responsibilities. He was also reluctant to take initiative in the formulation of broad national policies. In the area of land reform he had no coherent, concrete proposals. As seen earlier, many of his first agrarian proposals were merely the revisions of existing laws. The land-tenure bill was a new program, but he was not personally involved in its formulation. He asked Congress in January 1955 to enact the bill, yet he remained silent on the measure for four months. Third, his legislative strategy showed a certain lack of sophistication and skillfulness. In May 1955, when he began actively seeking the passage of the bill, he tended to exert his pressure on Congress openly and did not seek, as a complementary tactic, to channel his influence through extensive personal consultations with members of Congress, a tactic which might have enabled him to obtain an early legislative victory. Instead, he experienced much delay and uncertainty. The regular sessions of Congress in 1954 and 1955 adjourned without enacting the land-tenure bill, and he finally obtained the passage of the measure only "in the last few minutes" of the special session of 1955.

And, finally, Magsaysay faced the problem of finding a way to translate his electoral strength into an effective instrument of political power. His split with the senior leaders of the Nacionalista Party denied him the opportunity to use the party fully as a means of mobilizing popular support. Partly because of this, and partly because of his predilection, he sought prompt enforcement of his rural programs by extensively using his executive authority. He personally initiated a Liberty Wells program (supported by voluntary donations) to provide water to rural residents, launched community rehabilitation programs in areas of Central Luzon that had been evacuated by the Huks, used his discretionary funds to create an Agricultural Tenancy Commission, and utilized non-governmental agencies to disseminate information about tenancy reform laws. In San Luis, Pampanga—the center of Huk rebellion and the home town of former Huk leader Luis Taruc—Magsaysay supervised the so-called "The President's San Luis Project," which opened up and redistributed 8,000 hectares of land to small farmers.[43] By following this course of action, Magsaysay made the impact of the Presidency widely felt in rural areas and succeeded in retaining peasant loyalty. But his impact would conceivably have been more endurable had he effectively organized the peasantry into a coherent political force. Similarly, the executive-initiated agrarian programs could have benefited far more farmers than they did in practice had Magsaysay tried to obtain full congressional endorsement.

With all these political limitations, Magsaysay's leadership nevertheless contributed far more to the passage of the 1955 law than any other factor. The fast pace at which he moved to secure the enactment of the land-tenure bill after he certified to Congress its urgency, his calling of a special session in the face of an impending election, his threat of calling another session if the special session failed to adopt the bill—all these manifestations of Magsaysay's commitment to the bill compelled many congressmen to face the difficult choice of either accepting the bill which they opposed at heart or rejecting the bill and thereby antagonizing a highly popular President. Since acceptance of the bill did not necessarily result in its effective enforcement, and since antagonizing the President might lead to a loss of rural strength in the 1955 or 1957 elections, many congressmen opted for the adoption of the bill. Magsaysay's use of confrontation tactics in his dealings with Congress not only secured him a victory in the battle for the bill; there was a consequence of perhaps far greater political significance. To a certain extent, Magsaysay was able to inject the peasant mind with political consciousness and to induce farmers to participate more actively in politics than before. As will be discussed in Chapter X, this was manifested in the 1955 election results.

[43] See *ibid.*, pp. 133 and 141; and Carlos P. Romulo and Marvin M. Gray, *The Magsaysay Story* (New York: The John Day Company, 1956), pp. 273–276.

RA 1400, The Land Reform Act of 1955[44]

As enacted, the Land Reform Act of 1955 is a short piece of legislation containing a total of thirty brief sections. It declared as its principal objective the creation of "family-size farms" through the opening up of public lands, purchase, and expropriation of private lands and their distribution to landless farmers. It provided for a Land Tenure Administration (LTA), directly under the President, to administer the law. With respect to *the expropriation of private land*, the government could acquire land only upon petition of the tenants on a landholding and only "as to the area in excess of three hundred hectares of contiguous area if owned by natural persons and as to the area in excess of six hundred hectares if owned by corporations." In areas "where justified [*sic*] agrarian unrest exists," lands might be expropriated regardless of size. Compensation was made wholly in cash unless the owner requested payment by land certificates.

With respect to *acquisition of land by purchase*, the LTA, upon the petition of a majority of the tenants on a landholding, would proceed to negotiate with the owner to obtain the land. When the owner and the LTA could not agree upon the price or the method of payment, the land was liable to expropriation proceedings. Compensation was to be made wholly in land certificates or partly in cash and partly in certificates. The owner was given the added option of negotiating with the LTA to exchange his land for government-owned "residential, commercial or industrial land."

The President was authorized to issue negotiable land certificates in the amount of ₱60,000,000 annually for the first two years, and ₱30,000,000 in each succeeding year. The Act alloted a sum of ₱100,000,000 from the bonds authorized under Republic Act 1000 for the purpose of carrying out land redistribution. In addition, ₱20,000,000 was to be appropriated annually for a sinking fund, and ₱300,000 for administrative expenses. Lands acquired were to be sold to tenants or qualified farmers "at cost." The farmer purchaser was to pay the government land price in twenty-five annual installments with a 6 percent annual interest. The law sought to create family farms "not exceeding six hectares each," but made no reference to any possible displacement of tenants.

Compared to its original version and to the numerous subsequent

---

[44] The text of the Act can be found in Appendix I, below.

amended versions, the enacted law was truly a compromise measure in regard to every one of its key provisions. One might say that the mere acceptance of the law was an important event, for the principle of compulsory redistribution was finally accepted by a Congress that had resisted it for so long. Upon close scrutiny of the provisions of the law, however, one finds a number of serious ambiguities and omissions. First, in using the term "contiguous area" to determine the size of exemption for individually owned land, the law could make available only a tiny portion of private land for redistribution. As the 1948 census of agriculture revealed, the total area of land worked by tenants on farms of 200 or more hectares was only 103,769.10 hectares. This amounted to 1.81 percent of the nation's total farm area of 5,726,583.64 hectares.[45] The area of tenanted land belonging to farms of 300 or more hectares must have been even smaller.

Second, in using the term "natural persons" to define individual landowners, the Act failed to specify whether a family was to be regarded as one owner or several. This lack of precision in the definition of ownership, as the Indian experiences have amply demonstrated, could critically curtail the area available for expropriation. It is conceivable that, before the LTA started expropriation proceedings, a family could divide its land possessions among its members—and perhaps among its relatives as well— to escape the liability of expropriation. The law permitted acquisition of land without regard to size in areas where "justified" agrarian unrest existed but did not lay down any criteria for declaring the existence of such a condition in a given area.

Third, as a precondition for the LTA to institute purchase or expropriation proceedings, a majority of the tenants on a landholding had to petition for governmental action. As the Philippine tenants were known to be very submissive to their landlords, few would have the courage to initiate the petition. The law did prohibit ejectment of tenants during the purchase or expropriation proceedings, but it did not prohibit ejectment once these proceedings conclusively determined that the government could not acquire the landholding in question. And finally, with respect to the compensation provisions, the law laid down no concrete, indisputable formula for determining the land price. As a consequence, the process

---

[45] The Philippines, Bureau of the Census and Statistics, *Summary Report on the 1948 Census of Agriculture* (Manila, 1952), p. 151.

of land acquisition would either entail prolonged court proceedings in settling a price, or end up paying the landowners a high price, or both.

The 1955 law was the most significant legislative enactment on land reform by the Philippine Congress up to that time. During some twenty years, the elite had negotiated continuously with the landed interests to improve reform legislation. It finally succeeded in winning the acceptance of the principle of compulsory expropriation of land. But the key provisions of the 1955 law remained weak and difficult to enforce. Following a gradualistic, bargaining approach, the elite was to seek further improvement in the future. This led to the passage of the 1963 Agricultural Land Reform Code.

VII

REDISTRIBUTIVE PROGRAMS: LAND REDISTRIBUTION AND TENANCY REFORM

Redistributive programs are intended to reallocate equitably the sources of agricultural income; they frequently include land redistribution and tenancy reform.

Land Redistribution

Whether intended for equalizing the size of farm holdings or for creating a total owner-farm system, land redistribution requires the compulsory transfer of land. As summarized in Tables 10 and 11, all eight countries under study have, in time, adopted this type of program.

PUBLIC, ROYAL, AND FOREIGN HOLDINGS

In countries where public, royal, or foreign holdings exist, it is logical and prudent for elites first to transfer these holdings to the cultivators. By redistributing public and/or royal land, the elites demonstrate their determination to carry out reform, thus setting an example for private holders to follow. While unable to argue openly and justifiably against a program to redistribute the land they do not own, private holders may even favor such a redistribution, in the hope that it might lessen the demand for their land.

In Taiwan in 1945, when the island was returned to China from Japan, public land amounted to 181,490 *chia* (176,045 hectares, about 21 percent of the farming area), with most of it leased to farmers at a preferential low rental of 25 percent of the farm produce. In 1951, the Taiwan Provincial Government, in order to pave the way for the subsequent land-to-the-tiller program and to finance land improvement projects, adopted a set of regulations for selling public land to its in-

TABLE 10

LAND REDISTRIBUTION LAWS, EIGHT COUNTRIES

	Colombia	India	Iran
Title and date of main law	Social Agrarian Reform Law, 1961	ª	Land Reform Laws, Decrees, and Regulations 1951, 1958, 1962, 1963, 1964
Application of law: Universal or piecemeal	Piecemeal	Piecemeal, by states	Universal
Methods of land acquisition	(a) Grant of public land (b) confiscation of holdings exceeding 2000 ha. and uncultivated for 10 years, (c) negotiated purchase, (d) expropriation	State governments (a) declare area of surplus land (i.e. above ceiling), (b) acquire it with compensation	(a) Donation of crown land by the Shah, (b) grant of public land, (c) expropriation of private land in excess of one village, (d) negotiation between farmer and owner in regard to private land below one village
Ceiling on private holdings	Each individual holder: 200 ha., of which no more than 100 ha. suitable as crop land	ª	(a) First stage: one village per individual holder, (b) second stage 20–150 ha. per holder
Allowance for family members	No	ª	No
Pre-enforcement alienation of private land	No provision, but alienation in places not yet designated as reform areas is permitted	ª	With regard to (a) ceiling above one village, void after approval of 1962 law, (b) ceiling below one village, void after submission of the 1964 regulations to the Majlis
Type of land exempted	See priorities	ª	Mechanized farms up to 500 ha.; orchards, tea plantations
Priorities of types of land to be redistributed	(a) Public land, (b) uncultivated private land, (c) inadequately farmed private land, (d) tenanted farm land, (e) properly farmed, owner-occupied land	(a) Surplus land (above ceiling), (b) land from land-gift movement, (c) cultivable waste land	(a) Crown land; (b) public land; (c) private land: (1) land above ceiling, (2) barren land, (3) uncultivated land

TABLE 10 (*Continued*)

	Colombia	India	Iran
Methods of redistribution	Government initiates acquisition proceedings and resells land to beneficiaries	State governments resell expropriated land to beneficiaries	(a) Crown and public land: sale to beneficiaries; (b) private land: (1) above one village, government resells to beneficiaries, (2) below one village, direct purchase by farmer from owner
Selection of beneficiaries	Incumbent farmers on public or private land	State practices vary, but generally (a) landless tenants, (b) small holders, (c) landless workers	Order of priority: (a) resident, incumbent farmer, (b) his (her) heir, (c) tenant, (d) farm worker, (e) other
Size of beneficiary holdings	Large enough to sustain the life of a normal-size family	Unspecified in most states; 1 to 3 family holdings in certain states; cooperative farming encouraged	Size unspecified; beneficiaries required to join cooperatives
Principal reform agencies	Instituto Colombiano de la Reforma Agraria (INCORA)	State land revenue agencies	Land Reform Organization

	Mexico	East Pakistan	West Pakistan
Title and date of main law	Article 27, Constitution of 1917; Agrarian Code, 1942	The East Bengal State Acquisition and Tenancy Act, 1950, amended, 1961	The West Pakistan Land Reforms Regulation, 1959
Application of law: universal or piecemeal	Universal	Piecemeal, by province	Piecemeal, by province
Methods of land acquisition	(a) Restitution, (b) "dotación," (c) amplification	Provincial government (a) declares area of surplus land (i.e. above ceiling), (b) acquires it with compensation	Same procedure as in East Pakistan

TABLE 10 (*Continued*)

	Mexico	*East Pakistan*	*West Pakistan*
Ceiling on private holdings	100–300 ha. per individual holder (crop land only)	1950–1961: 110 *bighas* (14.7 ha.) per family 1961–: 375 *bighas* (50.6 ha.) per family	500–1,000 acres (202.5–405 ha.) per individual holder
Allowance for family members	No	No	Owner may transfer to heirs up to a total of one-half of ceiling area; in addition, to each female dependent one-sixth of ceiling area
Pre-enforcement alienation of private land	After the initiation of acquisition proceedings, alienation of land must be approved by government	No information	(a) Originally, void after October 8, 1958; (b) Amendment of April 9, 1960: alienation before this date was valid provided it would not result in excessive division of land
Type of land exempted	Generally non-food crop land (up to specified limits), buildings, hydraulic works	Tea, coffee, sugarcane, rubber, mechanized farms, orchards, dairy farms, etc.	Land belonging to charitable, religious, educational institutions, stud and livestock farms, orchards (up to 150 ha.)
Priorities of types of land to be redistributed	(a) Public land, (b) private land	(a) *Zamindari* land, (b) private surplus land	Private surplus land
Methods of redistribution	(a) Restitution: restoration of land to original owner with proved title, (b) "dotación" and amplification: petition by farmers, approval by government, free grant of land	Government resells surplus land to beneficiaries	Government resells surplus land to beneficiaries

TABLE 10 (*Continued*)

	Mexico	*East Pakistan*	*West Pakistan*
Selection of beneficiaries	(a) Restitution: original owner or descendant (b) "dotación" and amplification: (1) farmers with family, (2) farmers without family, (3) others	Cultivators holding less than 3 acres (1.2 ha.) of land	(a) Incumbent tenants, (b) others
Size of beneficiary holdings	Before 1943: 4–8 ha. 1943–1947: 6–12 ha. 1947– 10–20 ha. Beneficiaries required to join *ejidos*.	Unspecified	Unspecified
Principal reform agencies	Federal Agrarian Department	East Pakistan Revenue Department	The West Pakistan Land Commission

	The Philippines	*Taiwan*	*U.A.R.*
Title and date of main law	The Agricultural Land Reform Code, 1963	Regulations on Sale of Public Land, 1951, The Land-to-the-Tiller Act, 1953	Agrarian Reform Law, 1952, as amended
Application of law: universal or piecemeal	Piecemeal	Universal	Universal
Methods of land acquisition	Expropriation of private land upon petition by one-third of lessees	Grant of public land, expropriation of tenanted private land	Confiscation of royal land; expropriation of private land
Ceiling on private holdings	75 ha. per individual or per corporation owner (limited to leased land only)	3–6 *chia* (2.9–5.8 ha.) per registered land holder (limited to tenanted land only)	1952–1961: 200 *feddans* (84 ha.); since 1961: 100 *feddans* (42 ha.) per individual holder
Allowance for family members	No	No	1952 law allows transfer of up to 100 *feddans* to children of owner
Pre-enforcement alienation of private land	Void, once petition for expropriation is filed	Void after April 1, 1952, except in legally specified cases	1952 law allows transfer within five years of excess land to small farmers and agricultural students; 1961 amendment allows transfer of excess land within a year

TABLE 10 (*Continued*)

	The Philippines	Taiwan	U.A.R.
Type of land exempted	"Lands under labor administration" [b]	(a) Tenanted land within area of city planning, newly developed land, experimental farm land, land for charitable use or educational use, land for industrial use. (b) Twice ceiling area for religious land	Reclaimed land, fallow or desert land being improved, land for industrial use, land of agricultural, scientific, benevolent societies, *wakf* (religious) land
Priorities of types of land to be redistributed	(a) Idle land, (b) leased land in excess of 1,024 ha., then of 500 ha., 144 ha., 75 ha.	(a) Public land, (b) tenanted private surplus land	Same priorities as in Taiwan
Methods of redistribution	Government resells surplus land to beneficiaries	Government sells both public land and expropriated private land to beneficiaries	Government resells expropriated land
Selection of beneficiaries	Order of priority: (a) original owner's relatives who are cultivators, (b) incumbent cultivators, (c) cultivators working on idle land, (d) small owner-farmers, (e) others	Incumbent cultivators	Cultivators with less than 5 *feddans* (2.1 ha.) of land
Size of beneficiary holdings	Family-size farm	Public land: $\frac{1}{2}$–4 *chia* (0.48–3.9 ha.); private land: unspecified	2–5 *feddans* (0.84–2.1 ha.); beneficiaries required to join cooperatives
Principal reform agencies	The Land Authority	The Ministry of the Interior and the Provincial Land Bureau	The Ministry of Agrarian Reform (Predecessor: The General Organization for Agrarian Reform)

[a] See Table 12.
[b] Sugarcane, coconut plantations, orchards, commercialized farms.
SOURCES: Primarily land reform laws, Appendix I, below.

TABLE 11

LAND REDISTRIBUTION LEGISLATION OF INDIA, STATES AND UNION TERRITORIES

Legislation	Ceiling[a] (in Acres)	Applied to Family or Registered Individual Holder	Allowance for Large Families	Pre-enforcement Alienation of Private Land	Types of Land Exempted[b]
The Andhra Pradesh Ceiling on Agricultural Holdings Act, 1961	27–324	Individual	For a family in excess of 5, each additional member may retain one ceiling area	Void after enactment	1–4, 7–10, 25, 26, 28
The Assam Fixation of Ceiling on Land Holdings Act, 1959	50	Family	No	Void after introduction of bill	1, 2, 4, 5, 26, 28
The Bihar Land Reform Act, 1961	20–60	Individual	For a large family, up to twice the ceiling area	Permissible to give land as gift to family members within 6 months after commencement of law.	1, 2, 21, 23, 25, 30
The Gujarat Agricultural Lands Ceiling Act, 1960	19–132	Family	No	Void after commencement of law, if without permission of the Collector of Revenue	6, 23–26, 28
Jammu & Kashmir, The Big Landed Estates Abolition Act, 1950	22¾	Individual	No	No provision	4, 14, 15, 26
The Kerala Agrarian Relations Act, 1960	15–37.5 (15)	Family	For large family, up to 1½ the ceiling area	Void after introduction of bill	2, 3, 7, 16, 17, 25, 26, 30

Act	Ceiling (acres)	Unit	Large family provision	Validity of transfers	References
The Madhya Pradesh Ceiling on Agricultural Holdings Act, 1960	25–75 (25)	Individual	For large family, up to twice the ceiling area	Valid within 2 years after commencement of law if land is transferred to reform beneficiaries or their organizations; void for all other transfers after publication of bill	1–4, 8, 23–28
The Madras Land Reforms Act, 1961	24–120 (30)	Family	Same as above	Void after publication of bill	1–4, 7, 9, 10, 14, 17, 19, 24–26, 29–31
The Maharashtra Agricultural Lands Act, 1961	18–126	Family	Same as above	Void after publication of bill	11, 23–26, 31
The Mysore Land Reforms Act, 1961	27–216 (27)	Family	Same as above	Valid after commencement of law until owner is notified to the contrary	1–4, 7, 9, 10, 13, 17, 28
The Orissa Land Reforms Act, 1960[c]	25–100 (25)	Individual	Same as above	No provision	1, 2, 4, 7–9, 16, 18, 22, 26–28
Punjab: (a) The Punjab Security of Land Tenures Act, 1955[c] (amended)	30–100 (30)	Individual	No	Void after April 15, 1953	2, 4, 26, 28, 31
(b) The Pepsu Tenancy and Agricultural Lands Act, 1955	30–100 (30)	Individual	No	Generally, void after introduction of bill	1, 4, 8, 9, 25, 26, 28, 31
The Rajasthan Tenancy Act, 1960 (amended)	22–336 (30)	Family	For large family, twice the ceiling area	Valid if land is "partitioned" or transferred to a landless person; void for all other transfers after Feb. 25, 1958	1, 8–12, 26, 28
The Uttar Pradesh Imposition of Ceiling on Land Holdings Act, 1960	40–80 (40)	Individual	For large family, up to $1\frac{6}{10}$ the ceiling area	Generally, void after introduction of bill	2, 3, 7, 9, 10, 12, 20, 23, 25, 32

TABLE 11 (*Continued*)

Legislation	Ceiling (in Acres)[a]	Applied to Family or Registered Individual Holder	Allowance for Large Families	Pre-enforcement Alienation of Private Land	Types of Land Exempted[b]
The West Bengal Land Reforms Act, 1955	25	Individual	No	Validity of alienation after May 5, 1953, to be determined by government	2, 4, 9, 10, 24–26
Union Territories:					
Delhi Ceiling on Land Holdings Act, 1960	25–60 (30)	Family	For large family, up to twice the ceiling area	Generally, void after government announced intention to propose law.	4, 8–10, 26–28
Himachal Pradesh Land Reforms Act, 1953	30	Individual	No	Void after April 1, 1952	4, 28
Manipur Land Revenue & Land Reforms Act, 1960	25	Family	For large family, up to twice the ceiling area	Void after Jan. 15, 1959	1–4, 7–10, 26, 28
Tripura Land Revenue and Land Reforms Act, 1960	25–75 (25)	Family	Same as above	Void after publication of bill	1–4, 7–10, 26, 28
Mean	26–105[d]				

[a] Most states and territories prescribe several ceilings, depending on the quality of land and accessibility of water. Only the lowest and highest ceilings are given. In many instances, ceilings are expressed in standard acres, which may be converted to ordinary acres in accordance with pre-established formulas. In such instances, two ceilings are indicated in the table, first in ordinary acres and then in standard acres enclosed in parentheses.

[b] Key to the types of land exempted from ceilings legislation:

1 sugar cane	2 tea	3 coffee
4 orchard	5 citrus	6 fruit tree
7 rubber	8 cattle-raising	9 dairy farming
10 livestock	11 stud farm	12 groves
13 pepper	14 fuel tree	15 grass
16 cashew nut	17 cardamom	18 casuarina
19 cinchona	20 pharmacological products	21 lac-brood farms
22 sisal		

23 specially approved leased farms
24 commercial or industrial undertakings
25 religious, charitable, educational, or medical institutions' land
26 cooperative farming society
27 government approved exempted area
28 "efficiently managed farms in compact blocks whose break-up . . . may result in the fall of production"
29 hill area
30 Gramdan Bhoodan (land gift organization) area
31 awarded for "gallantry"
32 miscellaneous

[c] The State assumes no responsibility for acquisition of surplus land for redistribution to farmers. Surplus land is to be transferred through direct negotiation between purchaser and owner.

[d] In ordinary acres.

SOURCE: India, Planning Commission, *Progress of Land Reform* (Delhi: The Manager, Government of India Press, 1963).

cumbent cultivators. The most crucial aspect of the program was the determination of a formula for appraising land value. The soundness of this formula not only materially affected the success or failure of the program but also had considerable bearing on the program for redistribution of private land, which was to use the same formula. The Taiwan Provincial Land Bureau proposed to calculate land value on the basis of 2.5 times the annual yield of the main crop of the land. This proposal had two principal merits. By setting land value at exactly 10 times the rent of the leased public land, the formula was simple to use and easy to understand. As land price was expressed in terms of farm products, it would not be subject to currency fluctuations. Though considerably underestimating the actual land value, this formula was adopted without much debate.[1] Under the program, farmers were to pay the land price in rice (for paddy field) or sweet potato (for dry land) within 10 years in 20 semi-annual installments without interest. Since 1951, there have been several sales of public land resulting in the transfer of 98,982 *chia* (96,012 hectares) to farmers.

In Iran, crown estates and public land, in the early 1950s, constituted about 10 percent of the agricultural area.[2] Taking the initiative in disposing of the crown land, the Shah issued a decree, in 1951, to sell the more than two thousand villages that he then owned. The incumbent farmers were eligible to purchase the land at a price 20 percent below the appraised value, and to make the payment in 25 annual installments, with a 1 percent service charge, for 15 years. The Bank-e-Omran (the Bank of Development and Rural Cooperatives) was created in 1952 to take charge of the sale program and to use the sale proceeds to provide agricultural loans and to finance rural improvement projects in the crown land area. In 1955, the Majlis enacted a law to sell the public land to the incumbent cultivators. Each of the farmers was eligible to buy 10 to 15 hectares and to pay the purchase price in 20 annual installments; half of the sale proceeds was to be turned over to the Agricultural Bank to support services similar to those of the Bank-e-Omran. After a cadastral survey and mapping of the public domain, actual sales began in 1958.

In Egypt, the estates of the royal family covered some 180,000 *feddans* (75,600 hectares) at the time of the coup in 1952. In the following year, the army regime issued a decree, Law No. 598, confiscating these royal

---

[1] See Article 20 of the Land-to-the-Tiller Act, 1953, in Appendix I, below.
[2] Mohammad Reza Shah Pahlavi, *Mission For My Country* (New York, 1961), p. 200.

estates, and sold them to the incumbenut cultivators. Initially, these estates were the primary targets of reform; even as late as 1960, they constituted 39 percent of the total redistributed area.[3]

In all these cases, the enactment of programs for redistributing public and royal holdings was accomplished with relative ease, encountering no undue delay and frustration. The adoption of a program to dispose of foreign holdings has often proved to be an even easier political task. Though the program may necessitate negotiations with foreign powers, it elicits no domestic resistance. Instead, it can sharpen the sense of national identity and enhance the popular image of the elite. In Mexico, as late as 1923, foreign holdings of no less than 17 nations covered 32 million hectares of land, or 20.1 percent of the country's total area.[4] Indeed, with non-Mexicans owning so much of Mexico, the revolution of 1910 "cannot be understood without an insight into the irritation produced by the foreign ownership of land in the country." [5] During the revolution, the elite was prompt in adopting measures severely restricting foreign land-ownership. Article 27 of the Constitution stipulates:

> Only Mexicans by birth or naturalization and Mexican companies have the right to acquire ownership of lands, waters, . . . The State may grant the same right to foreigners, providing they agree . . . to consider themselves as nationals in respect to such property, . . . Under no circumstances may foreigners acquire direct ownership of lands or waters within a zone of one hundred kilometers along the frontiers and of fifty kilometers along the shores of the country.

With the adoption of this law, the Mexican government gradually took over the foreign possessions and transferred them to the *ejidos*.

In Egypt, foreign-owned land has dwindled since the beginning of this century, but in 1950 it still amounted to 215,783 *feddans* (90,628 hectares), about 3.6 percent of all private land.[6] After the 1952 revolution, the Egyptian government did not immediately prohibit foreign possessions but applied the ceiling provisions of the reform decree to these

[3] Gabriel S. Saab, *The Egyptian Agrarian Reform, 1952–1962* (London, 1967), pp. 21–22.

[4] Frank Tannenbaum, *The Mexican Agrarian Revolution* (New York, 1929), pp. 360, 365–366.

[5] Frank Tannenbaum, *Mexico: The Struggle for Peace and Bread* (New York: Alfred Knopf, 1950), p. 140.

[6] In 1910, foreigners owned 720,230 *feddans* (302,569 hectares) of land in Egypt, about 13.2 percent of all private land, a record high for this century. Gabriel Baer, *A History of Landownership in Modern Egypt, 1800–1950* (London, 1962), p. 230.

possessions and limited land recipients to Egyptians. In 1963, the government adopted Republican Decree No. 15, banning foreign landownership altogether; all the 140,000 *feddans* (60,800 hectares) remaining in foreign hands were taken over by the goverment, and a substantial portion was redistributed.

PRIVATE HOLDINGS[7]

To redistribute private holdings, of course, constitutes by far the most formidable task for political elites. They must resolve two central issues. One relates to the amount of land an owner is permitted to retain, and the other concerns the financing of the program.

The Issue of Ceilings

The task of determining the amount of land that an owner is permitted to retain requires the imposition of ceilings on landownership; these should be low enough to enable a large number of farmers to acquire land and high enough to avert excessive division of land. In performing this task, elites are influenced by political considerations. With the landed class removed from the position of power, *separated elites* in rural areas can seek only the peasants as their allies. These elites, therefore, are likely to take a stance in favor of small farmers. As a rule, they encourage broad sharing of landownership, thus prescribing low ceilings. Still seeking to preserve the interests of landowners, *cooperative elites* are not particularly interested in promoting equalization of landownership; they tend to establish high ceilings outright or to prescribe low ones with generous concessions to landowners.

To compare the ceilings of the eight countries under study one can use either of the following two measurements: the ceilings as prescribed by reform laws, and the ratio of the prescribed ceilings to the pre-reform average size of farm holdings of the country. Since this latter measurement can indicate the extent to which prescribed ceilings can potentially contribute to the equalization of landownership in the post-reform period, it will be used in the comparison. All eight countries, it is necessary to point out, have prescribed more than one ceiling—for different regions, different types of land, or over different periods of time. In order to make the

---

[7] For the sake of brevity, the term refers hereafter to individual holdings of a country's nationals, excluding those of foreigners.

comparison manageable, only the latest and uppermost ceilings of these countries have been selected for study. The pertinent data for the eight countries are presented in Table 12.

When all other conditions are equal, the country that has a low ceiling-to-pre-reform-average-size-of-farm-holding ratio is likely to make available a large proportion of its farm land for redistribution. A detailed examination of the results of land redistribution in Chapter IX will substantiate this point. At present, for purposes of illustration, the cases of Mexico and West Pakistan, which possess respectively the lowest and the highest ratio among countries in Table 12, may be mentioned. As will be seen later in Table 31, as of 1960, Mexico provided to its reform beneficiaries 10,329,000 hectares, or 43.28 percent of a total crop area of 23,816,900 hectares; in contrast, as of 1965, long after the completion of its reform program, West Pakistan had acquired for redistribution only 2,220,-718 acres (898,725 hectares), or 5.99 percent of a total crop area of 37,037,-000 acres (14,988,874 hectares).[8] Table 12 also shows that generally the ratio is lower in countries ruled by separated elites than in countries ruled by cooperative elites. The cases of Colombia and India stand as exceptions. Governed by cooperative elites, these two countries have a lower ratio than does the U.A.R., where a separated elite exercises power. However, a further inquiry into the ceiling programs of the eight countries will much reduce the significance of these exceptions.

Application of programs. The manner in which a ceiling program is applied to a country's territory will affect the amount of land available for redistribution and the length of time needed to complete the program. There are two approaches. A country can adopt a piecemeal approach: either it assigns responsibility for reform to its local government units with each unit enacting and applying a separate program; or, it enacts a uniform national program, but first applies the program to selected areas, gradually extending it to the entire national domain. In India, the states and union territories enacted twenty separate acts applying ceiling legislation to their respective geographical domains. In Pakistan, the East Wing applied legislation enacted in 1950, as the West Wing enforced a program under the material law decree of 1959. In Colombia and the Philippines, uniform national programs were enacted but could only be applied to selected project areas as decreed by government. A country can also follow a universal approach in the application of its program, i.e. it applies

[8] See Table 31, below.

TABLE 12

CEILING OF RETAINED PRIVATE LAND AND THE CEILING-
TO-AVERAGE-FARM-HOLDING RATIO, EIGHT COUNTRIES

Country (A)	Ceiling of Retained Land[a] Year (B)	Ceiling of Retained Land[a] Area (C)	Size of Average Farm Holding[b] Year (D)	Size of Average Farm Holding[b] Area (E)	Ratio of Ceiling to Average Size of Farm Holding (C) ÷ (E) (F)	Rank of Countries, Low to High Ratio (G)
Mexico	1942	300 ha.	1930	153.35 ha.[c]	1.96	1
Taiwan	1953	6 chia (5.8 ha.)	1952	1.33 chia[d] (1.29 ha.)	4.51	2
Colombia	1961	200 ha.	1960	22.65 ha.[e]	8.83	3
India	1950–1961	105 acres (42.5 ha.)	1953–1954	7.53 acres[f] (3.05 ha.)	13.94	4
U.A.R.	1961	100 feddans (42 ha.)	1950	6.1 feddans[g] (2.6 ha.)	16.39	5
Philippines	1963	75 ha.	1960	3.59 ha.[e]	20.89	6
Iran	1964	150 ha.	1960	6.05 ha.[e]	24.79	7
E. Pakistan	1961	125 acres (50.6 ha.)	1960	3.5 acres[h] (1.4 ha.)	35.71	8
W. Pakistan	1959	1,000 acres (405 ha.)	1960	9.8 acres[i] (4.0 ha.)	102.04	9

[a] See Tables 10 and 11.

[b] An effort has been made to make use of data which are *properly* dated. That is, of a given country the "holding" data should, insofar as possible, closely predate the "ceiling" data. One exception to this rule is found in the case of West Pakistan. But, since the dates of the holding data and the ceiling data of West Pakistan are very close, and since it is known that not so much land was transferred within these dates as to affect appreciably the average size of agricultural holding, the holding data are still useful for present purpose.

[c] Based on FAO, *World Agricultural Structure, Study No. 1, General Introduction and Size of Holdings* (Rome, 1961), Table 3, p. 55.

[d] Based on China, Executive Yuan, *Taiwan Statistical Data Book, 1965* (Taipei, Taiwan 1965), p. 20.

[e] From Table 3, above.

[f] P. S. Sharma, "A Study of the Structural and Tenurial Aspects of Rural Economy in the Light of 1961 Census," *Indian Journal of Agricultural Economics*, XX (October-December 1965), 71.

[g] Gabriel S. Saab, *The Egyptian Agrarian Reform, 1952–1962* (London 1967), p. 10.

[h] Pakistan, Planning Commission, Agriculture & Food Section, *Handbook of Agricultural Statistics* (Karachi, 1964), Table 85.

[i] *Ibid.*, Table 87.

one uniform program throughout the national domain simultaneously. Iran, Mexico, Taiwan, and the U.A.R. followed this approach.

Advocates of the piecemeal approach often contend that, since the implementation of land redistribution creates a heavy demand on public funds and on administrative and technical personnel, an orderly transfer of land and adequate public assistance to the beneficiaries require a gradual, area-to-area application of the program. In reality, this contention frequently hides the intention of frustrating the process of implementation. For adequacy of financial, administrative, and technical preparations for reform is a relative matter. As will be elaborated later, if the elite is willing, a country following the universal approach but with less preparation on all these counts than a country adopting the piecemeal approach can, nevertheless, achieve greater implementation of its program.

The piecemeal approach harbors two basic pitfalls which obstruct land redistribution efforts more than inadequacy of preparation. One is the possibility—legally sanctioned and encouraged—of evasion. In countries where the piecemeal approach is adopted, landowners in areas not yet covered by a ceiling program can conceivably dispose substantially or completely of their surplus land prior to the application of the program to their areas. The longer the time needed for the program to reach the entire national domain, the smaller the amount of land that is available for redistribution. The other pitfall is that this approach will inevitably lead to a serious delay in the completion of the redistribution program. The fact is that every country following this approach has not provided a terminal date for its program; and in every instance in which a program was to be extended to a new area, a new battle for the program—in either the legislative or the executive branch of the government—had to be waged. In India, each of the twenty states and union territories had to enact a reform bill of its own; it took the nation eleven years to complete the legislative phase of reform. In Pakistan, the East Wing adopted a reform law in 1950, but the West Wing did not have a reform program until nine years later. In Colombia and the Philippines, the reform laws failed to provide clear, definite criteria for the selection of reform areas. The speed at which the programs proceed, and the number of reform areas actually selected are supposedly matters within the discretion of executive officials. But, facing both the pressure of the landed interests to slow down implementation and the competing demands for funds and personnel from other public programs, these officials cannot really use their discretionary authority to act expeditiously on reform.

The universal approach can avoid both pitfalls. By following this approach, a country can deprive the landlords of a major opportunity for evasion. Generally, the country will not grant its executive officials discretionary authority as to where and when to start implementing reform, but will place them under statutory obligation to take over all surplus land everywhere. Thus, relatively prompt completion of the program is possible. In Iran, Taiwan, and the U.A.R., once the ceiling programs went into effect, lands above the ceiling limit—whenever located—were taken over by the government and transferred to incumbent cultivators. Each ceiling program was concluded within a few years. In Mexico, petition by prospective beneficiaries was necessary for the initiation of redistribution proceedings, but no geographical and administrative limitations were imposed on these proceedings. Nevertheless, partially because of this requirement and partially because of the very large size of the nation's farm area, the ceiling program had gone on for decades before it was substantially completed.

Concessions to landowners. Concessions to landowners under a land redistribution program can assume three forms: permission of pre-enforcement alienation of land in excess of the ceiling limit, allowance of additional land for family members of owners, and exemption of certain lands from redistribution. As seen in Tables 10 and 11, among the eight countries studied four permit various forms of pre-enforcement alienation of surplus land: Colombia, the Philippines, India, and the U.A.R. The first two countries appear to be most generous in this aspect. Since the laws of both countries apply to only declared reform areas, landowners in all other areas can dispose of their surplus land in any way they please. They can sell it, divide it among their family members, present it as a gift to others, or change its crop pattern so that it can qualify for exemption when reform is enforced in their area. Even in the declared reform areas, landowners are still free to transfer their land until it is actually subject to expropriation proceedings. In India, among the 20 states and union territories, 12 prohibit pre-enforcement alienation of land, 6 give limited permission for such a proceeding, and 2 make no reference to the issue. Of the 12 states and territories that prohibit pre-enforcement alienation, 9 enacted ceiling programs from 1959 to 1961, long after the country had set out on the course of reform. Conceivably, many a landowner in these 9 states and territories, in anticipation of the adoption of the ceiling programs, could have transferred his surplus land before the actual adoption of the legislation. In the U.A.R., private transfer of land before expropriation was permitted, but the land had to be transferred to specified recipients within specified time limits.

As to allowance for family members, only three of the eight countries studied make such a provision. In India, 13 states and union territories permit large families to retain land in excess of the ceiling limit—mostly twice that limit. West Pakistan allows a landowner to transfer land to his heirs up to half of the ceiling limit and also to each female dependent up to one-sixth of such a limit. U.A.R.'s 1952 law permitted an owner to transfer land to his children up to half of the original ceiling limit. With respect to exemptions, the practice of the countries under study is uniform in one aspect. They generally exclude from redistribution orchards and tea plantations, which are not suitable for physical division. However, there is one significant difference between the countries ruled by separated elites and those ruled by cooperative elites: the former generally do not exempt commercialized, mechanized farms from redistribution, whereas the latter generally do.

Priority of types of land for redistribution. All eight countries allow landowners to select the best land, within the ceiling limit, to retain, but differ in the order of priority regarding the type of private land to be expropriated. The pertinent provisions of the ceiling programs of Taiwan, Mexico, the U.A.R., and Iran are clearly in favor of the reform beneficiaries. In the first three countries, the only type of private land subject to expropriation is well-farmed crop land. In Iran, the expropriation of well-farmed crop land takes precedence over barren and uncultivated land. In these four countries, most of the land actually expropriated for redistribution was from the areas in which reform beneficiaries were incumbent farmers. In the other four countries, the order of priority of land redistribution favors landowners. In India and Pakistan, though the laws generally designate well-farmed crop land as the major type of land for expropriation, the land actually liable to expropriation includes a large proportion of uncultivated or waste land unsuitable for redistribution. This is so because the possibility of pre-enforcement alienation of surplus land, the special allowance for large families, and high ceilings have all considerably reduced the amount of well-farmed land available for expropriation. In Colombia and the Philippines, the order of priority regarding the type of private land to be expropriated is unmistakably devised to protect the interests of landowners. In Colombia, the government can, as a rule, expropriate owner-occupied, properly farmed holdings within a reform area only after the exhaustion of "uncultivated land," "inadequately worked land," and tenanted land of that area. In the Philippines, the order of priority of expropriation in a reform area is as follows: idle or abandoned land, and then well-farmed land of decreasing size—holdings over 1,024 hectares, 500 to 1,024 hectares, 144 to 500 hectares, and finally 75 to 144 hectares.

Taken together, the prescribed ceilings and the major provisions governing actual land transfer in the programs of the eight countries studied indicate that countries ruled by separated elites are liable to make available more promptly to the landless farmers a larger amount and a better quality of farm land than those ruled by cooperative elites. Thus, it may now be noted that though the U.A.R. has a higher ceiling-to-average-farm-size ratio than Colombia and India, the U.A.R. can nevertheless achieve greater implementation of redistribution. For the ratio of the U.A.R. is not significantly higher than that of Colombia and India, but the provisions governing the transfer of land in the two countries are more restrictive than those in the U.A.R.

The Issue of Financing

If the ceiling provision of a reform program is the principal determinant of the *potential availability* of land for redistribution, the financing provision of a program is a major factor affecting the amount of land *actually transferred*. The issue of financing land redistribution involves technical and political questions.

Technical aspects of financing

Technically, the formula for the appraisal of land value, the form of compensation to landowners, the terms of payment by the beneficiaries, and the possibility for channeling landowners' compensation earnings into industrial investment must be careful studied and decided upon. Although highly varied and complex in detailed formulations, the methods devised by the eight countries to resolve the technical questions of financing can be summarized in Tables 13 and 14 and in the following notations.

Appraisal of land value. To appraise land value, a multiple-factor formula is generally utilized. A country may select a particular basis for land valuation and have it multiplied by one or more prescribed factors. For Colombia, Iran, Mexico, and the U.A.R. the basis of land valuation is land tax; for East Pakistan, landowner's income from land; for West Pakistan and Taiwan, the production of land; and for the Philippines, rental income. The states and union territories of India cover virtually all

TABLE 13

Land Redistribution Programs, Financial Provisions, Seven Countries

(A) Valuation of Land[a]

Countries	Date	Formula	Remarks
Colombia	1962	130% of cadastral value of the land	Law provides for three land valuers; their function is unclear No compensation for land uncultivated for ten years
Iran	Since 1963 1962	Self-valuation by landowner 105–180 times land tax	Depending on date of tax assessment, type of land, rental rates, etc. Land tax is one-tenth of net rental income of landlords
Mexico	1917	110% of assessed tax value of the land	No compensation for usurped land
E. Pakistan	1950	"5 times the net annual profit from the land"	
W. Pakistan	1959	Land value converted to equivalents of produce index units. For the first 18,000 units—Rs. 5 per unit; for next 24,000 units —Rs. 4; for next 36,000 units—Rs. 3; for next 72,000 units—Rs. 2; for the rest—Rs. 1	
Philippines	1963	Land authority negotiates with owner about land price, subject to court approval	One suggested basis for appraising land value: the authorized rent capitalized at a rate of 6%. Authorized rent = 25% of net annual yield of the land
Taiwan	1953	2.5 times the annual gross yield of the main crop of the land	Annual gross yield refers to that which was appraised and fixed in 1949
U.A.R.	1952	70 times land tax	Land tax is one-seventh rent

[a] Refers only to value of farm land, not including that of farm accessories.
Source: Primarily Appendix I.

TABLE 13

(B) COMPENSATION TO LANDOWNERS: STATUTORY PROVISIONS

Countries and Types of Land[a]	Date of Law	Forms of Compensation			Remarks
		Cash	Bonds[b]	Other	
Colombia					
Type (1)	1961	No	Class B, 25–Year, 2% (N)	—	Bonds may be used by INCORA to finance all its activities and may be used by landowners for purchase of public land and for paying off debts to INCORA
Type (2)	1961	Yes[c]	Optional, Class A, 15–Year, 7%	—	
Type (3)	1961	Yes[d]	Optional, Class A, 15–Year, 7%	—	No compensation for land uncultivated for 10 years
Iran	1962	6.67%	10–Year, 3% (N)	Stocks of government corporations optional	(a) 1962 law applies to surplus land above one-village limit. Payment period was originally set for 15 years. First year payment in cash with the rest in 14 annual payment orders of the Agricultural Bank. This period was reduced in 1964 to 10 years
	1964	one-third	10–Year, (N)		
					(b) 1964 law applies to surplus land below one-village limit
Mexico	1920	No	20–Year, 5% (N)	—	No compensation for usurped land. Bonds may be used for tax payment and for purchase of public land
E. Pakistan	1950	Yes	40–Year, 3%	—	Cash or bonds or both
W. Pakistan	1959	No	25–Year, 4%	—	Bonds are heritable, transferable, but not negotiable
Philippines	1963	10%	25–Year, 6% (N)	—	Bonds may be used in exchange for stocks of government corporations, Japanese reparation goods, public land, government real properties Owners may request that 30% of compensation be paid in preferred stocks of Land Bank, with 6% interest

TABLE 13 (*Continued*)

Countries and Types of Land[a]	Date of Law	Forms of Compensation			Remarks
		Cash	Bonds[b]	Other	
Taiwan					
Type (4)	1953	No	10–Year, 4%	Stocks in government corporations	Compensation: 70% in bonds and 30% in stocks. Rice bonds for Type (4) land, and sweet potato bonds for Type (5). When redeemed, the former is paid in rice; the latter in cash.
Type (5)	1953	No	10–Year, 4%		
U.A.R.	1952	No	30–Year, 3%	—	
	1958	No	40–Year, 1.5%		
	1961	No	15–Year, 4% (N)		

a Types of land (1) idle land, (2) poorly farmed land, (3) well-farmed land, (4) paddy field, (5) dry land.

b Bonds are not negotiable unless symbol (N) appears. Both length of maturity and interest rates are indicated.

c If compensation is to be paid entirely in cash, 20 percent will be given for the first payment, the rest in 8 annual installments with 4% interest.

d Same as above, except that after the first payment, the rest is to be paid in 5 annual installments with 6% interest.

SOURCE: Primarily Appendix I.

(C) COMPENSATION TO LANDOWNERS: ACTUAL PAYMENT

Countries	As of	Payment
Colombia	Dec. 31, 1966	A total of ₱897,817,000 worth of bonds were issued. Land purchased and expropriated: 107,555 ha. Information on the portion of bonds issued for the purpose of land redistribution is not available
Iran	Apr. 12, 1967	Total cost of compensation 8,878,595,462 rials; first payment in cash: 2,802,076,304. Total land expropriated: 14,834 villages
Mexico	Dec. 31, 1959	1920 law authorized to issue ₱50 million worth of bonds; actually issued: ₱24,426,800. Total amount of land for which compensation was paid: 222,797 ha.
E. Pakistan	. . .	. . .
W. Pakistan	Dec. 31, 1965	Land Commission paid out Rs. 92,545,794 (principal) and more than Rs. 10 million (interest). Land expropriated: 2,220,718 acres (898,725 ha.)

TABLE 13 (*Continued*)

Countries	As of	Payment
Philippines	Dec. 18, 1968	Land Authority paid out ₱2,393,032 (10% in cash, the rest in bonds) for expropriation of 703.90 ha. of land. (For the 1963 program only.)
Taiwan	June 30, 1954	814,557 M/T worth of rice bonds (91.6% of the total volume to be issued) and 276,591 M/T worth of sweet potatoes (87.5% of the total volume to be issued), and NT$659,774,640 worth of stocks of government corporations were given to landowners. Land expropriated: 143,000 ha.
U.A.R.	1962	£E50,084,252 worth of bonds were issued. Total amount of land expropriated for which compensation was paid: 257,258 *feddans* (108,074 ha.)

Symbols: ₱ = peso
Rs. = Rupee
NT$ = New Taiwan dollar
£E = Egyptian pound
M/T = metric ton
(N) = negotiable bond

SOURCES: Colombia, INCORA, *5 Años de Reforma Social Agraria: Informe de Actividades en 1966* (Bogota: INCORA, 1967), pp. 15 and 34; Iran, Land Reform Organization, *Land Reform in Iran* (Tehran, [1967]), p. 19; Edmundo Flores, "On Financing Land Reform: a Mexican Casebook," *Studies in Comparative International Development*, Vol. III, No. 6. (1967–1968), 119–20; Pakistan, Land Commission of West Pakistan, *Implementation of Land Reform Scheme in West Pakistan: Appraisal Paper for World Land Reforms Conference to Be Held in Rome (Italy) from June 20 to July 2, 1966* (Lahore, 1966), *passim;* "Report on Landed Estates Acquired by Land Bank," Memorandum of the National Land Reform Council, the Philippines, December 19, 1968; China, JCRR, *JCRR Annual Reports on Land Reform in the Republic of China from October 1948 to June 1964* (Taipei, Taiwan, 1965), pp. 77–78; U.A.R., Ministry of Agrarian Reform and Land Reclamation, *Agrarian Reform and Land Reclamation in Eleven Years* (Cairo: General Organization for Government Printing Office, [1963]), p. 30.

(D) PAYMENT BY BENEFICIARIES

Countries	Date of Law	Terms[a]	Remarks
Colombia	1961	Compensation cost plus overhead and survey cost, 15–year, 4%	—
Iran	1962	(a) Compensation cost plus 10%, 15–year, no interest	(a) For surplus land above one-village limit

TABLE 13 (*Continued*)

Countries	Date of Law	Terms[a]	Remarks
	1964	(b) Compensation cost plus 10%. First annual payment: 30% of the total purchase cost to be loaned by government, with the rest paid in 10 annual installments. Terms of loan: 15–year, 3%	(b) For surplus land below one-village limit
Mexico	1917	Beneficiaries receive land free	—
E. Pakistan	1950	Compensation cost	—
W. Pakistan	1959	Compensation cost, with interest	—
Philippines	1963	Compensation cost, 25–year, 6%	Part of the interest payment covers administration cost
Taiwan	1953	Compensation cost, 20 semiannual installments, 4%	Payment shall be made in rice or sweet potatoes
U.A.R.	1952	Compensation cost plus 10%,[b] 40–year, 1.5%	1964 Law applies only to future land purchases
	1961	Unpaid balance reduced by 50%	
	1964	One-fourth of compensation cost, 40–year, no interest	—

[a] Unless indicated otherwise, payment is made in cash and in annual installments. Length of payment period and interest rates are indicated.

[b] In 1952, this extra charge was 15% of the compensation cost. A 1958 decree reduced it to 10%.

SOURCES: Primarily Appendix I; and Gabriel S. Saab, *The Egyptian Agrarian Reform, 1952–1962* (London 1967), p. 186.

(E) PUBLIC EXPENDITURE

Countries	Authorization	Actual Expenditure
Colombia	(a) ₱1,000 million worth of class A bonds and ₱200 million class B bonds (b) no less than ₱100 million to be appropriated for INCORA (c) INCORA may contract loans, impose taxes, receive donations and payment for the land it sells and the services it performs	As of December 31, 1966: INCORA's total disposal assets were ₱975,899,637.67, including ₱897,817,000 worth of agrarian bonds
Iran	(a) allocate in the national budget funds to cover the difference between compensation cost and payment by beneficiaries	See Table 13 (C), above

TABLE 13 (*Continued*)

Countries	Authorization	Actual Expenditure
	(b) allocate from the development funds at least 1 billion rials annually to be used as loans to beneficiaries to purchase land	
	(c) authorize in the 1962 budget a sum of 2 billion rials to underwrite the payment orders of the Agricultural Bank	
Mexico	(a) 1920 law authorized the issue of agrarian bonds for ₱50,000,000 to finance land redistribution	(a) actually issued as of Dec. 31, 1959 ₱24,426,800
	(b) 1932 law authorized the issue of bonds for ₱30,000,000 to pay compensation for land taken from small landowners	(b) no information
	(c) 1941 decree authorized the issue of bonds for ₱10,000,000 to exchange for (a) bonds;	(c) ₱8,989,600
	(d) 1951 decree authorized the issue of bonds for ₱50,000,000 to pay credits arising from claims in respect of small agricultural properties	(d) ₱48,169,700
E. Pakistan	. . .	. . .
W. Pakistan	Proceeds from sale of expropriated land to form a fund to finance payment of compensation	See Table 13 (C) above
Philippines	1963 law authorized a capital stock of ₱1.5 billion for the Land Bank, of which the government was to subscribe ₱900,000,000, with the remaining ₱600,000,000 to be issued in preferred stocks with 6% interest. The law also appropriated for the Land Authority ₱5,000,000. (Other authorizations relating to land reform but not specifically to land redistribution are not listed here)	(a) Land Bank: 1963–1964, none; 1964–1965, ₱700,000; ₱2.2 million as of Aug. 8, 1966 (b) All reform agencies: 1963–1964, ₱14,926,831; 1964–1965, ₱28,662,798; 1966–1968, ₱18,000,000 annually
Taiwan	(a) 1953 law authorized the use of proceeds from sale of expropriated land to finance land bonds	See Table 13 (C), above
	(b) 1953 law also authorized the sale of stocks of government corporations	
U.A.R.	1952 law authorized the establishment of an Agrarian Reform Fund through contributions from proceeds of sale of expropriated land, and budgeting appropriations	See Table 13 (C), above

SOURCES: Same as those of Table 13 (C), above, and Concordia G. Palacios, "Financing the Land Reform Program," *Philippine Journal of Public Administration*, X (January 1966), 22; Manuel P. Manahan, "The Prospects for Land Reform," *Solidarity*, II (July-August 1967), 14; and Edward R. Kiunisala, "Victory for Land Reform?" *Philippines Free Press*, December 6, 1969, p. 6.

TABLE 14

LAND REDISTRIBUTION PROGRAM OF INDIA: FINANCIAL PROVISIONS

States & Union Territories	Compensation to Owners		Purchase Price Payable by Tenants	
	Scale of Compensation[a]	Mode of Payment[b]	Purchase Price	Terms of Payment
Andhra Pradesh	5 to 3 times annual gross income; depending on size of land, progressively decreasing rate of compensation	Cash or bonds or both	12 times the rent (in Telangana area)	
Assam	50 times the land revenue[c] for cultivated land; 25 times for fallow land	Cash in a lump sum or in up to 5 annual installments (2½%)	15–20 times the land revenue	5 annual installments
Bihar	Rs. 900–Rs. 50 per acre, depending on type and quality of land	Cash or bond (30-year, 2½%)	(a) For occupancy under-raiyat, $\frac{3}{4}$ of the compensation to owner (b) For non-occupancy under-raiyat, $\frac{7}{8}$ of the compensation to owner	Lump sum with a 10% rebate, or 30 annual installments
Gujarat	(a) 12–200 times the assessed land value for dry land, depending on location (b) increase (a) 1½ times for seasonally irrigated land and increase (a) 3 times for perennially irrigated land (c) reduce (a) or (b) by $\frac{1}{4}$ to $\frac{1}{8}$ for land held by under-raiyat	Cash or bonds (up to 20-year, 4½%) or both	20–200 times the land revenue (but 6–12 times the rent in the Kutch area)	12–16 annual installments
Jammu & Kashmir	No provision	—	No provision	No provision
Kerala	60%–25% of marketing value, progressively decreasing rate of compensation	Cash or bonds (10-year, 4½%) or both	16 times the fair rent[d] or 12 times the contract rent	Lump sum with a 25% rebate, or 16 annual installments

TABLE 14 (Continued)

| States & Union Territories | Compensation to Owners | | Purchase Price Payable by Tenants | |
	Scale of Compensation[a]	Mode of Payment[b]	Purchase Price	Terms of Payment
Madhya Pradesh	50–20 times the land revenue progressively decreasing rate of compensation	Up to Rs. 1000 in cash with the rest in 19 annual installments (3%)	15 times the land revenue	Lump sum with a 10% rebate, or 5 annual installments
Maharashtra	(a) 55–195 times the land revenue for dry land, depending on location (b) increase (a) by 25–100% for irrigated land, depending on extent of irrigation (c) reduce (a) by various proportions for misc. lands	—	(a) 20–200 times the land revenue (in former Bombay area) (b) 12 times the rent (in Marathawada and Vidarbha)	12–16 annual installments
Mysore	10 times the average net annual income of land	Cash in a lump sum or up to 20 installments (4½%)	15 times the net rent (i.e., rent minus land revenue)	20 annual installments
Orissa[e]	To be negotiated by purchaser and owner, or to pay market value of land	Cash in 3 annual installments	Market value	Negotiation between the owner and the tenant
Punjab (a) Punjab[e] Area	No provision	No provision	¾ of the market value	10 semi-annual installments
(b) Pepsu Area	(a) Cultivated land—progressingly decreasing rate of compensation: first 25 standard acres—12 times fair rent;[f] second 25 standard acres—9	Cash or bonds or both	90 times the land revenue or Rs. 200 per acre, whichever is less	6 annual installments

State	Basis / rate of compensation	Form of payment	Rate	Mode of payment
Rajasthan	times fair rent; remaining land—90 times the land revenue (b) 45 times the land revenue for barren land; 35–20 times rent, progressively decreasing rate of compensation with respect to increasing size of land	Cash or bonds or both	15–20 times the land revenue	10 annual installments
Uttar Pradesh	(a) For *Bhumidhars* (owners)—80 times the land revenue or 40 times the hereditary rate, plus 20 times the difference between the land revenue and the hereditary rate (b) For *Sirdas* (who have permanent and heritable right to land)—20 times the hereditary rate, plus 20 times the difference between this rate and the land revenue (c) For *Asamis* and other tenants without permanent rights—5 times the rent	Cash or bonds (3½%)	10 times the rent	Lump sum
West Bengal	20–2 times the net income of land, progressively decreasing rate of compensation	Cash and bonds (3%)	Tenants (not including sharecroppers) given ownership of land free	—
Union Territories: *Delhi*	20 times the net annual income	Cash in a lump sum or in installments, or bonds (10-year, 2½%)	Same as compensation to owner	10 annual installments

TABLE 14 (Continued)

States & Union Territories	Compensation to Owners		Purchase Price Payable by Tenants	
	Scale of Compensation[a]	Mode of Payment[b]	Purchase Price	Terms of Payment
Himachal Pradesh	(a) 48 times the land revenue for cultivated land (b) 4 times the land revenue for land uncultivated for 6 years	Cash or bonds (up to 24 semi-annual installments, 2½%) or both	(a) For occupancy tenants (i) those paying produce rent—24 times the land revenue, (ii) those paying cash rent —12 times the land revenue (b) Non-occupancy tenants, 48 times the land revenue	10 semi-annual installments
Manipur & Tripura	20 times the net annual income	Cash in a lump sum or in up to 20 annual installments or bonds (20-year, 2½%)	30 times the land revenue	10 annual installments

[a] For farm land only, not including fixtures, implements, buildings, and other accessories.
[b] Percentage in parentheses refers to interest rate.
[c] Land revenue = land tax.
[d] Fair rent in Kerala varies from $\frac{1}{16}$ to $\frac{3}{4}$ of the gross produce, depending on location, type, and crops of land.
[e] The State assumes no responsibility for acquisition of surplus land and for its redistribution. Transfer of surplus land is a matter of direct transaction between the purchaser and the owner.
[f] Fair rent in Pepsu = $\frac{1}{3}$ of the gross produce.

SOURCE: India, Planning Commission, Progress of Land Reform (Delhi, 1963).

the above categories—and more. Thus, in Bihar the government prescribes outright a number of basic unit prices for land which are multiplied by the amount of expropriated land, and in Kerala and Orissa, the bases of land valuation are respectively the partial and full market value of the land. As to the prescribed factors that multiply the bases of land valuation, the countries studied again vary in details. Colombia, Mexico, East Pakistan, the Philippines, Taiwan, and the U.A.R. adopt what may be called a single-factor formula. That is, a country prescribes one uniform multiplying number. As an illustration, in East Pakistan the basis for land valuation is the "net annual profit from the land"; the land value is obtained by simply multiplying this annual profit by a factor of five—regardless of the type and locality of the land. In contrast, Iran and West Pakistan adopt a variable factor formula, i.e. a set of multiplying numbers that vary with one or more characteristics of the land. In Iran, the multiplying numbers range from 105 to 180, depending on the date of tax assessment, type, rental rates, and distance to market of the land. In West Pakistan, the multiplying numbers decrease in value as the sizes of the "produce index units" (bases for land valuation) increase, resulting in a formula of progressively decreasing rates of compensation for expropriated land. In India, some states and territories adopt the single-factor formula, others the variable-factor formula.

Forms of compensation. The eight countries pay compensation to landowners in the form of bonds, cash, or stocks of government corporations, or a combination of these, with bonds representing the most common form. The popularity of payment in bonds owes, of course, to the fact that the issuance of bonds allows the government to start a land redistribution program without having to raise a large fund immediately. It also has the advantage of avoiding the possibility of creating inflation, which a total cash payment for compensation is likely to bring about. Mexico, West Pakistan, and the U.A.R. use bonds as the exclusive form of compensation; Colombia, Iran, East Pakistan, the Philippines, and most Indian states combine bonds with cash for compensation; and Taiwan pays landowners with bonds and stocks of government corporations. Only in two states (Assam and Mysore) and three union territories (Delhi, Manipur, and Tripura) of India are landowners compensated with cash in a lump sum.

Among all forms of payment mentioned here, those adopted in Taiwan are perhaps the most remarkable. The compensation consists of 70 percent in bonds and 30 percent in stocks of government corporations. The value of the bonds is expressed in terms of two crops: rice and sweet potato. When redeemed, the rice bond is paid in rice; and the sweet potato bond in cash. Involving minimal cash transaction and creating little financial burden for the government, this method of payment was adopted specifically to avoid inflation. In taking this precaution, Taiwan benefited from the post–World War II reform experience of Japan where compensation by cash contributed much to the depreciation of Japanese currency. Payment in the form of stocks of public enterprises is also worth noting. Intended to induce the flow of surplus rural capital to industries, the scheme was pioneered in Taiwan with considerable success. In 1954, one year after the commencement of the land-to-the-tiller program, the government transferred to landowners in the form of compensation payment NT$659,-774,640 worth of stocks in four public corporations—the Paper and Pulp Corporations, the Cement Corporation, the Industrial and Mining Corporation, and the Agriculture and Forestry Corporation. The shares of stocks were originally distributed on the basis of a par value of NT$10 each. Ten years later, in 1964, their average stock-exchange prices were NT$32.94, NT$31.04, NT$18.46, and NT$17.60 in the order listed above. Since the average commodity prices

> rose from 1953 to 1964 by about 100 percent, and . . . [since] the shares of the first two companies accounted for . . . [70 per cent of the total] shares of the four companies, the shares turned out on balance to have provided a capital gain in real terms to the landowners, . . . From the viewpoint of a Government seeking to denationalize certain industries, the procedure provided a large group of potential stockholders despite the absence [until 1962] of a developed market for shares.[9]

Taiwan's successful experimentation with compensation in stocks led other nations to adopt the same scheme. The 1963 land reform law of the Philippines, for instance, allowed landowners to exchange the bonds they received as compensation for shares in five government-owned or controlled corporations: The National Development Company, the Cebu Portland Cement Company, the National Shipyards and Steel Corporation, the Manila Gas Corporation, and the Manila Hotel Company. These companies were to negotiate with bondholders about the price and conditions

---

[9] These data were derived from the Taiwan Stock Exchange Report of September 1964, pp. 9–12, quoted in U.N., *Land Reform, Fourth Report*, p. 111; see also JCRR, *JCRR Annual Reports on Land Reform*, p. 78.

for the sale of shares. In Iran, a decree of January 1963 provided for the sale of 205 government factories to finance land redistribution then in progress. The sale of these factories, whose capital value was estimated at 11.9 billion rials, was expected to raise about one-sixth of the required fund.[10]

Terms of payment by beneficiaries. Most land redistribution programs require beneficiaries to pay for the land they receive. Only in Mexico and in West Bengal, India, are farmers granted land free of charge. In all other cases, beneficiaries must meet two terms of payment. One term of payment relates to the purchase price. In Colombia, Iran, and the U.A.R. the purchase price is the same as the compensation cost plus administrative charge; in East and West Pakistan, the Philippines, Taiwan, and Delhi, India, the beneficiaries pay only the equivalent of the compensation cost. Some Indian states require the beneficiaries to pay a fixed portion of the compensation cost (e.g. Assam), while other states adopt a payment formula for the beneficiaries entirely unrelated to the formula for compensation (e.g. in Rajasthan, compensation is paid in an amount equivalent to 20 to 35 times the *rent of the land*, but the beneficiaries pay the equivalent of 15 to 20 times the *land revenue* as purchase price). Another term of payment concerns the methods and forms in which the purchase price is paid. Taiwan requires a payment in twenty semi-annual installments and in kind (rice for paddy field and sweet potato for dry land). Colombia, Iran, Pakistan, the Philippines, the U.A.R., and most Indian states require a payment in installments of various lengths and in cash. In addition, there are still more variations in payment schemes in Indian states. In Bihar, Kerala, and Madhya Pradesh beneficiaries have the option between installment payments and a lump sum payment with a discount; in Orissa, landowners and beneficiaries are to negotiate the terms of payment.

Public expenditure. In general, land redistribution involves two financial transactions: government purchase of expropriated land, and resale of the land to beneficiaries. To underwrite the cost of compensation and to provide the needed administrative services in the transfer of land, governments must authorize funds. But authorization of funds and

---

[10] The 205 government enterprises "comprise 24 agricultural factories, 42 foodstuffs, nine textiles, two wood, five printing and allied factories, four pharmaceutical and chemical, seven non-metal and mining, four ice plants, and 108 electric power stations. . . . Many of these are running at a loss of between 80 and 100 million rials a year." *Iran Almanac 1963*, p. 394, and UN *Land Reform, Fourth Report*, p. 23.

the actual public outlay are two different things. In certain countries, for example, the Philippines, governments are generous in authorization but reluctant to expend the authorized funds. In certain other countries, for example, the U.A.R., and Iran, governments are willing to use regular budgetary resources to pay part of the purchase price for the beneficiaries. A further discussion of this subject will be found in the following section.

Political aspect of financing

All these technical aspects of financing land redistribution programs are very complicated and, at times, confusing. But by no means do they raise insoluable problems. On the other hand, the political aspect of financing involves a relatively simple and straightforward question: how to devise a financing arrangement beneficial to the landless, acceptable to landowners, and realistic in terms of the government's capacity for compensation payment? Much of the difficulty in the formulation of a redistribution program may relate to this simple question. In resolving this question, separated and cooperative elites take basically different courses of action. Undeterred by the landed interests, *separated elites* tend to adopt a stand favorable to the reform beneficiaries; concerned with the continual support of the landed interests, *cooperative elites* seek to protect the interests of the landowners.

In Mexico, the revolutionary leadership originally intended to place the land redistribution program on a more or less self-supporting basis, with the beneficiaries paying the purchase cost, and the government compensating owners with agrarian bonds. On January 31, 1919, the National Agrarian Commission issued Circular 34 requiring the prospective beneficiaries "to pay the Nation the value of lands which they were going to receive by donation, in accordance with the indemnity which the Nation must pay to the proprietors of the land expropriated; . . . "[11] But, in 1921, President Alvaro Obregón, a man closely identified with the agrarian cause, rescinded the circular. Thereafter all beneficiaries received land free. To provide compensation to the landowners, the government decided to pay the land price entirely in bonds. Reaffirming the intention of indemnification that had been mentioned in the land-reform decree of January 6, 1915, and in Article 27 of the constitution, the Agrarian Debt Law of January 10, 1920, authorized the issuance of Agrarian Debt Bonds

[11] Eyler N. Simpson, *The Ejido, Mexico's Way Out* (Chapel Hill, 1937), p. 225.

up to ₱50 million to be redeemed in twenty years at 5 percent annual interest. This intention, however, was by and large unfulfilled. As of June
1933, only ₱24,426,800 worth of bonds were actually delivered to a total
of 170 landowners, covering 222,797 hectares of expropriated land. According to an estimate by Minister of Agriculture Manuel Pérez Treviño, as
of December 1930, the value of the expropriated land was around ₱800
million. According to another estimate, as of December 1931, the total area
of expropriated land to which compensation was due was slightly less than
6.6 million hectares.[12] As of the early 1930s, therefore, the ₱24,426,800
worth of agrarian bonds paid by the government amounted to only 3.05
percent of the total value of the expropriated land, and the 222,797
hectares of land for which compensation was paid amounted to about 3.4
percent of the total expropriated area. The government simply defaulted
in the payment for the rest of the expropriated land. With no agrarian debt
bond issued since 1931, Mexico's land redistribution program—which was
much expanded in the 1930s—practically resulted in the confiscation of
private land.[13]

In the U.A.R., the compensation price was fixed at 70 times the land
tax and payable in bonds only. Gabriel S. Saab has estimated that this
land price amounted on the average to about 50 percent of the market
value of the land and that certain landlords suffered as much as an 80
percent loss.[14] Farmers purchasing land, who had been required under the
1952 decree to pay over a forty-year period the full price assessed for
compensation plus a 15 percent charge to cover the administrative cost,
have benefited from several reductions of payments afterward. Since 1964,
they have been paying only one-fourth of the compensation cost. The
author has calculated that the first annual purchase payment by reform
beneficiaries was about 14 percent below the pre-reform rent in value and,

---

[12] See *ibid.*, pp. 109–110.
[13] See comments to this effect in James G. Maddox, "Mexican Land Reform,"
American Universities Field Staff Reports, Vol. 4, No. 5 (July 3, 1957), pp. 11–12;
William H. MacLeish (ed.), *Land Liberty* (New York, 1962), p. 5; and Edmundo
Flores, "On Financing Land Reform: a Mexican Casebook," *Studies in Comparative
International Development*, Vol. III, No. 6 (1967–1968), 118–120. According to
Flores, the 222,797 hectares of land for which conpensation was paid in the early
1930s remained the only land provided with compensation three decades later. It
amounted to "less than 0.5 percent of the total of 55 million hectares distributed until
1960 (p. 120)."
[14] Saab, *op. cit.*, p. 24.

since 1964, 64 percent below the rent.[15] Thus, the Egyptian reform beneficiaries will, in forty years, become full owners of the land they till by
paying a price amounting to only a fraction of their previous rent. The
government, shouldering the increased cost resulting from payment reductions, has generally kept its pledge to honor its financial obligations to the
owners of expropriated land.

In Taiwan, the formula for computing compensation to landowners
as well as the purchase price by the beneficiaries is the same: 2.5 times
the annual yield of the main crop of the land. The author estimates that
this formula resulted in an undervaluation of the land by 29 to 47 percent.[16]

---

[15] This calculation is based on an estimate by Saab of the value of annual purchase
payments by reform beneficiaries during various periods of time in which reductions of
purchase payment took place. Saab's estimate, expressed in terms equivalent of land tax,
is as follows:

    1952–1958   6 times land tax
    1958–1961   5 times land tax
    1961–1964   3.5 times land tax
    1964–   2.5 times land tax

(Ibid., pp. 43–45, 185–186). Since land tax equals one-seventh of the rent, the annual
purchase payments for the periods listed above amounted respectively to 86 percent, 71
percent, 50 percent, and 36 percent of the rent.

[16] According to a study of the Chinese Research Institute of Land Economics, the
average value of private farmland on the Chinese mainland before the Communist rule
was found to be seven times the farmer's rent. As Taiwan's rental rate of private land
was limited in 1949 to 37.5 percent, land price in Taiwan would be 2.626 (3.75%
× 7) times the farm produce. Mainly on the basis of this finding, the compensation
for the expropriated land was fixed at 2.5 times the annual main crop yield. Hui-sun
Tang, *Land Reform in Free China* (Taipei, Taiwan, 1954), p. 15. However, the rental
rate of mainland China before 1949 was roughly 50 percent, not 37.5 percent. Thus,
accepting the Institute's finding, one should obtain a land price of 3.5 (50% × 7)
times the value of farm produce, not 2.5 times. The compensation price is, therefore,
about 29 percent below the land's actual value.

This compensation price also appears to be below the value of land as stipulated
by a national law. Article 110 of the Chinese Land Law of 1930 fixed rental rates at
8 percent of the value of land. From this Article, a formula for calculating land value
may be derived. If L = land price, R = rent, and AP = annual produce, the following
equation is obtained:

$$\frac{R}{L} = \frac{8}{100}$$

$$L = \frac{100R}{8} = \frac{100 \times 37.5\% \text{ AP}}{8} = 4.7 \text{ AP}$$

The land value under this national law should then be 4.7 times annual produce. The
compensation payment is then 47 percent below the value of the land according to this
law.

Reform beneficiaries paid the government the purchase price in twenty semi-annual installments in a ten-year period. Since payment was made in rice or sweet potato (the crops the purchasers actually produce), and since the amount of annual payment was less than a year's rent,[17] tenant farmers were transformed in ten years into full owners without paying anything more than the equivalent of rent.

Colombia, India, Iran, Pakistan, and the Philippines have generally adopted financing arrangements favorable to the original landowners. Most of these countries set the compensation price near the market value of the land. With the exception of West Pakistan, all these countries provide some form of cash compensation to landowners; except in some Indian states where reform beneficiaries pay a purchase price below the compensation cost, in all these five countries, land recipients have to shoulder the cost in full; and, except for Iran, none of these countries has appropriated a fund sufficient for the transfer of a large amount of land.

The cases of Colombia, the Philippines, and Iran may be particularly noted. The Colombian land reform law of 1961 stipulates that INCORA shall negotiate, on the basis of the land valuation by three appraisers (appointed respectively by INCORA, the landowner, and the Augustín Codazzi Geographical Institute), with landowners about the compensation price. As the law failed to prescribe a basis or method for land valuation, a decree (No. 1904) was adopted in July 1962, setting the compensation price at 130 percent of the cadastral value of the land. But since the cadastral value was known to be much lower than the actual worth of the land, this decree was subject to immediate attack by landowners and the powerful *Sociedad de Agricultores Colombianos*. In November 1963, a new decree (No. 2895) was issued, allowing the owners to make valuations of their land—for compensation as well as tax purposes—by themselves, subject to revaluation every two years. The rationale of the self-valuation method is that such a method assures accurate assessment of the value of the land. The owners will not undervalue their land for fear of low compensation; nor will they overvalue their land for fear of high tax. However, because of the piecemeal application of the reform law in Colombia, this justification for self-valuation really does not have much validity. A landowner outside a land-reform area can conceivably undervalue his land to enjoy low taxes and revalue it to a higher level just before the application of reform to reap high compensation. As the process,

---

[17] See Article 20 of the Land-to-the-Tiller Act, 1953, in Appendix I, below.

of establishing land-reform areas is frustratingly slow, the fact that the landowner can revalue his land every two years affords him an opportunity to strike the best deal for himself.[18] While the formula for land valuation is favorable to landowners, the terms of compensation appear very generous. Apart from land uncultivated for ten years consecutively, which is to be confiscated, only idle land is compensated in long-term (25 years), low-interest (3 percent) bonds; but both poorly farmed and well farmed lands must be compensated in cash unless the owners request payment in short term (15 years), high interest (7 percent) bonds.[19] In purchasing the land, the reform beneficiaries have to shoulder in full this high compensation price and, additionally, the overhead and survey cost of up to ₱10 per hectare.

Some scattered evidence indicates that INCORA, while possessing limited financial resources, has engaged in rather expensive land acquisition transactions. "In the 6 months from July to December, 1962, INCORA began 510 proceedings again 136,000 hectares valued at 51 million pesos, but acquired only 3 parcels totaling 618 hectares and valued at 924,000 pesos."[20] Thus the acquisition cost came to about ₱1,500 a hectare. In August 1966, INCORA negotiated with General Gustavo Rojas Pinilla, a former President and a presidential candidate in the 1970 election, to purchase 2,428 hectares of his cattle and cotton lands. The purchase cost for these lands was about ₱2,000 per hectare.[21] In 1968, INCORA resold to a reform beneficiary three hectares of orchard land (from the property it had earlier purchased from private owners) at a price

[18] Self-valuation presents landowners with a number of other opportunities for undermining land redistribution. Owners may be willing to pay a high tax by declaring a high value for desirable land so as to compel the reform agency to acquire only undervalued undesirable land; they may be "willing to invest one or two years in land taxes on high declared values (but usually low rates), in order to collect excessive compensation"; or they may declare "high values, and then prompt their tenants to demand immediate expropriation." U.N., Land Reform, Fourth Report, p. 104. In short, this scheme of land valuation affords the maximum protection to the landowners, reduces the effectiveness of the reform agency, converts land expropriation proceedings to a commercial transaction, and practically leaves the reform beneficiaries voiceless.

[19] This type of Colombian bond has the highest interest rate of any bonds issued by the countries under study. In part this high interest is justified by the high rate of inflation in the country.

[20] Pat M. Holt, Colombia Today—and Tomorrow (New York, 1964), p. 93.

[21] The New York Times, September 4, 1966, p. 22. Original data were expressed in acres and in U.S. dollars which have been converted respectively into hectares and pesos.

of ₱8,030 per hectare.[22] While facing these high acquisition costs, INCORA has, from the beginning, experienced financial trouble. Though the 1961 reform law authorized an annual appropriation of ₱100 million for reform, the agency received only ₱20 million in 1962; and much of this amount was used to finance INCORA's activities other than land redistribution. Recently, through foreign loans and increased appropriations, INCORA has improved its financial capacity,[23] but it does not appear likely that the agency will possess in the foreseeable future "resources necessary to ensure the success of a nationwide program of agrarian reform." [24] According to one author, because of its limited financial resources, INCORA can perhaps, at best, settle annually only one-third of the 20,000 new farm families added to the country every year.[25] Under the circumstances, what INCORA can do in land redistribution is not even enough to prevent the problem of maldistribution of land from worsening, let alone resolve the problem.

In the Philippines, the 1963 reform law authorized the Land Authority to negotiate with landowners, subject to court approval, as to the compensation price of the expropriated land. Though the law suggested the authorized annual rent—capitalized at the rate of 6 percent a year—as one basis of land valuation, the actual compensation price still much depended on negotiation between the parties, which tended to favor landowners. In negotiating with the Land Authority, landowners were able to obtain with ease a desirable valuation; if not, they could still reject a low valuation by appealing to the court for redress.[26] Thus assured of a satis-

[22] *Ibid.*, June 12, 1968, p. 20. Original data were expressed in acres and in U.S. dollars which have been converted respectively into hectares and pesos.

[23] The United States has provided INCORA a loan of $18.5 million to support the supervised credit program, and INCORA's budget was reportedly tripled to an equivalent of US$18.5 million a year in 1968. See *ibid.* and Ernest A. Duff, *Agrarian Reform in Colombia* (New York, 1968), p. 168.

As seen in Table 13 (C) and (D), INCORA had issued ₱897,817,000 worth of bonds as of the end of 1966. However, an overwhelming portion of these bonds was used for financing INCORA's various activities other than land redistribution, as compensation for expropriated land was generally paid in cash.

[24] Duff, *ibid.*, p. 169.

[25] Ernest Feder, "When Is Land Reform a Land Reform? The Colombian Case," *American Journal of Economics and Sociology*, XXIV (April 1965), 134.

[26] The courts in the Philippines have taken the position that just compensation must be provided for expropriated land and that just compensation means "a fair and full equivalent for the loss sustained" by the owner from the act of expropriation (Don M. Ferry, "The Constitutional and Social Aspects of Land Reform," in Gerardo P.

factory land price, the landowners also enjoyed favorable terms of compensation. One-tenth of the compensation had to be paid outright in cash, and the rest in 25–year negotiable bonds at 6 percent interest. These bonds could be used for various purposes: to be exchanged at par value for stocks of government corporations, Japanese reparation goods, public land, or government real properties. Landowners were given the additional option of receiving 30 percent of the compensation in preferred stocks of the Land Bank. All these compensation costs would be eventually borne by reform beneficiaries, who would have to pay the government a purchase price in 25 annual installments at a 6 percent interest. (This interest rate is higher than the rate paid by reform beneficiaries of any other country under study.) To compensate landowners, the reform law of 1963 authorized an impressive fund. The Land Bank was to issue over a period of years a capital stock of ₱1.5 billion, ₱900,000,000 of which was to be subscribed by the government, with the remaining ₱600,000,000 to be issued in preferred stocks at 6 percent interest. In addition, a total of ₱377,000,000 was appropriated for the Land Authority and other related agencies, viz., the Agricultural Credit Administration, the Court of Agrarian Relations, and the Office of Agrarian Counsel.[27] The actual release of funds, however, fell far short of the statutory appropriations. By August 1966, the government should have subscribed, as authorized by law, to ₱400,000,000 in Land Bank stocks. But only ₱2.2 million was made available to the bank. The total budget for all land-reform agencies in recent years amounted to about ₱18 million annually; of this sum the share for the Land Authority—the principal agency in charge of land redistribution—was often smaller than that for either the Agricultural Credit Administration or the Agricultural Productivity Commission.[28] And

---

Sicat [ed.], *The Philippine Economy in the 1960's* [Quezon City, 1964], pp. 143–144). The courts have enforced this interpretation with persistence and vigor. For instance, in 1957 the Land Tenure Administration, the predecessor of the present Land Authority, expropriated three estates under the Land Reform Act of 1955. Eight years after the event, in July 1965, the Supreme Court ruled the earlier compensation payment inadequate. In 1967, the Land Authority was ordered to make an additional payment to two owners totaling ₱4,230,940.35, "of which one-half . . . was paid in cash and the other half in treasury notes redeemable after one year with 6 per cent interest." The third owner received an additional payment of ₱38,637.21 in cash. As of the end of 1967, these additional payments for land expropriated under the 1955 reform amounted to 13 times the total compensation for land expropriated under the 1963 reform law. The Philippines, National Land Reform Council, Plans and Programs Office, *An Evaluation on Land Reform Operations* (Diliman, Quezon City [1968]), Annex A, p. 3.

[27] Ferry, *op. cit.*, p. 126.

[28] See, for instance, the budgetary allocations for the second half of 1967 among

TABLE 15

COMPENSATION FOR LAND ACQUIRED FOR REDISTRIBUTION UNDER
THE PHILIPPINE AGRICULTURAL LAND REFORM CODE, 1963

As of December 1968

Estates	Location	Area (hectares)	Compensation
Evangelista	Pampanga	108.8483	₱380,900
Manapat	Pampanga	136.3909	613,700
Manapat	Pampanga	28.6983	129,000
Castillo	Pampanga	158.2725	791,000
Trillana	Pampanga	217.2324	260,600
Cabrera	Pampanga	54.4582	217,832
Total		703.9006	₱2,393,032

SOURCE: "Report on Landed Estates Acquired by Land Bank," Memorandum of
the National Land Reform Council, the Philippines, December 19, 1968.

much of this meager fund for the Land Authority was used to finance
the leasehold conversion programs. Deficient in fund, and yet required to
pay a high compensation price, the Land Authority obviously could do
very little land redistribution.[29] As seen in Table 15 from 1963 to December
1968 the government acquired, at very high cost, a tiny amount of land
for redistribution.

For about 704 hectares of land the government paid out over ₱2.3 million
(10 percent in cash and 90 percent in bonds), averaging about ₱3,400 (or
about US$850) a hectare.

In Iran, the compensation price for expropriated land is equivalent to
105 to 180 times the land tax; this is contrasted to the compensation price
for the U.A.R., which has set it at 70 times the land tax. If land tax in both

the Land Authority and other reform agencies, in the Philippines, *An Evaluation on
Land Reform Operations*, Table 9.

[29] In an interview with the author, Conrado F. Estrella, National Land Reform
Administrator and Governor of the Land Authority, expressed the view that the single
most serious problem confronting Philippine land reform was a shortage of funds. The
1963 law authorized billions of pesos for land redistribution, but he calculated that altogether only ₱80 million had been released in the five years since the operation of the
law. Interview in Diliman, Quezon City, the Philippines, January 24, 1969.
A government publication has projected that in twenty years the entire land-reform
program would require a fund of about ₱3.677 billion. (See Ferry, *op. cit.*, pp. 125–
126.) But if the reform fund is released in the future at the same rate as in the five
years since 1963, it would take the government 229 years to provide the required fund!

countries is converted to the equivalent of rent, the Iranian compensation price would equal to 10.5 to 18 times the rent, as compared to 10 times the rent in the case of the U.A.R.[30] While willing to pay a high compensation price, Iran is the only country among those ruled by cooperative elites that has made ample financial provisions to fulfill its obligation to the landowners. As seen in Table 13 (E), the government is willing not only to use its regular budgetary resources but also to allocate from "development funds"—funds originally earmarked for economic development projects— a billion rials annually to pay the landowners. In addition, it has decided to sell over 200 government-owned factories to finance the redistribution program. A year after the beginning of the program, "the total value of the villages purchased by the Land Reform Organization by September 1963 amounted to 4.7 billion rials or about 63 million [U.S.] dollars. This is equivalent to one-fifth of the annual revenue of Iran from the oil industry . . . [or] 8.8 per cent of the national budget of Iran." [31] By April 1967, the total compensation cost had increased to 8,878,595,462 rials (or about US$160 million) of which the government had paid 2,802,076,304 rials (about US$36.6 million) in cash as the first payment.[32]

Tenancy Reform

Judging by the criteria of social justice and agricultural production, tenancy may be considered inferior to the owner-farm system. As rentals can and do become excessive, tenancy symbolizes an exploitative situation. With limited incentive, security, and capacity for capital formation, tenants generally are less oriented than owner-farmers toward increasing production. However, in view of the low land-man ratio in the developing countries, to eliminate the tenancy system once and for all would require inordinate coercion and result in serious disruption of production. In areas where the incidence of tenancy is high, it seems appropriate that the system be preserved and improved upon so as to complement a program of land redistribution or to facilitate eventual transition to a full owner-farmer system. Whether tenancy remains a permanent or transitory in-

[30] As seen in Table 13(A), in Iran, land tax equals one-tenth of the rent, and in the U.A.R., one-seventh the rent.

[31] [The Iranian Agricultural Economics Research Group, Institute for Economic Research], "A Review of the Statistics of the First Stage of Land Reform," *Tahqiqat é eqtesadi*, II (March 1964), 145.

[32] *Land Reform In Iran*, p. 19.

stitution, its reform requires the removal of exploitative interests and the adoption of measures to improve tenant productive capacity. The abolition of the *zamindari* system in India and Pakistan represents a major effort toward achieving the first objective of tenancy reform, while rental reduction and provisions for tenant security are measures aimed at attaining the second.

THE ABOLITION OF THE ZAMINDARI SYSTEM

As mentioned earlier, with his right to receive rent derived directly from his role as revenue collector, the *zamindar* was, strictly speaking, only an intermediary between the government and the cultivating farmers, without landownership rights.[33] When India and Pakistan adopted programs to abolish the *zamindari* system, these programs spoke of the resumption by government of the land from the *zamindars* together with their rent-receiving interests, without granting the cultivators any economic benefits and, in most cases, landownership. The reform merely sought to create a direct relationship between the government and the cultivator by eliminating the intermediary.

In East Pakistan, the East Bengal State Acquisition and Tenancy Act of 1950 abolished the *zamindari* system and transferred the rent-receiving interests to the provincial government. The *zamindars* were to be compensated on a decreasing scale from ten times net annual income (for income not exceeding Rs. 500) to twice that income (for income exceeding Rs. 100,000), in non-negotiable bonds carrying 3 percent interest payable in not more than 40 annual installments.[34] The tenants of the former *zamindari* lands were to receive permanent, heritable, and transferable occupancy rights to the lands, and to pay the government the same amount of rent as they used to pay the *zamindars*. According to the Land Revenue Department of East Pakistan, the government began acquisition proceedings against the *zamindars* in 1951 and had taken over "443 big estates with [a] total rent roll of Rs. 47,427,207 per annum" by March 1956.[35] For

[33] The word *zamindar* is only the most popular name for all those people who received during the British rule land revenue and rent on behalf of the government. In India and Pakistan, these people were also known as *jagir, malguzar, inam, kadar, alamilkiat, muafi,* etc.—altogether under a dozen different names.

[34] "The net income is determined by deducting from the estimated gross receipts of the rent receiver the various charges payable or costs incurred, like land revenue, rent, cesses, agricultural income tax, maintenance of irrigation works, and collection charges." Pakistan, National Planning Board, *The First Five Year Plan 1955–60* (Karachi: The Manager, Government of Pakistan Press, 1957), p. 314.

[35] *Report of the Land Revenue Commission, East Pakistan,* 1959, p. 7.

two reasons, later acquisition proceedings were slowed down. Initially, the legality of the program was challenged, and not until January 1957 did the Supreme Court rule in favor of the government. Then, the inadequacy of administrative arrangements for the programs and the lack of accurate land records prevented the program from reaching an early conclusion.[36]

In West Pakistan, the abolition of the intermediary interests, primarily the *jagirs*, took place after the issuance of the 1959 land-reform decree. With respect to those *jagirs* who possessed merely rent-receiving interests, their interests were taken over by the government without compensation; with respect to *jagirs* who held proprietary right, the decree allowed them to retain the same amount of land as private landowners under the ceiling program, but confiscated their land in excess of the ceiling. All lands taken over from the intermediary interests were to be resold to small farmers in accordance with the procedure for redistribution of expropriated private land. As of 1965, the government acquired a total of 316,930 acres (128,262 hectares) of *jagiri* land, amounting to 14 percent of the 2,220,718 acres (898,725 hectares) of land expropriated under various provisions of the 1959 decree.

Compared to that of Pakistan, the *zamindari* system of India was very broad in scope and complex in structure; the abolition of the system, therefore, represented a very significant aspect of India's land-reform policy. At the time of independence, intermediary tenure existed throughout India, but heavily concentrated in the states of Uttar Pradesh, Bihar, West Bengal, Punjab, Madhya Pradesh, and the former states of Madras, Hyderabad, and Saurashtra. Occupying about 40 percent of the total area of India, the tenure covered 172 million acres of agricultural land.[37] After

[36] The inadequacy of administrative arrangement was especially evident with regard to the assessment, preparation, and auditing of compensation payments. As a result, with a total compensation estimated at Rs. 75 million, the government had not paid by 1959 "any amount as final compensation to the rent-receivers, who have been deprived of their property long ago." With respect to the poor state of land records, the Land Revenue Commission of East Pakistan has commented that "a large number of mistakes has [sic] crept into the records and that these mistakes, if left uncorrected, will not only materially hamper collection [of rent] but will also create serious troubles between tenants and tenants in the future." *Ibid.*, pp. 18 and 35.

[37] India, Planning Commission, *Progress of Land Reform* (Delhi, 1963), p. 3; and M. L. Dantwala, "Financial Implications of Land Reforms: Zamindari Abolition," *Indian Journal of Agricultural Economics*, XVII (October-December 1962), 1. For a table showing the distribution of *zamindari* and other tenures in Indian states, see India, Ministry of Food and Agriculture, *Agricultural Legislation in India*, Vol. IV: *Land Re-*

independence, all the states with a heavy concentration of *zamindari* tenure took a lead in enacting reforms laws to abolish the tenure, completing the legislative work in the period from 1949 to 1952. Within the next few years, reform laws were adopted throughout India. The basic features of these laws are as follows:

State governments were to take over the following possessions of the *zamindars*: tenant-cultivated land, waste land, communal land, forests, mines, minerals, rivers, and fisheries. The *zamindars* "were permitted to retain land under their personal cultivation, variously known as *sir*, *khudkasht, gharkhed,* or *khas* land. Except in Assam, Kashmir, Himachal Pradesh, Bengal and Saurashtra, no limit has been placed on the area of such land which may be retained by *zamindars*. The limit is 133 acres in Assam, 28 acres in Bengal and up to 3 economic holdings in Saurashtra." [38]

Except Jammu and Kashmir, where intermediary interests were resumed by the government without compensation, all states were to pay the *zamindars* a compensation that was computed on the basis of "net income," "net assets," or "basic annual revenue." In certain states, such as Uttar Pradesh and Madhya Pradesh, the basis of compensation was multiplied by a flat rate, while in other states, such as Bihar and Madras, the basis was multiplied by a variable rate on a sliding scale according to the income of the *zamindars*. Where a flat rate was adopted, the *zamindars* were also provided with a "rehabilitation grant." Compensation was payable in some cases in cash but mostly in transferable and negotiable bonds, with interests, redeemable over a period ranging from five years in Madras to forty years in Uttar Pradesh. The assessment of compensation and actual payment were the responsibilities of the state revenue administration.[39]

The acquired common land, waste land, and forests were placed under the direct management of the state government and, in certain cases, village councils. With respect to the acquired tenant-cultivated lands, the cultivators in most states acquired permanent, heritable, transferable occupancy rights to the land they used to work and had to "pay the State Government the same amount in rent as they were paying the *zamindars*." [40] In some states, for example, Uttar Pradesh, Madhya

---

forms (Abolition of Intermediaries) (Delhi: The Manager of Publications, 1953), Appendix I.

[38] Dantwala, *op. cit.*

[39] For details of the compensation scheme, see *ibid.*, pp. 2–11.

[40] *Ibid.*, p. 5.

Pradesh, and Mysore, tenants were granted the option of acquiring owner-ship rights. In Uttar Pradesh, to illustrate, tenants could acquire full proprietary rights on a payment to the government equalling 10 times the rent in a lump sum or 12 times the rent in installments. The rent or pur-chase payments from the tenants received by the government were to be used to finance compensation to the *zamindars*.

The program for the abolition of the *zamindari* system was virtually concluded in the late 1950s. The total compensation payable to the *zamindars* was estimated at about Rs. 6.1 billion (including rehabilitation grant and interest) as of 1968; Rs. 2.7 billion (Rs. 1.4 billion in bonds and Rs. 1.3 billion in cash) had been paid out.[41] About 20 million culti-vators were beneficiaries of the program, with most remaining as tenants.[42]

The fact that most cultivators in the former *zamindari* areas remain today as tenants rather than owners is frequently cited by critics as a major weakness of the reform. They contend that since these cultivators still have to pay the state government the same rent as they previously paid the *zamindars*, the program resulted merely in a substitution of one big public landlord for many small private ones. Moreover, while the cultivators received no reduction of rent under the program, the government stood to gain financially because the rent the tenants paid to the *zamindars* was larger than what the *zamindars* used to deliver to the government.

The program has also been criticized for the favoritism it showed to the *zamindars* and to other non-cultivating interests. Many states allowed *zamindars* to retain numerous categories of land; the standard ones include "home-farm land" and land under "personal cultivation." But the statutory definition of these terms was either absent or very loose so that *zamindars* had ample opportunity for evading the reform. In the West Bengal Estates Acquisition Act of 1953, for instance, there was no specification as to the meaning of "homesteads" or of "personal cultivation." The West Bengal Land Reforms Act of 1955 offered a redress with respect to the latter term. " 'Personal cultivation,' " the act stated, "means cultivation by a person of his own land on his own account—(a) by his own labour, or (b) by the labour of any member of his family, or (c) by servants or

[41] India, Chief Ministers Conference on Land Reform, 1969. Notes on Agenda, p. 7. Cited in Gene Wunderlich, "Land Reforms in India," U.S., Agency for Inter-national Development, *Spring Review*, Country Paper (June 1970), p. 46.

[42] Exactly how many tenants have acquired landownership under the *zamindari* abolition program is not known. But the figure is likely to be very small since the num-ber of tenants in both *zamindari* and non-*zamindari* areas who had acquired landowner-ship by 1966 was only 3,056,000—out of a total of more than 72 million cultivators.

labourers on wages payable in cash or in kind or both." [43] One wonders if there is any essential difference between tenants or sharecroppers and the tenure status of persons in category (c) above. This contrived legal laxity not only resulted in a substantial reduction of the land area liable to government acquisition but led to a wave of evictions of tenants by zamindars who pretended to retain land for personal cultivation. In all states, the zamindari land acquired by the government was supposedly given to tenants for cultivation. In reality, some "tenants" receiving land, like the zamindars who retained land for personal cultivation, were not truly cultivators. In India the term cultivator

> refers more to the position a person occupies in the social hierarchy than to the economic functions he performs. A member of the numerous castes and sub-castes traditionally held to be cultivators [sic] regards himself as a "cultivator" whether he performs any farm work or not. . . . The transfer of land from intermediaries to "cultivators" was therefore far from being a transfer to the actual tillers of the soil. [44]

In most cases, zamindari abolition, in the opinion of Gunnar Myrdal, amounted to a transfer of land rights from one non-cultivating interest to another. "Generally speaking, sub-tenants—that is unprivileged tenants and sharecroppers—drew no benefit from these reforms." [45] While cultivating tenants received no genuine economic benefits from the zamindari abolition, some intermediaries also suffered from insufficient compensation. As in East Pakistan, there were in India problems of inadequate administrative preparation for the program. Land-revenue agencies were generally much understaffed to handle the gigantic financial tasks that a basic transformation of 40 percent of India's agricultural land required. "Delays in the payment of compensation have occurred," the Indian Planning Commission reported, "mainly on account of difficulties arising

[43] See the two acts of West Bengal in Appendix I, below.
[44] Gunnar Myrdal, Asian Drama: an Inquiry into the Poverty of Nations, II (New York: Pantheon, 1968), 1308.
[45] Ibid., p. 1309. Commenting on this point, the Indian Planning Commission stated somewhat circumspectly: "The elimination of intermediaries is a far-reaching change in the economic life of rural India. But the tenants holding land under intermediaries were not in all cases cultivating their lands. The intermediaries also do not always cultivate their home-farm lands. Considerable areas have thus been leased out to subtenants. On the abolition of intermediaries, the sub-tenancies generally remain." India, Planning Commission, Progress of Land Reforms (Delhi, 1955), p. 11, quoted in Myrdal, op. cit., pp. 1308–1309.

out of assessment of compensation. . . . In many States survey and settlement had not been made over large areas or was out of date. In many
cases there was hardly any revenue administration at the village level and
annual land records were not being maintained." [46]

Despite all its deficiencies, India's *zamindari* abolition program must
be considered a major political and social accomplishment of the Congress
Party. The termination within a decade of a 150-year old agrarian institution that encompassed nearly half of India's land is an extraordinary
act that required the political elite to demonstrate unusual resolution.
Having now carried out a pledge it made two decades ago, the Congress
Party can justifiably claim that the program stands as at once a symbol of
freedom from the British raj and a concrete step toward rural egalitarianism. Spurious "personal cultivation," it is true, is tolerated in practice,
but the program did break down the concentration of landownership that
once characterized many *zamindari* areas. Though the bulk of cultivators
under reform are now only tenants of state governments, their rental payment is fairly low. This is so partly because they are now relieved from
the illegal payments exacted by *zamindars* and partly because the rental
rates, which were fixed a long time ago, are not high. Also, most cultivators
have acquired a permanent, heritable occupancy right to their land, a right
which makes them nearly full owners; and some have gained at a modest
cost proprietary rights to their land. Though sub-tenancy still exists today,
the majority of the cultivating farmers in the former *zamindari* areas are
no longer subject to multiple exploitation. While compensation payments
to *zamindars* were insufficient, the government did pay off more than 40
percent of its financial obligations to these intermediaries. On balance,
one may conclude, the program has made a very significant contribution
toward the creation of equitable land tenure in India.

TENANCY IMPROVEMENT MEASURES

Measures to improve tenancy usually include conclusion of contracts
with fixed terms, guarantee against unwarranted eviction of cultivators,
and reduction of high rentals. These measures are designed to replace
tenancy relations characterized by exploitation and antagonism with ones
of fairness and cooperation, so that both the tenant and the landlord
can be motivated to make a maximum contribution to the increase of
production. Generally, it is not very difficult to incorporate some of these

[46] India, *Progress of Land Reform* (1963), p. 5.

measures into land reform-laws, irrespective of the type of elite in power. In fact, in the debates over the issue of land reform, these measures rarely constitute a hotly contested issue; and, in countries like India and the Philippines, many tenancy laws were enacted without much difficulty. A number of reasons may account for this. In the developing countries, the prevailing tenancy conditions—the high rentals, the extra dues, and the free labor service that the tenant is required to provide; the ease with which the landlord can take back his land; and the tenants' perennial indebtedness—are so obviously abusive and morally indefensible that their amelioration can hardly be challenged by the landlord class. Moreover, the measures to improve tenancy do not as vitally affect the interests of the landlord class as does land redistribution, thus arousing not as much vigorous opposition. The central issue in land reform remains the question of land ownership, not land use. Finally, the landlord class frequently accepts a tenancy reform law with a justifiable conviction that it can easily be evaded in practice. Unlike a land redistribution program, which is a transaction requiring intensive government supervision for a relatively short period of time, tenancy reform is a continuous process demanding that the government enforce crop divisions, settle tenancy disputes, and uncover evasions. The limited administrative capacity of the government to perform these tedious and complex tasks, the weak bargaining position of the tenant, and the undiminishing heavy demand for land after reform— all these factors explain why a tenancy reform law is easier to enact than to enforce.

This being so, the kind of tenancy reform law introduced by one type of elite differs, nevertheless, substantively from that adopted by another. Among the eight countries studied, Mexico does not have a high incidence of tenancy (see Table 3) and does not have a tenancy reform law. East Pakistan, where tenants outside the former *zamindari* areas are relatively few, does not have a tenancy reform law separate from the *zamindari* abolition program. Colombia has only very recently adopted some tenancy improvement measures, but it has not begun to implement them on any large scale. INCORA reported in 1970 that its present tenancy reform program involved principally the registration of tenants and sharecroppers in reform areas, the extension of contracts to these cultivators, and the investigation of tenancy conditions. As of November 1969, a total of 76,497 cultivators, working on 545,683 hectares of land, have registered with the agency. As its major task in the second stage of tenancy reform, INCORA has planned to negotiate with owners of tenanted land to transfer some

land to the incumbent tenants and sharecroppers.[47] All other countries
have enacted and put into effect comprehensive tenancy reform laws
whose major provisions are summarized in Tables 16 and 17. As with land
redistribution legislation, India's tenancy programs are highly complex.
In order to appreciate this complexity and also to compare the programs
of India with those of other countries, the program of one Indian State,
West Bengal, is included in Table 16 with the reform laws of the other
countries. The programs of all Indian states and union territories are
shown separately in Table 17. To appreciate the major differences among
these tenancy reform programs, a number of key provisions may be selected
for comparison.

Tenancy contract. Where tenancy reform is necessary, it is intended
to improve the position of the tenant *vis-à-vis* the landlord. The primary
instrument for carrying out this intent is the tenancy contract. Two pro-
cedural matters deserve attention: the form and the term of the contract.
A contract can assume either a written or an oral form. The merit of a
written contract lies in the fact that the document can unequivocally state
the full benefits of the reform and make it difficult for landlords to resort
to evasion; a violation of the contract can be identified and corrected with
the backing of the law. On the other hand, an oral contract has a number
of disadvantages. With such a contract, the tenant's chance of getting the
legally allowable benefits is much dependent upon the goodwill of the
landlord, something that is not always forthcoming. Moreover, since the
content of an oral contract cannot be objectively ascertained, such a contract is bound to give rise to confusion and disputes. Furthermore, the
landlord, who used to respect an oral contract before reform, may be
tempted to subvert one that is concluded in accordance with a reform
program that reduces his benefits and privileges.

When a tenancy contract is concluded, the length of time it covers is
also of importance. If it is a long-term contract, the tenant will have a
sense of security with respect to his rights. On the other hand, the landlord may conclude a short-term contract, leaving the tenant constantly
uncertain as to his future working conditions. Conceivably, the landlord
may also offer a long-term contract but demand the tenant to make certain concessions that he would not make otherwise. Wishing to avoid the
trouble of frequent renegotiations that a short-term contract necessitates,

[47] Colombia, INCORA, Secretaría de Organización y Sistemas, *La Reforma Agraria
en Colombia* ([Bogotá], 1970), pp. 16–17.

TABLE 16

TENANCY IMPROVEMENT PROGRAMS, SIX COUNTRIES

	West Bengal, India	Iran
Law	The West Bengal Land Reforms Act	Regulations
Year	1953	1964
Applicability	Land cultivated by *bargadars* (sharecroppers)	All tenanted land that landowners choose to lease to tenants
Contract		
Written or oral	No regulation	Landowners have the option to draw up lease papers
Term	No regulation	30 years. Rent renegotiated every 5 years
Renewal	No regulation	Not specified
Security of tenants from eviction	Grounds for eviction: (a) *bargadar* fails to cultivate land as agreed (b) *bargadar* does not personally cultivate land (c) *bargadar* violates this law (d) landowner resumes land for personal cultivation	Grounds for eviction: (a) tenant fails to pay rent, after a 3–month grace period, (b) tenant dies without an heir to farm the land
Rent		
Cash or kind	Kind	Cash, unless both parties agree otherwise
Fixed or share		Fixed
Level (rate)	40% to 50% of gross produce[a]	Average net receipts (rent less tax) of landowners in previous 3 years
Compensation for improvement	No regulation	Not specified, but tenant may make improvement with consent of owner or of Land Reform Organization
Future ownership for tenants	No regulation (for *bargadars*)	If landowner decides to sell land, tenant may purchase the land with a public loan to pay one-third of cost
Disputes	State government may appoint officer to settle disputes	Land reform officials settle disputes, subject to a final review by a commission of three officials of agricultural departments
Other provisions	*Bargadars* shall not cultivate more than 25 acres (8.1 ha.)	Tenants and landowners of a village may jointly manage their land if both sides agree

TABLE 16 (*Continued*)

	West Pakistan	The Philippines
Law	The West Pakistan Land Reforms Regulation[b]	The Agricultural Land Reform code
Year	1959	1963
Applicability	All tenanted land	Tenancy in proclaimed land-reform areas will be converted to leasehold
Contract		
Written or oral	No regulation	Either, as agreed by both parties
Term	No regulation	Continuous until terminated, or as specified in written contract
Renewal	No regulation	See "term"
Security of tenants from eviction	Grounds for eviction—to be ascertained in revenue court: tenant (a) fails to pay rent, (b) does not use land for agreed purpose, (c) fails to farm land, (d) sublets land, (e) fails to farm land according to local custom	Grounds for termination of leasehold or eviction (a) if tenant abandons land, voluntarily surrenders land, fails to comply with lease contract, uses land not for agreed purpose, neglects land, fails to pay rent, or sublets land; (b) if landowner or member of family resumes land for personal cultivation; tenant entitled to "disturbance compensation"
Rent		
Cash or kind	Not specified	Either, as agreed by both parties
Fixed or share	Not specified	Fixed
Level (rate)	Not specified	Maximum: 25% of yield less cost of seeds, harvesting, processing
Compensation for improvement	No regulation	Half value of "useful and necessary improvements"
Future ownership for tenants	Tenants may purchase government expropriated land	Tenants have right of preemptive purchase and are entitled to purchase government expropriated land
Disputes	The West Pakistan Land Commission to settle disputes	Court of Agrarian Relations—with tenants represented by Agrarian Counsel—to settle disputes
Other provisions	—	—

TABLE 16 *(Continued)*

	Taiwan	U.A.R.
Law	The Farm Rent Reduction to 37.5% Act;[c] Land to the Tiller Act	Agrarian Reform Law and Regulations
Year	1951 and 1953	Law No. 178 of 1952, No. 148 of 1962, and No. 17 of 1963
Applicability	All tenanted private land	All tenanted land
Contract		
Written or oral	Written and registered	Written and registered
Term	Minimum, 6 years	Minimum, 3 years
Renewal	Automatic, unless landowners resume land for personal cultivation (see below)	Not specified, but cooperative society is generally charged with the responsibility to work out contract
Security of tenants from eviction	Landowners may resume land if tenant sublets land, dies without an heir, waives right of cultivation, or fails to pay 2 years' rent. Landowner cannot resume land for personal cultivation if he does not personally cultivate, has sufficient income to support his family, or leaves tenant without means of subsistence	Grounds for eviction: Tenant (a) refuses to sign contract, (b) breaks contract, (c) violates law
Rent		
Cash or kind	Either, to be specified in contract	Either
Fixed or share	Fixed	Fixed
Level (rate)	37.5% of annual yield of the principal product of the main crop	Seven times land tax for tenants, one-half of produce for sharecroppers
Compensation for improvement	Landlord to pay compensation for improvement when he resumes land. Tenant has to notify landlord about improvement	Landlord to provide compensation for "necessary improvement"
Future ownership for tenants	Tenant has right of preemptive purchase of tenanted land when it is for sale. He can also purchase government expropriated land	Tenant may purchase government expropriated land
Disputes	Farm Tenancy Committees settle disputes subject to judicial review	"Committee for Statuting on the Conflicts Connected with Agriculture" to settle disputes, subject to judicial review

TABLE 16 (*Continued*)

	Taiwan	U.A.R.
Other provisions	Farm tenancy committees appraise annual yield of principal product of the main crop	Penalty is provided for landlords' overcharge of rent and tenants' negligence of land

ᵃ If landowner supplies plough, cattle, manure, and seeds, 50%; if not, 40%.

ᵇ The provisions pertaining to tenancy in this Regulation are the only ones applying to the whole of West Pakistan. There were also tenancy laws applying to some regions of West Pakistan, for example, the Sind Tenancy Act of 1950, the Punjab Tenancy Acts of 1950 and 1952. After the issuance of the reform regulation of 1959, the legal status of these regional laws is unclear. In any case, they have not been implemented. See West Pakistan, Land Reforms Commission, *Report of the Land Reforms Commission for West Pakistan* (Lahore, Pakistan, 1959), pp. 50ff, and Pakistan, National Planning Board, *The First Five Year Plan 1955–60*, pp. 315–317.

ᶜ First enforced as administrative regulations in 1949.

SOURCE: Primarily Appendix I.

the tenant may be tempted to accept a long-term, but excessively burdensome, contract.

As seen in Table 16, only Taiwan and the U.A.R., where separated elites rule, require a written contract of a fixed term. The other four countries, where cooperative elites rule, do not require a written contract. The reform laws of India and West Pakistan do not specify what form a tenancy contract should take, and those of Iran and the Philippines either explicitly or implicitly let the landlord choose the form. Among these four countries, only Iran prescribes a definite contract period. India and West Pakistan have no regulation on the matter, and the Philippines only vaguely stipulates that the contract will be in effect continuously until terminated or modified.

Security from eviction. To the tenant, security of tenure is a *basic* right which any tenancy reform must provide. If assured of the right to continue working on his land, the tenant can be motivated to increase production. On the other hand, if the landlord can easily terminate the contract and freely eject the tenant from the land, any meaningful implementation of reform will become extraordinarily difficult, if not totally impossible. Under the threat of eviction, certain tenants, in order to retain the land, may have to collude with their landlords by abiding by the law on the surface but in reality paying illegal exactions. Other tenants, who insist on receiving the full benefits under the law, may end up losing their

TABLE 17

Main Features of Indian Tenancy Laws

States and Union Territories	Regulation of Rent: Rates of Fair Rent (Gross Produce)[a]	Right of Resumption of Land by Owners for Personal Cultivation[b]	Restriction on "Voluntary Surrender" by Tenants	Future Ownership for Tenants[c]
Andhra area Andhra Pradesh	45%–50%	[d]	No	No provision
Telangana area Andhra Pradesh	$\frac{1}{5}$–$\frac{1}{4}$	Yes, till 1959	No	Purchase right provided
Assam	$\frac{1}{5}$–$\frac{1}{4}$	Yes & No[e]	No	No provision[f]
Bihar	$\frac{1}{4}$–$\frac{1}{2}$	Yes & No[e]	Registration & review required	No provision[f]
Gujarat	$\frac{1}{6}$	Yes & No[e]	Registration required	Purchase right provided
Jammu & Kashmir	$\frac{1}{4}$–$\frac{1}{2}$	Yes	No	No provision
Kerala	$\frac{1}{16}$–$\frac{1}{3}$	Yes	No	Purchase right provided
Madhya Pradesh	[g]	Yes	Registration & review required	Purchase right provided
Madras	$\frac{1}{3}$–$\frac{2}{5}$	Yes	No	No provision
Maharashtra	$\frac{1}{6}$	Yes & No[e]	Registration required	Purchase right provided
Mysore	$\frac{1}{5}$–$\frac{1}{4}$	Yes	Registration & review required	Purchase right provided
Orissa	$\frac{1}{4}$	Yes	No	Purchase right provided
Punjab	$\frac{1}{3}$	Yes	No	Purchase right provided
Rajasthan	$\frac{1}{6}$–$\frac{1}{3}$	Yes	No	Purchase right provided
Uttar Pradesh	[h]	No	No	Purchase right provided
West Bengal	$\frac{2}{5}$–$\frac{1}{2}$[i]	Yes & No[e]	No	[j]
Union Territories				
Delhi	$\frac{1}{5}$	No	No	[j]
Himachal Pradesh	$\frac{1}{4}$	Yes	No	Purchase right provided

TABLE 17 (*Continued*)

States and Union Territories	Regulation of Rent: Rates of Fair Rent (Gross Produce)[a]	Right of Resumption of Land by Owners for Personal Cultivation[b]	Restriction on "Voluntary Surrender" by Tenants	Future Ownership for Tenants[c]
Manipur	$\frac{1}{5}-\frac{1}{4}$	Yes	Registration & review required	Purchase right provided
Tripura	$\frac{1}{5}-\frac{1}{4}$	Yes	Registration & review required	Purchase right provided

ᵃ Where rental rates vary, the variations are due to many factors: the extent of irrigation, the size of holdings, the types of rent (in cash or in kind), the locations of land, the crops grown, the classes of land, and whether or not landowner supplies cattle, ploughs, etc.

ᵇ "Personal cultivation" generally means cultivation by landowners or by persons hired by landowners paid in cash or in kind. For a survey of the definitions of this term in all Indian states and Union territories, see *ibid.*, pp. 49–55.

ᶜ With respect to non-resumable land (i.e. tenanted land not liable to resumption by owners for personal cultivation) and government acquired *zamindari* land.

ᵈ No tenants could be ejected until May 31, 1963.

ᵉ Yes—with respect to land cultivated by non-occupancy tenants; no—with respect to land cultivated by occupancy tenants (i.e., tenants with permanent heritable, transferable right).

ᶠ But tenants may purchase land above ceiling limits.

ᵍ Two to four times the land revenue.

ʰ No rates have been prescribed.

ⁱ Data pertain to land cultivated by sharecroppers, not by tenants.

ʲ Ownership of government-acquired *zamindari* land was already conferred on tenants, but not on sharecroppers.

SOURCE: India, Planning Commission, *Progress of Land Reform* (Delhi, 1963).

land. Under these conditions, tenancy reform may even work to the disadvantage of the tenants: because of reform they may be reduced to farm laborers or become unemployed.

Among the six countries appearing in Tables 16 and 17, Taiwan imposes the most stringent conditions on tenant evictions, whereas India makes it easiest for the landlord to reclaim his land. In Taiwan, a landlord cannot resume his land for personal cultivation if, by resuming the land, he leaves the tenant without a means of subsistence. Since an overwhelming majority of Taiwanese tenants do depend on land to make a living, their landlords simply cannot exercise the resumption right. In India, no meaningful limitation is imposed on landlords' resumption rights. As personal cultivation can mean cultivation through hired persons paid in cash or in kind, the landlord is given, in fact, a free rein in removing tenants and letting others work for him. In addition, all tenancy reform laws of India allow tenants to give up their tenancy rights through "voluntary surrender." In only a few states, "voluntary surrender" proceedings must be registered with the government—in some states, also subject to official review—before such surrender can be legally recognized. Most states impose no restriction at all. As to the remaining four countries, the Philippines and West Pakistan provide more grounds for eviction than Iran and the U.A.R. Consequently, tenants face a greater possibility of losing their land in the former two countries than in the latter.

Rent reduction. As tenants in most of the countries studied have traditionally paid high rent, tenancy reform normally should seek a reduction of this burden. This reduction is intended partially to improve the well-being of the cultivator and partially to make it possible for him to accumulate savings necessary for financing agricultural improvement projects. If a tenancy reform law does not seek to alleviate the heavy burden of the tenant, such a reform merely regularizes tenancy relations without yielding any benefits to either the cultivators or to the agricultural economy as a whole.

As seen in Tables 16 and 17, among the four cooperative-elite-ruled countries, Iran and West Pakistan have not reduced rental payments, and India has found itself in a complex situation. In most Indian states, the level of rent is limited to from one-fifth to one-fourth of the annual gross produce, with the rest varying around this level. The result is that in some states there has been a moderate to considerable reduction of rent, whereas in others the reduction has been either insignificant or non-existent. The Philippines is the only one of these four countries providing for a major reduction of rent—limiting it to 25 percent of the gross produce minus the cost of production. Both of the two separated-elite-ruled countries have effected a significant reduction of rent. In Taiwan, rent is limited to 37.5 percent of the annual gross produce, which represents a 25 percent reduction from pre-reform rentals. In the U.A.R., rent is set at seven times the land tax. Estimates by specialists regarding Egyptian rental reduction from the pre-reform level range from 25 to 33 percent.[48]

---

[48] See Donald C. Mead, *Growth and Structural Change in the Egyptian Economy* (Homewood, Ill., 1967), p. 77; and Saab, *op. cit.* (n. 3 above), p. 144.

It appears evident that the tenancy reform programs of the cooperative-elite-ruled countries are generally less favorable to tenants than those of the separated-elite-ruled countries. To appreciate fully the significant differences between tenancy reform programs formulated by these two types of elite, the programs of the Philippines and Taiwan will be singled out for further comparison. Both countries have experienced serious tenancy problems, and both have placed a great deal of stress on tenancy reform programs. With little activity in land redistribution, the Philippines now concentrates its land-reform effort almost entirely on the creation of a leasehold system in tenancy areas. In Taiwan, the rent-reduction program of 1949 was the KMT's very first measure to restructure the island's land tenure system, and its success was critically important to the introduction of subsequent reform measures. Yet, despite these similarities, the two countries adopted markedy different tenancy reform programs.

The Philippines Program

The Philippine Agricultural Land Reform Code of 1963 envisaged as its principal objective the substitution of leasehold for tenancy. The origin of the leasehold provisions of the 1963 code can be traced to a number of earlier tenancy reform laws, including the Philippine Tenancy Act of 1933 (CA 4054), the Philippine Rice Share Tenancy Act of 1946 (RA 34), and the Agricultural Tenancy Act of 1954 (RA 1199). With respect to provisions on conclusion of contract, tenure security, and rental rates, the 1963 code made some slight improvement over the 1946 and 1954 laws. The two earlier laws covered rice land, whereas the 1963 code extended to farms planted with other crops. The two earlier laws assigned 30 percent of the produce of tenanted land as rent in cases in which landlords contributed merely land to the productive process, whereas the 1963 code reduced the percentage to 25. Other than these changes, the later law is not significantly different from the earlier ones.

The 1963 code provides that "the agricultural lessor [i.e. landowner] and the agricultural lessee [i.e. tenant] shall be free to enter into any kind of terms, conditions or stipulations in a leasehold contract, as long as they are not contrary to law, morals or public policy (Section 15)." Thus, either a written or oral contract is permissible, and "in the absence of any agreement as to the period, the terms and conditions of a leasehold contract shall continue until modified by the parties (Section 16)." Grounds for eviction and termination of contract are numerous, and some contracts are loosely written. As in India, the landowner in the Philippines is entitled to resume land for personal cultivation or for non-agricultural uses, provided that the tenant on a farm with five hectares or less of land be given one year's advance notice and that the tenant on a larger farm be entitled to a "disturbance compensation equivalent to five years' rental (Section 36)." The tenant may terminate leasehold through "voluntary surrender of the landholding (Section 8)," and he will lose the right to work the land if he "failed to adopt proven farm practices (Section 36)." As to the level of rent, the law stipulates that it "shall not be more than the equivalent of twenty-five *per centum* of the average normal harvest during the three agricultural years . . . [immediately before the establishment of leasehold] after deducting the amount used for seeds and the cost of harvesting, threshing, loading, hauling and processing . . . provided . . . that if capital improvements are introduced on the farm not by the lessee to increase its productivity, the rental shall be increased proportionately to the consequent increase in production due to said improvements (Section 34)." Leasehold can be established "in any region or locality . . . when the National Land Reform Council proclaims that all the government machineries and agencies in that region or locality relating to leasehold envisioned in this Code are operating . . . (Section 4)." Agrarian Counsels are to help tenants in the exercise of their legal rights, and Courts of Agrarian Relations are to settle landlord-tenant disputes.

The Taiwan Program

In Taiwan, the Farm Rent Reduction to 37.5% Act of 1951 requires that all farm lease contracts be made in writing and that the parties jointly register with the government "in the signing, revision, termination, or renewal" of their contracts (Article 6). The contract shall last for a minimum of six years and shall be automatically renewable unless the tenant subleases the land, dies without an heir, waives his right of cultivation by migrating elsewhere, changes his occupation, or has failed to pay rent for two years (Articles 16 and 17). The landowner cannot resume land for personal cultivation under any one of the following conditions: if he does not cultivate the land himself, if his income is adequate to support his family, or if his resumption of the land would deprive the tenant's family of its means of subsistence. The tenant is to pay the landowner 37.5 percent of the annual yield of the main crop; "the amount, kind, quality and standard of" rentals are to be specified in the contract and will not be changeable for the duration of the contract. Enforced throughout the island within one year, the program involved direct participation of farmers in its implementation. The Farm Tenancy Committees (and their predecessors, the Rent Reduction Committees), whose members included as many tenants as the landlords and owner-farmers combined, helped provide information concerning the program, appraise rentals, and settle landlord-tenant disputes.

A Comparison

As can readily be seen, the Taiwan program is more beneficial to the tenant and better formulated than its Philippine counterpart. A comparison of three major provisions of the two programs will illuminate this point.

Forms of contract. The 1963 Philippine law does not require a written contract with a specified term to effect a leasehold. This stands as a major loophole through which landlords can evade many provisions of the law. As a Philippine official report on land reform has stated:

> When an area is proclaimed a land reform district, all share-tenants are supposed to be automatically transformed into lessees. Actually, however, there are still farmers practicing the old tenurial system of sharecropping.
>
> Written leasehold contracts is [sic] one of the indicators that lease-hold is existing. But the law permits oral agreements, too. A situation then arises wherein a farmer and a landowner may have an oral contract, but actually they are practicing share-tenancy.[49]

The report contains the following statistics on the leasehold program: as of December 1967, in all the 19 proclaimed land-reform districts of the country, there were 26,628 share tenants, 12,876 (or 48.4 percent) of whom had been converted to lessees. Of a total of 15,827 contracts that had been concluded or under negotiation, only 6,602, or 41 percent, were written ones.[50] Thus, even in the limited number of reform areas, tenants still outnumbered lessees; and lessees entered more oral contracts than written ones.

In Taiwan, a written tenancy contract is required. Initially, landowners also attempted to evade the reform, and some even refused to sign a contract. But landowners soon realized that their right to receive rentals

---

[49] The Philippines, *An Evaluation on Land Reform Operations*, p. 27.
[50] *Ibid.*, pp. 29–30.

depended on the conclusion of written contracts; practically all of them complied with the law and signed contracts in 1949.[51]

Level of rent. Under the Philippine program, the level of rent is established at 25 percent of the produce minus the cost of operation. This appears fairly low. But this is true only when the landlord merely furnishes land. In practice, however, the landlord furnishes something more. As is typical in the country's high tenancy area—Central Luzon—the landlord and the tenant generally share equally "the costs of seed, fertilizer, and irrigation; in addition, they share equally the costs of harvesting and threshing which vary from 15 to 20 percent of the gross harvest." [52] For these additional contributions the landlord receives additional rent. Moreover, it is generally known that the landlord has traditionally provided the tenant with loans at an extremely high interest rate, and that the tenant has been in perennial debt.[53] Since the credit supplied by the land-reform agencies (principally the Agricultural Credit Administration) is totally inadequate for the tenant's need,[54] the landlord—though legally prohibited from imposing a loan on the tenant—still supplies a major share of private farm credit. For this service, he can claim still more of the tenant's produce. Partially for this reason, the enforcement of tenancy reform becomes very difficult. As Conrado F. Estrella has commented: "the *tao*, or peasant, depended on the landlord for everything. For loans between crops, for a good word with the police or the politicians, for orders on what to plant and when to plant it. He didn't know what it was to think for himself." [55]

---

[51] In 1949, 296,043 tenant families—44.5 percent of all farm families—concluded 377,364 contracts, covering an area of 264,514 *chia* (251,598 hectares), or 38.1 percent of the total private farm land. Official data did not reveal how many of these 296,043 tenant families were "pure" tenant families and how many part-tenant and part-owner families. But one can assume all of the 239,939 pure tenant families existing in 1949 concluded written contracts. See Tang, *op. cit.* (n. 16 above), pp. 46–47; and Chen Cheng, *Land Reform in Taiwan* (Taipei, Taiwan, 1961), p. 308.

[52] Generosa F. Rivera and Robert T. McMillan, *An Economic and Social Survey of Rural Households in Central Luzon* (Manila, 1954), pp. vi–vii.

[53] See *ibid.*, p. 104; *Hardie Report*, pp. v–vi; and Napoleon G. Rama, "The Liberation of the Filipino," *Philippines Free Press*, February 9, 1963, p. 63. For a detailed survey of rural indebtedness in the Philippines, see "Borrowing Practices of Farm Households," *The Philippine Statistical Survey of Households Bulletin*, Series No. 12, May 1961.

[54] In 1968, about 15 to 18 percent of the farmers in reform areas could obtain some credit from public institutional channels. The Philippines, *An Evaluation on Land Reform Operations*, p. 37.

[55] *The New York Times*, April 12, 1968, p. 14.

So much depended upon the landlord that the tenant could not but abide by the wish of the landlord as to how much rent he actually paid, whatever the law prescribed.

Taiwan prescribes a higher level of rent than the Philippines. But rent reduction in Taiwan is genuine. The tenant has to pay only 37.5 percent of the annual produce of the main crop; all other forms of levies by the landlord—advance rent, security deposits, gifts, payment of farm by-products, charges for tenant dwellings—are prohibited. Moreover, the exact amount of rent payable to the landlord was fixed on the basis of the average crop yield of the three years prior to 1949. This feature of the program, which allows the subsequent increase of yield to accrue to the tenant, is the single most important source of incentive for the tenant to increase production. The Taiwanese tenants, who were traditionally as dependent on the landlord for their credit needs as were their Philippine counterparts, can now go to the Farmers' Associations to obtain low-interest loans. Controlled by the cultivators, these associations are fully capable of meeting the major credit requirements of the farming community. (See Chapter XII, below.) Consequently, the landlord in Taiwan can no longer employ usury as a means of obtaining extra rental from the tenant.

Application of reform law. In the Philippines, the piecemeal application of the 1963 law has so far excluded an overwhelming majority of the tenants from receiving the benefits of the law. The legal requirement that a leasehold system can be created only in areas where "all the government machineries and agencies" relating to the system are operating provides executive and administrative officials with an excuse for going slow with implementation. For the authority to create these machineries and agencies is discretionary, and if in a given area the government chooses not to exercise such authority, there will be no reform in that area. As will be elaborated in Chapter IX, only a small proportion of the tenancy areas has been declared under reform, and traditional share-tenancy still prevails in most parts of the country. Even in the declared reform areas, some of the governmental instrumentalities responsible for the implementation of the 1963 law appear very weak. For example, the Offices of Agrarian Counsel and the Courts of Agrarian Relations, the principal legal agencies to help the tenants assert their rights and to settle their disputes with the landlords, are much under-staffed and are less helpful to the tenants than expected. The law authorizes the creation of eighty agrarian counsels and fifteen agrarian courts to cover the whole country, with all counsels and judges appointed by the President. "It is doubtful," a United Nations report noted, that this complement of legal personnel "will prove adequate to enforce the [leasehold] provisions, and in some respects, there is doubt whether the provisions are enforceable." [56] A tour by the author of the South Nueva Ecija Land Reform District on January 30 and 31, 1969, provided a glimpse into the problems encountered by the legal personnel. In the Office of Agrarian Counsel in Gapan, Nueva Ecija, 6 officers were assigned to serve 26,000 farmer clients. One woman legal officer revealed that the recommended ratio of legal officer to farmers was 1:400, but she covered as many as 8,000 farmers. Inundated with cases, the officers just could not make adequate preparations in assisting the tenants in conciliatory or judicial proceedings. The Court of Agrarian Relations for the district, also located in Gapan, appeared to be similarly over-burdened. From October 22, 1968, to January 31, 1969, a total of 244 cases were placed on the judicial docket. Of these, 136 were pending, 27 newly filed, 73 assigned for hearing and investigation, and only 8 disposed. While the court was immobilized by an ever-increasing backlog of cases, the judges, who were political appointees of the President, were not always scrupulously judicious in handling the court proceedings. Both land-reform officials and farmers interviewed by the author claimed that some of the judges were landowners themselves whose impartiality was at times doubt-ful.

The experience of Taiwan in this regard is completely different. The rent-reduction law was simultaneously applied to every locality in 1949. Thus, practically all farmers of private tenanted land immediately bene-fited from the program. At the same time, tenant participation in the enforcement of the program relieved much of the administrative burden of the government. In regard to tenancy disputes, farmers did not have to depend on officials to defend their views and interests but could rely on their own representatives on the Farm Tenancy Committees to articu-late their cases. As a reconciliatory instrumentality, the committees both alleviated the need for a large complement of legal personnel and assured impartial execution of the reform.

[56] U.N., *Land Reform, Fourth Report*, p. 29.

VIII

DEVELOPMENTAL PROGRAMS: COOPERATIVE FARMING AND PUBLIC LAND SETTLEMENT

Seeking to increase farm output through efficient utilization of existing agricultural resources and to expand farm areas, developmental programs include cooperative farming and public land settlement projects.

Cooperative Farming

As a policy for promoting the pooling of resources and mutual aid among farmers, a cooperative program has much to offer. Indeed, virtually all people concerned with agricultural development consider it necessary and desirable to integrate the farming community into cooperative societies for purposes of credit provision, rural extension, marketing, and other services. However, once a cooperative scheme is proposed for farming operations, it immediately becomes a divisive issue. Proponents of the scheme regard land reform as incomplete and inadequate if it stops at land redistribution and tenancy improvement measures. Only through cooperative farming can the two principal objectives of land reform—productivity and equity—be really accomplished. On the other hand, many who warmly endorse redistributive reform programs reject cooperative farming as impractical and disruptive. They prefer to preserve the family-farm system.

Ideologically, cooperative farming is often identified as a socialist scheme that stresses egalitarianism, group action, and some form of common ownership of land. Practiced on a large scale mainly in Communist countries and also in Israel, this scheme, its advocates believe, is particularly appropriate for the developing countries. Since most farms in these countries are small and fragmented—a problem that land redistribution is likely to intensify—these farms should be consolidated so that under joint management they can benefit from economies of scale; experimentation with cropping patterns; mechanization; efficient allocation and utilization of labor, water, and inputs; bulk purchasing and bulk marketing. Moreover, as fatalism and alienation, which characterize the attitude of traditional farmers, are a barrier to the emergence of an enterprising peasantry, cooperative schemes should be adopted to promote mutual assistance and group activity.

Opponents of cooperative farming contend that the scheme deprives farmers of a sense of independence, and contains disincentives for production. Agricultural production, they argue, involves a highly dispersed process of on-the-spot decision-making by individual farmers. Central management, which is appropriate for the operation of industrial factories, becomes inefficient and cumbersome in farm operations. Thus observed John Stuart Mill in his *Principles of Political Economy*:

> The superiority of the large system in agriculture is by no means so clearly established as in manufactures. The combination of labour of which agriculture is susceptible is chiefly . . . that [of] several persons helping one another in the same work, at the same time and place. . . . There is no particular advantage in setting a great number of people to work together in ploughing or digging or sowing the same field, or even in mowing or reaping it unless time presses. A single family can generally supply all the labour necessary for these purposes.[1]

Opponents contend further that if incentive is the driving force for increasing agricultural production, it can come primarily with ownership of land (at least substantial control of land) which directly relates one's reward to one's work. Under a cooperative scheme, a farmer's income is only indirectly related to his labor input; and his interest in raising the group output cannot be very high. Moreover, as has been amply shown in Chapter V, agricultural productivity tends to vary inversely with the size of holdings. This is mainly because the existence of surplus rural labor on small holdings induces the owners to adopt labor-intensive practices. It is true that by consolidating small holdings into a large area, a cooperative farm can increase its *labor productivity* through mechanization. But, then, it will exacerbate the problem of surplus rural labor without perhaps increasing *land productivity*. Furthermore, a cooperative farm faces a dilemma in the selection of a manager. If the cultivators choose their manager from among themselves, he frequently does not have the adequate

---

[1] Cited in Kenneth H. Parsons, *The Owner Cultivator in a Progressive Agriculture, An FAO Land Tenure Study* (Rome, FAO, 1958), p. 37.

administrative and technical competence to run a large farm. If they select a competent outsider as the manager, they lose even more the sense of ownership of their pooled land. In such a case "some of the basic decisions in farming," as Theodore W. Schultz has observed, "are made under *absentee* conditions." [2] That is, farmers working in the field do not make basic decisions; others do. Finally, opponents of cooperative farming believe that only under one of the following two conditions can cooperative farming be productive: when farmers voluntarily organize a cooperative farm in which all members show a strong sense of empathy—the ability to "widen sympathies"; and when farmers are more or less forcefully inducted into a cooperative, disciplined by the government. However, because farmers in the developing countries seldom engage in activities beyond the village, and because they often nurture a strong sense of family- or clan-centered isolation, they tend to be indifferent or suspicious toward large and impersonal organizations. And to place cooperative farms under rigid state control would not only build into the farms strong disincentives but also seriously overburden the administrative capacity of the government.

How do these conflicting views on cooperative farming relate to reality? Three countries—India, Mexico, and the U.A.R.—have made major efforts toward creating cooperative farms. Based on divergent organizational principles, the cooperative farms of these countries have achieved different results.

THE INDIAN MODEL

In India, the Congress Party gave its first endorsement to the "cooperative farming" idea as far back as 1936 when it adopted the Faizpur Agrarian Programme.[3] Since then, the party has repeatedly advocated the idea, considering cooperative farming to be a "higher," "socialist" form of production, best capable of coping with such typical Indian rural problems as farm fragmentation, low level of agricultural technology, and scarcity of material inputs.

After independence, the Planning Commission recommended, through the five-year plans, the establishment of cooperative farms throughout the nation. The First Five Year Plan suggested: "It is important that small and middle farmers, in particular, should be encouraged and assisted to

[2] Theodore W. Schultz, *Transforming Traditional Agriculture* (New Haven and London: Yale University Press, 1964), p. 121 (original italics).

[3] See H. D. Malaviya, *Land Reforms in India* (New Delhi, 1954), pp. 63–64.

group themselves voluntarily into cooperative farming societies." [4] The Second Five Year Plan proclaimed in 1956 that India was "to take such essential steps as will provide sound foundations for the development of co-operative farming, so that over a period of 10 years or so a substantial proportion of agricultural lands are [to be] cultivated on co-operative lines." The plan recommended three methods for pooling the land:

(1) The ownership of land may be retained by individuals but the land may be managed as one unit, the owners being compensated through some form of ownership dividend;

(2) The land may be leased to the co-operative society for a period, the owners being paid agreed rents or rents prescribed by law, or

(3) Ownership may be transferred to the cooperative society but shares representing the value of land may be given to individuals. [5]

Meanwhile, the Indian government's effort to develop cooperative farms was strengthened when, in 1957, the Indian Delegation to China on Agrarian Cooperatives reported favorably on the Chinese Communist experiences in this regard. The Congress Party soon adopted the 1959 Nagpur Resolution confidently declaring that "the future agrarian pattern should be that of cooperative joint farming." Village *panchayats* (councils) were to operate joint farming cooperatives; farmers were to pool their land under joint management but retain their ownership; they were to receive dividends in addition to remuneration for work done. As a first step, ceilings legislation under the land redistribution program was to be completed within the year so that all surplus land could be vested in *panchayat* cooperatives which would consist "of landless laborers and small peasants." [6]

Various types of cooperative society have since been created in many parts of India. These include (1) tenant farming and better farming societies, (2) collective societies, and (3) joint farming societies. Members of the first type of society work on individual plots and cooperate only in obtaining loans and grants; farmers of the second type work collectively on land which they do not individually own (land may belong to the government or the cooperative society); and members of the third type— the only one envisaged by the Nagpur Resolution—hold individual owner-

---

[4] Cited in India, Planning Commission, *Progress of Land Reform* (Delhi, 1963), p. 225.

[5] Cited in *ibid.*, p. 251.

[6] For the text of the resolution, see A. M. Khusro and A. N. Agarwal, *The Problem of Co-operative Farming in India* (New York: Asia Publishing House, 1961), pp. 36–38.

ship of land, which is pooled together under joint management.[7] As of 1965, an official source of information revealed there were a total of 4520 cooperative societies of all types with 86,986 members covering 488,130 acres of land.[8] Obviously, the Indian cooperative farming movement has proceeded at a very slow pace. Ten years after the publication of the Second Five Year Plan in 1955, India had not reached the goal of placing "a substantial proportion of agricultural lands . . . on cooperative lines." Instead, at best only 488,130 acres, or 1.52 percent, of India's total cultivated land of 320 million acres were managed by cooperative societies.

An official assessment of the cooperative movement, which was made some time ago but still holds true today, asserts that "very little has . . . been done so far, and few planned experiments have been taken." And "the reasons for insufficient progress in cooperative farming have been largely psychological and organisational." [9] The Indian cooperative farming scheme derives from the ideas of such men as Gandhi and Nehru without enthusiastic support from the rank and file of the Congress Party, much less from the farming community. Often farmers have been initiated into a cooperative farming society without adequate psychological preparation. They possess no attachment to the society to which they happen to belong; they have no identity of interests among themselves.

Though the government constantly renews its pledge to cooperative farming, it does not appear to have a definitive policy on the subject. In fact, within the government there has been some opposition to the cooperative farming idea. For instance, Gulzari Lal Nanda, a member of the Planning Commission, has expressed the view: In India "there is a strong attachment to land among peasants and, therefore, cooperative farming cannot be brought about on any large scale except through coercion or force, which has to be ruled out in any democratic country; the cooperative farming would retard initiative and hamper the growth of farmer's personality; it may even hinder the development of democratic institutions." [10] In a 1960 survey of the attitudes of 224 Congress members in parliament

        [7] For a detailed description of these societies, see India, Planning Commisson, Reports of the Committees of the Panel on Land Reforms (Delhi: Government of India Press, 1959), pp. 210–211; and Khusro and Agarwal, op. cit.
        [8] India, Ministry of Information and Broadcasting, India, A Reference Annual, 1966 (Delhi: The Manager, Government of India Press, 1966), p. 247.
        [9] India, Reports of the Committees of the Panel on Land Reforms, p. 177.
        [10] Quoted in Myron Weiner, The Politics of Scarcity: Public Pressure and Political Response in India (Chicago: The University of Chicago Press, 1962), p. 154. Cf. Doreen Warriner, Land Reform in Principle and Practice (Oxford, 1969), pp. 174–175.

toward cooperative farming, Stanley A. Kochanek found that, though there was considerable support for the idea, this support was much less than that for land redistribution, and that the respondents' conceptions of cooperative farming were quite divergent, "which could mean anything from the kind of extreme joint co-operative introduced by the Chinese during the great leap forward to the establishment of service cooperatives." [11]

Cooperative farming in India encounters other problems too. Since the ceiling laws were defectively written, the total land available for cooperatives is extremely limited. Also, cooperative societies have admitted as members all types within the farming population, including farm laborers, tenants, owner-farmers, and landlords. Several adverse consequences have emerged. Certain cooperatives are merely family enterprises of large landowners established for the purposes of evading land redistribution laws and of obtaining government loans and subsidies.[12] In other societies, large landowners clearly dominate the rest. Thus, Daniel Thorner has observed, "Firmly lodged in the chief positions of village power today, the dominant families stand ready to seize the lion's share of the vast programme of cooperative development. As the peasants say: 'Jis ke pas jitna hai, utana use milta hai.' (To him that hath much, much shall be given.)" [13] The emerging pattern is that whereas "the management is invariably in the hands of the biggest" resident landowners, many other owners "live away from the farm and they do neither manual nor managerial work. . . . Most of these cooperative farms are thus really large capitalist farms or estate farms and have been constituted with motives other than genuine co-operation." [14]

Because of its failing experience in cooperative farming, the Indian government has gradually lost its enthusiasm. Though still endorsing cooperative farming as an idea, the Third Five Year Plan, 1960–1965, approached the matter with considerable caution. Indian peasant-proprietors "are to be encouraged and assisted in organising themselves in voluntary co-operative bodies for credit, marketing, processing and distribution and,

[11] Stanley A. Kochanek, "The Relation between Social Background and Attitudes of Indian Legislators," *Journal of Commonwealth Political Studies*, VI (March 1968), 44.

[12] See Daniel Thorner, *Agricultural Cooperatives in India, A Field Report* (London: Asia Publishing House, 1964), pp. 35–36; and Khusro and Agarwal, *op. cit.*, p. 40.

[13] *Op. cit.*

[14] Khusro and Agarwal, *op. cit.*, pp. 40–41.

with their consent, progressively also for production." [15] In the 1967 election, the Congress Party's "Manifesto" upheld the aim of building a "Democratic Socialist Society," but none of its six land policy planks referred to cooperative farming. Pointing to the failure of Congress's cooperative policy, the Samyukta Socialist Party declared in its manifesto:

> The ruling party had contested the 1962 general elections on the slogan of cooperative farming. But after five years, less than three lakh [300,000] acres of land have come under cooperatives, out of a total of 32 crore [320 million] acres of cultivated land. At this speed, the policy would need 5,000 years for its implementation. Nowhere else has such gross violation of an election promise taken place. . . .[16]

THE MEXICAN MODEL

Compared with the Indian cooperative farm, the Mexican *ejido* system has a very impressive record. Embracing half of the Mexican farming community, the system is an institution of indigenous origin and long history.[17] It was revived in response to popular demand and is strongly defended by the vast number of its own members (the *ejidatarios*) and their intellectual and political allies.

The demand for the revival of the *ejido* system to administer the redistribution of land was an important objective of the Mexican revolution. "In ideology and in practice," Eyler N. Simpson observed in 1935, "the principal evidence of progress has been the emergence of the *ejido* as the major objective of the agrarian revolution as a whole and as the fundamental method and immediate aim of land reform in particular." [18] The 1915 land reform decree acknowledged that the despoiled Indian land

[15] India, Planning Commission, *Third Five Year Plan* (New Delhi, 1961), p. 221.

[16] For the text of the manifestoes of these two parties, see M. Pattabhiram (ed.), *General Election in India 1967, An Exhaustive Study of Main Political Trends* (Bombay: Allied Publishers, 1967), pp. 169–178, 197–203.

[17] The *ejido* literally refers to the land lying outside the village. In pre-Spanish Mexico, a communal land-tenure system prevailed among Indian communities. The aggregate of all lands belonging to a village was then known as the *altepetalli*. A portion of the *altepetalli* was held in common by the village for supporting the village chief, and for public functions, with the rest allotted among kinship groups, known as *calpulli*. The land of a *calpulli* consisted of two categories: the untilled category, for miscellaneous uses held in common by the *calpulli*, and the cultivated category, which was further divided into small plots, called *tlatimilli*, with each family of the *calpulli* assigned one plot to which a family had only an inheritable, usufruct right. The present *ejido* system is a reconstruction of this pre-Spanish communal system. See Eyler N. Simpson, *The Ejido, Mexico's Way Out* (Chapel Hill, 1937), pp. 4–5.

[18] *Ibid.*, p. 77.

traditionally belonged to villages, which, "following ancient and general custom," had held it in common. The decree promised to return all illegally alienated lands, forests, and waters to the villages, and pledged that "villages which, need . . . [ejidos but] do not have [them] . . . shall have the right to obtain a sufficient portion of land to reconstruct them." [19] The decree further stipulated that a village Ejido Executive Committee be formed to petition for land and to redistribute the land granted. Repeating these provisions, Article 27 of the 1917 Constitution specifically stressed the communal character of the ejido: It "shall have legal capacity to enjoy common possession of the lands, forests, and waters. . . ." Both the 1915 decree and the 1917 Constitution, however, were unclear as to whether the ejido was a governing institution among all recipients of land, and were unspecific as to its organization. The first major law on ejidos, the Ley de Ejido of December 28, 1920, was not helpful either. It remained for an administrative regulation of the National Agrarian Commission, Circular 51 of October 11, 1922, to set forth the guiding principles. According to this circular, "ejido villages must be organized along strictly cooperative and communal lines," namely: "distribution of profits in proportion to work contributed; . . . equal rights for members . . . following the formula: 'one member one vote' "; and the right of one-fifth of the membership to exercise the privileges of initiative, referendum, and recall. Each ejido was to establish an administrative committee of three members as its governing authority.[20] In 1925, the Law of Ejido Patrimony was enacted which deemphasized the collectivist character of the ejido by allowing most ejidatarios to work individually on separate plots rather than to farm on a collective basis. This law, slightly modified several times afterwards and then absorbed successively by the agrarian codes of 1934 and 1942, laid down the basic framework of the ejido organization, which remains largely unchanged to this day.

As the system now stands, a minimum of twenty individuals eligible to receive land, usually heads of families, may form an ejido. Each ejido consists of a general assembly, an executive committee (comisariado ejidal), and a vigilance committee (consejo de vigilancia). The general assembly, consisting of all ejido members, is empowered to elect and remove the members of the executive and vigilance committees, to approve the decisions of the executive committee, and to rule upon matters relating to commonly held ejidal lands. The executive committee, comprising three

[19] Quoted in ibid., pp. 56–57.
[20] Quoted in ibid., pp. 319–320.

members and three alternates elected for three-year terms, is responsible for the management of the *ejido* farms. The vigilance committee, also consisting of three members elected for three-year terms, watches over the activities of the executive committee to ensure that the latter complies with governmental agrarian regulations and carries out the General Assembly decisions.

Since the beginning of the Mexican land redistribution program several decades ago, the *ejido* system has been gradually extended to all parts of Mexico. With all land recipients required to become members, the *ejido* system accounts for about 44 percent of the cultivated area of Mexico and over 53 percent of all farm families.[21]

The *ejido* is of two types: individual and collective. The former, covering over 95 percent of the *ejido* land, is characterized by commmunal ownership of land, individual operation of separate plots, and centralized credit and marketing. The land worked by *ejidatarios* cannot be "alienated, ceded, transferred, leased, mortgaged or otherwise encumbered wholly or in part (Article 138 of the 1942 Agrarian Code)." The collective *ejido*, covering less than 5 percent of the *ejido* land, requires joint farming of undivided land. It requires total collectivization of farming operations from planting and harvesting to marketing of crops. The profits are distributed among *ejidatarios* in the form of money income or social benefits or both, in proportion to their work. These two types of *ejido* are organized similarly, except that the collective *ejido* maintains a foreman and several assistants (appointed by the General Assembly) who manage the daily operation of the farm. Both types of *ejido* receive government financial and other assistance through *ejidal* banks and other public institutions.

The *ejido* system was initially thought to have created a genuine cooperative organization which combined rational land use with experimentation in rural democracy. As an institution created by and closely iden-

---

[21] In 1950, there were 17,579 *ejidos* with 1,552,926 farm families (53.2 percent of the total farm families) and 39 million hectares of farm land (about 44 percent of the total farm land). In 1960, the *ejidos* increased to 19,220 with 2,169,485 families and 50.2 million hectares of land. The proportions of *ejido* families and land remained substantially the same in 1960 and in 1950. The cited information is derived from James G. Maddox, "Mexican Land Reform," *American Universities Field Staff Reports*, Vol. 4, No. 5 (July 3, 1957), pp. 17, 19; and Mexico, Secretaría de Agricultura y Ganadería, et al., *Projections of Supply and Demand for Agricultural and Livestock Products in Mexico to 1970 and 1975* (Mexico City, 1965), p. 161; and Inter-American Committee for Agricultural Development, *Inventory of Information Basic to the Planning of Agricultural Development in Latin America: Mexico* (Washington, D.C.: Pan-American Union, 1964), p. 51.

tified with the Mexican revolution, the *ejido* has profoundly changed the agrarian structure of Mexico. It has definitely eliminated the feudalistic *hacienda* system; it has converted millions of former serf-like peasants into free and secure landholders. As Jesús Silva Herzog observed: When the Mexican peasant

> was a peon on the hacienda, his opinion counted for nothing in the politics of his locality or of the State, and even less nationally. [But] since the agrarian reform he is obliged to take part in elections of the Ejidal Comisariado and of the Vigilance Committee of the ejido [and] to manage it and defend its interests; he may become part of the directive mechanism; is a member of the General Assembly . . . ; is affiliated with the National Peasant Confederation . . . ; and he can vote in favor of those who guarantee the maintenance of an agrarian policy of economic and social progress.[22]

It has created a democratic framework for rural organization, and the *ejidatarios* have, on the whole, manifested interest in participating in its operations.[23] Directly and indirectly, it has significantly contributed to the agricultural expansion of Mexico in recent decades.

However, after half a century of existence the *ejido* shows signs of weakening. Its towering façade cannot hide the strains of its internal structure. Today, the *ejido* has raised farming efficiency, production, and income, but its economic performance cannot match that of the medium-sized private farm.[24] Though the *ejido* elects its own managerial staff, the actual operation of the farm, from planting of crops to marketing of pro-

---

[22] *El Agrarismo Mexicano y la Reforma Agraria* (México—B.A., Fondo de Cultura Económica, 1959), pp. 327–328. Quoted in Lowry Nelson, "Some Social Aspects of Agrarian Reform in Mexico, Bolivia and Venezuela" (Washington, D.C.: Pan American Union, 1964; mimeo.), p. 68.

[23] While it is known that certain *ejidatarios* have lost interest in the activities of their organizations, most *ejidatarios*, experienced observers agree, attend *ejido* meetings with regularity and participate in discussions with eagerness. Clarence Senior noted that in his visit to the Laguna region he "has attended many elections of *ejido* officials. He was accompanied at two by the president of the Farmers' Union of a midwestern state [of the United States]. 'If I had one-tenth of my membership able to conduct meetings in such a responsible manner and participate with such wisdom,' said the official after the second meeting, 'I would have the most important farmers' organization in the United States.' The writer [Senior] has been similarly impressed at the overwhelming majority of the meetings he attended." *Land Reform and Democracy* (Gainesville, Fla., 1958), p. 187. Cf. Henrik F. Infield and Koka Freier, *People in Ejidos* (New York, 1954), *passim*.

[24] An analysis of the record of production in *ejido* and non-*ejido* lands will be provided in the next chapter.

duce, is greatly under the influence of the *ejidal* bank, whose supply of credit keeps the farm going. With this external control, many *ejidatarios* have lost the feeling of independence, becoming, in fact, workers for the bank.[25] In the individual *ejidos*, the small size of the plots causes diseconomies of scale, making it difficult to modernize farming. The prohibition of renting and selling of land punishes the industrious farmers by preventing them from acquiring more land, and tolerates the wasteful use of land by the indolent. The lack of title by many *ejidatarios* engenders a sense of insecurity and prevents them from easy access to government credit.

In the collective *ejidos*, the organizational defects are even more pronounced. As reviewed by Nathan L. Whetten, there is, first of all, "the lack of adequately trained local leadership" with the kind of managerial and technical competence necessary for operating a large cooperative farm. Secondly, there is the problem of discipline. As managers and foremen are elected and removed by majority vote, they tend to sacrifice efficiency for popularity. Since "each *ejidatario* has the right to share permanently in the use of the land and can be deprived of this right only by presidential decree, . . . it is difficult to require that he perform the task actually assigned to him if he decides to do something else instead." And there are other problems, such as the sharing of profits without regard to differences in work, widespread and persistent internal dissension, the lack of a sense of landownership and, hence, the absence of incentives for increasing production.[26]

The low productivity and organizational deficiencies of the *ejido* are widely acknowledged facts, and the fate of the *ejido* has long been a matter

[25] Since its creation in 1936, the *Ejidal Banco*, because of frequent payment defaults by *ejidatarios*, often operated at a huge loss. From 1936 to 1960 it loaned a total of ₱8,536,649,000 with a loss of ₱2,063,750,000. Emilio Romero Espinosa, *La Reforma Agraria en México: A Medio Siglo de Iniciada* (Mexico: Cuadernos Americanos, 1963), p. 111. To insure recovery of its loans, the bank has instituted rigid control over the operation of the *ejidos*, particularly the collective ones. Usually, in extending a loan the bank requires the *ejidatarios* to plant specified crops, periodically inspects the farm operations, and receives a portion of the harvest as repayment for loans. "The peasants will soon learn," Clarence Senior has commented, "they have exchanged their old bosses for a single new one. And the new one will be impersonal and heartless." *Op. cit.*, p. 97. See also *The New York Times*, June 9, 1966, p. 14.

[26] See Nathan Whetten, *Rural Mexico* (Chicago, 1948), pp. 212–214. Cf. Michael Belshaw, *A Village Economy: Land and People of Huecorio* (New York: Columbia University Press, 1966), pp. 22–23. For a summation of problems of the *ejidos*, see Rodolfo Stavenhagen, "Social Aspects of Agrarian Structure in Mexico," *Social Research*, XXXIII (Autumn 1966), 469–477.

of official concern. Differences within the revolutionary elite over the direction of development of the *ejido* occurred as early as in 1925 when the Law of *Ejido* Patrimony was enacted. But it was the celebrated interview in 1933 between former President Plutarco Elías Calles and Ezequiel Padilla that initiated a formal debate between what Eyler Simpson has called the *veteranos* and the *agraristas*, the two factions within the elite respectively opposing and supporting the *ejido*. Calles, speaking for the *veteranos*, conceded that it was necessary to break up the large estates, and regarded the creation of the *ejidos* as "one of the most solemn promises of the Revolution." But he believed that the creation of the *ejido* was a transitory step leading to the creation of family farms. If provided with holdings larger in size then the *ejido* parcels, these farms would better utilize modern farming techniques, induce the enterprising farmers to increase production, and hence be much more suited to the needs of Mexico. He proposed to end—in the presidential term of Cárdenas—further creation of *ejidos* and to concentrate on establishing family farms.[27]

The *agraristas*, while agreeing with the *veteranos* on the failure of the *ejido* system, claimed that the system had not functioned well because of the lack of full acceptance of "the principle of socialization of the land." The continual existence of private farms and the advocacy of the reversion of *ejido* land to individual ownership were evidence that Mexican agrarian policy was, in practice, antagonistic to this principle. To the *agraristas*, the collective interests of the nation should take precedence over individual profits, and the "false capitalistic concept of free competition" should be supplanted by "the concept of social necessity." They contended further that the *ejido*, with its implicit principle of egalitarianism, was the institution closely identified with the agrarian revolution, something that had to be defended at all costs. This institution had prevented the recurrence of land concentration and, with it, economic exploitation. They suggested that the *ejido* system be universally established to replace all private holdings, and that land redistribution be speeded up.[28]

Much of the substance of these arguments has been repeated in subsequent debates on the role of the *ejido*, and there may have been, at times, a polarization of views. Jorge Vera Estañol, for example, wrote in the mid-1950s, "We have condemned with all the force of our convictions the appearance of the medieval institution of the *ejido*. The communal form

[27] Simpson, *op. cit.*, pp. 440–442. See also Whetten, *op. cit.*, pp. 126–127.
[28] See Simpson, *op. cit.*, pp. 442–451.

of property creates neither interest in nor love for the land, the fundamental basis of agriculture. . . . *The ejido must be destroyed.*" [29] In defending the *ejido* system, Cárdenas, who created a larger number of *ejidos* than any other Mexican president, expressed the view, in 1952, that the *ejido* system was a valuable, dynamic institution with a capacity to correct its own minor organizational difficulties. The real rural problem of Mexico was the lack of land, credit, and water. Nothing short of the extension of the *ejido* system to the whole country could solve Mexico's farm problems.[30]

These debates aside, the *ejido* system has, in fact, become a stagnant social institution holding half of the Mexican farming population to a subsistence level. Yet, because the *ejido* is regarded as the heart of the Mexican revolution, "an end in itself and an institution in its own right," [31] the government has neither found it politically feasible to abolish the system nor devised means to reinvigorate it. The government seems to have taken the expedient course of aiding the more productive middle-sized private landowners by expanding rural public works, leaving the present state of the *ejido* undisturbed. This policy has had the effect of accentuating the income disparity between the *ejido* and prosperous private farmers. It may, of course, further weaken the *ejido* system. Working on tiny pieces of land under less than favorable conditions, many *ejidatarios* have illegally rented out their land or abandoned it altogether.[32]

Indian and Mexican experiences with cooperative farming indicate that, despite high official expectation, joint cultivation of land is, in fact, not practiced on any large scale, that economic advantages expected of the cooperative farm are not realized, that the internal organization is

---

[29] Jorge Vera Estañol, "The Results of the Revolution," in Stanley R. Ross (ed.), *Is the Mexican Revolution Dead?* (New York: Alfred A. Knopf, 1966), p. 214 (original italics).

[30] See Infield and Freier, *op. cit.*, pp. 146–150.

[31] Simpson, *op. cit.* (n. 17 above), p. 450.

[32] For a series of revealing reports on this subject, see the dispatches by Henry Giniger in *The New York Times*, May 5, 6, 13, 16, 17, 26, 29, 1966; and June 8, 9, 11, 1966. "In the state of Sinoloa," Giniger reported in one dispatch, "a member of one organization of small farmers said the proportion of ejido farmers who had abandoned their holdings to landowners might be as high as 70 per cent (May 17, 1966)." In another dispatch he wrote, "Even in areas where the land is well irrigated and highly productive, the ejidos present a problem. . . . [In] the southern part of the state of Sonora, Mexico's biggest wheat and cotton producer, it is estimated that half the ejido lands there have been illegally rented to private farmers (June 9, 1966)."

defective, that members of the cooperative have no incentive for increasing production, and that private landowners have no desire to join the system.

The unsatisfactory performances of the Indian and Mexican cooperative systems, however, should not obscure two important differences between them. First, in the Indian cooperative society the lumping together of all types of farmers and the resulting dominance of the society by the larger landowners constitute an inherent deterrence to the very aim that the society attempts to attain—cooperation among its own members. In the Mexican *ejido*, all members possess equal social status and the same rights within the cooperative. None can dominate or exploit the other. The primary source of discontent lies perhaps less in the internal arrangements of the cooperative than in the *ejido's* perennial dependent relationship on an external agent, the *ejidal* bank. Secondly, the Indian cooperative system was created because of the appeal of the cooperative idea to the policy makers, rather than because of the yearnings of farmers. Covering only a tiny fraction of the country's rural land, and having no genuine support either within the system or the government, the Indian system is incapable of creating an identity of its own and has not shown a prospect for sustained growth. Its future remains uncertain. On the other hand, the Mexican *ejido* was created in response to the insistent demands of Mexican farmers, violently expressed through the Zapata movement. With all the beneficiaries of Mexico's very extensive land redistribution program as members, the *ejido* system has grown to enormous size within the Mexican agrarian structure. Despite all its weaknesses, the *ejido* remains a secure institution. With two and a half million *ejidatarios* as its staunchest defenders, the system can only be improved, but not abolished.

Neither the government nor the *ejidatarios* can remain indifferent for too long to the present state of the *ejido*. Some innovations are possible. The government may have to increase its aid to the *ejido* in the form of expansion of irrigation facilities, supply of fertilizers, and credit. The *ejidatarios* may have to readjust their agricultural pattern so as to combine individual incentive with some joint farming. In a limited way, this has taken place. In the Laguna region in central Mexico, Clarence Senior has reported, many collective *ejidos* have changed into a mixed system, under which the *ejidatarios* work collectively only from the beginning of the agricultural season to the stage of crop planting; they subsequently work on individual plots chosen by lot. The *ejidatarios* receive wages for work in the first period, and in the second period, in crops they actually produce. "In this way," an *ejidatario* in La Partida, Laguna explained,

> at the time of harvest, each man reaped his just reward without being required to toil for the indifferent or indolent. . . . Human nature is what it is, and always will be. In a collective system if a man does not feel like working, well and good. But then what? The group suffers. In a mixed system, on the contrary, if a man does not feel like working, it is he, and he alone, who pays the price for it, and no one else. In a collective system one man may work sixty-five days and another only thirty. Should they both in the end receive the same share? [33]

Senior cited estimates indicating that 95 percent of the *ejidos* of the Laguna region operated on this basis.[34] Other authors reported that this mixed system had won the tacit approval of the government.[35]

THE EGYPTIAN MODEL

The Laguna experiment in Mexico is a pragmatic innovation by the *ejidatarios* with neither official sponsorship nor doctrinal justification. Its significance is that it demonstrates the feasibility of the mixed cooperative. It is now appropriate to examine a third model of cooperative farming: the Egyptian supervised cooperative system. For it offers convincing proof that a mixed cooperative system is not only experimentally feasible but can be adopted on a broad scale with considerable success. The Egyptian cooperative may yet be one of the more promising models to which the agricultural patterns of other developing countries may profitably adapt.

In Egypt, all beneficiaries of the land redistribution program were required to join the integrated cooperative societies. The activities of these societies range from the supply of inputs, rural extension, credit, and marketing to joint farming. With an average membership of 300 farmers, and normally covering about 1,000 *feddans* of land, an Egyptian cooperative society in the land-reform area elects its own administrative board and

---

[33] Infield and Freier, *op. cit.*, pp. 136–137.

[34] *Op. cit.* (n. 23 above), p. 113.

[35] Infield and Freier, *op. cit.*, p. 137. For a recent study of the economic performance of the *ejidos* in Laguna, including the mixed system, see Shlomo Eckstein, "Collective Farming in Mexico, the Case of the Laguna," in Rodolfo Stavenhagen (ed.), *Agrarian Problems and Peasant Movements in Latin America* (Garden City, N.Y.: Doubleday & Company, 1970), pp. 290ff.

appoints its own *mushrif ta'awuni* (manager). The manager and his administrative and technical staff, in reality selected and controlled by the Cooperative Administration in the Ministry of Agrarian Reform, are responsible for the operations of the farm. The most notable feature of the cooperative society is the compulsory triennial rotation of crops. Land of a society is consolidated into compact blocks; each block is divided into three large *tagmi'a* (fields); each cooperative member receives a piece of land in each of the three fields; and one field is planted with one type of crop, the second with another, and the third left fallow. The rotation takes place continuously so that three crops can be grown in a two-year cycle. The society decides, through its manager, the pattern of crop rotation, field layout, and the allocation of farm equipment. Farmers work collectively in ploughing, applying fertilizers and pesticide, watering, and harvesting, while each cultivator is responsible for his own pieces of land in sowing, weeding, hoeing, and daily care. Crops are marketed partly by the society and partly by the farmers themselves. Initially limited only to cotton, the crops marketed by the society now include cereals, fibers, vegetables, fruit, and flowers. Unlike collective farms in other countries where labor input is the basis of compensation, the Egyptian cooperative farm pays each individual member according to his actual output.

In 1959, 312 cooperative societies in land-reform areas were organized, covering nearly 520,000 *feddans* (218,452 hectares) of land; by July 1966, the number of societies had grown to 565 with 303,624 members.[36] The system registered a striking success. It must be recalled that Egyptian soil was extremely productive before land reform;[37] hence, some feared a major alteration of land tenure might lead to a sharp decline in production. But in the post-reform period, with a temporary decrease of production in certain former large estates, the overall production of the cooperative farms has been on the rise. Between 1952 and 1959, cotton production rose by 45 percent in cooperative areas, as compared to a 15

[36] M. Riad El Ghonemy, "Economic and Institutional Organization of Egyptian Agriculture Since 1952," in P. J. Vatikiotis (ed.), *Egypt Since the Revolution* (New York: Frederick A. Praeger, Publishers, 1968), p. 71.

[37] "The Nile valley holds the world's land productivity record. Cropping rates are high. . . . On four-fifths of the land (the area perennially irrigated) three crops a year can be harvested, though in fact the average cropping rate is five crops in two years. Yields are high, the cotton yield being the world's highest and maize yield as high as the United States level, while wheat yields are comparatively low, though they exceed the European average." Doreen Warriner, *Land Reform and Development in the Middle East* (London, 1962), p. 19.

percent rise for Egypt as a whole.[38] The performance of the cooperative system must be considered unusually successful.

The success of the supervised cooperative system in land-reform areas has led the government to extend the system to non-reform areas. In 1956, the government undertook a pilot project in Nawag, a non-reform area with an acute land fragmentation problem, to consolidate the land into large blocks. Instead of holding several plots in different blocks, as in the reform areas, farmers in Nawag grouped all their land within one block. Triennial rotation farming was practiced; farmers exchanged with each other the crop they needed but did not grow. The project led to an impressive rise of yield. Average net income of farmers rose by roughly 50 percent one year after the beginning of the project, and yield of all corps averaged at least 20 percent higher than that of the neighboring small holdings. By 1960, 103 villages had adopted the scheme. In 1959, the government also extended membership of the supervised cooperatives to all small owner-farmers in the vicinity of reform areas.[39]

Many factors have contributed to the success of the Egyptian system. The government's readiness to extend low-interest credit, the fairness of the marketing process, and the dedication of the farmers are all very important. But two other reasons for the success appear more fundamental. The first relates to organizational principles. The cooperative system combines the efficiency of large-scale farming with the incentive of the family farm. It offers a major solution to the problem of land fragmentation, while preserving small ownership in a large farm area. Moreover, by relating reward directly to output, the Egyptian system provides a strong stimulus to farmers for increasing production. As Doreen Warriner has summarized so succinctly: the system "reconciles individual incentive and the growth of cooperative spirit with large scale operation." [40] The second reason concerns the "skilled management" of the agrarian reform administration. The administrative and technical personnel operating the cooperative societies were generally competent and efficient.[41]

The Egyptian supervised cooperative system, however, suffers from one principal disadvantage. The attempt to create a self-reliant peasantry has not been entirely successful. Instead of being subservient to landlords,

[38] *Ibid.*, pp. 201–202.

[39] For details of the Nawag project, see Gabriel S. Saab, *The Egyptian Agrarian Reform, 1952–1962* (London, 1967), pp. 190–196.

[40] *Op. cit.*, p. 203.

[41] *Ibid.*, and Keith Wheelock, *Nasser's New Egypt* (New York, 1960), pp. 92–93.

members of the system are now dependent upon the state. With its management under government control, the system enjoys neither internal autonomy nor external independence. But, on balance, the Egyptian cooperative, as one observer has put it, "stands out as one of the most positive contributions to the general theory of agrarian structure." [42] The system can reap the benefits of joint farming without suffering from its disadvantages. The compulsory character of the system and the dominance of the government in its management may well be the critical condition that assured it a successful beginning. As General Mohammed Naguib has pointed out:

> Our co-operative programme is said to smack of authoritarianism. Perhaps it does, but who but the Government in Egypt is able and willing to take measures necessary to ensure the land reform's success. . . . It can be argued that compulsion and cooperation are contradictory concepts, and that cooperatives, ideally, should be voluntary associations. Given the deplorable conditions of life in Egyptian villages, however, the distinction between compulsion and co-operation is irrelevant. The average *felláh* has fallen too low to be able to help himself without a great deal of compulsory assistance from the Government. . . .[43]

In the long run, however, the maintenance of the system's vitality probably depends as much on the profitability of its undertakings as on state paternalism. The demonstrable benefits that the system can bring to its membership form the cement tying them together and the force driving them to exert ever greater efforts in their work. This fact explains, at least partially, why the Egyptian cooperative is vigorous and expanding and why the Mexican *ejido* is relatively stagnant, even though governmental intervention in internal operation is evident in both systems.

Designating the Egyptian cooperative system as an "individualistic" oriented model, as distinct from a strictly collective cooperative, one expert on the cooperative movement contends that the Egyptian system may best suit the agricultural needs of a developing country such as India.[44] In the opinion of another specialist, the Egyptian cooperative system shows basically similar features to the highly successful Israeli cooperative

---

[42] Saab, *op. cit.*, p. 79.

[43] Mohammed Naguib and Leigh White, *Egypt's Destiny* (New York, 1955), pp. 166–167.

[44] Otto Schiller, "Two Ways of Cooperative Farming," *Indian Journal of Agricultural Economics*, XVII (April-June 1962), 50–53.

farms.[45] In fact, one can argue that Israel's cooperative farm system is better organized but less applicable to other developing countries than the Egyptian. Israeli cooperatives are socially and economically integrated institutions organized largely on a voluntary basis; they enjoy almost complete independence from the government. But they were created under rather unique conditions. First, Israeli farmers were immigrants who obtained and operated their land in a hostile environment. They had to maintain a high degree of internal cohesion in order to survive. Second, Jewish culture may be said to exhibit a strong strain of communal solidarity, thus favoring group activity. Finally, many Israeli immigrants are ideologically attuned to the socialist way of production.[46] These conditions generally do not exist in the developing countries; hence the applicability of the Israeli cooperative experiences to these countries is much limited.

Among the three models of cooperative farming examined in this chapter, the Indian system appears to be merely an aspiration that has vaporized; the Mexican system is an institution large in size but weak in structure; the Egyptian system appears to be the only one that deserves imitation by other countries.

Public Land Settlement

Like cooperative farming, public land settlement (or colonization) is an attractive idea. To settle people on new land and to develop it for agricultural use does not involve any basic alteration of the property rights of existing landowners; hence a public-land-settlement program will generate no opposition from the landed class. The program may yield a number of important benefits, such as the alleviation of population pressure from congested rural areas, the expansion of farm acreage, and increased agricultural production. In fact, farmers in many developing countries, driven by poverty and land shortage, have already moved spontaneously into unsettled areas and engaged in colonization out of their own resources. But since spontaneous colonization cannot be undertaken on a large scale

[45] Melvin Albaum, "Cooperative Agricultural Settlement in Egypt and Israel," *Land Economics*, LXII (May 1966), 221–225.

[46] For descriptions of some of these conditions, see A. Granott, *Agrarian Reform and the Record of Israel* (London: Eyre & Spottiswoode, 1956), chap. i, "Land as the Basis of the Upbuilding"; and Haim Halperin, *Changing Patterns in Israel Agriculture* (London: Routledge and Kegan Paul, 1957), pp. 201–205ff.

and since it frequently creates conflicts over land titles and entails un-economical use of resources, it cannot substitute for a publicly planned and publicly directed land settlement program.

However, as soon as land settlement is adopted as part of a compre-hensive land-reform system, much of its attractiveness is lost. Many land-lords who support the program in the belief that it may be a substitute—or substantially alleviate the need—for land redistribution soon find such a belief unfounded, and their enthusiasm for the program disappears. In reality, of course, the landed class is never genuinely interested in a full-scale public land settlement program, either as a supplement or as an alternative to land redistribution. For such a program is bound to require considerable public funds, to which the landed class and other vested interests are not willing to contribute. Aside from the lack of genuine political support, a program faces a number of serious difficulties. There are such essential pre-settlement tasks as land surveys; soil analysis; the selection of enterprising, cooperative settlers among the poor farmers, who are known to be passive and fatalistic; and the creation of a rudimentary rural infrastructure. Most developing countries simply do not have the administrative and financial capacity to undertake all these technically demanding and time-consuming tasks.

TAIWAN AND THE U.A.R.

Despite these difficulties, five of the countries studied have tried to institute land-settlement programs as a part of their reform effort. Among these countries, Taiwan and the U.A.R. have a limited area of undeveloped agricultural land and both countries have conceived their land-settlement projects merely as extensions of their land-redistribution programs. Long after the conclusion of the land-to-the-tiller program, Taiwan tried to de-velop its tidal land along the island's west coast. If fully developed, this land could accommodate some 30,000 farm families of 180,000 people.[47] After successfully undertaking a demonstration project in Hsinchu County in 1961, the government decided to develop up to 16,900 hectares of tidal land. The Taiwan Land Development Corporation, a public corporation created in December 1964, was put in charge of the program. The devel-oped land was distributed to participating farmers in accordance with the appropriate provisions of the land-to-the-tiller programs. The corpora-

[47] Kiang Hung, "Tidal Land Development and Planning," *Land Reform Monthly* (in Chinese), XII (June 1962), 19; and *Central Daily News* (Taipei, Taiwan), June 18, 1963, p. 3, and December 22, 1963, p. 4.

tion's first project, covering 1,600 hectares of land, was in Tainan County. In addition to the tidal land projects, development of mountain land began in 1961, when the Provincial Mountain Resources Development Bureau was created to formulate a comprehensive developmental program. The program made a modest start in 1964 by designating for reclamation 8,496 hectares of hilly land in 16 counties and municipalities.[48] The government also sought to develop animal husbandry on Taiwan's slope land. To this end, the government concluded with the United Nations Special Fund in January 1965 a five-year technical assistance agreement, under which the United Nations was to contribute US$880,200 to help formulate developmental plans.[49] The developed mountain land was to be distributed to farmers according to the appropriate provisions of the early land-redistribution program.

In the U.A.R., colonization efforts are directed at the reclamation of land in desert areas and along the Nile Valley. Three government agencies —the Egyptian General Organisation for Land Rehabilitation, the Egyptian General Organisation for the Rehabilitation of the Deserts, and the Egyptian General Organisation for Land Reclamation—are in charge of these projects. The first two agencies engage directly in colonization activities, while the third purchases land developed by private land development companies. In addition, there is a separate project for Al-Tahrir (Liberation) Province. The reclamation projects are scattered in Upper and Lower Egypt; in general, reclaimed land is distributed to beneficiaries according to the land redistribution program of 1952. As of November 1963, these projects achieved the results shown in Table 18.

COLOMBIA

Unlike Taiwan and the U.A.R., where undeveloped agricultural land is quite limited, Colombia, the Philippines (and, at one time, Mexico) possess quite extensive uncultivated arable areas. In Colombia, along the Cauca and Magdalena River valleys, there are potentially fertile fields yet to be converted into farms. In addition, the vast *Llanos Orientales* (Eastern Plains) remain practically untouched. This is a region covering nearly two-thirds of Colombia's total territory but with less than 0.02 percent

---

[48] *Central Daily News*, September 15, 1964, p. 4.

[49] *Ibid.*, January 29, 1965, p. 2, and January 30, 1965, p. 3. For an assessment of the prospect for the development of Taiwan's mountain land by a JCRR consultant, see Randolph Barker, "Development of the Slopeland Region of Taiwan" (Taipei, Taiwan: JCRR, 1963; mimeo.).

TABLE 18

DISTRIBUTION OF RECLAIMED LAND IN THE U.A.R.

As of November 1963

Name	Area (in feddans)	Number of beneficiaries
Land Rehabilitation Organisation	4,441 (1,786 ha.)	893
Desert Rehabilitation Organisation	18,762 (7,544 ha.)	3,924
Land Reclamation Organisation	56,610 (22,763 ha.)	18,354
Al-Tahrir Province	8,953 (3,600 ha.)	1,247
Total	88,766	24,418

SOURCE: U.A.R., *Agrarian Reform and Land Reclamation in Eleven Years* (Cairo [1963]), pp. 40–41.

of the country's population, as of the early 1960s.[50] Stretching eastward to Venezuela and southward to Brazil and Peru, this area of vast mountain slopes, broad rivers, grasslands, and forests contains, according to one estimate, "not less than ten million forested hectares with good soil, suitable for agricultural purposes." [51]

In these and other parts of Colombia, most of the undeveloped land lies in the public domain, and the government has made many attempts to colonize these areas. There were numerous programs in the last century to encourage colonization by immigrants;[52] but the country's current colonization effort started in 1948 when, in the aftermath of the infamous Bogotá riots, the Institute of Colonization, Parcelization, and Forest Defense was created. Launched with fanfare and enthusiasm, the institute soon found itself incapable of developing new land on any large scale, as it lacked both funds and personnel to engage in preparatory and developmental

[50] Pat M. Holt, *Colombia Today—and Tomorrow* (New York, 1964), pp. 2–3.

[51] U.N., Economic Commission for Latin America, *Economic Development of Colombia* (*Analysis and Projection of Economic Development*, III) (Bogotá, 1955), pp. 71–72.

[52] From 1823 to 1870, Colombia adopted at least fifteen laws to make available land to foreigners, primarily Europeans and North Americans, for colonization and settlement. See T. Lynn Smith, *Colombia, Social Structure and the Process of Development* (Gainesville, Fla., 1967), pp. 98–101.

work. In 1953, after General Gustavo Rojas Pinilla seized power, a new agency was created absorbing the functions of the earlier institute. The Institute of Colonization and Immigration, reviving the efforts of the last century to attract Europeans to settle on Colombia's public land, "formulated ambitious and expensive plans for setting up 'colonization centers.' " But "under inexperienced management, with hardly any prior study, the Institute plunged into several colonization ventures, built airstrips, bought machinery to set up sawmills, brought volunteer settlers to work poor soils in inhospitable climates and . . . met with total disaster." [53] The intended European beneficiaries of the colonization program did not become land developers but urban residents instead; and the Institute made available only some 3,000 small farm plots to Colombian citizens during its brief period of existence.[54]

In 1956, the Institute was abolished, with the *Caja de Crédito Agrario, Industrial y Minero* (the Bank of Agricultural, Industrial, and Mining Credit, popularly known as the *Caja Agraria*) taking over its colonization activities. Law 20 of 1959 authorized the *Caja Agraria* to finance land-settlement projects through sales of bonds to commercial banks up to an amount equivalent to 10 percent of the banks' savings deposits. The *Caja Agraria* began its first land-settlement project along the valley of the Ariari River in the Department of Meta in the *Llanos Orientale*, and later expanded to include four other settlement areas. Attempting to operate these projects on a fully reimbursable basis, the *Caja Agraria* provided 50 hectares of land to each settler, who had to be a Colombian citizen between the ages of twenty-one and fifty-five and experienced or knowledgeable in agriculture. Farmers losing land during *la Violencia* were given preference in settlement areas. The settler was charged ₱2,500 for the price of the land, payable in ten years. The *Caja Agraria* provided the settler an initial loan of up to ₱5,000 and another ₱5,000 when the settler showed evidence of satisfactory performance and staying capacity. In the first two years of the Ariari project, the bank extended about ₱1.8 million in credit to 471 families (comprising 4,341 persons) and invested ₱3 million in physical facilities.[55] By late 1961, when *Caja Agraria* ceased to operate colonization projects, it had resettled about 2,000 families in five

---

[53] Albert O. Hirschman, *Journeys Toward Progress* (New York, 1963), p. 139.

[54] Robert C. Eidt, "Modern Colonization as a Facet of Land Development in Colombia, South America," *Yearbook of the Association of Pacific Coast Geographers*, Vol. 29, 1967, pp. 26–27.

[55] Holt, *op. cit.*, p. 79.

project areas; in contrast, 4,500 families had come as spontaneous settlers.[56] Instead of achieving financial self-sufficiency, the *Caja Agraria* projects appeared in the end to have incurred high public expense and few beneficial results.

Colombia's public land settlement experience up to the early 1960s showed a number of problems. Official commitment to the program was neither fully spelled out nor sustained for a long duration. The agencies created to administer the program were poorly organized, poorly prepared, and poorly financed to do the work. Moreover, in colonization areas the problem of title conflicts was widespread, causing, at times, armed clashes between squatters and pretentious landowners. Furthermore, many settlers worked on rather small pieces of land that could barely sustain life, while others could not endure the harsh conditions of the colonies and abandoned their plots to more prosperous neighbors. As a result, "a *minifundia-latifundia* appears to be developing in the colonization areas." [57] Finally, despite official encouragement and costly public assistance, settlers under government-administered projects were fewer and were less successful economically than the spontaneous settlers.

In 1961, Colombia made a fresh start at public land settlement. With the passage of the Social Agrarian Reform Act, INCORA was created, absorbing *Caja Agraria's* colonization program. The new land-reform organization is authorized to grant public land to individual farmers as well as to organized settlement projects. In making individual grants, INCORA can make available to each settler up to 450 hectares of land and, in special areas where accessibility is difficult and where soil is poor, up to 3,000 hectares (Articles 29 and 30). In organized settlement areas, INCORA is to grant land that is easily accessible and "suitable . . . for small scale crop-farming, and stock-breeding." In these areas, the agency is to maintain "reserve zones" where such community facilities as demonstration farms, schools, health centers, and agricultural services may be established. INCORA shall sell land to small-scale settlers but grant land free to "poor or relatively poor workers" to create family farms (*unidades agrícolas familiares*) (Article 45).

In spite of these legal provisions, INCORA, conscious of the costly failures of past colonization ventures, decided from the beginning to

---

[56] *Ibid.*, p. 82.

[57] For a description of these problems, see Joseph R. Thome, "Title Problems in Rural Areas of Colombia," *Inter-American Economic Affairs*, XIX (Winter 1965), 84, 93, and 96–97. Quotation appears on p. 96.

sponsor no more new colonization projects. Instead, it has concentrated on assisting the ongoing public land-settlement projects and private spontaneous colonization activities through the building of access roads and irrigation facilities, the extension of credit, and the award of land titles.[58] According to Robert C. Eidt, as of 1967 there were six INCORA land settlement projects (in Caquetá, Ariari, Sarare, El Lebrija, Carare, and Galilea), most of which had been initiated by the *Caja Agraria*. These settlement projects operated within an aggregate area of 1,231,125 hectares, but only 4000 families have obtained titles to their land. "An estimated 40,000 to 50,000 'spontaneous' families have arrived on their own in these official colonization zones." [59]

Colombia's experiences with colonization definitely indicate that for some time to come land settlement cannot in any way alleviate the need for meaningful land redistribution. In the words of a report of the Colombian National Agrarian Committee:

> It is frequently said that the possibility of occupying public domain lands . . . makes it unnecessary to utilize, for the purpose of carrying out the agrarian social reform, lands that are today in private hands. The most superficial analysis would be sufficient to dissipate so erroneous an opinion. . . . The cost of colonization is extremely high and the obstacles . . . notorious. . . . We do not ignore the large contribution it can make but it is evident for us that the social-agrarian reform could not be confined within its limits.[60]

THE PHILIPPINES

Like Colombia, the Philippines possesses quite extensive potentially arable public land. Vast underpopulated areas exist on such islands as Palawan, Mindoro, and Mindanao. For some time, colonization on these islands has been strongly recommended as a means of reducing the need

---

[58] Colombia, INCORA, *Informe de Actividades en 1963*, p. 57, and *Informe de Actividades, 1964* (Bogotá 1964), pp. 3–4.

[59] Eidt, *op. cit.*, p. 30. How much farm land was actually assigned to the settlers—government-directed or spontaneous—is not known.

[60] Quoted in Ernest A. Duff, *Agrarian Reform in Colombia* (New York, 1968), p. 101. Similarly, in assessing Colombia's economic plan, the Organization of American States specifically cautioned Colombia against large-scale colonization. The O.A.S. only endorsed public assistance to colonization projects in areas where infrastructure already existed. Organization of American States, Ad Hoc Committee to Study the General Program of Economic and Social Development of Colombia, *Evaluation of the General Economic and Social Development Program of Colombia: Report . . .* , July 1962 (Washington, D.C., 1962), p. 158.

for redistribution of existing farms, of relieving population pressure from Luzon, and of expanding agricultural acreage. Mindanao, the second largest island in the nation, has been particularly attractive to colonists. Nine-tenths the size of Luzon (the largest island of the Phillippines) but with only half its population, Mindanao possesses broad plains, many rivers, and a rather evenly distributed rainfall—the kind of conditions appropriate for agricultural pursuits. The government's land-settlement program in Mindanao started in 1913, and within four years seven colonies were established; but none was successful. Many colonists moved elsewhere or returned to their home towns. Cautioned by this initial failure, the government limited subsequent colonization operations to the provision of free transportation to selected qualified settlers without giving them financial assistance. From 1918 to 1939, the colonization program was administered by the Inter-island Migration Division of the Bureau of Labor. Again the program failed to achieve any significant result. "By 1936, only 30,000 to 35,000 persons remained in the government's agricultural colonies in Mindanao." [61] In 1939, the National Land Settlement Administration (NLSA) was created to coordinate colonization projects. With its activities suspended during the Second World War, NLSA had resettled a total of 8,300 families by 1950, when the agency was replaced by the Land Settlement and Development Corporation (LASEDECO). This new agency succeeded in resettling 1,500 families before it was superseded by the National Resettlement and Rehabilitation Administration (NARRA) in 1954. During its tenure, from 1954 to 1963, NARRA administered a total of 23 projects—including those established by the previous agencies—in Mindanao, Palawan, and other scattered areas. These projects covered roughly 161,500 hectares of land and 30,686 families. Only half of the settlers moved to the settlement areas under the sponsorship of the government, and the rest came by themselves. The results of all these government organized settlement projects are summarized in Table 19.

Aside from the settlement projects sponsored by the civilian agencies, the Philippine army initiated a colonization program as part of its anti-Huk campaign. In 1951, the Economic Development Corps of the Armed Forces of the Philippines (EDCOR) was created to rehabilitate captured

---

[61] Frederick L. Wernstedt and Paul D. Simkins, "Migrations and the Settlement of Mindanao," *The Journal of Asian Studies,* XXV (November 1965), 88. See also Karl J. Pelzer, *Pioneer Settlement in the Asiatic Tropics: Studies in Land Utilization and Agricultural Colonization in Southeast Asia* (New York: American Geographical Society, Special Publication No. 29, 1945), p. 132.

TABLE 19

PUBLIC LAND SETTLEMENT PROJECTS IN THE PHILIPPINES, 1918–1963

Agency	Period	Families Resettled
Inter-island Migration Division, the Bureau of Labor	1918–1939	30,000 to 35,000 (persons)
National Land Settlement Administration	1939–1950	8,300
Land Settlement and Development Corporation	1950–1954	1,500
National Resettlement and Rehabilitation Administration	1954–1963	30,686

SOURCES: Frederick L. Wernstedt and Paul D. Simkins, "Migrations and the Settlement of Mindanao," *The Journal of Asian Studies*, XXV (November 1965), 92; and Robert E. Huke, *Shadows on the Land: an Economic Geography of the Philippines* (Manila: The Bookmark, Inc., 1963), p. 167.

and surrendered Communist guerrillas by settling them on public land. A brilliant idea implemented with considerable publicity, the rehabilitation program showed very meager results, as seen in Table 20. In eleven years of operation, EDCOR managed to resettle only 1,554 families on 8,892 hectares of land. The idea of rehabilitation of former Huks was, by and large, unrealized. In 1959, of the 1,046 settlers in EDCOR project areas only 221 were "ex-Huks." [62]

With the reform law enacted in 1963, the responsibility for resettlement of farmers was transferred to the newly created Land Authority and Land Bank. Under Article 3 of the law, the two agencies surveyed and made available suitable public agricultural land to small settlers; provided these settlers with transportation, a ten-year interest-free loan, farm equipment, supplies, housing facilities; and established community services. Public land could also be sold to large landowners whose lands had been expropriated for redistribution. To encourage development of large-scale farming of virgin land, a holder of agrarian bonds was allowed to purchase up to 144 hectares of public land in the case of individuals and up to 1,024 hectares in the case of corporations.

After the enactment of the 1963 reform law, little implementation of the colonization provisions took place. The lack of official interest in this

[62] Maynard Weston Dow, *Nation-Building in Southeast Asia* (Rev. ed.; Boulder, Colo.: Pruett Press, 1965), chap. iii, "EDCOR Resettlement Projects and the Philippine Huk Rebellion," Table 12, p. 124.

TABLE 20

EDCOR RESETTLEMENT PROJECTS, THE PHILIPPINES, 1951–1963

Project Name	Municipality, Province, Island	Year Founded	Cultivated Area (ha.)	Number of Families	Settler Population	Administrative Status as of 1963
Arevalo	Kapatagan, Lanao, Mindanao	1951	646	115	690	Civilian as of July 1, 1958
Gallego	Parang, Cotabato, Mindanao	1951	1,250	223	1,398	Army
Peredo	Angadanan, Isabela, Luzon	1953	390	75	450	Transferred to NARRA, July 1, 1958
Genio	Libungan, Cotabato, Mindanao	1954	6,602	1,070	6,420	Army
Tawi-Tawi	Balimbing, Sulu, Tawi-Tawi	1955	. . .	. . .	. . .	Abandoned Feb. 1, 1958
Catanauan	Catanauan, Quezon, Luzon	1963	4	71	426	Army
Total		—	8,892	1,554	9,384	—

SOURCE: Maynard Weston Dow, *Nation-Building in Southeast Asia* (Rev. ed.; Boulder, Colo.: Pruett Press, 1965), chap. iii, "EDCOR Resettlement Projects and the Philippine Huk Rebellion," Table 9, pp. 102–03.

aspect of land reform resulted from the government's deep dissatisfaction with past failures and from the absence of any public conviction that the new program could perform any better.

The difficulties the Philippine land settlement programs encountered are many and serious. Instances of land speculation were frequently reported: non-cultivators bought land at a nominal price from the government and left it idle; when the unknowing farmers occupied it and developed it into arable acreage, the original buyers would claim the land and reap all the benefits.[63] The goal of relieving population pressure from Central Luzon and other high-tenancy areas was not achieved. One estimate

[63] See David Wurfel, "Philippine Agrarian Reform under Magsaysay," *Far Eastern Survey*, XXVII (January 1958), 7–8; and Frank H. Golay, *The Philippines: Public Policy and National Economic Development* (Ithaca, N.Y.: Cornell University Press, 1961), p. 281.

indicated that in June 1955 only 37 percent of the settlers had come from high-tenancy provinces,[64] while another revealed, in the late 1950s, that "not more than perhaps 5 percent of the resettled families have originated from the overcrowded high tenancy areas of Central Luzon, the region at which the program was aimed." [65] Insofar as the resettlement projects in Mindanao are concerned, two authors commented in 1965: "Using the most liberal measures of the number of families resettled and the growth of families after settlement, less than 10 percent of the net migration to Mindanao can be accounted for by settlers in government-sponsored projects." [66] The idea of creating an all owner-farmer system in settlement areas was also not realized. Because of lack of credit and other difficulties, some settlers who had come as independent colonists later became tenants. For instance, "In Mindanao, in the area of Kidapawan alone, it has been found that of the tenants . . . settled in that area . . . 26 per cent have reverted to share tenancy." [67] Finally, the resettlement operations were very expensive. According to one estimate, the average cost for resettling one family was ₱1,325 for the National Land Settlement Administration projects (1939–1950) and ₱2,329 for the Land Settlement and Development Corporation projects (1950–1954),[68] and the average cost for settling one family under the EDCOR projects was reportedly in excess of ₱10,000.[69] Much of the expenditures on the public resettlement programs involved administrative and overhead costs and subsistence aid rather than productive investment. Aware of the financial problem, former Senator Raul S. Manglapus, a main architect of the 1963 reform law, declared: "It has been shown that resettlement in public land cost the NARRA ₱43 million to resettle 30,000 tenants and that at this rate, it would cost the Philippine Government ₱19 billion to resettle the 1,200,000 tenant families of this country. . . . We do not have this 'kind of money.' " [70] Measured by any criterion—the effect on reduction of tenancy, the relief of population pressure, the increase of food supply—the result of public land resettlement in the Philippines has not justified the cost.

[64] Wurfel, op. cit., p. 9.

[65] Hugh L. Cook, "Land Reform and Development in the Philippines," in Walter Froelich (ed.), Land Tenure (Milwaukee, 1961), p. 174.

[66] Wernstedt and Simkins, op. cit.

[67] Raul S. Manglapus, "Land, Industry and Power," Larawan, Series IX, No. 10 (September 19, 1963), 5.

[68] Robert E. Huke, Shadows on the Land (Manila, 1963), p. 166.

[69] Golay, op. cit., p. 284.

[70] Manglapus, op. cit. Cf. Concordia G. Palacios, "Financing the Land Reform Program," Philippine Journal of Public Administration, X (January 1966), p. 27.

MEXICO

Compared to the preceding countries, Mexico has made truly impressive progress in public land settlement. The country's colonization effort has been comprehensive in scope, including projects administered under the land redistribution (*ejido*) program, publicly sponsored colonies in non-*ejido* areas, and land developed under public irrigation projects.[71]

Under the colonization law of August 2, 1923, national lands were to be granted to farmers who had been occupying and tilling them for a number of years—with an upper limit of 25 hectares for irrigable land or 200 hectares for non-irrigable land per person. New colonization laws of 1926 and 1946 created the National Colonization Commission and then the Department of Agrarian and Colonization Affairs to administer publicly sponsored land settlement projects. As discussed in the last chapter, under the land redistribution program, land may be granted through "restitution," "dotación," and "amplification." When land is exhausted under these procedures, prospective land recipients (i.e. those with a reserve right to receive land, *campesinos con derechos a salvo*) may be transported to a new area where land is made available for distribution. The new land may belong to public or private holdings with a size in excess of the prescribed ceilings. A group of twenty-five *campesinos* may apply for settlement in a new area; the *campesinos* will first build, by themselves, their living quarters—eventually to be used as a schoolhouse—using local materials and machinery lent by the Agrarian Department. Later settlers will then come to build family houses, receive land, clear the fields, and start cultivating the farms. Until the first harvest, settlers will receive a daily wage, which, together with transportation costs and other expenditures incurred by the public, will eventually be repaid to the government. Until 1963, new settlements could be organized in private colonies or set up in *ejidos*. In the case of private colonies, land recipients had to pay the cost of land, but considerably below the market price. In the case of new *ejidos*, land was granted free. In 1963, a law was adopted, limiting future land settlement projects to *ejidos*.

The fact that publicly developed lands were provided to different types of settlers (individual farmers, existing *ejidos*, as well as organized private colonies) makes its difficult to estimate accurately the total area of land

---

[71] The following description of the Mexican colonization programs is based on U.S., Department of Agriculture, Foreign Agriculture Service, *Land Redistribution in Mexico* (Washington, D.C., 1962), pp. 3–5; Whetten, *op. cit.* (n. 27 above), pp. 168–171; and Simpson, *op. cit.* (n. 18 above), p. 86.

TABLE 21

PUBLIC LAND SETTLEMENT PROJECTS IN MEXICO, 1916–1943

Year	Number of Colonies	Number of Settlers	Number of Hectares	Average Number of Ha. per Settler
1916–1919	2	389	26,658	68.5
1920–1924	9	879	101,839	115.9
1925–1929	3	288	38,508	133.7
1930–1934	64	4,092	269,527	65.9
1935–1939	54	6,453	411,924	63.8
1940–1943	28	1,026	123,649	120.5
Unknown	17	619	275,702	445.4
Total	177	13,746	1,247,807	90.8

SOURCE: Nathan Whetten, *Rural Mexico* (Chicago, 1948), p. 171.

colonized under governmental sponsorship. The information cited in Table 23 pertains only to part of the results of the public colonization effort. During 1916 to 1943, according to Nathan L. Whetten, the government organized a total of 177 colonies in which 13,746 colonists were settled on 1,247,807 hectares of land (see Table 21).

Since the end of the Cárdenas administration in 1940, the land redistribution program has dwindled, while colonization projects have made considerable progress. From 1958 to 1959, for example, a total of 555,912 hectares were delivered to new population centers and private colonies, as compared to the 508,167 hectares granted under the land redistribution program.[72] During the Adolfo López Mateos administration, 1958–1964, the pace of colonization accelerated. There were then 1,173 colonization projects benefiting some 360,000 persons and involving an expenditure of ₱5 billion.[73]

In addition to land settlement projects, the Mexican government has, in recent decades, vastly expanded its irrigation areas, particularly in the country's northwest region. Through the extension of water resources, much arid, uncultivated, or underutilized land was developed into productive farms, most of which were made available to existing private landholders or to new private settlers.[74] From 1928 to 1944 a total of 801,379

[72] U.S., Department of Agriculture, *Land Redistribution in Mexico*, p. 8.
[73] Mexico, Departmento de Asuntos Agrarios y Colonizacion, *Seis Años de Política Agraria del Presidente Adolfo López Mateos* (Mexico, D.F.: Editora Sol, 1964), *passim*.
[74] The Mexican irrigation "programme includes not only solving the ancient prob-

TABLE 22

LAND UTILIZATION IN MEXICO, 1940, 1950, AND 1960

Year and Category	Crop land		Pasture land		Forests	
	Area Million ha.	Percent	Area Million ha.	Percent	Area Million ha.	Percent
Land in farms						
1940	14.9	50.8	56.2	65.6	38.1	57.6
1950	19.9	67.9	67.4	78.6	38.8	58.6
1960	23.8	81.2	79.0	92.2	43.7	66.0
Land not yet in farms						
1960	5.6	18.8	6.7	7.8	22.5	34.0
Total land, 1960	29.4	100.0	85.7	100.0	66.2	100.0

SOURCE: United States, Department of Agriculture, Economic Research Service, *Summary and Evaluation of Projections of Supply and Demand for Agricultural Products in Mexico to 1965, 1970 and 1975* (Washington, D.C., 1968), p. 47.

hectares of land was developed through the irrigation projects and delivered to 107,742 recipients.[75] This was at a time when public irrigation projects expanded at a moderate pace. Subsequently, these projects made the most dramatic expansion. According to one source, from 1926 to 1946 the government extended irrigation areas by 419,900 hectares and improved existing areas by 396,400 hectares; but in the following two decades, 1947–1967, new and improved irrigation areas gained respectively by 1,254,000 hectares and 528,000 hectares.[76] A large proportion of these areas consisted originally of uncultivated public and private land.

One can gain a measure of understanding of the very significant expansion of publicly developed land in Mexico by looking at the country's land utilization data for the last three decades, in Table 22.

---

lems of insufficient water in thirsty zones, and floods and an over-abundance of water in others, but such modern objectives as the development of large new habitats endowed with communication networks, schools and other amenities. . . . [The programme] is the greatest in Latin America for the creation of reclaimed and irrigated land, . . ." Howard F. Cline, *Mexico, Revolution to Evolution* (London, 1962), pp. 68–69.

[75] Whetten, *op. cit.* (n. 27 above), p. 591.

[76] Eduardo L. Venezian and William K. Gamble, *The Agricultural Development of Mexico, Its Structure and Growth Since 1950* (New York: Frederick A. Praeger, Publishers, 1969), p. 99.

As seen in Table 22, in this period land potentially suitable for agricultural purposes has been rapidly converted to actual use. Between 1940 and 1960 nearly one-third of Mexico's crop area and slightly more than one-fourth of the pasture area were added to the country's farms. Much of this expansion of agricultural area was directly or indirectly sponsored and financed by the government. Mexico's colonization effort must be considered the most successful among all the countries studied.[77]

These discussions of public land settlement projects in the five countries lead to two general observations. First, cooperative elites are as unproductive in their colonization efforts as in their other reform programs. In Colombia and the Philippines, abundance of potentially arable lands in the public domain and the elites' repeated advocacy for colonization of these lands has produced no significant results. In contrast, separated elites in countries with new land resources are capable of achieving considerable progress in public-land settlement—just as they are in other programs. The results of colonization in Taiwan and the U.A.R. are not impressive, mainly because the new land available for development is very limited. But Mexico, where new land is relatively abundant, has registered an impressive record. Second, a developing country in need of land reform must weigh the cost and benefit of large-scale public colonization projects against those of other reform programs, particularly land redistribution. In most countries, the high administrative and financial cost of colonization projects simply precludes them as substitutes or even companion measures for land redistribution. Only after land redistribution has been substantially enforced can a country move into expensive public colonization adventures. Mexico's experience in colonization, which took place on a large scale only in the last two or three decades (after the broad land redistribution program of Cárdenas), is a case in point.

[77] For two case studies on Mexican colonization projects, see Thomas T. Poleman, *The Papaloapan Project, Agricultural Development in the Mexican Tropics* (Stanford: Stanford University Press, 1964); and Alfred H. Siemens, "New Agricultural Settlement along Mexico's Candelaria River: Implications of Increased Commitment to Planning and the Ejido," *Inter-American Economic Affairs*, XX (Summer 1966), 23–39.

IX

POLITICAL COMMITMENT,
IMPLEMENTATION, AND RESULTS

After a reform program is formulated, the process of implementation, of course, determines the actual impact of the reform. A combination of a well-formulated program with ineffectual implementation can create little impact; a vigorous enforcement of a relatively poorly written reform law may achieve considerable results. Factors affecting the implementation of a given country's reform program are numerous. They may include the administrative competence and financial capacity the elite commands, the presence or absence of political stability in the country, the extent of landlord resistance, the awareness of the peasantry, and the degree of political commitment to reform. The third hypothesis of this book is that *political commitment to reform—i.e. the willingness and readiness of the political elite to mobilize all available resources to carry out a reform program—is of critical importance, outweighing all other factors. With strong political commitment, a country is likely to achieve extensive implementation of its program even though some of the other factors are unfavorable. Without strong political commitment, a country cannot effectively implement its program even if some of the other factors are favorable.*

Countries with a Strong Political Commitment to Reform

Mexico, Taiwan, the U.A.R., and Iran appear to be the countries that have demonstrated strong political commitment to land reform. In the first three countries, this can be attributed partially to the type of elite in power. Having severed relations with the landed class, these elites can retain the confidence of their new allies in the countryside—the peasants—only by promptly carrying out their programs. The strong political commitment of these countries, it should be noted, owes also to the timely emergence of individual political leaders—in contrast to the elite as a collectivity—fervently devoted to the welfare of the peasantry and personally identified with the reform effort. In the case of Iran, where the dominant elite is in power, a total personal identification by the Shah with the country's reform movement probably constitutes the most vital political commitment on which the progress of reform depends.

In these four countries, the need for a vigorous espousal of reform by individual political leaders may be explained by two considerations. First, as elites in these countries generally do not include representatives of the peasantry, personal identification with reform by political leaders can create a visible link between the elites and the peasantry. Second, and more important, a political leader of resolute will and dynamic personality, with compassion for the peasantry, can energize the reform movement, provide it with spirit, and dramatize its results. In doing so, such a political leader can help generate popular enthusiasm for reform and weaken landlord resistance.

MEXICO: OBREGÓN, PORTES GIL, CÁRDENAS, AND LÓPEZ MATEOS

In Mexico, in the half century since the issuance of the land-reform decree of 1915, over 60 million hectares of land have been distributed to the *campesinos*. But the pace of land redistribution has never been steady, proceeding haltingly some of the time and advancing boldly at other times. Although all twelve presidents from 1915 to 1964 were committed to land reform, they differed in the degree of commitment and in their emphasis on productivity or equity as the primary reform objective. As noted before, President Carranza issued the 1915 decree out of political-military necessity. Having neither an interest in taking "any bold steps in the field of agrarian reform" nor a "great faith in the ability of the . . . peasant to boost agricultural production," [1] Carranza redistributed merely 224,393 hectares of land during his five-year term—the lowest monthly rate of land redistribution in the reform history of Mexico (see Table 23). In fact, much of this land had already been seized by the *campesinos* before the actual redistribution. By comparison, all subsequent presidents have provided more land to the *campesinos*, but four of these appear to have made the greatest contribution to the country's reform movement.

[1] Charles C. Cumberland, *Mexico, The Struggle for Modernity* (New York: Oxford University Press, 1968), p. 296.

TABLE 23

LAND REDISTRIBUTION IN MEXICO BY PRESIDENTIAL TERM, 1915–1964

President	Term	Months in Office	Total Ha. Distributed[a]	Average Ha. per Month	Total Number of Beneficiaries
Venustiano Carranza	1915–1920	63.5	224,393	3,535	59,848
Adolfo de la Huerta	1920	6	157,533	26,256	17,355
Alvaro Obregón	1920–1924	48	1,677,067	34,939	158,204
Plutarco Elias Calles	1924–1928	48	3,310,577	68,970	318,030
Emilio Portes Gil	1928–1929	14	3,036,842	216,917	213,981
Pascual Ortiz Rubio	1929–1932	31	1,203,737	38,830	84,009
Abelardo L. Rodríguez	1932–1934	27	2,094,638	77,579	161,327
Lázaro Cárdenas	1934–1940	72	20,072,957	278,791	774,000
Manuel Avila Camacho	1940–1946	72	5,327,943	73,999	112,447
Miguel Alemán	1946–1952	72	3,844,745	53,399	85,026
Adolfo Ruiz Cortines	1952–1958	72	3,198,781	44,278	55,929
Adolfo López Mateos	1958–1964	72	16,004,170	222,280	80,000[b]
Total	—	—	60,153,383	100,591	2,120,156

[a] Refers to total farm land redistributed, including crop and non-crop land.

[b] Author's estimate.

SOURCES: Ing. Marte R. Gomez, *La Reforma Agraria de México Su crisis durante el período 1928–1934* (México, 1, D.F.: Libreria de Manuel Porrua, S.A., 1964), Appendice; and México, Departamento de Asuntos Agraria y Colonizacion, *Seis Años de Política Agraria del Presidente Adolfo López Mateos, 1958–1964* (México, D.F.: Editora Sol, 1964), p. 16.

⌊The first is General Alvaro Obregón. A man possessing at once the ruthlessness of a tough military commander, the pragmatism of a politician, and the idealism of a revolutionary leader,⌋Obregón, at one time or another, collaborated with Villa, Zapata, and Carranza, and fought against them all.⌋ Though changeable in his devotion to political allies, Obregón was persistent in his advocacy of land reform. Ironically, while in 1919 Zapata died an enemy of the Carranza regime in which Obregón served as War Minister, Obregón later definitively implemented Zapata's reform idea. When Obregón broke with Carranza in 1920, he immediately won over the political allegiance of the Zapatistas. While Gildardo Magaña—Zapata's successor—joined Obregón's revolt against Carranza, Antonio Díaz Soto y Gama —another Zapatista leader—formed the *Partido Nacional Agrarista* (National Agrarian Party) to campaign for the election of Obregón as president. The union of the Obregonista and Zapatista forces proved mutually beneficial. Within the year, Obregón became president, and the Zapatistas gained strong influence within the new government. To proceed with land reform, Obregón secured, in 1920, the enactment of the Uncultivated Lands Law and the Ejido Law. In 1921, he decided to grant land free to *campesinos* by rescinding an earlier circular of the National Agrarian Commission which had required land recipients to pay a purchase price. He carefully framed a program to avoid the danger "of serious disturbance of agricultural production . . . [resulting from] excessive distribution of land" and, at the same time, to step up the pace of reform "in those rural areas of greatest discontent." [2] During his four-year term, Obregón delivered 1,677,067 hectares of land to 158,204 *campesinos*—over five times the land distributed and twice the number of reform beneficiaries as under the combined programs of the two previous presidents, which lasted five years (see Table 25). Thus, if Carranza first legally committed the nation to land reform through the 1915 decree and the 1917 Constitution, it was Obregón who first gave substance to the commitment. In distributing so much land at a decisive moment in modern Mexican history when the nation was passing through the military phase of the revolution to national consolidation, Obregón insured the survival of the agrarian cause and built a momentum for land redistribution which future presidents had to sustain.

This momentum received a major impetus during the administration of Emilio Portes Gil, 1928–1929. As governor of his home state Tamaulipas in 1924, Portes Gil established his "reputation of being a radical agrarian." [3] He started land redistribution in the state, promoted rural education, and organized the Tamaulipas Peasant League. In 1928, when president-elect Obregón (for a second term) was assassinated, the National Agrarian Party immediately launched a drive to make Portes Gil provisional president, seeing in him "the best guarantee for a continuation of the agrarian reform programme. . . ." [4] This expectation he fulfilled. During his brief presidential tenure, he made Marte R. Gómez, adviser of the National Peasant League, his Minister of Agriculture and drastically expanded the reform program. In a little over a year, he provided the *campesinos* with more than three million hectares of land, nearly equal to the total land distributed by his predecessor, President Plutarco Elias

---

[2] L. Vincent Padgett, *The Mexican Political System* (Boston: Houghton Mifflin Company, 1966), p. 27.

[3] Gerrit Huizer, *On Peasant Unrest in Latin America* (Washington, D.C.: CIDA, 1969, mimeo.), p. 61.

[4] *Ibid.*, p. 62.

Calles, in four years. He moved at an unprecedented pace, distributing on the average over 200,000 hectares of land a month—thrice the comparable rate of the Calles administration. After he stepped down from the presidency, Portes Gil remained active in the promotion of peasant welfare. In 1935, as president of the official party *Partido Nacional Revolucionario* (PNR, the National Revolutionary Party), he helped organize state peasant leagues which became the building stones of the future national peasant confederation.

Like Portes Gil, Lázaro Cárdenas had been closely associated with the land-reform movement before becoming president. While governor of his home state Michoacán from 1928 to 1932, he formed a confederation of peasants and workers to propagate the agrarian cause and to help distribute land. Wresting farms from *haciendas,* he granted more land to the villages in Michoacán than all his predecessors combined. In the 1933 presidential campaign, he won the united support of all peasant organizations, labor, the military, and retired President Calles. In December, the national convention of the PNR nominated him by acclamation as the presidential candidate and adopted a Six-Year Plan declaring, among other things: "The only limit to the distribution of land and waters shall be the complete satisfaction of the agricultural needs of the centers of rural population." [5] Though virtually assured of electoral victory after the PNR nomination, Cárdenas campaigned far and wide in the country seeking direct contact with the people. He pledged: "If I am elected president, there will be no one who can stop me until the peasant has received the best lands and the State has given him all financial, moral and material aid possible." [6]

True to his pledge, Cárdenas established a land-reform record during his presidential term of 1934 to 1940, unmatched by any president either before or after him. He moved on many fronts. He armed the peasant to defend against the "White Guards" of *hacendados.* "I always maintained," Cárdenas declared, "that only by giving arms to the agrarian elements which have been, are and will be the firm supporters of the Revolution, one can teach them to continue accomplishing their apostolate. . . . I will give to the peasants the Mausers with which they made the Revolution, so they can defend it and the *ejido* and the school." [7] In 1940, at the end of the Cárdenas regime, the armed peasant reserve force numbered

[5] Quoted in *ibid.,* p. 72.
[6] Quoted in Cumberland, *op. cit.,* p. 298.
[7] Quoted in Huizer, *op. cit.,* p. 74.

60,000 men. Cárdenas also organized all land recipients into a massive peasant organization (the *Confederacion Nacional Campesina*, CNC), integrated the CNC into the reorganized official party, *Partido Revolucionario Mexicano*, removed all legal restrictions on the right of resident peons (*acasillados*) to receive land,[8] and created the *Banco Nacional de Credito Ejidal* to assist the *ejidos*. Most important, he launched a fervent drive to distribute land. During his presidential term, he spent almost as much time in the villages as in the capital. Cutting through red tape, he granted land on the spot, personally ordered the construction of wells and dams, and much excited the enthusiasm of the villagers. In six years he provided three-quarters of a million peasants with some 20 million hectares of land—more than the land distributed by all his predecessors combined; alone, Cárdenas was responsible for one-third of the results of Mexico's land redistribution program in the half century from 1915 to 1964. For such magnitude of accomplishment, he was "glorified, exalted—indeed, virtually deified by the masses." [9]

In word and in deed, Cárdenas was truly the foremost Mexican president dedicated to the agrarian cause. In the two decades following his administration, Mexican presidents displayed, in their attitude toward land reform, a declining interest in redistributive measures and placed increasing emphasis on measures seeking to stimulate agricultural growth. As a result, from 1940 to 1958 there was a persistent downward trend in Mexican land redistribution. Not until the Adolfo López Mateos administration was this downward trend reversed. Not a participant in the revolution, but a product of the political Establishment, López Mateos revived official interest in land reform partly because of rising rural discontent among millions of landless *campesinos*, and partly because of "the leftward tendencies of the [ruling] Revolutionary Coalition" in recent years.[10] In the 1958 presidential election, López Meteos campaigned extensively in the

[8] Up to 1934, all peons residing on *haciendas* had not been accorded the right to receive land under the land-reform program. The 1934 Agrarian Code, enacted under the administration of Abelardo L. Rodríquez, first extended this right to the peons, but with many restrictions. In 1937, Cárdenas issued a decree abolishing these restrictions and putting peons on an equal footing with the free *campesinos* in receiving the benefits of reform. This change led Padgett to comment: "Perhaps the resident peon provision more than any other single provision was basic to the great expansion of agrarian land redistribution under the Cárdenas government." *Op. cit.*, p. 192.

[9] Frank Ralph Brandenburg, *The Making of Modern Mexico* (Englewood Cliffs, N.J.: 1966), p. 131.

[10] Padgett, *op. cit.*, p. 42.

countryside, conveying to the rural electorate his concern for its welfare and his identification with land reform. He won the election with considerable rural votes. But López Mateos was not another Cárdenas. He did not place egalitarian consideration above a concern for economic growth; to the new president, the pace of land reform must be accelerated, but not at the expense of agricultural production. Thus, in his 1960 annual report to Congress "he summarized the [agrarian] policies of his administration . . . by saying that it was redistributing all lands legally disposable, developing ejidos based on cattle-raising and on forest products, and aiding productivity to bring greater economic returns to ejidatarios." [11] In 1963, López Mateos reaffirmed these policies by declaring: "Agrarian Reform forges ahead. It will forge ahead inexorably. No one can stop it or deviate [from] it; neither those who seeking to protect their own interests say that it has failed and must end or move back, nor those who pretend to believe that it is not moving ahead and that laws must be changed to carry it through." [12] To balance the need for equity and productivity, López Mateos sought to satisfy the peasant demand for land by expanding public land settlement programs but refrained from distributing medium-sized, highly productive private farms. He opened up federal, state, and municipal lands for the enlargement of existing *ejidos* and for the creation of new population centers. He also obtained legislation, in 1963, limiting future land grants in new settlement areas to *ejidos*, and created livestock and forestry *ejidos* through expropriation of those private ranches and forestry lands that had previously been designated as temporarily unexpropriable. With persistence and devotion, he established a record of land redistribution second only to that of Cárdenas. In his final state-of-the-union message in 1964, he observed: "It had been affirmed for years that lands susceptible of distribution in accord with law no longer existed or were on the point of disappearing. My government, in six years, has distributed more than a third of the lands distributed during the forty-four years that the Agrarian Code has been enforced . . ." [13] (see Table 23).

TAIWAN: CHEN CHENG

Compared to the prolonged course of reform in Mexico, the period in which Taiwan's principal reform programs were implemented was short,

[11] Howard F. Cline, *Mexico, Revolution to Evolution* (London, 1962), p. 214.

[12] President Adolfo López Mateos, *State of the Union Message*, 5th September 1963 (Mexico City [English translation], n.d.), pp. 35-36.

[13] Quoted in Padgett, *op. cit.*, p. 195

lasting only five years. But the case of Taiwan also reveals that the success of reform crucially depended upon the dedication of political leaders. From 1949 to 1953, when the rent-reduction program, the sale of public land programs, and the land-to-the-tiller programs were successively introduced, all KMT leaders—both at the national and provincial levels—demonstrated single-minded determination to carry out the party's first major social policy in Taiwan.

Among these leaders, General Chen Cheng proved to be the most vital force in the process of implementation. Raised in a farm family of meager income, Chen was exposed to rural poverty in his boyhood and subsequently showed considerable empathy with the peasants. In his long military-political career, Chen consistently demonstrated a concern for popular welfare and a penchant for social reform. In the 1930s, while in charge of the Nationalist military campaign against the Communists, "he was much impressed by the way in which the Communists used . . . [social and economic] reforms to win widespread support among the peasants." [14] Though never wavering in his anti-Communist position, "he contented himself with publishing and distributing at his own expense Communist documents having to do with social and economic reform which his troops had captured. . . ." [15] In the 1940s, when he was Governor of Hupeh Province, he enforced with considerable vigor a sweeping tenancy reform program which came to be the prototype for the Taiwan rent-reduction program.

A man of forceful personality, incorruptible character, and unswerving loyalty to Chiang Kai-shek, Chen became Governor of Taiwan in 1949, Premier in 1950, and Vice President in 1954. In these years, in the councils of both the KMT and the government, he established himself as the strongest advocate for land reform, and demonstrated his capacity for effective implementation of the programs. The implementation of the first of these programs—rent reduction—was the most difficult and hazardous. It was initiated in 1949, at a time when the civil war was still raging on mainland China. Conditions on the island were highly unstable; resistance of landlords to the measure could not be ruled out; and the administrative personnel were ill-equipped for the task. In the midst of all this chaos and uncertainty, Chen resolutely pushed the program. To generate public

[14] Donald G. Gillin, "Problems of Centralization in Republican China: The Case of Ch'en Ch'eng and the Kuomintang," *The Journal of Asian Studies*, XXIX (August 1970), 844.

[15] *Ibid.*, 845.

enthusiasm, he held numerous meetings with the concerned leaders within and without the government. With respect to the members of the Provincial Assembly, where landlords were influential,

> General Chen took special pains to see them either individually or in groups so as to enlist their support. Many observers ridiculed his efforts and thought he was, as a Chinese proverb goes, "asking the tiger for its hide." However, he . . . acted energetically to overcome all opposition through forceful reasoning and compelling persuasion.[16]

He was successful in this persuasion only because he was disposed to proceed with the reform even without the support of the local leaders and was quite ready to crush any opposition. The program was promptly implemented and concluded without any known overt resistance. Chen reminisced:

> The Chinese Government began to make the necessary arrangements in January, 1949. Actual enforcement started in April of the same year and was concluded in September. It took only a few months to finish an unprecedented and difficult task. The speed with which the work was completed and the smoothness with which it was carried out were, it must be confessed, entirely unexpected.[17]

After the conclusion of this program, Chen went ahead with land redistribution through the sale of public land and the land-to-the-tiller programs. In speech after speech, he told the farming community of his determination to complete these programs and to punish those who might frustrate the effort. For instance, in a 1953 speech concerning the land-to-the-tiller program, Chen declared:

> I am thoroughly determined to make this program fully implemented. The people of this island have always abided by the law; they will support this program. If there are a few unscrupulous persons trying to obstruct the enforcement of the program, I will apply the law with the fullest force so that the selfish few will not be able to harm the interest of the majority.[18]

---

[16] T. H. Shen, "Land Reform and Its Impact on Agricultural Development in Taiwan," in James R. Brown and Sein Lin (eds.), *Land Reform in Developing Countries,* 1967 International Seminar on Land Taxation, Land Tenure, and Land Reform in Developing Countries, Sponsored by The Lincoln Foundation, Phoenix, Arizona, at Taipei, Taiwan, December 11–19, 1967 (The University of Hartford, 1968), pp. 359–360.

[17] Chen Cheng, *Land Reform in Taiwan* (Taipei, Taiwan, 1961), p. 21.

[18] Quoted in Têng, A *Factual Report on the Enforcement of the Land-to-the-Tiller Program* (Taipei, Taiwan, 1955), p. 9 (my translation from the Chinese).

His demonstrated commitment to reform and the tight control of the island by the army were conditions sufficient for the rapid conclusion of the programs. One is inclined to agree with the assessment of Chen's role in the process of implementation by an experienced observer. There were a number of factors, Wolf Ladejinsky has written, responsible for the effective enforcement of Taiwan's reform programs:

> The . . . prevalent belief among the Nationalist politicians that the Communists won [the civil war on the mainland] because . . . the promise of land to the tillers played a crucial role in creating the favorable climate. Certain elements in the Nationalist ideology worked to the same end, especially when the beleaguered government realized it needed greater social stability as a means to military security. But none of these factors might have sufficed were it not for the fact that General Chen Cheng . . . had resolved that rural Taiwan was to undergo a thorough change. . . . [He] left no doubt in the mind of the opposition that he was ready to proceed with a good deal of "unceremonious vigor." [19]

Chen's identification with Taiwan's reform is not only recognized among experienced observers, but also firmly established among the peasants. Because of what he did for them, many villagers developed an affection for him, preferring to call him—during his last years of life—"Uncle Chen." When he died in 1965, numerous farmers from all over the island attended the funeral to pay their last homage.[20]

A rural survey conducted by the author in Tainan, Taiwan, in December 1968, provides a clear indication of the high level of awareness by this predominantly agricultural community of Chen's role in land reform. Of the 550 respondents in the Tainan survey, 404 (or 73.46 percent) identified Chen as having made the greatest contribution to the cause of land reform in Taiwan. (Detailed results of the response are provided in Table 24.)

---

[19] Wolf Ladejinsky, "Agrarian Reform in Asia," *Foreign Affairs*, XLII (April 1964), 457 and 459.

[20] Shen, *op. cit.*, p. 360; and *The New York Times*, March 6, 1965, p. 25. In an interview with the author in December 1968, Chiang Shui-hsiang, a farmer and village councilman in Tainan, Taiwan, indicated that he had received 1.2 *chia* of land from the government. In the conversation, Chiang paid special tribute to Chen for this beneficence, and said he had since 1965 taken three special trips to visit Chen's grave to express his gratitude. Other farmers interviewed unanimously showed affection for Chen.

TABLE 24

RURAL PERCEPTION OF CONTRIBUTORS TO LAND REFORM
IN TAIWAN,
TAINAN SURVEY, 1968

Question: "*Who has made the greatest contribution
to the cause of land reform in Taiwan?*"

	Respondents	
Contributor	Number	Percent
Sun Yat-sen	4	0.73
Chiang Kai-shek	13	2.36
Chen Cheng	404	73.46
Others	10	1.82
Don't know	2	0.36
No answer	117	21.27
Total	550	100.00

SOURCE: See Appendix III.

THE U.A.R.: NAGUIB AND NASSER

In the U.A.R., the first post-revolution Prime Minister, Ali Maher had practically no interest in redistribution of private estates. A liberal politician in the old regime, Ali Maher had long preferred a mild agrarian policy to comprehensive tenurial changes. He advocated a progressive tax on large landowners and a minimum size for holdings.[21] In August 1952, he declared that, although he supported "those who agree to the establishment of a limit to the size of large land holdings, I do not wish to subject the country to a violent economic upheaval, especially at this time." [22] Maher's disinterest in reform was one of the principal reasons for his break with the Free Officers and for his dismissal in September. Replacing Maher as Prime Minister, General Mohammed Naguib immediately expressed the Free Officers' concern for peasant welfare: "We officers, though no longer peasants ourselves, were deeply in sympathy with the plight of the peasants whose sons made up our ranks." [23] He emphasized the significance of land reform in these terms:

[21] See Gabriel Baer, A *History of Landownership in Modern Egypt 1800–1950* (London, 1962), p. 208.

[22] *Ibid.*

[23] Mohammed Naguib and Leigh White, *Egypt's Destiny* (New York, 1955), p. 13.

What better means is there of raising a peasant's morale, and thereby his initiative, than by making it possible for him to buy a piece of land? The landless peasant is a demoralized and defenseless person. A landed peasant is a man of spirit who will defend his land, if necessary, with his life. The difference between a landless and landed peasant is the difference between a two-footed animal and a man.[24]

Naguib promptly started the reform movement and led it with considerable zeal.

His successor, Nasser, provided the movement with even greater and more sustained support, and much expanded its scope. Nasser conceived the Egyptian revolution as consisting of two dimensions: political and social. Political revolution was the prerequisite for social revolution; and social revolution was the justification of political revolution. To Nasser, land reform was a movement in which the two revolutions coincided. In 1961, he gave substance to the newly proposed ideology, "Arab Socialism," by lowering the ceiling of private farms from 200 *feddans* to 100 (84 to 42 hectares). By 1964, through a series of decrees, he reduced three-fourths of the payment obligations of farmers who had purchased land under the reform. He assembled "a highly competent administrative team to manage the Agrarian Reform Program" and entrusted Sayed Marei, the Director of the Higher Committee for Agrarian Reform, with the responsibility for operating the programs.[25] To establish a permanent link with the peasantry, Nasser followed the route of Mexico's Cárdenas by incorporating farmers into a massive political organization, the Arab Socialist Union, and by guaranteeing them definite representation in the government. Thus Nasser's devotion to the agrarian cause resulted in not only a substantial increase of the economic benefits of reform but also an integration of the peasantry into the political system.

IRAN: THE SHAH AND ARSANJANI

The critical importance of political commitment to implementation is perhaps most dramatically demonstrated in the case of Iran. Among the five countries ruled by cooperative elites, Iran is the only one that has achieved substantial results in reform, and this has been done even with,

---

[24] *Ibid.*, p. 166.

[25] Keith Wheelock, *Nasser's New Egypt* (New York, 1960), pp. 78, 92–93. Cf. Doreen Warriner, *Land Reform and Development in the Middle East* (London, 1962), pp. 42, 44–45, 47, 202–203.

initially, strong opposition within the government.[26] Also, the 1962 law was poorly formulated and its provisions were generally more favorable to the landed interests than were the reform laws adopted by separated elites. Yet Iran was able to achieve results quite comparable to those of Mexico, Taiwan, and the U.A.R. Without doubt, the single most important factor that made this possible was the determined and vigorous role played by the Shah. It was out of his perception of a political need that the 1962 reform decree was born; it was under his personal guidance that the program advanced at a rapid pace.

With an early sympathy for peasant welfare,[27] the Shah demonstrated a strong disposition to effecting land reform in a number of ways. He once declared that "it was no glory for me to reign over a people who are poor and probably hungry. . . . In a country where 75 percent of its inhabitants dwell in rural areas, surely the bulk of the monarch's responsibilities should be towards them." [28] He relinquished his vast royal estates, distributed public land, and created agricultural banks. He suspended the Majlis and abandoned his traditional political ally, the large landlord class, all in order to redistribute private farms. After issuing the land reform decree in January 1962, he personally launched, two months later, the first project in Maragheh, Azerbaijan Province. Touring the country extensively, he aroused warm peasant response to his program. Denouncing the obstructing landlords as "arch reactionaries," he spoke passionately of his program: "Nothing can hold the land reform. . . . Even if I, its initiator, were to change my mind, it could not stop." [29]

Most instrumental in the actual administration of the program was Hassan Arsanjani, the Minister of Agriculture from 1961 to 1963. A man experienced in agricultural credit and a liberal politician with a lifelong

[26] When the 1962 land-reform decree was referred to the Cabinet for consideration, the Ministers of Finance, Justice, Interior, and War refused to give their consent. Through the pressure of the Shah, the Cabinet later reluctantly approved it, but still delayed providing the necessary funds. See Kenneth B. Platt "Land Reform in Iran," U.S. Agency for International Development, *Spring Review* (June 1970), pp. 71–72.

[27] "When I was still a student in Switzerland," the Shah recollected, "I became seriously concerned about the plight of Persia's peasants. My ideas continued to develop, and after my father left, I issued a decree handing over all my farm lands to the Government." *Mission for My Country* (New York, 1961), p. 201.

[28] Quoted in Platt, *op. cit.*, p. 44.

[29] Quoted in E. A. Bayne, "Persian Kingship Revisited, Part II, A King's Program," *American Universities Field Staff*, Report Service, Southwest Asia Series, XII (October 1963), 2.

interest in land reform,[30] Arsanjani pushed the program with energy and drive, as if he was launching a genuine rural revolution. He declared: "In these reforms . . . we are facing the reactionary front which has wasted 50 years of Parliamentary regime and have [sic] now confronted us with the choice of a 'red' or 'white' revolution. If things continue as they are, the country will explode." [31] Determined to destroy the landed aristocracy, he set out on a course of speedy redistribution to stun the opponents. Less concerned with the rights of the landowners than with the enthusiasm of the peasants, he forcefully persuaded the reluctant cabinet to appropriate an initial fund of a billion rials. He quickly assembled a Land Reform Organization with a skeleton staff, whose members he specially trained and indoctrinated to promote rural reform; organized a nation-wide peasant cooperative congress; and plunged into the countryside to divide farms. With a relatively small complement of field personnel, he proceeded at fantastic speed. Forty days after the initiation of the program in Maragheh in March 1962, 33 villages were distributed to 2,259 farmers.[32] By September 1963, the Land Reform Organization with a field staff of 1,159 had distributed a total of 8,042 villages (see Table 25).

Arsanjani resigned as Minister of Agriculture in March 1963. He was criticized for pushing the program too fast, and he was suspected of attempting to use land reform for personal political gains. But he had certainly carried out a task that a man with less devotion and drive could not have accomplished. He made the reform movement irreversible and created an atmosphere for urgent action. Many prominent political leaders with vast landholdings were thus persuaded of the need for reform and gave up their land voluntarily. For instance, Ali Amini, the Prime Minister during whose term Arsanjani served as Minister of Agriculture, was one of the wealthiest landowners of the country. But he once warned the landlords: "Divide your lands or face revolution—or death." He gave up his land. His successor, Assadollah Alam, and Arsanjani's successor, General Ismail Riahi, both pledged to carry forward the program. The latter commented that land reform "is the force of the times," and that "any opposition will

---

[30] In 1947, because of his strong advocacy for reform he was unseated from the Majlis, to which he had been elected in 1946. "The landowners succeeded in getting his credentials . . . rejected." Doreen Warriner, Land Reform in Principle and Practice (Oxford, 1969), p. 117.

[31] See Echo of Iran, Iran Almanac and Book of Facts, 1963 (3rd ed.: Tehran, n.d.), p. 388.

[32] Platt, op. cit., pp. 72–73.

TABLE 25

SPEED OF LAND REDISTRIBUTION IN IRAN, MARCH 1962–SEPTEMBER 1963

Province	No. of villages purchased	Time taken for distribution, days	Average days per village	No. of officials	No. of vehicles
Khorasan	1,133	358	0.3	50	36
Fars	989	461	0.4	147	65
East Azarbayjan	1,184	597	0.5	76	36
Khoozestan	459	283	0.6	71	30
Kermanshahan	631	461	0.7	81[a]	17
Kerman	359	291	0.8	76	32
Central Regiohan	337	273	0.8	106	26
Zanjan	399	370	0.9	14	7
Kurdestan	325	377	1.1	15	19
Esfahan	284	335	1.2	90	27
Mazandaran	261	315	1.2	88	7
Tehran	240	290	1.4	64	22
Arak	291	477	1.4	64	22
Gilan	305	492	1.6	75	5
Hamadan	196	331	1.7	81[a]	8
West Azarbayjan	285	579	2	48	21
Salas	129	327	2.5	54	11
Ghazvin	159	482	3	17	5
Persian Gulf Coast	58	296	5	18	21
Omman Coast	16	280	17.5	9	7
Baluchestan and Sistan	2	235	117.5	32	10
Yazd	– – –	300	—	11	1
Total	8,042	—	—	1,159	423

[a] The same 81 officials worked in the two provinces jointly.

SOURCE: Research Group, "A Review of the Statistics of the First Stage of Land Reform," *Tahqiqat é eqtesadi*, II (March 1964), 146.

be crushed."[33] An additional contribution of Arsanjani to reform implementation concerned his success in energizing the administrative officials. As one observer has pointed out, "these officials have been devoting themselves to land reform with a zeal not often seen among civil servants in this part of the world."[34]

[33] See John A. Hobbs, "Land Reform in Iran: A 'Revolution from Above,'" *Orbis*, VII (Fall 1963), *passim*, and John Hanessian, Jr., "Iranian Land Reform," *American Universities Field Staff*, Report Service, Southwest Asia Series, XII: No. 10 (April 1963), 1, 15–16.

[34] Hanessian, *ibid.*

OVERCOMING DIFFICULTIES

As their political leaders were firmly committed to land reform, Mexico, Taiwan, the U.A.R., and Iran could substantially carry out their respective programs. The crucial importance of political commitment is also revealed in the way in which political elites deal with factors unfavorable to implementation. In Mexico and Iran, the lack of a prereform comprehensive land survey and accurate land records posed serious problems impeding orderly transfer of land. But to undertake this preparatory work prior to implementation would have entailed prohibitive financial and administrative costs and would have taken so much time that it would have jeopardized the entire program. This was especially true in Iran, where no standardized units for measuring land have ever been adopted. The Ministry of Agriculture has estimated that a comprehensive survey of Iran's farm land would cost about U.S. $80 million. Such an expenditure is equivalent to half of the compensation payment for all expropriated land up to 1967. The task of land surveying, mapping, and recording would also require "years of preparation and, with the vagaries of political life, would have doomed the [land reform] programme right from the start." [35]

To overcome this difficulty, both Mexico and Iran adopted "short-cut" methods. In Mexico, *campesinos* could obtain land through three alternatives: *restitución, dotación,* and *ampliación.* That is, they could, with proof of title, recover their land from those who had illegally occupied it; they could acquire land from large holdings located within a seven-kilometer radius of the village in which they lived; or they could expand the area of land they received under the two previous procedures through additional grants by the government. In all cases, the government provided the land to the farming community *en bloc,* without having to award individual titles. With four-fifths of Mexico's redistributed land coming through *dotación,* [36] the government could launch the reform program without being bogged down in a detailed land survey.

[35] *Ibid.,* p. 4; and Dayush Homayoun, "Land Reform in Iran," *Tahqiqat é eqtesadi,* II (Sept. 1963), 23.

[36] Of all land redistributed in Mexico from 1916 to 1944, 6 percent was granted through restitution, 79 percent through *dotación,* and a little less than 15 percent through amplification. Nathan Whetten, *Rural Mexico* (Chicago, 1948), pp. 129–130. The proportion of land through *dotación* remained unchanged subsequently, about 80 percent around 1960. U.S. Department of Agriculture, *Land Redistribution in Mexico,* p. 2.

In Iran, the landlord was simply allowed to retain one "village," while all incumbent cultivators obtained the rest of the land they had been working on. This explains why the Land Reform Organization could implement the program with such dispatch.

To deal with the shortage of public funds, Mexico made extremely limited compensation payments to some landlords, while practically confiscating the estates of all the rest. In Taiwan, the government paid landlords primarily in crops and stocks of public corporations, thus entailing few cash transactions. In Iran, the government reallocated its budget, diverting to the Land Reform Organization a substantial portion of the oil income originally assigned to the Plan Organization for economic development.[37]

The presence of civil war and the threat of political instability did not prevent Mexico and Taiwan from launching their reform programs. In Mexico, over 5 million hectares of land were distributed from 1916 to 1928, when the country was engulfed in repeated internal fighting. In Taiwan, the 1949 rent-reduction program was enforced at a critical time when the island enjoyed a measure of tranquility only on the surface. The civil war was not yet concluded; and not until 1950 was the island immune from the threat of Communist underground organizations and of an invasion from the mainland. Indeed, some members of the KMT leadership had expressed strong reservations about the rent-reduction program, considering that it might have strong destabilizing consequences. But in spite of the inauspicious circumstances and the presence of internal dissension, the KMT decided to move forward with reform and concluded the program with unusual dispatch.[38]

[37] Arsanjani estimated that the total cost of Iran's land reform would be 70 billion rials (about U.S. $930 million), half of which would hopefully come from the Third Five Year Plan (1963–1968). Hanessian, *op. cit.*, p. 9. By September 1963 the cost of the "villages" purchased through land reform had amounted to 4.7 billion rials, equaling one-fifth of Iran's annual oil income, or 12.5 percent of the national budget for 1963. Research Group, "A Review of the Statistics of the First Stages of Land Reform," *Tahqiqat é eqtesadi*, II (March 1964), 145.

[38] Thus, Hui-sun Tang, a senior JCRR official, has written: "When the rent limitation program was being initiated in Taiwan, certain conservative people were rather skeptical of its advisability. They considered it unwise for the Government to speak of land reform when the military situation was yet precarious, because any such idea would only tend to alienate the landlords. Much opposition was heard from all sides, similar to what we had experienced in the past on the mainland. But the responsible authorities were convinced that national and social security could not possibly be achieved by always following the old ruts, that there must be reform and progress, . . ." *Land Reform in Free China* (Taipei, Taiwan, 1954), p. 31.

To cope with the problems of peasant indifference and landlord ob-structions, the countries with a strong political commitment adopted two solutions. The elites of Mexico and Taiwan allowed the peasants to par-ticipate in the process of implementation, and institutionalized the bene-ficiaries into permanent organized forces. In Mexico, the procedures for land redistribution required villages petitioning for land to form Agrarian Executive Committees which were composed of villagers themselves, ap-pointed by the state governors. These Committees represented the villages in the entire redistribution proceedings. The petition for land was sub-mitted to the state governors who referred it to the Agrarian Mixed Commission for proper action. The Commission—consisting of five mem-bers, of which two represented the federal government, two the local authorities, and one the reform beneficiaries—was the principal agency for the implementation of reform. In addition to allowing the *campesinos* to maintain direct representation in the process of implementation, the Mexican elite also organized them into a nation-wide federation, which was incorporated into the official party. This move heightened the political awareness of the *campesinos* and enabled them to resist the landlords' retaliations.

In Taiwan, a host of semi-governmental agencies were created or reorganized to publicize the reform and to involve the beneficiaries in the administration of programs.[39] Among these, the one performing the most vital role was the Farm Tenancy Committee system. Created in 1952, the system maintained one committee for each farming community, which consisted of eleven members—two members from the local government, five tenant farmers, two owner-farmers, and two landlords. The committee system performed five major categories of functions:

1. Information, assistance, and supervision in the implementation of rent reduction.

2. Appraisal of the standard amount of total annual yield of the principal product of the main crop.

3. Investigation of crop failures and decision on such remedial meas-ures as reduction or exemption of rent.

4. Conciliation of tenancy disputes.

---

[39] These agencies include the 37.5 Rent Campaign Committees, the Committees for the Establishment of Owner-Farmers, the Farm Tenancy Committees, the Farmers Associations, and the Irrigation Associations.

5. Recommendation as to the land to be retained by landlords, and assessment of land value under the land-to-the-tiller program.

With the committees assuming these responsibilities, the government could promptly and effectively implement the reform programs. At the same time, the tenants and small owner-farmers, possessing a decisive advantage in committee membership, could avail themselves of the full benefits of reform and could prevent the landlords from resorting to sabotage, evasion, or resistance. Throughout the reform period of 1949 to 1953, there was not a single known instance of violence. In no small measure the committee system contributed to the successful enforcement of Taiwan's programs.

In Egypt and Iran, the elites preferred to dramatize their role by taking swift and drastic action against the obstructionists. On September 10, 1952, one day after the issuance of the Egyptian reform decree, Adli Lamlúm, owner of an 810-hectare estate in Upper Egypt, threatened to use force to prevent division of his land. The government dispatched troops the next day and forcefully arrested Lamlúm and his followers. On October 8, a military tribunal sentenced the owner to life imprisonment, and five others to jail terms of from five to fifteen years.[40] Thereafter scarcely any physical opposition occurred. Thus demonstrating their serious intention to carry out reform, the military went immediately into action throughout the country, and "the pace of movement was too fast for effective opposition. . . . By November, 1952, the first 187,000 feddans [78,559 hectares] of excess lands, belonging to 112 of the largest landowners, were requisitioned for redistribution. . . . What little resistance had remained up to that point dissolved in a panic of price-breaking private sales of excess holdings as permitted by the law, . . ."[41]

In Iran, the initial resistance to land reform was violent and widespread. From Maragheh, the first declared reform district, to other parts of the country numerous instances of obstruction were reported. Landlords, individually or collectively, expelled peasants, destroyed their houses, damaged ganats (irrigation canals), and uprooted trees. Some landlords intimidated or attempted to bribe land-reform officials to prevent them from functioning in their areas; others armed themselves and threatened

---

[40] Naguib, op. cit. (n. 23 above), pp. 174–175.
[41] Kenneth B. Platt, "Land Reform in the United Arab Republic," Agency for International Development, Spring Review, Country Paper (June 1970), pp. 43–44.

"to take to the hills and start a rebellion"; still others plotted with Moslem mullahs to incite riots and demonstrations. These violent activities gradually accelerated and, in November 1962, a land reform official, Malek Abedi, was murdered in Fars Province, where the landlords attempted to launch a concentrated drive against reform. In June 1963, landlord-instigated and mullah-sponsored riots took place in Tehran and other cities, posing a severe threat to the government.[42]

The government retaliated with strong measures. The Shah personally castigated the "black reaction" and "pseudo-clergymen." On one occasion, he declared: "Black reaction's mentality has not changed for a thousand years. It just cannot understand (reforms). . . . What kind of respect can people who exploit their fellow men have for religion?" On another occasion, he warned the landlords that if they "do not wake up, . . . their lands will be freely distributed among the landless peasants. Any person caught in a subversive act, or found destroying the crop, will be severely punished by the security forces and judiciary."[43] Many landlords were arrested and jailed; some were banished from their towns; land of some resistant landlords was confiscated; and demonstrations were ruthlessly suppressed. With respect to the murder incident in Fars, the government reacted by imposing martial law on the province, declaring a day of national mourning, severely punishing the perpetrators—the number of people implicated in the case reached one hundred and fifty—and actually speeding up the process of implementation. As the government had clearly demonstrated its resolve to remove the forces of obstruction, the landlords made no further effort at a concerted and sustained struggle, and accepted the reform with apparent resignation.

Countries Without a Strong Political Commitment to Reform

In India, Pakistan, Colombia, and the Philippines, the elites have not demonstrated a sustained commitment to reform. Though a number of political leaders in these countries have consistently stressed the need for tenurial changes, some have failed to exert a lasting impact on their countries' agrarian policy, while others have not really been willing to re-

[42] For various accounts of landlords' resistance to reform, see *Iran Almanac 1963*, pp. 398–400; "Iran: Murder v. Reform," *Time*, LXXX (November 23, 1962), 19–20. *The New York Times*, June 6, 1963, pp. 1, 8; and June 7, 1963, pp. 1, 3; and Peter Avery, "Trends in Iran, the Past Five Years," *World Today*, XXI (July 1965), 283.

[43] *Iran Almanac 1963*, pp. 399, 400.

duce substantially the interest of the landed class for the benefit of the peasantry.

INDIA: THE FAILING SUPPORT OF CONGRESS

During the nationalist movement in India, Mahatma Gandhi, the foremost champion of agrarianism, enthusiastically embraced all reform programs the Congress offered. In word and deed, he clearly identified himself with the rural masses. But his untimely death prevented him from influencing the post-independence reform programs. His successor, Nehru, abolished the *zamindari* system and constantly pushed further reforms. But in personality, temperament, and mannerism, he was totally different from his political mentor. He effectively assumed Gandhi's leadership position, but not the latter's image as a man of the peasantry. Moreover, Gandhi and Nehru apparently held different views toward reform. The former favored confiscation of the land of large owners, thus implying giving land free to the peasants; whereas the latter considered it essential to give some compensation.[44] The Gandhian approach to reform, motivated by the thought of reviving the pre-modern Indian social system, attached primary importance to the idea of giving land to the landless. "Land and all properties is his who will work it," Gandhi declared.[45] Nehru and other "modernists" in the Congress, in contrast, conceived tenurial changes as a vital part of the process of economic development, in which the increase of production was the governing consideration. In effecting agrarian programs, the Congress should "think more and more from the point of view of an economy of abundance," Nehru emphasized.[46] After the death of Gandhi, his agrarian views found expression in the privately initiated land-gift movement, which, despite the energetic drive by Bhave, had only meager results. The government's land reform programs, formulated in accordance with the modernist conception, were comprehensive in scope but were not given any effective central direction or the necessary political support to bring them to a successful conclusion.

This is clearly seen in the administrative machinery utilized by the

[44] See H. D. Malaviya, *Land Reforms in India* (New Delhi, 1954), pp. 20, 70–71, and 74.

[45] Quoted in *ibid.*, p. 70.

[46] Quoted in Susanne H. Rudolph, *Some Aspects of Congress Land Reform Policy* (Cambridge, Mass., MIT, Center for International Studies, 1957, ditto), p. 15. For an incisive analysis of the differences in the approaches of the Gandhians and Modernists to India's agricultural policy, see *ibid.*, pp. 10–16.

Congress for enforcement of reform. Entrusting the responsibility for formulation and execution of programs to the states, the Congress created no special national agency to provide the necessary overall guidance and supervision. Instead, it relied on the Planning Commission to perform these vital tasks. Preoccupied with the process of formulation and evaluation of economic plans, understaffed in its Land Reform Division,[47] and lacking enforcement powers, this agency was simply too ill-equipped, unprepared, and impotent to do the job. In dealing with the states about land reform, the Commission merely outlined broad principles and reviewed the progress of implementation. Thus, during a parliamentary inquiry on November 18, 1965, B. R. Bhagat, the Minister of Planning, declared in the Lok Sabha:

> The proposals relating to land reforms in the Five Year Plans are in the nature of a broad, common approach, which have to be adapted and pursued in each State with due regard to local conditions and in response to local needs. The measures adopted in the States have been reviewed in the Midterm Appraisal and the Planning Commission publication "Progress of land reforms." [48]

The national leadership of the Congress was fully aware, of course, that to let each state, where the landed interests were entrenched, pursue form "with due regard to local conditions and in response to local needs" was simply to permit these interests to delay reform. The leadership persistently tolerated this delay but continuously ignored a 1949 recommendation of the Congress Party's Agrarian Reforms Committee that Central Land Commissioners be appointed, vested "with necessary powers," and "charged with the task of quickening up the pace of the agrarian reforms." [49] This was clear testimony to the leadership's disinterest in serious implementation.

An independent agency for land reform did not exist in the national government, and the states did not maintain such an agency either. Instead,

---

[47] Among the twenty or so administrative units of the Planning Commission, there is one "Land Reform Division" with a staff of about twelve members.

[48] India, Parliament, *Lok Sabha Debates*, Thirteenth Session, Third Series, Vol. XLVIII (1965), No. 11, c. 2573–2574.

[49] Indian National Congress, *Report of the Agrarian Reforms Committee* (New Delhi: All-Indian Congress Committee, 1949), p. 13. The leadership also ignored a similar recommendation of the First Five Year Plan (1951–1956), for the creation of a "Central Organisation of Land Reforms" to oversee implementation in states. See India, Planning Commission, *Progress of Land Reform* (Delhi, 1963), p. 229.

the Revenue Administration was assigned the responsibility for enforcement of reform laws. Having long been susceptible to the influence of big landlords, this Administration could hardly be expected to show eagerness and impartiality in discharging its added responsibility. Already heavily burdened by its own working load, the Administration was supposed to perform a host of exacting and complex tasks in connection with various reform programs: assessment and payment of compensation to landowners, collection of payment from beneficiaries, maintenance of land records, conduct of land surveys, and administration of land settlement. It just could not adequately perform these tasks, even if it had been willing and dedicated to doing so.

To this day, the administrative mechanisms for reform enforcement are still extremely weak and excessively decentralized. And the Congress leadership has not developed strong peasant organizations to complement the government machinery. The Congress was eager and effective in mobilizing the peasantry into the nationalist movement but reluctant to bring the same force into the process of implementation of its agrarian policy. As a result, the enforcement of India's reform programs—which, if genuinely carried out, would be a revolutionary transformation of rural India—falls entirely on the shoulders of the reluctant bureaucrats.

Since its independence in 1947, India has perhaps enacted more land-reform laws than any other country in the world. But what is the record of performance? This can best be seen in a government document on the subject. In November 1963, the Indian National Development Council created an Implementation of Land Reform Committee to review the progress of reform in the states. After extensive study in the field, the committee issued a report in 1966 containing the following principal findings:

> (i) Administrative arrangements for enforcement and supervision are often inadequate and public opinion has not been sufficiently built up to quicken the pace of reforms. . . .
> (ii) Records of tenants do not exist in several States and are often incomplete and out of date even when they do. For effective enforcement of tenancy reform, it is imperative that records of tenancies should be prepared and kept up to date whatever the difficulties in the way. . . .
> (iii) The economic condition of tenants, even where they have been conferred permanent rights, still continues to be weak. It is important to confer on them the right to make permanent improvements

to the land and to ensure adequate compensation to them in the event of eviction. . . .

(iv) In some States, such as Andhra Pradesh, Assam, Bihar, Madras and West Bengal (in respect of Bargadars), the existing provisions for security of tenure are of a temporary nature. Comprehensive measures for converting tenants and sharecroppers into owners have not yet been adopted. Delay in enacting comprehensive legislation creates a great deal of uncertainty which is inimical to efforts for increasing agricultural production. Speedy action is called for to rectify this situation.

(v) Even the apparently restricted right of resumption for personal cultivation has, in practice, widened the scope of ejectments. Besides, such resumption upsets the economy of small owner-cum-tenant farmers who had leased in small areas to make up viable units of cultivation. . . .

(vi) Numerous ejectments of tenants have occurred under the guise of "voluntary surrenders." This has tended to defeat one of the major aims of land reforms, namely, providing security of tenure for the tiller of the soil. . . .

(vii) The rents as fixed by law are still too high in Adhra area, Jammu and Kashmir, Madras, Punjab and West Bengal and should be brought down to the level recommended in the [Five Year] Plans —to one-fourth or one-fifth of the gross produce. . . .

The programme of ceilings set out in the Plan has been diluted in implementation. There were deficiencies in the law and delays in its enactment and implementation resulting in large scale evasions. . . .[50]

Such is the record of performance. One must note that these findings, which were also contained in previous official reports and numerous scholarly studies,[51] were issued after the Congress leadership had repeatedly pledged—through five-year plans, policy statements, official reports, and Congress resolutions and manifestoes—to devote an increasing effort to implementation of reform. But the leadership has never made good its

[50] India, Planning Commission, *Implementation of Land Reforms: A Review by the Land Reforms Implementation Committee of the National Development Council* (New Delhi, 1966), pp. 279–281.

[51] See, for instance, India, Planning Commission, *Reports on the Committees of the Panel on Land Reforms* (Delhi, 1959), p. 65; India, Planning Commission, *Memorandum on the Fourth Five Year Plan* (New Delhi, 1964), p. 37. Wolf Ladejinsky, *A Study on Tenurial Conditions in Package Districts* (India, Planning Commission, 1965), *passim*; *Indian Journal of Agricultural Economics*, XVII (January–March 1962), entire issue; and, J. S. Uppal, "Implementation of Land Reform Legislation in India—A Study of Two Villages in Punjab," *Asian Survey*, IX (May 1969), 359–372.

pledge. Recently it stressed again the need for intensifying the enforcement effort. In November 1969, Prime Minister Indira Gandhi told the
chief ministers of the states: "No single program so intimately affects so
many millions of our people as land reform." She demanded they " 'act
now when there is still time and hope' to effectively implement the land
reforms as part of the new agricultural strategy." [52] In the following month,
she exhorted a Congress Party convention, " 'as a matter of urgency,' . . .
the state governments implement existing laws on land reform by no
later than 1971." [53] Judging by the failures of the Congress Party in the
past, and by the fact that "the chief ministers of most of the nation's 17
states depend heavily on landed class for their . . . [political] support," [54]
one wonders if this latest verbal affirmation for reform can lead to serious
action. Perhaps there still is *time* for India to implement effectively its
reform laws, but there is no *hope* that this can be done.

PAKISTAN: A MEAGER PROMISE

In India, the lack of commitment to reform has resulted in a hopeless
delay in the implementation of programs; in Pakistan, the lack of such
commitment has much reduced the *scope* of implementation. The only
Pakistani leader who demonstrated a concern for reform was Ayub Khan.
Unlike his civilian predecessors, who expressed interest in reform in words
but never in deeds, General Ayub Khan was definitely ready to put his
programs into effect. As the *Khyber Mail,* a newspaper in Peshawar, West
Pakistan, commented in an editorial of January 27, 1959, "Time and again
a successive chain of political parties and politicians promised to introduce
land reforms but none had the courage to . . . [face up to] an extremely
difficult and complicated problem." In contrast, the paper continued, "The
President has proved beyond doubt that he is essentially a man of action
and does not believe in making promises which cannot be fulfilled." [55]
However, his promises were never generous. When he took over power,
Ayub Khan became preoccupied with the task of restoration of political
order and stability, leaving the crucial tasks of formulation and implementation of reform to civil servants. The West Pakistan Land Reforms Commission he created to draft a reform decree was conservative in outlook

[52] *India News,* December 12, 1969, p. 1.
[53] *The New York Times,* December 28, 1969, p. 9.
[54] *Ibid.*
[55] Quoted in Pakistan, Planning Commission, *Land Reform in Pakistan* (1959), pp.
59–60.

and biased in favor of the landed interests. Under Ayub Khan's instructions
that it should seek to preserve and improve but not to alter fundamentally
the existing land-tenure system, the Commission came to recommend a
set of ceilings of landownership much higher than those endorsed by the
pre-coup civilian government. In advocating reform, Ayub Khan expressed
his admiration for the Egyptian model and considered it worth imitating.
Yet he nearly quadrupled East Pakistan's ceiling of landownership (from
33 to 125 acres) in 1961—the very year in which the Egyptian ceiling was
lowered to half of the 1952 level (from 200 to 100 *feddans*).

With a professed concern for the preservation of the rural middle
class, and conceding that his reform in West Pakistan could affect only
some six thousand of a total of five million landowners in the province,
Ayub Khan precluded any large-scale reform even before the program
started. Yet he made the claim: "We have done all that could possibly be
done for . . . [the tenants] in our present situation." [56]

In 1965, after more than a decade's reform in West Pakistan, the
Pakistani Planning Commission, apparently considering it desirable to
expand the scope of the 1959 program, proposed to reduce the ceilings of
landownership from 500 acres to 250 for irrigated land, and from 1,000
acres to 500 for non-irrigated land. [57] The Ayub Khan regime scratched the
proposal without even any serious discussion.

COLOMBIA: THE RELUCTANT ELITE

In Colombia, as one observer has aptly noted, "the ruling groups have
accepted the principle of land reform reluctantly, and there are strong well-
organized groups opposed to more than token implementation." [58] Many
reform administrators, in fact, come from the same economic and social
class as the reform opponents. As required by the 1961 law, the Managing
Board of INCORA consists of equal membership of the Liberal and
Conservative Parties, including representatives from such organizations of
the landed interests as the Colombian Agricultural Society (SAC), and
the Colombian Cattlemen's Confederation (*Confederación Colombiana
de Ganaderos,* CCG). [59] The maintenance of political parity in the distribu-

---

[56] Ayub Khan, *Speeches and Statements,* Vol. I (Karachi, n.d.), p. 51.

[57] Pakistan, National Planning Board, *The Third Five Year Plan 1965–70,* pp. 426–
427.

[58] Cole Blasier, "Power and Social Change in Colombia," *Journal of Inter-American
Studies,* III (July 1966), p. 393.

[59] Other members of the board are representatives from the Ministry of Agriculture,
the Ministry of Public Works, the *Caja Agraria,* the National Supplies Institute, the

tion of the board membership practically prevents INCORA from follow-ing an independent and active policy, while the presence of SAC and CCG representatives serves as a restraint to any attempt to restrict ef-fectively the landed interests. To mobilize local resources for the admin-istration of the program, and to publicize INCORA'S activities, the 1961 law provides for the creation of regional councils to be organized accord-ing to the same principles as the national board (Article 101). Observers on the scene have discovered that in their initial operations a number of councils were not properly functioning, while others "had started to manifest themselves as spokesmen of the landed interests in order to make life more difficult for the central administration." [60] While the landed in-terests were represented in the national and local administrative structure of INCORA, the peasants were not brought into the implementation process. There are no *campesino* organizations created specifically to repre-sent the farmers and to participate in the execution of the reform law.[61] By building into the administrative process an active force in opposition to reform and by failing to enlist a potential force of support, the elite's intention cannot be plainer. It is to retard rather than to facilitate im-plementation.

Within the elite, a few leaders have shown a greater concern for reform. It is largely due to the efforts of these individuals that Colombia has been able to achieve a modest record in enforcing certain aspects of the 1961 law. For some time, former President Carlos Lleras Restrepo was intimately associated with the country's reform movement. He chaired the committee that drafted the 1961 reform bill; he actively campaigned both within and without Congress for the passage of the law; he was a member of the INCORA board; and during his presidential tenure, 1966–1970, he earnestly sought to expand the financial resources of INCORA,

Augustín Codazzi Geographical Institute, the Agricultural Cooperatives, the agricultural workers, the Catholic Social Action, the Armed Forces, and two Senators and two Rep-resentatives from the Congress. In 1965, there were a total of twenty-three members.

[60] See the remarks by Albert O. Hirschman and Charles W. Anderson on this sub-ject in Land Tenure Center, *Land Reform and Social Change in Colombia*, p. 10. See also Ernest Feder, "The Rational Implementation of Land Reform in Colombia," *Amé-rica Latina*, VI (Jan.–March 1963), 94.

[61] It is true that rural cooperatives and agricultural workers have representatives on the national managing board and the regional councils of INCORA. But they are se-lected by the government, not by the peasants. Unlike the farmers of Mexico and Tai-wan who were organized to participate in the execution of reform programs, the bulk of the Colombian *campesinos* remains totally unorganized, playing no role in either the selection of INCORA representatives nor in the execution of program.

and managed to obtain a new tenancy reform law. But, as the head of a coalition government, he could not personally exercise a decisive influence on any national policy that the evenly divided Congress (between the Conservatives and Liberals) chose not to support. Enrique Peñalosa Camargo, the first director of INCORA till 1969, was a man of energy, dedication, and outstanding administrative competence. Appointed to the position at the age of thirty-one, Peñalosa promptly assembled an able staff, created a rather efficient organization, moved boldly on various fronts, and launched more than forty projects in the country, at least one in each department. Considering the political restraints to which he was subject, one must say he achieved an impressive record of service. But as an administrator, he had to act within the basic policies charted by the top political elite. Like Lleras, Peñalosa could serve, but not challenge, the interest of the elite. He could actively push land reform, but only within the given mandate.

The 1961 law is rather comprehensive in scope, involving both redistributive and developmental measures. To the reform proponents, the redistributive measures, particularly the redistribution of private farms, were clearly of primary importance. This was the intention of the National Agrarian Committee that provided the preliminary draft of the 1961 law. As enacted, the law declared the elimination of inequitable concentration of ownership as its very first objective (Article 1). Initially, Peñalosa firmly held this view and announced, in 1962, a large-scale "parcelization" of farms as INCORA's primary activity. He emphasized that INCORA would acquire private land through purchase if possible, but through expropriation if necessary. The elite held a different view. It believed that the reform agency should place emphasis on neither the redistribution of private farms nor a broad-scale developmental program. Instead, the effort should be directed at those projects least disturbing to the existing land tenure and involving minimal cost. This belief, manifested primarily through the type and amount of funds appropriated by the Congress, led gradually to a change of orientation in INCORA. Indicative of such a change was a statement by Peñalosa during a press interview in January 1967. He enunciated three reform objectives: "First, to supply the growing domestic demands [for food]; second, to provide substitutes for current imports of foodstuffs, and third, to increase exports of foodstuffs." [62] Im-

[62] Quoted in Ernest A. Duff, *Agrarian Reform in Colombia* (New York, 1968), pp. 120–121.

plying that the increase of production of food could best be accomplished by emphasizing the *present* INCORA approach to reform, he made no mention of land redistribution during the entire interview. What was the *present* INCORA approach to land reform? This can be seen in the principal categories of activities of the agency as summarized in Table 26.

Among INCORA's principal activities, redistribution of private land has clearly achieved the least results. The amount of redistributed land (125,051 hectares) accounted for about only 2 percent of the total area of land affected by INCORA's various activities. Among INCORA's other activities, the extinction of ownership of uncultivated private land is of no major significance, because much of this land has never been utilized and is not presently suitable for agricultural use. The grant of land titles to farmers in the public domain has been an important accomplishment, for it has greatly alleviated the problems of insecurity and conflicts of claims. This activity, it should be noted, involved no transfer or grant of land; it merely legalized the status quo. In that sense, it is not a land redistribution program. At present, INCORA clearly concentrates efforts on the extension of credit, the expansion of irrigation areas, and the provision of basic agricultural services to the settlers in reform project areas. As of 1968, a government document reported, "approximately 44% of . . . [the INCORA's] funds are for farm improvement projects, primarily supervised for developing existing small farms; 40% for capital-intensive land reclamation projects, such as irrigation, drainage and flood

TABLE 26

PRINCIPAL ACTIVITIES AND RESULTS OF INCORA, 1962–1969

Principal Activities		Results
Redistribution of private land	7,594 families	125,051 ha.
Extinction of ownership of un-cultivated private land	247 properties	3,462,650 ha.
Grant of land titles in the public domain	87,656 titles	2,775,340 ha.
Extension of loans, general	33,000 families	₱827,240,000
Extension of loans, cattle		₱193,955,000
Expansion and improvement of irrigated land		44,770 ha.
Cooperative societies created	31 societies	20,231 members

SOURCE: INCORA, Secretaría de Organización y Systemas, *La Reforma Agraria en Colombia* (Bogota, 1970).

control; and 16% for colonization." [63] But even with these activities, only a small number of farmers who happen to be in the project areas have benefited, with the bulk of the Colombian *campesinos* totally unaffected.

THE PHILIPPINES: ABSENCE OF SUSTAINED COMMITMENT

In the Philippines, Ramon Magsaysay was undoubtedly a strong advocate for reform. His sponsorship of the Economic Development Corporation as a means to pacify the Huks was an important indication of his understanding of the political significance of the land issue. Declaring "that he would live like Mexico's Cárdenas, 'who always stayed with the people to learn their problems and their needs . . . ,' " [64] Magsaysay exacted from a reluctant Congress three major reform bills and personally launched the San Luis Project to distribute land in the former Huk-controlled area. Magsaysay's death in 1957, however, left much of his program unimplemented, and with the passage of time his brief but strong rural impact has gradually receded into the background.

Magsaysay's political successors managed to enact a new law in 1963, much expanding the scope of the earlier program. But some of the people who shared Magsaysay's devotion to the peasantry have been out of office, while those in office do not possess the kind of reform spirit Magsaysay once generated. Raul S. Manglapus and Manuel P. Manahan, two former Senators closely identified with Magsaysay's rural-reform movement, bowed out of politics in 1967. President Diosdado Macapagal, during whose administration the 1963 reform law was adopted, and the present President, Ferdinand Marcos, have emphasized their support for reform, but have both viewed reform as a means to serve their immediate political ends rather than as a program with a purpose of its own. When elections approached, or when the Huk movement became threatening, a token effort at implementation would be made; at other times, both Presidents would give verbal endorsement to reform and become reluctant to provide the necessary financial support.

From the enactment of the Philippine Rice Share Tenancy Act of 1946, the Philippine land-reform movement has stretched over twenty-five years. Yet not a single national leader has been clearly recognized by the rural population as the movement's principal driving force. The rural

[63] Colombia Information Service, *Colombia Today*, IV (March 1969), no page number.
[64] Francis L. Starner, *Magsaysay and the Philippine Peasantry* (Berkeley, 1961), p. 39.

survey the author conducted in 1969 in the Luzon provinces, in which the Philippines' present reform effort is concentrated, reveals that as many as three-fourths of the 407 respondents either failed to identify a major contributor to the country's reform or did not know any. (In contrast, it may be recalled, about the same proportion of the rural respondents in the Taiwan survey singled out Chen Cheng as the principal reform leader there.) Of all Philippine respondents, only 26 (or 6.39 percent) identified Presidents Magsaysay, Macapagal, and Marcos. A same number named "farmers and tenants" as the major contributors.

In the Philippines, without a commitment from the top leadership, but facing the determined opposition of the landlords in the field, those responsible for program administration were seriously inhibited from playing an active role. Conrado F. Estrella, the Governor of the Land Authority (LA), as demonstrated his devotion to reform by voluntarily placing his large landholdings in leasehold and by tirelessly preaching the cause of agrarian change in Manila and in the barrios. Similarly, like their

TABLE 27

RURAL PERCEPTION OF CONTRIBUTORS TO LAND REFORM IN
THE PHILIPPINES,
LUZON SURVEY, 1969

Question: *"Who has made the greatest
contribution to the cause of land reform in the Philippines?"*

	Respondents	
Contributor	Number	Percent
Ramon Magsaysay	2	0.49
Diosdado Macapagal	6	1.47
Ferdinand E. Marcos[a]	18	4.42
Conrado F. Estrella	2	0.49
Farmers and tenants	26	6.39
Others	43	10.57
No one	3	0.74
Don't know	12	2.95
No answer	295	72.48
Total	407	100.00

[a] Including such answers as "national government" and "the present administration."

SOURCE: See Appendix III.

counterparts in Columbia, the administrative and technical personnel of the LA are intelligent, dedicated, and competent men. But they, likewise, had to work within the limitations imposed by the national political leadership. The 1963 law provides that, before an area can be proclaimed a land reform district, all relevant "government machineries and agencies" must be ready to operate in the area, and the government must have fully "considered factors affecting feasibility and funding requirements . . . (Sec. 128)." These provisions practically leave everything to the discretion of the President. In interviews with officials of the LA in 1969, the author gathered the distinct impression that while the LA was enthusiastically recommending the creation of new reform districts, the number of districts actually created always fell far short of its expectations. In trimming down the number of recommended districts, President Marcos invariably pleaded that he could not spare enough personnel and funds to meet the LA's recommendations. In January 1969, over five years after the passage of the 1963 land-reform law, President Marcos, announced: "We raised the land reform program to the level of serious action for the first time. . . . As of today, land reform covers 60 municipalities and two cities in 12 provinces, and involves 86,939 farmers." [65] But the nation then had 1,379 municipalities and 50 cities in 59 provinces, and over 2,000,000 farm families. If the progress of reform in the future proceeds at this pace, it will require at least another 110 years for the law to extend to all of the nation's territory.

The absence of commitment to reform has not only severely restricted the geographical coverage of the 1963 law but also hampered effective implementation in declared reform districts. With respect to the land redistribution program, the total affected area of land in all reform districts from 1963 to 1968 was not more than 6,100 hectares, an insignificant amount in a country with over 7,000,000 hectares of farm land. As to the leasehold program, the progress of implementation was faster, but only slightly so. As it now stands, the program applies to only palay (rice) land, excluding from its coverage land planted with other crops. From 1963 to 1968, the program covered a total of 86,618 farmers and 216,526.66 hectares of land, amounting to 8.22 percent of the total palay farmers and 7.13 percent of the total palay land of the nation (see Map 1 and Table 28). The ineffective implementation of the program is also

[65] Ferdinand E. Marcos, New Filipinism: the Turning Point, State of the Union Message to the Congress of the Philippines, 27 January 1969 (Manila, [1967]), pp. 9, 94.

LAND REFORM IN THE PHILIPPINES, 1968,
REGIONS AND PROVINCES

Regions are designated by number; names of provinces are identified below each designated region; arabic numerals above the star refer to the number of municipalities declared as land-reform districts in each region.

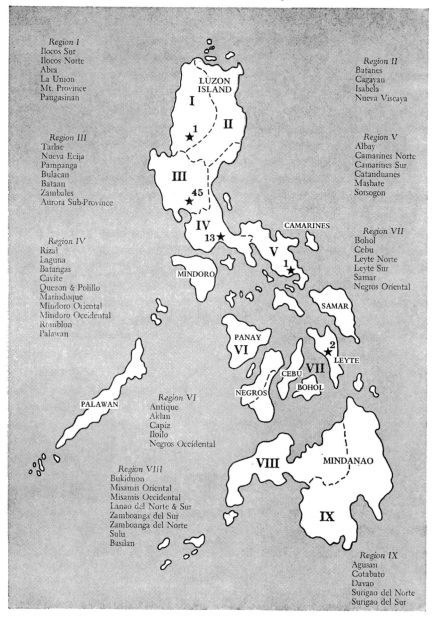

Region I
Ilocos Sur
Ilocos Norte
Abra
La Union
Mt. Province
Pangasinan

Region III
Tarlac
Nueva Ecija
Pampanga
Bulacan
Bataan
Zambales
Aurora Sub-Province

Region IV
Rizal
Laguna
Batangas
Cavite
Quezon & Polillo
Marinduque
Mindoro Oriental
Mindoro Occidental
Romblon
Palawan

Region VI
Antique
Aklan
Capiz
Iloilo
Negros Occidental

Region VIII
Bukidnon
Misamis Oriental
Misamis Occidental
Lanao del Norte & Sur
Zamboanga del Sur
Zamboanga del Norte
Sulu
Basilan

Region II
Batanes
Cagayan
Isabela
Nueva Viscaya

Region V
Albay
Camarines Norte
Camarines Sur
Catanduanes
Masbate
Sorsogon

Region VII
Bohol
Cebu
Leyte Norte
Leyte Sur
Samar
Negros Oriental

Region IX
Agusan
Cotabato
Davao
Surigao del Norte
Surigao del Sur

LUZON ISLAND

CAMARINES

MINDORO

SAMAR

PANAY

LEYTE

CEBU

NEGROS

BOHOL

PALAWAN

MINDANAO

TABLE 28

PROGRESS OF LEASEHOLD CONVERSION IN THE PHILIPPINES, 1963–1968

Region	Number of Munici- palities	Number of Palay Farmers Converted to Lessees	Area of Land Affected in ha.	Proportion of Coverage			
				Percent of Whole Region		Percent of Whole Nation	
				Farmers	Area	Farmers	Area
Region III[a]	46	75,843	195,852.49	31.33	33.07	7.20	6.45
Region IV	13	6,954	14,376.67	5.38	3.72	0.66	0.47
Region V	1	1,137	2,166.80	1.53	1.00	0.11	0.07
Region VII	2	2,684	4,130.70	3.33	1.75	0.25	0.14
Total	62	86,618	216,526.66	. . .	. . .	8.22	7.13

[a] Central Luzon, including one municipality in Region I.

SOURCE: [Philippines, National Land Reformation Council], *The Philippine Land Reform Program* [1968].

indicated by the fact that, even in declared reform districts, tenants yet to be benefited from the program far outnumber those having been converted to lessees. For instance, in Nueva Ecija Province—a principal reform area—there were a total of 47,920 palay farmers. As of 1968, the tenure status of these farmers was as follows: 4,076 owner operators; 6,065 lessees; 36,823 tenants; and 956 farmers of unspecified status.[66] Thus the number of tenants was six times that of lessees.

It should be noted that, in the declared reform districts, resistance to the leasehold system was widespread. In Tarlac Province, for example, Governor Eduardo Cojuangco, the land baron of the province, expressed his objection to the leasehold program to LA Governor Estrella when the latter toured the area. "I'm against land reform," he said. The lessees "won't be able to hold onto the land. . . . [With] one bad crop . . . they'll be out of business. In ten years there will be just a few big holdings again. Wait and see." [67] Unlike the large landholders who openly questioned the 1963 law, smaller landlords preferred to sabotage leasehold through evasion and subterfuge. LA Governor Estrella has summarized some of their major methods. Landlords might offer their tenants certain favors—for example, interest-free credit—to induce the latter not to seek

[66] The Philippines, National Land Reform Council, Plans and Programs Office, *Land Reform Statistical Digest*, No. 5 (June 1968), Table 3.

[67] *The New York Times*, April 12, 1968, p. 14.

TABLE 29

LEASEHOLD CONTRACTS AND LESSEES, THE PHILIPPINES,
as of December 31, 1968

Contracts and Lessees	Number
Registered contracts[a]	5,175
Lessees[a]	3,928
Written contracts due for registration	3,407
Lessees	2,902
Oral contracts	7,539
Lessees	7,081
"Compromise agreements" [b]	1,139
Lessees	1,139
Cases under mediation	2,809
Cases waiting for court action	1,720

[a] Original data did not differentiate between oral and written contracts, but it can be safely assumed that the number of written contracts did not constitute the majority of the registered ones.

[b] Meaning unexplained in original data.

SOURCE: The Philippines, National Land Reform Council, Plans and Programs Office, *Quarterly Report, October–December 1968*, Table 1.

to convert to lessees. If unsuccessful, they might harass the tenants by "threats of ejectment and withdrawal of farm implements and work animals loaned to the tenants." They might also change the type of crops to qualify for exemption. "The change is usually from rice to sugar cane, because the latter does not fall within the purview of a general leasehold proclamation." If all these forms of resistance were unavailing, there was still the possibility of continuing the "tenancy relationship between a lessee and a landowner despite the presence of a signed and registered leasehold contract. . . . Under this anomalous arrangement, the lessee gives the landowner, . . . extra *cavans* [a unit of weight] of palay in addition to what is actually stipulated in the leasehold contract." [68]

In addition to these problems, there is the widespread practice of concluding leasehold contracts in oral form instead of written form. Table 29 indicates that as of December 31, 1968, in the declared reform districts, oral leasehold contracts were more than twice as numerous as written ones. Since even written contracts cannot prevent disguised

[68] Conrado F. Estrella, "The Philippine Land Reform Program, A Country Statement" (Diliman, Quezon City, 1966), pp. 36–38.

tenancy, it is extremely questionable that oral contracts can really do so. One can summarize the Philippine leasehold experiences by saying: the program applied to an insignificant number of areas; in these areas tenants outnumbered lessees; and lessees concluded more oral contracts than written ones.

INADEQUATE UTILIZATION OF RESOURCES

One consequence of the lack of strong political commitment in India, Pakistan, Colombia, and the Philippines is the inadequate utilization of available resources in carrying out programs. Though the elites of these countries often complain about the shortage of public funds, they appear to command greater financial resources than those elites that have demonstrated a strong commitment to reform. Consider, for instance, the gross domestic product (GDP) and the government revenue of the eight countries under study. As seen in Table 30, if Mexico is excluded from con-

TABLE 30

FINANCIAL RESOURCES, EIGHT COUNTRIES, 1958

| | Gross Domestic Product | | | | |
| | Total | | Per capita | | |
Country	In million U.S. $	Rank	In U.S. $	Rank	Government Revenue or Expenditure as a Percent of GDP
India	28,224	1	68	7	11.01[a,b]
Mexico	9,832	2	292	1	4.58[c]
Pakistan	5,889	3	66	8	8.91[c,d]
Philippines	5,118	4	198	3	11.25[a]
Colombia	3,197	5	221	2	11.21[a]
U.A.R.	2,724	6	110	5	5.46[b,c]
Iran	2,079[e]	7	108	6	10.07[c]
Taiwan	1,310	8	133	4	25.65[a,f]

[a] Government revenue.

[b] Percentage derived from net domestic product.

[c] Government expenditure.

[d] 1962.

[e] Gross national product, 1957. Mikoto Usui and E. E. Hagen, *World Income 1957* (Cambridge, Mass., 1959), cited in Bruce M. Russett, et al., *World Handbook of Political and Social Indicators* (New Haven and London: Yale University Press, 1964), pp. 153, 156.

[f] 1959.

SOURCE: Except noted otherwise above, U.N., *Yearbook of National Accounts Statistics 1966* (New York: United Nations, 1967).

sideration (for much of the country's land redistribution program was carried out without compensation), it appears that the U.A.R., Iran, and Taiwan—the three countries with extensive land redistribution—possessed smaller financial capacity than the other countries. In terms of the total GDP, these three countries occupied the three lowest positions among the eight countries. In terms of per capita GDP, they fell considerably behind Colombia and the Philippines. In terms of government revenue or expenditure as a percentage of GDP, Taiwan's figure is very large, but as much as 80 percent of the central government's budget has been for years devoted to defense.[69] Iran's figure is smaller than that of the Philippines, Colombia, and India, and only slightly larger than that of Pakistan. The U.A.R.'s figure is the smallest among all these countries (excluding Mexico). Thus, the financial resources commanded by the U.A.R., Iran, and Taiwan were not large. Reading all these data together, one gathers the distinct impression that, in the countries with limited reform implementation, what retards progress is not lack of funds (which is a problem common to all eight countries), but political willingness to allocate a sufficient share of relatively abundant financial resources to reform.

This impression is strengthened as one looks at the budget allocations for land reform in Pakistan and the Philippines, two of the countries without strong commitments to reform. In Pakistan during the Second Five Year Plan, 1960–1965, the total projected expenditure for agriculture was Rs. 2,515 million; of this amount only Rs. 71.8 million, or 2.8 percent, was assigned to land reform. During the Second Five Year Plan, 1965–1970, the corresponding figures were Rs. 5,083.43 million, Rs. 11 million, 0.2 percent. In both plans, land reform was among the few agricultural programs that consistently received the lowest financial allocations—allocations amounting to only a tiny fraction of the funds assigned to "manures and fertilizers," "animal husbandry," and "plant protection." [70] In the Philippines, to promote agricultural development, the Marcos Administration adopted a rural "infrastructure" program and created a Barrio Development Fund—a kind of rural pork-barrel program practically allowing

[69] See Hung Chao Tai, "The Kuomintang and Modernization in Taiwan," in Samuel P. Huntington and Clement H. Moore (eds.), *Authoritarian Politics in Modern Society* (New York, 1970), p. 424.

[70] See Pakistan, Planning Commission, *Handbook of Agricultural Statistics June 1964* (Karachi, 1964), pp. 10–11; and Pakistan, *The Third Five Year Plan 1965–70*, pp. 459–460.

the President to dispense freely ₱2,000 to each barrio. Both of these programs entailed considerable expenditure. But land reform was given
comparatively little financial support. As one observer has put it: "Compared to the infrastructure budget, the allocation for land reform is a
drop in the ocean. The smelly Barrio Fund amounted to four times more
than the land reform budgets for the past four years combined. The
tobacco subsidy is three times as large as the land reform allocation." [71]

With respect to the administrative and technical personnel required
for implementing reform, available information on three countries—Iran,
Colombia, and the Philippines—makes a rough comparison possible. In
September 1963, the Land Reform Organization of Iran had a field staff
of 1,159 persons scattered over the country's 22 provinces and territories.
Proceeding with unusual speed (see Table 25), they redistributed in over
one year's time 8,042 villages, or about one-sixth of Iran's total rural area.
Colombia and the Philippines maintained a comparable number of field-
staff members; Colombia's INCORA had 1,215 officials in 1966, and
the Philippines LA employed 1,143 in 1967.[72] Yet, in five years' time,
these two countries covered only an extremely small fraction of the
farm land.

In fact, in both Colombia and the Philippines, there was a rather
high density of technical staff in the reform districts. In the 1960s,
INCORA employed over 400 agronomists and over 300 engineers. As one
observer has noted, deploying the technicians in the limited number of
reform districts, INCORA had more technical expertise than it could
utilize. "Any problems the reform may encounter are not due to a lack
of technical knowledge. . . . Any 'unreadiness gap' has been effectively
closed." [73] Much the same situation existed in the Philippines. A Philippine
Land Reform Project Team, normally working within a declared reform
district, consisted of five administrative officers, and one each of the following categories of personnel: credit officer, fertilizer agent, extension super-
visor, farm management technician (FMT), home management technician
(HMT), rural youth officer (RYO), cooperative officer, and legal officer.
The maintenance of such an elaborate staff on a project team raised a

[71] Edward R. Kiunisala, "Victory for Land Reform?" *Philippines Free Press*, December 6, 1969, p. 6.

[72] See Colombia, INCORA, *5 Años de Reforma Social Agraria, Informe de Actividades en 1966* (Bogotá, 1967), p. 38; and the Philippines, National Land Reforms Council, *An Evaluation on Land Reform Operations* (Quezon City, [1968]), Tables 4, 5,
and 6.

[73] Duff, *op. cit.* (n. 62 above), p. 134.

number of problems. First, this limited the government's capacity to expand the geographical coverage of the program.[74] Second, these officers were drawn from different agencies—the Agricultural Productivity Commission, the Agricultural Credit Administration, the Office of the Agrarian Counsel, and the Land Bank—over whom the Land Authority had only a coordinating authority. As a result, inter-service conflicts and complaints were frequently reported, leading to lower efficiency of the project team. And third, the high staff density have resulted in excessive official intervention in the farming practices of the reform beneficiaries. Thus, an official report commented:

> In land reform areas, one FMT [for example,] is assigned to every 75 to 100 farmers. If . . . [this] ratio is maintained throughout in all land reform areas, it may appear that the administration is pampering our farmers too much and results may then be contrary to what is envisioned in the [land reform] code. . . . This situation holds true also [in the case of] the HMTs and RYOs.[75]

The report recommended a reduction of these types of personnel.

Evidently, the slow progress in reform in Colombia and the Philippines cannot be attributed to the lack of administrative and technical personnel but to the failures of the elites to make proper use of available manpower.

Results of Reform: Achieving Equity and Productivity

After implementing their reform programs for various lengths of time, what results have the eight countries studied achieved? Are there any basic differences in the results achieved between the countries with strong political commitment and those without it? These questions will be answered in the following pages. Since all countries regard equity and productivity as their reform objectives, the results of their programs can be compared by assessing the extent to which these programs fulfill these objectives. The equity effect can best be ascertained through an examination of the impact of reform on the landholding pattern, and the productivity effect

---

[74] "In one [reform] district, two credit officers, costing some $U.S. 1,600–1,700 per year in salaries and expenses, were wholly employed in handling about $U.S. 9,000 worth of loans to some 500 farmers. . . . At this rate of staffing density, it is estimated that 50,000 officials would be needed to extend the provisions of the [land reform] Code to the whole country." U.N., *Land Reform, Fourth Report*, p. 27.

[75] The Philippines, *An Evaluation on Land Reform Operations*, pp. 43–44.

by an analysis of the general trends of agricultural growth in the post-reform period.

IMPACT OF LAND REFORM ON LANDHOLDING PATTERN

Land Redistribution and Landholding Pattern

In a given country and within a specific period of time, the proportion of the total farm land that was redistributed and the proportion of the total farm families receiving land indicate the degree of change in the landholding pattern brought about by land redistribution. In the eight countries studied, the redistributed land covers public, private, royal, and foreign holdings as well as newly developed land under the public land-settlement programs. Table 31 presents the data.

This table reveals the sharp contrast in the results of land redistribution between Iran, Mexico, Taiwan, the U.A.R., on the one hand; and Colombia, India, Pakistan, and the Philippines, on the other. The reforms in the first group of countries affected much larger amounts of land and benefited far greater numbers of farm families than the reforms in the second group of countries, thus fulfilling to a greater extent the objective of equity. In terms of land redistributed or to be redistributed as a percentage of the total farm land, Column (E), the smallest in the first group of countries (the U.A.R.) is two and a half times the size of the largest in the second group (West Pakistan). This contrast would be even sharper if one took into account only the land actually redistributed. As seen in Appendix II, below, the areas of land listed under the first group of countries, with the exception of the U.A.R., pertain to the land already transferred; whereas the areas of land listed under the second group refer to the land acquired for redistribution, including a portion not yet transferred. The percentage of West Pakistan in Column (E), for example, would be lowered to 2.68 percent if only land actually redistributed were considered; the comparable percentage of the U.A.R. would be lowered to 13.72. Then the U.A.R. figure would be over five times as large as the West Pakistan figure.

As for the beneficiaries of reform, as seen in Column (H), the proportion of farm families receiving land in the U.A.R. (the country with the smallest proportion among the first group of countries) is over twice as large as that in India (the country with the largest proportion among the second group).

Table 31 also reveals the dramatic difference in the results of reform in a number of countries achieved within approximately the same length of time. From 1962 to 1967 Iran redistributed 30.53 percent of its farm land among 18.26 percent of its farm families. In contrast, the comparable percentages for Colombia from 1962 to 1969 are 0.81 and 2.93 percent; for West Pakistan, from 1959 to 1965, 5.99 and 1.52 percent; and from 1963 to 1968, the Philippines redistributed no more than 0.08 percent of its land.

It should be noted that Iran, where a dominant elite is in power, has achieved more extensive land redistribution than the U.A.R., where a revolutionary elite controls the government. Two factors may account for this fact. First, the Shah of Iran has been eager to see quick results, whereas in the U.A.R., reform seems to proceed at a steady pace over a long period. More important, Iran enjoys a much more favorable land-man ratio than does the U.A.R., thus is in a better position to accommodate the interests of both peasants and landowners.[76]

Decline in Land Concentration

As it aims at a more equitable landholding pattern, land reform leads to a decline in land concentration. The equity effect of reform can, therefore, also be seen in the degree of decline in land concentration. Land concentration can be conveniently measured by Gini index. In a given country, this index indicates the difference between the existing land distribution—i.e. the distribution of the area of farm land among the number of farm holdings—and a hypothetical equal land distribution. The greater the index, the greater the inequality of the existing land distribution, or the greater the concentration. Table 32 presents the Gini index numbers of the eight countries under study. Where possible, comparable data of two different dates are included so as to show trends of change.

As seen in this table, the six countries with two Gini index numbers showed a decline in land concentration. It is not, however, ascertainable precisely how much of this decline in each case was due to land reform. With respect to Colombia, India, and the Philippines, where only very limited amounts of land were redistributed, the slight declines in land concentration must have been primarily influenced by factors other than land reform, such as the extension of farming areas. In the case of Mexico, Taiwan, and the U.A.R, the periods in which the decline occurred co-

[76] See Table 3.

TABLE 31

AGGREGATE RESULTS OF LAND REDISTRIBUTION, PRIVATE, PUBLIC, ROYAL, FOREIGN, AND NEWLY DEVELOPED LAND, EIGHT COUNTRIES

Countries	Period	Area of Crop Land Acquired for Redistribution or Actually Redistributed	Total Area of Crop Land	Land Redistributed or to Be Redistributed as a Percent of Total Cropland $100 \times (C) \div (D)$	Farm Families Who Acquired Land	Total Farm Families[a]	Farm Families Who Acquired Land as a Percent of Total Farm Families $100 \times (F) \div (G)$
(A)	(B)	(C)	(D)	(E)	(F)	(G)	(H)
With Extensive Redistribution							
Iran	1962–1967	14,834[b] villages	48,592[e] villages (1963)	30.53[d]	587,566[b]	3,218,460[e] (1960)	18.26
Mexico	1915–1960	10,329,000[b] ha.	23,816,900[b] ha. (1960)	43.36	1,523,796[b,g]	2,870,238[f] (1960)	53.09
Taiwan	1951–1963	242,550[b] chia	899,264[h] chia (1963)	26.97	360,266[b]	824,560[h] (1963)	43.69
U.A.R.	1952–1964	944,457[b] feddans	6,122,000[i] feddans (1964)	15.43	263,862[b]	3,143,000[i] (1964)	8.40
With Limited Redistribution							
Colombia	1962–1969	222,471[b] ha.	27,399,772[j] ha. (1960)	0.81	35,000[k]	1,193,837[l] (1960)	2.93
India	1951–1966	8,450,400[b] acres	329,585,000[m] acres (1961–1962)	2.56	3,056,000[b]	72,466,000[n] (1961–1962)	4.21

E. Pakistan	1950–1960	292,849[o] acres	21,726,000[p] acres (1960)	1.35	...	...	...
W. Pakistan	1959–1965	2,220,718[b,q] acres	37,037,000[r] acres (1960)	5.99	56,906[b]	3,757,000[r] (1960)	1.52
Philippines	1954–1968	209,060[b] ha.	7,772,485[s] ha. (1960)	2.70	...	...	...
Philippines	1963–1968	6,000[b] ha.	7,772,485[s] ha. (1960)	0.08	...	...	...

[a] Numerals in parentheses in this column refer to year or years of data.

[b] See Appendix II, below.

[c] Research Group, "A Review of the Statistics of the First Stage of Land Reform," *Tahqiqat é eqtesadi*, II (March 1964), 141.

[d] The size of Iranian villages varies. In the absence of precise information on the extent of land redistributed, this percentage can at best be an approximation.

[e] Iranian Embassy to the United States, *Facts about Iran* (January 24, 1966), p. 4. Data were calculated on the basis of pilot surveys in 1960.

[f] Hiroji Okabe, "Agrarian Reform in Mexico: An Interpretation," *The Developing Economies*, IV (June 1966), 189. Information is based on the 1960 agricultural census.

[g] The total number of *ejidatarios*.

[h] China, *Taiwan Statistical Data Book 1965* (Taipei, Taiwan, 1965), p. 20; data relate to public and private land.

[i] U.A.R, Central Agency for Public Mobilisation and Statistics, *Statistical Handbook of the United Arab Republic 1952–1964* (Cairo, 1965), *passim*.

[j] See Table 3.

[k] This is the author's estimate. Data do not include the number of *campesinos* who had been in the public domain before the enactment of the 1961 law and who received titles from INCORA afterwards.

[l] CIDA, *Tenencia de la Tierra y Desarrollo Socio-Economico del Sector Agricola; Colombia* (Washington, D.C, 1966), p. 68.

[m] Information, dated December 8, 1966, supplied to the author by the Indian Planning Commission. This area refers to only cultivated land.

[n] Same source as above. This refers to farm households, including those of farm laborers.

[o] Pakistan, Planning Commission, *Papers Pertaining to Preparation of Second Five Year Plan in the Agriculture Sector*, Vol. III, *Land Reforms and Colonization* (Karachi, 1962), p. 49. This refers to the amount of land acquired under the 1950 act. Because much of the massive seizure of the former Hindu *zamandari* land went unrecorded, the exact amount of all land that changed hands is not known.

[p] Pakistan, Planning Commission, *Handbook of Agricultural Statistics, June 1964* (Karachi, 1964), p. 174.

[q] Including land not appropriate for cropping.

[r] Same source as note [p], pp. 176–177.

[s] The Philippines, *Census of the Philippines 1960: Agriculture*, Vol. II, *Summary Report* (Manila, 1965), p. 2.

TABLE 32

GINI INDEX OF LAND CONCENTRATION, EIGHT COUNTRIES[a]

Country	Year	Gini Index	Year	Gini Index	Decline in Gini Index, in Percentage $\dfrac{(C) - (E)}{(C)} \times 100$
(A)	(B)	(C)	(D)	(E)	(F)
Colombia	1960	0.864[b]	1969	0.818[b]	5.32
India	1953–1954	0.628[c]	1960–1961	0.589[c]	6.14
Iran	1960	0.652[d]	. . .	. . .	. . .
Mexico	1930	0.959[e]	1960	0.694[f]	27.64[g]
E. Pakistan	1960	0.511[h]	. . .	. . .	. . .
W. Pakistan	1960	0.615[i]	. . .	. . .	. . .
Philippines	1948	0.576[j]	1960	0.534[k]	7.26
Taiwan	1952	0.618[l]	1960	0.457[m]	26.08[n]
U.A.R.	1952	0.810[o]	1964	0.674[o]	16.74

[a] For a detailed description of the method of Gini index calculations, see Richard L. Merritt and Stein Rokkan, *Comparing Nations, The Use of Quantitative Data in Cross-National Research* (New Haven: Yale University Press, 1966), pp. 359–365. All the Gini indices of this table were calculated by the author on the basis of data from sources identified below.

[b] Departamento Administrativo Nacional de Estadística "La reforma agraria in cifras," *Boletín Mensual de Estadística*, No. 222, Bogota (enero 1970). Cited in Herman Felstehausen, "Agrarian Reform and Development in Colombia" Agency for International Development, *Spring Review*, Country Paper (June 1970), "Critique" by USAID/COLOMBIA, p. 13.

[c] India, National Sample Survey, Eighth Round, 1953–54, and Seventeenth Round, 1960–61. Data relate to land distribution by operation. Information, dated December 8, 1966, supplied to the author by the Indian Planning Commission.

[d] U.S. Department of Agriculture, *Changes in Agriculture in 26 Developing Nations, 1948–1963* (Washington, D.C. 1965), pp. 43–44. Data relate to land distribution by operation.

[e] FAO, *World Agricultural Structure, Study No. 1: General Introduction and Size of Holdings* (Rome, 1961), p. 62. Data relate to distribution of farm land by ownership. No comparable data for the time prior to 1930 are available. The impact of Mexican land reform on the land distribution pattern as indicated in the present table, therefore, does not reflect the changes in land tenure between 1916, when land redistribution started, and 1930. The amount of land distributed from 1916 to 1930, however, is not very large, about 16 percent of the total amount of land distributed from 1916 to 1964.

[f] Mexico, *Censo Agricola y Ganadero de 1960*, Direccion General de Estadistica. Data include both *ejido* and *non-ejido* holdings but relate only to cultivated crop land.

[g] Since Mexico's Gini indices of land concentration in 1930 and 1960 are calculated on the basis of, respectively, farm land and cultivated crop land, and since in Mexico the cultivated crop land forms only one-sixth to one-fifth of the farm land, this per-

TABLE 32 (*Continued*)

centage can only be suggestive of what may be the actual decline of concentration in crop-land holdings.

[h] Pakistan, Planning Commission, *Handbook of Agricultural Statistics June 1964* (Karachi, 1964), p. 174. Data relate to land distribution by operation.

[i] *Ibid.*, p. 178–179. Data relate to land distribution by operation.

[j] The Philippines, *Summary Report on the 1948 Census of Agriculture* (Manila, 1952), pp. 136 and 151. Data relate to land distribution by operation.

[k] The Philippines, *Census of the Philippines 1960: Agriculture*, Vol. II, *Summary Report* (Manila, 1965), pp. 3, 12. Data relate to land distribution by operation.

[l] JCRR, *Abstract of Land Statistics, Taiwan Province* (Taipei, Taiwan, 1963), pp. 23 and 27. Data relate to land distribution by ownership.

[m] Taiwan, *General Report on the 1961 Census of Agriculture* (Taichung, Taiwan, 1963), pp. 28–29 and 50. Data relate to land distribution by operation.

[n] This is an approximate figure, because in Taiwan the data on land distribution in 1952 and 1960 relate respectively to owner farm holdings and operation farm holdings.

[o] U.A.R., *Statistical Handbook of the United Arab Republic 1952–1964*, pp. 40 and 43.

incided with those in which extensive land redistribution took place. It can safely be said, therefore, that in these three countries the decline was due mainly to land reform.

As to the countries with one Gini index number, it may be said that in Iran extensive land redistribution since 1962 must have led to a notable decline in land concentration, and that in Pakistan the very small amount of land redistributed must have made no major contribution to the decline of land concentration, if any.

It is significant to note that though Iran, Mexico, Taiwan, and the U.A.R. have extensively implemented land redistribution and substantially reduced land concentration, these countries have not reduced the number of small-farm holdings. Holdings below five hectares still constitute an overwhelming proportion of farms in these countries (see Table 33). What these countries have achieved is primarily the elimination of excessively large holdings, not the removal of very small farms. As a result, in all these countries, the post-reform landholding pattern is characterized by a combination of a very large number of small holdings and a small number of holdings of moderate size.

IMPACT OF LAND REFORM ON AGRICULTURAL PRODUCTION

In the absence of comprehensive, comparable data, the impact of reform on agricultural production cannot be measured in terms of the individual programs of the eight countries studied. The impact will have to be analyzed in terms of the total change in agricultural production

TABLE 33

SMALL–FARM HOLDINGS, FOUR COUNTRIES

		Below five hectares	
Country	Year	Number of Holdings as a Percent of Total Holdings	Area of Holdings as a Percent of Total Area of All Holdings
Iran[a]	1960	66.00	18.00
Mexico[b]	1960	59.90	12.20
Taiwan[c]	1960	99.39	95.41
U.A.R.[d]	1964	98.80	73.40

[a] See Table 2. The absence of a post-reform agricultural census makes it necessary to cite pre-reform data on small holdings in this table. These data are still useful for the purpose of identifying the number of small holdings in the post-reform period. This is so because the Iranian reform generally allowed incumbent cultivators to take over the land exceeding the established ceilings on which they had been working. It is not likely that the number of small holdings would decline as a result.

[b] Mexico, *Censo Agrícola y Ganadero de 1960.*

[c] Taiwan, *General Report on the 1961 Census of Agriculture* (Taichung, Taiwan, 1963), pp. 28–29, and 50.

[d] U.A.R., *Statistical Handbook of the United Arab Republic 1952–1964*, p. 43. Data relate to holdings with a size below 4.201 hectares.

brought about by all programs. This analysis will first begin with a comparison of the pre- and post-reform growth trend of agriculture in these countries in general, then proceed to study this trend in Taiwan in detail, and finally compare the productive records of reform areas and non-reform areas in two selected countries, the U.A.R. and Mexico.

General Trends of Agricultural Growth

In all eight countries, agricultural production has for some time been following an upward trend. However, only four countries have experienced both comparatively high agricultural growth rates and a faster rate of increase in agricultural production than in population. This is seen in Table 34.

From 1952/53 to 1964/65 Mexico, Taiwan, the U.A.R., and Iran experienced more satisfactory agricultural growth than the remaining countries, and it is in these same four countries that more extensive land redistribution took place. To discern how reform affected production it

TABLE 34

AVERAGE ANNUAL GROWTH RATE OF AGRICULTURAL
PRODUCTION AND POPULATION 1952/53–1954/55 TO
1962/63–1964/65

Country	Average Annual Rate of Growth, Compound Interest	
	Agricultural Production	Population
Mexico	6.3	3.1
Taiwan	4.3	3.4
U.A.R.	3.7	2.5
Iran	3.3	2.5
Philippines	3.2	3.2
India	2.7	2.2
Colombia	2.4	2.8
Pakistan	2.2	2.4

SOURCE: FAO, *The State of Food and Agriculture 1966*,
(Rome, FAO, 1966), p. 19.

is appropriate, then, to concentrate the present inquiry on the agricultural performance of these countries.

Mexico. In Mexico, agricultural production suffered a prolonged period of decline after implementation of the 1915 decree, but its subsequent rise was also most impressive. Available information indicates that not until the late 1930s did agricultural output show signs of recovery. After an extensive study of Mexican agricultural production records, James G. Maddox revealed that, with 1893 as a base year, the index number of agricultural production was 143.4 in 1910, 109.3 in 1925 (no data for the period between 1910 and 1925), 106.3 in 1935; by 1945 it had recovered from the post–1910 slump, reaching 153.5; and in 1955 it registered at 342.3, a spectacular gain.[77] Similarly, in examining the output of nineteen principal crops, Nathan Whetten found that in the 1940 to 1944 period as many as fourteen of these crops reached beyond the production level of a pre-reform period, 1903–1907.[78] For instance, wheat rose by 38 percent, cotton 45 percent, sugar cane 236 percent, and rice 298 percent; but corn

[77] James G. Maddox, "Mexican Land Reform," *American Universities Field Staff Reports*, Vol. 4, No. 5 (July 3, 1957), p. 26. Cf. Eduardo L. Venezian and William K. Gamble, *The Agricultural Development of Mexico* (New York, 1969), p. 53.

[78] Nathan Whetten, *Rural Mexico* (Chicago, 1948), p. 253.

remained at 72 percent of the pre-reform level and beans 93 percent. Since much of the increase in the output of these crops took place from 1940 to 1944, a period following the very extensive land redistribution by the Cárdenas administration (1934–1940),[79] land redistribution could not be considered a factor responsible for the pre–1930 output decline. As a number of specialists have observed, this decline was caused more by the devastations of the civil war and by the uncertainty of the direction of the government's agrarian policies than by reform.[80]

Taiwan. In Taiwan, the 1949 rent-reduction program and the sale of public land in 1951 apparently had no adverse effect on production at all. In 1948 to 1952 the output of rice, the island's most extensively planted crop, rose by 47 percent.[81] However, the land-to-the-tiller program of 1953 led to a fall of total agricultural output for two years. With 1952 as a base year, the index number of agricultural production was 113.3 in 1953; it declined to 112.0 in 1954, and 111.4 in 1955; then it rose to 119.0 in 1956, 138.3 in 1960, and 168.9 in 1964.[82]

U.A.R. In the U.A.R., agricultural production fell slightly in the first year following the 1952 reform. With 1952 as a base year, the index number of production declined to 99 in 1953, but rose to 109 in 1954, 135 in 1959, and 166 in 1964.[83]

Iran. In Iran, the production records of a number of principal crops show that in the first three years following the 1962 reform there was a sharp drop in wheat and barley output and a modest to impressive increase in rice, sugar beet, and cotton production.[84] The overall production showed a decline in 1964 but it rose above the pre-reform level in the following year. With 1952 to 1956 as a base period, the index number of agricultural

[79] The area of land distributed by Cárdenas in 1934–1940 was a good deal more than the distributed acreage in 1916–1934 (see Table 23 above).

[80] See, for instance, Maddox, *op. cit.*, pp. 25–26; and Eyler N. Simpson, *The Ejido, Mexico's Way Out* (Chapel Hill, N.C., 1937), p. 507.

[81] Chen, *op. cit.* (n. 17 above), p. 309.

[82] China, Executive Yuan, *Taiwan Statistical Data Book 1965* (Taipei, Taiwan, 1965), p. 21.

[83] U.A.R., Central Agency for Public Mobilization and Statistics, *Statistical Handbook of the United Arab Republic 1952–1964* (Cairo, 1965), p. 18. Cf. Donald C. Mead, *Growth and Structural Change in the Egyptian Economy* (Homewood, Ill., 1967), pp. 318–320.

[84] In 1962 to 1965 wheat and barley respectively declined by 18 and 28.2 percent, and rice, sugar beet, and cotton increased by 7.9, 31.8 and 246.67 percent. *Iran Almanac 1966*, p. 409.

production was 130 in 1962, 138 in 1963, 135 in 1964, 147 in 1965, and 159 in 1967.[85]

A conclusion can clearly be drawn from the post-reform agricultural growth patterns of Mexico, Taiwan, the U.A.R., and Iran. Extensive land reform has had only a temporarily adverse effect on agricultural output. After regaining the pre-reform level, production in these countries has shown a very strong capacity for rapid and continuous growth. In the long run, therefore, land reform must be considered a significant factor contributing to the increase of agricultural production.

Reform and Rise of Agricultural Productivity: Taiwan

The post-reform increase of agricultural production in the four countries, it must be cautioned, can also be attributed to a number of factors other than land reform. Obviously, it is difficult to measure separately the precise contribution to increased outputs by land reform and by such other factors as extension of cultivated land and greater and better agricultural inputs and services. But experiences in Taiwan do indicate that the special stimulant effect of reform on production can clearly be discerned, if not accurately measured. The sense of security and incentive, and the economic benefits that the island's reform brought to tenants and small owner farmers have induced them to improve agricultural productivity. Two studies provide some insight into this development. A 1965 survey of 110 farm families in seven Taiwanese townships showed increases in both land and labor productivity for four principal crops (rice, sweet potatoes, sugar cane, and bananas) between a pre-reform year, 1948, and a post-reform one, 1963. The detailed data are found in Table 35. In this period the increase of land productivity ranged from 13 percent for sweet potatoes to 54 percent for sugar cane; the increase of labor productivity from 5 percent for bananas to 47 percent for sweet potatoes. A study of the productivity of all crops throughout the island for 1950 to 1962 yielded further information on changes in agricultural productivity. In this period, "the aggregate resource productivity" of Taiwan's agriculture (i.e. the productivity of land, labor, and capital) rose by 27 percent, but land and labor productivity advanced by 60 percent and 37 percent respectively, while capital productivity dropped by 33 percent (see Table 36).[86] "This

---

[85] FAO, *Production Yearbook 1968* (Rome, 1969), Table 10, p. 30.

[86] The decline of capital productivity, of course, does not indicate the decline of capital input, which, in fact, rose consistently after reform. See E. L. Rada and T. H.

TABLE 35

LAND AND LABOR PRODUCTIVITY, SEVEN TOWNSHIPS, TAIWAN,
PRE- AND POST-REFORM, 1948 AND 1963

Crops	Year	Yield Per Hectare		Yield Per Man-Labor-Day	
		Kilogram	Index	Kilogram	Index
Rice	1948	2,655	100	44.6	100
	1963	3,225	122	56.3	126
Sweet potatoes	1948	13,110	100	213.7	100
	1963	14,770	113	312.8	147
Sugar cane	1948	38,544	100	218.7	100
	1963	59,283	154	271.2	124
Bananas	1948	5,603	100	15.1	100
	1963	7,468	133	15.9	105

SOURCE: Yen-Tien Chang, "Land Reform and Its Impact on Economic and Social Progress in Taiwan; in Memory of [the] Late Vice President Chen Cheng," *Industry of Free China*, XXIII (April 1965), 24–25.

suggests that farmers used their land and labor more intensively after the reform." [87] This post-reform intensive use of land and labor is most clearly seen in the effort to raise agricultural output through the extension of multiple cropping practices. Between 1946 and 1950 and 1956 to 1960, the total cultivated area rose by 22,986 hectares (from 852,911 to 875,897), but the harvest area gained 287,541 hectares (from 1,288,308 to 1,575,849), a jump in the multiple-cropping index of 16 percent.[88]

Reform v. Non-Reform Areas: the U.A.R. and Mexico

A comparison of the agricultural output in the reform areas and the non-reform areas of the U.A.R. and Mexico will help further identify the contribution of reform to production. In Chapter VIII, the successful economic performance of the Egyptian supervised cooperative system in

Lee, *Irrigation Investment in Taiwan—An Economic Analysis of Feasibility, Priority and Repayability Criteria* (Taipei, Taiwan: JCRR, 1963), Table 3, p. 17.

[87] Young-chi Tsui, "A Preliminary Assessment of the Impact of Agrarian Reform on Taiwan's Agricultural Economy," *Industry of Free China*, XXIII (February 1965), 28. Taiwan's main reform programs, it may be recalled, were introduced in 1949 to 1953.

[88] S. C. Hsieh and T. H. Lee, "The Effect of Population Pressure and Seasonal Labor Surplus on the Pattern and Intensity of Agriculture in Taiwan," *Industry of Free China*, XXIII (February 1965), 6. Cf. Charles Hsi-Chung Kao, "An Analysis of Agricultural Output Increase on Taiwan, 1953–1964," *The Journal of Asian Studies*, XXVI (August 1967), 619.

TABLE 36

INDICES OF RESOURCE PRODUCTIVITY IN AGRICULTURE, TAIWAN
1952 = 100

Year	Land Productivity	Labor Productivity	Capital Productivity	Aggregate
1950	91	97	121	99
1952	100	100	100	100
1954	113	111	93	107
1956	121	117	93	112
1958	135	120	91	118
1960	138	121	93	120
1962	151	134	88	126

SOURCE: Young-chi Tsui, "A Preliminary Assessment of the Impact of Agrarian Reform on Taiwan's Agricultural Economy," *Industry of Free China*, XXIII (February 1965), 28.

reform areas was referred to. A 1966 survey of three reform areas by the U.A.R. Ministry for Agrarian Reform revealed further that since the beginning of the implementation of the 1952 decree a number of main crops registered greater increases in output in these areas than in the nation as a whole. As seen in Table 37, except for rice, the yield of all crops was lower in reform areas than the national average *before the implementation of reform* (1951/52). Again, except for rice, the yield of all crops rose significantly above the national averages *after the implementation* (1962). The positive impact of reform on crop output is, therefore, clearly visible.

As in the case of the U.A.R., Mexican land-reform areas have, over the years, seen a considerable increase in agricultural production. But unlike the U.A.R.'s experience, Mexican reform areas generally have a lower productive record than the non-reform areas. Various studies comparing the output of *ejidos* (reform areas) and private farms (non-reform areas) —dealing with either all crops or the principal ones, and covering selected areas or the entire nation—unanimously indicated that reform areas have been on the whole not as productive as private farms; this is most evident in the years around 1950.[89]

[89] See, for example, Whetten, *op. cit.*, p. 248; Maddox, *op. cit.*, pp. 28, 30; Clarence Senior, *Land Reform and Democracy* (Gainesville, Fla., 1958), p. 189; W. Whitney Hicks, "Agricultural Development in Northern Mexico, 1940–1960," *Land Economics*, XLIII (November 1967), 396; and Donald K. Freebairn, "Relative Production Efficiency between Tenure Classes in the Yaqui Valley, Sonora, Mexico," *Journal of Farm Economics*, XLV (December 1963), 1156.

TABLE 37

INCREASE OF CROP OUTPUT IN THREE LAND-REFORM AREAS AND
IN THE NATION, U.A.R., 1951/52–1962,
Index: 1951/52 = 100

	Increase of Crop Output[a]									
	Cotton[b]		Wheat		Maize[b]		Rice		Sugarcane	
U.A.R.	Kg. per ha.	In- dex	Kg. per ha.	In- dex	Kg. per ha.	In- dex	Kg. per ha.	In- dex	Kg. per ha.	In- dex
Land- Reform Areas										
1951/52	551	100	615	100	705	100	1,622	100	37,000	100
1964	969	176	1,200	195	1,485	211	3,053	188	51,200	140
The Nation										
1951/52	662	100	765	100	945	100	1,340	100	39,000	100
1964	851	129	1,095	143	1,035	110	2,488	186	44,100	113

[a] Data originally were in Egyptian weight units.
[b] Averages for two sample land reform areas.
SOURCE: M. Riad El Ghonemy, "Economic and Institutional Organization of Egyptian Agriculture Since 1952," in P. J. Vatikiotis (ed.), *Egypt Since the Revolution* (New York: Frederick A. Praeger, Publishers, 1968), p. 75.

Corroborating the findings of these studies is an analysis by Folke Dovring of the overall impact of Mexican land reform on productivity from 1940 to 1960 which, together with tenure data on *ejido* and private farms, is summarized in Table 38. In terms of the *total output of all crops*, *ejido* farms more than doubled in this period, doing much better than small private farms (with a size of five or less hectares), which experienced a 45 percent rise. But output of *ejido* farms fell considerably behind that of medium to large private farms (with a size over five hectares), which increased more than three times in the same period. As to the *average output of all crops per hectare of land*, i.e. land productivity, 1960 data indicate that the *ejido* output was about 91 percent of that of the medium to large private farms, and 87 percent that of the small private farms. However, with respect to *the per hectare output of eight main crops*, the relationship between the *ejido* and private farms is neither entirely clear nor consistent. Except for the 1950 data, which showed that the *ejido* fell behind the medium to large private farms in respect to the output of every one of the eight main crops, ejidos actually led private farms in the output of four crops in 1940 (corn, beans, sugar cane, and bananas), and still retained their leading position in the output of sugar cane and bananas in 1960. Moreover, insofar as the 1960 data are concerned, the productive capacity of the ejidos and private farms are generally comparable, the differences being not very significant. These data on output of main crops led Dovring to conclude: "The often-made charge that the land reform, and especially the ejido system, has been a detriment to Mexico's economic development is thus without foundation." [90] Dovring does concede, however, that even if only 1960 data are taken into account, the ejidos fell considerably behind private farms in terms of the output of all crops, either in aggregate output or per hectare output.

The apparent discrepancy between the output of all crops and main crops with respect to the ejidos and private farms can be explained by two factors. One relates to the output of secondary crops in the ejidos and in the private farms. Dovring has suggested that private farms possessed a larger share than the ejidos of some of the high-yield secondary crops such as agaves.[91] Another factor may be the inadequacy of the productivity data of different categories of farms. The lumping together of all private farms over five hectares in the computation of per hectare output for the principal crops makes it impossible to differentiate land productivity of farms of rather large size (50 or more hectares) which are known to be very high, from that of medium-sized farms (5 to 50 hectares). Conceivably, large private farms may contribute a larger share of the total output than medium-sized ones.

A number of specialists have argued that in cases in which the ejidos are known to be less productive than private farms, it is because the large private farms are more capitalized, more irrigated, more mechanized, provided with more chemical fertilizers, and, significantly, are more *labor-*

[90] Folke Dovring, *Land Reform and Productivity* (Urbana, Ill., 1966), p. 17. See also Solomón Eckstein, *El marco macroeconómico del problema agrario mexicano* (Washington, D.C.: CIDA, Trabajos de investigación sobre tenencia de la tierra y reforma agraria, No. 11, January 1969), pp. viii, 119 *sq.*; and R. Hertford, "Sources of Change in Mexican Agricultural Production, 1940–1965" (unpublished Ph.D. dissertation, University of Chicago). Both works were cited by Dovring in another study, "Land Reform in Mexico," Agency for International Development, *Spring Review*, Country Paper (June 1970), 52, 58. For an analysis comparable to Dovring's, see Marnie W. Mueller, "Changing Patterns of Agricultural Output and Productivity in Private and Land Reform Sectors of Mexico, 1940–1960," *Economic Development and Cultural Change*, XVIII (January 1970), 252–266.

[91] Dovring, *Land Reform and Productivity*, pp. 7–8.

TABLE 38

DATA ON LAND TENURE AND CROP OUTPUT, MEXICO, 1940, 1950, 1960

Holdings and Crops	Ejido Farms			Non-Ejido, Private Farms					
				5 ha. & Under			Over 5 ha.		
	1940	1950	1960	1940	1950	1960	1940	1950	1960
Number of farm holdings	1,222,859[a]	1,378,326[a]	1,523,796[a]	928,593	1,104,835	899,108	290,336	360,798	447,334
(1) Percent of all holdings, for each year	50.08	50.23	53.09	38.03	36.62	31.33	11.89	13.15	15.58
(2) Index: 1940 = 100	100	113	124	100	108	97	100	124	154
Area of cropland, in ha.	6,696,273	8,457,488	9,807,167	1,074,190	1,219,807	1,189,918	6,251,147	9,421,756	11,509,682
(1) Percent of all cropland, for each year	47.76	44.28	43.58	7.66	6.39	5.25	44.58	49.33	51.14
(2) Index: 1940 = 100	100	116	146	100	114	111	100	150	184
Average size of holding, in ha.	5.48	6.14	6.44	1.16	1.21	1.32	21.53	26.11	25.72
Index of total crop output 1940 = 100	100	125	212	100	135	145	100	195	323
Average crop value per ha. in ₱	...	...	568.3	...	...	653.8	...	...	630.4
Main crops output, kg. per ha. Index 1940 = 100, in parentheses									
(1) Corn[b]	692 (100)	741 (107)	842 (122)	...	...	846	624 (100)	855 (137)	839 (135)

(2) Cotton[c]	705	889	1,380	...	1,473	919	999	1,378
	(100)	(126)	(196)			(100)	(109)	(150)
(3) Coffee[d] (Index: 1950 = 100)	321	1,386	1,375	...	1,348	474	1,439	1,588
		(100)	(99)				(100)	(110)
(4) Wheat	738	816	1,066	...	1,137	828	1,039	1,522
	(100)	(111)	(143)			(100)	(126)	(184)
(5) Beans	450	352	554	...	830	417	427	559
	(100)	(78)	(123)			(100)	(102)	(134)
(6) Sugar Cane	49,298	52,122	48,630	...	48,271	32,789	67,127	44,879
	(100)	(106)	(99)			(100)	(205)	(137)
(7) Henequen[e] (Index: 1950 = 100)	502	39.0	45.0	...	[f]	867	47.2	44.6
		(100)	(115)				(100)	(95)
(8) Bananas	4,796	4,274	6,739	...	6,367	4,509	6,719	6,454
	(100)	(89)	(141)			(100)	(149)	(143)

[a] Number of ejidatarios.
[b] Common corn grown alone.
[c] Row cotton.
[d] Clean beans, 1940; pulp 1950, 1960.
[e] Data in kg, 1940; in 1,000 raw leaves, 1950, 1960.
[f] Small numbers.

SOURCES: Data on holdings are from Mexico, Censos agropecuarios: Totales comparativos en 1930, 1940 y 1950 (1959); and Panorama economico latinoamericano, No. 171, La Habana, 1965, pp. 15–20; data on crop production from Folke Dovring, Land Reform and Productivity: the Mexican Case, a Preliminary Analysis, Department of Agricultural Economics, Agricultural Experiment Station, University of Illinois (Urbana, Illinois, 1966), pp. 6, 9; and Eduardo L. Venezian and William K. Gamble, The Agricultural Development of Mexico, Its Structure and Growth Since 1950 (New York: Frederick A. Praeger, 1969), p. 78.

intensive than the *ejidos*.[92] The greater availability of material inputs to the large private farms has stemmed from the governmental policy to aid these farms. The greater labor intensification on large private farms results partially from a greater natural increase of population on these farms and partially from the willingness of the farmers, encouraged by a favorable public policy, to exert an increasing effort to raise production.[93] In contrast, the *ejidatarios*, discriminated against by the government in the allocation of material inputs, and experiencing organizational deficiencies in the *ejido* system, which were reviewed in Chapter VIII, have a generally lower motivation than private farmers to devote extra energy and time to their farms.

The preceding discussions on the agricultural production of the Mexican *ejidos* and private farms warrant two generalizations. First, the *ejidos* have materially increased their productive capacity. The doubling by these farms of the total crop output in the period from 1940 to 1960 is an impressive record, which the traditional *hacienda* system—had it not been replaced by the *ejidos*—could not have achieved. Second, on the whole, the *ejidos* are less productive than private farms, particularly the large ones. But it must be recalled that if Mexico's large holdings are now highly productive, they were not so before reform; also, as has been amply demonstrated, today, in countries where over-concentration of landownership persists, large holdings are still proportionally less productive than small ones. Thus, to make large landowners more conscious of the need to increase production, and to induce absentee landlords to become enterprising farmers may well be a very significant indirect contribution of Mexican land reform to the country's agricultural growth.

From the foregoing analysis one can discern that the countries with a strong commitment to reform (Mexico, Taiwan, the U.A.R., and Iran) have achieved much greater implementation of the programs than have the countries without such a commitment (India, Pakistan, Colombia, and the Philippines). The first group of countries have experienced a greater reduction of land concentration and enjoyed a higher growth rate in agriculture, thus fulfilling to a greater extent both reform objectives of equity

[92] For this type of argument, see *ibid.*, *passim*; Dovring, "Land Reform in Mexico," pp. 44 *sq.*; Hiroji Okabe, "Agrarian Reform in Mexico," *The Developing Economies*, IV (June 1966), 188, 190–192; Hicks, *op. cit.*, pp. 396, 402; Freebairn, *op. cit.*, pp. 1156–1157; and Maddox, *op. cit.*, p. 30.

[93] Dovring, *Land Reform and Productivity*, pp. 12–13.

and productivity, than have the second group of countries. It is true that decline of production often immediately follows extensive implementation of reform, but this is analogous to the situation in which the health of a patient is weakened immediately following major surgery. The productive capacity of agriculture will in due course recover and advance just as the patient will in time recuperate and improve his physical well-being after a successful operation.

PART TWO

The Political Effects of Land Reform

Introduction

In the following chapters an attempt will be made to assess systematically the political effects of land reform in the eight countries studied. In making this assessment, two basic limitations must be noted. One relates to the inadequacy of data explicitly relevant to the political impact of land reform, and the other concerns the difficulty of devising appropriate methods to appraise such an imapct. One can perhaps appreciate these problems by considering for a moment the troubles besetting an analysis of the economic effects of land reform. As a United Nations report has commented: "Time series of an aggregative type permitting comparison of national [agricultural] output before and after land reform are rarely if ever available, while cross-section comparison [i.e. comparison of different sections of the economy] tend to be inconclusive." [1] In addition to this problem, there is the difficulty of separating the economic effects of tenurial reform from those of non-tenurial changes. "Frequently it will be impossible," an FAO study has commented, "to fix the causal connection betwen an individual program and a very distinctly defined effect; . . . The [economic] effects of any development or reform program are necessarily the results of more than one factor." [2] When assessing the *political effects* of land reform, one encounters even more serious informational and methodological problems. In almost all countries where land reform has taken place, pertinent political information is often less available than the admittedly scarce economic data, and the tools for political analysis are even more inadequate.

[1] U.N., *Progress in Land Reform, Third Report,* p. 8.
[2] Eric H. Jacoby, *Evaluation of Agrarian Structures and Agrarian Reform Programs, a Methodological Study* (Rome: FAO, 1966), pp. 33–34.

In view of these difficulties, it is necessary to utilize in the following discussions a considerable amount of data on political development in general. Some of these data—including survey results, electoral statistics, and opinions of specialists—may not appear to be immediately relevant to land reform, but an interpretative analysis of these data may hopefully shed light on the subject. If subsequent chapters appear to contain too much information of this type, this is dictated by the consideration that a guilt of inclusion is preferable to a guilt of omission. The intention is to open wide the net to catch possibly unseen fish.

To deal with the methodological problem, it has been decided to analyze the effects of reform on five selected subjects: political participation, national integration, rural institutionalization, stability, and Communism. A series of analytic schemes will be adopted as standards of measurement. It must be stressed, in this connection, that while land reform may create an impact on participation, integration, institutionalization, stability, and Communism, these latter subjects may themselves affect land reform. It is not assumed, therefore, that land reform and these latter subjects stand in a simple cause-effect relationship. Rather, land reform is viewed as just one factor affecting these subjects, and the proposed analytic schemes will provide only some rough indication of the extent of the impact.

In this analysis it is useful to contrast, in most cases, the countries showing extensive reform results (Iran, Mexico, Taiwan, and the U.A.R.) with those countries showing limited results (Colombia, India, Pakistan, and the Philippines). This procedure will make it possible to identify and explain the primary differences in the political impact of reform between the two groups of countries. Thus, if this impact cannot be measured in fine gradations, it can at least be seen in its broad outline.

X

POLITICAL PARTICIPATION

If land reform derives is principal impetus from the effort of the political elite to mobilize rural support for the government, to what extent will land reform affect rural political participation? The rural population, like its urban counterpart, may get involved in the political process in several ways. It may participate in elections, join the government, organize interest associations, and, under certain circumstances, resort to violent behavior as a form of political expression. Here, the first two of these forms of participation are examined, and the rest will be left for subsequent analysis.

Common Trends and Different Patterns

In the eight countries under study, two common trends in rural politics appear to be observable. One relates to certain electoral changes. Because of the adoption of universal suffrage and the rapid growth of population, the electorate has experienced a significant expansion since World War II. At the same time, political elites find the rural voters less docile than before, but still more manageable than their urban counterparts. They must, therefore, seek and expand rural votes to compensate for possible losses in the cities.[1] As a consequence, rural voters, in their aggre-

[1] For instance, the governing parties of Colombia (the ruling factions of the National Front), India (the Congress party), Mexico (the PRI), Pakistan (during the Ayub Khan's rule, the Pakistan Muslim League), and Taiwan (the Kuomintang) generally received more votes in rural areas than in urban or metropolitan areas in recent presidential or legislative elections. See respectively Ronald H. McDonald, "Political Protest and Alienation in *Voting*: The Case of Colombia," *Inter-American Economic Affairs*, XXI (Autumn 1967), 16 and 21; Myron Weiner, *The Politics of Scarcity, Public Pressure and Political Response in India* (Chicago, 1962), p. 31; Linda S. Mirin, "Mexico's PRI: How Much Democracy?" a paper prepared for the Symposium on the Evolution of Established One Party Systems, Timber Cove, California, April 5–7, 1968,

gate, have considerably increased their political weight compared to earlier times and to urban voters. This is not to suggest, of course, that the rural electorate expands at a faster pace than the urban, but the fact is that the former is still decisively larger. Recognizing this, politicians have begun to tap vigorously this large reservoir of votes.

The other trend concerns the change of political orientation. Having passed from a traditional to a modernizing stage of development, these countries are experiencing a transformation from what Gabriel A. Almond and Sidney Verba called the parochial type of political culture to the subject type.[2] The rural populace of these countries has gradually become conscious of its political interests but is unable to articulate them effectively; it is concerned with the outcome of public policies but is unable to influence their formation.

In general, these two trends prevail in all eight countries but, because of these countries' different experiences with land reform, the two trends are manifested in two essentially different patterns. In one group of countries—Iran, Mexico, Taiwan, and the U.A.R.—where land reform has resulted in the substitution of the peasantry for the landed class as a source of rural power, only the peasantry has significantly gained political influence, and the elites must now go directly to the peasants to seek support. In the other group of countries—Colombia, India, Pakistan, and the Philippines—where land reform has not basically altered the distribution of rural power, the landed class remains numerically strong and politically dominating. The elites must continue to solicit peasant votes through landlords as intermediaries.

Moreover, the two groups of countries differ in their response to rising rural electoral strength. Though rural populations everywhere look for increased government output in the countryside, the governments of the first group of countries have, over the years, sought both to readjust rights and interests derived from land and to provide all cultivators with material benefits; in the second group, the governments have emphasized only the provision to rural areas of goods and services that tend to benefit the well-to-do farming interests rather than the mass peasantry.

---

p. 20; Sharif Al-Mujahid, Pakistan's First Presidential Elections," *Asian Survey*, V (June 1965), 292; and Hung Chao Tai, "The Kuomintang and Modernization in Taiwan," in Samuel P. Huntington and Clement H. Moore (eds.), *Authoritarian Politics in Modern Society* (New York, 1970), pp. 419–421.

[2] *The Civic Culture: Political Attitudes and Democracy in Five Nations* (Princeton, N.J.: Princeton University Press, 1963), pp. 17–21.

These differences lead one to suggest that in Iran, Mexico, Taiwan, and the U.A.R., a functionally aggregative and geographically integrative pattern of political participation may gradually emerge on the rural scene. Peasants, who perform similar economic functions, will develop a common political identification and common electoral preferences, regardless of the locations of their residences. In Colombia, India, Pakistan, and the Philippines, the functionally non-aggregative and geographically isolated pattern of rural political participation that operated in the past persists to this day. That is, peasants cannot be politically united throughout the villages, though they all perform the same economic activities. Dictated by the preferences of their landlords, tenants of one village vote for the candidates of one political party or political faction and the tenants of another village vote for the candidates of another party or another faction. These contrasting patterns of rural political participation can be analyzed by reference to the peasants' relationships with the elites, and the peasants' representation in public institutions.

The Aggregative Pattern

IRAN

In Iran, the peasant acquired voting rights as early as 1906, "but he lacked both interest in and awareness of the meaning of his new privilege. Bewildered, he marched obediently to cast his vote for the candidate of his landowner." [3] With the coming of land reform, peasant political subservience was gradually lessened. Accompanying the disappearance of the larger landlords and the dwindling of political influence of the smaller ones was a deliberate attempt by the political elite to bring the peasants onto the national scene. Under the 1962 land-reform decree, the beneficiaries were required to join rural cooperative societies. In January 1963, Hassan Arsanjani, the Minister of Agriculture, organized the First Rural Cooperative Congress to bring together in the national capital some 4,800 peasant delegates from various parts of the country. Arsanjani expressed the belief: "The land reforms would have remained fruitless without this great gathering in Tehran. The land reforms, through the co-

---

[3] Richard W. Cottam, *Nationalism in Iran* (Pittsburgh, 1964), p. 35. In the early history of the Majlis peasants were excluded from political representation as they did not constitute one of the six classes—i.e. "aristocrats, dignitaries, religious leaders, traders, guilds, and landlords"—from which Majlis membership was selected. See *Iran Almanac 1966*, p. 126.

operative societies, linked all the Iranian farmers together, and this Congress was linking all the rural cooperatives under one roof. . . ." [4] When the Congress convened, the Shah utilized the occasion to announce his intention of holding a national referendum on his six-point program, the most vital part of which was land reform.

"The holding of the Congress," as an observer has commented, "was a successful part of a drive by the Shah to win the support of the nation's peasants and to counter opposition to the reforms." [5] The delegates to the Congress, on their part, adopted a number of resolutions in which they pledged "to protect and safeguard the constitutional monarchy of Iran; to carry out the well-wishing instructions and the progressive orders of His Imperial Majesty the Shahanshah . . . [to] confirm and approve the six laws offered to referendum by His Imperial Majesty . . . [and to] appeal to all the farmers of this country to discharge their national duty by participating in the national referendum and by voting for these laws which will consolidate their freedoms." [6] When the referendum was held in the same month, "workers, farmers, and shop-keepers waved banners and sang in the streets, shouted slogans praising the Shah, and gave an unmistakable affirmative vote [5,598,711 to 4,115] for the Shah's program." [7] The referendum approved, among other things, a change in the social basis of political representation. "Social classes mentioned in Article 14 of the Majlis Election Law were changed; two classes (aristocrats and landlords) were deleted and replaced by workers and peasants. The new classes are now: clerical, businessmen, guilds, farmers, workers, and peasants." [8] In preparation for the forthcoming parliamentary election, the government sponsored in Tehran in August 1963 a Congress of Free Men and Women which nominated 193 candidates for the 200 seats of the Majlis. Boycotted by many middle-class elements, the National Front, and clergymen, the September Majlis election had a small voter turnout. But, with the support of peasants and workers, the Congress's nominees won 90 percent of the contested seats. For the first time in the history of the Majlis, small farming interests gained direct representation and a

[4] *Iran Almanac 1963*, p. 391.

[5] John Hanessian, Jr., "Iranian Land Reform," *American Universities Field Staff*, Report Service, XII, No. 10 (April 1963), 7–8.

[6] *Iran Almanac 1963*, p. 392.

[7] John Hanessian, Jr., "Reform in Iran by Decree and Referendum," *American Universities Field Staff*, Report Service, Southwest Asia Series, XII, No. 9 (April 1963), 5.

[8] *Iran Almanac 1966*, p. 126.

measure of influence. Of the 196 newly elected members, 6 were peasants, 7 were small-farm holders, and 19 were land-reform officials, as contrasted to only 4 small landlords who were elected as individuals rather than as representatives of their class.[9]

MEXICO

If Iranian land reform was part of a "White Revolution," a revolution from the top which the peasants did not initiate, Mexican land reform resulted from a revolution in which large numbers of peasants were directly involved from the beginning. The impact of Mexican land reform on peasant political participation is thus more far-reaching. "The giving of land to rural communities of Mexico," one observer has noted, "has released energies long latent and aroused hopes long dormant. These energies need to be directed and these hopes enchanneled."[10] And it is with the CNC and the PRI—and its predecessors—that the beneficiaries of land reform have established their political identification. "In promoting the organization and growth of the *Confederación Nacional Campesina* as one of the corporate sectors of the Revolutionary party," two authors have pointed out, "the government had both established a principle of solidarity among the formerly disunited rural population and provided the *ejidatarios* an instrument for more effective political action. Thereby the rural population was brought into an unprecedented participation in national political processes where it could exert a continuing, if varying, pressure for steps to improve the agricultural sector."[11]

As a nationwide organization with over 2.5 million *ejidatarios*, the *Confederación Nacional Campesina* forms the single largest component of the PRI. (See Table 39.) This massive rural organization, together with the labor and popular sectors of the PRI, provides the Mexican ruling party with invincible electoral strength, and has enabled it to obtain continuous sweeping victories in all electoral contests since the party's formation over three decades ago. Indeed, the almost automatic electoral support that peasants and others have provided the PRI led the party leadership to believe that it could select candidates for high offices with considerable discretion. The way in which Gustavo Díaz Ordaz was chosen in 1964 as the party's presidential candidate, and the warm but ritualistic

[9] *Ibid.*, pp. 129–131.

[10] Eyler N. Simpson, *The Ejido* (Chapel Hill, N.C., 1937), p. 352.

[11] William P. Glade, Jr. and Charles W. Anderson, *The Political Economy of Mexico* (Madison: The University of Wisconsin Press, 1963), p. 63.

TABLE 39

SECTORS AND MEMBERSHIP OF THE PARTIDO REVOLUCIONARIO
INSTITUCIONAL, C. 1958 ('000 OF MEMBERS)

Organization	Abbreviation	Members
I. THE FARM SECTOR		
1. National Peasant Confederation	CNC	
A. CNC Proper		2,500
B. Peasant Union		150
2. Mexican Agronomists' Society	SAM	10
Totals, FARM SECTOR		2,660
II. THE LABOUR SECTOR		
1. Workers' Unity Bloc		
(affiliates)	BUO	
Mexican Labour Confederation	CTM	1,500
Regional Confederation of		
Mexican Workers	CROM	35
General Confederation	CGT	25
Railway Workers' Union	STFRM	102
Mining and Metal Workers' Union	STMMSRM	90
Petroleum Workers' Union	STPRM	85
Telephone Workers' Union	STRM	10
Motion Picture Workers' Union	STPCRM	6
Various independent		20
Bloc sub-total		1,873
2. Anti-Unity Bloc affiliates		
Revolutionary Confederation of		
Workers and Peasants	CROC	150
Revolutionary Confederation	CRT	25
Electrical Workers' Union		50
Various independent unions		15
Bloc sub-total		240
Totals, LABOUR SECTOR		2,113
III. THE POPULAR SECTOR	CNOP	
1. Civil Servants		
Bureaucrats' Unions	FSTSE	300
Teachers	SNTE	55
2. Co-operatives		
National Federation of Co-operatives		275
National Co-operative League		3
3. Small Farm Proprietors		
National Confederation of Small		
Owners		850
National Growers' Association		15
4. Small Merchants/Industrialists		40
5. Professional/Intellectual Groups		55

TABLE 39 (*Continued*)

Organization	Abbreviation	Members
6. Youth		75
7. Artisans/Service (non-salaried)		70
8. Women's Groups		
Society of Technicians/Professions		25
Other (auxiliaries, &c.)		10
9. "Diverse Persons" (not otherwise		
specified		75
TOTALS, POPULAR SECTOR		1,848
NATIONAL REVOLUTIONARY PARTY,		
ALL SECTORS		6,621

SOURCE: Robert E. Scott, *Mexican Government in Transition* (Urbana, Ill., 1959), pp. 166–167.

response of peasants and others toward him illustrates this point. "Although Díaz Ordaz was then holder of the top job in the cabinet [Interior Minister], he was little known to the Mexican people. That changed overnight. The following day, as word was passed that Díaz Ordaz was the choice, the entire nation rushed forward to acclaim him as the only possible candidate. Unions, peasants' confederations, social clubs, teachers' organizations, government workers, all pledged him support." [12]

In certain instances in which the PRI faced some political challenge, the party could always count on the rural votes to win the political contest. This is strikingly seen in the following case. In March 1967, the PRI leaders in the state of Sonora abruptly cut off an open competition within the party for the gubernatorial nomination and selected Faustino Félix Serna, a friend of the incumbent governor Luís Encinas Johnson, as the candidate. Later, "when the three main sectors of the party, the peasants, labor and the public [i.e. popular], met separately . . . in accordance with the party's nominating procedure, there was no debate, merely a ratification of the Félix nomination." [13] Students in the capital city Hermosillo became dissatisfied with the arbitrary manner of selecting the PRI candidate and staged a prolonged demonstration against the government, leading to riots, loss of life and property. To maintain order, in May the

[12] "Mexico—a Model for Latin America," *U.S. News and World Report*, LX (January 24, 1966), 59.

[13] *The New York Times*, March 27, 1967, p. 8; and March 29, 1967, p. 15.

federal government had to impose martial law in the state. Despite all this, Félix remained on the ballot and ran a close race with the National Action Party candidate, Gilberto Suarex Arvizu. In the end, Félix won the election, "as rural majorities cancelled out a probable opposition lead in Hermosillo. . . ." [14]

Like their counterpart in Iran, Mexican peasants collaborate with the political elite because such collaboration entitles them to continual representation in the party and in the government. *Ejidatarios* and other small farmers enjoy a guaranteed share of seats in the PRI hierarchy, from the national central executive committees down to the municipal and district committees. Similarly, *ejidatarios* maintain representation on all levels of the government hierarchy. Robert E. Scott has estimated that, as a rule, the farm sector of the PRI occupies about 40 percent of all elective offices of the nation.[15] Another account indicated that, in the federal legislature, the CNC normally occupies about one-fifth of the 60 senatorial seats and 40–odd of the 178 seats in the lower house.[16]

TAIWAN

In Taiwan, land reform has resulted in the complete removal of the large landed gentry and a continuous decline in the number of small landlords.[17] Though landlords still retain today a measure of influence in community affairs, as a class their political strength is definitely waning. The 1968 Tainan survey conducted by the author provides some evidence to this effect. Whereas rural residents in Tainan had traditionally regarded landlords as *ipso facto* local leaders, these residents no longer considered landlords to possess such a privilege. When asked to evaluate the political influence of eight groups of community leaders, the Tainan respondents ranked landlords the seventh, next to the lowest. It is of considerable interest to point out that the findings of this survey are in sharp contrast to those of the survey the author conducted in Luzon, the Philippines, in

[14] *Ibid.*, July 4, 1967, p. 7. See also *Christian Science Monitor*, May 19, 1967, p. 4.
[15] Robert E. Scott, *Mexican Government in Transition* (Urbana: The University of Illinois Press, 1959), p. 89.
[16] Frank Ralph Brandenburg, *The Making of Modern Mexico* (Englewood Cliffs, N.J., 1964), pp. 155–156.
[17] As of 1969, the number of landlords in Taiwan was estimated at 69,000, renting out a total of about 60,000 hectares of land. These landlords constituted less than 10 percent of all farm households and possessed less than 10 percent of all private farm land. See China, Nei Cheng Pu [and] Nung Fu Hui, *Taiwan Nung Ts'un Ti Chu Tien Nung Ching Chi T'iao Ch'a Yen Chiu* (Ministry of the Interior and JCRR, *A Survey of the Rural Economy of Taiwanese Landlords and Tenants*) (Taiwan, 1969), p. i.

TABLE 40

RANKINGS OF POLITICAL INFLUENCE OF COMMUNITY LEADERS,
TAINAN, TAIWAN; AND LUZON, THE PHILIPPINES,
TAINAN SURVEY, 1968; LUZON SURVEY, 1969

	Tainan 1968		Luzon 1969	
Community Leaders	Rank	Regarded as influential by percent of respondents	Rank	Regarded as influential by percent of respondents
Local governmental officials	1	97.40	1	93.63
Party leaders	2	97.29	2	84.28
Teachers	3	94.04	5	43.68
Businessmen	4	82.29	8	34.98
Lawyers	5	78.21	4	47.24
Physicians	6	75.84	6	40.59
Landlords	7	63.29	3	54.44
Clergy	8	59.76	7	38.83

SOURCE: See Appendix III. Respondents giving "no answer" or "don't know" to survey questions were excluded from the data of this table.

1969. Because of lack of effective land reform in the Philippines, the landlords there still retained their traditional political influence. When the Luzon respondents were asked to assess the influence of the same eight groups of community leaders as those in the Tainan survey, landlords were ranked the third, next to the two highest. The pertinent data of both surveys are presented in Table 40.

Other evidence indicates that since the beginning of land reform, Taiwanese landlords have lost interest in politics and have voluntarily withdrawn from leadership positions. Martin M. C. Yang reported in a 1964 rural survey a drastic decline in the interest of landlords in local politics. About "70 per cent of the 575 former landlord households," Yang observed in his survey, "said they had become either less interested or had felt no interest at all in the community's local politics since land reform. Only 25 percent said they were as interested as before." [18] Similarly, in a 1957 to 1958 field study of Hsin Hsing Village in west central Taiwan, Bernard Gallin discovered that "the Land Reform Program . . .

[18] Martin M. C. Yang, Socio-Economic Results of Land Reform in Taiwan (Honolulu: East-West Center Press, 1970), p. 483. For a description of the Yang survey, see note to Table 59, below.

has led many landlords to withdraw their interests from [leadership positions of] the rural villages. . . ." [19]

While leading to political inactivism by landlords, land reform in Taiwan has much stimulated the interest of farmers in politics. Since the late 1940s, the rural electorate has continuously expanded, and farmers are increasingly represented in local government and rural organizations. A survey of seven townships in Taiwan shows that farm voters of various tenure groups rose by 30 to 40 percent between the elections held before land reform (1948 and earlier) and those held afterwards (the early 1960s). Table 41 presents the detailed data.

Unlike the PRI in Mexico, the KMT in Taiwan has not formally incorporated the peasants into the party's structure. But a kind of mutually dependent relationship between the party and rural voters seems to have been established. On the one hand, the KMT depends more upon rural support than upon the urban electorate to maintain its dominant position.[20] On the other hand, farmers who seek elective positions in the provincial and local governments must obtain the blessing of the KMT. This mutually dependent relationship has led to a continuous growth of farmer representation in public institutions.

The general trend toward increasing farmer political representation in Taiwan is affirmed in the Tainan survey of 1968. As seen in Table 43, nearly half of the 487 officials interviewed in the community were either present or former farmers. The survey also brought to light the farmers' own appraisal of the impact of land reform on political participation. More than two-thirds of the 280 farmer respondents considered land reform to have helped them to get involved in local government (see Table 44). A further finding of the survey is worth noting. In contrast to the pre-reform pattern of electoral participation, in which farmers habitually voted for landlord-candidates, there was in the post-reform era a clear trend toward increasing electoral identification between farmers and candidates from their own rank. When asked in the survey to indicate their

[19] Bernard Gallin, Hsin Hsing, Taiwan: A Chinese Village in Change (Berkeley: The University of California Press, 1966), pp. 115–117; quotation on p. 117.

[20] See Tai, op. cit. (n. 1 above), pp. 419–421. It is true that among Taiwan's rural residents, many were not direct beneficiaries of land reform, and that many rural voters supported the KMT because of the rural-development programs rather than because of land reform. But the very large number of reform beneficiaries, their direct participation in the execution of reform laws, and the fact that rural development programs were adopted largely after the introduction of a policy of tenurial changes suggest that land reform must have had the primary energizing effect of rural political participation.

TABLE 41

PERCENTAGE OF RURAL VOTER TURNOUT IN PROVINCIAL AND LOCAL ELECTIONS, IN SEVEN TOWNSHIPS, TAIWAN, BEFORE AND AFTER LAND REFORM[a]

Voters by Tenure Group	Provincial Assembly		Hsien Assembly		Hsien Magistrate		Township Assembly		Township Chief		Village Head	
	Before	After	Before	After	Before	After	Before	After	Before	After	Before	After
Owner	38.6	81.9	41.6	81.3	38.0	80.1	21.7	49.4	32.5	81.9	42.2	77.7
Part owner	42.3	88.5	46.2	84.6	50.0	92.3	26.9	53.9	42.3	84.6	38.5	76.9
Tenant	25.0	64.3	28.6	67.9	32.1	67.9	21.4	50.0	17.9	82.1	42.9	78.6
Average	37.3	80.5	40.5	80.0	38.6	80.0	22.3	50.0	31.8	82.3	41.8	77.7

[a] Elections before land reform refer to the ones held before 1948, and those after land reform in the early 1960s.

SOURCE: Adapted from Yen-tien Chang, "Land Reform and its Impact on Economic and Social Progress in Taiwan; in Memory of [the] Late Vice President Chen Cheng," *Industry of Free China*, XXIII (April 1965), 36–37.

TABLE 42

FARMER REPRESENTATION IN PUBLIC OFFICES AND RURAL ORGANIZATIONS,
TAIWAN, BEFORE AND AFTER LAND REFORM

	Before Reform	After Reform				
Offices and Organizations	1948	1953	1958	1959	1960	1962
Village, precinct, or neighborhood chiefs						
Total number	86,908	90,186	94,278	95,122	95,804	97,165
Farmers, number	4,737	6,998	11,206	14,615	14,730	17,000
Percent of total	5.4	7.7	11.8	15.3	15.3	17.4
District or township chiefs						
Total number	359	360	361	361	319	
Farmers, number	0	2	7	30	42	
Percent of total	0	.55	1.93	8.31	13.16	
Members of *Hsien* or municipal assemblies						
Total number	523	860	1,025	1,025	1,025	
Farmers, number	15	58	122	117	114	
Percent of total	2.87	6.74	11.90	11.41	11.12	
Members of Provincial Assembly						
Total number	37	55	66	66	73	18,413[a]
Farmers, number	0	1	3	2	4	
Percent of total	0	1.81	4.54	3.03	5.47	
Civil servants and teachers in public schools						
Farmers, number	3,673	6,820	9,778	10,168	10,648	
Members of Farm Tenancy Committees						
Farmers, number	10	594	840	1,047	1,071	
Delegates and officers of Farmers' Associations						
Farmers, number	395	1,823	1,516	5,538	5,865	
Total farmer-held offices	8,830	16,296	23,472	31,517	32,474	35,413

[a] Total number of farmers who held office for the categories covered.

SOURCES: Chen Cheng, *Land Reform in Taiwan* (Taipei, Taiwan, 1961), p. 314; U.N., *Land Reform, Fourth Report,* p. 155; and Taiwan, Taiwan Sheng Ti Fang Tsu Ch'ih Chih Yao Pien Chi Wei Yuan Hui, *Taiwan Sheng Ti Fang Tsu Ch'ih Chih Yao (Compendium on Self-Government in Taiwan;* Taichung, Taiwan, China, 1965), *passim.*

TABLE 43

Offices	Total Officials Interviewed		Officials Who Were Farmers	
	Number	Percent	Number	Percent Interviewed
Village Officials	25	100	12	48.00
Township Council, members	80	100	50	62.50
Township Chiefs	6	100	4	66.66
Members of *hsien* assembly	11	100	8	72.73
Civil servants and teachers in public schools	260	100	85	32.69
Officials of Farmers' Associations	105	100	76	72.38
Total	487	100	235	48.25

SOURCE: See Appendix III. Total number of farmer respondents, 280. Total number of all categories of respondents, 550.

TABLE 44

FARMER APPRAISAL OF THE IMPACT OF LAND REFORM ON LOCAL-
POLITICAL PARTICIPATION, TAINAN, TAIWAN,
TAINAN SURVEY 1968

Question: *"Do you consider the enforcement of land reforms helps
you get involved in local government?"*

Response to Question	Respondents	
	Number	Percent
Yes	199	71.07
No	23	8.21
Don't know	21	7.50
No answer	37	13.22
Total	280	100.00

SOURCE: See Appendix III. Total number of farmer respondents, 280.

TABLE 45

FARMER PREFERENCES FOR CANDIDATES FOR PUBLIC OFFICE ACCORDING TO
OCCUPATIONAL BACKGROUND, TAINAN, TAIWAN,
TAINAN SURVEY, 1968

Question: *"There are four candidates running for two public offices.
The candidates have similar qualifications but belong to different
occupations. For which two are you going to vote?"*

Candidate's Occupational Background	Respondents' Choices		
	Frequency	*Percent*	*Preference Rank*
Farmer	252	90.00	1
Worker	40	14.29	2
Businessman	28	10.00	3
Landlord	27	9.64	4
No Answer	17	6.07	

SOURCE: See Appendix III. Total number of farmer respondents, 280.

electoral preferences by choosing two among four candidates with four
different social backgrounds, the farmers responded with a 90 percent
preference for the farmer-candidate but only a 9.64 percent for the landlord candidate. The other two types of candidates—worker and business-
man—received a combined total of 24.29 percent. This finding shows that
an aggregative pattern of rural political participation has definitely emerged
in Tainan and, one can safely say, also in Taiwan as a whole.

THE UNITED ARAB REPUBLIC

In the U.A.R., land reform has created an impact on rural political
participation similar to that in Mexico. Reform left in the countryside a
large number of small landlords, but they are, by and large, denied political representation; on the other hand, the elite has made repeated
efforts to integrate the peasantry into political institutions. The successive
political organizations sponsored by the regime—the Liberation Rally created in 1953, the National Union in 1958, and the Arab Socialist Union
(ASU) in 1962—made special provisions for the inclusion of reform
beneficiaries and other small farmers. At present, the Arab Socialist Union,
which "runs parallel to and interlocks with the structure of the state at
every level of government," guarantees workers and farmers half of the
seats on its committees at all levels, and only farmers owning less than

25 *feddans* (10.5 hectares) of land can become ASU members.[21] Similarly, in governmental institutions farmers and workers are given preferred treatment. In the various national legislatures created since the late 1950s—the Parliaments of 1957 and 1960, the Preparatory Committee of 1961, the Congress of Popular Forces of 1962, and the National Assembly of 1964—farmers have been allocated an increasingly large share of representation, ranging from 19.8 percent of the seats in 1957 to 38.1 percent in 1964.[22] The Provisional Constitution of 1964 provided, in Article 49, that "one half of the members of the [National] Assembly at least must be workers and farmers." In the National Assembly election of March 1964, in which only ASU members and people owning less than 25 *feddans* of land could be candidates, 114 farmers and 75 workers—together accounting for 54 percent of the total of the 350 elected members—won seats.[23] Writing in the late 1960s, M. Riad El Ghonemy estimated: "Since 1963, about 25 percent of the members of the Egyptian National Assembly have been elected from among beneficiaries of land reform." [24] In the provincial and local governments, farmers and workers, through their affiliation with the ASU, apparently are given representation as well, though there is no specific allocation of seats for them.[25]

Thus, through land reform and deliberate induction of the peasantry into the U.A.R.'s political framework, the elite has established a strong hold over rural areas. Peasants have gradually become identified with the regime,[26] and, as in the case of Mexico, they delivered in national elections

[21] Patrick O'Brien, *The Revolution in Egypt's Economic System From Private Enterprise to Socialism, 1952–1965* (London: Oxford University Press, 1966), p. 290. Cf. Peter Mansfield, *Nasser's Egypt* (Baltimore: Penguin Books Inc., 1965), pp. 199–201.

[22] For statistical data on occupational distribution of these legislative bodies, see Leonard Binder, "Political Recruitment and Participation," in Joseph La Palombara and Myron Weiner, *Political Parties and Political Development* (Princeton, N.J.: Princeton University Press, 1966), pp. 235–237.

[23] Fayez Sayegh, "The Theoretical Structure of Nasser's Socialism," in Albert Hourani (ed.), *Middle East Affairs, Number 4* (London: Oxford University Press, 1965), p. 38.

[24] M. Riad El Ghonemy, "Economic and Institutional Organization of Egyptian Agriculture Since 1952," in P. J. Vatikiotis (ed.), *Egypt Since the Revolution* (New York, 1968), p. 72.

[25] Law 24 of 1960 stipulates: the provincial Governorate Council shall consist of 11 ex-officio members appointed by the central government, 5 ASU members, and 4 elected members; the City Council, 6 appointed members, 5 ASU members, and 20 elected members; and the village council, 6 appointed members, 2 ASU members, and 28 elected members. O'Brien, *op. cit.*, p. 285.

[26] Thus, Leonard Binder observed in the early 1960s: "Members of the rural lower classes and those more recently arrived in the city from rural areas can . . . identify

a very large number of votes almost unanimously supporting the official candidates. The solidarity between the peasants and the political elite is not only manifested in elections but also revealed in time of crisis. When President Nasser offered his resignation in June 1967, following the U.A.R.'s defeat by Israel, peasants participated in mass rallies in his favor leading to the withdrawal of his resignation. When, in February, 1968, students demonstrated against the government because of lack of democracy—an episode quite similar to the student protests in Sonora, Mexico—Nasser came to the defense of the political system he had created. As a conciliatory measure, he reorganized the cabinet and held a national referendum, but he did not abolish the ASU or the National Assembly, as the students had demanded. He stressed that in the National Assembly "50 percent of the seats were allocated to 'workers and farmers' in order to 'foil the forces of the counterrevolution.' " [27] Again, when Nasser suddenly died in September 1970 in the midst of the volatile and seemingly irresolvable Middle East crisis, the demonstrated loyalty of the peasantry became an important factor that steadied the shocked nation and facilitated the transition of leadership. In the following month, many *fellahin* joined in Nasser's "tumultuous, frenzied funeral procession," in Cairo, evincing a strong feeling of national solidarity. Within the month, when the election was held to name Anwar Sadat as the new president, peasants all over the country furnished the bulk of votes ratifying the choice.[28]

The foregoing discussion makes it apparent that the peasantry in Iran, Mexico, Taiwan, and the U.A.R. has gradually developed a common political identity, formed a direct relationship with the national elite, and obtained considerable representation in public institutions. The emergence of this pattern of rural political participation, of course, owes as much to the broad effort of the national elite to mobilize the masses into the established political order as to the specific policy for tenurial changes. But tenurial changes are undoubtedly a crucial prerequisite for successful peasant mobilization. Without land reform, the landed class would have

---

themselves with the President and with the leadership of the United Arab Republic. Nasser is one of them. He can and often does speak to them in their own language." "Egypt: the Integrative Revolution," in Lucian W. Pye and Sidney Verba (eds.), *Political Culture and Political Development* (Princeton, N.J., 1965), p. 405.

[27] *The New York Times*, March 8, 1968, p. 9; March 17, 1968, p. 12; and March 21, 1968, p. 24.

[28] See *The New York Times*, October 2, 1970, pp. 1, 16; October 15, 1970, p. 4; and October 17, 1970, p. 3.

continued to interpose itself between the peasantry and the national elite making all but impossible a genuine union between the latter two forces on a nationwide basis. Only when the landed class is removed through reform can the national elite's political solicitations receive broad, positive peasant response.

The Non-Aggregative Pattern

In the remaining four countries the political influence of the landed class appears somewhat diminished, but remains dominant in the villages. Dictated by the political preferences of this class, the peasantry follows a non-aggregative pattern of political participation. Instead of achieving a common political identity, peasants find their voting strength to be geographically dispersed and aligned with different parties and factions. They are able neither to form a direct relationship with the national elite nor to acquire their own representation in the government.

COLOMBIA

In Colombia, the Social Agrarian Reform Act of 1961 has not attracted the attention of most *campesinos*, much less served as an instrument for uniting them. As a critical Congressman said of the reform law on the occasion of its passage: "Here we are at the feast of agrarian reform, and look who's present: All the people from the city, all the bourgeoisie; absent are all the people from the countryside to press for a real agrarian reform." [29]

This pungent remark has, perhaps, certain applicability to the recent pattern of electoral participation in Colombia as well. While many peasant voters stayed away from the polls, politicians in the cities eagerly contended for public offices. Since the formation of the National Front in 1957 the country has seen a striking, persistent decline in voter turnout in elections and, paradoxically, a fair amount of competition among can-

[29] Quoted in *Land Reform and Social Change in Colombia*, the University of Wisconsin, Land Tenure Center, Discussion Paper 4 (November 1963), p. 7. Alfonso López Michelson, leader of the radical *Movimiento de Revolucionario Liberal* (MRL), criticized the law in a similar vein: "I wish the defenders of the project [the reform law] to answer these objections, that they point out to me one other nation in which the announcement of an agrarian reform has produced so much enthusiasm, so much support, and so much prosperity among the landowners (as it has in Colombia)," Quoted in University of Wisconsin, Land Tenure Center, *Prospects for Political Stability in Colombia with Special Reference to Land Reform*, Discussion Paper 1 (Jan. 1963), p. 8.

TABLE 46

DECLINE OF ELECTORAL PARTICIPATION IN COLOMBIA,
REGISTERED AND ACTUAL VOTERS, 1957–1966

Election	Year	Registered Voters	Actual Voters	Actual Voters as Percent of Registered Voters
Plebiscite	1957	6,080,342	4,397,090	72
Congressional	1958	5,365,191	3,693,939	69
Presidential	1958	5,365,191	3,108,567	58
Congressional	1960	4,397,541	2,542,651	58
Congressional	1962	5,338,868	3,090,203	58
Presidential	1962	5,404,765	2,634,840	49
Congressional	1964	6,135,628	2,261,190	37
Congressional	1966	7,126,980	2,843,450	40
Presidential	1966	7,126,980	2,593,705	36

SOURCES: *Colombia Election Factbook March–May, 1966* (Washington, D.C.: Institute for the Comparative Study of Political Systems, 1966), p. 16; and Robert H. Dix, *Colombia: The Political Dimensions of Change* (New Haven: Yale University Press, 1967), p. 162. Original data on the 1966 elections are based on estimates.

didates. As seen in Table 46, after establishing a high mark in the 1957 plebiscite, voter participation in Colombian elections followed a continuously downward trend, reaching the lowest point in the 1966 presidential election, in which nearly two-thirds of the qualified voters did not appear at the polls. In the same period, while both the Conservative and Liberal parties experienced constant factional splits and fluctuation of factional representation in the national legislature,[30] "the factions of the two major parties . . . are remarkably competitive throughout most of Colombia's departments." [31] Under these conditions, one may agree with the observation: "Rather than to view Colombia as a 'two-party system' . . . , it might be more reasonable [to] view it as a multi-party system with alliances." [32] Electoral politics was essentially a process of multi-faction competition.

One explanation for the coexistence of the two political phenomena —the decrease of voter participation and the persistence of political competitiveness—lies in the fact that the elite did not represent the popular

[30] For the fluctuations of factional strength in Congress in the first decade of the National Front government, see Pat M. Holt, *Colombia Today—and Tomorrow* (New York, 1964), p. 57; and McDonald, *op. cit.* (n. 1 above), p. 19.

[31] McDonald, *ibid.*

[32] *Ibid.*

interests. Assured of a political monopoly under the arrangements of the National Front, the two political parties did not have a felt need to recruit elements of the lower social strata.[33] To many voters, elections presented no meaningful choices; abstention was only natural. At the same time, with each party allocated half the legislative seats, contention among factions within a party grew.

One has to await detailed analysis of rural electoral data to discern the precise extent of peasant abstention in recent elections. One also has to await comprehensive field studies to estimate how much of this abstention reflected peasant dissatisfaction with the existing land-tenure system. However, a recent rural survey in one department of Colombia appears to have shed some light on the subject. In 1968, John D. Powell conducted for the Center for Rural Development, Cambridge, Massachusetts, a series of interviews with 168 peasants in the Department of Cundinanarca. The resultant data revealed two findings relevant to the present discussion. An overwhelming majority of these peasants considered the land problem in the survey area very serious, and many expressed a strong feeling of anger toward the problem. At the same time, they continued to regard the landed class as politically dominant and socially influential. These findings are presented in Tables 47 and 48.

The Powell Survey revealed that, after six years of enforcement, land reform in Cundinanarca has neither alleviated the land problem nor made a dent on the power position of the landed interests. The land-tenure problem in Cundinanarca, it should be noted, is rather typical of entire rural Colombia.[34] The department is also particularly involved in the activities of land reform. A number of projects operate in the department, and INCORA headquarters, in Bogotá, is also located within the department's boundary. If reform has failed to alter in any way the power position of the landed class here, there is reason to believe such a failure has also occurred throughout rural Colombia.

Today, as in the past, the national elite of Colombia has neither established a firm identification with the peasants nor formally incorporated them into the existing political parties. Both the Conservatives and the

[33] Cf. John D. Martz, "Political Parties in Colombia and Venezuela: Contrasts in Substance and Style," *The Western Political Quarterly*, XVIII (June 1965), 318 and 322; and Jeanne Kuebler, "Smoldering Colombia," *Editorial Research Report*, August 4, 1965, p. 569.

[34] For a detailed description of the tenure problems of the area, see Lawrence H. Davis, "Economics of Property Tax in Rural Areas of Colombia" (unpublished Ph.D. dissertation, University of Wisconsin, 1968).

TABLE 47

PEASANT EVALUATION OF LAND PROBLEM,
CUNDINANARCA, COLOMBIA, 1968

Evaluation	Number	Percentage
Gravity of the Problem		
Grave	136	80.95
Minor	14	8.33
No problem	16	9.52
No answer	2	1.20
Total	168	100.00
Feeling about the Problem		
Angered	87	51.79
Bothered	43	25.60
No feeling	29	17.26
No answer	9	5.35
Total	168	100.00

SOURCE: John D. Powell, *Organizing Colombian Peasants: a Research Report* (Cited hereafter as *Powell Survey;* Cambridge, Mass.: The Center for Rural Development [1968]), Appendix A.

The Survey, conducted in June and July 1968 by John D. Powell with the assistance of six local researchers, covered thirteen villages in eight *municipios* (counties) in the Department of Cundinanarca, Colombia. The land tenure of the surveyed area was typically characterized by the *latifundia-minifundia* complex. About 97 percent of all farms were under 10 hectares, with a combined acreage of less than 50 percent of the total land. On the other hand, about 6 percent of the landowners possessed one half of the land. The sample of the survey consisted of 168 peasants representing 42 percent of the households of the villages. Interviews were conducted on the basis of a questionnaire (in Spanish) formulated by Powell and John R. Mathiason.

Liberals, it is true, possess secure rural constituencies; and many peasants are intensively partisan. But the leadership of both parties reaches the rural electorate largely via the big landed gentry which is found in both parties. The intensity of peasant partisanship owes, of course, to the prolonged interparty feud rather than to an identification of basic interests between the peasants and the two parties. With no effective link with the national elite, and dispersed in their electoral power, peasants can neither exert influence on public policies nor obtain representation in public institutions.

TABLE 48

PEASANT RANKINGS OF STATUS OF COMMUNITY LEADERS,
CUNDINANARCA, COLOMBIA, 1968

Community Leaders[a]	Over-all Rank	Respect		Influence		Service		Leadership	
		Per-cent	Rank	Per-cent	Rank	Per-cent	Rank	Per-cent	Rank
Landlord	1	41.0	1	42.3	1	17.9	1	20.3	1
Priest, School teacher	2	13.7	2	7.7	2	1.8	6	3.0	5
Leader of local organization	3	4.8	4	6.5	3	12.5	2	5.4	2
Local government official	4	9.5	3	5.4	4	5.4	3	4.8	3
Peasant	5	4.8	4	3.8	6	4.8	4	3.6	4
Storekeeper, other	6	4.8	4	4.2	5	2.4	5	3.6	4
"No one"		11.3		12.5		38.7		36.9	

[a] Not a complete enumeration of all categories of community leaders, with "no answer" excluded.

SOURCES: Adapted from *Powell Survey*, Table 16, p. 48. With respect to the four specific status categories—"Respect," "Influence," "Service," and "Leadership"—the questions in the survey were as follows: "Whom do you consider to be the most respected person in the community?"; "Who is the person that has the most influence in the community?"; "Who is the person that does the most to resolve community problems?"; and "Who is the most distinguished leader in your community?"

INDIA

In India, the two phases of land reform seem to have had basically different impacts on rural politics. In the phase of reform ending with the abolition of the *zamindars,* one detects a tendency toward the emergence of an aggregative pattern of rural political participation. *Zamindar* abolition represented the culmination of a long series of actions taken by the Congress Party to enlist peasant loyalty for the nationalist movement. Through the initiation of the rural *satyagraha* (non-cooperative movement) in Bihar in 1917, the invitation of *kisan* delegates to the Congress's annual session in 1918, the launching of a no-rent campaign in the United Provinces in 1930, the organizing of *kisan* councils in the 1930s, the adoption of the resolution abolishing *zamindars* in 1935, and the final implementation of that resolution in the 1950s the Congress Party mobilized a sizable number of peasants into the political process and created a cooperative relationship with them. Seeking to improve their economic plight through participation in these Congress-sponsored activities, the peasants in the scattered Indian villages were galvanized into a national force.

This tendency toward an aggregative pattern of rural political participation failed to gain momentum as India moved into the second phase of land reform in the aftermath of the *zamindar* abolition. The post-abolition reform measures led to neither a substantial reduction of the power of the landed interests nor the creation of an independent peasant political force. Indian *kisans* participated in the elections in large numbers,[35] but they followed essentially a non-aggregative pattern. In today's rural India, the landowning interests and such other parochial entities as caste, religious, and linguistic groupings are the potent local forces commanding the *kisans'* voting preferences.[36] Because faction politics in India is both vigorous and widespread, rival politicians seeking elective offices and local leaders of parochial groupings tend to form a system of "vertical faction chains," whereby the former trade political favors for the latter's votes.[37] But as both factional and parochial conflicts are persistent and pervasive, the *kisans*, divided in their factional and parochial loyalties, cannot achieve any measure of political unity among themselves. If, in the independence movement, the *kisans* could be united behind the Congress Party in opposition to the *zamindars*, today they cannot join together and

[35] The level of voter participation in India's four general elections has been fairly high. In the first general elections (1951–1952), 60.7 percent of the eligible voters voted; in the second (1957), 47.7 percent; in the third (1962), 51.9 percent; and in the fourth (1967), about 60 percent. Richard L. Park, *India's Political System* (Englewood Cliffs, N.J.: Prentice-Hall, Inc., 1967), pp. 59–63. About 80 percent of the population resided in rural areas in these years.

[36] One may say with fairness that the following observation, which was made in reference to a rural district in Andhra Pradesh, is applicable to the entire countryside of India: "It is clear that to be successful in politics in this rural district . . . one must be a landowner, middle-aged, educated, and a member of one of the dominating landowning castes . . ." Hugh Gray, "The 1962 General Election in a Rural District of Andhra," *Asian Survey*, II (September 1962), 35.

[37] A vast amount of literature exists on this subject. Some of the representative writings may be cited. Rajni Kothari, "The Congress 'System' in India," *Asian Survey*, IV (December 1964), 1161–1173; Myron Weiner, "India's Third General Elections," *Asian Survey*, II (May 1962), 3–18; and "Village and Party Factionalism in Andhra: Ponnur Constituency," *The Economic Weekly*, XIV (September 22, 1962), 1509–1518; A. H. Somjee, "Groups and Individuals in the Politics of an Indian Village," *Asian Survey*, II (June 1962), 13–18; D. F. Miller, "Factions in Indian Village Politics," *Pacific Affairs*, XXXVIII (Spring 1965), 17–31; and Ramashray Roy, "Intra-Party Conflict in Bihar Congress," *Asian Survey*, VI (December 1966), 706–715.

be identified with a single party or with a single political faction in opposition to the landlords.

As the governing party, Congress seems at present to rely on its ability
to deliver public goods and services to rural areas and on the *kisans'*
memories of its historical role in the independence movement to retain
their sympathies. But the Congress may not entirely succeed in this effort.
The *kisans* are aware that the public goods and services benefit the landowning interests far more than the small farmers, and their memory of
Congress's historical accomplishment may erode in intensity with the
passage of time. For years, the strength of the Congress in the Lok Sabha
and in state legislatures has been steadily declining, reaching the lowest
point in the 1967 election.[38] In this election, the Congress failed for the
first time since independence to retain a majority in the legislatures of
more than half of India's states; and it lost, among others, Rajasthan,
Uttar Pradesh, Kerala, and Bihar—states generally with a greater farming
population than most of the remaining states.[39] *Kisan* disaffection for the
party must have been substantial.

Because of the dispersion of their vast electoral strength, Indian *kisans*
cannot obtain any meaningful representation in the Lok Sabha and in
state legislatures. Even in the *panchayat* system, the revival of which was
primarily intended to stimulate the rural masses to participate in village
government, the *kisans* find themselves continuously subject to the dominant influence of the well-to-do landed interests. The *panchayat* system

---

[38] In the four general elections held from 1950/51 to 1967, the share of the total
seats in the Lok Sabha won by the Congress declined from 74.4 percent in 1950/51 to
53.93 percent in 1967; in the same period Congress's share of the total legislative seats
declined from 68 percent in 1952 to 47.7 percent in 1967. Throughout these years,
Congress's share of the total popular vote in both Lok Sabha and state legislative elections never exceeded 50 percent. See Park, *op. cit.*, pp. 60–63; Myron Weiner, *Party
Building in a New Nation, The Indian National Congress* (Chicago: The University
of Chicago Press, 1967), p. 55; and *Weekly Indian News* (Washington, D.C.) March
10, 1967, p. 6.

[39] Many believe that, following the 1967 elections, the dominant one-party system operating in India since independence has been replaced by a plural party system
on the state level, and may be so replaced on the union level in the future. Michael
Brecher, "Succession in India 1967: The Routinization of Political Change," *Asian
Survey*, VII (July 1967), 424; and Paul Wallace, "India: The Dispersion of Political
Power," *Asian Survey*, VIII (February 1968), 89ff. For urban and rural population
distribution of Indian states, see Myron Weiner, "Political Development in the Indian
States," in Weiner (ed.), *State Politics in India* (Princeton, N.J.: Princeton University
Press, 1968), p. 33.

has brought the peasantry into the political framework of the village, but has not brought about participatory democracy at the local level.[40] Of the 160,000 *panchayats* established by 1957, an official document reported, "possibly not more than 10 percent . . . are functioning effectively, roughly one-half are average, and the remaining 40 percent are working unsatisfactorily." [41] One of the main reasons for this failing performance was that "often the *panchayats* consisted mostly of the wealthy and influential persons. . . . In general *panchayats* cannot be said to command the loyalty of all sections of the community, especially the poorer peasants, the landless . . . ; in practice the economically weaker sections have as yet little voice in the affairs of the *panchayat*." [42] Little has changed since the issuance of this report.[43]

THE PHILIPPINES

Philippine experiences with land reform and rural political participation show certain parallels with those of India. The electoral process in the Philippines is competitive, and politicians are keenly aware of the great weight of the rural electorate. Moreover, if in the past the Indian

[40] The *panchayat*, an ancient Indian village organization, is literally a council of five members exercising, collectively, administrative, financial, and judicial authorities. Once called by Sir Charles Metcalfe the "little republics," and viewed by others as the origin of Indian rural democracy, the *panchayats* were revived in 1947. See Carl C. Taylor *et al.*, *India's Roots of Democracy: A Sociological Analysis of Rural India's Experience in Planned Development since Independence* (New York: Frederick A. Praeger, Publishers, 1965), pp. 29ff. When revived, the institution was conceived to be "a village organization representing the community as a whole . . . which brings the people into common programmes to be carried out with the assistance of the administration." India, Planning Commission, *The First Five-Year Plan* (New Delhi, 1953), p. 133. The *panchayat* system is a three-level rural government. At the village level a *panchayat* of up to fifteen members is elected by the village residents; at the block level there is a *panchayat samiti* consisting of heads of village *panchayats* of the block and covering about 60,000 people; and at the district level there is a *zilla parished* composed of *samiti* presidents of the district.

[41] India, Committee on Class Projects, *Report of the Team for the Study of Community Projects and National Extension Service* (Team leader: Balvantary G. Mehta, New Delhi, 1957), II, 1.

[42] *Ibid.*, 2.

[43] Cf.: "My own observation is that in certain States the [*panchayats*] are largely, and in some areas entirely, dominated by the landed elements in rural society. . . ." Ralph H. Retzlaff, *Village Government in India* (London: Asia Publishing House, 1962), p. 10. Cf. also B. Maheswari, "Role of the Administrator in Panchayati Raj," *The Economic Weekly*, XV (June 15, 1963), 959–964; and Iqbal Narain, "The Concept of Panchayati Raj and Its Institutional Implications in India," *Asian Survey*, V (September 1965), 456–466.

TABLE 49

THE PHILIPPINE ELECTORATE, 1951–1967

Year	Registered Voters			Actual Voters	Actual Voters as Percent of Registered Voters
	Total	Provincial	City	Actual Voters	Registered Voters
1951	4,754,307	4,146,196	608,111	4,391,109	92.36
1953	5,603,231	4,717,809	867,372	4,326,706	77.20
1955	6,487,061	5,543,313	943,748	5,046,448	77.80
1957	6,763,897	5,750,200	1,013,697	5,108,112	75.52
1959	7,822,472	6,652,564	1,169,908	6,393,724	81.74
1961	8,483,568	7,091,933	1,391,635	6,738,805	79.43
1963	9,691,621	8,030,009	1,661,612	7,712,019	79.57
1965	9,962,345	8,188,478	1,773,867	7,610,051	76.39
1967	9,744,604	7,795,912	1,948,692	7,957,019	81.66

SOURCES: The Philippines, Commission on Elections, *Reports of the Commission on Elections* (Manila, 1960, 1965, 1969).

nationalist movement could help create a common identity among the *kisans* and establish a direct cooperative relationship between them and the Congress Party, there were indications in the Philippines that peasants, if led by a political movement strongly committed to the resolution of the land issue, could also be united on the basis of this issue and could consciously align themselves with the leadership of the movement. But, again as in India, land reform in the Philippines has failed to weaken the political influence of the landlords; peasant voters still follow a non-aggregative pattern of political participation.

Since independence, Philippine politics has been characterized by a rapid expansion of the electorate, a high rate of voter participation, great fluidity in party alignments, and a strong sense of independence among the voters. As indicated in Table 49, from 1951 to 1967, the total number of registered voters rose from 4,754,307 to 9,744,604, an increase of 105 percent. In a comparable period, from 1948 to 1966, the population of the country rose from 19,234,182 to 33,345,000, a gain of 74 percent.[44] The rate of electoral expansion was, therefore, considerably higher than that of population growth. Table 49 also reveals that a very large proportion (from three-fourths to four-fifths) of the registered voters actually cast their ballots in elections. While voter participation was high, party

[44] The Philippines, Department of Commerce and Industry, Bureau of the Census and Statistics, *Yearbook of Philippine Statistics 1966* (Manila, 1966), pp. 2–3.

discipline was weak and factional politics prevalent. Presidential aspirants often switched party affiliation to win nomination; turncoat candidates often won elections;[45] and not until 1969 had any Philippine President been elected twice.[46] These features of the Philippine electorate show that the voters were capable of exercising discriminating political choices irrespective of party label and incumbency of high office-holders.[47]

As is also evident in Table 49, though the number of rural voters (those in the provinces) increased at a slower rate than that of urban voters, they still constituted, as of 1967, the dominant component of the national electorate (about 80 percent). More notably, in all elections since independence the rural areas had a consistently higher voter turnout than the cities (the average rate of voter turnout in the elections of 1949 to 1965 was 79.8 percent for the rural electorate, as against 72.5 percent for the urban).[48] The numerical weight of the rural voters, together with such typical characteristics of the Philippine electoral process as the grassroots style of presidential campaigns and keen bipartisan competition,[49] has strongly motivated politicians to seek the rural voters.

[45] Thus, in 1946, Manuel A. Roxas bolted the Nacionalists Party, became the presidential candidate of the Liberal Party he helped organize, and won the election against the Nacionalista candidate Sergio Osmeña. In 1953, Ramon Magsaysay, the Liberal Defense Minister under President Elpidio Quirino, became Nacionalista presidential candidate and won the election against the Liberal candidate Quirino. In 1965, Ferdinand E. Marcos, Liberal President of the Senate, became Nacionalista presidential candidate and defeated incumbent Liberal President Diosdado Macapagal.

[46] In 1969, President Marcos broke the tradition by winning reelection.

[47] One, perhaps revealing, instance illustrating the Philippine voters' sense of political selectivity was provided in the 1957 presidential election. The voters elected Nacionalista Garcia as president by 2,072,257 votes but chose Liberal Macapagal as Vice President by a larger number of votes, 2,189,197. See Quentin Reynolds and Geoffrey Bocca, Macapagal the Incorruptible (New York: David McKay Company, 1965), p. 133.

[48] Hirofumi Ando, "Voting Turnout in the Philippines," Philippine Journal of Public Administration, XIII (October 1969), 432.

[49] In the 1953 presidential election, Magsaysay's barrio-to-barrio campaign contributed a great deal to the awakening of rural political consciousness. Of Magsaysay's political appeal, Jose V. Abueva has said: "Everywhere Magsaysay went he raised people's expectations of what government under his leadership would do for them. . . . By his acts and by sheer force of his personality, he brought to popular consciousness the promise and potentialities of popular government. . . . He has established an irreversible trend of public expectations of government." "Ramon Magsaysay, Third President of the Republic—an Estimate," Philippine Journal of Public Administration, I (April 1957), 93. See also Jorge R. Coquia, The Philippine Presidential Election of 1953 (Manila, 1955), pp. 220–224. Macapagal carried on this populist approach to politics with intensity and vigor. "In less than four years [while he was Vice President, 1958–1961] he visited . . . virtually every Filipino barrio (of which there are at

In certain limited instances, peasants responded to the appeals of politicians by aligning themselves with those supporting agrarian changes. As discussed in Chapter IV, before the Second World War the peasantry in Central Luzon gave considerable electoral support to the radical, peasant-oriented *Sakdalista* Party, enabling its candidates to win a number of contests at all levels of government. In the 1946 election, "Central Luzon . . . threw 33 percent of its votes to the left wing Democratic Alliance while giving 56 percent of its presidential vote to the Nacionalista presidential candidate, Sergio Osmeña, who was thought to have more sympathy for the peasantry than his opponent." [50] A much broader appeal to the peasants was made, of course, by Magsaysay in his presidential campaign in 1953. It should be pointed out that while some peasants voted for him because of his stand on the issue of land reform, many more endorsed him primarily because of the popularity of the former defense minister and the personal integrity of the man. In fact, as Frances L. Starner has observed, an analysis of the 1953 electoral statistics and the tenancy rates of the nation would indicate that "there is no correlation between the distribution of Magsaysay's voting strength in 1953 and the incidence of tenancy either in the Philippines as a whole or in Central Luzon specially." [51] In Central Luzon, Magsaysay's voting strength varied. For instance, in Nueva Ecija, where the incidence of tenancy was rated the second highest in the nation and where there was a very impressive increase of voters, Magsaysay's majority margin was smaller than his national average;[52] this was also true in such other high tenancy provinces as Pangasinan and Tarlac. In other words, in the 1953 election Magsaysay's

least 23,000), including many previously regarded as inaccessible. His strategy [in the 1961 election] was aimed at obtaining the support of a majority of the rural votes. . . ." Martin Meadows, "Philippine Political Parties and the 1961 Election," *Pacific Affairs*, XXXV (Fall 1962), 272. Cf. R. S. Milne, "From Magsaysay to Macapagal," *Parliamentary Affairs*, XV (Autumn 1962), 12–13. Macapagal's 1965 campaign was similarly penetrative, reaching out to many outlying islands to meet the people. See Albert Ravenholt, "Democracy in Action on Remote Philippine Islands," *American Universities Field Staff*, Report Service, Southeast Asia Series, XIII, No. 7 (April 1, 1965).

[50] Carl H. Landé, *Leaders, Factions, and Parties: The Structure of Philippine Politics* (New Haven, 1965), p. 122.

[51] Frances L. Starner, *Magsaysay and the Philippine Peasantry* (Berkeley, Calif., 1961), p. 48.

[52] In 1953, 79.4 percent of the registered voters in Nueva Ecija actually voted in the presidential election as compared to 61.6 percent in 1949. In the 1953 election, Magsaysay won 58.8 percent of the presidential vole in Neuva Ecija as against 68.9 percent of the vote of the whole nation.

personality, rather than his program, was a decisive factor attracting the peasant vote. It is significant, therefore, to note that after two years in office and after exacting from the Congress a number of land-reform bills, Magsaysay could induce peasants to make electoral choices on the basis of issues. Campaigning in the 1955 local and senatorial elections, he helped elect many of his supporters. "In areas of Central Luzon where he had made his poorest showing in 1953, he appeared to have made extensive inroads by late 1955; and responses in these areas indicated that the President's land reform program was perhaps the most important factor in the gains he had made." [53]

After Magsaysay's death, his close associates who were sympathetic with the peasantry consistently showed their strength in Central Luzon. In the 1957 presidential election, the newly-formed Progressive Party of the Philippines, "the only party which campaigned actively for more rapid land reform, . . . placed third in the nation with slightly more than one million votes. However, it placed first or second in the provinces of Central Luzon. . . ." [54] Running as the presidential candidate of the party, Manuel Manahan, once considered Magsaysay's political heir, received more votes than Carlos P. Garcia (the winner of the election) in 12 out of a total of 53 Philippine provinces. Of these 12 provinces, 9 were in Central and Southern Luzon, the area with the highest concentration of tenancy in the nation.[55] In the 1961 presidential election, Emmanuel Pelaez, "another Magsaysay lieutenant . . . who ran as Liberal Party vice presidential candidate, also made a somewhat better showing in Central Luzon than in the nation as a whole (43 percent against 38 percent)." [56]

These are the few instances in which the peasants appear to have gathered their electoral strength on the basis of the land issue. But no agrarian movement leading to the establishment of a common identity

[53] *Ibid.*, p. 83.

[54] David Wurfel, "Philippine Agrarian Reform under Magsaysay," *Far Eastern Survey*, XXVII (February 1958), 30.

[55] In Pampanga, Nueva Ecija, Bulacan, and Tarlac—four Central Luzon provinces where the incidence of tenancy was rated, in 1948, in successive order, from the highest to the fourth highest in the Philippines—Manahan received a total of 142,677 votes against 111,374 for Garcia. See The Philippines, Commission on Elections, *Report of the Commission on Elections to the President of the Philippines and the Congress on the Manner the Elections Were Held on November 12, 1957* (Manila, Bureau of Printing, 1958), pp. 208–211. For geographical distribution of tenancy rate, see Starner, *op. cit.*, pp. 10–12.

[56] Landé, *op. cit.*

between the peasantry and the elite has ever gained ground. To a certain extent this is because those who appealed to and won peasant support entered the electoral campaign largely as unorganized individuals. But, basically, this is because the two established parties are allied with the landowning interests. The Philippine two-party system, as former Senator Raul S. Manglapus has commented, "is in fact a system of one party with two factions that are assured of perpetual alternation in power." [57] The elite controlling both parties is almost identical in social composition and political outlook. As landlords form a part of the national elite and domi-nate in local politics, politicians of both parties find it necessary to form, in the words of Carl Landé, vertical dyadic electoral alliances with the local landed gentry. In a given locality, as one party is allied with one prominent gentry leader who controls peasant votes, the other party must cooperate with another gentry leader. Through this alliance the parties and the landowners exchange political favors for peasant votes.[58] As the 1969 Luzon Survey has indicated (see Table 42, above), rural respondents still ranked landlords third among the eight categories of community leaders, in terms of the political influence they commanded. Only local government officials and party leaders had a higher rating. But then these were mostly landowning politicians who forged the vertical dyadic alliance.

Like the "vertical faction chains" operating in rural India, the vertical dyadic alliances of the Philippines assure a large voter turnout at election time. In both instances, this system of vertical political alliance is rein-forced by parochial ties: the caste, religious, linguistic identities in India, and kinship in the Philippines. However, in the Philippines one does not see a rise of peasant protest votes against the existing political parties, as in the case of India, nor does one see a decline of total rural votes, as in the case of Colombia. Unlike India, where political parties are relatively differentiated from each other in terms of ideology, Philippine parties show no basic difference on issues. To express their dissatisfaction, Indian voters can vote against parties; whereas Philippine voters can oppose only individual candidates. Also, unlike Colombia where the arrangements of the National Front deprive voters of a sense of political efficacy, Philippine voters have proved quite independent and capable of throwing politicians

[57] Quoted in *The New York Times*, November 14, 1967, p. 9.

[58] Landé, *op. cit.*, pp. 1 and 28. Cf. Mary R. Hollinsteiner, *The Dynamics of Power in a Philippine Municipality* (Quezon City: University of the Philippines, Com-munity Development Research Council, 1963) pp. 188–189.

out of high offices. Peasant disaffection in the Philippines is, therefore, not manifest in the electoral process, but reveals itself, as will be discussed later, largely in the revival of Huk strength.

PAKISTAN

In Pakistan, the pattern of electoral participation during Ayub Khan's rule was to a large extent shaped by the former President himself. Under the system of Basic Democracies (first introduced in 1959 and formally embodied in the 1962 constitution), an elaborate government structure was erected through indirect elections. The populace could directly elect only members of Union Councils. These Councils constituted the Electoral College of Pakistan as well as the pyramidal base of the country's local government system. As electors, the members of Union Councils, called Basic Democrats, would choose, on behalf of the people, the President of the nation and members of the National Assembly and the provincial assemblies of East and West Pakistan. The elected members of the Union Councils, along with appointed officials, also formed the first tier of local government. By cooptation, and again along with appointed officials, the Basic Democrats formed government at higher levels: *Tehsil* (in West Pakistan) and *Thana* (in East Pakistan) Councils as the second tier, District Councils as the third, Divisional Councils as the fourth, and the Provincial Development Advisory Councils as the highest.

The introduction of the system of Basic Democracies, Ayub Khan often explained, was for the purpose of developing a grass-roots leadership which would "bridge the gap between the people and the officials. . . ." [59] The system, he emphasized, should "grow and evolve from the very first ring of the political ladder so that it finds its roots deep among the people starting at the village level in rural areas and at the mohalla [a subdivision of town] level in towns." [60] Not "foisted upon the people from above . . . [but working] from below . . . [and] free from the curse of party intrigues, political pressures and tub-thumping politicians," the system "will be truly representative of the people themselves." [61] Ayub Khan envisioned the relationship between the Basic Democracies and land reform to be a

[59] Quoted in West Pakistan, Information Department, The Directorate of Publications, Research and Films, *West Pakistan Year Book 1965* (Lahore, Pakistan, n.d., p. 43.

[60] Quoted in Herbert Feldman, *Revolution in Pakistan* (London, 1967), pp. 103–104.

[61] Ayub Khan, *Speeches and Statements*, II (Karachi, n.d.), 34–35.

complementary one. Basic Democracies should become "the pivots of all-purpose welfare units which . . . [would help solve] our rural problems . . . both in the local and the national context." And, in this context "the land reforms should [help] . . . abolish the time-honored distinction and antagonism between the 'feudal lords' and the middle-class landowners. This ought to open a new chapter of equality, fraternity and cooperation in their mutual relationship and pave the way for . . . the development and progress of our country." [62]

So much for the structural characteristics of the Basic Democracies and the purposes for which the system was created. What was the system's performance? In particular, to what extent has land reform affected its operations? Available evidence indicates that the level of voter participation in the first Basic Democracies election in 1959 to 1960 was fairly high for the nation as a whole, though there was a larger voter turnout in West Pakistan than in the East Wing, and a heavier rural vote than urban. Of the 32 million registered voters, over 20 million (or about 63 percent) came to the polls: 9 million (or about three-fourths) of the registered voters in West Pakistan and about 12 million (or a little over half) of the registered voters in East Pakistan.[63] Illustrative of the low turnout in cities was the voting in Karachi—the largest urban area of the country—where only 35 percent of the registered voters voted.[64]

The system of Basic Democracies appears to have stimulated rural involvement in politics. "Of the 80,000 Basic Democrats elected in 1959–60, the overwhelming majority . . . were occupied with agriculture. For the country as a whole 50,000 . . . were classified as agriculturally employed. . . . Another 12,000 were classified as small landholders and small businessmen. . . ." [65]

As members of the Electoral College, the 80,000 Basic Democrats voted Ayub Khan in as President in January 1960, and elected the first provincial legislative assemblies of the East and West Wings in a nonpartisan contest in 1962 (parties were then prohibited). In the presidential election of 1965, of the 79,700 valid ballots cast by the Basic Democrats, 49,951 (or 62.7 percent) were for Ayub Khan and 28,691 (or 36 percent)

[62] Ibid., p. 20.

[63] Douglas E. Ashford, National Development and Local Reform, Political Participation in Morocco, Tunisia, and Pakistan (Princeton, N.J.: Princeton University Press, 1967), p. 125.

[64] Ibid.

[65] Ibid., p. 128. Cf. Khalid B. Sayeed, The Political Systems of Pakistan (Boston, 1967), pp. 251–252.

for the late Miss Fatima Jinnah (presidential candidate of the Combined Opposition Parties).[66] It is of interest to take note of the relative distribution of electoral strength of the two candidates. Miss Jinnah had a comparatively large amount of support in urban areas and in East Pakistan, capturing Dacca and Karachi, the largest cities in the East and West Wings respectively. In contrast, Ayub Khan retained a massive hold on rural areas and on West Pakistan.[67] In the assembly elections of 1965 (which were contested on a partisan basis as party systems had been revived in late 1962), the Basic Democrats provided the ruling party, the Pakistan Muslim League (PML, headed by Ayub Khan), a large majority of seats in the National Assembly and a small one in the West Provincial Assembly, but a smaller number of seats in the East Provincial Assembly than those of independents and opposition parties combined.[68] PML's strength was also stronger in the West Wing than in the East, and in rural areas than in urban.[69]

It is not to be concluded that the fairly high level of rural voter participation in the Basic Democracies elections, and Ayub Khan's and the PML's apparent political hold in the countryside reflected either a change in the non-aggregative pattern of rural electoral participation toward an aggregative one or a close identity between the peasantry and the political elite. Rural votes were still to a large extent dictated by the wishes of the landed interests whose "power and prestige . . . remained unaffected" by land reform.[70] Toward the end of the Ayub Khan regime, these interests continued to possess a large share of representation in the national and provincial legislatures, with the peasants unrepresented at all. For instance, in the 1962 to 1965 National Assembly, according to the Election Commission statistics, 40 (33 from West Pakistan and 7 from East Pakistan) of the total of 156 members were landlords.[71] Another source

[66] Al-Mujahid, *op. cit.* (n. 1 above), p. 292.

[67] See *Ibid.*; Karl von Vorys, *Political Development in Pakistan* (Princeton, N.J., 1965), p. 288; and Sayeed, *op. cit.*, p. 250.

[68] The legislative seats of the PML and other parties elected in 1965 were as follows: National Assembly—PML, 120; opposition parties, 16; West Provincial Assembly—PML, 96; Independents, 49; Jamaat-i-Islami, 1; East Provincial Assembly—PML, 66 seats; Independents, 58; and opposition parties, 23 seats. Sharif al-Mujahid, "The Assembly Elections in Pakistan," *Asian Survey*, V (November 1965), 547–548.

[69] Cf. Sayeed, *op. cit.*, pp. 114–115 and 230–233.

[70] Mushtaq, Ahmad, *Government and Politics in Pakistan* (Karachi, 1963), p. 246.

[71] Cited in Sayeed, *op. cit.*, p. 114.

estimated the landlord strength as high as 70 (58 from the West Wing and 12 from the East).[72] In the 1962 to 1965 West Pakistan Provincial Assembly 77 out of a total 155 members were landlords.[73]

At the lower level of the government, the political dominance of the landed class was even more pronounced. Though the Basic Democrats consisted of a large number of "agriculturalists," "the term *agriculturalist* in West Pakistan, so far as the membership of the Union Councils was concerned, meant that the councillors were large landlords.[74] To a lesser extent, this was also true in East Pakistan. And in both East and West Pakistan, the Union Council chairmanship belonged to the landowning class. Together with government officials, the large landowners practically reduced the Basic Democracies to the status of administrative agencies in which they enjoyed privileged treatment. To the peasants, the system of Basic Democracies was—contrary to the intention of Ayub Khan—an institution imposed from above, to which they had little attachment.[75] To the landlords, the system was the new instrument through which they could both obtain material benefits from the government and extend their control over the peasants. To the national elite, the system was a means of securing massive rural electoral support. "The government, under the present circumstances, would lend support only to that landlord who

[72] Ahmad, *op. cit.*, p. 273.

[73] Sayeed, *op. cit.*, p. 115.

[74] *Ibid.*, p. 252. An observer on the scene has noted that "some Union Councils in the Punjab and Sind [in West Pakistan] were controlled by old factions of *zamindars* (landlords). . . . This is especially true in Sind . . . where land reform has little penetrated." Louis Dupree, "A Note on Pakistan," *American Universities Field Staff*, Report Service, South Asia Series, Vol. II, No. 8 (1963), 23. In a dispatch from Baidyer Bazar, East Pakistan, *The New York Times* commented on how influential a Basic Democrat such as Bahauddin Ahmed was. "When people here refer to his role as a Basic Democrat or as chairman of the Union Council (on which the eight Basic Democrats in the neighborhood sit), they do so deferentially, attaching the traditional honorific, 'sahib'. By local standards, chairman sahib and all the members sahibs are positively well-to-do, as are 75 per cent of the 35,000 Basic Democrats in the province. . . . The bitterly disaffected and virtually disenfranchised clerks, students, and professionals of East Pakistan's towns and cities tend to see it [the system of Basic Democracies] all as one giagantic patronage system with the Basic Democrats, representing the traditional landed interests, as the main beneficiaries." August 8, 1968, p. 7.

[75] A survey of village life in Lahore district found that "to most villagers a Union Council appeared to represent more a court of law than a corporate representative body capable of undertaking social welfare activities in the area. . . . The village folk are predominantly non-political in their process of thinking." Quoted in Ashford, *op. cit.* (n. 63 above), p. 123. Cf. Sayeed, *op. cit.*, pp. 253–258.

impressed [it] through the number of Basic Democrats he controlled in an area or a district." [76] These arrangements much resemble the vertical alliance system prevailing in India and the Philippines. But unlike the peasants in India and the Philippines whose direct participation in the rather competitive electoral process compelled the elites to be attentive to the land issue, the peasants in Pakistan had only indirect suffrage in the national and provincial elections, and thus left politicians virtually free to ignore the issue.[77] The Pakistani peasants could vote directly for the Basic Democrats, but the latter were by and large landlords. There was no way for the peasantry of Pakistan to reach the national elite.

In all eight countries studied, the enlargement of the rural electorate is a rather common trend which took place independently of land reform. But in some of these countries, certain significant changes within the rural electorate have occurred which can be directly attributable to tenurial reform. In countries with limited implementation of land reform, the traditional, three-tier relationship in the rural electorate persists today. *The national elite* has inducted *the peasantry* into the political process but exerts control over the peasantry via *the landed class*. The continual interposition of this class between the national elite and the peasantry in the political process is the single important factor that disperses peasant electoral strength and renders it difficult for the peasants to make concerted electoral choices. Consequently, the political system is accountable to the landed class, but not to the rural masses. So long as this condition exists, the transformation of the peasants from a "subject" status to a full "participant" status in the political system will be extremely difficult.

In countries with extensive implementation of land reform, the traditional three-tier relationship in the political process has been reduced to a two-tier one. With the landed class disappearing or considerably weakened, the national elite and the peasantry have come to face each other directly. The union of the peasantry on a nationwide basis, and the identification of the peasantry with the national elite are the common

---

[76] Sayeed, *op. cit.*, p. 232.

[77] In an analysis of the themes of speeches of Ayub Khan and Jinnah in the 1965 presidential election, von Vorys reported that the two candidates were primarily concerned with the overriding issue of the desirability of the political system that Ayub Khan had created, with relatively little attention paid to other issues. *Op. cit.*, pp. 280–287. There was barely a reference to land reform in Ayub's election manifesto, implying that it was an accomplished fact, which was in no need of any further attention. Al-Mujahid, *op. cit.* (n. 1 above), 286.

goals of both groups. The peasants are assimilated into the political system and may, in time, obtain a measure of influence over the system. For, in the long run, the political hold of the elite in rural areas depends much more on the mass peasantry than on the disappearing landed class. The significance of land reform on rural political participation in these countries does not lie, then, in the acceptance by the elite of the peasantry as a part of the political system, but in the future possibility that the peasantry may become an effective part.

XI

NATIONAL INTEGRATION

To what extent can land reform contribute to the integration of isolated peasant communities into a national whole? National integration may be said to consist of two dimensions: a territorial extension of the authority of the central government of a country from the capital to the periphery, and a growing psychological identification by the populace with the nation. The above question, then, may be answered in terms of the territorial and psychological dimensions of national integration.

In countries where the landed class wields a political influence over the peasantry roughly comparable to the influence of the national government over the landed class itself, a direct exercise of authority by the national government over the peasantry will, of course, result in the diminution of the political influence of landlords. Hence, if a land-reform program helps extend national authority directly to rural masses it will make a positive contribution to territorial integration.

As land reform is generally initiated by the national government, an enforced program will create an impact on the peasant's attitude toward the nation. In countries dominated by the landed gentry, a United Nations report has observed, "the redistribution of land may represent the first occasion in which the central . . . Government makes any impact on the farmer's consciousness, and this, . . . can lead to the spread of a national consciousness, which is a necessary precondition for a 'popular National Government' to be possible." [1] The impact of a reform program on psychological integration of the peasantry can, therefore, be assessed by reference to peasant perception of the program. Perception involves two aspects: the awareness of the program by the peasantry as a whole and the evaluation of the program by its beneficiaries. The greater the number

---

[1] U.N., *Land Reform, Fourth Report*, p. 161.

of peasants aware of the program and the more favorable the evaluation of it by its beneficiaries, the greater the contribution of reform to psychological integration.

Territorial Integration: the Flow of National Authority

In most of the eight countries under study, government officials administering land reform in the field have brought about, in varying degrees, a flow of national authority into rural areas. However, two differing patterns of flow have emerged. In Iran, Mexico, Taiwan, and the U.A.R., where the elites have been strongly committed to reform, a "conflicting" pattern prevailed. That is to say, in the implementation of land reform the flow of national authority was basically in conflict with the political strength of the landed class. In Colombia, India, Pakistan, and the Philippines, where the elites had no intention of carrying out large-scale reform, a "complementary" pattern operated. The extension of national authority and the continuation of the political hold of the landed class in rural areas were mutually supporting.

It appears that these two patterns can be conveniently discussed in the light of only four of the eight countries studied. As seen earlier, in Mexico the political power of the *hacendados* was the very thing the revolutionaries sought to destroy. In Taiwan, as a non-indigenous elite determined to consolidate its rural hold and to ward off Communist penetration, the KMT leadership could not tolerate the continuation of the rural power of landlords in rivalry to its own authority. In both places, the extension of national authority in the process of reform implementation was completely at the expense of the political influence of the landlords. In Colombia and the Philippines, land reform was introduced by elites that included the landed interests. The primary purpose of the elite was to curb rural violence, but not to destroy the power of the landed class. Today, as the landlords' rural influence remains largely intact in both countries, further implementation of land reform clearly requires some mutual accommodation between the national government and the landlords in the countryside. The existence of two contrasting patterns of flow of national authority in Mexico, Taiwan, Colombia, and the Philippines is too obvious to require further analysis. In Iran, the U.A.R., India, and Pakistan, land reform has resulted in the removal of the largest landlords but left a very substantial number of smaller landlords. It is here that a detailed inquiry is needed in order to see how differences in the attitude of the elites toward these remaining landlords crucially affect the patterns of flow of national authority.

As suggested earlier, in post-reform Iran, the Shah was generally cooperative toward the small landlords. However, the monarch perceived his cooperative relationship with the small landlords mainly in terms of tolerating their continued possession of some large tracts of land, not in terms of the perpetuation of their feudalistic influence. In other words, the Shah respected the *economic privileges* of the small landlords but repudiated their *political power*.

In fact, the effort at assertion of national authority at the expense of the feudal landlords started with the rule of Reza Khan Shah, the father of the present monarch. To the late Shah, the possession by the landed aristocracy of near-governmental authority in rural Iran reflected to a considerable extent the administrative incapacity of the central government.

> The presence of the landlords as the intermediary between the government and the masses has resulted in the administrative machinery of the government and its relations with the agricultural population remaining to an astonishing degree as primitive as it was several centuries ago. For the existence of the landlord and his headmen in the village dispense[d] with the need for extensive administrative organization.[2]

To introduce greater administrative control into the rural areas, Reza Khan established in 1926, one year after he ascended to the throne, a uniform land tax system with a 3 percent levy on crops (later increased to 8 percent), and a 5 percent charge on the water revenues of landowners.[3] To demonstrate his determination to channel national influence into the villages, Reza Khan broke up many large estates and forcefully suppressed resistant landowners.[4] During the latter part of his reign he also personally acquired from the disgruntled landlords 2000 villages with

---

[2] Dayush Homayoun, "Land Reform in Iran," *Tahqiqat é eqtesadi*, II (September 1963), 21.

[3] John Hanessian, Jr., "Yosouf-Abad, an Iranian Village, Part V: Land Reform and the Peasant's Future," *American Universities Field Staff*, Report Service, Southwest Asia Series, XII (January 1963), 3.

[4] Richard W. Cottam, *Nationalism in Iran* (Pittsburgh, 1964), pp. 47-49, 99-100.

nominal compensation and, in certain instances, virtually by confiscation.[5]

Through these measures, Reza Khan somewhat subdued the landed aristocracy; but once this objective was accomplished, he had no intention of reducing further the power of the aristocracy. There was neither a modification of the tenure structure on which the aristocracy's political influence rested nor an attempt to improve the life of the peasantry. On the contrary, the Reza Khan regime strengthened the hands of the landlords by legalizing a privilege that they had previously exercised as a matter of customary practice. Traditionally, in a village owned by a landlord, the *kadkhuda* (the village head) was a personally named representative of the landlord. "This role was recognized by law in 1935, and in 1937 a bill passed by the Majlis stated that a *kadkhuda* was to be appointed by the local governor from among the inhabitants of the village, upon the recommendation of its owner." [6] During the reign of Reza Khan, therefore, the extension of national authority from Tehran to the countryside was intended to assert the monarchical power *over and above* the rural influence of the landed aristocracy but not to *replace that influence.*

To the peasants, the presence of the national authority was not a blessing. Government officials were dispatched to rural areas largely to extract from peasants, by legitimate or illegitimate means, a revenue that had previously been under the exclusive domain of the landed aristocracy. The result "was for the countryside to be invaded by a horde of governmental officials, most of whom are inadequately paid. At best they live on the country and at worst look upon the office as an opportunity to grow wealthy." [7] In such a situation "the peasant fears personal contact with government officials. He has learned that justice is influenced by bribery, extortion, and other dishonest practices." [8]

These rural conditions continued to exist toward the early 1960s when land reform started, and one suspects that they still exist in certain parts of Iran today. But the reform initiated by the present Shah resulted in the emergence of a pattern of flow of national authority basically different from that which had prevailed during his father's reign. Iran's extensive land redistribution resulted in the disappearance of the big landed aristocracy and, with it, its feudalistic power. With respect to the small land-

[5] Ann K. S. Lambton, *Landlord and Peasant in Persia* (London, 1953), p. 256.

[6] Donald L. Wilber, *Contemporary Iran* (New York, 1963), pp. 42–43.

[7] Lambton, *op. cit.*, p. 385.

[8] John Hanessian, Jr. "Yousouf-Abad, an Iranian Village, Part IV: the Peasant and his Landlord," *American Universities Field Staff*, Report Service, Southwest Asia Series, XII (January 1963), 2.

lords, the Shah's regime tolerated their retention of certain economic privileges but did not permit them to keep political power. Thus, unlike Reza Khan's Iran, where territorial integration was achieved by the fusion of the national and the landed authorities, today's Iran has seen the union of the countryside with Tehran through the displacement of the landed authority by the national. Moreover, if in the past "the gendarmes and the tax collectors have long been the only signs of the central government at Tehran [in the countryside, and their activities] . . . have not been of a welcome nature," [9] in today's Iran, land-reform officials, the Literacy Corpsmen (public personnel dispatched to villages to spread literacy), and other government personnel have established in rural areas a national presence that generally is beneficial to the peasantry. Critics of the Shah's regime have contended that the presence of these officials in rural Iran has led to the replacement of a peasantry subservient to the landed aristocracy with one subordinate to the government.[10] If this is so, it signifies that land reform has made a considerable contribution to territorial integration in Iran.

In implementing land reform in the U.A.R., the elite stopped short of achieving equality of landownership, and economic restrictions on the remaining landlord class were only gradually introduced. The 200 *feddans* of land that a landowner was allowed to retain under the land-reform decree of 1952 was nearly 33 times larger than the average farm size of that time; only in 1961 was the retention limit reduced to 100 *feddans*. With respect to rent control, the 1952 decree set the rent at seven times the land tax, and not until 1958 was the rent reduced to six times the land tax.[11]

In contrast to its relative tolerance of the continued existence of economic privileges for the small landlord class, the elite's effort to eradicate the political privileges of the big landed aristocracy was uncompromising from the beginning. With land reform came a direct confrontation between the national authority based in Cairo and the rural power of the aristocracy in the countryside. The swift, strong enforcement action by the military regime against landlords obstructing reform and the outright confiscation of royal land gave substance to the slogan, often

---

[9] Wilber, *op. cit.*, p. 10.

[10] See, for instance, Hossein Mahdavy "The Coming Crisis in Iran," *Foreign Affairs*, XLIV (October, 1965), 141–142.

[11] Gabriel S. Saab, *The Egyptian Agrarian Reform, 1952–1962* (London, 1967), pp. 46–47.

chanted by the Free Officers in the initial phase of reform, "We have wiped out agrarian feudalism (*igtā'*) in order to eliminate political feudalism." [12]

Further attesting to the serious intention of the national elite to terminate the rural power of the landed class was the renewed drive in 1966 against the "feudalists." In two months' time the government was reported to have seized 50,000 acres of land from 106 families of the old aristocracy and to have dismissed "939 mayors, security chiefs and provincial police . . . as a result of alleged collusion with 'feudalists.'" Concurrent with these governmental activities, the Arab Socialist Union made an inquiry into "village councils and rural cooperatives for [uncovering] 'infiltrators.'" [13]

With the rural power of the remaining small landlord class removed, the national elite made strenuous efforts to extend public authority into the villages. The induction of the masses into the electoral process, the organization of rural cooperatives under close national supervision, and the systematic integration of the rural population into local government and the Arab Socialist Union—all these measures broke the traditional physical and social isolation of the peasants and engendered among them some sense of national awareness. Writing in the 1930s, Henry Habib Ayrout observed: "The *fellahin*—walled in by their habits as well as their villages . . .—[were] closer to the soil they understand than the State of which they knew nothing. . . . Though [the peasant] is more truly Egyptian than many political figures, he is still not conscious of belonging to a nation." [14] Such parochialism and ignorance that once characterized the traditional Egyptian *fellahin* have ceased to be applicable today. Like their counterparts in Iran, Egyptian *fellahin* have been freed from the domination of the landed gentry but have become dependent on the government; and the government has become a centripetal force pulling together the geographically scattered peasantry into a national community.

THE "COMPLEMENTARY" PATTERN: INDIA AND PAKISTAN

In Iran and the U.A.R., the elites have sought through land reform to destroy the feudalistic influence of the landed gentry but have allowed

---

[12] Quoted in Gabriel Baer, A *History of Landownership in Modern Egypt* (London, 1962), pp. 220–221.

[13] *The New York Times*, June 25, 1966, p. 2.

[14] *The Egyptian Peasants* (Boston, 1963), pp. 3–4, 109.

the small landlords to continue to enjoy their economic privileges. In India and Pakistan, in contrast, the national elites have removed neither the political power nor the economic privileges of the existing landed class. In rural India and Pakistan, the flow of national authority and the continual exercise of political influence by the landed class are complementary.

In India, the movement for abolishing the *zamindar* system resulted in a complete breach between Congress leaders and the established landed gentry, but post-*zamindar* land reform has not led to a confrontation between the national elite and the present landed class. In adopting the post-*zamindar* reform programs, Congress leadership was motivated partially by the thought of assuring the *kisans'* continual loyalty to the party and partially by the party's ideological commitment to the creation of a democratic socialist order. But it was never the intention of the Congress to carry on the tradition of agrarian struggle by setting the *kisans* against the remaining landlords who, compared to the *zamindars*, were very numerous, but held relatively few land possessions.

To retain the loyalty of both the *kisans* and the remaining landlords, the party sought, through its agrarian policy, to achieve "rural harmony" rather than a "rural class struggle." [15] This policy consisted of three aspects. First, the party laid down only a general framework for agrarian changes, without spelling out the details. Second, the party assigned to the states responsibility for actually formulating and enforcing reform programs. This permitted agrarian changes to be effected in tune with local conditions without undue interference from the Union Government. And third, the Congress attempted to enforce reform laws through more or less voluntary compliance by the peasantry and the landed class, without having to assert public authority on behalf of the prospective beneficiaries.

In India today, without a single national agency exclusively concerned with the coordination of reform laws or the presence in the countryside of any Union personnel to enforce them, the most the Union Government can do to prompt the states to carry out reform is to withhold from the recalcitrant states material benefits that are due them under economic development plans. Within state governments there are also no special agencies or special personnel to enforce reform laws. The transfer of land from the landlord to the peasants, according to the ceilings provisions of

[15] Myron Weiner, *The Politics of Scarcity* (Chicago, 1962), pp. 144–145.

reform laws, is a transaction between the parties concerned, without the government acting as intermediary; and tenant farmers really have to rely on themselves to obtain benefits under tenancy reform laws. The state revenue administration, an agency supposedly responsible for enforcement of reform laws, is too understaffed to be able to execute the laws and too amenable to the pressure of the landed class to accord the peasants the full benefits to which they are entitled. Frequently, either through family connections or by common interest, landlords can tacitly collaborate with *patwaris* (village officials who keep land records and revenue rolls) and other revenue officials to conform with reform laws on the surface but to render them ineffectual in practice. This they can do by resorting to such tactics as division of land among family members, "voluntary surrender" of land by tenants, resumption of land for self-cultivation by landlords, and evasive measures against rental control laws. Thus, admitted the Indian government: "Frequently at the lower levels of the administration, collusion and evasion have gone unchecked," resulting in ineffective implementation of programs.[16]

As an idea, land reform in India emanates from the central government, but the flow of national authority in connection with the enforcement of reform programs is channeled through state and local agencies where landowning interests are dominant. To assure the continuous supply of public material benefits, state governments can cooperate with the central government by passing reform laws without seriously implementing them. Thus in India, to the extent that land reform contributes to territorial integration, this contribution is seen in the fusion of the national elite with the local landowning interests, but not in the union of the government in New Delhi and the mass peasantry in the villages. One is inclined to agree with Myron Weiner who has written: "In general, . . . one might say that at the village level neither loyalty to political movements on the basis of policies nor loyalty to India in a territorial sense is well developed."[17]

In Pakistan, the land-reform programs in the two wings of the country have had different impacts on territorial integration. In East Pakistan, where the big Hindu landowners fled the province, the adoption of the

[16] India, *Third Five Year Plan*, quoted in India, *Progress of Land Reform* (1963), p. 262.

[17] Weiner, "India: Two Political Cultures," in Lucian W. Pye and Sidney Verba, (eds.) *Political Culture and Political Development* (Princeton: Princeton University Press, 1965), p. 213.

East Bengal State Land Acquisition and Tenancy Act of 1950 legalized the forceful takeover of the holdings of large owners and symbolized the removal of their power. In West Pakistan, where a few very big landlords gave up their land, the political hegemony of the landowners was only "curtailed [but] not destroyed." [18] Unlike the reform program in the East Wing, which has no stated purpose other than that of sanctioning a *fait accompli*, the reform program in the West Wing was a comprehensive program consciously introduced by the Ayub Khan regime as a vital part of its nation-building effort. An assessment of the impact of land reform in Pakistan on territorial integration may, therefore, be more meaningfully done by limiting attention to the West Wing.

In the formative stage of West Pakistan's reform program it was already apparent that the Ayub Khan regime had no serious intention of breaking up the political power of the landlord class. As noted in Chapter V, the Land Reform Commission appointed by Ayub Khan to formulate a program stated quite explicitly in 1959 that it did not aim at "breaking up the power of the 'old ruling oligarchy with its roots in big estates.'" Since the Commission included members of the landed gentry, and since it understandably recommended a very mild program, no major reduction of the economic and political privileges of the landlord class could be expected. In implementing this program, the government did extend the authority of the national government into rural areas. But it failed to undercut the power of the landlord class as a whole. From the point of view of Ayub Khan, the enforcement of a mild program had gained him the support of the peasants without jeopardizing his backing from the landlords. From the point of view of the landed gentry, the acceptance of the program had not led to substantial economic losses and had assured the support of the regime for the gentry's remaining economic and political privileges. Thus commented Khalid B. Sayeed:

> So far as the President's political support from West Pakistan is con-
> cerned, it rests on some of the well-known landowning families, some
> of the Punjabi and Sindhi *pirs* (spiritual guides), and several *maliks*
> (tribal chiefs) from the Tribal Agencies of the Frontier. The Presi-

---

[18] Herbert Feldman, *Revolution in Pakistan* (London, 1967), p. 62. A total of 910 landowners surrendered over 2.2 million acres of land. Some of the largest surrenders may be illustrated in the following instances: The Nawab of Hoti, 8,000 acres; Colonel Amir Khan, 13,500 acres; three members of the Daultana family, 16,000 acres; 37 landlords in the Multan District, 40,500 acres; 154 landlords in the Hazara District, 68,000 acres, *ibid.*, p. 60.

dent exercises his control over these landlords through the Governor of West Pakistan. The Governor, in his turn, operates through the Deputy Commissioners without whose good will and support it would be difficult for many landlords to carry on their activities and control their tenants. It is often said that many of the Punjabi and Sindhi landlords still carry on their activities in a semifeudal fashion, but it may be pointed out that the sort of feudal control they exercise over their tenants largely exists because successive governments have found it convenient to exercise their control over the rural society of West Pakistan through such feudal intermediaries.[19]

As in the case of India, the complementary pattern of flow of national authority in Pakistan led to the union of the national elite and landed gentry, without integrating the peasantry into the political system.

The foregoing analysis warrants one generalization. In Iran and the U.A.R., land reform has led to the removal or substantial weakening of the political power of the landlords and has facilitated the effort of the elites to bring the peasantry into the fold of the national government. In India and Pakistan, land reform has not significantly reduced the political power of the landlords and has perpetuated the union of the national and landed authorities. The former two countries have thus achieved greater territorial integration than the latter two.

Psychological Integration: Peasant Perception of Reform

As noted earlier, the extent to which the land-reform program of a country contributes to the peasants' psychological integration with the national community is determined by their perception of the program. Perception involves both awareness and evaluation. The most important factor affecting peasant awareness of a program is, of course, the extent of the program's implementation. The greater the implementation, the greater the awareness. Other factors affecting awareness include the publicity given to a program, the manner in which the elite overcomes the resistance of the landed class, and the degree of involvement of the peasants in the process of implementation. As to the evaluation of a reform program, it is seen primarily in the changes in income and well-being of the beneficiaries.

[19] *The Political Systems of Pakistan* (Boston, 1967), p. 114.

COLOMBIA AND THE PHILIPPINES

Of the eight countries under study, Colombia and the Philippines have so far been the countries with the fewest reform results. As a consequence, peasant awareness of reform appears to be low. In Colombia, the ordinary *campesino* outside the limited number of land-reform areas does not appear to have knowledge of the 1961 reform law. To publicize its programs, INCORA has adopted two measures. One is to set up at least one land-reform project per department, so as to create nationwide peasant awareness. The other is to decentralize INCORA's administrative structure. Regional land reform committees have been formed in order to induce local participation in program implementation. Neither measure has produced the expected results. The Powell survey in the Department of Cundinanarca, cited in the previous chapter, indicates that an extraordinarily large proportion of the peasant respondents had no conception of the 1961 land-reform program and that many of these respondents thought the existing land-reform agencies unhelpful in the solution of their problems. As seen in Table 50, over 90 percent of the peasant respondents in Cundinanarca were completely unaware of the 1961 reform law. Some of these respondents did know of the existence of the two principal reform agencies, INCORA and the *Caja Agraria*. However, as indicated in Table 51, merely about 26 percent of the respondents considered INCORA helpful in resolving their problems, and less than 16 percent had ever had

TABLE 50

PEASANT AWARENESS OF LAND REFORM, CUNDINANARCA, COLOMBIA, 1968

Question: *"What is the Social Agrarian Reform Law recently passed by the Congress?"*

	Peasant Respondents	
Response to the Question	Number	Percent
Correct	3	1.79
Partly correct	4	2.38
Incorrect	8	4.76
Don't know	152	90.48
No answer	1	.59
Total	168	100.00

SOURCE: *Powell Survey*, Appendix A.

TABLE 51

PEASANT EVALUATION OF AND CONTACT WITH LAND REFORM AGENCIES
CUNDINANARCA, COLOMBIA, 1968

	Peasant Respondents			
	With Reference to INCORA		With Reference to Caja Agraria	
Evaluation and Contact	Number	Percent	Number	Percent
Helpfulness of Reform Agency in Solving Problems				
Much	20	11.90	82	48.81
Little	25	14.88	44	26.19
None	91	54.17	35	20.83
Don't know	28	16.67	4	2.38
No answer	4	2.38	3	1.79
Total	168	100.00	168	100.00
Contact with Agents of Reform Agency				
Never	142	84.52	92	54.76
Annually	19	11.31	43	25.60
Several times a year	2	1.19	16	9.52
Monthly	2	1.19	6	3.57
Weekly	1	0.60	7	4.17
Inapplicable	2	1.19	4	2.38
Total	168	100.00	168	100.00

SOURCE: *Powell Survey*, Appendix A.

contact with the agency's personnel. The respondent's evaluation of the rural credit agency, the *Caja Agraria*, was more favorable. A fairly large proportion (three-quarters) of the respondents regarded the *Caja Agraria* as helpful, but over 54 percent never availed themselves of the agency's services. The apparent discrepancy between the usefulness of the services of the *Caja Agraria* as perceived by the peasants and their actual utilization of such services may be explained by the fact that while the agency was generally considered helpful because it made public credit available to the rural community, its operations tended to benefit the well-to-do farming interests more than the small *campesinos*. As Powell noted in his report, during the field survey in Cundinanarca, "there were a large number of marginal comments [by the respondents] taken down by our interviewers which qualified the help which the Caja gave as help 'for the rich,' or 'if you are rich.' " [20]

It must be recalled that the Department of Cundinanarca is an area of major importance in Colombia's present land-reform activities, and that INCORA has created several reform projects in this department as well as in the neighboring departments. Thus, if most Cundinanarca peasants displayed low awareness and gave an unfavorable evaluation of Colombia's reform program, one cannot expect the peasants of the country as a whole to perceive the program any differently.

A case study of the land settlement program in the Department of Caqueta in East Colombia sheds more light on peasant perception of reform. In the early 1960s, Ronald L. Tinnermeier made a comparative study of colonization experiences of *campesinos* under an INCORA project and spontaneous settlers in the same area. The study found that among both the INCORA-directed settlers and the spontaneous settlers, most appeared willing to continue their life in Caqueta—95 percent of the directed settlers and 82 percent of the spontaneous settlers indicating their preference to stay on their new farms. However, half of the land in the INCORA project area has been abandoned; and 65 percent of the directed group, as contrasted to 25 percent of the spontaneous group, indicated that their present earnings were less than their previous ones. (These findings are summarized in Table 52.) The paradox is that nearly all of the directed settlers wished to remain in the INCORA project, yet the project had a very high land-abandonment rate. Tinnermeier explained that this might be due to the concern of most of the present settlers that an indication of intention to leave might prompt INCORA to react unfavorably toward their future requests for assistance.[21] It is also possible that many of the present settlers, arriving homeless as victims of *la Violencia*, preferred poverty to insecurity. In any case, from the point of view of the settlers, Tinnermeier concluded, the government resettlement program in Caqueta was not a successful experience.[22]

In the Philippines, because the land-reform issue has been constantly

[20] John D. Powell, *Organizing Colombian Peasants: A Research Report* (cited hereafter as *Powell Survey*; Cambridge, Mass.: The Center for Rural Development [1968]), p. 29.
[21] Ronald L. Tinnermeier, "New Land Settlement in the Eastern Lowlands of Colombia," The University of Wisconsin, Land Tenure Center, Research Paper No. 13, 1964, p. 10.
[22] *Ibid.*, p. 49.

TABLE 52

CONDITIONS OF SETTLERS IN COLONIZATION PROJECT, CAQUETA, COLOMBIA

Conditions	INCORA-Directed Settlers[a]	Spontaneous Settlers[b]
Average size of holdings	60.4 ha.	75 ha.
	Percentages	
Willing to stay	95	82
Abandoning land	50	. . .[c]
Present home compared to previous one		
Worse	47	30
Equal	23	29
Better	30	41
Present earnings compared to previous earnings		
Less	65	25
Equal	13	30
Greater	22	45

[a] Total number 100.

[b] Total number 84.

[c] Tinnermeier did not indicate the land abandonment rate in the area of spontaneous settlers; it was apparently thought very low.

SOURCE: Ronald L. Tinnermeier. "New Land Settlement in the Eastern Lowlands of Colombia," The University of Wisconsin, Land Tenure Center, Research Paper No. 13, 1964, *passim*.

raised in electoral campaigns, the peasants have become familiar with the issue; but their awareness of the government's specific programs remains low. Citing a Robot-Gallup survey of the rural Philippines, one study indicated, in 1965, that less than 40 percent of the tenant families interviewed knew about the 1963 reform law.[23] At the same time, the intended beneficiaries of the law apparently did not have a high regard for it. In declared land-reform districts, a sizable number of farmers were reported to have shunned the benefits of the law by refusing to convert a tenancy to a leasehold system. For instance, in the Province of Bulacan, Albert Ravenholt reported in 1965, 145 tenants shifted to leasehold, while 56 did not.[24] Similarly, the United Nations reported in 1966 that "in some districts as many as a third have declined the chance to acquire the status

[23] Albert Ravenholt, "The Promise of Philippine Land Reform," *American Universities Field Staff*, Report Service, Southeast Asia Series, XIII (April 2, 1965), 12.

[24] *Ibid.*, p. 11.

TABLE 53

FARMER AWARENESS OF LAND REFORM, TAINAN, TAIWAN; AND LUZON,
THE PHILIPPINES, TAINAN SURVEY, 1968; LUZON SURVEY, 1969

Questions: *"Do you know of Taiwan's land-reform programs and the years in which they started?" "Do you know the year in which the Philippine Agricultural Land Reform Code was enacted?"*

Response	Tainan Respondents		Luzon Respondents	
	Number	*Percent*	*Number*	*Percent*
Correct	75	26.79	30	11.41
Partially correct	65	23.21		
Incorrect	4	1.43	52	19.77
Don't know or no answer	136	48.57	181	68.82
Total	280	100.00	263	100.00

SOURCE: See Appendix III. Taiwan adopted three principal reform programs—each in a different year. Respondents able to identify all three years are tabulated as "correct" in the response column; those correctly identifying only one year or two are tabulated as "partially correct." This latter category of response does not apply to the Luzon respondents, who were asked only to identify the year in which the 1963 Philippine reform law was enacted.

of protected lessees under the law." [25] The findings are substantially reaffirmed in the 1969 Luzon survey conducted by the author. As seen in Tables 53 and 54, nearly 90 percent of the 263 farmer-respondents in Luzon could not identify correctly the year in which the present reform law was adopted. For purposes of comparison, it may be noted that half of the 280 farmer respondents in Tainan could identify completely or partially the years in which the three Taiwanese reform programs were adopted. Only about 47 percent of the Luzon respondents considered the Philippine land reform "very successful" or "successful." The corresponding proportion of the Tainan respondents was over 85 percent.

[25] U.N., *Land Reform, Fourth Report*, p. 27. In an interview with the author in Nueva Ecija in January 1969, Estrella, the Governor of the Land Authority, a number of land reform field workers, and local government officials all acknowledged that, though the number of tenants refusing to become lessees was declining, some farmers still preferred to remain as tenants. These officials estimated that these farmers accounted for 5 to 10 percent of the total.

TABLE 54

FARMER EVALUATION OF LAND REFORM IN TAIWAN AND THE PHILIPPINES,
TAINAN SURVEY, 1968; LUZON SURVEY, 1969

Question: *"Do you think land reform in this country successful?"*

	Tainan Respondents		Luzon Respondents	
Response	Number	Percent	Number	Percent
Very successful	103	36.79	28	10.65
Successful	137	48.93	95	36.12
Not successful	9	3.21	39	14.83
Don't know	13	4.64	88	33.46
No answer	18	6.43	13	4.94
Total	280	100.00	263	100.00

SOURCE: See Appendix III.

INDIA AND PAKISTAN

In India and Pakistan, land-reform results are more extensive than those in the Philippines and Colombia. One can presume that there is also a keener peasant perception of reform programs in the former two countries. For want of pertinent information, Pakistan's peasant experiences with land reform will not be discussed. In India, the *kisans* appear to be well aware of the program for abolition of the *zamindar* system, and the 20-million beneficiaries seem to be relatively satisfied with their new lives. Though most of these farmers remain as tenants, they appear to enjoy security in their land rights and low rents. Subsequent reform programs, however, have not been well received by the supposedly more numerous beneficiaries. In 1956, the Indian Planning Commission reported that "ignorance of the people about . . . the land reform enacted was a major problem in the process of implementation." [26] In 1961, the Third Five Year Plan attributed the lack of progress of reform to, among other things, "the failure to enlist the support and sanction of the village community in favour of effective enforcement of legal provisions." [27]

Because of faulty formulation of the law, ineffective implementation, and the continued political and economic dominance of the landlords,

[26] India, Planning Commission, *Reports of the Committees of the Panel on Land Reforms* (Delhi, 1959), p. 65.
[27] Cited in India, *Progress of Land Reform* (1963), p. 262.

Indian *kisans* frequently declined to avail themselves of benefits under the reform programs. Tenants refused to become owners or to seek rental reductions under the law. For instance, from 1957 to 1961, of a total 10,459 tenants in Padra Taluq in the State of Gujarat 1,552 became owners under the tenancy reform law of 1956, while 203 refused the opportunity.[28] From 1957 to 1958 in the West Gadvari District in the State of Andhra Pradesh, 249 cases were recorded in which tenants obtained fixed rental rates according to the Tenancy Act of 1956, but there were also 486 cases of termination of leases, resulting in the ejection of many tenants.[29] The continual high rate of lease termination in the district in later years (241 in 1958 to 1959; 518 in 1959 to 1961) had a depressing effect on tenants seeking to establish fixed rentals. Thus from 1957 to 1958 there were 249 cases in which rentals were fixed; from 1959 to 1961, there were only 43.[30] As a result, many tenants in the district believed that "it was very difficult for them to get land for cultivation, and the reluctance of the landlords to give land was attributed to the passing of the Tenancy Act."[31] And there is considerable evidence that evictions of tenants in consequence of reform are a nationwide phenomenon.[32] The conclusion is inescapable that, in many instances, reform in India brought not benefits but disadvantages to the intended beneficiaries. The evaluation of the reform experiences by the beneficiaries cannot be expected to be favorable.

IRAN AND THE U.A.R.

If, in the countries discussed thus far, peasant perception of land reform has generally been characterized by ignorance or negativism, or both, in Iran and the U.A.R., the peasantry has shown greater awareness of and enthusiasm for the reform programs. In both Iran and the U.A.R. —particularly in Iran—forceful clashes between the national elites and

[28] M. B. Desai and R. S. Mehta, "Abolition of Tenancy Cultivation," *Indian Journal of Agricultural Economics*, XVII (January-March 1962), 132.

[29] L. Krishnamurty, "Land Leglislation in Andhra—The Tenancy Act of 1956 and the Andhra Pradesh Ceiling on Agricultural Holdings Act of 1961," *Indian Journal of Agricultural Economics*, XVII (January-March 1962), 165.

[30] *Ibid.*

[31] *Ibid.*, p. 167.

[32] See India, *Reports of the Committees of the Panel on Land Reforms*, p. 36. Kusum Nair, *Blossoms in the Dust: The Human Factor in Indian Development* (New York: Frederick A. Praeger, Publishers, 1961), pp. 58–62; and A. M. Khusro, *Economic and Social Effects of Jagirdari Abolition and Land Reforms in Hyderabad* (Hyderabad: Osmania University, Department of Publications and University Press, 1958), p. 163.

the landlords in the initial phases of reform not only demonstrated to the peasantry the serious intent of the elites with regard to reform, but also helped focus the attention of the farming communities on the programs. The crushing of the resistant landlords and the personal distribution in the countryside of land titles by the Shah and Nasser constituted a very effective information campaign for reform, a campaign that might otherwise have required a large amount of administrative manpower. Today, as reform areas have spread all over Iran and the U.A.R., it is not likely that any large segment of the farming communities in these countries is unaware of the tenurial changes sponsored by Tehran and Cairo.

The beneficiaries of reform in Iran and the U.A.R. appear to have favorably evaluated their new life. The acclaim that the Shah and Nasser received from the villages during their extensive tours in rural areas did contain a genuine sense of peasant appreciation for these rulers' concern with peasant welfare. Available evidence—fragmentary in nature but uniform in content—shows that reform beneficiaries in both countries experienced a rise of income and expressed some satisfaction with being new landowners.[33]

For instance, in the Iranian village of Hosseinabad, the increase of peasant income after reform was reflected in such "prestige and leisure" spendings as those on "radios, finer clothes and better housing, and in some cases [acquiring] more wives, a pilgrimage to Meshed or . . . Mecca." [34] In another Iranian village, Hakimabad, a land recipient, Ali Hussein, expressed satisfaction with paying the government a land price less than the rent he had previously paid to the landlord, and with being his "own boss." Another farmer, Yahya Gudzari, observed that "my income is three times what it was three years ago." [35] In still another village, Kohanz, farmer Hussein Sanandajy said in an interview: "I am glad, very glad, to have my own land and to know that I am working for

---

[33] See William Green Miller, "Hosseinabad, A Persian Village," *The Middle East Journal,* XVIII (Autumn 1964), 483–498; and Hedrick Smith, "Watermelon Village Races Against Time," *The New York Times Magazine,* August 28, 1966, pp. 30ff. In addition, articles by John Hanessian, Jr., on village life in Yosouf-Abad, Iran, referred to several times earlier; Arnold Hottinger, "Land Reform in Iran," *Swiss Review of World Affairs,* XIII, No. 8 (November 1963), 7–10; and No. 9 (December 1963), 17–18; Gadalla's book, *Land Reform in Relation to Social Development, Egypt* (Columbia, Mo., 1962), and a number of newspaper accounts to be cited below; all contain information supporting this observation.

[34] Miller, *op. cit.,* 493.

[35] *The New York Times,* December 27, 1966, p. 30.

myself"; while "village elders shouted that they were 'a hundred per cent'
behind 'Shahanshah'—the King of Kings." [36]

Similarly, the beneficiaries—new owners, tenants, and colonists—of
the U.A.R.'s land-reform program have considerably improved their lives.
A number of studies done in the early 1960s indicated that since the beginning of reform the average income of new owners had risen by at
least 50 percent.[37] With respect to the increase in the income of tenants,
estimates varied. But it appears safe to agree with Donald C. Mead that
"average rents paid to [landlords] declined by some 25 percent" in 1951
to 1961, with the savings accruing to tenants.[38]

Egyptian farmers themselves also gave some information regarding
the benefits they experienced under reform. In 1962, in a land-reform
area in Enchass, one new owner received, after paying the land price and
all operational expenses, a net income of about US $175 as compared to
the national per capita income of US $118.[39] In the village, Kafr el
Battikh, Mahmamoud Rizek Hussein, a previous tenant with 10 acres of
land who became an owner of 2.5 acres under the 1952 reform, said in
1966 that his income had been doubled and that his affiliation with the
government-sponsored cooperative was "a definite advantage to him." [40]

[36] Ibid., September 25, 1967, p. 18.

[37] Doreen Warriner, Land Reform and Development in the Middle East (London,
1962), p. 37; Peter Mansfield, Nasser's Egypt (Baltimore, 1965), p. 177; Saab, op. cit.,
p. 121. Cf. Gadalla, op. cit., pp. 53, 76–77.

[38] Growth and Structural Change in the Egyptian Economy (Homewood, Ill.,
1967), p. 77. Mead indicated that the total rent payment in Egypt constituted 13.1
percent of the national agricultural income in 1950, and that it declined to 7 percent
in 1960. Ibid., p. 78. Warriner, citing official information dated 1955, estimated that
there was a 50 percent increase of tenant income since 1952, and that about four
million farmers had been benefitted. Op. cit., p. 39. Saab reported that in 1953 tenant
income had risen by 23 percent. Op. cit., p. 144. The United Nations reported in 1966
that "incomes of tenant-farmers in the United Arab Republic have, in some cases,
risen by more than 50 per cent at the expense of the landlords." U.N., Land Reform,
Fourth Report, p. 151. Cf. Gadalla, op. cit., pp. 54–55. The variations in these estimates in the rise of tenant income may be due to the differences in time periods which
these estimates cover. Rental rates were reduced twice, once in 1952 and again in 1958.

[39] The New York Times, May 21, 1962, p. 12.

[40] Smith, op. cit., p. 70. Farmers settling on newly colonized land seem to have
also improved their income and well-being. For a report on the life of a farm family
in a land settlement project in the Tahrir (Liberation) Province, see John K. Cooley,
"It's a Life Full of Work and Full of New Things, The Rashids of Lower Egypt,"
Christian Science Monitor, February 16, 1967, p. 9.

MEXICO AND TAIWAN

For a number of unique reasons, peasants in Mexico and Taiwan appear to have a keener perception of land reform than those in any other nation discussed above. In Mexico, the agrarian origin and character of the revolution is undoubtedly responsible for the *campesinos'* total awareness of the land-reform issue. It was the *campesinos,* not Madero and other political leaders, who first raised the issue in the revolution. It was under the forceful pressure of the *campesinos* that the 1915 reform decree came into being; it is they who are the beneficiaries of probably the largest land-reform program in the non-Communist world; and it is they who, through their association with the official party, have provided a sustained impetus for reform over half a century.

Despite criticism of the *ejido* system by others, most of the *ejidatarios* themselves have taken genuine pride in their membership in the *ejidos* and feel relatively satisfied with their economic conditions. This is an assessment to which scholars with field experience would readily agree.[41] For purposes of illustration, a 1966 study of rural organization in Taretan in the State of Michoacan may be cited. It was found that this farming community accorded *ejido* membership a high social standing. As seen in Table 55, *ejidatarios* were ranked first or second among four social groups in terms of social respect. The Taretan study also indicated that most *ejidatarios* were satisfied with the services of various rural organizations to which they belonged. "Seventy-seven percent of the members of ejidal credit societies included in our sample," the authors of the study reported, "said they were either 'fairly well satisfied' . . . or 'totally satisfied' with the overall functioning of their organizations; . . ." Relatively large proportions of the various groups of *ejidatarios* also favorably evaluated the services of the Agrarian Department of the federal government, the principal agency in charge of land reform—50 to 75 percent considered the department to have done "a good deal" or have done "much" for them. The *ejidatarios'* evaluation of the services of the Ejidal Bank, also a federal

[41] See Clarence Senior, *Land Reform and Democracy* (Gainesville, Fla., 1958); Eyler N. Simpson, *The Ejido, Mexico's Way Out* (Chapel Hill, N.C., 1937); James G. Maddox, "Mexican Land Reform," *American Universities Field Staff,* Report Service (Vol. 4, No. 5, July 3, 1957); Nathan Whetten, *Rural Mexico* (Chicago, 1948); Henrik F. Infield and Koka Freier, *People in Ejidos* (New York, 1954). For further discussion on this subject, see the next chapter.

TABLE 55

Social Status of Occupational Groups, Taretan, Michoacan, Mexico, 1966

Question: *"Which groups are most respected by everyone in Mexico?"*

	Rank of Occupational Groups				
Respondents	Ejida-tario	Factory Worker	Small Landowner	Farm Laborer	(N)
Ejidatarios	1	2	3	4	(86)
Sugar-mill workers	2	1	3	4	(21)
Small landholders	2	1	3	4	(18)
Farm laborers	1	2	3	4	(20)

Source: Adapted from Henry A. Landsberger and Cynthia N. Hewitt, "A Pilot Study of Participation in Rural Organizations: 'Political Socialization' in Mexico" (Ithaca: Cornell University, New York State School of Industrial and Labor Relations, 1967, mimeo.) p. 38a.

agency, however, was less favorable. The corresponding percentages ranged from 26 to 41.[42]

The total awareness of land reform on the part of Mexican farmers and the favorable evaluation by *ejidatarios* of their own experiences have much heightened the national consciousness of Mexico's rural communities. As James G. Maddox has observed: "Mexico has made giant strides in becoming a nation, . . . and in raising the levels of living of at least 95 percent of her people, precisely because of her Revolution. . . . And the Revolution would probably not have been possible without land reform." [43]

If, in Mexico, the long historical experience of revolution has increased the awareness of land reform, in Taiwan, the small size of the island, coupled with a well-developed transportation system and readily available communications media, considerably facilitated the efforts of the government to publicize the reform programs. Moreover, during the period of reform, while the countryside was inundated with government workers and inspectors to enforce reform laws,[44] the beneficiaries played an effec-

[42] Henry A. Landsberger and Cynthia N. Hewitt, "A Pilot Study of Participation in Rural Organizations: 'Political Socialization' in Mexico" (Ithaca: Cornell University, New York State School of Industrial and Labor Relations, 1967; mimeo.), pp. 50a, 51a, and 56.

[43] Maddox, *op. cit.*, 22–23 (original italics).

[44] Under the rent reduction program, 4257 staff workers and over 3000 inspectors were mobilized for the task. The working staff for the land-to-the-tiller program to-

tive role in the implementation process. Through their representation on the Farm Tenancy Committees, tenants and small owner-farmers not only helped settle reform-related problems, but also, in the process of doing so, became familiar with reform laws and regulations. As cited earlier in Table 53, the Tainan survey indicated a high awareness on the part of farmers of Taiwan's various reform programs.

Tenants and new owner-farmers also generally expressed satisfaction with the reform results. The United Nations reported in 1966 that the rise of tenant income in consequence of the rent-reduction program of 1949 varied from 11 to 37 percent.[45] According to a 1951 government report, the increased income was immediately reflected in new rural spending. "The farmers humorously called the cattle they bought . . . 37.5% cattle; the houses they built . . . 37.5% houses and even the brides they had married . . . 37.5% brides—in commemoration of the reduced farm rent." [46] A 1952 rural survey of sixteen townships conducted by JCRR revealed that "in all the townships studied, the local leaders spoke in appreciation of the advantages of the rent reduction program to the tenants. . . . Of 857 heads of farm households interviewed, 76 percent said that they thought the program had raised general living conditions." [47] In 1959, JCRR made another survey in these same sixteen townships and two additional ones. It reported that of the 1,350 households surveyed 54 percent considered the rent reduction program to have raised their living stands; about 13 percent indicated no difference; 31 percent could not make any comparison, and 2 percent felt they had experienced a lowering of their living conditions. With respect to the land-to-the-tiller program, the survey showed that 52 percent indicated an improvement of their living conditions; less than 4 prcent held to the contrary; 12 percent felt no change; and 32 percent were unable to evaluate.[48]

Two other surveys, of more recent date, yield further information on this subject. As seen in Table 56, the 1968 Tainan survey conducted by

talled 32,902 persons. Both the national and provincial governments also dispatched observation teams checking out enforcement results. See Hui-sun Tang, *Land Reform in Free China* (Taipei, Taiwan, 1954), pp. 40, 45, 97–98, 118. Cf. Chen Cheng, *Land Reform in Taiwan* (Taipei, Taiwan, 1961), pp. 73–74.

[45] U.N., *Land Reform, Fourth Report*, p. 151. Cf. Chen, *op. cit.*, p. 43.

[46] *Findings of the Cabinet Rent Reduction Inspection Team*, cited in Chen, *op. cit.*, pp. 44–45.

[47] Arthur F. Raper, *Rural Taiwan—Problem and Promise* (Taipei, Taiwan, 1953), p. 170.

[48] E. Stuart Kirby, *Rural Progress in Taiwan* (Taipei, JCRR, 1960), pp. 138–140.

the author revealed that of six factors considered significant to the rural prosperity of Taiwan, land reform was ranked first by the farmer respondents. A 1964 survey by Martin M. C. Yang of the entire island assessed specifically how the two categories of farmers—new owner-farmers and tenants—felt about land reform. From 82 to 90 percent expressed a "happy feeling toward the Rent Reduction and the Land-to-the-Tiller programs." (See Table 57.)

The preceding analysis has sought to identify the impact of land reform on national integration, in its territorial and psychological dimensions. Because of lack of data in certain instances, this analysis is less precise and detailed than it ought to be; and because certain cited evidence is not amenable to statistical comparison, the task of achieving a comparative evaluation on this subject involves some arbitrary judgment. With due recognition of this limitation, Table 58 has been constructed to indicate the broad variations in the contribution of land reform to national integration in the eight countries studied.

TABLE 56

FACTORS IDENTIFIED BY FARMERS AS HAVING CONTRIBUTED TO RURAL STABILITY
AND PROSPERITY IN TAIWAN, TAINAN SURVEY, 1968

Question: *"Would you identify up to three factors that have contributed to
rural stability and prosperity of Taiwan?"*

	Frequency of Factor Identified		
Factors	*Number*	*Percent of total respondents*	*Rank*
Land reform	141	50.36	1
Improvement of seedling	95	33.93	2
Development of water resources	93	33.21	3
Services of Farmers' Associations	63	22.50	4
Replotting of farm land	44	15.71	5
Services of JCRR[a]	42	15.00	6
Don't know	4	1.43	
No answer	11	3.93	

[a] JCRR performs vital services for Taiwan's farming communities both before and after land reform. But these services are principally channeled through farmers' organizations, particularly the Farmers' Associations. This accounts for farmers' low estimation of the usefulness of JCRR.

SOURCE: See Appendix III. Total number of farmer respondents, 280.

TABLE 57

EVALUATION OF LAND-REFORM PROGRAMS BY BENEFICIARIES, TAIWAN, 1964

	Beneficiaries	
Evaluation	Number	Percent
New owner-farmers		
Feeling toward the Rent-Reduction Program		
Happy	1,120	89.60
Indifferent	111	8.88
No answer	19	1.52
Total	1,250	100.00
Feeling toward the Land-to-the-Tiller Program		
Happy	1,030	82.40
Not happy	216	17.28
No comment	4	0.32
Total	1,250	100.00
Present Tenants		
Feeling toward the Rent-Reduction Program		
Happy	226	90.40
Indifferent	19	7.60
No answer	5	2.00
Total	250	100.00

SOURCE: Adapted from Martin M. C. Yang, *Socio-Economic Results of Land Reform in Taiwan* (Honolulu: East-West Center Press, 1970), pp. 138, 140, and 145. The data in this table were derived from a survey conducted in 1964 by a team of interviewers under the direction of Yang. The sample, drawn from farm families from 36 townships in 5 regions of Taiwan, consisted of a total of 3075 households. These households were broken into six categories: (1) new owners (former tenants who became owners through land reform), 1250 households; (2) present tenants, 250; (3) owner farmers who did not acquire land under reform, 250; (4) present farmer laborers, 250; (5) landlords whose land was expropriated under reform, 575; and (6) non-farmers, 500. Only data pertaining to the households of the first two categories are presented in this table.

TABLE 58

LAND REFORM AND NATIONAL INTEGRATION

Countries	Extent of Contribution of Land Reform to National Integration
Colombia	Negligible
Philippines	Negligible
Pakistan	Small
India	Small
Iran	Moderately great
UAR	Moderately great
Mexico	Great
Taiwan	Great

XII

RURAL ORGANIZATIONS: THE PROCESS OF INSTITUTIONALIZATION

The Concept of Institutionalization

In the course of land reform, nations often create new rural organizations or revamp existing ones in order to facilitate the implementation of programs and to render services to the beneficiaries.[1] Many of these organizations are not merely private associations seeking to articulate and promote the interests of their membership. Some of them have been made part of the administrative machinery for the execution of reform laws and regulations; some have acquired government-like authority in dealing with the reform beneficiaries; some have formed special relationships with the governing political parties and become principal supporters and defenders in the countryside of existing regimes.

How do the experiences of land reform in the eight countries under study affect the functioning and evolution of rural organizations? This question may be answered by identifying the extent to which a reform program contributes to the institutionalization of rural organizations. Institutionalization, to paraphrase a statement of a political scientist, refers to a process by which organizations become stabilized and rationalized.[2] An organization achieves stability through the growth of its membership and the acquisition of value to its members. The growth of the membership of an organization will enhance the viability of the organization, and

---

[1] The term, *rural organizations*, refers to associations that operate in the countryside with a membership composed primarily of farm cultivators. Excluded from this definition are city-based agricultural producer's associations that consist mainly of landlords (for example, the National Sugarcane Planters Association of the Philippines and *Sociedad de Agricultures de Colombia*).

[2] Samuel P. Huntington defines institutionalization as "a process by which organizations and procedures acquire value and stability." *Political Order in Changing Societies*, (New Haven, 1968), p. 12.

a growing organization will in time reach a point where its membership will accept it as a lasting institution. Acquisition of value signifies that the membership of an organization has accepted a set of common goals to be pursued.[3] Value forms the psychological bond of the membership and the cohesive force of the organization.

The rationalization of an organization denotes a process of maximization of the goal-achievement capacity of the organization.[4] It involves two dimensions: differentiation and adaptability.[5] Differentiation refers to the degree to which the interests of an organization are specified; and adaptability, the capacity of an organization to innovate in response to the challenges of a changing environment. The more differentiated and the more innovative an organization is, the more rationalized it is. To sum up, institutionalization involves four aspects: membership growth, acquisition of value, differentiation, and adaptability.

In a given country, the impact of land reform on the membership growth of rural organizations is seen in the number of reform beneficiaries that have joined existing or newly constituted rural institutions. The impact becomes significant when the number of these members is so large that it assures the viability and permanence of existing or new rural institutions.

[3] Sociologists often employ the term *legitimation* to describe the process of infusion of value into a social system and consider "institutionalization" identical with or instrumental to legitimation. For example, Talcott Parsons defines legitimation as a process of diffusion of values among the subsystems of a society and of maintenance of nexus between values and the society. Values refer to "modes of normative orientation of . . . a social system." Legitimation is carried out through institutionalization. *Structure and Process in Modern Societies* (New York: The Free Press, 1960), pp. 171, 176–177. Similarly, Marion Levy, Jr., states, "The terms legitimate and illegitimate with regard to power and responsibility refer to the factor of institutionalization or its absence." Institutionalization is achieved when members of a social system comply with "a given normative pattern . . . of action." *The Structure of Society* (Princeton, N.J.: Princeton University Press, 1952) pp. 102–104, 496. Thus defined by sociologists, the term legitimation differs from the concept of legitimacy as used in the present study, which signifies the popular support that a political elite commands.

[4] In this sense, rationalization is meant to achieve efficiency. As Robert A. Dahl and Charles E. Lindblom have said, "An action is rational to the extent that it is 'correctly' designed to maximize goal achievement, . . . The more rational action is also the more efficient action. The two terms can be used interchangeably. Stripped of prejudicial inferences, efficiency is the ratio between valued input and valued output." *Politics, Economics, and Welfare: Planning and Politico-Economic Systems Resolved into Basic Social Processes* (New York: Harper & Row, 1953), pp. 38–39.

[5] For a discussion of these two concepts in the context of modernization, see S. N. Eisenstadt, *Modernization: Protest and Change* (Englewood Cliffs, N.J.: Prentice-Hall Inc., 1966), pp. 2–7, 38–43. Cf. Huntington, *op. cit.*, pp. 12ff.

As a value to be acquired by rural organizations, land reform has both moralistic and materialistic goals: to promote social justice in the rural community through equitable sharing of the sources of agricultural income, and to advance the welfare of farmers through the improvement of their productive capacity. The effect of a reform program on the acquisition of value by rural organizations is indicated by the degree to which these organizations have come to espouse these two reform goals. The effect becomes significant when the espousal is so firm as to prompt rural organizations to push vigorously for the expansion of reform areas and for the enlargement of reform benefits. In many cases, it should be noted, the concept of land reform derives from official ideology, and the elite frequently strives to inculcate into the consciousness of the membership of rural organizations the specific ideological component that justifies reform. The success or failure of this effort is indicated by the acceptance or ignorance of the official ideology on the part of members of these organizations.

With respect to the contribution of land reform to the differentiation of rural organizations, the main consideration is whether reform has brought about a separation of interests between the cultivating farmers and the non-cultivating landlords, thereby removing the former's subservience to the latter. The separation of interests and the removal of subservience can be achieved through the creation of separate organizations for reform beneficiaries and landlords. Alternatively, in organizations that consist of reform beneficiaries and landlords alike, provisions can be made to insure equitable representation for both groups and the safeguarding of their respective interests.

As to the impact of land reform on the adaptability of farmer organizations, one can assess it only when the post-reform period is sufficiently long to permit rural organizations to experience challenges brought about by changing times. In such a situation, adaptability is indicated by the ability of rural organizations to rely on their own resources to meet the challenges, and the flexibility with which they operate. The more land reform helps enhance the self-reliance and operational flexibility of an organization, the greater its contribution to adaptability.

The preceding paragraphs have set forth the criteria for evaluating the contribution of reform programs to the institutionalization of rural organizations.[6] In accordance with these criteria, one may say that in as many

---

[6] Lest it be misunderstood, the intention here is merely to assess the extent of the contribution of land reform to institutionalization of rural organizations. It is not im-

as six of the eight countries studied land reform has failed to achieve any substantial impact on the institutionalization of rural organizations. These include Pakistan, the Philippines, Colombia, India, Iran, and U.A.R. In the first four countries, land reform has not contributed to the institutionalization of rural organizations mainly because the reform programs of these countries have not produced any large number of beneficiaries to become members of rural organizations. In the last two countries, land reform has resulted in the creation of farm cooperatives encompassing a sizable number of beneficiaries, but these cooperatives are much under the domination of the government. They have yet to create an identity of their own. The membership, lacking a genuine feeling of participation in the management, looks upon the cooperatives not so much as institutions articulating and promoting their interests as public instrumentalities performing functions vital to farm operations in reform areas. In short, the cooperatives serve, but do not represent, the reform beneficiaries.

For these reasons, it appears appropriate in the following analysis to forego further discussion of these six countries and to concentrate on Mexico and Taiwan where the institutionalization process has achieved considerable progress.

Patterns of Institutionalization: Mexico and Taiwan

Fully developed and well-structured rural organizations exist in both Mexico and Taiwan. These organizations possess the largest membership of any occupational groups in the respective countries; they have been in existence over several decades; they have effectively served the interests of their members; they have fully implemented democratic principles of organization; and they have proved effective in mobilizing rural votes. To a considerable extent, the growth of the institutional strength of Mexican and Taiwanese rural organizations can be attributed to land reform. Mexico's largest rural organization, the *Confederacion Nacional Campesina*, was created to integrate all recipients of land, the *ejidatarios*. In Taiwan, while new rural organizations were formed specifically to facilitate implementation of reform, existing agricultural institutions were revamped to improve services for the beneficiaries as well as for other farming interests.

However, despite these similarities, the patterns of evolution of the

---

plied that land reform is necessarily a prerequisite to institutionalization of all rural organizations.

rural organizations of the two countries are basically different. These can be comparatively analyzed by reference to the four aspects of institutionalization.

Mexico: The Turbulent Evolution of CNC

The movement for organizing the Mexican *campesinos*, like the making of modern Mexico, followed a turbulent and agonizing course. In the quarter of a century from 1910 to 1935, Mexican *campesinos* fought on different sides in the prolonged civil war; they became the target of intense competition among rival politicians, generals, and political parties; and they were engaged in wide-spread internecine struggle. Hundreds of thousands of them lost their lives; numerous acts of cruelty and atrocity were committed; and inestimable losses of private property and farm production were incurred throughout the nation.

In the initial phase of the revolution, many *campesinos* rose in rebellion because of their deep dissatisfaction with the prevailing land-tenure system. But soon the *campesinos* joined in the fighting merely to assure survival. As Marjorie Ruth Clark has observed.

> Agricultural production was so interrupted and so at the mercy of the revolutionary armies and the innumerable bands of marauders and bandits, the conditions of the workers on the *haciendas* so unbearable that thousands of them joined the armies as the only remedy against starvation. That was, very often, the strongest argument in favor of fighting, nor did it make much difference on which side they fought if they were promised land.[7]

Thus, for instance, in the State of Morelos, the center of the Zapatista movement, *campesinos* waged pitched battles against federal troops under the command of, successively, Presidents Porfirio Diaz, Francisco I. Madero, Adolfo de la Huerta, and Venustiano Carranza. They suffered severe losses from the treacherous invasions of General Victoriano Huerta in 1911, the devastating depopulation campaign of General Juvenico Robles in 1912 to 1913, and the savage campaign of extermination of General Pablo Gonźales in 1916 to 1919.[8] It was a war without compro-

---

[7] Marjorie Ruth Clark, *Organized Labor in Mexico* (Chapel Hill: University of North Carolina Press, 1934), p. 151.

[8] For a vivid portrayal of this ferocious fighting, see John Womack, Jr., *Zapata and the Mexican Revolution* (New York, 1969). The damages done on Morelos by Generals

mise. " 'Peace at any cost' was the cry of the successive governments; 'land at any cost' was the reply of the south." The human toll was fantastic. In these nine years, one third of Morelos' total population was destroyed.[9]

In the north, Pancho Villa fought against the same forces as Zapata did in the south. He engaged in a see-saw battle between his home state, Chihuahua, and Mexico City. Elsewhere, in the northern states of Baja California, Sonora, Sinaloa, Coahuila, Nuevo León, Tamaulipas, and the central states of Michoacán, Guerrero, Puebla, San Luis Potosí, and Veracruz, the peasant forces and their allies fought the federal forces and, sometimes, fought among themselves. These wars spread ruin in the countryside, but they also swelled the peasant army. A remark by John Womack referring to conditions in Morelos certainly applies to much of rural Mexico: "Desolating village after village, federal commanders drove people into new associations: neighborhoods and families disappeared, their refugee parts to be swallowed up in roving rebel armies." [10]

The *campesinos* not only fought against those in control of government but also were subject to the oppressive assaults of the *hacendados* who were frequently supported by federal forces. In 1925 in the State of Aguascalientes, the *jefe de operaciones* (local military commander), General Rodrigo Talamantes, "in connivance with the large landlords . . . used his forces to drive peasants off their *ejidos*. More than one head of a

---

Robles and Gonzáles were particularly heavy. Pursuing his "resettlement" plan, Robles decreed in 1913, "all inhabitants of pueblos, ranchos, and smaller hamlets had to 'reconcentrate' in the closest district seat, or in one of a few other major towns. Pueblos suspected as 'nests of Bandits' would be burned and razed; and anyone caught in the countryside without a license would be summarily tried and executed." As a result, "everywhere in Morelos communities disintegrated. . . . [Within] months Robles and his henchmen shredded the tough fabric of provincial society that would have required decades of peaceful development to unravel." *Ibid.*, pp. 167, 170. Waging an even more ruthless campaign, Gonzáles' soldiers wantonly ransacked the countryside, leaving a Morelos with "pueblos completely burned down, timber leveled, cattle stolen, crops that were cultivated with labor's sweat . . . [filled] the boxcars of their long trains and . . . sold in the capital." Continuing the drive of "resettlement," the "constitutionalist" forces under Gonzáles drove people like "a herd of pigs" to train stations and shipped them to Mexico City, where they were left scattered in slums, absolutely destitute. In terms of the atrocity committed, "Robles, damned a thousand times, is little in comparison" with Gonzáles. Letter by Juan Espinosa Barreda, an eyewitness of the rampage, to Alberto Paniagua, March 30, 1917. Quoted in Womack, *op. cit.*, p. 268.

[9] Frank Tannenbaum, *Peace by Revolution: Mexico After 1910* (New York: Columbia University Press, 1933; paperback edition, 1966), p. 179.

[10] *Op. cit.*, p. 170.

village committee he strung to a convenient *pirú* tree." [11] In Yucatan, Felipe Carrillo Puerto, an agronomist strongly advocating the peasant cause, became governor in 1922 and much expedited land redistribution among the Maya Indians. "But Carrillo Puerto's governorship lasted less than two years. As soon as the landholding elite got a chance for revenge, during the military coup of Adolfo de la Huerta, Carrillo Puerto was shot with three of his brothers and nine other leaders, in January 1924. Actual power was regained by the *hacendados*." [12] In Veracruz, "the large owners . . . formed a Revolutionary Junta with [the] help of the military commander [General Guadalupe Sánchez] and armed their serfs. The peasants . . . were practically defenseless against the cavalry of General Guadalupe Sánchez, and the armed serfs and the cattle herds of the landowners, when these destroyed the harvests of the *ejidos*, and burnt the houses of the *ejidatarios*." [13] In Michoacán, "as a counter measure against . . . land reform, the Sindicato Nacional de Agricultores, the association of large landholders . . . started to form 'white syndicates' . . . under the motto: 'Justice and Charity (Justicia y Caridad).' " The soldiers and the "White guards" attacked the *campesinos* and assassinated their leaders.[14]

Similar repressive activities against the *campesinos* were carried on in many parts of the country, and did not subside even during the presidency of Cárdenas. In the first eighteen months of the Cárdenas administration fifty-three battles between agrarianists and their opponents occurred. Many *campesinos* petitioning for land were assassinated by men hired by the landowners—2,000 in Veracruz alone. To provide protection to the *campesinos*, Cárdenas armed the villagers. At the end of his term in 1940, the rural force thus created consisted of about 70 battalions and 75 cavalry regiments, a total of 60,000 men.[15]

While fighting federal forces and the *hacendados*, the *campesinos* were compelled to organize themselves in order to hold on to their newly received land. With the assistance of the regional branches of the National Agrarian Commission, leagues of agrarian communities (*Ligas de Communidades Agrarias*) emerged in Morelos, Veracruz, Yucatan, Puebla,

[11] Ernest Gruening, *Mexico and Its Heritage* (New York: Appleton-Century-Crofts, Inc., 1928), p. 324.

[12] Gerrit Huizer, *On Peasant Unrest in Latin America* (Washington, D.C., 1969), p. 50.

[13] *Ibid.*, p. 54.

[14] *Ibid.*, pp. 56–59.

[15] *Ibid.*, pp. 82–84.

Michoacán, Tamaulipas, and various other states. Moving toward establishing a nationwide organization, these leagues and other associations held the I *Congreso Nacional Agrarista* in May 1923. Under the sponsorship of the newly founded *Partido Nacional Agrarista* (PNA), with 1,078 delegates participating in its proceedings, the Congress expressed firm support for the land redistribution program then in progress. In November 1926, another effort was made to unite the state peasant leagues when the First National Congress of Leagues was held in Mexico City. Claiming to represent 300,000 *campesinos* from 16 of the 27 states of Mexico, the 158 delegates to the Congress decided to form a *Liga Nacional Compesina* (the National Peasant League, LNC). They reaffirmed their faith in the provision of the constitution that guaranteed peasant rights, and advanced a number of proposals with socialistic tendencies.[16] Despite these moves, however, unity among peasant organizations was far from a reality. On the contrary, division among the peasants was intensified because of the conflicts among different organized groups that sought to identify with the peasant cause. Thus, there was the competition for peasant support by the *Partido Nacional Agrarista* and the *Confederación Regional Obrera Mexicana* (Regional Confederation of Mexican Workers, CROM). To promote the "Land for the People" idea, and to elevate itself from a sectional political group into a strong national political party, the PNA tried vigorously to incorporate all peasant organizations into its structure. The CROM, formed in 1918 by Luis Morones, was primarily an industrial labor organization, but, recognizing the potential political strength of the *campesinos*, it sought to enlist agricultural workers as members. The CROM claimed, in 1926, to represent 1,500 peasant workers' syndicates as affiliates.[17] While engaged in the competition for recruitment of *campesinos*, the PNA and CROM extended their rivalry into the political sphere. As discussed earlier, the PNA forged an alliance with General Alvaro Obregón through which it helped to further the General's presidential aspirations; in turn, the party was promised speedy implementation of land redistribution, then stalled. The PNA gained ascendancy during the presidency of Obregón, but gradually lost influence when Plutarco Elias Calles became president, with whom the CROM was identified. When Calles' term came to a close in 1928, the PNA backed Obregón for reelection and, in the aftermath of the assassination of Obregón, supported Emilio Portes Gil for the presidency. In the meantime, Calles,

[16] *Ibid.*, p. 60.
[17] *Ibid.*, p. 47.

still commanding much political influence in the country, founded the official party, *Partido Nacional Revolucionario* (PNR) in 1929. Through his new institution, Calles "was able to split the Agraristas, purge his opponents and add the party [PNA] to the PNR coalition." [18] Absorption by the PNR still did not lead to unity among the peasant organizations. In fact, the official party's intensive drive to gain control of the *Liga Nacional Campesina* resulted in a split of that organization in 1930.[19] One small group joined the PNR; another affiliated with the Mexican Communist Party. The majority of the *Liga's* membership, however, remained politically independent and formed, under the leadership of the founder of the *Liga*—Ursulo Galván—a *Liga Nacional Campesina "Ursulo Galván."*

The mixing of agrarian movements with politics further stimulated the proliferation of peasant organizations. As agrarianism became a kind of political game, Marjorie Ruth Clark observed, "it makes little difference to the peasant which of the many organizations he joins. He must take care to belong to the one which is strongest in his region, if he wishes to escape persecution." [20] Quoting from a report of a zonal representative of the National Agrarian Commission, Eyler N. Simpson made a similar observation: "The greatest difficulties in the ejidos of this zone came from political parties. . . . Each group tries at all costs to maintain control of the ejido and of the ejidatarios in order to . . . place in office its own members." [21] Simpson continued: "There is hardly a state without an assortment of Agrarian Leagues, Peasant's Syndicates, and Ejido Parties, organized and led by astute politicians. . . ." [22]

It was not until the presidential term of Lázaro Cárdenas in the late 1930s that the divergent agrarian organizations moved decisively toward

[18] Peter P. Lord, "The Peasantry as an Emerging Political Factor in Mexico, Bolivia, and Venezuela" (Madison: The University of Wisconsin, The Land Tenure Center, Paper No. 35, May 1965), p. 9.

[19] The government's attempt to control the LNC became very evident at the VI Convention of the Liga, in 1930. "The first directive board of the convention, . . . was replaced by one more favorable to governmental control. Members were forced to disarm before entering the meetings, and police were stationed everywhere throughout the meeting place in a twofold attempt to prevent violence and to make obvious the determination of the government to have a part in the proceedings." Clark, *op. cit.* (n. 7 above), p. 157.

[20] *Ibid.*, pp. 161–162.

[21] Eyler N. Simpson, *The Ejido, Mexico's Way Out* (Chapel Hill, N.C., 1937), pp. 335–336.

[22] *Ibid.*, p. 350.

the goal of unification. Most instrumental to this unification drive was, of course, Cárdenas himself, who, upon nomination for the presidency by the PNR in 1934, was determined to turn the war-wrecked country into a united nation and to construct the political framework on which to integrate the disparate forces of the revolution. "He recognized in his people a deficiency of civic spirit and a lack of awareness of difference between liberty and license, but he believed that these obstacles would be overcome in time if the masses as well as the elite groups in society possessed strong, permanent organizational mechanisms through which their demands would reach the government directly." [23] It was in this belief that Cárdenas helped create, early in his presidential term, the *Confederación Nacional Campesina* and, sought, through the affiliation of the rural organization with the governing party, to establish a direct, permanent, nation-wide link between the revolutionary elite and the mass peasantry. To Cárdenas, the organizing of the CNC was also necessary for a number of other reasons. The CNC was expected to sustain and complement the massive land redistribution program he was soon to launch, to be instrumental in wresting power from the "old guard" Calles, and to serve as a counterweight against the increasingly influential labor organization, the *Confederacion de Trabajadores de Mexico* (CTM).

In a decree of July 10, 1935, Cárdenas first instructed the National Executive Committee of the PNR to organize a league of agrarian communities in every state. Then he directed Portes Gil to launch a massive drive to integrate these leagues into a national whole. He personally attended the conventions of the state leagues and pledged his support. In August 1938, the CNC was formally baptized, extending its membership automatically to every *ejidatario*. In the same year, the PNR was renamed the *Partido de la Revolucion Mexicana* (PRM), encompassing four sectors: labor (CTM), peasant (CNC), popular, and military.[24] The military sector was later dropped from the official party, and the CNC gradually evolved into the largest and the most effectively organized rural institution in Mexico, and one of the three most vital pillars of the official party.

The CNC has developed an elaborate nation-wide structure parallel

---

[23] Frank Ralph Brandenburg, *The Making of Modern Mexico* (Englewood Cliffs, N.J., 1964), p. 83.

[24] "The Constituent Congress of the PRM was composed of 393 members, 100 from workers' organizations, 96 from peasant organizations, 96 from the middle class (teachers, petty industrialists, artisans) brought together into the 'popular sector,' and 101 from the army." Huizer, *op. cit.* (n. 12 above), p. 82.

to that of both the government and the PRI, and has staffed this massive structure with peasants and peasant-elected representatives. At the foundation of this structure is, of course, the *ejido* system. The *ejidos* at the village level elect five representatives every three years, who constitute a regional committee; 512 such regional committees are grouped into 32 *Ligas de Comunidades Agrarias y Syndicatos Campesinos* at the state level. At the top of the CNC is a national convention, made up of the executive committees of all the state *ligas*, which elects a 14–member National Executive Committee. Acting as the national spokesman for the CNC is the Secretary-General.

The pattern of evolution of Mexico's CNC has thus been marked by persistent and many-sided armed struggles, intense competition among different political groups, and politicization of the peasantry. Throughout this process of peasant mobilization, land reform has remained the catalyst, stimulating the *campesinos* to organize and to integrate themselves into a permanent institution.

Taiwan: The Orderly Growth of Rural Organizations

The growth of Taiwan's rural organizations in the post-World War II era has followed a different pattern of evolution from that of Mexico's. If the CNC is a product of revolution and civil strife, rural organizations in Taiwan emerged peacefully and experienced an orderly growth. Of all Taiwan's rural organizations, three are most important: the Farmers' Associations, the Irrigation Associations, and the Farm Tenancy Committees. The first two are of long standing, but they were reorganized in the midst of reform specifically to meet the needs of the beneficiaries and of other farming interests. "To coordinate with the implementation of the Land-to-the-Tiller policy," declared President Chiang Kai-Shek in August 1953, "reform of the farmers' associations and irrigation associations is of paramount importance." [25]

The farmers' associations have a long history, dating back to Japanese rule. In 1900 in San-hsin Village of Taipei district, the first agricultural association (nōkai) "was organized by the [Japanese] administration under the leadership of local officials in cooperation with landlords and wealthy farmers; . . ."[26] Under the supervision of the government's agricultural

[25] Quoted in T. H. Shen, *Agricultural Development on Taiwan Since World War II* (Ithaca, N.Y.: Comstock Publishing Associates, 1964), p. 130.

[26] Ramon H. Myers and Adrienne Ching, "Agricultural Development in Taiwan under Japanese Colonial Rule," *The Journal of Asian Studies*, XXIII: 4 (August 1964),

experimental station, the association provided to its membership fertilizers, tools, seeds, and extension services. In the following two decades the San-hsin model was gradually extended to every administrative district on Taiwan.[27] All these associations were service-oriented, somewhat technical, and under the strict control of the Japanese administration, with local landlords exercising a measure of influence.[28] With the departure of the Japanese from Taiwan after the Second World War, these associations "became organizations of the local gentry and landlords." [29]

During land reform, the Chinese Nationalist government undertook to reorganize these associations so that they would continue to provide essential agricultural services to the farming community but would not be subject to the manipulation of the landlords.

The reorganized associations have two main features. First, the entire system of associations is formed through cooptation. Each association possesses an assembly of representatives, a board of directors, and a board of supervisors. The membership of an association at a lower level elects its own assembly of representatives, who, in turn, choose among themselves the members of the two boards and also representatives of the association at the next, higher level. The board of directors, composed of ten to twenty-one members, is the governing organ of the association and manages the routine business through an appointed manager and other administrative personnel. The board of supervisors, consisting of three to seven members, has the principal responsibility of auditing the financial transactions of the association. Second, cultivating farmers are assured of the right to control the operation of the association through the following provisions:

1. Membership is divided into two categories: active and associate. The former is limited to one member per farm family. A farm family is one that derives 50 percent or more of its income from actual cultivation

---

562. See also China, Taiwan Sheng Ti Fang Tsu Ch'ih Chih Yao Pien Chi Wei Yuan Hui, *Taiwan Sheng Ti Fang Tsu Ch'ih Chih Yao* (*Compendium on Self-Government in Taiwan Province*) (Taichung, Taiwan, China, 1965), p. 891.

[27] In 1918, "the total number of district officials involved in administering these associations was 620. . . . Colonial officials recognized the *nokai's* role as a transmission belt to introduce new technology into agriculture through its strategic link between the administration and the farming community." Myers and Ching, *op. cit.*, 563.

[28] "The Japanese Governor-General was chairman of the Provincial Farmers' Association, and the local magistrates were chairmen of the local associations. These associations were instruments of the Japanese administration in matters relating to agricultural production." Shen, *op. cit.*, p. 49.

[29] Chen Cheng, *Land Reform in Taiwan* (Taipei, Taiwan, 1961), p. 107.

of the land. Associate membership may be acquired by people with less than 50 percent of their income derived from farming.

2. At least two-thirds of the representatives of a farmers' association and of the members of the board of directors of the association must consist of owner-farmers, tenants, and farm laborers.

3. Associate members enjoy all the rights of active members, except that they cannot vote in association elections. They can, however, be elected to up to one-third of the membership of the board of supervisors.

Today the association system consists of 1 association at the provincial level (i.e., for the whole island), 22 at the county (*hsien*) and municipal level, and 340 at the township level. At the base of the system are 5,035 Small Agricultural Units, each of which consists of association members of a village or hamlet. As of 1965, the total membership of the farmers' associations was 845,650, including 751,035 active members, who had elected 23,480 representatives, 4,555 directors, 1,266 supervisors, 5,035 chairmen, and 5,035 vice chairmen of Small Agricultural Units.[30]

In the several elections held so far, cultivating farmers have gained a dominant share of all elective positions in the associations on every level of the hierarchy. This was the case in the elections of 1956, 1959, and 1962. As of 1965, owner-farmers, tenants, and farm laborers contributed 98.93 percent of the representatives, 99.13 percent of board directors, and 73.87 percent of the board of supervisors.[31]

The history of Taiwan's irrigation associations is even longer than that of the farmers' associations.[32] During the Ch'ing Dynasty (1644–1911), under Chinese rule, large landowners and other private interests built, with official financial assistance, a number of reservoirs. The owners operated these reservoirs through hired managers, who actually supervised water distribution among farmers. In the Japanese period (1896–1945), irrigation associations were established under government auspices, with their operations remaining in private hands. This state of affairs lasted until the time of land reform. After implementing the land-to-the-tiller program in 1953, the Chinese government began to reorganize the associations. The island was divided into twenty-six irrigation districts, each with one association.

The association admitted both owners and users of irrigation facilities

[30] *Compendium on Self-Government in Taiwan Province*, p. 896.

[31] *Ibid.*, p. 895.

[32] See Myers and Ching, *op. cit.*, 569 and *Compendium on Self-Government in Taiwan Province*, p. 949.

as members, who elected an assembly of representatives for a three-year term. These representatives, in turn, elected a board of councilors and a president, also for three-year terms respectively. Two-thirds of the representatives had to be tillers of land. In 1957, a Federation of Irrigation Associations for the whole island was created with presidents of the twenty-six district associations as members. As of 1965, these associations consisted of 848,901 members.[33] Cultivating farmers obtained a large proportion of the elective positions. For instance, in the election of 1956, cultivators won 1,121 (or 79 percent) of the total of 1,426 representatives, 137 (or 57 percent) of the total of 240 councilors, and 1 presidency.[34]

Today, the assembly of an irrigation association serves as a policy-making organ whose decisions are executed by a full-time, salaried president. In discharging his responsibilities, the president is assisted by an appointed general manager and administrative and technical staff members. To facilitate water distribution, an association is geographically divided into several areas, each with an irrigation working station, which is further divided into small irrigation groups. The principal functions of an association include management, improvement and regulation of irrigation facilities, settlement of water disputes, and water conservancy.

Of Taiwan's three principal rural organizations, the Farm Tenancy Committees are most directly related to land reform. The farmers' associations and irrigation associations existed prior to reform, and they were merely reorganized to ensure equitable representation of the beneficiaries. The farm tenancy committees, however, were created during reform and regarded as vital instruments in the implementation of reform.

The origin of the farm tenancy committees is also traceable to Japanese experiences. In 1949, at the invitation of the JCRR, Wolf Ladejinsky, an expert with extensive experience with the Japanese land-reform program, visited Taiwan and recommended the creation of a landlord-tenant organization to deal with the tenancy disputes then arising during the enforcement of the rent-reduction program. Accepting the recommendation, the Chinese government wrote into the Rent Reduction Act of 1951 a provision authorizing the creation of Farm Tenancy Committees. To protect the interests of the tenant, the law provided that "the number of members representing tenant farmers on the Committee shall be no fewer

[33] *Compendium on Self-Government in Taiwan Province*, p. 951.
[34] Shen, *op. cit.*, pp. 132–133.

than the total number of members representing landlords and owner farmers." [35] When the Land-to-the-Tiller Act was enacted in 1953, it declared specifically the committees "shall assist in the execution of this Act."

Closely resembling the Japanese Land Commissions,[36] the Farm Tenancy Committees of Taiwan consist of one committee for each of the 22 counties (*hsien*) and municipalities and the 319 townships and villages. Every committee consists of 11 members; 2 *ex-officio* members appointed by the government at the appropriate level, 5 representatives of tenants, 2 of owners, and 2 of landlords. In a hamlet, people with different tenure status elect separately their representatives; then through a system of cooptation, the committees at the higher levels of the system are formed.

The first committee elections were held in 1952, producing a total of 3,032 members; of this total 1,686 (or about 56 percent) were tenants, 673 (or 22 percent) owner farmers, and 673 (or 22 percent) landlords. In assisting in the execution of the rent reduction and land-to-the-tiller programs, the Farm Tenancy Committees perform a variety of functions. In the main, the committees provide farmers with information on reform programs, appraise the value of appropriated land and buildings, investigate crop failures in tenanted farms, decide whether delay or reduction of rent is justified, and settle tenant-landlord disputes (for details, see Chapter IX, above). As an indicator of the extensiveness of the committees' activities, from 1952 to 1956 (when tenant-landlord conflicts were most intense and frequent), the committees settled a total of 62,645 disputes.[37] By providing the reform beneficiaries with important roles in the process of implementation, these committees have been most effective in dispelling peasant indifference and in curbing the landlords' evasive and resistant tactics. By assuring the tenants and owner-farmers a privileged position

[35] See Appendix I.

[36] The Japanese Land Commissions were responsible for carrying out "most of the practical business of the [Japanese land reform] program. . . . [These Commissions were] organized in the villages, towns, and cities which were comprised of members elected publicly with membership allotted to persons according to tenure status: five persons representing the tenants, three persons representing the landlords, and two persons representing the owner-cultivators." M. Kaihara, "On the Effects of Postwar Land Reform in Japan," in Walter Froehlich (ed.), *Land Tenure, Industrialization, and Social Stability* (Milwaukee, 1961), p. 146.

[37] H. S. Tang and S. C. Hsieh, "Land Reform and Agricultural Development in Taiwan," in Froehlich, *op. cit.*, p. 127. For a brief description of types of disputes that the committees ordinarily dealt with, see E. Stuart Kirby, *Rural Progress in Taiwan* (Taipei, JCRR, 1960), p. 96.

vis-à-vis the landlords, these committees have also "raised the social status of" the cultivators.[38]

ACQUISITION OF VALUE

If the pattern of evolution of rural organizations in Mexico and Taiwan are totally different, the ways in which the organizations of the two countries acquired value are no less different: Mexican rural organizations embraced the Mexican ideology that gave justification to land reform because their members actually helped shape that ideology. Taiwanese rural organizations accepted *The Three Principles of the People* as a basis of reform in Taiwan largely because of indoctrination by the KMT.

Mexico: "Land and Liberty"

As mentioned in Chapter IV, the Mexican revolution was initially aimed at political change and was without social content. Madero's slogan "Effective Suffrage, No Reelection" was designed primarily to overthrow the Porforian regime. Incidental to this central objective was the idea of the restitution of usurped Indian lands. But it was in response to this idea that the *campesinos* joined the upheaval, adding a new meaning to the revolution. Henceforth land reform became the instrument that fused a political movement for governmental change with a social movement for agrarian transformation. "*Tierra y Libertad* (Land and Liberty)" was the motto that symbolized the union of political leaders and the *campesinos* and replaced "Effective Suffrage, No Reelection" as the ideology of the revolution.[39]

Unlike the political doctrines motivating or justifying other revolutions (for instance, Marxism in the case of the Russian revolution of 1917), which are theories formulated preceding the upheavals, the Mexican ideology derived its content from the practical experiences of the revolutionaries. It is a concept that came largely from the peasants and was consecrated with their blood.

In November 1911, the Zapatistas declared their reform idea in the *Plan de Ayala*. In regard to "the fields, timber, and water which the landlords, cientificos, or bosses have usurped, the pueblos or citizens who have the titles corresponding to those properties will immediately enter into possession of that real estate of which they have been despoiled by the

[38] Tang and Hsieh, *op. cit.*, p. 128.
[39] On the origin of the phrase, "Land and Liberty," see Womack, *op. cit.* (n. 8 above), pp. 193, 398.

bad faith of our oppressors, maintaining at any cost with arms in hand the mentioned possession." The *Plan* continued, "there will be expropriated the third part of those monopolies . . . with prior indemnization, in order that the pueblos and citizens of Mexico may obtain ejidos, colonies, and foundations for pueblos . . . and [that] the Mexicans' lack of prosperity and well-being may improve in all and for all." [40]

With unswerving dedication to this pronouncement, the Zapatistas "considered the Plan a veritable catholicon, much more than a program of action, almost a Scripture. . . . The Ayala Plan became famous as the premier banner of modern Mexico's most remarkable and controversial experiment, agrarian reform." [41] During the revolution, "in each town which was conquered by the peasant troops all the records of landownership were purposely destroyed and practically all the lands of the State of Morelos, fifty-three haciendas, farms and ranches, were given to the peasants." [42] The Zapatista force, Frank Tannenbaum has vividly described,

> was an army without an encampment; when a battle was to be fought, the soldiers gathered in response to a call; when a battle was over, the soldiers went back to their villages, hid their rifles, and turned to tilling the soil. A federal column could find no soldiers to fight, only unarmed peasants who humbly worked the land. When a campaign was on, the soldiers of Zapata would change every three months, some going home, others joining the army. So it went for nine years.[43]

Parallel to the Zapatistas' reform effort in the south was Pancho Villa's drive for land redistribution in the north. In the latter region, the division of the immense *latifundios* into small lots for peasants, rather than the restitution of land, constituted the most acute issue of the day. In May 1915, Villa put forth his agrarian law, declaring that large holdings would be expropriated with compensation and sold, in parcels of no larger than twenty-five hectares, to peasants.[44] Roaming, raiding, and plundering in the northern states, with occasional intrusions into Mexico City and the United States, the Villistas fought to enforce their idea of land reform.

---

[40] *Ibid.*, Appendix B, pp. 402–403.

[41] *Ibid.*, p. 393.

[42] Huizer, *op. cit.* (n. 12 above), p. 14.

[43] Tannenbaum, *op. cit.* (n. 9 above), pp. 178–179.

[44] Jesús Silva Herzog, *El Agrarismo Mexicano y la Reforma Agraria* (Fondo de Cultura Económica, Mexico, 1959), pp. 238–239. Cited in Huizer, *op. cit.* (n. 12 above), pp. 26–27.

In response to these peasant pressures, the revolutionary elite accepted land reform as a political necessity and wrote it, through a series of political proclamations and legal acts, into the Mexican revolutionary ideology. In the "Sovereign Revolutionary Convention" in Aguascalientes, convened by General Carranza in October 1914 and participated in by the delegates of the Villa and Zapata forces, the delegates approved the main provisions of the Ayala Plan.[45] On December 12, 1914, Carranza proclaimed his *Plan de Veracruz* promising to carry out land reform.[46] Then, on January 6, 1915, he issued the land-reform decree recognizing "the necessity for returning to the villages the lands . . . as an elementary justice, as the only way of insuring peace and as a method for promoting the welfare . . . of our poor classes." [47] Finally, the constitution of 1917 gave formal sanction to reform through the incorporation of the 1915 decree into Article 27.

In the following decades, as land reform was implemented throughout the country, "Land and Liberty" became an idea firmly lodged in the consciousness of the *ejidatarios;* and their organization, the CNC, became the strongest defender of land reform. In retrospect, one sees that the acquisition of land reform as a value by Mexican rural organizations was a result of the physical experiences of their membership, as well as the consummation of a legal process. Today, over half a century after the issuance of the 1915 decree, the *ejidatarios* remain highly cognizant of land reform as an integral part of Mexican revolutionary ideology. The Taretan study, cited earlier, reveals, for example, that when asked "what were the principal aims of the Revolution?" 80 percent of the *ejidatario* respondents replied either *tierra* or *libertad,* or both.[48] This high level of awareness of revolutionary ideology by the *ejidatarios* is matched by the intensity of their feelings toward the preservation of the *ejido* system. As reported in the Infield and Freier study, when an *ejidatario* was asked to comment on the idea of abolition of the system,

> Sr. Morones [the *ejidatario*] . . . broke into a smile, then with a slashing movement of his hand across the throat, he pronounced the classical words: "*Sobrarán sombreros,*" which, translated literally, mean: there would be a surplus of hats, or, in other words, heads would roll. While the others nodded their assent, he added seriously

[45] See Womack, *op. cit.* (n. 8 above), pp. 217–218.
[46] Simpson, *op. cit.* (n. 21 above), p. 54.
[47] Quoted in *ibid.,* p. 57.
[48] Henry A. Landsberger and Cynthia N. Hewitt, "A Pilot Study of Participation in Rural Organizations" (Ithaca, N.Y., 1967, mimeo.), p. 41.

and with deep conviction: "It is simply impossible to do away with the *ejidos*. Why, the whole economy of the country would collapse. Anybody with eyes in his head can see the progress this country has made since 1936, and this [progress is possible] only because of the work done by the *ejidos*.[49]

Taiwan: The Three Principles of the People

It seems clear that in Mexico the enthusiastic endorsement by *ejidatarios* of the concept of "Land and Liberty" and their strong identification with the *ejido* as an institutional expression of that concept resulted mainly from their active, prolonged involvement in the shaping and enforcing of this concept. This is in contrast to the experiences in Taiwan. The Taiwanese rural population appears to have accepted *The Three Principles of the People* as the theoretical foundation of the land-reform programs, but this KMT ideology was almost exclusively formulated by one man, Dr. Sun Yat-sen. Moreover, as is implicit in the discussion above, with its emphasis on restitution of Indian lands, Mexican land-reform— at least for the greater part of the post–1910 period—had social justice as its central objective. As elaborated at some length in Chapter IV, KMT ideology seems to place equal emphasis on social and economic considerations. Furthermore, the content of Mexican ideology was gradually crystallized during the course of the revolution; the formulation of KMT ideology antedated the reform in Taiwan by several decades. It was through an intensive, systematic campaign that KMT ideology was inculcated into the peasant political consciousness.

This campaign was prompted by two considerations. The first concerns the KMT's incipient effort to establish a permanent link with the peasantry. In 1949, when the KMT started the rent-reduction program, the party came into direct contact with the peasants for the first time in its history. To inform the rural populace about Dr. Sun's land-reform theory, the KMT reasoned, would strengthen the impression that land reform was introduced to Taiwan by the party not on the spur of the moment, but on the basis of the party's long-term ideological commitment. The campaign would, therefore, not only facilitate the implementation of reform but also create a sympathetic understanding of the party by the peasant. The other consideration relates to the KMT's effort to draw a basic distinction between the programs the party introduced in Taiwan

[49] Henrik F. Infield and Koka Freier, *Peoplei n Ejidos* (New York, 1954), pp. 140–141.

and those enforced on mainland China by the Communist regime. This could best be done by identifying the different intellectual bases of the two sets of reform programs. After the reform programs were successively carried out in Taiwan, the Kuomintang remained enthusiastic about stressing the ideological aspect of these programs. The party, now adopted a stance in favor of recovering the mainland by political means, considering that its success in land reform in Taiwan provided it with a propaganda weapon to win the sympathy of the peasantry on the mainland. "The enforcement of the Land-to-the-Tiller Program," two authors in Taiwan have maintained, "is a concrete realization of Dr. Sun's policy for agricultural land. . . . [The enforcement of the program] not only helps make Taiwan a model province under *The Three Principles of the People* but also enables [us] to call upon the farmers on the mainland to rise up against the Communists." [50] Expounding a similar thesis, *The Central Daily News*, the opinion organ of the KMT, commented in 1963 in an editorial:

> The land problem is of both economic and political significance. In the long history of China, the land problem was a vital factor affecting the operation of the cycle of political uprisings and stability. . . . Realizing this fact, the Chinese Communists have utilized the land problem as their political capital of subversion. Land reform, therefore, is a major battle field in the long struggle between the Communists and us. We must maintain this perspective when viewing our achievements in land reform in Taiwan, . . .[51]

The campaign to propagate KMT ideology in the countryside was conducted in two ways. The first was to indoctrinate land-reform personnel. In 1949, before the rent-reduction program was formally implemented, the government offered a series of training courses to 4,257 reform officials and workers at every level of the provincial government.[52] When the land-to-the-tiller program was launched in 1953, the training process was drastically expanded to include many non-officials. In February and March 1953, training courses were offered to 10,259 government workers, 3,032 farm tenancy committee members, and 19,611 representatives of

---

[50] Ch'ang-hsi Wang and Wei-kuang Chang, *Taiwan Tu Ti Kai Keh* (*Land Reform in Taiwan*) (3rd ed., Taipei, Taiwan: Hsin Tung Li Ch'u Pan Shê, 1953), p. 160. My translation from the Chinese.
[51] *The Central Daily News*, July 25, 1963, p. 2. My translation from the Chinese.
[52] Wang and Chang, *op. cit.*, p. 8.

tenants, owner-farmers, and landlords—totalling 32,902.[53] In all these courses, the participants, while receiving instructions on how to enforce reform laws and regulations, learned about the KMT theory underlying the programs. It was partly through the indoctrinated personnel that the KMT hoped to carry its political message to the villagers.

The other way to instill KMT ideology into the peasant mind was a massive information drive to bring the ideology directly to the farmers. Utilizing every conceivable communications media—public announcements, leaflets, posters, radios, and village meetings—the government and the KMT explained in detail to the rural communities the basic principles and content of the programs.[54]

The indoctrination of reform officials and the provision of massive quantities of reform information in rural Taiwan resulted in a high awareness by the farmers of the contents and theoretical foundations of the reform programs. The effectiveness of this propaganda campaign can be seen in the results of the 1968 Tainan Survey conducted by the author. Over a decade and a half after the implementation of the land-to-the-tiller program, the Tainan rural respondents were still highly cognizant of KMT ideology as the basis of the program. When asked to identify the content of *The Three Principles of the People*, a large proportion in every category of respondents gave the correct answer. The results of the survey are shown in Table 59.

It is to be noted that most of the respondents (the first three categories in Table 59), were either cultivating farmers or landowners. They were thus either active or associate members of farmers' associations. Hence one can assume that these associations have come to be identified with KMT ideology.

DIFFERENTIATION OF INTERESTS

In the farming community, the interests of cultivators and non-cultivators are basically different. Cultivators make economic gains through active *utilization* of factors of production (land, capital, labor), whereas non-cultivators obtain wealth through the *supply* and *manipulation* of two of these factors, land and capital. Under a normal land-tenure system, the interests of cultivators and non-cultivators are different but complementary, the relationship between them being analogous to that be-

[53] Hui-sun Tang, *Land Reform in Free China* (Taipei, Taiwan, 1954), p. 118.
[54] For a description of the scope and intensity of the informational activities of the KMT, see *ibid.*, p. 70; Wang and Chang, *op. cit.*, pp. 14–16.

TABLE 59

RURAL AWARENESS OF KUOMINTANG IDEOLOGY, TAINAN, TAIWAN,
TAINAN SURVEY, 1968

Question: "What are the three principles
in 'The Three Principles of the People'?"

| | Response to Question | | | | | | | | | |
| Status of Respondents | Correct | | Partially Correct | | Incorrect | | No Answer | | Total | |
	Num- ber	Per- cent	Num- ber	Per- cent	Num- ber	Per- cent	Num- ber	Per- cent	Num- ber	Per- cent
Cultivating farmers	203	72.50	20	7.14	1	0.36	56	20.00	280	100
Landlords	28	71.79	4	10.26	0	0.00	7	17.95	39	100
Non-farmers, but family owning land	114	95.00	2	1.67	0	0.00	4	3.33	120	100
Non-farmers, owning no land	33	76.74	2	4.65	1	2.33	7	16.28	43	100
Status unidenti- fied	55	80.88	5	7.35	0	0.00	8	11.76	68	100
Total	433	78.73	33	6.00	2	0.36	82	14.91	550	100

SOURCE: See Appendix III. N = 550

tween industrial manufacturers and bankers. In the case of a defective land-tenure system the two interests are different and conflicting. Non-cultivators tend to exploit cultivators, and cultivators frequently become subservient to non-cultivators.

In reforming their tenure systems, both Mexico and Taiwan have clearly taken cognizance of the difference in the interests of cultivators and non-cultivators and have terminated the traditional, exploitive-subservient pattern of relationship between them. The two countries differ, however, in their approach to the creation of new patterns of relationship.

Mexico: Differentiation Through Separate Organizations

In Mexico, the ill-feelings between landowners and landless *campesinos* generated by the traumatic experiences of revolution precluded any possibility of collaboration between these farming interests. In the face of this situation, Mexico simply created separate rural organizations for the reform beneficiaries and for all others having an interest in agriculture. The *ejidatarios* formed the *Confederación Nacional Campesina*, which became the largest group within the farm sector of the PRI. Private landowners organized the *Confederación Nacional de la Pequeña Propiedad Agrícola* (the National Confederation of Small Agricultural Proprietors, CNPPA), which, with a membership of 850,000, constituted the most numerous group within the PRI's popular sector. For several decades, the CNC has placed pressure upon the government to accelerate land redistribution and to allocate more public funds to *ejidos*. The CNPPA, on the other hand, has repeatedly sought through the federal Congress to raise the ceiling of private holdings and to provide protection to these holdings against land-invasion activities. For instance, landowners in Taretan, Michoacán, formed in 1965 an *Asociacion de Pequeños Propietarios*. "Its thirty members joined for only one reason—to protect themselves against the possibility of invasion of their land by ejidatarios. They hope to receive counselling on legal steps necessary to safeguard their property as well as representation before governmental agencies in Morelia if such an invasion occurs." [55]

Though working at cross purposes, the CNC and the CNPPA show no serious hostility toward each other, for they belong to the same political party, and use relatively little violence to advance their respective claims. However, the differentiation of rural interests in Mexico reaches beyond the bifurcation of the rural community into the CNC and the CNPPA. Differentiation is also evident in the multiplication of other rural organizations, each of which attempts to articulate a particular interest. Maintaining nation-wide—or at least strong regional—membership and structure, these other organizations include the *Confederación Nacional de Ganaderos* (the National Cattlemen Association), the Mexican Agronomists' Society, the *Unión General de Obreros y Campesinos de Mexico* (the General Union of Workers and Peasants of Mexico, UGOCM), and the *Central Campesina Independiente* (CCI). The last two organizations deserve further attention, for the appearance of these organizations not only signifies an intensification of the conflict between the *campesinos* and the large landowners, but also a split within the ranks of the *campesinos*. Radical in their tactics and maintaining no ties with the PRI, the UGOCM and the CCI pose a challenge to both the large landowning interests and the established peasant organization, the CNC.

---

[55] Henry A. Landsberger and Cynthia N. Hewitt, "Preliminary Report on a Case Study of Mexican Peasant Organization" (Ithaca: Cornell University, New York State School of Industrial and Labor Relations, 1966, mimeo.), p. 59.

The UGOCM, founded by the Communists in 1949 but never legally recognized by the government, is perhaps the largest rural dissident group in Mexico. Its peasant strength is found primarily in the agriculturally more developed regions of Veracruz, Sonora, and Laguna.[56] For years, the organization has criticized the inadequacies of the services of the ejidal bank, agitated for forceful and speedy land redistribution, and organized large-scale land invasions. Led by Communist leaders Jacinto López (the Secretary-General of the UGOCM) and Ramón Danzos Palomino, the peasants attempted during 1958 to invade the 400,000 hectares of land of the American-owned Cananea Cattle Company and actually seized the company's radio station. In the same year, the UGOCM led squatters to invade lands in Culiacán Valley in Sinoloa, the Mexicali region in Baja California, Norte, and threatened to seize all lands held by foreigners along the frontier. In each instance, the government acted with swift retaliation by forcefully removing the invaders, and imprisoned Jacinto López and other leaders. But also in 1958, the government expropriated the Cananea land for redistribution and bolstered the CNC's local branch in the area through increased credits and other benefits, thus enabling the CNC to win over from the UGOCM a sizable number of the Cananea peasants. López renewed his agitational activities in 1959, when he came out of jail after the Cananea episode, organizing 3000 squatters to seize land in Ciudad Obregón in the State of Sonora. The invaders were again repulsed, but the Agrarian Department "promised a solution of the land problem within the law." In 1961 and 1962, the UGOCM and a number of other rural organizations sponsored several "hunger caravans" to march to Mexico City in demand for land.[57]

Pursuing the same line of agitational activity, the *Central Campesina Independiente* came into existence in January 1963. Formed by twelve peasant unions, with participation by the Communists and, initially,

[56] The precise number of the members of the UGOCM is not known. Estimates varied widely. Vicente Lombardo Toledano indicated in 1961 that the organization had 77 regional federations, 6 state federations with a total membership of about 300,000, of which 70 percent were peasants. Another account stated that initially the UGOCM and its affiliates had as many as 500,000 members, but the membership soon diminished considerably. Still another study revealed that the UGOCM had 20,000 members in the mid-1950s. And a report of the United States Bureau of Labor Statistics noted in 1963 the UGOCM membership had declined to about 10,000. Huizer, *op. cit.* (n. 12 above), pp. 111 and 113; and Lord, *op. cit.* (n. 18 above), p. 14.

[57] For a description of the organization and activities of the UGOCM, see Karl M. Schmitt, *Communism in Mexico: A Study in Political Frustration* (Austin: The University of Texas Press, 1965), pp. 178–182; and Huizer, *op. cit.*, pp. 111–116.

endorsed by Lázaro Cárdenas, the CCI consisted of many dissident peasant leaders who were previously affiliated with the CNC and the UGOCM. Though claiming to be a nationwide organization, the CCI limited its operations largely to Mexico's north and northwest regions and Laguna. Since its founding, the CCI organized land invasions in Baja California and Chihuahua and led a peasant march to Mexico City. Its effectiveness, however, was curtailed by internal rivalries. One faction, led by Alfonso Garzón, the former CNC leader in Baja California, preferred to pursue a radical agrarian policy but without antagonizing the PRI and the CNC. The other faction, headed by Communist Ramón Danzos Palomino, formerly of the UGOCM, insisted on carrying on massive agitational activities, effecting a clear break with the PRI and the government.[58]

It is hard to assess precisely the degree of impact of the activities of these radical organizations on the government's rural policy. But they appear to have prompted the government to adopt a more positive attitude toward the problem of the landless *campesinos*. Referring to one of these organizations, Karl M. Schmitt has commented:

> In March the Attorney General reported that his office had about two thousand complaints against the squatters under study. The government in most instances has moved swiftly with a combination of force and concessions to head off these demonstrations before serious violence developed. The UGOCM may not be able to take credit for all agrarian agitation, but it has done more than any other organization in Mexico to point up the needs of the Mexican peasant and to do something about them.[59]

Similarly, the CCI has been able to obtain some satisfaction for its demands. For example, partially in response to CCI agitation activities, the Diaz Ordáz administration reached an agreement with the United States to reduce salination of the Colorado River, which had severely damaged

---

[58] For information on the CCI, see Schmitt, *op. cit.*, pp. 245–246; Huizer, *op. cit.*, pp. 116–117; and Bo Anderson and James D. Cockroft, "Control and Cooptation in Mexican Politics," *International Journal of Comparative Sociology*, VII (March 1966), 19, and 24–26. According to Schmitt, the formation of the CCI has absorbed many of the activities of another radical organization, the *Unión Central Sociedades de Credito Colectivo Ejidal* (the Central Union of Credit Societies of Collective Ejidos, UCSE). With its headquarters in La Laguna, the UCSE first sought to increase credit supply and to strengthen the *ejido*. Increasing dissatisfaction with the government's credit program, however, radicalized the UCSE. The organization also sponsored land invasions. See Schmitt, *op. cit.*, pp. 186, 245. Cf. Huizer, *op. cit.*, pp. 132–139.

[59] Schmitt, *op. cit.*, p. 182.

the agricultural land of the Mexicali Valley. In addition, the government has promised funds for rehabilitation of the land ruined by salt water.[60] Thus, Mexico has seen, in recent years, a division of the agricultural communities into roughly three broad sections: the *ejidatarios*, the private landowners, and the landless *campesinos*. Each section has its own organizations, goals, and tactics. But all are concerned with the pace and scope of land reform.

Taiwan: Differentiation Through Equitable Representation

Precisely the opposite pattern of differentiation of interests operates in Taiwan. Without creating an organization exclusively for the reform beneficiaries, Taiwan in the post-reform era envisioned continued—or renewed—cooperation within the same rural institutions between the cultivators and non-cultivators. Of course, during the implementation of land reform, the interests of the landlords, on the one hand, and the tenants and farm laborers, on the other, were clearly antagonistic. One's gain was precisely the other's loss. But for a number of reasons, the enmity of these different tenure groups did not carry on into the rural organizations of the post-reform era. First, as Taiwan's land-reform program was thoroughly implemented, it practically reduced the farm community to one of small but productive farmers. In the post-reform era, Taiwan has a lower Gini index of land concentration than any country studied here. (See Table 32, above.) There is no longer a landlord class opposed to a tenant one. Second, as noted in Chapter III, the island suffered more from the problem of land fragmentation than from extreme inequality. *Haciendas* of the type prevalent in Latin America never existed in Taiwan, nor did the deep-seated antagonisms between landlord and tenant. Aside from an extremely small number of absentee landlords, the bulk of the cultivating farmers possessed a mixed-tenure status. Tenants might own some tiny pieces of land; owner-farmers might rent out part of their holdings; landlords might work on part of their own land; farmer laborers might sometimes rent or even own some land; and joint ownership was widely practiced. Somewhat simplified by reform, this complex system persists today. The lack of clear demarcation of Taiwan's tenure groups naturally softened inter-group contention both before and after reform. Third, during reform, animosity between the reform beneficiaries and the landowners was kept to a minimum and was short-lived. The fact is that the beneficiaries

[60] Anderson and Cockroft, *op. cit.*, p. 25.

made only modest gains, and the landowners lost relatively little. The reduction of rent and the transfer of landownership during the reform period were done promptly, peacefully, and in an orderly way. These proceedings are contrasted to the drawn-out, violent, and chaotic process of land redistribution in Mexico, which prolonged inter-group animosity. Finally, there was an awareness on the part of all those having a stake in farming—tenants, owner-farmers, farm laborers, landlords—that their cooperation within the same rural institutions was in their common interest. The agricultural community in Taiwan is small in size and resources. To separate the beneficiaries and other farming interests—all of whom contained a substantial portion of farmers of mixed-tenure status—into different organizations would be a proposition difficult to realize. Even if it were implemented, it would lead to waste in the utilization of resources and duplication in programs. The integration of farmers of different tenure groups into the same rural organizations that perform services and functions beneficial to all was, therefore, a much more practicable and desirable approach.

After all, land reform is not aimed at perpetuation of rural antagonism but at the accommodation of different agricultural interests. As Chen Cheng has put it,

> Everybody strives for "self-interest," which is a sin only when it is promoted at the expense of others. The interests of farmers are identical. With the elimination of exploitation by landlords there is no reason why farmers should not cooperate with one another closely. For these reasons, self-governing bodies organized by farmers themselves and devoted to the promotion of their own interests will be more efficient than government bureaucracies.[61]

The important point is, of course, that these organizations must be self-governing entities in which inter-group exploitation no longer exists. This is precisely what has been accomplished by the creation of the Farm Tenancy Committees and the reorganization of the Farmers' Associations and the Irrigation Associations. The statutory assurance as well as the practical establishment of adequate and fair representation for all tenure groups in these organizations make them truly institutions of all farmers (broadly defined here to include landlords), for all farmers, and by all farmers. This is in sharp contrast, it might be pertinent to note, to the Indian rural cooperatives, which admit all tenure groups without provid-

---

[61] *Op. cit.* (n. 29 above), p. 107.

ing adequate safeguards and representation to the small *kisans*. The Indian cooperatives, consequently, become rural organizations of all farmers but serve only the well-to-do.

The foregoing discussion leads to one general observation. Taiwanese rural organizations seem to have achieved both differentiation of interests as well as their accommodation. Mexican rural organizations have preserved differentiation of interests but have perpetuated their antagonisms. (Indian rural organizations sought neither differentiation of interests nor removal of antagonisms.)

ADAPTATION

The principal rural organizations of Mexico and Taiwan are responsible for the execution of reform programs as well as for the provision of services to reform beneficiaries. These organizations are the CNC of Mexico, the Farm Tenancy Committees, the Farmers' Associations, and the Irrigation Associations of Taiwan. The following discussion will be limited to these institutions, as they are the largest, oldest, and most important of all rural organizations in Mexico and Taiwan respectively.

In the past decades, these organizations appear to have performed their functions with considerable success. The CNC has seen to it that nearly half of Mexico's cultivated land was placed in the hands of its membership. It has secured peasant representation on all levels of government and obtained many public material benefits for the *ejidatarios*. Similarly, in Taiwan, the Farm Tenancy Committees, the Farmers' Associations, and the Irrigation Associations have helped create a system of small but vigorously growing farms. They have likewise obtained for the farmers a major share of representation in local government. It should be noted that though both Mexican and Taiwanese rural organizations have demonstrated a capacity for growth and change, the CNC has lately appeared to be less adaptable to rural needs than have the three organizations in Taiwan.

Mexico: Stagnancy of the CNC

In Chapter VIII, the organizational difficulties of the *ejido* (the basic component of the CNC) have already been discussed. In the following analysis, the activities of the CNC itself will be reviewed. Though maintaining a nation-wide structure parallel to the governmental hierarchy, the CNC has not been particularly effective in channeling and articulating *campesino* demands. The CNC does channel *campesinos'* complaints and requests to the government, but these complaints and requests are frequently individually transmitted without much coordination. Governmental agencies thus do not feel as obliged to respond positively to *campesino* pressures as when these are well articulated and presented with the backing of the entire *campesino* community. This is one principal reason why the *ejidatarios*, who form the largest bloc in the PRI, cannot exert political influence on the party commensurate with their numerical strength.

The foremost concern of the CNC is to bring land to the landless. Over the years, many *campesinos* have obtained land, but the CNC could have exerted greater pressure on the government to extend the scope of reform. To illustrate, the Agrarian Department has reported that for 1940 to 1943, of the 1,112 petitions for land, 691 were denied; and in the same period, while about 500,000 hectares of land were expropriated, almost 2,400,000 hectares, nearly five times the expropriated land, were declared "*inafectabilidad* (not subject to expropriation)." In 1940, about 1.5 million *campesinos* had received land, but an equal number had not.[62] Twenty-eight years later, in 1968, Noberto Aguirre, Chief of the Department of Agrarian Affairs and Colonization, reported that there remained in the country some 25 million hectares of undeveloped land, of which only 800,000 were suitable for farming. He "estimated that these 25 million hectares would support only 300,000 campesinos, or 15 per cent of the 2 million now waiting for land." [63]

The shortage of farm land for redistribution to the landless is only partially caused by the exhaustion of potential farm land. It is also caused by the relatively high ceilings established for private holdings. As seen in Chapter VII, Mexican law prescribes a set of ceilings for so-called small farm properties (*pequeña propiedad*) which range from 100 to 300 hectares of crop land. However, the law has a different prescription for future grants to *campesinos*: a minimum of 10 hectares of irrigated land or 20 hectares of seasonal land. In reality, this is the *maximum* any *campesino* waiting for land can hope to receive. To put it simply, a double standard is established for the allocation of Mexico's land: 10 to 20 hectares for the *campesinos* and 100 to 300 hectares for the "small proprietors." That this glaring discrepancy can be written into the law reflects to a certain extent the ineffectiveness of the CNC in articulating and protecting the interests of the *campesinos*.

[62] Mexico Departmento Agrario, *Primer Congreso Nacional Revolucionario de Derecho Agrario* (Memoria, Mexico, D.F., 1946), pp. 330–331. Cited in Huizer, *op. cit.*, p. 95.
[63] *The New York Times*, August 12, 1968, p. 10.

The incompetence of the CNC is manifested not only in its acquiescence with this abnormality but also in its permissiveness in allowing small proprietors to recover an important legal right—the right to seek an injunction (*ampro*) in land expropriation proceedings. After the initiation of land reform, this right was first abolished because *hacendados* had used it to delay implementation. But in 1947, a constitutional amendment was adopted granting private landowners injunction rights in regard to properties declared not liable. When this right was restored to the landowners, the CNC protested the action but did little else. In fact, some deputies in the federal Congress and representatives of the CNC "noted at times quite openly that it was not convenient to bother the peasants with the details of [the] legislation, even if disadvantageous, in order to avoid agitation in the countryside which was considered bad for the country as a whole." [64] Similarly, Frente Zapatista, a group of followers of Zapata closely related to the PNR and the CNC, commented: "The political moment is not fit for discussion of [agrarian changes], because the simple announcement that the Agrarian Code . . . [would] be reformed in a sense favorable to the creation of new latifundios has provoked unrest among the peasants, unrest, which if not soothed, may disturb the huge and patriotic plans of work which the government of President [Miguel] Aleman is realizing." [65] Thus, for the peace and welfare of all people but the peasants, peasant interest had to be sacrificed by their own representatives!

Under the circumstances, it is not surprising to find that some "small proprietors" have become very large landowners. It was reported in 1960 that "there were still some estates of more than a million acres, that 551 haciendas had from 123,500 to 247,000 acres each, and that all in all, 9,600 private owners possessed a total of over 197 million acres." [66] After an extensive tour of the farm areas in the country's northwest, Henry Giniger observed in 1966 that "in Sonora a few small landowners have become big ones. . . . In the land registry offices each holding of 250 acres is in the name of a different person, often all of them members of one family. Cases of babies with land titles are not unknown. . . . Some of the holdings, commonly termed here 'family latifundia' go up to 5,000 acres." [67] Referring to the reappearance of *latifundia*, François Chevalier noted that

[64] Huizer, *op. cit.*, p. 104.
[65] Quoted in *ibid*.
[66] Brandenburg, *op. cit* (n. 23 above), p. 253.
[67] *The New York Times*, May 17, 1966 p. 17.

"small proprietors," acquired through the assistance of friendly government officials large commercial farms and became so-called "nylon farmers." [68] Many of them also bought farms for speculation rather than for agricultural pursuits.[69] All of these irregularities took place under the eyes of the CNC, but it did little to correct them.

The CNC's failings are not limited to its inability to bring land to the landless *campesinos*, who are its prospective members. The *ejidatarios*, who are the CNC's present members, also suffer from the laxity and impotence of the organization. The CNC has not been helpful in inducing the government to resolve a problem prevalent in the *ejidos*. Today, after half of a century of reform, only 15 percent of the *ejidatarios* have received legal title to the lands on which they have been working. To many *ejidatarios*, lack of title is a major economic liability, for it is difficult for them to obtain agricultural loans to be used on farms to which they have no title. More important, in regard to another matter—the competition for public funds for rural investment—the CNC has frequently lost out to its rival, the National Confederation of Small Agricultural Proprietors (the CNPPA). The different rates of expansion of publicly financed irrigated areas in *ejido* and private farms (i.e. "small agricultural properties") provide a clear illustration. In 1940, 994,320 hectares of *ejido* land were irrigated, as compared to 905,770 hectares of private land; in 1950, 1,221,-000 hectares of *ejido* land were irrigated as against 1,788,000 hectares of private land; in 1960, the respective areas were 1,428,000 and 2,087,000 hectares.[70] In two decades, the irrigated area in *ejido* land expanded by 43.6 percent; the corresponding figure for private land is thrice that, or 130 percent.

The CNC's loss to the CNPPA in the competition for public rural investment funds is paralleled by the decline of CNC representation in the federal Congress and the rise of political strength of the popular sector of the PRI, of which the CNPPA is the largest constituent unit.[71] Thus, in 1943 the farm sector of the PRI, of which the CNC was the dominant

[68] François Chevalier, *Ejido y Estabilidad en México*, CIENCIAS POLITICAS Y SOCIALES, año XI, No. 42, Oct.-Dic. 1965, UNAM, Mexico, pp. 429–430. Cited in Huizer, *op. cit.*, p. 108.

[69] Manuel Gonzales Ramirez, *La Revolución Social de México*, Vol. III, *El Problema Agrario* (México, Fondo de Cultura Economica, 1966), p. 397. Cited in Huizer, *op. cit.*, p. 109.

[70] Chevalier, *op. cit.*, p. 429. Cited in Huizer, *op. cit.*, p. 108.

[71] The Mexican Congress consists of a 178–member Chamber of Deputies and a 60–member Senate.

part, maintained 46 seats in the Lower House of Congress while the popular sector occupied 78; in 1952, the former had 36 seats, the latter 75; in 1958, the farm and labor sectors of the PRI shared a total of 84 seats, the popular sector alone had 78. A similar trend prevailed in the Senate. In 1943, the farm and labor sectors together controlled slightly less than a majority of seats, while the popular sector had the rest; in 1952, out of the PRI's 58 senatorial seats, the farm sector had 14, the labor sector 5, and the popular sector 39; in 1958, out of the PRI's 60 seats, the farm sector had none, the labor sector 21, and the popular sector 39.[72]

The reasons for the decline in the effectiveness and representativeness of the CNC as a farmer organization appear to lie primarily in the pattern through which the organization has evolved. The politicization of the CNC's leadership, on both national and local levels, has considerably undermined the autonomy of the organization. The fusion of the *campesino* organization and the governing party has frequently led CNC officials to view their offices as sources of power and wealth rather than as vehicles for articulation of *campesino* interests. "Control of the regional machinery of the CNC," L. Vincent Padgett has explained, "in conjunction with the governmental machinery of the *municipio* provides the prospect of influence as well as financial rewards which are difficult to overlook. In a rural *municipio* the CNC organization may well be the only organized interest. Control of that organization is an important step in the formation of a local machine on the basis of which a man can become the boss or *cacique* of the *municipio* for a long time." [73] A new rule of "caciquismo" is now being followed. Having once occupied a position of power, CNC officials would like to perpetuate themselves in office. Through cultivated "friendships" and connections with government officials, and circumventing by various ruses the legal prohibition against re-election, they can continuously keep themselves in power. *Caciquismo* and *continuismo* dictate that CNC officials be more submissive to PRI and government officials, who have the authority in the allocation of rural public funds, than to their constituents, the CNC membership.[74] CNC officials have in time become more concerned with their personal interests than with those of the

[72] Lord, *op. cit.* (n. 18 above), pp. 25–26.

[73] L. Vincent Padgett, *The Mexican Political System* (Boston, 1966), p. 113.

[74] For a case study on the evolution of *caciquismo* and *continuismo* in *ejidos* of Ignacio Romero Vargas in the Municipio of Cuatlancingo, Puebla, see *ibid.*, pp. 114–120. Another case study, indicating an oligarchial tendency in an *ejido* organization in Taretan, Michoacán, can be found in Landsberger and Hewitt, "A Pilot Study of Participation in Rural Organizations," (n. 48 above), pp. 35–36.

organization that they represent. When personal interests and organizational interests are not in accord, it is the latter that receive less attention. In short, the absorption of the CNC by the PRI leads to a subordination of the former to the latter, and this subordination restricts the freedom of the CNC to respond effectively to the needs of its own membership.

The failings of the CNC are not due to the lack of organizational autonomy alone. They can also be explained by the fact that strong ideological infusion into the peasant organization leaves the CNC with little operational flexibility, particularly at its bottom level, the *ejido* organization. Though obviously suffering organizational deficiencies, the *ejido* cannot be reformed. Any tampering with this sacred creature of the revolution would have grave political consequences. At the same time, the government is not willing to break up the well-managed medium and large farms and to convert them into *ejido* holdings, for these farms are the most productive. Facing this dilemma, the government has followed, since the 1940s, a basic policy: it preserves the *ejido* system while making available more public funds to private holdings. Unable to persuade the government to alter this discriminatory policy because it cannot make *ejido* land more productive, the CNC can in no way bring adequate credits, water, and other material inputs to *ejido* areas. Unlike Taiwan, where one rural organization serves farmers of different tenure groups, Mexico has basically two tenure groups, *ejido* and non-*ejido* private holdings, served respectively by two rural organizations, the CNC and the CNPPA. The Mexican arrangement is evidently less rational, for the two Mexican rural organizations, performing essentially the same functions, naturally tend to compete, rather than to collaborate, leading to wasted resources and inter-group jealousies and tensions. The Mexican arrangement is also unfair, for one organization is given preferential treatment and the other practically left stagnant. But for Mexico to follow the Taiwan model is neither desirable from the point of view of the *ejido* and the private farmers nor practicable in light of the almost unbridgeable cleavage between the two tenure groups. Such a fundamental dilemma has not only led to a decline in the CNC's strength and effectiveness in the past, but also perhaps left the organization's future innovative capacity permanently restricted.

Taiwan: Dynamic Growth of Rural Organizations

If the CNC has shown a tendency toward stagnancy and ineffectiveness, the rural organizations of Taiwan have demonstrated a capacity for vigorous growth. Illustrative of the accomplishments of these organizations

TABLE 60

ECONOMIC ACTIVITIES OF TAIWAN FARMERS' ASSOCIATIONS, 1953–1962

Items	1953	1957	1962
	In New Taiwan Dollars		
Business[a]	71,555,428	229,573,934	493,960,652
(Index)	(100.0)	(320.8)	(690.3)
Savings deposits	102,296,878	375,278,464	1,374,202,763
(Index)	(100.0)	(366.9)	(1,343.3)
Loans	81,375,212	290,587,329	983,243,697
(Index)	(100.0)	(357.1)	(1,208.3)
Expenditures			
on extension	12,329,631	35,300,249	71,191,832
(Index)	(100.0)	(286.3)	(577.4)

[a] Purchasing, marketing, storaging, processing and related transactions.

SOURCE: Min-hioh Kwoh, *Farmers' Associations and Their Contribution Toward Agricultural and Rural Development in Taiwan* (Bangkok: FAO, Regional Office for Asia and the Far East, 1964), pp. 10–12.

are the economic activities of the Farmers' Associations. As seen in Table 60, in the ten years after the implementation of the land-to-the-tiller program, these associations, registered phenomenal expansion in every category of economic undertaking—business, savings deposits, loans, and expenditures on agricultural extension. For instance, the expenditure on agricultural extension grew 5.7 times in the period under review, and the volume of saving deposits increased 13.5 times.[75] These statistics indicate the very broad scope and range of services the associations render to the members. They also reflect a growing confidence by the membership in the associations. Whereas the *ejido* and the CNC have had to depend on government banks and agencies for credits, water, and material inputs, the Taiwanese Farmers' Associations together with the Irrigation Associations can now fully meet the farmers' needs out of their own resources.

The economic vitality of the Farmers' Associations also impressed the author during the Tainan survey in 1968. In every one of the sixteen townships of the Tainan *hsien*, the tallest, newest, and most modern building (by local standards) invariably belonged to the Farmers' Associations. Interviews with farmer and non-farmer respondents and inspections of the

[75] The rate of inflation in Taiwan in this 10–year period was mild. One U.S. dollar was equivalent to NT $40 throughout the period.

TABLE 61

Officials of Rural Organizations Serving as Government Officials
Tainan, Taiwan, 1968

Government Officials	Number Interviewed	Farm Tenancy Committees	Farmers' Associations	Irrigation Associations	Total
Hsien	53	2	5	1	8
Township	260	6	48	10	64
Village	25	0	7	2	9
Total	338	8	60	13	81

Source: See Appendix III.

business accounts of these associations clearly indicated that these associations were the most prosperous enterprises in the countryside and that their services were genuinely appreciated. By and large, what was true of the Farmers' Associations in the Tainan *hsien* was also true of those in Taiwan's other fifteen *hsien*.

The growing economic strength of the Farmers' Associations was paralleled by their rising representation in the government. The Tainan survey revealed, for instance, that of the 338 government officials interviewed (on the *hsien*, township, and village levels) 81 (or about one fourth) were either present or former officials of the Farmers' Associations, the Irrigation Associations, or the Farm Tenancy Committees (see Table 61).

Available information indicates that the political strength of these organizations was even greater in Taiwan as a whole than in Tainan. For instance, in 1964, a JCRR official with extensive rural experiences reported that "five of the sixteen [*hsien*] magistrates, one of the five [city] mayors, eleven of the seventy-four members of the Provincial Assembly, over forty per cent of the township office heads, and thirty per cent of the members of the county [*hsien*] and city assemblies were former elected officers of the Farmers' Associations." [76] As of 1968, another informed observer has noted, over 800 Farmers' Association officials were concurrently representatives in the Provincial, County, and Township Assemblies, and 11 were speakers or vice speakers of County Assemblies. "The General Manager

[76] Min-hioh Kwoh, *Farmers' Associations and their Contribution toward Agricultural and Rural Development in Taiwan* (Bangkok, 1964), p. 74.

and three members of the Board of Directors . . . of the Provincial Farmers' Association are Provincial Assemblymen." [77]

In recent years, the Farmers' Associations have gradually made some appearance in the national government. In 1969, when an election was held to fill vacancies in the National Assembly and the Legislative Yuan (parliament), the Farmers' Associations obtained three out of a total of fifteen seats in the National Assembly and one out of a total of eleven seats in the Legislative Yuan.[78] Farmer voters displayed considerable interest in the contest. Either in terms of absolute numbers or in terms of the number of actual voters as a percentage of eligible voters, farmers cast more ballots than practically any other occupational group in the election.[79]

While this trend of growing political representation by rural organizations heartened the farmers, it caused concern in official quarters. Some JCRR officials believed "that since the local FA [Farmers' Association] likely will be financially stronger than the township government, political involvement will lead to the diversion of FA resources to 'pork barrel' activities alien to its charter responsibilities." [80] Sharing this belief, the provisional government adopted a regulation in 1966 prohibiting FA officials from concurrently holding elective positions in the government and offices in the FA.

Mexico and Taiwan Compared

It is of interest to note that though this political restriction on the FA in Taiwan has been criticized as hampering the normal development of institutional links between legislators and farmers,[81] in Mexico, precisely because of its strong politicization, the CNC has lost some of its effectiveness and representativeness as a peasant organization. This seems to account for the relative stagnation of the Mexican CNC and the dy-

[77] Richard Lee Hough, "AID Administration to the Rural Sector: the JCRR Experience in Taiwan and Its Application in Other Countries" (Washington, D.C.: Agency for International Development, Discussion Paper, No. 17, 1968), p. 28.

[78] *The Central Daily News*, December 21, 1969, p. 1. Among the Farmers' Association officials elected to national offices were Wan-cheng Chu and Chi-yo Lui, respectively the President and the General Manager of the Provincial Farmers' Association.

[79] Both territorial (regional) electorates and occupational electorates were established for the election. For an analysis of voter turnout by region and occupation, see *ibid.*, December 30, 1969, p. 3.

[80] Hough, *op. cit.*, p. 28.

[81] See, for instance, Richard Lee Hough's view in *ibid.*, p. 29.

namic growth of Taiwanese rural organizations. As an integral part of the PRI, the CNC has not been able over the years to assert its organizational autonomy or to promote its interests independent of those of the official party. It is an organization *of* the farmers, not *for* the farmers. The Taiwanese FA, in contrast, maintains an identity separate from the KMT and autonomy in its operations. As a number of field observers have commented, land reform and the development of rural organizations in Taiwan *"improved the capacity of local institutions to articulate the interests of the rural population; . . . and . . . generated rural capacities and attitudes that are substantially independent of the politics of the central government."* [82] Commented another observer: "Notwithstanding their non-political origins, [the rural] organizations had increasing political implications. . . . Indeed, it appeared that the stirrings of a . . . democratic order were manifest at the local level, particularly in rural communities among Farmers' and Irrigation Associations. . . . The Farmers' Associations were, to a considerable extent, based upon local initiative, management, and control." [83] Thus, these organizations can innovate and change, always trying to preserve the interests of their own membership.

In sum, rural organizations in both Mexico and Taiwan appear much more institutionalized than their counterparts in the six other countries examined in this book. But the differences between the rural organizations of Mexico and Taiwan are still notable. Taiwanese rural organizations seem to have a more rational structure and a greater capacity for innovation. In addition, Taiwanese rural organizations first acquired their service functions before acquiring political functions, and the latter have been kept subordinate to the former. Mexican rural organizations acquired political functions before they became service-oriented, and their political role may well be a major factor restricting their capacity for growth and change.

[82] John D. Montgomery, Rufus B. Hughes, and Raymond A. Davis, "Rural Improvement and Political Development: the JCRR Model" (Washington, D.C.: Agency for International Development, 1964 mimeo.), p. 7 (emphasis original).

[83] Neil H. Jacoby, *U.S. Aid to Taiwan: a Study of Foreign Aid, Self-Help, and Development* (New York: Frederick A. Praeger, Publishers, 1967), pp. 113–14.

XIII

RURAL STABILITY

In what way does land reform affect rural stability? Two conflicting opinions on this subject are often advanced. On the one hand, many assume that since a defective tenure system is a source of peasant discontent and rural tension, a public program seeking to correct tenure defects will alleviate such discontent and tension, thus orienting the farming community toward peaceful agricultural pursuits. On the other hand, it may be said that as a program entailing drastic, compulsory changes in the tenure system, land reform will result in the immediate disturbance of established relationships among the peasants, the landlords, and the government. Land reform, one can argue, may actually exacerbate the tension between peasants and landlords, invite landlords to defy public authority, and incite peasants to make excessive demands upon society. Thus land reform has the potential for great instability.

This division of opinion is more apparent than real. For both opinions may be valid and compatible, and the difference between them can be attributable to the different time perspectives from which the impact of reform on stability is assessed. One opinion is concerned with the long-term consequences of land reform; the other deals with its short-term impact. To appraise the effect of land reform on stability, it appears useful to discuss first the concept of stability.

The Concept of Stability

In today's developing world, where economic, social, and political transformations are factually and aspirationally a given condition, stability defined as the continuation of the status quo is no longer a relevant concept. More appropriately, stability may be considered a situation in which a community can purposefully adjust itself to a continuously changing environment. As Lucian W. Pye has put it, stability is the ability to adapt to change, not to prevent it.[1] One "crucial aspect of modernization," S. N. Eisenstadt has similarly observed, is "the ability to maintain 'sustained' growth in the major institutional spheres and to develop an institutional structure capable of absorbing such changes with relatively few eruptions and breakdowns."[2] In short, stability signifies adaptability. In contrast, instability may refer to a condition in which the rigidity of a social system provokes the forces of change to resort to large-scale violence to achieve their intended objectives.

Two well-known theories explaining massive violence or revolution are relevant to the present inquiry. The Marxian theory suggests that a prevalent feeling of economic deprivation may occasion a revolution. Proceeding from the class-struggle theory, Karl Marx and Friedrich Engels asserted, over a century ago, that "the proletariat alone is a really revolutionary class." This was so because, as "the lowest stratum of our present society," "the proletariat . . . cannot stir, cannot raise itself up, without the whole superincumbent strata of official society being sprung into the air. . . . The proletarians have nothing to lose but their chains."[3] In contrast, the Tocquevillean theory holds that it is not absolute poverty but a general improvement of well-being after a prolonged period of economic deprivation that will give rise to revolution. In analyzing the French revolution, Alexis de Tocqueville argued:

> It was precisely in those parts of France where there had been most improvement [before the revolution] that popular discontent ran highest. . . . For it is not always when things are going from bad to worse that revolutions break out. On the contrary, it oftener happens that when a people which has put up with an oppressive rule over a long period without protest suddenly finds the government relaxing its pressure, it takes up arms against it.[4]

Both of these theories share the supposition that the gap between people's economic aspirations and economic reality is the major source of instability.[5] Aspirations are what people expect to be due them; reality refers

[1] *Aspects of Political Development* (Boston, 1966), p. 75.

[2] "Breakdowns of Modernization," *Economic Development and Cultural Change*, XII (July 1964), 347.

[3] Karl Marx and Friedrich Engels, *Manifesto of the Communist Party* (New York: International Publishers Co., 1948), pp. 19–20, 44.

[4] Alexis de Tocqueville, *The Old Regime and the French Revolution*, trans. Stuart Gilbert (Garden City, N.Y.: Doubleday & Co., 1955), p. 176.

[5] Raymond Tanter and Manus Midlarsky call this gap as "revolutionary gap" and suggest that "the larger the revolutionary gap, the longer and the more violent the

to what they are actually given. The widening of the gap will result in an enlargement of the number of people susceptible to the persuasion of violent change. When the gap widens to the breaking point, massive violence occurs. It may well be that this breaking point can be reached as a consequence of rapidly deteriorating economic reality, or of fast-rising aspirations, or of both. Therefore, to preserve stability the essential task is, at least, to prevent the gap from widening and, at best, to close the gap. This is a delicate and very difficult task. For in the developing countries today both aspirations and economic reality constantly change. To achieve stability requires not only that economic and social adjustments be continuously forthcoming but also that they come at the proper time. To meet this requirement, the government of a developing country must have a keen perception of the direction of social change and a capacity for innovation. But these are qualities that governments of most developing countries do not possess. Consequently instability becomes a perennial and widespread phenonmenon in these countries.

Defective Land Tenure and Instability

Does a defective land-tenure system bear a positive relationship to political instability? Many consider so. For instance, in a comparative study of the land-tenure systems, political instability, and economic conditions of forty-seven countries—including developing, developed, Communist, and non-Communist ones—Bruce M. Russett first hypothesized: "Inequality of land distribution does bear a relation to political instability, but that relationship is not a strong one, . . ." [6] However, he later added

---

revolution may be." "A Theory of Revolution," *Journal of Conflict Revolution*, XI (September 1967), 270–271. At the time of final revision of this manuscript, I became aware of a number of other works closely parallel to the discussion here. Though much more elaborate than the present chapter, these works substantiate the argument that the aspiration-reality gap is the source of instability. See Ted Robert Gurr, *Why Men Rebel* (Princeton, N.J.: Princeton University Press, 1970), and Gurr's article on "A Comparative Study of Civil Strife" and an article on "Social Change and Political Violence: Cross-National Patterns" by Ivo K. Feierabend, Rosalind L. Feierabend, and Betty A. Nesvold, in *Violence in America, Historical and Comparative Perspectives*, A Report to the National Commission on the Causes and Prevention of Violence by Hugh Davis Graham and Ted Robert Gurr, Vol. II (Washington, D.C.: U.S. Government Printing Office, 1969).

[6] Russett, "Inequality and Instability, The Relation of Land Tenure to Politics," *World Politics*, XVI (April 1964), 449. Russett's data include the following categories: Gini index of land distribution; percentage of landowners who hold, in aggre-

an important qualification. In a poor, predominantly agricultural society where inequality of land distribution is combined with a high tenancy rate, instability is very likely. In such a case, he went on to say, a large number of people possessing little land and no alternative sources of wealth besides agriculture are condemned to permanent poverty.[7] In other words, defective land tenure creates a situation in which the aspirations of a large number of farmers can easily exceed what their economic pursuits can offer them. They can be persuaded to resort to arms to improve their economic plight. In their study of revolution, Raymond Tanter and Manus Midlarsky advanced a similar hypothesis: "Where the 'revolutionary gap' between aspiration and expectations is largely due to a high level of inequality of land distribution, we would expect an increase in the probability of revolution."[8] Collating Russett's land-tenure statistics with their own data on political instability, the two authors concluded that "revolutions occurred in those societies with a higher degree of land inequality."[9]

Obviously the mere existence of a land-tenure-created aspiration-reality gap represents only an instability potential. It is only when this gap suddenly widens that the instability potential is likely to be converted into an actuality.[10] Historically, the widening of this gap has been due mainly to a deterioration of the economic reality brought about by natural or historical disasters, such as persistent and widespread drought, flood, pest, famine, or war. It was under these conditions that politically ambitious men found it easy to incite the mass peasantry to arms. Rural rebellion represented a rejection of a worsening economic reality, but it did not necessarily result in the change of the tenure system, which remained in the post-rebellion era as a continued source of the aspiration-reality gap. When the gap widened again under similar catastrophic conditions, another rebellion would be likely. The long history of China

---

gate, a half of the total farm land; tenancy rate; changeover of executive personnel; number of internal wars (actual and attempted); death rate in internal civil strife; gross national product; proportion of labor force in agriculture. The time periods of these data varied, but most were between 1945 and the early 1960s.

[7] *Ibid.*, 452.

[8] Tanter and Midlarsky, *op. cit.*, 276. It should be pointed out that the authors used the term "expectations" to describe what is called "economic reality" in the present study. See *ibid.*, 270–271.

[9] *Ibid.*, 277.

[10] Cf. Donald Hindlay, "Political Conflict Potential, Politicization, and the Peasantry in the Underdeveloped Countries," *Asian Studies* (The Philippines), III (December 1965), 470–489.

provides the most pertinent example.[11] In contemporary times, in contrast, the widening of the gap is largely due to the rise of aspirations rather than to the deterioration of reality. This rise of aspirations is, in turn, caused partially by the increase of peasant political consciousness and partially by the efforts of those movements that constantly emphasize to the peasants the undesirability of the existing land-tenure system and the need for its change. Rural violence is a forceful expression of the need to improve a stagnant economic reality. These two patterns—historical and contemporary—of conversion of rural instability potential to reality are graphically depicted in Figure 1.

Short-Term Destabilizing Consequences of Land Reform

If a defective land-tenure system has an instability potential, does land reform assure stability? As mentioned earlier, the advocates of reform often assume it does. The reality, however, is more complicated than this assumption implies. In fact, under certain specified conditions, land reform may negatively affect stability, creating destabilizing consequences.

First, to introduce land reform during civil war may intensify or extend the conflict. The reason is simple. During a civil war, the government of a developing country often finds it necessary to rely upon landlords to preserve tranquility in remote areas where government authority cannot reach. Hence, when confronted with the necessity for initiating land reform, the elite becomes very cautious. It is aware of the danger that to introduce a drastic reform program is to reduce the power of landlords, therefore freeing certain peasants from the control of both the landlords and the government. Concerned with the loyalty of both landlords and peasants, the elite generally cannot offer a reform program more beneficial to the peasants than what the rebels can promise. This was the case with

---

[11] Barrington Moore, Jr. has advanced the hypothesis that in a rural society in which there is a diffusion of power, peasant rebellion is not likely, whereas an agrarian society tightly controlled by a centralized bureaucracy is vulnerable to such outbreaks. *Social Origins of Dictatorship and Democracy: Lord and Peasant in the Making of the Modern World* (Boston: Beacon Press, 1966), p. 459. This hypothesis seems to explain very well the agrarian movements in historical India and China, the two countries that are included in Moore's study. But it does not appear to explain fully the cases of the Huk rebellion in the Philippines and *la Violencia* in Colombia; in both of these countries the rural power structure was rather diffuse. One may more appropriately argue that when in an agrarian society the aspiration-reality gap suddenly widens, peasant rebellion becomes likely, irrespective of the nature of the political system operating in the society.

FIGURE XIII-1

DEFECTIVE LAND TENTUBE AND RURAL INSTABILITY: MAJOR PATTERNS
OF CONVERSION OF INSTABILITY POTENTIAL TO ACTUALITY

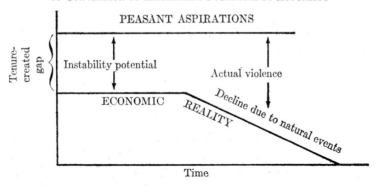

HISTORICAL PATTERN

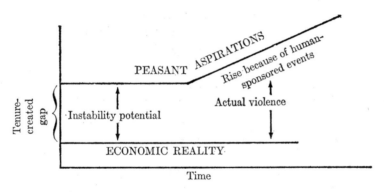

CONTEMPORARY PATTERN

the Kuomintang during its mainland rule, the Madero government in
Mexico, and the South Vietnamese Government today.[12] Either taking

[12] In a statistical study of the land-tenure conditions and the Viet Cong insurgency
in twenty-six South Vietnamese provinces, Edward J. Mitchell concluded: "From the
point of view of government control, the ideal province in South Vietnam would be
one in which few peasants farm their own land, the distribution of landholdings is
unequal, no land redistribution has taken place, . . ." In other words, a relative
stability existed in areas where there was no land reform. This was so, Mitchell explained, because "there exists in [these] areas . . . a powerful landlord class exercising
firm control over a conservative peasantry which has thoroughly rationalized the in-
evitability of the existing situation. It is not these peasants who revolt, but those who"
have been freed from the control of their landlords. Edward J. Mitchell, "Inequality

little action beyond verbal advocacy for reform, or implementing only a modest program, the ruling elites saw the Communists, the Zapatas, and Viet Cong win peasant support by offering more radical programs. In these cases, the ruling elites excited peasant aspirations to a level that they could not satisfy. This is a working of the Tocquevillean hypothesis. At the same time, the peasants, already in the midst of a state of armed conflict, were easily persuaded of the value of violent change. They joined the battle, extending the scale of conflict. This is not to suggest that the ruling elite should or should not introduce land reform during a civil war, or that if it introduces one, it will necessarily lose the war. Thus in the Mexican civil war, Madero (who first advocated land reform) lost, but his successor Carranza (who actually launched the reform) won. What is suggested here is that in initiating reform during a civil war the elite must be prepared to face the destabilizing consequences the program can create.

Second, land reform may also lead to instability when the government, after having engaged in reform measures for a period of time, is unable to make reform benefits available to a growing peasantry, or is too slow in doing so. As a result of the agitations of radical movements, the disaffected peasant may resort to such measures as land invasions, violent protests, or demonstrations. The recent experiences of Mexico and India show this. As mentioned in the last chapter, because of the shortage of land for redistribution and because of the swelling ranks of the landless *campesinos*, Mexico has since the late 1950s seen some of these farmers being led by the UGOCM, the CCI, and other left-oriented organizations to launch demonstrations, "hunger caravans," and *paracaidismo* (parachuting, i.e., land invasion). In recent years, these forceful actions have spread to many places including Sinaloa, Sonora, Baja California, Zacatecas, San Luis Potosí, and Guerrero.[13] Similar events also occurred in

---

and Insurgency, a Statistical Study of South Vietnam," *World Politics*, XX (April 1968), 421–438, at 437–438. Applying this thesis to his study of the Huk insurgency, Mitchell elaborated: "It can be argued that an external threat to the community in the form of a disciplined guerrilla force can best be handled when the structure of authority is simple. Landlords, with clear interests in defending the village, may be able to efficiently organize their tenants and debtors into a resistance. A more democratic community of small independent farmers may prove indecisive and incapable of organizing a defense." Mitchell, "Some Econometrics of the Huk Rebellion." *The American Political Science Review*, LXIII (December, 1969), 1170.

[13] Gerrit Huizer, *On Peasant Unrest in Latin America* (Washington, D.C., 1969), pp. 114–116; Thomas F. Carroll, "Land Reform as an Explosive Force in Latin

India, "Because of the government's failure to act on land reform and other problems," former Indian Deputy Premier Morarji Desai said in 1970, India was going through a period of lawlessness. Thus, led by the Communists and socialists, tens of thousands of farmers started a nation-wide "land grab" movement in 1969. They took "up their pitchforks and hoes and sticks to seize the land of the jotedars, or big farmers. In the last year [1969] more than 300,000 acres have been taken this way." These activities were intensified in 1970. The farmers seized "farms, landed estates, . . . golf courses and a race track in a campaign to force land reform on the Indian government." From August 1969 to August 1970, about 20,000 demonstrating farmers were arrested.[14] Ironically, the Green Revolution which has begun to alleviate the Indian food crisis, heightened the level of rural discontent. Commented *The New York Times* in an editorial entitled "A Green Revolution Turns Red":

> The explanation [for this ironic development] is that in nations like India where there has been little effective land reform, the benefits of larger yields accrue to a relatively few landowners. . . . They are . . . investing in tractors and other devices that lower the demand for farm labor and thus aggravate the problem of the dispossessed.
>
> As a result, the green revolution has been turning red in wide-spread areas of rural India where landless peasants have turned on the landlords under the leadership of India's several Communist factions. There are indications that something similar may be developing in Pakistan, the Philippines, parts of Latin America and other places. . . .[15]

All the land-seizure activities in Mexico and India, it should be noted, were intended to achieve an explicit purpose: to push for greater or faster land reform. To a certain extent, such rural disturbances are analogous to instabilities in labor relations in urban areas. After having won the right to organize unions, workers may, at the instigation of their leaders, seize the plants in which they work in order to satisfy their wage demands.

America," in John J. Tepaske and Sidney Nettleton Fisher (eds.), *Explosive Forces in Latin America* (Columbus, Ohio, 1964), p. 118; and "Under the Lid in Mexico," *U.S. News and World Report*, May 2, 1966, pp. 50–51.

[14] For reports on these "land grab" activities, see *The New York Times*, March 31, 1970, p. 2; and August 21, 1970, p. 3; and *The Detroit News*, August 16, 1970, p. 2A.

[15] *The New York Times*, January 8, 1970, p. 38. Cf. Clifton R. Wharton, Jr., "The Green Revolution;" *Foreign Affairs*, XLVII (April 1969), 468.

Force is consciously and temporarily used as a means to achieve a specified end.

Finally, tenurial changes may lead to instability when resistant landlords clash with the peasants or the government in order to frustrate implementation. In most cases, *prolonged* landlord-peasant clashes in consequence of land reform do not occur. This is so because if the peasants are provided with public protection with regard to their rights under reform, they will not need to fight against the landlords. The government will. If there is no such protection, the peasants often lose out to the landlords when the latter use intimidation, eviction, and similar measures. Armed resistance by landlords to a reform-minded government, particularly when they suspect the government's serious intent to carry out the reform, is a greater possibility. As mentioned in Chapter IX, the experiences of Iran and Egypt demonstrate this point.

Viewing the destabilizing consequences of land reform from the perspective of time, one may suggest that these consequences are of short-term significance. When a land-reform program is introduced during a civil war, its destabilizing consequences cannot long outlast the war itself. In countries where disaffected farmers participate in land invasions and demonstrations in order to widen an implemented reform program, these farmers may under certain circumstances obtain some satisfaction. If not, they cannot stage an armed rebellion of any long duration. To do so they would not only confront the forces of the government, but also find themselves opposed by a large number of reform beneficiaries who have a vested interest in the preservation of the status quo. And the case of a *lengthy* armed resistance by landlords against the government hardly exists anywhere. The reasons are simple. The strength that the landlords have is primarily in wealth, not in armed might. In fighting against public authority they can neither match the government's physical force nor expect the peasantry to supply them with manpower. Also, landlords, who are already fewer than the peasants, cannot hope to maintain internal unity in the struggle. Certain landlords may have developed non-agricultural sources of income which they do not want to lose in fighting, while others may fear that the peasantry will win more of their land possessions if they persist in opposition. Consequently, when confronted with a government determined to carry out reform, the resistant landlords will find their ranks dwindling and will soon cease their violent activities.

Long-Term Stabilizing Consequences of Land Reform

To suggest that land reform under specified circumstances may create short-term destabilizing consequences is to imply that reform generally tends to generate long-term stabilizing consequences.

To assess the positive contribution of land reform to stability, one must first recognize the interrelationship of the economic and political dimensions of land reform. In essence, a reform program is a major instrument in closing the aspiration-reality gap among the peasantry. By helping develop greater economic opportunities and by making them available to a wider segment of the farming community, land reform may thus dissuade the discontented farmers from resorting to force as a means to improve their life. Land reform, in short, is an investment in rural stability as well as in peasant economic welfare.

From the point of view of stability, land reform is a profitable investment, for the cost-benefit ratio is favorable. Today, peasant aspirations, while rising continuously, remain low; and they rise at a slower rate than the expectations of urban residents. Apathy and fatalism still much characterize peasant behavior in the developing countries. The typical small peasant certainly wants to be a landowner, but he is not without scruples when taking over another's land. His demand for reform benefits frequently tends to be low, and hence relatively easy to satisfy. Scattered evidence in rural Colombia, the Philippines, and India confirms this analysis. In his survey in Cundinanarca, Colombia, John Powell found that though most peasant respondents considered land problems in the survey area to be very serious, two-thirds of the respondents regarded "respect for the property of others" as among the most important of civic duties, and that there were more respondents in favor of "petition for land" as the main function of rural organizations than those supporting "land invasion" (88.7 percent as against 61.9 percent).[16] In the Philippines, a rural survey found that a substantial number of farmers had very moderate views on the issue of land redistribution and tenancy reform. Of the total of 1,290 peasants surveyed (consisting of farmers with different types of tenure status) 42 percent thought that a landowner should be allowed to retain "any land other than that which he cultivated himself"; 40 percent thought he should not; and 18 percent did not know whether he should. On the issue of the need for written tenancy contracts to protect the tenants, of the total sample of 1,293 peasants (again, with

[16] Powell, *Survey*, pp. 40, 44.

various types of tenure status) interviewed, only 60 percent considered that there was an absolute need. When only the answers of the 326 tenants of the total sample were taken into account, the percentage was even lower, 49.[17] Though this survey was published in the early 1950s, it may still have some relevance today. For that was a time when the land issue had already occupied the attention of the Philippine nation, and the Huk movement had gained a wide following by exploiting the issue. In a single-person tour over a vast part of rural India, Kusum Nair found that peasant demand for land was extremely meager. In a village in Madras (now Tamilnadu), for example, she reported that when a number of farmers—all with large families—were asked how much land, if offered free, they would desire, the amount of land they wanted ranged from one and one-third to three acres. Most of these farmers were also willing to take in only 50 to 60 percent of the crops, leaving the rest to the original owners.[18]

A re-examination of the land-redistribution data of the present study reveals that in countries where the beneficiaries have favorably evaluated their reform experiences—Iran, Mexico, Taiwan, and the U.A.R.—the amount of land the farmers actually received was very small, particularly when compared to the amount of land that the landlords were allowed to retain. On the basis of the information in Tables 12 and 31, the following data may be obtained: the average amount of land received by a reform beneficiary was about 6.5 hectares in Mexico, 0.7 hectare in Taiwan, and 1.5 hectares in the U.A.R. The amount of land a landowner was permitted to retain ranged from 9 times the average amount of redistribution land in Taiwan to 46 times in Mexico. Data on Iran are not comparable, but the average amount of land the reform beneficiaries received was not large either. Evidently then, it takes relatively little land to satisfy peasant demands.

While land reform as a program of investment in stability requires a moderate expenditure, the returns are high. This is so for three reasons. First, the mode of agricultural life is generally conservative. Once assured of an income from the land, the peasant will focus his time, energy, and wealth on it. He will develop, in due course, a sense of identification with his reformed status and be prepared for its defense when it is challenged or threatened. Insofar as farming is a year-round undertaking, the farmer will

---

[17] Generoso F. Rivera and Robert T. McMillan, *The Rural Philippines* (Manila, 1952), p. 169.

[18] Nair, *Blossoms in the Dust* (New York, 1961), pp. 30–31.

be continuously tied up with it, having little opportunity for other time-consuming undertakings, peaceful or violent. Land reform, in this sense, must be frankly recognized as a program for investment in immobility and conservatism.[19] As a study on the land-reform programs of Venezuela, Bolivia, and Mexico has suggested:

> There is the long term benefit of increasing the political influence of a basically conservative sector of the population [the peasants]. . . . The new owner of a five-hectare parcel of land will probably put just as strong a value on private property and individual rights as the owner of five thousand hectares. Our data have indicated that this is a very real consequence of land redistribution in all three countries.[20]

Second, land reform may contribute to long-term stability because it may lead, as seen in the last chapter, to the development of institutional channels through which rural demands and complaints can be continuously brought to the attention of the government. Remedial actions may, therefore, be taken before rural discontent develops serious proportions. Thus, on the one hand, land reform may be perceived as a program to implant in the farmer the potential for stability; on the other hand, it can be seen as an instrument to reduce his propensity for instability. When the farmer goes to the government demanding more land, water, and inputs, or when he asks the government for a redress of certain grievances, he posits a hope in the existing political system. So long as this feeling persists, he is not likely to take his demands and complaints to a movement that seeks the overthrow of the system. In Morelia, Mexico, for instance, "peasants in white shirts and pants and straw hats come daily [to government offices] to defend their holdings from hungry neighbors or to try to get some land

---

[19] This is to assume that no socialized or totally collectivized farming is going to take place in the non-Communist developing countries, and that family farming, with or without some cooperative undertaking, remains the dominant system. On the relationship between family farming and stability Erven J. Long has commented: "A system of owner-operated farms of such size as to require family labor only would contribute the maximum toward political and social stability." "The Economic Basis of Land Reform in Underdeveloped Economies," *Land Economies* XXXVII (May 1961), 115.

[20] Charles J. Erasmus, "Agrarian Reform: A Comparative Study of Venezuela, Bolivia, and Mexico," in Dwight B. Heath, *et al., Land Reform and Social Revolution* (Madison: The University of Wisconsin, Land Tenure Center, 1965, mimeo.), pp. 708–709. Lowry Nelson, in his study on the land reform of these same three countries, has reached a similar conclusion. See "Some Social Aspects of Agrarian Reform in Mexico, Bolivia and Venezuela" (Washington, D.C., 1964), pp. 68–69.

to work of their own." [21] In Iran, in "the office of the director of land reform in Tabriz," a peasant beneficiary of the reform "demanded immediate action to settle a dispute with a neighbor, also a new owner." [22] In Taiwan, farmers, through the farmer's associations, complained to the government about the unfavorable ratio at which government-supplied fertilizers were exchanged for their rice.[23] In each of these instances, the farmers lodged with the government their specific demands or complaints; at the same time, they had to accept the institutional restraints that are inherent in a government.

It is only from this perspective that one can fully understand the political behavior of the less privileged Mexican peasants: the small *ejidatarios* and the landless farmers. Compared to the middle-sized private farmers, the *ejidatarios* cannot be considered well treated. But since the *ejidatarios* did obtain a substantial amount of land, they are content to let any further improvement of their well-being go through the channels of the PRI and the government, where demands of private farmers and other groups also compete for attention. The *ejidatarios* may press for their demands; so may other groups. In reality, all groups must accept the political system as the framework within which they compete for the satisfaction of their respective interests. As Robert E. Scott has observed: "It is neither the PRI itself nor any individual president, so much as the need for adjustment among the competing interests which both serve, that motivates interest associations to act within the official party or to accept its part in the decision-making process. . . ." [24] As to the landless farmers, who are outside both the *ejido* and the PRI, possible benefits under the Mexican land-reform program remain an inducement to them to moderate their actions. As mentioned earlier, land invasions were organized to prod the government to provide the landless with land. These activities formed pressure exerted upon the government to heed their demand for land, not an effort to seek its overthrow. Though physical clashes and bloodshed did occasionally take place, by and large the participants of land invasions and demonstrations were willing to withdraw from these activities when confronted with firm action from the government. The government, after quelling the protesters, often took compensatory measures. Beginning with

[21] *The New York Times*, May 5, 1966, p. 14.

[22] *Ibid.*, May 12, 1963, p. 28.

[23] T. H. Shen, *Agricultural Development on Taiwan Since World War II* (Ithaca, N.Y., 1964), p. 335.

[24] *Mexican Government in Transition* (Urbana, Ill., 1959), p. 175.

the López Mateos administration (1958–1964), Mexico accelerated the pace of land redistribution, presumably in response to the pressure of the landless. In 1967, "President Gustavo Díaz Ordaz gave land titles for more than 2.5 million acres of [cattle ranch land] to 9,600 peasant families [in Chihuahua]. It was officially described as the biggest single distribution of land in Mexican history." [25]

Finally, land reform may in the long run contribute indirectly to rural stability by helping reduce urban instability. In at least four of the eight countries under study—Iran, Mexico, Taiwan, and the U.A.R.—urban instability in the form of mass demonstrations or attempted or actual coups had taken place before these countries implemented their land reform programs. In these countries today, urban instability either does not exist at all or has become insignificant. Obviously one cannot attribute the presence of urban stability in these countries primarily to land reform, for many other factors are also involved. But land reform may have contributed to the lowering of the urban instability potential in at least two ways. First, land reform may provide the national elite with a feeling of mass rural support so that it may confidently deal with urban problems.[26] In the case of Iran, the conflict between the Shah and the political force representing the urban middle-class interests—the National Front—is of such intensity and endurance that the Shah practically has to write off the political support of that class. It is land reform that gave the Shah the political capital with which he could effectively counteract some of his opponents in the cities. Similarly, as mentioned in Chapter X, the political elites of both Mexico and the U.A.R. relied on rural support to cope with the student challenges in the cities. The case of Mexico may be further noted. When the authoritarian practices of the PRI were challenged by students in Sonora, Mexico, in 1967, the party simply mobilized the rural voters to sanction these practices. When the government faced almost nation-wide student unrest in the fall of 1968, President Gustavo Díaz Ordaz took stern measures against the demonstrators, using the police and the army to smash disturbances. On October 2, just days

[25] *The New York Times*, October 30, 1967, p. 1.

[26] "In a radical praetorian society," Samuel P. Huntington has cogently argued, "the city cannot furnish the basis for governmental stability. The extent of the instability depends upon the extent to which the government is able and willing to use the countryside to contain and to pacify the city. If the government can build a bridge to the countryside, if it can mobilize support from the rural areas, it can contain and ride out the instabilities of the city." *Political Order in Changing Societies* (New Haven, 1968), p. 209.

before the opening of the Olympic Games in Mexico, the troops opened fire on the rebelling students at Tlatelolco Square in Mexico City, killing at least 49 people; and hundreds of students were arrested and imprisoned. By ruthless action the government effectively silenced the dissident students. That the government could do this is in large part attributed to the fact that the government, not the dissidents, retained the sympathy of the masses. During the midst of the 1968 crisis, the students once attempted to bring "workers and peasants into the fight, but only slight headway had been made. Trade unions [in Mexico] . . . are part of the establishment through their membership in the Institutional Revolutionary Party, . . . The same is true of peasant organizations. Their memberships have sought to keep their ranks free of student influence, which they regard as subversive." [27] The students have done little since to stir "protests by either organized labor or the peasants." [28] In Taiwan, the KMT has not faced a student challenge in urban areas, but it has confronted keen electoral competition in the cities. For years, it relied heavily on rural votes to maintain a commanding position in electoral contests. Such a position to a certain extent must have convinced the urban population of the desirability of accepting the political leadership of the KMT.

The other way in which land reform contributes to the lowering of urban instability is concerned with the restraining effect of reform on the outflow of people from the countryside. Unlike the growth of cities in Western countries, which took place gradually and was accompanied by a rise in employment opportunities, "urbanization in [most] newly developing countries is taking place at an unusually rapid pace," a pace that exceeds the rate of industrialization.[29] Consequently, there are unemployment, shanty towns, over-population in the cities—the very conditions conducive to urban instability. In the event that land reform leads to an increase of rural income and economic opportunities, it will help slow down rural emigration, thereby reducing the strains on urban stability. It is not possible to measure precisely the restraining effect of land reform on the outflow of rural population, for it is extremely difficult to isolate this effect from the "pulling effect" that urbanization exerts upon potential migrants. However, evidence in Taiwan and Mexico indicates that

[27] *The New York Times*, September 9, 1968, p. 25.
[28] *Ibid.*, January 19, 1970, p. 18.
[29] Gerald Breese, *Urbanization in Newly Developing Countries* (Englewood Cliffs, N.J.: Prentice-Hall, Inc., 1966), p. 134.

reform has appreciably strengthened the population-retaining capacity of rural areas. In Taiwan, as a government economic official has observed,

> Because of land reform, our wealth is much more evenly distributed across the country, possibly more than in any other Asian country. The movement to the cities [from the countryside] has been slowed because the disparity between rural and urban living standards is less. The average farmer probably lives better than the average industrial worker in the city.[30]

The slowing of urban migration in Taiwan is not only due to the narrowing of the gap between urban and rural life, but is also due to the emergence of a system of small farms in the post-reform era. "A peasant small holding system," a United Nations document has explained, "is more likely to retain population than a capitalist-farming wage-labour system, not only because it leads to a more intensive input of labour, but also because the farmer's personal stake in the land provides a psychological anchor—the weight of which is greater the more secure his tenure." [31] This explanation applies precisely to Taiwan. The security of holding that small owner-farmers enjoy, and the low rental payments that the tenants have to make—tangible benefits of reform—have induced the Taiwanese farmers to resort to land- and labor-intensive practices. The data relevant to this point have been cited in Chapter IX.

The same can be said of Mexico. Despite its phenomenal urban growth and industrialization in recent decades, the country still found, in 1960, over half of the population engaged in agriculture (see Table 1, p. 21). The explanation lies in increased demands for labor in rural areas in the post-reform period. Folke Dovring has found that from 1930 to 1960, of all the Mexican labor force 12 years of age and over, those in agriculture rose from 3,580,000 to 5,481,000 while those in non-agricultural occupations from 1,401,000 to 3,816,000. The non-agricultural labor force rose much faster than the agricultural, but the latter was still much larger in absolute size.[32] This is the basis of the claim by an FAO study of urbanization in Latin America that Mexico suffered less from the adverse consequences of urban growth than many other countries on the continent. In Mexico "large numbers of moderately populated agricultural villages pro-

[30] *The New York Times,* August 21, 1968, p. 26.
[31] U.N., *Land Reform, Fourth Report,* p. 145.
[32] Folke Dovring, *Land Reform and Productivity,* p. 12.

vide an alternative to urban migration. . . . The program of agrarian reform has probably contributed to this staying power." [33]

By strengthening the political position of the elite in the cities, and by reducing the population strain on urban areas, land reform can help improve the over-all political conditions of a country. In this sense, the contribution of land reform to urban stability has a feedback effect on the countryside.

In concluding the discussion of the effect of land reform on rural stability, one may note that of the eight countries under study, the four with more extensive reform—Iran, Mexico, Taiwan, and the U.A.R.— have all experienced rural stability since their respective programs were substantially implemented; and all indicators are that this condition will last. The Mexican case is perhaps the most revealing one. In the two decades following 1910, hundreds of thousands died in the revolution and civil war; military dictatorship and almost intermittent assassinations of Presidents dominated the political scene; and comparatively little land was redistributed. But beginning around 1930, when there was drastic expansion of the *ejido* system, and when peasants and others were assimilated into the governing party, peace and stability gradually prevailed.[34] For more than three decades, Mexicans regularly elected their Presidents; and the Presidents, all of whom have been civilians since 1946, have filled out their terms. In the countryside, though land invasions do occasionally occur, no general restlessness has been evident. In the *ejido* communities, stagnation instead of instability seems to be the problem.

India and West Pakistan did not have as extensive reform programs

[33] Quoted in Frances M. Foland, "Agrarian Reform in Latin America," *Foreign Affairs*, XLVIII (October 1969), 104.

[34] On this point three writers have commented. Martin Needler has suggested that it was as early as the 1920s, when President Alvaro Obregón took a stand favorable to the workers and the farmers, that stability was beginning to take root. "By favoring labor organization and land reform, Obregón had given peasants and workers a stake in the preservation of the regime. From that time on revolts against the regime became progressively weaker until they disappeared altogether; . . ." "Mexico" in Needler (ed.), *Political Systems of Latin America* (Princeton, N.J.: D. Van Nostrand Co., 1964), p. 5. Arthur P. Whitaker and David C. Jordan have thought that real stability began around 1929 when "Mexico's new revolutionary ruling class took its first step toward establishing internal stability and regularity by conciliating the social forces that had shown the greatest capability for organized violence. These groups had been the military, labor and peasants." *Nationalism in Contemporary Latin America* (New York: The Free Press, 1966), p. 44.

as the four above-mentioned countries, but the programs implemented were of such magnitude that they made large-scale rural instability unlikely. Only in Colombia and the Philippines, where land reform has made the least progress, does a threat to rural stability exist. In Colombia, banditry and Communist guerrilla activities prevailing in certain rural areas are insignificant in scale as compared to *la Violencia*, but the persistence of this lawlessness is symptomatic of the existence of a high potential for rural instability. In the Philippines, the current revival of Huk strength in Central Luzon is almost exclusively due to the inability of the elite to resolve the land issue. This will be taken up in the next chapter.

XIV

LAND REFORM AND COMMUNISM

The relationship between land reform and Communism is ambivalent. On the one hand, because the Communists everywhere embrace fundamental tenurial changes as an indispensable part of their economic and social program, they have effectively identified themselves with the land-reform movement. As is well known, during the first stages of the Communist revolutions in China and Cuba, certain liberals in the West accepted the followers of Mao Tse-tung and Fidel Castro as nothing more than land reformers. Ironically, this view was to a certain extent shared by some conservative forces in the developing countries. As mentioned in Chapters V and VI, during the legislative debates over the reform laws in Colombia, Iran, and the Philippines, some opponents of reform branded all attempts to bring about compulsory land redistribution as a Communist inspired conspiracy. While land reform is thus regarded as closely identified with the Communist movement, many supporters of land reform regard it as the best—at least, the necessary—means to deter the Communists from penetrating into rural areas. Landlords must relinquish some of their possessions through peaceful change in order to avoid the loss of them all in violent revolution.

These conflicting opinions aside, the reality in the developing countries is that the Communists attempt to ride to power on the land issue, whereas the non-Communists seek to resolve the issue to save their power. It is appropriate, therefore, to analyze briefly how the Communists in some developing countries approach the land issue, before proceeding to assess the impact of land reform on Communism in the countries under study.

Communist Approaches to the Land Issue

In the developing countries today, the Communists appear to follow three approaches to the land issue. They may resort to guerrilla warfare, political agitation, or parliamentary action.

GUERRILLA WARFARE

This approach usually consists of several distinct steps. First, the Communists must build a rural guerrilla base largely through their own efforts and resources. Urban in background, few in number but tightly disciplined and totally dedicated to the overthrow of the existing political order, Communist guerrillas have to identify and propagate an anti-government cause, develop an incipient military force, and create a zone of operation within an area which government forces cannot easily reach. They have to do all these things without the assistance or participation of the rural residents. Second, they seek to expand their base and extend their operation by recruiting the peasants. It is at this stage that they attempt to identify themselves with the land issue. This they do by negatively stirring up rural grievances against the existing land-tenure system and by positively offering peasants a program for land redistribution. And third, after capturing power, they impose a Marxist solution on the farm problem by collectivizing the land. Both Mao Tse-tung and Fidel Castro followed these steps. In recent years, guerrillas in Bolivia, Venezuela, Colombia, and the Philippines have attempted to pursue this course of action.[1] Communist experiences in the last two countries may be particularly noted.

Long steeped in the tradition of rural violence and political warfare, Colombia has for decades seen an assortment of guerrilla movements operating in the Andes. These movements show considerable divergence in duration, composition, and orientation. At first there were armed village partisans of the Liberals and Conservatives who fought prolonged fratricidal wars before and during la Violencia. This kind of intermittent rural conflict gradually subsided in the late 1950s, and small bands of outlaws now rove the countryside as a manifest legacy of la Violencia. Then there are "peasant leagues" and "independent republics" that came into existence in the 1930s. Consisting of poor campesinos and directed by the Communists, these organizations operated in the mountain districts of Cundinanarca, Tolima, Meta, and Caqueta, on both sides of the eastern cordillera of the Andes. Originally these Communist-controlled enclaves were not centers of aggressive activities but self-contained peasant zones

[1] See James Petras, "Revolution and Guerrilla Movements in Latin America: Venezuela, Colombia, Guatemala, and Peru" in James Petras and Naurice Zeitlin (eds.), Latin America: Reform or Revolution? (Greenwich, Conn.: Fawcett Publications Inc., 1968), pp. 329–369; Richard Gott, Guerrilla Movements in Latin America (New York: Doubleday & Co., 1971); and the discussions below.

in which the former *colonos* defended their forcefully occupied farms against the *hacendados* and the government. In recent years, however, a number of activist Communist organizations have pursued a militant course of action, seeking to convert the peasant defense zones into bases of guerrilla activities. These movements have enlisted people with extremely divergent backgrounds, including such disparate groups as students, priests, peasants, and, of course, the Communists themselves.[2] Of various ideological persuasions, all these movements seek to overthrow the government through revolution and war.

Estimates of the strength of these movements in Colombia vary. Robert Dix indicated that in the early 1960s there were about half a dozen Communist-operated areas, with altogether a few thousand *campesinos*.[3] William O. Galbraith cited estimates indicating that Communist guerrillas varied from 5,000 to 30,000 men.[4] Still another source of information, *The Economist*, published a map in 1965 depicting the sites of five "independent republics," five "new Castroite guerrilla cells," and eight centers of "peasant activitists."[5] The latest account on the subject came from *The New York Times*.[6] The paper reported in early 1971 that there were three principal guerrilla organizations operating in Colombia. The first was a Castroite organization known as the Army of National Liberation (*Ejercito de Liberación Nacional*, ELN). With about 80 men, the ELN came into being in 1963 and operated in the middle Magdalena Valley in the northern part of the country. The second group, the Army of Popular Liberation (ELP), started in 1968 as a Maoist group. Consisting of 150 members, the ELP based its operation in the Central range of the Andes. And the third, the largest, insurgent group, the Colombian Revolutionary Armed Forces (*Fuerzas Armades Revolucionarias de Colombia*, FARC), was under the wing of the pro-Russian Colombian Communist Party. With 400 guerrillas, this group began its activities in 1966 in the eastern foothills of the Andes. The first two groups included a good portion of former

---

[2] See Pierre Gilhodès, "Agrarian Struggles in Colombia," in Rodolfo Stavenhagen (ed.), *Agrarian Problems and Peasant Movements in Latin America*, pp. 407–451; and Orlando Fals Borda, *Subversion and Social Change in Colombia*, trans. by Jacqueline D. Skiles (New York: Columbia University Press, 1969), pp. 118 ff.

[3] Robert H. Dix, *Colombia: The Political Dimensions of Change* (New Haven, 1967), p. 275.

[4] William O. Galbraith, *Colombia: A General Survey* (London: Oxford University Press, 1966), pp. 154–55.

[5] "Murders Yet to Come," *The Economist*, August 28, 1965, pp. 772, 777.

[6] *The New York Times*, February 24, 1971, p. 25. See also Gilhodès, *op. cit.*

students, disaffected professionals, and reformist priests;[7] whereas the last group had peasants as its basic contingent. According to the government, its anti-guerrilla campaign in 1970 resulted in killing 134 insurgents, wounding 9, and capturing 201. The casualties of the Colombian army included 25 soldiers killed and 38 wounded. Other casualties inflicted by the guerrillas were as follows: officials, 13 killed and 18 wounded; civilians, 108 killed and 38 wounded.[8]

Few in number, fragile in overall strength, and constantly haunted by the government's counter-insurgency forces, the guerrillas have fought tenaciously in the hills. Adopting a stance in favor of radical land reform, they have tried vigorously to capture the sympathy of the poorest stratum of the peasantry—the tenants, sharecroppers and *colonos*.[9] At the moment, they are still fighting a highly mobile war, without fixed bases. Their hope for expansion of their zones of operation remains distant.

In the Philippines, the Huk movement now follows a similar course of action, but its origin is different from that of the Colombian guerrillas. Created as the People's anti-Japanese Army under Communist auspices, the Huks developed their rural strength during the Second World War. By linking the land issue to its anti-Japanese campaign, the Huks firmly established bases in Central Luzon, the crowded tenancy area. During the war, as Chester Hunt has observed,

> The Japanese had effectively occupied the cities, but never had sufficient troops to garrison the entire country and suppress guerrilla opposition. Under these circumstances, a major technique of guerrillas was the effort to prevent the Japanese troops from securing a normal share of the harvest. Since the landlord was well known and could not openly defy the Japanese, the guerrillas encouraged the *taos* to seize the crops themselves rather than follow the usual procedures of marketing. This meant that the landlord was almost inevitably placed

[7] A celebrated case involving the participation of a prominent Catholic priest in guerrilla activities occurred in the mid-1960s. Father Camilo Torres Restrepo, a former chaplain of the National University and a former member of the governing board of INCORA, organized in 1965 a People's United Front (*Frente Unido del Pueblo*, FUP) to "unite the lefts," joined the ELN as a guerrilla fighter later in the year and was killed in action in 1966.

[8] *The New York Times*, February 24, 1971, p. 25.

[9] In 1952, the Colombian Communists and other Leftists organized a National Conference of Guerrillas seeking to "inject . . . agrarian reform into the guerrilla resistance." Dix, *op. cit.*, p. 371. Though having never been able to create a unified command, the various guerrilla movements have been united in their support of land invasion and land redistribution activities.

in the position of either collaborating with the Japanese or of giving up his usual source of income. . . . [Hence, by using this technique, the guerrillas] combined the element of patriotic opposition to an occupying power with a long standing resentment of tenants against farm owners.[10]

The Huk's anti-Japanese and anti-landlord stance enabled the guerrillas to expand their rural following. When they rose in rebellion in the late 1940s they made a strenuous effort to retain this following by stressing their identification with the land-reform movement. After suffering a serious defeat in the early 1950s they appeared to revive their strength in the 1960s. Sensing the gravity of the reemergence of the Communist challenge, the Senate Committee on National Defense and Security of the Philippine Congress conducted a detailed investigation in 1967 of the Huk movement. In its report (which was partially written by Alfredo B. Saulo, a former Huk leader), the committee found the Huks to have established an "invisible government" commanding the obedience of considerable masses in Central Luzon, with a Communist takeover as their supreme goal. The insurgents consisted of 156 armed Huks, 136 combat supporters, 950 service support or legal cadres, and 30,000 in mass support. "While the Huk leaders are either communists or have communist leanings," the committee noted, "the rank and file of the organization is made up of poor, unschooled, landless peasants. The latter don't even know the difference between democracy and communism, and . . . [all they want is to] have lands of their own. . . . It was this hunger for land of the peasants which the communists have exploited to win their faith and confidence." Thus, "in the short range program of the Communist Party of the Philippines," the committee further noted, "the number one goal or objective is to give land to the landless farmers. The poor, illiterate peasants who have joined the Huk movement don't even bother to question the sincerity of their leaders on this score. Nobody has informed them of the fact that in all communist countries not a single farmer can boast of a farm under his name. . . ." In the committee's view, the Huk movement "is following the tradition set by the communists in China where the peasantry, . . . became the main force of the revolution. It is reminiscent of the Chinese communist strategy of winning first the surround-

[10] Chester Hunt et al., Sociology in the Philippine Setting (Manila: Alemar's, 1954), p. 356.

ing rural areas before launching the final struggle against the established order in the urban stronghold." [11]

While engaged in guerrilla warfare against the government, the Huks at present also undertake a whole range of illicit activities, including political assassinations, kidnappings, smuggling, banditry, and manipulating elections in their areas of operation.[12] There are also incipient indications that the guerrillas have tried to extend beyond their traditional area of operation, Central Luzon, and make inroads into the island of Negros in the south, where disaffected farm laborers have long harbored grievances against sugar plantations.[13]

In face of the renewed Huk challenge, the government has expanded its counter-insurgency operations and scored a number of very significant victories. In May 1964, the Communist Party's Secretary-General Jesus Lava was captured; in September 1970, Faustino del Mundo, alias Commander Sumulong, second in command in the Huk movement, was appre-

[11] The Philippines, Congress, the Senate Committee on National Defense and Security, *Committee Report No. 1123, On the Security Problems Posed by the Huk Movement and on the Government's Performance in Central Luzon* (Manila, 1967). All the above quotations appear on pp. 8–10.

[12] With respect to the Huk's guerrilla operations, the Senate Committee report referred to above listed the following casualties: in 1965, there were "12 incidents involving 14 killings, 2 wounded and 2 kidnappings. . . . In 1966, there were 64 incidents, 83 killings, 21 wounded and 20 kidnappings. . . ." Among the principal victims were majors, barrio officials, including Anastacio Gallardo, Mayor of Candaba, Pampanga, and also President of the anti-Huk Mayor's League of Pampanga. *Ibid.*, p. 26. According to a recent report, the Huks stepped up their activities in subsequent years, resulting in killing "196 persons in 1969, double the figure for 1968. In the first two months of this year [1970], 54 persons were reported killed by Huks." *The New York Times*, October 19, 1970, p. 12. With respect to Huk control of local elections, the police reported in 1967 that 19 of the 21 mayors in Pampanga assisted "the Huks in return for political support. One provincial governor in Central Luzon privately admits that he cannot be elected without Huk support." *Ibid.*, April 16, 1967, p. 11.

[13] There were Huk-sponsored unrests on Negros island in 1969. In August, the New People's Army, a sect of the Huks, began their operations there by killing several policemen and officials. *Ibid.*, March 8, 1970, p. 14, and *The Manila Times*, August 25, 1969, pp. 1A and 6A. On September 22, 1969, the latter newspaper published an open letter from Amado Guerrero, who claimed to be chairman of the Central Committee of the Communist Party of the Philippines. In the letter, Guerrero pointed up the exploitive conditions on the sugar plantations in Negros and excessive concentration of landownership. The letter listed in detail the names of landlords and their possessions, with 728 landlords owning a total of 117,255.5 hectares, ranging from 50 to 1000 hectares each. *Ibid.*, September 22, 1969, p. 4A.

hended. In the following month, Pedro Taruc, Secretary-General of the Communist Party since 1964 and the Supreme Commander of the Huks since 1954, was slain in Angeles, Pampanga. These severe losses in the leadership of the Huk insurgents, however, did not appear to weaken seriously the overall strength of the movement. For several years, the Huk forces have been decentralized because of the existence of factions. Before they fell victim to the government's anti-guerrilla drive, Taruc and Sumulong were reported leaders of one faction, controlling "256 armed men and 200 combat support troops plus 43,000 members." A stronger faction, according to the Philippine government, was the "Re-established Communist Party of the Philippines" and its military arm, the New People's Army. Based in Tarlac Province, and under the leadership of Bernabe Buscayno, alias Commander Dante, this faction was Maoist in orientation and had "a hard core of 400 men, about 400 combat support troops and 41,000 members." In the opinion of the Philippine Constabulary, after the removal of Taruc and Sumulong as Huk leaders, their followers would very likely join the Dante group and hence would bolster its strength. There was also a third faction, the *Partido Komunistang Philipinas*, which commanded "100 armed men with 100 combat support troops and a base of 37,000 members. The leaders of this faction . . . are believed to include intellectuals from the universities." [14]

In terms of numerical strength, the Huk movement does not seem to present a serious threat to the nation, particularly since the recent losses in its top leadership. But the close connection between the land issue and the movement is as clear today, when the movement has revived, as it was in the 1940s, when the movement first resorted to arms. Consequently, as long as the issue is not substantially resolved, it will continue to provide a cause to insurgents, sustaining their protracted war against the government.

In the Philippines, as in Colombia, one can say with certainty that the result of the political and military contest between the government and the rural guerrillas will greatly hinge upon which of the two can offer a solution to the problem of the landless.

POLITICAL AGITATION

In certain instances, the Communists may resort to agitational activities in approaching the land issue. Agitational activities and guerrilla war-

[14] *The New York Times*, October 19, 1970, p. 12.

fare both involve in varying degrees the use of mass violence, but these are essentially different tactics. When the Communists employ the former, they often do not have the intention of launching a full-scale rebellion against the government, and they lack the military training and organization necessary for the conduct of guerrilla warfare. When the Communists employ the latter tactic, they usually avow the total destruction of the existing political system, and they have already gained some elementary experience in fighting a mobile war.

In following the approach of political agitation, the Communists frequently concentrate on organizing one particular category of peasant: landless farm workers. Generally numerous, insecure in employment, inadequately paid, and often the most neglected among all types of farmers by land-reform programs, the landless workers can congregate with much less difficulty than those who own land; they have greater grievances than other farmers, and are quite susceptible to Communist persuasion. They are the exact counterpart of the urban proletariat. For this reason, the Communists can apply, with some adjustments, their tactics of urban mass agitation to the rural scene. By organizing unions, sponsoring strikes, staging land seizures, and raiding local authorities, they hope to inject into these farmers a class consciousness and a sense of militancy. They attempt to forge a force of peasant poletarians against the rural well-to-do.

Communist experiences in Colombia, Mexico, and India provide some illustrations of this approach. In 1928, an incipient Communist organization in Colombia, *Grupo Comunista,* taking advantage of rising rural discontent, organized (American) Indian agricultural workers on the banana plantations in the Department of Tolima, sponsored a strike, and clashed with the intervening army, causing "hundreds of fatalities." [15] Continuing the effort of politicizing and unionizing the agricultural workers, the newly organized Communist Party of Colombia (created in 1930) applied in the early 1930s in rural areas "its urban syndicalist criteria." [16] It made strong demands for improving the working conditions on the *haciendas,* organized further strikes, and vigorously sought to enlist Indian workers.

> The first secretary of the Communist Party was an Indian from Cauca who had strong ties with the Cacique Quintín Lame, an Indian leader who headed an uprising in Cauca, the north of Huila, and the south

[15] Gilhodès, *op. cit.,* p. 413; and Robert J. Alexander, *Communism in Latin America* (New Brunswick, N.J.: Rutgers University Press, 1957), pp. 245–247.

[16] Gilhodès, *op. cit.,* p. 414.

of Tomila. Thus it was that on the first of May 1931, the Indians occupied Coyaima, raised the red flag, and established a soviet, presided over by one of their number, Ismael Díogenes Contreras.[17]

These agitational activities, it should be noted, were largely confined to limited Communist-controlled areas in the Andes; the Colombian Communists have not, since the early 1930s, utilized this tactic to develop a broad rural following. In contrast, the Communists in Mexico have recently become interested in agitating the landless *campesinos* and galvanizing them into a massive force to challenge the PRI. As mentioned in Chapter XII, the waves of land invasions and demonstrations in many parts of the country have been organized under Communist auspices. The *Union General de Obreros y Campesinos de Mexico*, the *Union Central de Sociedades Ejidales*, and the *Central Campesino Independiente* are all Communist organizations actively involved in these activities.

A further illustration of the agitational approach may be furnished by the experiences of the Communists in India. For a few years after independence the Communist Party of India (CPI) attempted to adopt a militant line of action in rural areas. In Telengana, Hyderabad (now Andhra Pradesh), the Communists staged bloody uprisings which almost assumed guerrilla war proportions. They raided villages, murdered people, attacked government officials and records, and forcefully seized land. These activities lasted into 1951.[18] The Communists also sought to organize *bargadars* (sharecroppers) in West Bengal and agricultural workers elsewhere in order to expand their rural following.[19] Since most agricultural laborers were "untouchables" or of low castes, hence the most socially and economically deprived people, the Communists considered them to be "the most militant section of the agricultural population." In 1954, the Indian Communist Party declared that it "must vigorously take up and champion the immediate demands of the agricultural laborers." [20]

In recent years, while the CPI has apparently opted for a less militant road to power, a new Communist movement has proclaimed its willing-

[17] *Ibid.*

[18] See M. R. Masani, *The Communist Party of India, A Short History* (New York: The Macmillan Company, 1954), pp. 93–94, 125; Gene D. Overstreet and Marshall Windmiller, *Communism in India* (Berkeley: The University of California Press, 1959), p. 246; and Zahir Ahmed, *Dusk and Dawn in Village India* (New York: Frederick A. Praeger, Publishers, 1965), *passim.*

[19] See Myron Weiner, *The Politics of Scarcity* (Chicago, 1962), pp. 139–141; and Overstreet and Windmiller, *op. cit.*, pp. 393–394.

[20] *Ibid.*, p. 394.

ness to start an agrarian revolution. Known as the Naxalites, the new Communist revolutionary group made its first appearance in 1967, when a radical faction of the Communist Party of India, Marxist (CPM)— itself a faction split from the CPI—staged a peasant uprising in Naxalbari in northern West Bengal. The CPM, then the principal governing party in the United Front government of West Bengal, sent the Eastern Frontier Rifles to the area and forcefully suppressed the revolt. Piqued by their former colleagues, the Naxalites formally severed relations with the CPM, denouncing it, together with the CPI and the Congress Party, as reactionary. Recruiting disaffected students and professionals as its followers, the Naxalite movement soon extended into the neighboring states of Bihar, Andhra Pradesh, and the traditional Communist stronghold of Kerala. On May 1, 1969, the Naxalites formally created the Communist Party of India, Marxist-Leninist (CPML). With a national membership estimated to be around 20,000, the CPML adopted Maoist orientation and strategy. Demanding that all Communists "reject the hoax of parliamentarism" and bring about "an immediate revolution . . . through a revolutionary people's war," the CPML declared: "today the basic task is to liberate the rural areas through . . . armed agrarian revolution and encircle the cities, and, finally, to liberate the cities and thus complete the revolution throughout the country." [21]

Limited in numerical strength, and heavily dominated by students, the Naxalites are not, however, launching an agrarian revolution. Their current activities are bisected into, "1) the organization and education of student groups on a number of Indian college campuses, and 2) party work in rural areas among tribal and landless laborers." [22] In essence, they conduct agitational activities in both cities and countryside. On the rural front, "the Naxalites have been . . . exploiting the Government's failure to enforce a law placing a ceiling on landholdings. Laborers in the movement are encouraged to seize land held by landholders in excess of the ceiling, . . ." [23] In addition, they resorted to terrorist tactics, "killing policemen, landowners, Left Communists and other political rivals," causing hundreds of deaths.[24] Presently without the capacity to start a guerrilla

[21] Quoted in Marcus F. Franda, "India's Third Communist Party," *Asian Survey*, IX (November 1969), 806.

[22] *Ibid.*, 807. For a recent portrayal of the Naxalite movement in colleges in Calcutta, the center of the movement, see Dom Moraes, "Indian Revolutionaries with a Chinese Accent," *The New York Times Magazine*, November 8, 1970, pp. 30 ff.

[23] *The New York Times*, May 27, 1970, p. 5.

[24] *Ibid.*, November 26, 1970, p. 4.

war, the Naxalites apparently wish to use these small-scale violent actions to appeal to India's "80 million landless peasants, including 30 million tribals who are traditionally militant." [25]

PARLIAMENTARY ACTION

In places where the Communists have some electoral strength, they may approach the land issue through the parliamentary process. Generally, their stand on the issue tends to be moderate, and the program they support is below the Marxist prescription. Their endorsement of a mild reform program usually represents an effort to establish a popular image in rural areas in which they have yet to develop a mass following. This endorsement is meant to obtain maximum support from the peasantry at a cost of minimum antagonism from others. To the Communists, such a program is a transitional step eventually leading toward collectivization of farms.

In the Philippines, before they rose in rebellion, the Huks had participated in the 1946 election and supported a rather mild land-reform program. This program consisted of three main items: an increase of the tenant's share of crops, a guaranteed minimum wage of three pesos for agricultural workers, and the purchase of large estates for redistribution.[26] Though this program was not adopted by the government, the Congress did respond to the Huks' "fair share" proposal by enacting a rice tenancy reform law in 1946, which reduced rentals from the prevailing 50 percent to 30 percent of the crop.[27] In Iran, when the Communist-dominated Democratic Party, with the backing of the Soviet Occupation forces, gained in 1945 the control of the provincial government of Azerbaijan, it immediately proposed a land-reform program with a mixture of moderate and radical features. The program would have included the passage of "a law regulating peasant-landlord relations, the distribution of estates belonging to 'reactionary' landlords." Such a program, with some modifications,

[25] *Ibid.*, June 15, 1969, p. 2.
[26] Erich H. Jacoby, *Agrarian Unrest in Southeast Asia* (New York, 1949), p. 195. Cf. Frances L. Starner, *Magsaysay and the Philippine Peasantry* (Berkeley, 1961), p. 17; and Luis Taruc, *Born of the People* (New York: International Publishers, 1953), pp. 210, 229. Taruc was the founder and the first Supreme Commander of the Huks.
[27] See Napoleon D. Valeriano and Charles T. R. Bohannan, *Counter Guerrilla Operations, The Philippine Experience* (New York: Frederick A. Praeger, Publishers, 1962), pp. 48–49, and the Philippines, the Senate, Committee on National Defense and Security, *Committee Report No. 1123*, p. 6.

won the endorsement of the central government in Tehran.[28] But when the Democratic Party later considered it necessary to avoid the antagonism of the landowners so as to broaden its base of support, it abandoned the program.[29] In Egypt, before it was banned by the army regime following the 1952 revolution, the Communist Party paid scant attention to the agrarian issue. Though it endorsed the idea of reform as early as the 1920s, the idea was never fully articulated. One Communist writer, Sadiq Sa'ad suggested in 1945 that 50 *feddans* be established as the ceiling of privately owned land, and the Communists and leftists supported a kind of "agrarian programme" that included the abolition of large estates.[30] In Mexico, though they still frequently organize land invasions, the Communists also attempt to exert electoral pressure on the PRI for the expansion of the *ejido* system, a system which they consider essentially a non-Marxist, though progressive, solution of the farm problem. Their ultimate goal remains, as the Communist-dominated National Peasant League has proclaimed, that of "socialization of the land and other means of production." And this goal cannot be achieved "without an alliance [by the peasants] with the urban proletariat." [31]

Communist utilization of the parliamentary approach to the land issue can be illustrated more fully in the case of India, where the Communists have long sought to develop their electoral strength. Since the early 1950s, the Communist Party of India (CPI) has not placed much emphasis on rural agitation or revolution as a means to achieve power. Instead, it seeks to align itself with the peasants in the electoral process by attacking landlordism and stressing the need for speedier implementation of the much-stalled land-reform programs sponsored by the Congress Party. The CPI has opted for this moderate course of action because it is politically more profitable to the party than a militant policy. Thus in the aftermath of the Telengana uprising, a CPI document declared: "It would be gross exaggeration to assert that India is on the verge of armed insurrection or revolution." In the view of the party, "the peasant movement in the country as a whole remains weak. . . . Premature uprisings and

[28] Sepehr Zabih, *The Communist Movement in Iran* (Berkeley: The University of California Press, 1966), pp. 103, 110.

[29] Richard W. Cottam, *Nationalism in Iran* (Pittsburgh, 1964), pp. 126–127.

[30] Gabriel Baer, *A History of Landownership in Modern Egypt* (London, 1962), pp. 214–215.

[31] A. F. Shul'govskii, "Communal Land Tenure and Agrarian Reform in Mexico," *Soviet Sociology*, IV (Spring 1966), 26.

adventurist actions" should be avoided.[32] The party considered that its central task in the rural areas was to popularize its stand on the land issue, a stand in favor of land to the tillers. In the 1952 election, "land reform has been claimed to be one of the main planks of the Communist programme in India and the slowness in achieving agrarian reform has constituted one of the strongest and most plausible grounds for Communist propaganda against the Congress administration. . . ."[33] This political stance was fruitful, and the Communists have gradually expanded their electoral strength. Fifteen years later, in the 1967 national election, both the CPI and the emerging militant CPM reaffirmed this stance. In its electoral manifesto the CPI announced its land policy: "The first and foremost requirement in this connection is to enforce effective and far-reaching land reforms which would break up the present land concentration, give full security of tenure to actual tillers. . . ." The CPM manifesto made substantially the same claim, though it displayed some militancy in language. It denounced the "Congress agrarian reformers . . . [as] a big hoax on the toiling peasantry" and demanded "taking over landlords' land and their distribution among agricultural labourers and poor peasants gratis, cancellation of debts owed by peasants, agricultural workers, small artisans to money-lenders and landlords, . . ." The party reaffirmed its ideological commitment to eventual implementation of socialism. Regarding itself as the only party that "stands firmly and consistently for Socialism," the CPM declared: "Socialism of means of production under a proletarian state alone will abolish exploitation of man by man and finally solve the problems of poverty and impoverishment."[34] Both Communist parties achieved significant electoral gains, and through the collaboration of other left parties they won control of a number of state governments, notably in West Bengal and Kerala. And in both states the Communist-dominated United Front governments made a much greater effort to carry out reform laws than the previous Congress administrations.

Despite their ideological differences, the CPI and CPM both strongly adhere to their parliamentary orientation. This they do even in face of the challenge of the aggressive Naxalites, who charged:

[32] Masani, op. cit. (n. 18 above), pp. 252–263.

[33] Ibid., p. 137.

[34] Quotations on manifestoes of the CPI and the CPM appear in M. Pattabhiram (ed.), General Election in India 1967 (Bombay, 1967), pp. 235, 249, 251, 268.

the "United Front" governments . . . are neither able nor willing to solve the basic problem, the problem of land. The experience of the "United Front" governments has once again demonstrated that without smashing the state machinery of the big landlords and the big bourgeoisie and without destroying feudalism in the countryside, no benefit can be rendered to the masses and the talk of "relief" or reform is pure deception.[35]

In answering this charge, the two "established" Communist parties stated that an electoral coalition of all leftist forces was, in fact, the most effective way to defeat the Congress government. From the point of view of the CPI leadership, "There is not a ghost of a chance for that type of a long drawnout armed guerrilla warfare which went on in China for 22 years to succeed in India. . . . In India any revolution can succeed only under the direct leadership of the proletariat, with cities as the leading center of revolution." [36] Before the advent of such a revolution, all Communists should be united in their effort to dislodge the Congress Party from power rather than be divided over a doubtful proposition of achieving power through agrarian revolution. Like the CPI, the CPM also insists on the current need for a parliamentary road to power. "The main pillar of our tactics," a resolution of the CPM Central Committee declared in 1967, "is [a] united front from below. That is so because there is a powerful urge for unity in the masses . . . ," and the Communists have to strengthen this unity and turn it into an active political force.[37] Unlike the CPI, which pins a distant hope on an urban proletarian revolution, the CPM adopts a "neo-Maoist" strategy, which calls for a two-stage revolution. The present united-front tactics, which seek to achieve the broadest alliance among all popular forces, including workers, peasants, petty bourgeoisie, and the anti-imperalist elements of the bourgeoisie, are appropriate for the first stage and preparatory to the second stage, which is consummated in a Communist revolution. The CPM regards its present task as the breaking of the monopoly of power of the Congress Party. "The bourgeoisie-landlord state power can never be broken," a CPM document stated in 1968, "except through a people's democratic revolution or social-

[35] *Liberation*, Vol. II, No. 3 (1969), 6. Quoted in Franda, *op. cit.* (n. 21 above), 810.

[36] C. Rajeswara Rao, "Naxalite Movement, Origin and Harmful Consequences," *New Age*, June 29, 1969, p. 9. Quoted in Franda, *op. cit.*, 809.

[37] Quoted in Franda, *ibid.*, 813.

ist revolution. But before that . . . breaking up the one-party monopoly of power is considered as an important step forward, . . ."[38]

Current Limitations to the Communist Approaches

In following the above three approaches to the land issue, the Communists appear to have made very modest gains. In the sense of developing a new, broad rural following for the Communists, these approaches have been generally unavailing. This is so because there are significant limitations to which these approaches are at present subject.

In the developing countries where Communist-sponsored guerrilla warfare is in the incipient phase, the applicability of this approach to the land issue faces two major limitations. One relates to the difficulties in the alteration of the Communist strategy of revolution, and the other concerns the split in Communist parties.

Most Communist parties possess an urban membership and an urban orientation. If the cases of Pakistan and Taiwan are excluded from consideration because no full-fledged Communist party has ever existed or been firmly established there, this Communist urban bias appears to be the case in most countries studied here.

In all Latin America "during most of its history . . . the Communist party, like most other parties in the area, was overwhelmingly urban in composition and outlook. Its leaders were neither able nor willing to sustain the effort required to surmount geographical and psychological barriers separating them from the peasantry . . . [and today] without exception the peasantry contributes only a small percentage of the Communist party rank and file."[39] This general characterization of Latin American Communists certainly applies to those in Colombia and Mexico. The Communist Party of Colombia, as one of its former officials observed, "was obsessed with being a working-class party, but it was basically a party of [urban] intellectuals."[40] Similarly, urban intellectuals, professionals, and lately, students, dominate the Mexican Communist Party. In Iran, though it occasionally sought to gain peasant backing, the Tudeh Communist Party primarily concentrated its attention on the cities; few

[38] Quoted in *ibid.*, 817.

[39] Rollie E. Poppino, *International Communism in Latin America: A History of the Movement, 1917–1963* (New York: Free Press, 1964), pp. 101, 109.

[40] José Gutiérrez, *La Rebeldía Colombiana* (Bogotá, Ediciones Tercer Mundo, 1962), pp. 36–37. Quoted in Dix, *op. cit.* (n. 3 above), p. 276.

rural residents contributed to its membership.[41] In Egypt, "in contrast with most other parties, the Communists have no roots in the villages." [42] Only in India and the Philippines, did the Communists have considerable rural participants. In India, it was during World War II that the Communists captured control of the All-India Kisan Sabha, which provided them with a rural base. However, it contrast to the party's membership, the CPI leadership consists largely of people of urban middle-class background.[43] Even the ostensibly rurally oriented CPML has not recruited enough peasants to change its basically urban complexion. The CPML has attracted "college students and the disenchanted urban middle class. Its leadership—is not yet derived from the lower classes and the disadvantaged." [44] In the Philippines, rural involvement in Communist activities grew out of the Huk guerrilla movement against the Japanese occupation forces, and only recently has the leadership group included a substantial portion of rural elements.

The reasons for the predominance of urban residents are well known. In addition to the fact that urban residents are more exposed than villagers to Communist influence, there is the classical Marxist line of belittling the revolutionary potential of the peasants. According to orthodox Marxist thinking, it is difficult to mobilize and politicize the peasants because they are inert, ignorant, and lack class consciousness. Communist revolution must rely upon the urban proletariat as its vanguard, and will first occur in cities. Traditionally, therefore, most Communist parties have devoted comparatively little effort to rural recruitment and to agitational activities in the countryside.

In recent years, in view of the developments in China and Cuba, many Communists have been tempted to modify their urban orientation and to follow a guerrilla strategy. This strategy requires them to perform a number of difficult tasks: to adjust their mentality and living habits to the rural environment, to change their organizational principles and agitational tactics, and to recruit a cadre from a population that has not been much exposed to their ideology. Régis Debray, the new apologist of guerrilla warfare, has commented on this point;

[41] Zabih, op. cit., pp. 249, 256–257; and Donald N. Wilber, Contemporary Iran (New York, 1963), p. 140.

[42] Baer, op. cit., p. 215.

[43] See Overstreet and Windmiller, op. cit. (n. 18 above), 357–358, 384–386; and Weiner, op. cit. (n. 19 above), pp. 134–135, 140.

[44] Franda, op. cit. (n. 21 above), 803.

Fidel [Castro] once blamed certain failures of the guerrillas on a purely intellectual attitude toward war. The reason is understandable: aside from his physical weakness and lack of adjustment to rural life, the intellectual will try to grasp the present through preconceived ideological constructs and live it through books. He will be less able than others to invent, improvise, make do with available resources, decide instantly on bold moves when he is in a tight spot. Thinking that he already knows, he will learn more slowly, display less flexibility.[45]

In addition to these difficulties, the Communists must face the challenge of developing a cause which will enable them to attract rapidly a sufficient rural following to withstand government counter-insurgency actions. It appears that in Asia as well as in Latin America the most apparent cause enabling the Communists to identify with the peasants has not been rural dissatisfaction with the land-tenure system. In the experience of Asian Communist parties, the cause is nationalism. A comparative study of Asian Communist parties shows that those parties with a "medium" or "strong" rural membership are very frequently the ones that developed their rural strength through their anti-Japanese activities during the Second World War. This is the case with the Communist parties of Burma, China, Indonesia, Korea, Outer Mongolia, the Philippines, and Vietnam.[46] It was through these activities against the Japanese that the Communists publicized their existence and facilitated their recruitment effort. Located in areas controlled neither by government forces nor by the Japanese, Communist guerrillas could cultivate and expand their military power with relative safety. Typically, only after they developed sufficient rural strength did the guerrillas begin to seize on the land issue. Thus, in Asia it was primarily nationalism that established a link between the Communists and the rural population at large, not the issue of land. In the experience of the Cuban Communist revolution, an anti-Batista-regime stance was the functional equivalent of Asian nationalism. It was the struggle against a highly corrupt and oppressive regime that

[45] Régis Debray, *Revolution in the Revolution? Armed Struggle and Political Struggle in Latin America*, trans. from the French by Bobbye Ortiz (New York: Grove Press, Inc., 1967), p. 21.

[46] Robert A. Scalapino, "Communism in Asia: Toward a Comparative Analysis," in Scalapino (ed.), *The Communist Revolution in Asia: Tactics, Goals, and Achievements* (Englewood Cliffs, N.J.: Prentice-Hall, Inc., 1965), pp. 32–33. Scalapino's classification of social background of Communist membership consists of the following categories: "Worker," "Farmer," "Intellectual," "Petit Bourgeoisie," "Other Bourgeoisie," and "Military."

celebrated the Castroites' cause and won for the revolutionaries popular sympathy. It was neither Communism nor the land issue per se that helped the revolutionaries win power.[47]

For Communists who have just begun to follow the guerrilla war approach the crucial question is: in the absence of nationalism or its funtional equivalent, can a large rural following be created by solely capitalizing on the land issue? One may also add the question: even in countries where governments are corrupt and oppressive, can an anti-government stance be an adequate cause for the Communists to gain rural followers? Or, again, is such a stance a functional equivalent of nationalism? It is partially over these questions that the Communists split apart.

This very split which exists in practically every Communist Party in the developing countries represents another limitation of the guerrilla approach. Those who do follow the approach fall into an extremely isolated position; they have to fight the government while competing with other Communists and non-Communist leftists. The ranks of Communists in these countries are already small; the split makes it even more difficult for the guerrillas to create a minimum core of cadres necessary for meeting basic operational requirements. Under the circumstances, as is often the case, the guerrillas can spare little time and personnel for recruiting indigenous peasants, let alone for finding and circulating a broad cause, identifying the land issue and offering a program, and reaching out to the broad rural population. It is true that some Communists can rely on foreign support; or a guerrilla war may even be started with foreign sponsorship and participation. But in such cases, guerrillas will find that nationalism deters rather than facilitates their cause.

Communist experiences in Bolivia in 1966 to 1967 illustrate these points with striking clarity. As the published accounts of Ernesto Ché Guevara's diary and documents have revealed, the Cuban-sponsored adventure in Bolivia engendered antagonism rather than cooperation from the local Communist Party, which followed the Moscow line. At its peak strength, the guerrilla movement consisted of 51 fighters: 18 Cubans, 29 Bolivians, 3 Peruvians, and 1 East German. They often engaged in heavy fighting without enough manpower to maintain logistics and communica-

---

[47] One scarcely needs to emphasize that the Castro movement was neither projected as a Communist inspired revolution before the fall of the Batista regime nor sponsored by the established Communist Party in Cuba. See Theodore Draper, *Castroism: Theory and Practice* (New York: Frederick A. Praeger, Publishers, 1965), pp. 3–56.

tions. Most significantly, there was a "complete lack of peasant recruitment" into the guerrilla movement, a violation of Guevara's own previously stated dictum: a successful guerrilla war must be a mass struggle incorporating the rural populace. Instead, in several instances, the peasants aided government forces, leading to losses for the rebels. These were the conditions that remained with the movement toward its end in October 1967.[48] The inability of the guerrillas to obtain the cooperation of the Bolivian peasants, is not difficult to understand when one recalls that in 1952 Bolivia experienced a revolution which brought a large-scale land redistribution program to the (American) Indian peasants on the Andes mountains. One may find some truth in former Bolivian President René Barrientos Ortuño's comment on the failure of the guerrilla movement: Guevara and the Cuban Communists were victims "of their own misinformation about the Bolivian reality." They failed to take into account that Bolivia had its own revolution and reform and "that the Indians of the region they hoped to conquer had benefited from our reforms and would be the first to turn their backs to a foreign invasion." [49]

If, for the reasons noted above, the Bolivian guerrilla movement failed, presumably for the same reasons, one can say, the Cuban-supported guerrilla movements in Colombia and Venezuela have not been able to gather momentum. These instances of guerrilla warfare seem to demonstrate that any intention of Communist groups to gain political power by a combination of guerrilla warfare and exploitation of the land question is currently futile. But what about the future? Can there be a change of circumstances that makes a violent course of action fruitful? Before answering this question, a discussion of the limitations of the other two Communist approaches is necessary.

In essence, the theoretical premise of the Communist agitational approach is the class-struggle theory. Farmers who do not have the means of production (land) must be organized in the struggle against those who have. The difficulty of this approach lies in the lack of relevance of its theoretical premise to the reality of the agricultural societies in the developing world. In these societies, inter-group differences are social as well as economic. The population can be differentiated not only according to tenure status but also according to such social identities as clan, religion,

---

[48] See Daniel James (ed.), *The Complete Bolivian Diaries of Ché Guevara and Other Captured Documents* (New York: Stein and Day, Publishers, 1968).

[49] Quoted in *The New York Times*, January 9, 1968, p. 14. Cf. Daniel James's introduction to Ché Guevara's diary in James, *op. cit.*, p. 59.

caste, and the like. Farmers of different types of tenure status may belong to the same social group; people belonging to different social groups may be of the same tenure status. In addition, in an agricultural society, the economic differences among farmers of various types of tenure status are not so sharply drawn as those between classes in an urban-industrial society. One can identify in almost all developing countries a sizable group of landless farmers, but there is a far larger group of small peasants which may be of some combination of the following: part-landlord, part-owner, part-tenant, and part-laborer. And the landless farmers may work for these *small peasants* as well as for the *large landowners*. These characteristics of agricultural society impose serious restrictions on the effectiveness of the agitational approach. To follow this approach, which posits essentially two classes, the Communists find themselves siding with the many landless farmers, but they also antagonize the far more numerous other farmers.

Indian Communist experiences may again illustrate these points. The Indian Communist "Party's quandary with regard to the landless agricultural workers," Gene D. Overstreet and Marshall Windmiller have observed, limited the party's success in rural areas. These "workers constitute, in some areas, as much as 37 percent of the total agricultural population, and are employed, frequently at starvation wages, by the peasants and landlords. But the effective organizing of these landless laborers to obtain higher wages would hurt the peasant far more than it would the wealthy landlords. A Communist Party which brought this about could hardly expect the support of the small landholder, let alone that of the more prosperous peasants. . . ."[50] Myron Weiner further elaborated on this subject. Though referring specifically to West Bengal, Weiner's comments apply as well to rural India in general:

> Firstly, there was no clear-cut peasant-landlord dichotomy, since a vast number of rent collectors existed between some cultivator and the *zamindar*. Moreover, caste and kinship ties between some cultivators and their rent collectors diminished the prospects for class struggle. Second, the Krishak Praja Party and later the Muslim League won the support of the Muslim peasantry in Bengal; community consciousness, not class consciousness grew. And third, attempts by Communist peasant political workers to organize the *bargardars* . . . and, to a lesser extent, agricultural laborers alienated some peasant cultivators for whom the *bargardars* and agricultural laborers worked. In short,

[50] *Op. cit.* (n. 18 above), pp. 393–394.

even among cultivating peasants, conflicts of interests existed; and any attempt to build a movement on the basis of class tended to alienate one section or another of the peasantry.[51]

In the light of these difficulties, it is not surprising to find that the CPI has abandoned the agitational approach and opted for a parliamentary approach.

But the parliamentary approach also faces some serious difficulties. First, only very rarely and in very few places are Communists able to gain power through the democratic process. Only in certain states of India, notably Kerala and West Bengal, have Communists been able to form coalition governments on the basis of electoral successes. Hence, most Communists do not have the opportunity to offer, through the parliamentary process, a land-reform program of their own. Second, those few Communists who have gained power through the electoral process also face a dilemma with regard to the type of program they are going to initiate or support. Their ideological commitment requires them to sponsor a program of expropriation of land without compensation, and then the socialization of farms. But any attempt to adopt such a program alienates the electoral support of many owner-farmers without necessarily winning the sympathies of the prospective beneficiaries—the landless farmers—who may aspire to be landowners. To avoid such a pitfall, the Communists have to endorse a mild program emphasizing equality of land, private ownership, and expropriation with compensation. But in doing so they simply advance a non-Communist program. When such a program is enforced on a broad scale, a large class of owner-farmers will be created; hence, the prospect for a transition to socialist farming will accordingly diminish. In such a case the Communists will, in effect, build in the rural population a strong opposition to the Communist system of farming, thus damaging their own cause. That is to say, their enforcement of a non-Communist land-reform program will only impede them from initiating a genuine Communist one. This will remain the case as long as the Communists continue to be a minority party nationally or a majority party regionally. Barring the unlikely event that farmers might express their preference through ballots for a collectivized farming system, which has not occurred in any Communist country,[52] the only way for

[51] Op. cit. (n. 19 above), p. 139.

[52] On the contrary, as is well known, in some eastern European countries where Communist regimes showed some deference to the wishes of farmers, decollectivization has occurred. This is obviously the experience of Yugoslavia, Hungary, and Poland. In

the Communists to install such a system is first to seize national power forcefully. But this will then mean an end of the parliamentary approach.

Impact of Land Reform on Communism

In light of the above discussion of Communist approaches to the land issue and of the limitations to which these approaches are currently subject, what will be the long-term impact on Communism of land reform sponsored by non-Communist governments in the developing countries? To answer this question one should first consider the situation in which a non-Communist government fails to effect reform when it faces simultaneously a serious land issue and a Communist challenge. Since the rural population in the developing countries will generally continue to grow in the foreseeable future, one can see rising population pressure on land and, consequently, a widening of the aspiration-reality gap in rural areas. In time, this development may lead to a situation in which the current limitations on Communist approaches to the land issue may become loosened or irrelevant. Thus, if the Communists decide to follow the guerrilla war approach, the continuously widening aspiration-reality gap will enable them to reach an ever broader segment of the discontented rural population, and to convince more of the city-oriented, orthodox Marxists of the need to go to the countryside. Hence, the problems relating to the recruitment of rural cadres and the supply of indigenous leadership that the Communist guerrillas now face will become easier to resolve. It is not inappropriate to emphasize the fact that today, almost one whole generation after they first capitalized on nationalism to develop their rural strength, the Huks in the Philippines depend exclusively on the land issue for their survival and revival, and that in the meantime the Huk leadership and cadres have developed a rural orientation.

In the long run, the failure to resolve the land problem will also facilitate the Communist agitational approach. As rural poverty spreads and intensifies, traditional patterns of social stratification—i.e. the division of a society according to such criteria as race, language, caste, etc.—will grow weaker as a factor mitigating the conflict resulting from the polariza-

---

the non-Communist world, only in Israel is there a large number of farmers who voluntarily opted for collectivized farming. But, as stated earlier, the circumstances under which the Israeli *Kibbutz* and *Kvutza* systems emerged and the conditions under which these systems operate are very unique, making the Israeli experience practically inapplicable to any other place.

tion of economic differences. The ratio of the landless to other types of farmers will increase, and, therefore, the theory of class struggle will be made meaningful to the rural population. Out of the necessity for survival, and emboldened by their swelling ranks, the landless peasants may start to strike the plantations, organize demonstrations against the public authorities, and forcefully seize the land. If the government and the landed class adopt a repressive policy toward these activities without offering some positive response to the land problem, some of the agitating peasants may possibly be persuaded to join the guerrillas. Some others may devote their loyalty to a Communist party that promises a solution to their problem through the electoral process. Thus, should the Communists opt for the parliamentary approach, the prospect of winning electoral support for a Communist farm system will be brightened. If the Communists still deem it tactically necessary to introduce a non-Communist type of farm program, the introduction of such a farm program will at the very least improve their overall electoral position, enabling them to grow into something more than an insignificant national party.

In short, in the face of the widening aspiration-reality gap within the rising rural population, government inaction toward the land issue will facilitate the efforts of the Communists, following whatever approach they may choose, to capitalize on the discontent and obtain rural support. Viewed in this light, the obvious effect of the kind of land reform discussed in this study on Communism is that it may prevent the Communists from seizing the land issue. As an alternative to a typical Marxist farm program, a non-Communist land reform program may help build into the rural community long-term immunity from Communism.

Non-Communist land reform and an authentic Communist farm program may share a number of common features. Both are publicly sponsored programs entailing compulsory, drastic, and rapid tenurial changes. But they show profound differences with respect to the issue of landownership, the question of compensation, the landowners' rights to retain land, and the control of land use after tenurial changes. By endorsing private ownership, providing compensation to landowners for land expropriated, allowing landlords to retain a portion of their property, and leaving the control of land use to the tillers, non-Communist land reform engenders minimum economic and social disruption, gives fair treatment to all concerned, and, most important of all, wins the support of the intended beneficiaries. A typical Communist farm program—characterized by collective farming, punitive measures against landlords by depriving them of compensation as well as of future means of living, and state control of land use—tends to generate social antagonisms that may require employment of considerable physical force to suppress; it will disrupt the productive capacity of agriculture and lose the sympathies of those who farm the land.

David Mitrany has suggested that, in light of Soviet experiences, Communist agrarian policies are basically antagonistic to the peasantry. In Russia, the Communists seized the land issue to gain power; they collectivized farms in order to secure control of the peasants and to subordinate farming to the requirements of industrialization. In Mitrany's words, "Communism first encouraged peasants to help themselves to land, so that it might have its hands free to grasp political power, and then used that political power to deprive the peasants of land." Soviet collectivization of farming was in essence a politically motivated economic revolution, a revolution "directed against the hardest working of all working sections," the peasants. "The process of collectivization, as part of an economy planned and controlled from urban centers, is at the same time binding the villagers together as they have never been before, on a professional and class basis." [53]

Mitrany's analysis may be too subtle for the peasants to understand. But to the elites of the developing countries the implication of this analysis should be obvious. If from a historical perspective Communist agrarian policies are politically and economically exploitive of the peasantry, non-Communist governments can best compete with the Communists in rural areas by offering land-reform programs that are genuinely beneficial to the peasantry. These programs should help create a large class of small owner-farmers and tenants with secure occupancy rights and should help assure peasants of rising incomes. Under such circumstances, the Communists will lose a large number of farmers as their target of appeal, while the government will win strong allies in defense of the reformed land-tenure system.[54] A brief examination of the reform experiences of the eight countries under study appears to support this observation.

In the four countries with more extensive reform results (Iran, Mexico, Taiwan, and the U.A.R), a rural Communist challenge is either non-existent or insignificant. In Iran, the Tudeh Party has not been able

[53] David Mitrany, *Marx against the Peasant, A Study in Social Dogmatism* (New York: Collier Books, 1961), pp. 208–209.

[54] For a leftist view on this point, see Al McCoy, "Land Reform as Counter-Revolution," *Bulletin of Concerned Asian Scholars*, III (Winter–Spring 1971), 14–49.

to present any threat to the government since the late 1950s. Its leaders either went abroad or remain inactive in the cities. In rural areas, where it never developed a following, the party maintains no presence at all. In Mexico, "after more than forty years of struggle . . . ," Karl M. Schmitt has written, "the Communist movement appears to be not just stalemated but in decline." [55] This is so, as Howard F. Cline has explained, because "Mexicans pride themselves on the fact that *their* Revolution antedated the Russian one by a number of years, . . . There is little in Communist ideology that cannot be paralleled, and at an earlier date, from Mexican Revolutionary slogans and documents." [56] As a reformed indigenous institution, the vast *ejido* system has made Communist efforts to penetrate the rural areas unavailing and the Communist theory of collective farming unappealing. Today, the Communists may resort to agitational activities, but their effort is aimed at the creation of more *ejidos*, not their substitution by a Communist system.

In Taiwan, the completion of the three reform programs resulted in the creation of a large number of owner-farmers and in the improvement of tenant income. There is also the absence of an internal Communist threat. Though the absence of such a threat may be attributed to the stringent security measures of the Nationalist Government, the peasants can be said to have developed so strong a commitment to the reformed land system that they are quite unlikely to opt for the Marxist type of farming, even if they were open to Communist influence. The government, seeking to reinforce this peasant commitment, has constantly stressed that its programs were clearly an alternative to "the Marxist Leninist programs" adopted on the mainland, and that the two sets of programs differed fundamentally in ideological foundation, purposes, methods, and objectives.[57] In the U.A.R., similarly, the regime has also considered its land-reform program an alternative to the Communist farming program. The reform decrees of 1952 and 1961 rested on a theoretical foundation the U.A.R. had itself developed, the concept of "Arab Socialism." This concept, Nasser explained, differs from Communism in that "Arab Socialism" accepts religion whereas the latter rejects it; "Arab Socialism" advocates national independence, whereas the latter tolerates international inter-

[55] *Communism in Mexico* (Austin, Texas, 1965), p. 220.

[56] *Mexico, Revolution to Evolution* (London, 1962), p. 178. Cf. Walter Washingto, "Mexican Resistance to Communism," *Foreign Affairs*, XXXVI (April 1958), 504–505; and Alexander, *op. cit.* (n. 15 above), pp. 348–349.

[57] See Chen Cheng, *Land Reform in Taiwan* (Taipei, Taiwan, 1961), pp. 112–129.

ference; and "Arab Socialism" stresses cooperation of all people, whereas the latter adheres to the dictatorship of the proletariat.[58] The supervised cooperatives and the system of compulsory triennial rotation farming, introduced with land reform, were the Egyptians' own creation. The reform programs are, therefore, more appropriate to rural Egypt than is the Marxist farm system. "Arab Socialism," William E. Griffith has commented, "has stripped Communism of most of its gospel and substituted a much more effective ideology of its own." [59] Nasser's land reform and his program of socialization of industries in 1961 gave him confidence to believe that the U.A.R. had grown immune from any influence the Egyptian Communist Party might attempt to exert. He formally disbanded the party in 1965, urging the Communists to join the Arab Socialist Union.[60]

Among the four countries with less extensive reform results, only Pakistan today faces no challenge of Communism in rural areas. But Pakistan is also the only country among the eight studied that did not face a Communist threat before land reform. Communism, therefore, has not been a factor in the politics of land reform. In India, the Congress Party appears to face continuous Communist electoral competition over the land issue. But since the Congress is credited with the abolition of the zamindar system and since the Indian Communists are seriously split into factions and are, therefore, incapable of offering any meaningful alternative to Congress's programs, the Communist challenge on the land issue is not likely to develop major proportions. The Philippines and Colombia have experienced the least progress in land reform. They are also the two countries facing a threat from rural guerrillas. It is here that the impact of land reform on Communism remains to be seen. But to the elites of the two countries the case of China should be highly instructive. When the Communists seized the land issue on the mainland, they won power there. When the Nationalists implemented land reform on Taiwan, they secured a strong rural base on the island. Land reform may facilitate or deter Communism, depending upon whether the Communists or the non-Communists can be first seriously identified with it. Such is the relationship between land reform and Communism.

[58] Jaan Pennar, "Moscow and Socialism in Egypt," *Problems of Communism*, XV (September–October 1966), 47. One additional major difference is that Arab Socialism accepts private land ownership whereas Communism rejects it. See Fayez Sayegh, "The Theoretical Structure of Nasser's Socialism," in Albert Hourani (ed.), *Middle East Affairs, Number 4* (London, 1965), pp. 33–34.

[59] Cited in Pennar, *op. cit.*

[60] *Ibid.*, p. 42.

XV

CONCLUSIONS

A Recapitulation

In analyzing the political processes of land reform, this book has proposed three hypotheses. The perception of the need for legitimacy prompts the political elite to initiate land reform; the relationship between the initiating elite and the landed class determines the manner of program formulation and the content of the adopted program; and the political commitment decisively affects the extent of program implementation. The evidence presented in Chapters IV through IX appears to have verified these hypotheses.

In assessing the political effects of land reform, this book has adopted a series of analytic schemes to gauge the impact of reform on five subject matters: (1) *rural political participation* can be ascertained by identifying whether, in the aftermath of reform, the rural population follows an aggregative pattern of participation or a non-aggregative one; (2) *national integration* can be assessed by reference to the territorial flow of national authority and the peasants' psychological reaction to the nation in consequence of reform; (3) *institutionalization of rural organizations* can be studied by examining the effect of reform on four aspects of these organizations: membership growth, acquisition of value, differentiation, and adaptability; (4) *rural stability* can be appreciated by discerning both the short-term destabilizing and long-term stabilizing consequences of reform; and on (5) *Communism* can be properly understood by analyzing the interaction between the Communist approaches to the land issue and the non-Communist response to the land problem. The analysis presented in Chapters X through XIV indicates that land reform has a definite and positive contribution to make to these aspects of political development and that generally the degree of the contribution varies with the extent of the program implementation.

These findings lead to a few broad conclusions which are relevant not only to the countries under study but also to other developing countries in need of reform.

The Efficacy of Political Systems in Reform

In the political processes of land reform the type of political system operating in a country is a significant variable. Political systems can be roughly divided into two types: competitive and non-competitive. A competitive political system is characterized by an institutionalized decentralization of political authority among different groups, whether they are political parties or factions. Working within the framework of a constitution, the parties or factions compete with each other in the electoral process and in the legislative arena. A non-competitive political system refers to a system in which political power is concentrated in a very narrow segment of the established political structure. In most cases, the executive branch of the government reigns supreme, with the electorate and the legislature playing a ritualistic or perfunctory role. Colombia, India, and the Philippines possess the first type of system; Iran, Mexico, Pakistan, Taiwan, and the U.A.R. the second.

The present study gives strong evidence that the competitive system is less efficacious than the non-competitive in bringing about reform. The first three countries have generally carried out reform programs at a slower speed, with narrower scope and more limited results than did the five other countries. Basically, this is because in a competitive system the decentralization of authority affords the landed class opportunities to frustrate reform, whereas in a non-competitive system the centralization of power denies that class such an opportunity. This is evident in the entire political process of reform, from initiation and formulation to implementation.

Both competitive and non-competitive systems initiate land reform because of the need for gaining legitimacy. However, the two systems differ in their appraisal of the need. In a competitive system, all groups aspiring to achieve power must reach out to the rural areas to enlist broad electoral support. In response to the competitive solicitation of politicians, the rural masses become aligned with different parties, factions, and candidates and turn out in elections in rather large numbers. But because their voting strength is dispersed by the intervention of the landed class, the rural masses can provide electoral support to the elite but cannot effectively participate in the policy process affecting their interests. Under this condition, rural grievances may actually accumulate, posing a threat to political stability. Within the elite there may be elements who see the political necessity of removal of these grievances through land reform. Many others, however, may entertain the thought that the regime is broadly based, hence, not amenable to a serious crisis of legitimacy. The landed class and their representatives can thus refute the reform advocates about the urgency of tenurial changes. Within the Conservative and the Liberal Parties of Colombia, the Nacionalista and the Liberal Parties of the Philippines, and the Congress Party of India reform opponents often pointed out to their adversaries that these parties already had secure rural constituencies and broad peasant electoral support. The need for introducing land reform to bolster the legitimacy of the established regimes was not particularly evident. On the contrary, reform might actually have disrupted the political hold of the governing parties. In a competitive system, therefore, the elite is divided over both the political utility and the urgency of reform.

In a non-competitive system, the regime, by comparison, is not broadly based. The elite assumes political authority not as a result of electoral contests but because of an effective manipulation of power. However, when it considers bringing about land reform, the elite, as a small cluster of power holders, often shares the view that it has a definite and immediate need for broadening the foundation of the regime by incorporating the peasants. The revolutionary elites of Mexico and the U.A.R. promulgated reform decrees in the midst of political and military upheavals. Unless they could promptly win over the peasantry through reform, these elites might have been unable to acquire power or to secure the power they had acquired. The Kuomintang introduced reform in Taiwan at the conclusion of the civil war on mainland China. It keenly needed the Taiwanese peasants' allegiance to avoid a repetition of the defeat on the island. In Iran, the Shah pushed reform at a time of cumulating political, economic, and personal crises. He earnestly sought peasant alignment to provide strength to a thinly based and crumbling monarchy. In Pakistan, the reform in the East Wing was to ratify what the peasants had accomplished by force, and the reform in the West Wing was designed to bolster a freshly born military regime. In all these cases, the elites, who could never before claim to possess a strong rural constituency, were highly sensitive to the political value of tenurial changes and the necessity of immediate action. They had to put forward hurriedly their reform proposals without careful deliberation.

The difference in efficacy of competitive and non-competitive systems in land reform is manifested more prominently in the stage of program formulation than in the stage of initiation. Generally speaking, in a competitive system, reform sponsors must fashion a program within the legislature where they are bound to encounter the determined, repeated opposition of the representatives of the landed interests. They have to seek compromise with their opponents with regard to all major principles, as well as to specific provisions. Often through laborious, protracted negotiation, reform sponsors can in the end enact only mild or perfunctory laws. As amply shown in Chapters V and VI, in Colombia, the Philippines, and India the present reform laws were adopted only after decades of bargaining between the sponsors and the opponents. By raising the issue of constitutionality of reform bills, demanding high compensation for the adversely affected interests, using parliamentary dilatory tactics, and introducing weakening amendments, reform opponents insured that the laws enacted afforded the maximum protection to the landed class.

Reform sponsors in a non-competitive system prefer to formulate a program within the executive branch of the government, with little or token legislative involvement. They generally follow a unilateral-decision approach in working out the detailed provisions of a program. Thus, neither subject to the restraints attending the parliamentary process, nor facing the obstruction of the landed interests, reform sponsors are able to bring forth speedily a program largely to their liking. In most cases this means a program in favor of the peasants.

In Mexico, Taiwan, and the U.A.R. the reform sponsors were elites who had severed ties with the landed class. They decided upon the principal features of their programs and left it to the bureaucracy to compose the specific provisions. Subsequently, the legislatures gave their approval without extensive debate or substantive revision. In all these activities the voice of the landed interests was either excluded or barely heard. The programs adopted provided small farmers and tenants with considerable benefits, usually at the expense of the former large landlords. In Iran and Pakistan, the elites maintained cooperative relationships with some of the landed interests. But with power concentrated in their hands, the reform sponsors refused to bargain with these interests, suspended the legislatures, and promulgated their programs through executive decrees.

The efficacy of competitive and non-competitive systems in land reform shows the greatest difference in the implementation stage. In a competitive system, the resources and instrumentalities for reform enforcement are controlled by different governmental institutions which are susceptible to the obstructing influence of the landed interests. The creation of a reform agency, the staffing of this agency with administrative and technical personnel, and the provision and allocation of funds often require the consent and cooperation of some or all of the following institutions: the legislature, the administration, the bureaucracy, and public financial agencies. The settlement of these matters by these institutions provides reform opponents with fresh opportunities to frustrate and delay enforcement.

In India, the implementation of reform programs was seriously hampered by the lack of both a national and state agency exclusively responsible for enforcement. The federal parliament did not enact a law to create a national agency because it regarded land reform as a state responsibility. State legislatures failed to create state agencies because they considered the state revenue administration adequate for assuming reform enforcement responsibilities. In reality, however, the revenue administration was too understaffed to be able to carry on effectively the additional work. Some of its personnel, such as the *patwaris*, who derived income from land or had maintained in the past an intimate relationship with the local gentry, could not be expected to execute reform laws with impartiality and dispatch.

In Colombia, a reform agency, INCORA, was created, but on both its national managing board and its regional committees large landowners' organizations were given guaranteed representation. The Congress enacted a very comprehensive, detailed reform code in 1961, but it never provided INCORA with enough administrative and financial support to enable it to carry on its projects on a broad scale. Similarly, in the Philippines the Congress adopted in 1963 a reform code with ambitious goals and broad scope. It created a Land Authority to administer the law throughout the nation, but this agency was so inadequately equipped that it could operate primarily in only one region of the country, Central Luzon. To fund the reform program the Congress authorized the Land Bank to raise within five years after the enactment of the 1963 law a capital of ₱1.5 billion, ₱900 million of which was to be subscribed by the government. But by 1966 the bank had only received from the government a total of ₱2.2 million.

In a non-competitive system the executive branch of government can discharge most of its reform enforcement responsibilities without new legislative authorization. Even in cases in which new legislation is needed, the legislature often defers to the wishes of the executive. The reform agency created in a non-competitive system as a rule does not provide representation to the landed interests, and its personnel are frequently recruited from among those with strong motivations for reform enforcement who are unwilling to collude with the obstructionists. In addition, in certain cases the peasants are directly involved in the enforcement process, able to assert and protect their interests. In a non-competitive system the government is never seriously handicapped by the financial burden of reform. In certain countries this burden is not heavy; in certain other countries the government has the ability to generate funds, sometimes from the non-agricultural sector of the economy.

Mexico, Taiwan, the U.A.R., and Iran have all created enforcement agencies of broad structure and generally adequate staff to carry out their tasks on a nation-wide basis. In these agencies, the landed interests have been excluded, and their administrative and technical personnel have proved to be highly faithful in the execution of laws. In Mexico, Taiwan, and the U.A.R. reform beneficiaries were specially organized by the governments to assist in the implementation process. Among the countries with non-competitive systems, only Pakistan did not have a national reform agency, and in the West Pakistan Land Reforms Commission—a provincial reform agency—the landed interests did maintain a presence.

With regard to financial support for reform, all these countries encountered no difficulties. Iran utilized its oil income; Taiwan sold its public industrial enterprises; the U.A.R. and Pakistan reallocated the government budget. Mexico did not need to raise a large reform fund because it acquired land for redistribution practically through confiscation.

The foregoing comparison of the reform performance of competitive and non-competitive systems leaves little doubt that it is easier for a non-competitive system than for a competitive system to effect meaningful tenurial reform. To the developing countries in need of reform it is evident that in those countries where a multiparty or biparty system reigns, the prospect for prompt, effective, and drastic land reform is generally not bright. In countries where political power is concentrated in one political party or a small group of leaders, and where the elites earnestly seek to broaden their rural base, the possibility of a relatively successful reform is great.

The Choice of Reform Programs

In Chapter V, the question of selection of productivity or equity as the primary objective of land reform was discussed. Seeking to expand and utilize efficiently agricultural resources, developmental programs are generally oriented toward raising productivity. Aiming at reallocation of landownership and farm income, redistributive programs stress equity. Often viewing these objectives as competitive, the elites of the eight countries studied had to choose one of the two as a matter of emphasis. In making the choice, the elites acted on the basis of their relation with the landed class. Cooperative elites preferred productivity; separated elites equity.

What are the consequences of the choice? Evidently most of the countries emphasizing productivity as the primary reform objective ended up with ineffectual implementation of programs and little, if any, rise in productivity. As analyzed at some length in Chapter IX, in terms of the impact of reform on landholding patterns and on agricultural output, all except one of the cooperative elite-ruled countries—Colombia, India, Iran, Pakistan, and the Philippines—experienced much less success than the separated elite-ruled countries—Mexico, Taiwan, and the U.A.R. The exception is Iran, which has achieved considerable results. In countries where equity was emphasized, the implications of the choice are complicated. Mexico, Taiwan, and the U.A.R. have all extensively implemented their redistributive programs; land concentration has been reduced; and agricultural output has risen continuously. However, in recent years there have been strong indications that the long accepted policy of giving land to the tillers is now of doubtful value. This also happened to Japan, whose land-reform programs predated and closely resembled the Taiwanese, and whose reform experiences are highly relevant to the subject matter under consideration here. The cases of Mexico, Japan, and Taiwan deserve a brief review.

In its first three decades of land reform, Mexico concentrated on the division of *haciendas* into *ejidos*. Today the *ejidos* have improved their productive capacity but have fallen behind medium and large *non-ejido* farms in agricultural output, and the *ejido* as an organization has become stagnant. To a considerable extent, the problems of the *ejido* can be attributed to the early reform policy that heavily stressed the idea of equity. The division of farm land into small units, the lack of genuine cooperation among the *ejidatarios*, and the prohibition of land transfers in the *ejido* place the *ejidatarios* in an unfavorable position. Being small farmers with large families, the *ejidatarios* lack means to purchase modern farm inputs. With tiny farming units, the *ejidatarios* cannot apply mechanization and make full use of advanced agricultural techniques. They cannot, therefore, match the productive record of middle and large *non-ejido* farmers who do not suffer these liabilities.

Mexico's land reform has left an ironic legacy. Though intended to benefit the *campesinos*, the reform actually made the land of the beneficiaries less productive than that of the non-beneficiaries. To the Mexican nation, this is a serious setback. Half of the country's agricultural land, which is in *ejidatario* hands, cannot improve its productive capacity because *ejidatarios* cannot efficiently utilize it and because productive *non-ejido* farmers cannot acquire it.

Post-World War II Japanese land reform also concentrated on redistribution of land. The 1952 Agricultural Land Act, which stabilized the post-reform status quo, established low ceilings, varying between 1.6 to 4.5 hectares among the prefectures. The entire farming community was reduced to one of small family-farms. While these farms considerably increased their productivity, industries grew at an even higher rate. Consequently there was a persistent and accelerating migration to the cities by the rural population. The resultant reduction of farm population created a host of problems.[1] Old farmers had difficulty in keeping the younger generation on their farms. Those who remained on the land could not significantly improve efficiency because the small size of their farms inhibited them from adopting mechanization and other modern practices. In addition, during farming seasons the farmers often had to pay hired hands at a rising rate to meet the inadequacy of family labor. The farmer's income was thus reduced. Unable to support themselves by farming alone, many farmers had to seek additional employment. By 1965, as many as 80 percent of Japanese farm households practiced part-time farming,[2] a practice that contained a disincentive for further agricultural improvement.

The logical solution of these problems lies in the enlargement of the size of the farm unit, hence making possible the creation of centrally managed, modernized farms. But this solution will weaken the small

---

[1] In 1968, Japanese farmers numbered about 10 million, or about 20 percent of the nation's labor force. Twenty years ago, 47.3 percent of the labor force was found employed in agriculture. *The New York Times*, March 21, 1968, p. 14.

[2] *Christian Science Monitor*, August 23, 1967, p. 4.

family farm system and lead to a reconcentration of land. In effect, this means a "reverse of the land reform program." [3] Unwilling at present to undertake this change of policy, in 1962 the Japanese government adopted amendments to the Agricultural Land Act allowing farmers to farm land beyond the established "ceilings if they could do so still relying 'mainly' on the labour of family members." [4] In addition, the government encouraged farmers to engage in cooperative farming while retaining their landownership and their income.

The pattern of agricultural development that prevailed in post-reform Taiwan is precisely the same as that in Japan. The reform programs of 1949 to 1953 created a small-farm system, with two-thirds of the island's farm families each having less than one hectare of land. These programs also contributed to a significant rise in agricultural output. But there were these developments: great industrial growth, relative decline of farm income, rural migration to cities, shortage of farm labor, and inability of small farms to modernize themselves.

To cope with these farm problems, the government adopted a number of measures. It initiated a program for replotting farm land, promoted light farm mechanization, and improved farm service organizations. But the basic problem of tiny farm units remains unresolved. In 1970, the Kuomintang appeared resolved to follow a new agricultural policy. In its "Outline for Present Rural Economic Reconstruction," adopted on March 31, the party decided upon a number of measures, including continuation of replotting of land, establishment of minimum size of farm parcels, promotion of cooperative cultivation of crops, and creation of a joint-family farm system. [5] The last two measures, already experimented with on a limited scale, represented a significant opening for enlargement of farm units. But like the Japanese government, the KMT was unwilling to adopt a policy in favor of outright combination of small farms. Concerned that such a policy would be interpreted to be a retreat from its land-to-the-tiller program, the KMT now recommended only voluntary adoption of joint farming practices and insisted that the farm family retain its landownership as well as its harvests.

In both Japan and Taiwan, the measures adopted to cope with the problem of small farms are temporary. As the progress of industrialization will further drain off rural population, and as urban demand for agricul-

[3] *The New York Times*, March 21, 1968, p. 14.
[4] U.N. *Land Reform, Fourth Report*, p. 88.
[5] *The Central Daily News*, April 1, 1970, p. 3.

tural products will increase, a definite and permanent change in the agrarian structure is necessary. Small, inefficient farms will have to be combined into large, efficient ones. In this case, the reform programs of the two countries, which have much stressed equity, will be replaced by ones emphasizing productivity.

To the developing countries yet to formulate land-reform programs, what lesson can the experiences of the countries just discussed provide? To opt for programs in favor of productivity would only result in their ineffectual implementation. To adopt programs in favor of equity would eventually require their replacement by those in favor of productivity. Which is a more desirable choice?

All things considered, the choice appears to lie in redistributive programs. To the developing countries in need of land reform, the adoption of programs emphasizing agricultural productivity will often not lead to a significant rise of productivity. This is because inequitable land-tenure arrangements are the inherent restraints on agricultural growth. They must first be removed before agriculture can fully respond to measures stimulating growth. On the other hand, though *in the long run* redistributive programs will hinder agricultural growth, *at present* they are timely and appropriate. Today, the farming community of the developing countries typically suffers underemployment or unemployment. As discussed in Chapter V, redistributive programs can alleviate this problem because, by assuring equitable ownership and farm income, they provide strong incentives for farmers to use labor-intensive techniques to increase production. If, in the future, industrial growth leads to a shortage of farm labor in some of these countries, redistributive programs will then have fulfilled their historical mission. They should then be replaced by programs in favor of productivity; more capital-intensive farming should replace the more labor-intensive techniques; and small farms should be consolidated into larger ones. These changes will, of course, entail considerable expenditure and social disruption, as unproductive small farmers will have to give up their land and find new employment. But the economic and social costs of these changes will be minor, compared to the long-term benefits flowing from a new farm system attuned to the needs of a higher stage of economic development.

One further point may be noted. The steps taken by Japan and Taiwan (and also the emergence of the mixed *ejidos* in Mexico) point up the value of a family centered cooperative farming system. In all these instances, farm families are encouraged to practice joint farming, from planting to harvesting of crops. This makes it possible for the economic allocation of labor and efficient utilization of modern farm inputs. At the same time, the farm family retains its landownership as well as its crops, hence maintaining an incentive in farming. To a considerable extent, these cooperative practices resemble the Egyptian supervised cooperative farm system, which was discussed in Chapter VIII. The Egyptian system has great merit. Though individually owned, the farm plots of the Egyptian cooperative system were combined into large compact areas during the time of land reform. Thus, the Egyptian system did not incur the cost and social disruption that a future consolidation of small farms in Japan and Taiwan will necessarily involve. It deserves the closest attention of the developing countries contemplating land reform.

Changing Relationship of Land and Politics[6]

From the perspective of world history, the developing countries really follow an already established pattern of economic development when they advocate land reform as a necessary step to economic modernization. When many of today's advanced countries began economic modernization, manifested by an attempt to achieve accelerated industrial development, they had to improve their agriculture by removing the institutional defects of the agrarian structure. An improved agriculture facilitates industrial development because it helps expand agricultural exports to pay for increased industrial imports, provides industrial centers with capital and food, and stimulates rural demand for non-agricultural goods and services. In England, the Enclosures furnished a major impetus to the Industrial Revolution. In the Soviet Union, the collectivization of agriculture was a prerequisite to forced industrial expansion. In Japan, the agricultural reforms in the Meiji period in the nineteenth century and again in the late 1940s ushered in periods of spectacular industrial growth.

However, if these countries' experiences demonstrate a pattern, they indicate that when a country advances on the road of economic modernization, the absolute size of its agricultural sector will continue to grow, but the agricultural share of its population, gross domestic product, and exports will all decline. Thus, if land reform hastens the process of economic modernization in the developing countries, it reduces the relative economic importance of agriculture. This also signifies a future reduction of the

[6] Cf. A. F. K. Organski, *The Stages of Political Development* (New York: Alfred A. Knopf, 1965), esp. Chap. iii–v.

relative political importance of land. For land, the foundation of agriculture, is a dominant source of wealth, which in turn is the foundation of political power. Hence, the political value of land declines with the reduction of its economic value. In contrast, industry, commerce, and the professions will acquire more economic weight and political significance. This will eventually lead to a basic alteration of the established relationship of land and politics. Land and politics will cease to be mutually dependent. The type of land-tenure system will cease to be a principal determinant of the pattern of power. Instead, politics will determine what type of tenure system is best suited to the requirements of economic modernization. The universal espousal, if not universal implementation, of land reform in the developing countries signifies a beginning of this change.

Ironically, in the context of history, the impact of land reform is not to enhance the economic and political value of land, but to reduce it.

APPENDIXES

APPENDIX I

LAND REFORM LAWS AND REGULATIONS: EXCERPTS AND SUMMARIES[1]

Colombia

    The Land Law of 1936 (Act No. 200)
    Social Agrarian Reform Law of 1961 (Act No. 135)

India

    The West Bengal Estates Acquisition Act, 1953
    The West Bengal Land Reforms Act, 1955

Iran

    Land Reform Law, 1962
    Supplementary Articles to the Land Reform Law, 1963
    Regulations for the Implementation of the Land Reform Law, 1964

Mexico

    Constitution of the United Mexican States, Article 27
    Agrarian Code of the United Mexican States, 1942

East Pakistan

    The East Bengal State Acquisition and Tenancy Act, 1950: A Summary

West Pakistan

    The West Pakistan Land Reform Regulation, Martial Law Regulation
        No. 64, 1959

The Philippines

    The Land Reform Act of 1955 (Republic Act No. 1400)
    The Agricultural Land Reform Code, 1963 (Republic Act No. 3844)

Taiwan

    The Farm Rent Reduction to 37.5% Act, 1951
    Regulations Governing the Sale of Public Farm Lands to Establish
        Owner-Farmers in Taiwan Province, 1951
    The Land-to-the-Tiller Act, 1953

The United Arab Republic

    Agrarian Reform Law of 1952 (Decree Law No. 178, as Amended)
    Presidential Decrees Amending the Agrarian Reform Law of 1952

---

[1] Editorial notations and summaries appear in brackets. All other materials below are quoted directly from sources, as indicated.

Colombia

ARTICLE 1. Presumed not to be public lands, but private property are the tracts occupied by private persons; it being understood that said possession consists of the economic exploitation of the soil by means of positive action on the part of the owner, such as planting or seeding, [care of] livestock, and other [occupations] of equal economic significance.

ARTICLE 2. Rural tracts not possessed in the manner specified in the preceding article are presumed to be public lands.

ARTICLE 4. [The application of the present law] shall not be prejudicial to persons who two years prior to the promulgation of this law may have established themselves, without recognition of any dominion other than that of the State, and not by precarious title, on lands that were unused at the time of occupation. . . .

ARTICLE 6. There is established in favor of the Nation the extinction of the right of dominion or property to rural tracts on which possession is not exercised in the form established by Article 1 of this law during the lapse of ten continuous years.

SOCIAL AGRARIAN REFORM LAW OF 1961 [3]
(ACT NO. 135)

Chapter II. Colombian Agrarian Reform Institute
(Instituto Colombiano de la Reforma Agraria, INCORA)

ARTICLE 3. It shall be the responsibility of the Colombian Agrarian Reform Institute to [administer nationally owned land, make grants of such land, terminate rights of land ownership in pursuance of Article 6 of Act No. 200 of 1936, administer the National Land Fund, carry out land surveys, clarify and regularize land titles, promote road construction, assist in land rehabilitation and conservation works, carry out land consolidation projects, etc.]

[2] [English translation from T. Lynn Smith, *Colombia: Social Structure and the Process of Development* (Gainsville, Florida: University of Florida Press, 1967), pp. 86–87. An original, Spanish version of the law can be found in Manifio Pinto, *Manual de Derecho Civil Colombiano para Uso de los Agricultores* (2nd ed.; Bogotá: Editorial Lumen, 1941), pp. 201–234.]

[3] [English translation from Food and Agriculture Organization of the United Nations, *Food and Agricultural Legislation*, Vol. X, No. 4, V/1 (June 1, 1962), 1–49. The original Spanish version of the law, consisting of 19 chapters, 111 articles, is found in Colombia, *Diario Oficial*, No. 30691, December 20, 1961, p. 801.]

ARTICLE 8. The Colombian Agrarian Reform Institute shall be managed and administered by a Managing Board, a general manager, and such other officials as are provided for in the statutes. The Managing Board shall ensure equal representation of political parties. . . .

Chapter V. National Land Fund

ARTICLE 14. The National Land Fund shall have the following revenues:

1. Funds amounting to not less than one hundred million pesos (100,000,000 Colombian pesos) shall be appropriated annually.
3. Agrarian Bonds.

Chapter VII. Termination of Rights of Ownership over Uncultivated Land

ARTICLE 22. All owners of farms of over two thousand (2,000) hectares shall submit to the Institute a certificate in respect of their lands issued by the Official Registrar. . . .

ARTICLE 23. [The Institute shall have authority to terminate rights of ownership over uncultivated land in accordance with the Land Law of 1936 and Decree No. 59 of 1938.]

ARTICLE 25. [The Institute shall have authority to take possession of such land.]

Chapter VIII. Nationally Owned Common Land

ARTICLE 29. As from the date of the entry into force of this Act no grants of common land may be made except to private individuals and for areas not exceeding four hundred and fifty (450) hectares. . . . Any person applying for common land must show that he is actively working at least two-thirds of the area the grant of which he is requesting.

Chapter XI. Acquisition of Privately Owned Land

ARTICLE 54. The Colombian Agrarian Reform Institute is hereby authorized to acquire privately owned land in [accordance with the provisions of this Act.] If the owners of land which it is deemed necessary to acquire fail to sell or transfer their land voluntarily, the Institute may compulsorily acquire such land in accordance with the provisions of the succeeding articles.

ARTICLE 55. If privately owned land has to be acquired, . . . this shall be done in accordance with the following order of priority:

1. Uncultivated land not covered by the rules on the termination of rights of ownership;
2. Inadequately worked land;

3. Agricultural land which is totally or very largely farmed by tenant farmers or share-croppers;

4. Properly farmed land not covered by sub-paragraph 3 above but whose owners are prepared to alienate it voluntarily in accordance with the terms of this Act.

ARTICLE 57. In matters pertaining to the acquisition of privately owned land, the Institute shall furthermore observe the following rules:

1. It shall give priority to those areas where concentration of land holdings is particularly high or where there is total or partial unemployment affecting a large rural population.

2. The Institute shall acquire only such land as is suitable for small-scale crop farming or stock-breeding.

ARTICLE 58. Well-farmed land may only be expropriated [for purposes of consolidating small-holdings; enabling tenants or share-croppers to acquire or extend the plots on which they have been working; providing land to small landowners, tenants, or share-croppers when their land is no longer to be farmed; executing paragraph 3 of Article 55, or facilitating development of rural public works.] Each owner subject to expropriation shall, however, be entitled to retain an area of one hundred hectares. This right shall also apply to the owners of inadequately farmed land which the Institute has decided to expropriate under this Article.

ARTICLE 59. Except as otherwise specified in the foregoing Article, owners of inadequately farmed land shall, in the event of expropriation proceedings being instituted against them, be entitled to retain an area of up to two hundred (200) hectares, not more than one hundred (100) of which may be suitable for crop farming.

ARTICLE 61. [When the Institute decides to acquire private land, it shall make a survey of the land concerned, have an estimate of the land value made by a body of experts, negotiate with the owner for the purchase price; and, if the negotiations fail, the Institute shall issue an order of expropriation which, if the owner requests, shall be placed before the appropriate Administrative Disputes Court (*Tribunal de lo Contencioso Administrativo*) for final decision.]

Valuation for the expropriation proceedings shall be carried out by three experts appointed [respectively, by INCORA, the owner of the land, and the Augustín Codazzi Geographical Institute.]

ARTICLE 62. Land acquired by the Institute as a result of voluntary sale or expropriation shall be paid in the following manner:

1. For uncultivated land, in class B Agrarian Bonds issued in pursuance of this Act.

2. For improperly farmed land, in cash. An amount equivalent to 20 percent of the price shall be paid on the date of the transaction. . . . The remainder shall be payable in eight successive annual instalments of an equal value, the first of which shall fall due one year after the date of the transaction.

3. For land not accounted for under the two preceding paragraphs, in cash. An amount equivalent to 20 percent of the price shall be paid on the date of the transaction. . . . The remainder shall be payable in five successive annual instalments of an equal value, the first of which shall fall due one year after the date of the transaction.

The Institute shall pay interest at the rate of 4 percent *per annum* on the amounts outstanding to its charge under paragraph 2 above and at the rate of 6 percent *per annum* on amounts outstanding under paragraph 3 of this Article.

The owners of land referred to in paragraphs 2 and 3 above shall be entitled to full payment by the Institute at the time of the conclusion of the transaction and to payment of any part outstanding to their credit thereafter in Class A Agrarian Bonds at face value.

Chapter XIII. Agrarian Bonds

ARTICLE 74. The Government is hereby authorized to issue Agrarian Bonds in the quantity and manner and of the type [as specified below:]

An issue shall be made to the value of one thousand million (1,000 million) Colombian pesos of Class A Bonds and of up to two hundred million (200 million) Colombian pesos of Class B Bonds.

ARTICLE 75. Agrarian Bonds shall be of the following types:

Class A carrying 7 percent interest *per annum* to be amortized over fifteen years.

Class B carrying 2 percent interest *per annum* to be amortized over twenty-five years.

ARTICLE 77. The Institute shall issue Class A Agrarian Bonds only when the owners of land which it acquires in pursuance of this Act request payment for their land in such Bonds or use them to pay off the credits made by the Institute as a result of the acquisition.

ARTICLE 78. Class A Agrarian Bonds shall be received by the Institute at face value as [payment for land purchased in organized settlement areas, land acquired in land partition or consolidation areas, or participation in land improvement projects sponsored by INCORA. Class B Agrarian Bonds shall be similarly received for the last mentioned purpose].

Chapter XIV. Land Partition

ARTICLE 81. Family farms established in partition areas may be sold only to poor or relatively poor persons. . . .

ARTICLE 82. Save as otherwise provided in [this Act], the sales price of the plot to the beneficiary may not exceed the amount paid for it by the Institute. . . . Overhead expenses and the costs of measurement work and setting up landmarks shall be payable by the plot holder up to ten (10) Colombian pesos per hectare. . . .

ARTICLE 83. The rate of interest to be paid by plot holders shall be 4 percent *per annum*. During the first two years only half this rate shall be collected. Purchasers shall meet the total cost of the plot and any interest thereon within a period of fifteen (15) years using the cumulative amortization system. The amount of the principal shall not, however, begin to be collected until after the third year.

India

Chapter II. Acquisition of Estates and of the Rights of Intermediaries Therein

SECTION 4. (1) The State Government may from time to time by notification declare that with effect from the date mentioned in the notification, all estates and the rights of every intermediary in each such estate situated in any district or part of a district specified in the notification shall vest in the State free from incumbrances.

SECTION 5. (c) Every non-agricultural tenant holding any land under an intermediary, and until the provisions of Chapter VI are given effect, to every raiyat holding any land under an intermediary, shall hold the same directly under the State, as if the State had been the intermediary, and on the same terms and conditions as immediately before the date of vesting;

(d) Every non-agricultural tenant holding land under an intermediary, and until the provisions of Chapter VI are given effect, to every raiyat holding under an intermediary, shall be bound to pay to the State his rent and other dues in respect of his land, accruing on and from the date of vesting, and every payment made in contravention of this clause shall be void and of no effect.

SECTION 5A. (1) The State Government may after the date of vesting enquire into any case of transfer of any land by an intermediary made between the 5th day of May, 1953, and the date of vesting, if in its opinion there are *prima facie* reasons for believing that such transfer was not *bona fide*.

(2) If after such enquiry the State Government finds that such transfer was not *bona fide*, it shall make an order to that effect and thereupon the transfer shall stand cancelled as from the date on which it was made or purported to have been made.

SECTION 6. (1) An intermediary shall . . . be entitled to retain with effect from the date of vesting—
(a) land comprised in homesteads;
(b) land comprised in or appertaining to buildings and structures owned by the intermediary;
(c) non-agricultural land in his khas [self-utilized] possession . . . not exceeding fifteen acres in area, and excluding any land retained under clause (a): Provided that the total area of land retained by an

---

[4] [Source: S. K. Basu and S. K. Bhattacharyya, *Land Reforms in West Bengal, a Study of Implementation* (New Delhi: Oxford Book Company, 1963), pp. 94–105. The Law consists of 6 chapters, 52 sections.]

intermediary under clauses (a) and (c) shall not exceed twenty acres, as may be chosen by him.

(d) agricultural land in his khas possession, not exceeding twenty-five acres in area, as may be chosen by him;

(e) tank fisheries

(f) land comprised in tea gardens or orchards or land used for the purpose of livestock breeding, poultry farming or dairy;

(g) land comprised in mills, factories or workshops;

(h) where the intermediary is a local authority—land held by such authority;

(i) land held in khas by [a religious or charitable] corporation or institution or [a person for religious or charitable purpose.]

(j) where the intermediary is a co-operative society . . . engaged exclusively in farming . . . , agricultural land in the khas possession of the society. . . .

SECTION 12. (1) Every intermediary whose estate or interests have been vested in the State . . . shall be entitled to receive in cash, in respect of such estate or interest at such time and in such manner as may be prescribed, an annual *ad-interim* payment of one-third of the net approximate annual income from such estates and interests calculated in the prescribed manner.

Chapter III. Assessment and Payment of Compensation

SECTION 17. (1) After the net income has been computed . . . the Compensation Officer shall proceed to determine the amount of compensation payable to intermediaries in accordance with the following table, namely:—

Net income	Amount of compensation payable
For the first Rs. 500 or less of net income	Twenty times of such net income
For the next Rs. 500 or less of net income	Eighteen times of such net income
For the next Rs. 1,000 or less of net income	Seventeen times of such net income
For the next Rs. 2,000 or less of net income	Twelve times of such net income
For the next Rs. 10,000 or less of net income	Ten times of such net income
For the next Rs. 15,000 or less of net income	Six times of such net income
For the next Rs. 80,000 or less of net income	Three times of such net income
For the balance of the net income	Twice such balance of net income

THE WEST BENGAL LAND REFORMS ACT, 1955 [5]

Chapter I. Preliminary

SECTION 2. In this Act, unless there is anything repugnant in the subject or context—

(2) "bargadar" means a person who under the system generally known as *adhi, barga* or *bhag* cultivates the land of another person on condition of delivering a share of the produce of such land to that person;

(8) "Personal cultivation" means cultivation by a person of his own land on his own account—

(a) by his own labour, or

(b) by the labour of any member of his family, or

(c) by servants or labourers on wages payable in cash or in kind or both;

(10) "raiyat" means a person who holds land for purposes of agriculture [or a person who received land under the program for the abolition of intermediaries].

Chapter II. Raiyats

SECTION 4. (1) Subject to the other provisions of this Act, a raiyat shall on and after the commencement of this Act be the owner of his holding and the holding shall be heritable and transferable.

(3) No raiyat shall be entitled to own more than twenty-five acres of land, excluding homestead;

SECTION 6. (2) In all cases where the State Government takes over any [raiyat] land . . . , there shall be paid to the raiyat as compensation an amount equal to the market value of the interest of the transferor in the land on the date of the transfer.

Chapter III. Bargadars

SECTION 16. (1) The produce of any land cultivated by a bargadar shall be divided as between the bargadar and the person whose land he cultivates—

(a) in the proportion of 50:50 in a case where plough, cattle, manure and seeds necessary for cultivation are supplied by the person owning the land.

(b) in the proportion of 60:40 in all other cases.

SECTION 17. (1) No person shall be entitled to terminate cultivation of his land by a bargadar except in execution of an order, made by such officer

[5] [Source: Basu and Bhattacharyya, *op. cit.*, pp. 106–119. The law consists of 7 chapters, 50 sections.]

or authority as the State Government may appoint, on one or more of the following grounds:—

    (a) that the bargadar has without any reasonable cause failed to cultivate the land; or has neglected to cultivate it properly, or has used it for any purpose other than agriculture;

    (b) that the land is not cultivated by the bargadar personally;

    (c) that the bargadar has contravened any provisions of this Act;

    (d) that the person owning the land required it *bona fide* for bringing it under personal cultivation.

    (4) No bargadar shall be entitled to cultivate more than twenty-five acres of land.

Chapter IV. Provisions as to Revenue

SECTION 22. (1) A raiyat shall be liable to pay such revenue for his holding as may be determined in accordance with the provisions of this Act; Provided that until revenue has been so determined, a raiyat shall be liable to pay the same amount as revenue which was payable by him as rent for his holding at the commencement of this Act.

Chapter V. Consolidation of Lands Comprised in Holdings, and Co-Operative Farming Societies

SECTION 43. (1) Any seven or more raiyats owning lands in a compact block or intending to acquire such land, may form themselves into a Co-operative Farming Society. . . .

    (3) When a Co-operative Farming Society has been registered, . . . all lands, excluding homesteads, belonging to the members thereof . . . shall vest in the society, and no member shall be entitled to hold in his personal capacity any land, excluding homestead, which together with any land belonging to him but vested in the society under the provisions of this sub-section exceeds twenty-five acres so long as he continues to be a member of the society.

    (4) When the lands belonging to a member of a Co-operative Farming Society vest in such society, there shall be allotted to him shares the value of which will, as far as possible, be equal to the value of the lands of the member vested in the society.

SECTION 48. (1) A Co-operative Farming Society established under this Act shall be entitled to such concessions and facilities from the State Government as may be prescribed.

    (2) Without prejudice to the generality of the foregoing provisions, such concessions and facilities may include—

    (a) such reduction of revenue as Government may allow;

    (b) free supply of seeds and manure for the first three years and thereafter at concessional rates;

(c) free technical advice by the experts of the State Government;

(d) financial assistance on such terms and conditions as may be prescribed;

(e) arrangements for better marketing.

Chapter VI. Principles of Distribution of Lands

SECTION 49. Subject to the provisions of this Act, settlement of lands which are at the disposal of the State Government shall be made, on such terms and conditions and in such manner as may be prescribed with persons who are residents of the locality where the land is situated and who intend to bring the land under personal cultivation and who own no land or less than two acres of land, preference being given to those among such persons who form themselves into a Co-operative Farming Society:

Provided that no premium shall be charged for such settlement.

Iran

LAND REFORM LAW, 1962 [6]

Chapter I. Definitions

ARTICLE 1. From the point of view of enforcement of this Act, terms used throughout the Act shall have the following definitions:

2. Peasant: A person who does not own the land but who farms directly the land owned by a landlord, with the help of his family, or by himself, and who provides one or more farming elements (seeds, oxen, etc.) and who pays part of the crop (in cash or kind) to the landlord.
10. Village: A center of population which is also the working place of a number of families who are engaged in farming on the lands of the same area and where the income of the majority of the inhabitants is derived from agriculture.

Chapter II. Ownership Limits

ARTICLE 2. The maximum landownership allowed to a person in any part of the country is an entire (six-dang) village. Landlords with more than one village may choose one of their villages to keep for themselves. The remainder shall be distributed in accordance with the provisions of this Act. [Revised below]

ARTICLE 3. Exceptions to the provisions of Article 2 shall be as follows:

1. Orchards, tea plantations and woodlots [that] . . . belong to one landlord, with the attached water rights, shall remain the property of the landlord.
2. All lands which, at the date of approval of this law, are farmed by mechanized methods, but with the employment of agricultural workers and without the use of peasants, shall remain exempt from the provisions of Article 2. . . .

Chapter III. Lands Subject to Distribution

ARTICLE 6. Lands to be distributed in accordance with the provisions of this Act shall be as follows:

a. Village lands which become surplus as a result of enforcement of Article 2 and 3 of this Act, whether or not such lands have been subject of application for registration by the landlord.

[6] [Source: Iran, Land Reform Organization. Unofficial translation. The law consists of 9 chapters, 38 articles. An English version of the law can be found in the Embassy of Iran, Washington, D.C., *State Visit of Their Imperial Majesties Mohammad Reza Shah Pahlavi, Shahanshah of Iran, and Queen Farah to the United States of America*, April 1962, pp. 28–34.]

b. Barren Lands (mavat).

c. Uncultivated lands.

Chapter IV. Assessment and Payment

ARTICLE 10. In any region where land distribution is authorized by order, the Agricultural Office shall, upon determination of maximum ownership in accordance with the provisions of this law, determine the value of distributable holdings on the basis of agricultural tax and land transactions coefficient which will be determined for each region by the Ministry of Agriculture in view of the date of the last tax assessment, type of farming, crop sharing pattern, and landowner rights, and notify the landowner [in accordance with this law].

ARTICLE 11. The price of land thus assessed shall be paid by the government through the agricultural bank in ten annual instalments. [Revised below]

Chapter V. Land Distribution and Transfer Regulations

ARTICLE 15. The Ministry of Agriculture is required to immediately transfer the purchased lands to qualified applicants at the cost price plus a sum not exceeding 10 percent of the paid price and to collect the price in fifteen equal annual instalments through the Agricultural Bank.

ARTICLE 16. Lands distributed in accordance with the provisions of this Act shall be transferred to the head of the family. The following priority shall be given in the distribution of land:
  a. The peasants of the village who operate on the same land and who live in the same village.
  b. The heirs of peasants who have operated on the same land who died within twelve months prior to the distribution of the land.
  c. Share-croppers who farm in the same village.
  d. Agricultural workers living in the area being distributed.
  e. Persons volunteering for agricultural work.

Note: Only persons who are members of the cooperative of the same village shall be eligible for land under this law.

Chapter VII. Landlord-Peasant Relationship

ARTICLE 22. All farmers who have been farming on the land on the date of approval of this law, shall be considered as inhabitants of the village where the land is situated. No landlord, under any circumstance or excuse, can expel a peasant from a village or land, or prevent him from farming.

Note: In case the landlord wishes to directly cultivate the land which is already being farmed by a peasant, or on which the peasant owns roots or growth, the landlord may do so subject to the satisfaction of the peasant and after purchasing the peasant's possessions and rights on the land, by registered document.

ARTICLE 24. The shares of the landlord and peasant in every crop shall be determined on the basis of local custom and tradition, but effective from the date of approval of this Law, the landlord shall give the peasant from his own share an additional 5 percent in the case of irrigated farming, and 10 percent in the case of dry farming in order to augment the peasant's share. This increase shall be applicable in all parts of the country. [Revised below]

Chapter VIII. Financial Regulations

ARTICLE 27. All title deeds and documents concerning transactions shall be deposited in trust with the Agricultural Bank. The said bank, acting on behalf of the Ministry of Agriculture, is required to collect the instalments on lands and to pay the annual instalments to landlords. Should the peasants' instalments be insufficient to pay the landlords, the balance shall be made up with Government grant, the amount of which shall be specified every year in the State Budget.

Chapter IX. Regulations Governing Technical Aid and Protection of Farmers and Peasants

ARTICLE 32. Communal affairs of the distributed villages (such as the maintenance of qanats, streams, the use of agricultural machinery, and pest control and the fight against animal disease, etc.) shall be handled by the village Cooperative Society.

SUPPLEMENTARY ARTICLES TO THE LAND REFORM LAW, 1963 [7]

ARTICLE 1. Landlords are required to act in one of the following three manners in the case of villages or farms which did not qualify for distribution and remained in private ownership. Under the revised Land Reform Law:

   a. Landlords shall lease their village to the peasants of the same village. . . .
   b. From this date, landlords may sell their arable lands to the peasants by mutual agreement. . . .
   c. Irrigated or dry lands may be divided between the local peasants and the owner or owners according to the customary ratios of landlord-peasant shares.

---

[7] [Source: Iran, Land Reform Organization. Unofficial translation. There are altogether four articles.]

ARTICLE 4. The payment period for the evaluated prices of the villages subject to Article 11 of the Land Reform Law shall be 15 years instead of 10.

REGULATIONS FOR THE IMPLEMENTATION OF THE LAND
REFORM LAW, 1964 [8]

Chapter I. Lease

ARTICLE 1. Any landlord wishing to lease out his land by virtue of the prerogative given him under . . . Article 1 of the Supplementary Articles to the Land Reform Law, has the option to draw up lease papers individually with the farmers who have land usage right, or any one of them having a person as guarantor.

ARTICLE 2. The rent shall be payable in cash, unless both sides agree to have the rent paid partly or all in kind, to be delivered by the lessee.

ARTICLE 3. The period of lease shall be thirty years, and the rent shall be subject to review at the end of every fifth year.

ARTICLE 4. The amount of the rental shall be based on the average net income of the landlord from the land during the past three years, with regard to the traditional incomes of the locality, and subject to the agreement of the farmers and landlord. If the two sides fail to agree, the average net income (coefficient) of the landlord during the three years shall be determined by the Land Reform Organization.

Chapter II. Purchase

ARTICLE 10. If the proprietor desires to exercise his option under Section (b) of Article 1 of the Supplementary Articles to the Land Reform Law, he may sell his land, upon mutual agreement, to the farmers holding right of use of land. . . .

Note 1—From the funds put at the disposal of the Agricultural Credit and Development Bank by the Government, ⅓ of the cost of land may be loaned to the farmer at his request. . . .

Note 2—For the implementation of Note 1, the Government is bound to allocate from the development funds the needed sum, which in any case shall be not less [than] one billion rials a year, . . . The said loans shall be amortized over 15 years at a rate of interest of 3 percent. Repayment shall begin from the sixth year and shall be effected in equal instalments paid over 10 years. . . .

[8] [Source: Iran, Land Reform Organization. Unofficial translation. The regulations consist of 4 chapters, 47 articles.]

Chapter III. Distribution

ARTICLE 15. In case the proprietor (of a six-dang village), or the majority of proprietors (majority as to proprietorship) desire to take advantage of the authority given in section (c) of Article 1 of the Supplementary Articles to the Land Reform Law and between them and the farmers agreement is not obtained as to the distribution of land, they must submit their proposal to the LRO [Land Reform Organization]. The LRO will divide the property, with its water rights, in proportion to the income of the proprietors on one side, and that of the farmers on the other, with observance of local conditions, in such a way and as far as possible that the share of each proprietor may be assigned in one place. . . .

ARTICLE 16. Two-fifths of the value of the land which is distributed and transferred to the ownership of the farmers under the provisions of Article 15 shall be assessed at the highest assessment rate (coefficient) for the region and shall be paid for in the following manner: ⅓ of the said price shall be paid by the Agricultural Credit and Rural Development Bank, by virtue of Notes 1 and 2 of Article 10 of the present Regulations; and the balance must be paid by the purchasing farmer in ten equal annual instalments to the landlord(s) during 10 years.

ARTICLE 17. If the majority of the farmers [tenants] and landlords of a village agree, the entire village may be operated as a joint stock unit managed by a board of managers composed of three persons: one farmer, one landlord and a third member selected by mutual consent. If the two sides cannot agree on the selection of the third member, he shall be selected by the Ministry of Agriculture.

Chapter IV. Miscellaneous and General Articles

ARTICLE 19. Mechanized agricultural land not exceeding 500 hectares in any single village or [possessed by] any single landlord shall not be subject to the provisions of Article 1 of the Supplementary articles to the Land Reform Law, . . .

ARTICLE 22. The Central Organization of the Rural Cooperatives of Iran, in the execution of the provisions of land reform [laws] is required to take action for the gradual setting up of rural and farm cooperatives in villages subject to land reform; to supervise these cooperatives and to extend to them all such technical and financial assistance as may be necessary; and to arrange for the training of farmers to establish and manage such cooperatives.

ARTICLE 44. The period of payment of the price of lands purchased by the Government before the date of approval of the Supplementary Articles to the Land Reform Law shall be ten years. . . .

ARTICLE 45. If the area of land owned by the landlord exceeds the maximum specified below, the landlord must act only according to Section (a) or (b) of Article 1 of the Supplementary Articles to the Land Reform Law. In case of a dispute between the landlord and farmers, the decision of the Land Reform Organization shall be final.

Schedule of Maximum Holding

1. Rice paddies in Gilan and Mazandaran   20 hectares
2. Suburbs of Tehran, Varamin, Damavand, Shahr Rey,   30   "
   Shemran, and Karaj
3. Other lands and villages in the above-mentioned Shahrestans   70   "
   (item 2)
4. Suburbs of provincial capitals, excluding those of Kerman,   50   "
   Sanandaj, and Zahedan
5. The Shahrestans of Gorgan, Gonbad; and the lands in Dashte   40   "
   Moghan; and non-rice paddy lands in Gilan and Mazandaran
6. Khuzestan, Baluchestan, and Sistan   150   "
7. Other parts of the country   100   "

Mexico

CONSTITUTION OF THE UNITED MEXICAN STATES [9]

Article 27

Ownership of the lands and waters within the boundaries of the national territory is vested originally in the Nation, which has had, and has, the right to transmit title thereof to private persons, thereby constituting private property.

Private property shall not be expropriated except for reasons of public use and subject to payment of indemnity.

The Nation shall at all times have the right to impose on private property such limitations as the public interest may demand, as well as the right to regulate the utilization of natural resources which are susceptible of appropriation, in order to conserve them and to ensure a more equitable distribution of public wealth. With this end in view, necessary measures shall be taken to divide up large landed estates; to develop small landed holdings in operation; to create new agricultural centers, with necessary lands and waters; to encourage agriculture in general and to prevent the destruction of natural resources, and to protect property from damage, to the detriment of society. Centers of population which at present either have no lands or water or which do not possess them in sufficient quantities for the needs of their inhabitants, shall be entitled to grants thereof, which shall be taken from adjacent properties, the rights of small landed holdings in operation being respected at all times.

VIII. The following are declared null and void:

(a) All transfers of the lands, waters, and forests of villages, *rancherías*, groups, or communities made by local officials (*jefes políticos*), state governors, or other local authorities in violation of the provisions of the Law of June 25, 1856, and other related laws and rulings.

(b) All concessions, deals or sales of lands, waters, and forests made by the Secretariat of Development, the Secretariat of Finance, or any other federal authority from December 1, 1876, to date, which encroach upon or illegally occupy communal lands (*ejidos*), lands allotted in common, or lands of any other kind belonging to villages, *rancherías*, groups or communities, and centers of population.

(c) All survey or demarcation-of-boundary proceedings, transfers, alienations, or auction sales effected during the period of time referred to in the preceding sub-clause, by companies, judges, or other federal or state authorities entailing encroachments on or illegal occupation of the lands, waters, or for-

[9] [Source: English translation from Pan American Union, *Constitution of the United Mexican States, 1917; as Amended* (Washington D.C., 1961).]

ests of communal holdings (*ejidos*), lands held in common, or other holdings belonging to centers of population.

The sole exception to the aforesaid nullification shall be the lands to which title has been granted in allotments made in conformity with the Law of June 25, 1856, held by persons in their own name for more than ten years and having an area of not more than fifty hectares.

X. Centers of population which lack communal lands (*ejidos*) or which are unable to have them restored to them due to lack of titles, impossibility of identification, or because they had been legally transferred, shall be granted sufficient lands and waters to constitute them, in accordance with the needs of the population; but in no case shall they fail to be granted the area needed, and for this purpose the land needed shall be expropriated, at the expense of the Federal Government, to be taken from lands adjoining the villages in question.

The area or individual unit of the grant shall thereafter be not less than ten hectares of moist or irrigated land, or in default of such land its equivalent in other types of land in accordance with the third paragraph of section XV of this article.[10]

XI. For the purpose of carrying out the provisions of this article and of regulating laws that may be enacted, the following are established:

(a) A direct agency of the Federal Executive entrusted with the application and enforcement of the agrarian laws;

(b) An advisory board composed of five persons to be appointed by the President of the Republic and who shall perform the functions specified in the organic laws;

(c) A mixed commission composed of an equal number of representatives of the Federal Government, the local governments, and a representative of the peasants, to be appointed in the manner set forth in the respective regulating law, to function in each State, Territory, and the Federal District, with the powers and duties set forth in the organic and regulatory laws;

(d) Private executive committees for each of the centers of population that are concerned with agrarian cases;

(e) A communal office (*comisariado ejidal*) for each of the centers of population that possess communal lands (*ejidos*).

XII. Petitions for a restitution or grant of lands or waters shall be submitted directly to the state and territorial governors.

The governors shall refer the petitions to the mixed commissions, which shall study the cases during a fixed period of time and render a report; the State governors shall approve or modify the report of the mixed commission

---

[10] [This paragraph was added on February 12, 1947.]

and issue orders that immediate possession be given to areas which they deem proper. The case shall then be turned over to the Federal Executive for decision.

Whenever the governors fail to comply with the provisions of the preceding paragraph, within the peremptory period of time fixed by law, the report of the mixed commission shall be deemed rejected and the case shall be referred immediately to the Federal Executive.

Inversely, whenever a mixed commission fails to render a report during the peremptory time limit, the Governor shall be empowered to grant possession of the area of land he deems appropriate.

XIV. Landowners affected by decisions granting or restoring communal lands and waters to villages, or who may be affected by future decisions, shall have no ordinary legal right or recourse and cannot institute *amparo* proceedings [injunction].

Persons affected by such decisions shall have solely the right to apply to the Federal Government for payment of the corresponding indemnity. This right must be exercised by the interested parties within one year counting from the date of publication of the respective resolution in the *Diario Oficial*. After this period has elapsed, no claim is admissible.

Owners or occupants of agricultural or stockraising properties in operation who have been issued or to whom there may be issued in the future certificates of non-affectability may institute *amparo* proceedings against any illegal deprivation or agrarian claims on their lands or water.[11]

XV. The mixed commissions, the local governments and any other authorities charged with agrarian proceedings cannot in any case affect small agricultural or livestock properties in operation and they shall incur liability for violations of the Constitution if they make grants which affect them.[12]

Small agricultural property is that which does not exceed one hundred hectares of first-class moist or irrigated land or its equivalent in other classes of land, under cultivation.

To determine this equivalence, one hectare of irrigated land shall be computed as two hectares of seasonal land; as four of good quality pasturage (*agostadero*) and as eight of *monte* (scrub land) or arid pasturage.

Also to be considered as small holdings are areas not exceeding two hundred hectares of seasonal lands or pasturage susceptible of cultivation; or one hundred fifty hectares of land used for cotton growing if irrigated from fluvial canals or by pumping; or three hundred, under cultivation, when used for

[11] [As amended on February 12, 1947.]
[12] [*Ibid.*]

growing bananas, sugar cane, coffee, henequen, rubber, coconuts, grapes, olives, quinine, vanilla, cacao or fruit trees.

Small holdings for stockraising are lands not exceeding the area necessary to maintain up to five hundred head of cattle (*ganado mayor*) or their equivalent in smaller animals (*ganado menor*—sheep, goats, pigs) under provisions of law, in accordance with the forage capacity of the lands.

Whenever, due to irrigation or drainage works or any other works executed by the owners or occupants of a small holding to whom a certificate of non-affectability has been issued, the quality of the land is improved for agricultural or stockraising operations, such holding shall not be subject to agrarian appropriation even if, by virtue of the improvements made, the maximums indicated in this section are lowered, provided that the requirements fixed by law are met.

XVII. The Federal Congress and the State Legislature, within their respective jurisdictions, shall enact laws to fix the maximum area of rural property, and to carry out the subdivision of the excess lands, in accordance with the following bases:

(b) The excess over the fixed area shall be subdivided by the owner within the time fixed by the local law, and these parcels shall be offered for sale under terms approved by the governments, in accordance with the aforementioned laws.

(d) The value of the parcels shall be paid by annual instalments which will amortize principal and interest, at an interest rate not exceeding 3 percent per annum.

(e) Owners shall be required to receive bonds of the local Agrarian Debt to guarantee payment for the property expropriated. For this purpose, the Federal Congress shall enact a law empowering the States to create their Agrarian Debt.

AGRARIAN CODE OF THE UNITED MEXICAN STATES, 1942 [13]

ARTICLE 46. The centers of population which had been deprived of their lands, woods or waters by any of the acts referred to in Constitutional Article 27 shall be entitled to have their property restored to them whenever it is proven:

I. That they are the owners of the lands, woods, or waters whose restitution is petitioned.

II. That they were despoiled of same by any of the following acts:

[13] [Source: English translation from Asociacion de Empresas Industriales y Comerciales, *Agrarian Code of the United Mexican States* (Mexico, D. F. [1950], Mimeographed). The original, Spanish version of the code is found in Mexico, *Diario Oficial*, April 27, 1943. The code has more than 367 articles.]

(a) Alienations made by Political Chiefs, State Governors or any other local authority, in violation of the provisions of the Law of June 25, 1856, and other relevant laws and rulings.

(b) Concessions granted or deals or sales made by the Ministry of Development, Ministry of Finance or any other Federal authorities, from December 1, 1876, to January 6, 1915, whereby the property whose restitution is petitioned was invaded or illegally occupied.

(c) Survey or demarcation of boundary proceedings, deals, transactions, transfers or auction sales effected during the period of time referred to in the preceding Sub-Clause, by Companies, judges or other authorities of the States or of the Federation, whereby the property whose restitution is petitioned was invaded or illegally occupied.

ARTICLE 50.   Centers of population which lack lands, woods, or waters, or which do not have sufficient for their requirements, are entitled to be granted same, provided [that] the center of population existed at least six months prior to the date of its application.

ARTICLE 52.   Centers of population having twenty or more individuals who lack a grant unit or plot are capacitated to petition an extension of their communal holdings.

ARTICLE 53.   Groups of twenty or more individuals who fulfill the requisites established in Article 54 have the right to petition the creation of a new center of population even though they belong to different villages.

ARTICLE 54.   Peasants who fulfill the following qualifications shall be eligible to obtain a grant unit or a plot of ground by means of a grant, extension, creation of a new center of population, or be eligible to be placed on excess communal lands:

    I. Mexican by birth.

    II. He or she must have resided in the petitioning village for at least six months prior to the filing of the petition or the institution of the routine proceedings, unless it is the case of creation of a new center of population or of peasants who must be located on the excess land of communal holdings.

    III. He or she must personally work the land as an habitual occupation.

    IV. He or she must not own in their own name nor hold lands having an equal or larger area than the grant unit.

    V. He or she must not possess capital invested in an industry or commercial activity exceeding 2,500 pesos or agricultural capital exceeding 5,000 pesos.

ARTICLE 56.   The peons or workers on haciendas are entitled to be considered as eligible to receive land in the manner set forth in Article 54.

They shall therefore be taken into account in the census made, in the agrarian proceedings instituted at their request, or in those instituted by centers of population located within the radius from which lands can be taken, in which cases the agrarian authorities shall proceed as a matter of routine. They are also entitled to be placed on excess lands restored or granted to a center of population and to obtain a grant unit free of charge in the centers of population set up by Federal and State institutions which are specifically authorized by the Federation for the purpose.

[Land Redistribution and Exemptions—Summary of Articles 104, 111, 115 and 117] [14]

The lands for redistribution to any given village are to be taken from public or private holdings located within a 7-kilometer radius of the center of the petitioning village. Wherever suitable federal, state, or municipal properties are available, these are to be taken in preference to private holdings, but, when not available, private properties may be expropriated. Any private holding within this radius is subject to seizure except for certain specified exemptions, which, in general, are as follows:

1. An area not exceeding 100 hectares of irrigated or humid land, or 200 hectares of seasonal land, or the equivalent in other types of land. For exemption purposes, each hectare of irrigated land is equivalent to 2 hectares of seasonal [land], 4 hectares of good pasture land, or 8 hectares of woodland or pasture land located in barren country.

2. Up to 150 hectares of land used for the cultivation of cotton, if irrigated by river water or by pumping system.

3. Up to 300 hectares with ordinary plantations of bananas, coffee, henequen, rubber trees, coconut palms, vineyards, olive trees, trees producing quinine, vanilla or cacao, or fruit trees.

4. Up to 5,000 hectares of land in the states of Aguascalientes, Coahuila, Chihuahua, Durango, Nuevo León, San Luis Potosí, and Zacatecas on which guayule shrubs are already being cultivated or may in the future be cultivated. The exemptions may cover a period of fifty years, at the end of which time it may be possible to extend the period for another twenty years. In order to secure exemption of the above land from seizure, certain specified practices must be followed.

5. Lands which are being replanted with trees in accordance with the forestry law and regulations.

6. Under certain specified conditions, lands devoted to the raising of cattle may be granted an exemption concession for a period of twenty-five

---

[14] [Quotation from Nathan Whetten, *Rural Mexico* (Chicago: The University of Chicago Press, 1948), pp. 133–134.]

years. Each such concession must be the subject of a presidential decree and shall never exceed 300 hectares of the most fertile or 50,000 hectares of the most barren land.

7. All buildings are exempt from expropriation, provided that they are not abandoned and provided that they do not serve in some way the needs of the property expropriated.

8. Hydraulic works, including dams, reservoirs, canals, drainage systems, wells, and pumping stations are exempt, provided that they are used only for irrigating lands which do not form part of the ejido holdings or serve for irrigating both the seized lands and those which still remain in possession of the owner.

ARTICLE 138. The rights to agrarian property acquired by centers of population shall be inalienable, imprescriptible, not subject to attachment and untransferable, and therefore, under no circumstances or in any manner, may they be alienated, ceded, transferred, leased, mortgaged or otherwise encumbered wholly or in part. Therefore, any operations, acts or contracts already entered into, or which it may be sought in the future to enter into in violation of this precept shall automatically be null and void.

ARTICLE 169. Ejidatarios shall lose their rights to plots and, in general, all rights as members of a center of communal population—except their rights to the house plots awarded them in the urbanized zone—on the sole and exclusive grounds furnished by failure to work their plots for two consecutive years or more, or for failure to do their part of the work if the holding is farmed on a collective basis.

East Pakistan

THE EAST BENGAL STATE ACQUISITION AND TENANCY ACT, 1950:
A SUMMARY [15]

1. All rent-receiving interests in all lands (agricultural and non-agricultural) are to be abolished by being acquired by the Government. The actual tillers of the soil will thus become direct tenants under the Government, virtually as peasant proprietors. All agricultural tenants (raiyats) in future will have permanent, heritable and transferable rights in their lands and will be entitled to use the land in any way they like. The tenants of non-agricultural lands also will have similar rights in their lands.

2. Subletting of land in future is strictly prohibited. Cultivation under the barga (crop-sharing) system is not, however, to be treated as subletting.

3. All khas cultivated lands of all persons (including lands cultivated through bargadars) in excess of 100 bighas (33 acres) per family or 10 bighas (3.3 acres) per member of the family, plus the area of homestead land up to a limit of 10 bighas, are to be acquired by the Government. This limit of 100 bighas is relaxable in cases of tea, coffee, sugarcane and rubber plantations, cassia leaf gardens, orchards, and large-scale farming by the use of power driven mechanical appliances, and large-scale dairy farming. [Revised below]

4. The excess khas lands thus acquired will be settled with *bona fide* cultivators holding less than 3 acres of land.

6. For the acquisition of the rent-receiving interests compensation is payable at a graduated scale ranging from 10 times the net annual income in cases of persons with a net income of Rs.500 or less per annum to 2 times the net annual income in case of persons with a net income of more than Rs.1 lakh per annum.

7. For the acquisition of the khas lands compensation is provided at the rate of 5 times the net annual profit from the land.

8. Compensation may be paid either in cash or in bonds or partly in cash and partly in bonds. The bonds will be non-negotiable and will be payable in not more than 40 annual instalments and will carry interest at 3 percent.

11. All tenants will pay rent at fair and equitable rates to the Government. The maximum rate at which the rent of agricultural tenants can be assessed in future is limited to 1/10th of the value of the annual gross produce of the land.

18. After State Acquisition no one except a *bona fide* cultivator holding less

[15] [Source: East Pakistan, Revenue Department, *Report of the Land Revenue Commission, East Pakistan, July 1959* (Dacca: The East Pakistan Government Press, 1959), pp. 3–4.]

than 100 bighas of land for himself and his family will be permitted to purchase or otherwise acquire additional lands. [Revised below]

REVISIONS IN 1961

[As recommended by the Land Revenue Commission appointed by the East Pakistan Government in 1958, the retention limit of *khas* land specified in the 1950 law was raised in 1961 to 375 *bighas* (125 acres) per family. The excess area already acquired on the basis of the old limit, but not permanently settled by the Government with others, was to be restored to the previous owners to the extent of the new limit. (Pakistan, The Planning Commission, *The Third Five Year Plan* 1965–70 [Karachi, West Pakistan, 1965], p. 425.)

West Pakistan

THE WEST PAKISTAN LAND REFORM REGULATION,
MARTIAL LAW REGULATION NO. 64, 1959 [16]

Part I. Preliminary

2. *Definitions:* In this Regulation, unless there is anything repugnant in the subject or context:

   (1) "Commission" means the West Pakistan Land Commission constituted under paragraph 4;

   (4) "Jagir" includes:

       (a) any grant of land by way of *jagir,*

       (b) any grant of money made or continued by or on behalf of the State which purports to be or is received out of land revenue,

       (c) any assignment or release of land revenue,

       (d) any estate in land created or affirmed by or on behalf of the State which carries with it the right to receive or collect land revenue or any portion thereof,

       (e) any assignment of dues recoverable, but for such assignment by the Government.

   (10) "Produce index unit" means the measure in terms of which the comparative productivity of an acre of land of a particular kind in a particular assessment circle or area is computed and expressed for the purposes of the scheme relating to the resettlement of displaced persons on land, and, in respect of the assessment circles and areas where no such unit exists, such measure as may be determined by the Commission.

Part III. Restrictions on Ownership and Possession of Land

8. *Limits on Individual Holdings:* Save as otherwise provided in this Regulation, no person shall, at any time, own or in any capacity possess land in excess of five hundred acres of irrigated land or one thousand acres of unirrigated land, or irrigated and unirrigated land the aggregate area of which exceeds five hundred acres of irrigated land, one acre of irrigated land being reckoned as equivalent to two acres of unirrigated land, and any reference in this Regulation to an acre of irrigated land shall be construed accordingly.

9. *Exemptions:* Notwithstanding the provisions of paragraph 8.

   (a) an existing owner may retain out of his present holding such additional area, if any, which would bring the total area retained by him to the equivalent of thirty-six thousand produce index units;

---

[16] [Source: Pakistan, Planning Commission, *Land Reforms in Pakistan* (March 1959), Appendix II, pp. 41–52. The Regulations consist of 9 parts, 29 paragraphs.]

(c) except in cases provided for in paragraph 10 the Government may allow charitable or religious institutions approved by it to own or possess any additional area.

(d) the Government may, in the public interest, allow owners, or operators of recognized existing stud and livestock farms to retain such additional areas under such farms as it considers necessary for the purpose, for so long as such areas are maintained as stud and livestock farms.

(e) an existing owner may retain, out of his present holding, such additional areas, not exceeding [one] hundred and fifty acres, as may be under orchard, for so long as it is maintained as such.

(f) an existing owner whose holding is greater than the area of five hundred acres of irrigated land or the equivalent of thirty-six thousand produce index units may transfer to any or all of his heirs such additional area, if any, as taken together with any area gifted by him to all or any of his heirs on or after the fourteenth day of August, 1947, and any area retained by him under Clause (e) above, would bring the aggregate area so transferred to the equivalent of eighteen thousand produce index units.

Provided that the maximum area permissible to be retained under Clause (e) shall, in no case, be treated as more than the equivalent of six thousand produce index units.

11. *Special provision for female dependents:*
    (1) The Commission may, on the application of an existing owner holding ancestral land allow him to transfer by way of gift, in addition to the area which he can give under paragraph 9 (f), a maximum area equivalent to six thousand produce index units to each of his female dependents.

Part IV. Declaration of Areas, Resumption and Vesting of
Excess Land in Government and Compensation Therefor

16. *Resumption and Vesting in Government of Excess Land:*
    (1) Land in excess of the area permissible for retention under Part III shall vest in and be resumed by the Government free from any encumbrance or charge.

17. *Scale and Payment of Compensation:*
    (1) In addition to any compensation which may be payable under paragraph 18, compensation for land resumed under paragraph 16, shall be paid according to the following scale, that is to say:
        (a) for the first 18,000 produce index units, at the rate of Rs. 5– per unit;

      (b) for the next 24,000 produce index units at the rate of Rs. 4–
per unit;

      (c) for the next 36,000 produce index units, at the rate of Rs. 3–
per unit;

      (d) for the next 72,000 produce index units, at the rate of Rs. 2–
per unit; and

      (e) for the balance, at the rate of Rs. 1–per produce index unit.

(2) Compensation payable under this paragraph shall be paid through heritable bonds which shall be transferable but shall not be negotiable through or with banks.

(3) All bonds shall bear taxable simple interest at the rate of four percent per annum payable annually in the prescribed manner.

Part V. Sale and Utilization of Resumed Land

19. *Sale of resumed land:*

(1) Land resumed under Part IV shall, in the first instance, be offered for sale, on such terms and conditions as may be prescribed, to the tenants who are in cultivating possession of it, and any such land not sold to such tenants, shall be offered for sale to such other persons, and on such terms and conditions, as may be considered suitable by the Commission.

(2) Interest may be charged on the price payable under sub-paragraph (1) at such rate or rates as may be prescribed.

Part VI. Abolition of Certain Interests

21. *Jagirs:*

(1) All *jagirs*, of whatever kind and by whatever name described, subsisting immediately before the commencement of this Regulation, shall, on such commencement, stand abolished, and, save as hereafter in this paragraph provided, any right, interest, or estate granted, assigned, released, created or affirmed by any such *jagir* shall revert to the Government free from any encumbrance or charge, and no compensation shall be claimed by, or paid to, any person affected thereby.

(2) If a *jagir* is, wholly or partly, in the form of a grant of land, the person in favour of whom the *jagir* subsisted, shall be entitled to retain, as full owner, the whole of such land if the area, together with any other area which he may own or possess in any other capacity, is equal to or less than five hundred acres of irrigated land, or thirty-six thousand produce index units, whichever is more, and if the area exceeds that limit, then such portion, not exceeding the limit, as he may select, and the excess land shall revert to the Government free

from any encumbrance or charge, without payment of any compensation, and shall be disposed of by the Commission in the manner provided by or under this Regulation.

22. *Intermediary interest: Ala-milkiat*, and similar other interests, subsisting immediately before the commencement of this Regulation, shall, on such commencement, stand abolished, and no compensation shall be claimed by, or paid to, any person affected by the abolition.

Part VIII. Miscellaneous

26. *Transitional:* Until any order is made under this Regulation for the resumption or utilization of land, no tenant shall be ejected unless it is established in a revenue court that he has:
   (a) failed to pay rent; or
   (b) used the land in a manner which renders it unfit for the purpose for which it was let; or
   (c) failed to cultivate the land without sufficient cause; or
   (d) sublet his tenancy; or
   (e) failed to cultivate the land, where rent is payable in kind in the manner or to the extent customary to the locality; and in the meantime, subject to the provisions of this Regulation, the landlord and the tenant shall continue to enjoy the rights and discharge the obligations as heretofore.

The Philippines

THE LAND REFORM ACT OF 1955 [17]
(REPUBLIC ACT NO. 1400)

The Land Tenure Administration

SECTION 3. *Creation and Composition.* For the purpose of carrying out the policy enunciated in this Act, there is hereby created a Land Tenure Administration, hereinafter called the Administration, which shall be directly under the control and supervision of and responsible to the President of the Philippines. . . .

SECTION 6. *Powers.* . . . the Administration is authorized to:

(1) Purchase private agricultural lands for resale at cost to *bona fide* tenants or occupants, or in the case of estates abandoned by the owners for the last five years, to private individuals who will work the lands themselves and who are qualified to acquire or own lands but who do not own more than six hectares of lands in the Philippines;

(2) Initiate and prosecute expropriation proceedings for the acquisition of private agricultural lands in proper cases, for the same purpose of resale at cost: Provided, that the power herein granted shall apply only to private agricultural lands as to the area in excess of three hundred hectares of contiguous area if owned by natural persons and as to the area in excess of six hundred hectares if owned by corporations: Provided, further, That land where justified agrarian unrest exists may be expropriated regardless of its area.

Negotiable Land Certificates

SECTION 9. *Issuance.* The President, for the purposes provided for in this Act and upon recommendation of the Secretary of Finance and concurred in by the Monetary Board, is hereby authorized to issue negotiable land certificates upon the request of the Administration: Provided, That only sixty million a year will be issued during the first two years, and thirty million each year during the succeeding years.

SECTION 10. *Uses of certificates.* Negotiable land certificates may be used by the holder thereof for any of the following purposes:

(1) Payment for agricultural lands or other properties purchased from the Government. . . .

(2) Payment for the purchase of shares of stock or of the assets of any

---

[17] [Source: Frances L. Starner, *Magsaysay and the Philippine Peasantry: The Agrarian Impact on Philippine Politics, 1953–1956* (Berkeley, Calif.: University of California Press, 1961), Appendix V, pp. 231–236. The law consists of 30 sections.]

industrial or commercial corporations owned or controlled by the Government;

(3) Payment of all tax obligations of the holder thereof. . . .

(4) As surety or performance bonds, in all cases where the Government may require or accept real property as bonds.

Negotiated Purchase of Private Agricultural Lands

SECTION 11. *Lands subject to purchase.* The Administration, acting for and on behalf of the Government, may negotiate to purchase any privately owned agricultural land when the majority of the tenants therein petition for such purchase.

SECTION 14. *Payment.* In negotiating for the purchase of agricultural land, the Administration shall offer to pay the purchase price wholly in land certificates or partly in legal tender and partly in land certificates: Provided, That the amount to be paid in legal tender shall in no case exceed 50 percent of the purchase price: Provided, further, That the landlord, if he desires and the Administration so agrees, may be paid, by way of barter or exchange, with such residential, commercial or industrial land owned by the Government as may be agreed upon by the parties.

Expropriation of Private Agricultural Lands

SECTION 16. *When proper.* The Administration may initiate and prosecute expropriation proceedings for the acquisition of private agricultural land subject to the provisions of section six, paragraph (2), upon petition of a majority of the tenants and after it is convinced of the suitability of such land for subdivision into family-size farm units, and that public interest will be served by its immediate acquisition, when any of the following conditions exists:

(1) That the landowner falling within the terms of section six, paragraph (2), continues to refuse to sell after all efforts have been exhausted by the Administration to negotiate for its purchase; or

(2) That the landowner is willing to sell under sections eleven and twelve but cannot agree with the Administration as to the price and/or the manner of its payment.

SECTION 19. *Payment.* After the court has made a final determination of the just compensation for the land expropriated, it shall be paid wholly in cash unless the landowner chooses to be paid wholly or partly in land certificates, in which case section fifteen shall apply.

THE AGRICULTURAL LAND REFORM CODE, 1963 [18]
(REPUBLIC ACT NO. 3844)

Chapter I. Agricultural Leasehold System

SECTION 4. *Abolition of Agricultural Share Tenancy.* Agricultural share tenancy, as herein defined, is hereby declared to be contrary to public policy and shall be abolished: *Provided,* That existing share tenancy contracts may continue in force and effect in any region or locality, to be governed in the meantime by the pertinent provisions of Republic Act Numbered Eleven hundred and ninety-nine, as amended [the Agricultural Tenancy Act of the Philippines, 1954], until the end of the agricultural year when the National Land Reform Council proclaims that all the government machineries and agencies in that region or locality relating to leasehold envisioned in this Code are operating, unless such contracts provide for a shorter period or the tenant sooner exercises his option to elect the leasehold system: *Provided, further,* That in order not to jeopardize international commitments, lands devoted to crops covered by marketing allotments shall be made the subject of a separate proclamation that adequate provisions, such as the organization of cooperatives, marketing agreements, or other similar workable arrangements, have been made to insure efficient management on all matters requiring synchronization of the agricultural with the processing phases of such crops. . . .

SECTION 5. *Establishment of Agricultural Leasehold Relation.* The agricultural leasehold relation shall be established by operation of law in accordance with Section four of this Code and, in other cases, either orally or in writing, expressly or impliedly.

SECTION 8. *Extinguishment of Agricultural Leasehold Relation.* The agricultural leasehold relation established under this Code shall be extinguished by:

(1) Abandonment of landholding without the knowledge of the agricultural lessor;

(2) Voluntary surrender of the landholding by the agricultural lessee, written notice of which shall be served three months in advance; or

(3) Absence of the persons under Section nine to succeed to the lessee, in the event of death or permanent incapacity of the lessee.

SECTION 11. *Lessee's Right of Pre-emption.* In case the agricultural

[18] [Source: The Philippines, *Agricultural Land Reform Code* (Republic Act No. 3844) (Manila, The Philippines: Bureau of Printing, 1963). The text of the law can also be found in Food and Agricultural Organization of the United Nations, *Food and Agricultural Legislation*, Vol. XIII, No. 2 (December 1964) V/1b, pp. 1–41. The law consists of 11 chapters, 173 sections.]

lessor decides to sell the landholding, the agricultural lessee shall have the preferential right to buy the same under reasonable terms and conditions. . . .

SECTION 15. *Agricultural Leasehold Contract in General.* The agricultural lessor and the agricultural lessee shall be free to enter into any kind of terms, conditions or stipulations in a leasehold contract, as long as they are not contrary to law, morals or public policy. A term, condition or stipulation in an agricultural leasehold contract is considered contrary to law, morals or public policy:

(1) If the agricultural lessee is required to pay a rental in excess of that which is hereinafter provided for in this Chapter;

(2) If the agricultural lessee is required to pay a consideration in excess of the fair rental value as defined herein, for the use of work animals and/or farm implements belonging to the agricultural lessor or to any other person; or

(3) If it is imposed as a condition in the agricultural leasehold contract: (a) that the agricultural lessee is required to rent work animals or to hire farm implements from the agricultural lessor or a third person, or to make use of any store or services operated by the agricultural lessor or a third person; or (b) that the agricultural lessee is required to perform any work or render any service other than his duties and obligations provided in this Chapter with or without compensation; or (c) that the agricultural lessee is required to answer for any fine, deductions and/or assessments.

Any contract by which the agricultural lessee is required to accept a loan or to make payment therefor in kind shall also be contrary to law, morals or public policy.

SECTION 16. *Nature and Continuity of Conditions of Leasehold Contract.* In the absence of any agreement as to the period, the terms and conditions of a leasehold contract shall continue until modified by the parties: *Provided,* That in no case shall any modification of its terms and conditions prejudice the right of the agricultural lessee to the security of his tenure on the landholding: *Provided further,* That in case of a contract with a period an agricultural lessor may not, upon the expiration of the period, increase the rental except in accordance with the provisions of Section thirty-four.

SECTION 31. *Prohibitions to the Agricultural Lessor.* It shall be unlawful for the agricultural lessor:

(1) To dispossess the agricultural lessee of his land-holding except upon authorization by the Court under Section thirty-six. . . .

(2) To require the agricultural lessee to assume, directly or indirectly, the payment of the taxes . . . ;

(3) To require the agricultural lessee to assume, directly or indirectly, any part of the rent, "canon" or other consideration which the agricultural lessor is under obligation to pay to third persons for the use of the land:

(4) To deal with millers or processors without written authorization of the lessee in cases where the crop has to be sold in processed form before payment of the rental: or

(5) To discourage, directly or indirectly, the formation, maintenance or growth of unions or organizations of agricultural lessees. . . .

SECTION 33. *Manner, Time and Place of Rental Payment.* The consideration for the lease of the land shall be paid in an amount certain in money or in produce, or both, payable at the place agreed upon by the parties immediately after threshing or processing if the consideration is in kind, or within a reasonable time thereafter, if not in kind.

SECTION 34. *Consideration for the Lease of Riceland and Lands Devoted to Other Crops.* The consideration for the lease of riceland and lands devoted to other crops shall not be more than the equivalent of 25 *percent* of the average normal harvest during the three agricultural years immediately preceding the date the leasehold was established after deducting the amount used for seeds and the cost of harvesting, threshing, loading, hauling and processing, whichever are applicable. . . .

SECTION 35. *Exemption from Leasehold of Other Kinds of Lands.* Notwithstanding the provisions of the preceding Sections, in the case of fishponds, saltbeds, and lands principally planted to citrus, coconuts, cacao, coffee, durian, and other similar permanent trees at the time of the approval of this Code, the consideration, as well as the tenancy system prevailing, shall be governed by the provisions of Republic Act Numbered Eleven hundred and ninety-nine, as amended.

SECTION 36. *Possession of Landholding; Exceptions.* Notwithstanding any agreement as to the period or future surrender of the land, an agricultural lessee shall continue in the enjoyment and possession of his landholding except when his dispossession has been authorized by the Court in a judgment that is final and executory if after due hearing it is shown that:

(1) The agricultural lessor-owner or a member of his immediate family will personally cultivate the landholding or will convert the landholding, if suitably located, into a residential, factory, hospital or school site or [put it to] other useful non-agricultural purposes: *Provided,* That the agricultural lessee shall be entitled to disturbance compensation equivalent to five years rental on his landholding in addition to his rights under Sections twenty-five and thirty-four, ex-

cept when the land owned and leased by the agricultural lessor is not more than five hectares, in which case instead of disturbance compensation the lessee may be entitled to an advanced notice of at least one agricultural year before ejectment proceedings are filed against him. . . .

(2) The agricultural lessee failed to substantially comply with any of the terms and conditions of the contract or any of the provisions of this Code unless his failure is caused by fortuitous event or *force majeure;*

(3) The agricultural lessee planted crops or used the landholding for a purpose other than what had been previously agreed upon;

(4) The agricultural lessee failed to adopt proven farm practices as determined under paragraph 3 of Section twenty-nine;

(5) The land or other substantial permanent improvement thereon is substantially damaged or destroyed or has unreasonably deteriorated through the fault or negligence of the agricultural lessee;

(6) The agricultural lessee does not pay the lease rental when it falls due. . . . or

(7) The lessee employed a sub-lessee on his landholding in violation of the terms of paragraph 2 of Section twenty-seven.

Chapter III. Land Authority

Article 1   Organization and functions of the land authority

SECTION 49. *Creation of the Land Authority.* For the purpose of carrying out the policy of establishing owner-cultivatorship and the economic family-size farm as the basis of Philippine and other policies enunciated in this Code, there is hereby created a Land Authority, hereinafter called the Authority, which shall be directly under the control and supervision of the President of the Philippines. . . .

SECTION 51. *Powers and Functions.* It shall be the responsibility of the Authority:

(1) To initiate and prosecute expropriation proceedings for the acquisition of private agricultural lands . . . for the purpose of sub-division into economic family-sized farm units and resale of said farm units to *bona fide* tenants, occupants and qualified farmers: *Provided,* That the powers herein granted shall apply only to private agricultural lands subject to the terms and conditions and order of priority hereinbelow specified:

(a) all idle or abandoned private agricultural lands [exception omitted].

(b) all private agricultural lands suitable for subdivision into economic family-sized farm units, owned by private individuals or corporations worked by lessees, no substantial portion of whose landholding in relation to the area sought to be expropriated is planted to permanent crops under labor administration in excess of seventy-five hectares, except all private agricultural lands under labor administration and lands acquired under Section seventy-one of this Code; and

(c) in expropriating private agricultural lands declared by the National Land Reform Council or by the Land Authority within a land reform district to be necessary for the implementation of the provisions of this Code, the following order of priority shall be observed:

1. idle or abandoned lands;
2. those whose area exceeds 1,024 hectares;
3. those whose area exceeds 500 hectares but is not more than 1,024 hectares;
4. those whose area exceeds 144 hectares but is not more than 500 hectares; and
5. those whose area exceeds 75 hectares but is not more than 144 hectares.

(3) To administer and dispose of agricultural lands of the public domain. . . .

(6) To give economic family-sized farms to landless citizens of the Philippines who need, deserve, and are capable of cultivating the land personally, through organized resettlement. . . .

(7) To reclaim lands and sub-divide them into economic family-sized farms. . . .

Article 2   Expropriation of private agricultural lands

SECTION 53. *Compulsory Purchase of Agricultural Lands.* The Authority shall, upon petition in writing of at least one-third of the lessees and subject to the provisions of Chapter VII of this Code, institute and prosecute expropriation proceedings for the acquisition of private agricultural lands and home lots enumerated under Section fifty-one. . . .

SECTION 56. *Just Compensation.* In determining the just compensation of the land to be expropriated pursuant to this Chapter the Court, in land under leasehold, shall consider as a basis, without prejudice to considering other factors also, the annual lease rental income authorized by law capitalized at the rate of 6 *percent per annum.*

SECTION 60. *Disposition of Expropriated Land.* After separate certificates of titles have been issued in accordance with [this Code], the Land

Authority . . . shall allot and sell each parcel or lot to a qualified beneficiary selected under [this Code] subject to uniform terms and conditions imposed by the Land Bank: *Provided,* That the resale shall be at cost which shall mean the purchase price plus not more than 6 *percent per annum,* which shall cover administrative expenses, and actual expenses for subdivision, surveying, and registration: *Provided, further,* That such cost shall be paid on the basis of an amortization plan not exceeding twenty-five years at the option of the beneficiary.

Chapter IV. Land Bank

SECTION 74. *Creation.* To finance the acquisition by the Government of landed estates for division and resale to small landholders, as well as the purchase of the landholding by the agricultural lessee from the landowner, there is hereby established a body corporate to be known as the "Land Bank of the Philippines," hereinafter called the "Bank". . . .

SECTION 76. *Issuance of Bonds.* The Land Bank shall . . . issue bonds. . . . Such bonds and other obligations shall be secured by the assets of the Bank and shall be fully tax exempt both as to principal and income. . . . These bonds and other obligations shall be fully negotiable and unconditionally guaranteed by the Government of the Republic of the Philippines and shall be redeemable at the option of the Bank at or prior to maturity, which in no case shall exceed twenty-five years. . . .

SECTION 77. *Issuance of Preferred Shares of Stock to Finance Acquisition of Landed Estates.* The Land Bank shall issue, from time to time, preferred shares of stock in such quantities not exceeding six hundred million pesos worth of preferred shares as may be necessary to pay the owners of landed estates in accordance with Sections eighty and eighty-one of this Code. . . . The shares of stock issued under the authority of this provision shall be guaranteed a rate of return of 6 *percent per annum.* . . .

SECTION 80. *Making Payment to Owners of Landed Estates.* The Land Bank shall make payments in the form herein prescribed to the owners of land acquired by the Land Authority for division and resale under this Code. Such payment shall be made in the following manner: 10 *percent* in cash and the remaining balance in 6 percent, tax-free, redeemable bonds issued by the Bank in accordance with Section seventy-six, unless the landowner desires to be paid in shares of stock issued by the Land Bank in accordance with Section seventy-seven in an amount not exceeding 30 *percent* of the purchase price.

SECTION 85. *Use of Bonds.* The bonds issued by the Land Bank may be used by the holder thereof and shall be accepted in the amount of their face value as any of the following:

(1) Payment for agricultural lands or other real properties purchased from the Government;

(2) Payment for the purchase of shares of stock of all or substantially all of the assets of the following Government-owned or controlled corporations: The National Development Company; Cebu Portland Cement Company; National Shipyards and Steel Corporation; Manila Gas Corporation; and the Manila Hotel Company.

(3) Surety or performance bonds in all cases where the Government may require or accept real property as bonds; and

(4) Payment for reparations goods.

Chapter VII. Land Reform Project Administration

SECTION 126. *Creation of National Land Reform Council.* There is hereby created a National Land Reform Council, hereinafter called the Council. . . .

SECTION 128. *Functions of National Land Reform Council.* It shall be the responsibility of the Council:

(3) To formulate such rules and regulations as may be necessary to carry out the provisions of this Code for (a) the selection of agricultural land to be acquired and distributed under this Code; (b) the determination of sizes of family farms as defined in Section one hundred sixty-six; and (c) the selection of beneficiaries to family farms available for distribution: *Provided,* That priority shall be given in the following order: First, to members of the immediate family of the former owner of the land within the first degree of consanguinity who will cultivate the land personally with the aid of labor available within his farm household; Second, to the actual occupants personally cultivating the land either as agricultural lessees or otherwise with respect to the area under their cultivation; Third, to farmers falling under the preceding category who are cultivating uneconomic-size farms with respect to idle or abandoned lands; Fourth, to owner-operators of uneconomic-size farms; and Fifth, to such other categories as may be fixed by virtue of this Code, taking into consideration the needs and qualifications of the applicants:

(5) To proclaim in accordance with the provisions of this Code . . . that all the government machineries and agencies in any region or locality relating to leasehold envisioned in this Code are operating: *Provided,* That the conversion to leasehold in the proclaimed area shall become effective at the beginning of the next succeeding agricultural year after such promulgation; *Provided, further,* That the

proclamation shall be made after having considered factors affecting feasibility and fund requirements and the other factors embodied in Sections one hundred twenty-nine, one hundred thirty and one hundred thirty-one.

SECTION 129. *Creation of Land Reform Districts.* The Council shall exercise the functions enumerated in the preceding Section for particular areas which the Council shall select and designate as land reform districts. A district shall constitute one or more land reform projects, each project to comprise either a large landed estate or several areas within small estates. . . .

Chapter IX. Courts of Agrarian Relations

SECTION 141. *Creation.* Courts of Agrarian Relations are hereby organized and established throughout the Philippines in conformity with the provisions of this Chapter.

SECTION 154. *Jurisdiction of the Court.* The Court shall have original and exclusive jurisdiction over:

(1) All cases or actions involving matters, controversies, disputes, or money claims arising from agrarian relations. . . .

(2) All cases or actions involving violations of Chapters I and II of this Code and Republic Act Numbered Eight hundred and nine; and

(3) Expropriations to be instituted by the Land Authority. . . .

Taiwan

THE FARM RENT REDUCTION TO 37.5% ACT, 1951 [19]

ARTICLE 2. The amount of farm rent shall not exceed 37.5 percent of the total annual yield of the principal product of the main crop. . . .

ARTICLE 3. A Land Commission[20] shall be established by each County or Municipal Government and by each District, Township or Urban District Office. The number of members representing tenant farmers on the Commission shall be no fewer than the total number of members representing landlords and owner-farmers. . . .

ARTICLE 4. The standard amount of the total annual yield of the principal article of the main crop of a farm land shall be appraised, with reference to the grade to which it belongs, by the Land Commission of the District, Township or Urban District Office, and the amount appraised shall be submitted to the Land Commission of the County or Municipal Government for confirmation, and to the Provincial Government for final approval.

ARTICLE 5. The period for which any farm land is leased shall not be shorter than six years. . . .

ARTICLE 6. After the enforcement of this Act, all farm lease contracts shall be made in writing, and the lessor and the lessee shall jointly apply for the registration of the signing, revision, termination, or renewal of their farm lease contract.

ARTICLE 7. The amount, kind, quality and standard of farm rent, the date and place of payment and other relevant matters shall be specified in the lease contract. If the rent payable in kind is to be delivered by the lessee, the lessor shall pay for the cost of delivery according to the distance covered.

ARTICLE 11. If a crop failure on any farm land is caused by natural disaster or other *force majeure*, the lessee may request the Land Commission of the District, Township, or Urban District Office to investigate and ascertain the extent of the crop failure and to decide on measures for the reduction of rent, and the Commission must take action within three days.

ARTICLE 14. The lessor shall not collect the farm rent in advance or demand any security deposit. . . .

[19] [Source: Chen Cheng, *Land Reform in Taiwan* (Taipei, Taiwan, China: China Publishing Company, 1961), pp. 191–197. The law consists of 31 articles. A decree having substantially the same provisions as the present law was enforced in Taiwan in 1949. The Act of 1951 was supposedly to be applicable to all China.]

[20] [Also known as Farm Tenancy Committee.]

ARTICLE 16. The lessee shall cultivate the leased land himself and shall not sublease the whole or part thereof to another person.

If the lessee violates the provisions of the preceding paragraph, the lease contract shall become null and void, and the lessor may take back the leased land for his own cultivation or lease it to another person. . . .

ARTICLE 17. Farm lease contracts shall not be terminated before the expiration of the period of the contracts, except under any one of the following conditions:

(1) If the lessee dies without leaving an heir.

(2) If the lessee waives his right of cultivation by migrating elsewhere or changing his occupation.

(3) If the cumulative amount of the farm rent the lessee has failed to pay is equivalent to the total of two years' rent.

ARTICLE 19. The lessor shall not take the leased land for his own cultivation on the expiration of the period of the lease contract under any one of the following conditions:

(1) Where the lessor is unable to cultivate the land himself.

(2) Where the lessor's total income is sufficient to support his family.

(3) Where the lessor's action in taking back the land will deprive the lessee's family of its subsistence.

In case the lessor's total income is insufficient to support his family and at the same time the situation mentioned in Section (3) of the preceding paragraph is bound to arise, he may request the Land Commission of the District, Township or Urban District Office for conciliation.

ARTICLE 20. If, on the expiration of the period of the farm lease contract, the lessee is willing to continue the lease, the contract shall be renewed, unless the lessor takes back the land for his own cultivation in accordance with the provisions of this Act.

ARTICLE 22. In any one of the following cases, the lessor shall be punished with imprisonment for a term of one year or less, or with detention:

(1) If he terminates the lease contract in violation of the provisions of Article 17.

(2) If he takes back the land for his own cultivation in violation of the provisions of Article 19.

(3) If he refuses to renew the lease contract in violation of the provisions of Article 20.

ARTICLE 26. If any dispute concerning the lease of farm land arises between the lessor and the lessee, it shall be submitted to the Land Commission of the District, Township or Urban District Office for conciliation. In case of the failure of conciliation, the dispute shall be submitted to the Land

Commission of the County or Municipal Government for reconciliation. In case of the failure of re-conciliation, the latter Commission shall transfer the dispute to the judicial authorities, who shall immediately deal with it without charging any judicial fees therefore.

REGULATIONS GOVERNING THE SALE OF PUBLIC FARM LANDS
TO ESTABLISH OWNER-FARMERS IN TAIWAN PROVINCE, 1951 [21]

ARTICLE 5. A Committee for the Establishment of Owner-Farmers shall be set up by each County or Municipal Government to assist in the sale of public lands to promote owner-farmers, and rules for the organization of the said Committee shall be separately prescribed.

ARTICLE 6. Public lands shall be sold to applicants according to the following order of priority:
(1) Present tenant cultivator of public land.
(2) Farm hand.
(3) Tenant who is cultivating insufficient land under lease.
(4) Part-owner-farmer who is cultivating insufficient land.
(5) Person who was originally an interested party in public land and who, having no land to cultivate now, is in need of some for cultivation.
(6) Person who changes his occupation and becomes a farmer.

ARTICLE 7. The standard area of public land to be purchased by a farming family shall be:
(1) One half to two chia (1.1988 to 4.7934 acres) of paddy field.
(2) One to four chia (2.3967 to 9.5868 acres) of cultivated dry land.

ARTICLE 8. The sale price of public land shall be calculated in terms of farm products at 2.5 times the total annual yield of the main crop fixed for each grade of such land.

The sale price referred to in the preceding paragraph shall be fixed by the local Committee for the Establishment of Owner-Farmers and reported through the County or Municipal Government to the Provincial Government for reference.

ARTICLE 9. The sale price of public land shall be paid by the purchaser in instalments over ten years, and each annual payment plus the farm land tax or the land tax shall not exceed 37.5 percent of the total annual yield of the main crop of the land purchased, . . .

ARTICLE 10. The land price shall, in general, be paid in farm products, but may be paid in cash by converting the amount payable in kind into

[21] [Source: Chen, *op. cit.*, pp. 198–201. The Regulations consist of 16 articles.]

monetary terms according to the market price announced by the local County or Municipal Government.

ARTICLE 11. The purchaser of public land shall be exempted from paying rent thereon from the year when the land is purchased, but he shall begin from the same year to pay the farm land tax or the land tax.

THE LAND-TO-THE-TILLER ACT, 1953 [22]

(AS AMENDED IN 1954)

Chapter I. General Provisions

ARTICLE 2. The responsible organs for enforcing this Act shall be the Ministry of Interior for the Central Government, the Land Bureau of the Department of Civil Affairs for the Provincial Government, and the County or Municipal Government for the County or Municipality.

ARTICLE 3. After this Act goes into effect, the present Land Commission[23] in each County or Municipal Government and in each District and Township Office shall assist in the execution of this Act.

Chapter II. Government Purchase of Cultivated Land

ARTICLE 8. Tenant cultivated land of the following categories shall be purchased by the Government for resale to the present tiller or tillers:

(1) Land owned by the landlord in excess of the retention acreage prescribed in Article 10 of this Act.

(2) Land under joint ownership.

(3) Private portion of any land owned jointly by private individuals and the Government.

(4) Land under Government trusteeship.

(5) Land owned by private individuals or family clans for purposes of ancestral worship, and land owned by religious institutions.

(6) Land owned by the *Shenming Hui*[24] and land owned by other juristic persons and corporate bodies.

(7) Land which the landlord does not wish to retain and requests the Government to purchase.

The land referred to in Sections (2) and (3) above may be retained upon Government approval, by its lessor in accordance with the retention standards set forth in Article 10 of this Act, if the lessor is old and infirm, widowed, orphaned, or disabled and depends upon the land for his or her livelihood; or

---

[22] [Source: Chen, *op. cit.*, pp. 202–212. The law consists of 5 chapters, 36 articles.]

[23] [Also known as Farm Tenancy Committee.]

[24] [A religious organization in Taiwan.]

if a joint ownership of the land originally under individual ownership is created by act of succession with the joint owners being husband and wife, or brothers and sisters of blood relationship.

The retention acreage for land owned for ancestral worship and land owned by religious institutions referred to in Section (5) above, shall be twice as much as the retention acreage allowed for individual landlord. . . .

ARTICLE 10.   After the effective date of this Act, the acreage of tenant cultivated land to be permitted to be retained by a landlord shall be 3 *chia* (7.1901 acres) of paddy field of 7th to 12th grade,[25] inclusive. Retention acreage for paddy field and dry land of other grades shall be converted according to the following scales [conversion table omitted]. The land to be retained shall be examined and defined by the District or Township Land Commission . . . , with the results thereof reported to the County or Municipal Land Commission for clearance and then forwarded to the County or Municipal Government for approval. The Land Commissions, in making the examination and clearance, may set the actual retention acreage at 10 percent more or less than the prescribed scales, as may be necessitated by the shape and terrain of the land in question.

ARTICLE 12.   One year after the effective date of this Act, the present tiller, if he wishes to purchase the landlord's retained land referred to in Article 10 of this Act, may request the Government for loans. . . .

ARTICLE 13.   Farmhouses, drying grounds, ponds, fruit trees, bamboos, woods etc., and sites thereof which are accessory to the land under Government purchase and are used by its present tenant farmer shall be purchased by the Government together with the land.

The purchase price of the above accessory properties and their sites shall be appraised by the District or Township Land Commission, agreed upon by the County or Municipal Land Commission, and approved by the Provincial Government. . . .

ARTICLE 14.   The purchase price of the land shall be 2.5 times the amount of its total annual main crop yield for the respective land grades.

The amount of the total annual main crop yield mentioned above shall be calculated according to the standards as appraised and approved in the various localities during the 37.5 percent rent reduction program period.

ARTICLE 15.   The purchase price for the land shall be paid 70 percent in land bonds in kind and 30 percent in Government enterprise stock shares.

---

[25] [Taiwan's paddy field and dry land are divided in terms of quality of soil into 26 grades. For the purpose of the present Act one *chia* of paddy field of a given grade is equivalent to two *chia* of dry land of the same grade.]

ARTICLE 16. Land bonds in kind shall be issued by the Provincial Government in accordance with the law. They shall bear interest at the rate of 4 percent in kind per annum and shall be redeemable in equal annual amounts over a period of ten years. The actual handling of the issuance, redemption, and interest payment of the land bonds shall be entrusted to the Land Bank in the province.

Chapter III. Resale of Government Purchased Land

ARTICLE 19. Cultivated land purchased by the Government shall be resold to the present tiller. The accessory properties and their sites purchased together with the land referred to in Article 13 of this Act shall also be resold to the present tiller.

ARTICLE 20. The resale price of the land shall be computed according to standards set up in Article 14 of this Act. The resale price, together with the price of accessory properties and their sites, shall bear interest at the rate of 4 percent in kind per annum. Beginning from the season in which the land is purchased, the purchaser shall pay the price and its interest in 10 annual equal installments in kind, or in those land bonds in kind falling due in the same period. The average annual burden to be borne by the purchaser shall not exceed the burden on the same grade of land presently borne by the tenant farmer under the 37.5 percent rent reduction program. . . .

Chapter IV. Restrictions and Penal Provisions

ARTICLE 30. The Government shall take back the land sold to a purchaser and shall not refund any purchase price already paid, if he is found to have committed any of the following acts:
(1) Used the name of another person to purchase the land;
(2) Leased out the land after purchase;
(3) Failed to make an installment payment for more than four months alter falling due.

The United Arab Republic

AGRARIAN REFORM LAW OF 1952 [26]
(DECREE-LAW NO. 178, AS AMENDED)

Part I. Limitation of Agricultural Land-holdings and Expropriation of Certain Lands for Distribution among Small Farmers

ARTICLE 1. No person may possess more than 200 feddans of agricultural land. Fallow and desert lands owned by any person are considered as agricultural lands. [Revised in 1961. See below.]

ARTICLE 2. The following are exempt from the foregoing provision:
  (a) Companies and Societies may own more than 200 feddans of land under reclamation for purposes of sale. . . .
  (b) Private individuals may possess more than 200 feddans of fallow or desert land for improvement.
  (c) Industrial Companies in existence before the promulgation of this decree may possess an area of agricultural land as may be requisite for industrial exploitation, even if such area exceeds 200 feddans.
  (d) Agricultural and scientific Societies in existence before the promulgation of this decree, may own an area of agricultural land as may be requisite for carrying on their research work even if such area exceeds 200 feddans.
  (e) Benevolent societies in existence before the promulgation of this decree may own an area of agricultural land even if it exceeds 200 feddans; provided that the area has not been increased since the promulgation of this law.
  (g) Private individuals may own more than 200 feddans if the ownership is the result of a bequest in a will, or inheritance, or the consequence of any procedure other than a contractual one.
  Wakf land is similarly exempt from the application of the provisions of the preceding Article.
  [All retention limits specified in this article were revised in 1961. See below.]

ARTICLE 3. During the five years following the coming into force of this Law, the Government shall requisition the area in excess of 200 feddans retained by the proprietor for himself. . . . [Revised below.]

ARTICLE 4. [The preceding article] notwithstanding, the owner may, within a period of five years from the date of enforcement of this law dispose

[26] [Source: The United Arab Republic, Ministry of Agrarian Reform and Land Reclamation, *Agrarian Reform and Land Reclamation in Eleven Years* (Cairo: General Organisation for Government Printing Office, 1963), pp. 223–267. The decree-law consists of 6 parts, 40 articles.]

by transfer of ownership of the part of his agricultural land which has not been expropriated and which exceeds 200 feddans, as follows:

(a) To his children, at a maximum rate of 50 feddans per child, provided that the total to be disposed of to his children does not exceed 100 feddans. [Revise below.]

(b) To small farmers. . . .

(c) To graduates of Agricultural Institutes. . . .

[Retention limits were subsequently revised. See below.]

ARTICLE 5. Any person whose land is requisitioned by the Government in accordance with the provisions of Article 1 shall be entitled to an indemnity equivalent to ten times the rent of such land, with the addition thereto of the value of any fixed or mobile installations and of trees. The rent shall be assessed at seven times the basic land tax. . . .

ARTICLE 6. The indemnity shall be in [the] form of State bonds, bearing an interest at 1.5 percent redeemable in forty years. These bonds shall be registered bonds and may not be disposed of except to Egyptians. [Revised below.]

ARTICLE 9. The land requisitioned in each village shall be distributed among small farmers so that each one of them shall have a small holding of not less than two feddans and not more than five feddans, according to the quality of the land.

Persons to whom the land shall thus be distributed must satisfy the following conditions:

(a) They must be Egyptians . . . who have not been convicted of any dishonorable crime.

(b) They must be working in agriculture.

(c) They must own less than five feddans of agricultural land.

ARTICLE 11. The value of the land distributed shall be estimated on the basis of the amount of the indemnity paid by the Government for the requisitioning with the addition there-to of:

(1) An annual interest of 1.5 percent.

(2) An overall sum equivalent to 10 percent of the prices, for costs of requisitioning, distribution and other expenses.

The total price shall be paid by equal annual instalments within a period of 40 years, from the date of enforcement of this law, if no part of it had fallen due before this enforcement. If a part of the price had fallen due before the law had come into force, the rest of the price will be paid in equal instalments within the period completing forty years.

ARTICLE 12. A general Organisation shall be established under the name of "The General Organisation for Agrarian Reform" [subsequently was replaced by the Ministry of Agrarian Reform] vested with a moral personality and attached to the Presidency of the Republic.

Part II. Agricultural Co-operative Societies

ARTICLE 18. By virtue of the Decree, an Agricultural Co-operative Society shall be constituted from among the farmers who acquired the requisitioned land in the same village, and who do not own more than five feddans in such village.

ARTICLE 19. Co-operative societies perform the following functions.
(A) Advancing agricultural loans of all kinds to members of the society according to the needs of their land.
(B) Providing farmers with the necessary requisites for the exploitation of their land, such as seeds, fertilizers, livestock, agricultural machinery and means of storage and transport of crops.
(C) Organising the cultivation and exploitation of the land in the most efficient manner, including seed selection, varieties of crops, pest control and the digging of canals and drains.
(D) Selling the principal crops on behalf of the members after deducting from the price of such crop instalments in respect of the price of the land, Government taxes, and agricultural and other loans.
(E) Rendering all other agricultural and social services required by members.

Part IV. Supplementary Taxes

ARTICLE 25. As from January 1953, a supplementary tax shall be imposed on land holdings in excess of 200 feddans, at the rate of five times the amount of the basic tax.

Part V. Regulation of Landlord-Tenant Relationship

ARTICLE 33. The rent of agricultural land may not exceed seven times the amount of the basic tax assessed upon such land. In the case of a rent based on crop-sharing the owner's share shall not exceed one half after deduction of all expenses.

ARTICLE 35. Leases of agricultural land may not be concluded for less than three years.

ARTICLE 36. The contract of lease, whether on the basis of rent or of crop-sharing, must be in writing, whatever its value may be. . . . [This version of the article was adopted in 1963 as an amendment to the original version.]

ARTICLE 37. Without prejudice to the owner's right to benefit from his agricultural land or from other lands of the same description, no person shall, starting from the agricultural year 1961/62, with his wife and minor children, exploit by means of renting or occupation or in any other way, an area of agricultural or similar lands not owned by him, in excess of fifty feddans. . . .

PRESIDENTIAL DECREES AMENDING THE AGRARIAN REFORM LAW OF 1952 [27]

Decree-Law No. 127 of 1961

ARTICLE 1. The text of Article 1 of the decree with Law No. 178 of 1952 alluded to is replaced by the following text: "No person is allowed to own more than one hundred feddans of agricultural lands. Fallow and desert lands in ownership of any person are to be considered as agricultural lands. Any deeds of transfer of property which contravene these stipulations are deemed nil and cannot be registered."

ARTICLE 2. If the property of any person exceeds the limit which can be legally owned, either as a result of inheritance or by testament or any means of acquisition of property other than by contract, the owner may dispose of such excess within one year from the date of ownership. . . .

ARTICLE 5. The compensation is to be given in nominal bonds on the treasury redeemable within fifteen years and rendering an interest of 4 percent yearly calculated from the date of requisitioning; such bonds are to be negotiable on the stock exchange. . . .

Decree-Law No. 128 of 1961

ARTICLE 1. The unpaid balances of the price of lands distributed or to be distributed to persons benefiting by the provisions of the decree with Law No. 178 of 1952 and Law 161 of 1958 alluded to, are reduced to one half. The interests due to the same persons are also reduced to one half.

Law No. 17 of 1963

ARTICLE 3. The contract of lease, whether on the basis of rent or of crop-sharing, must be in writing, whatever its value may be, the contract should be at least in triplicate, a copy of which is to be delivered to each of the contracting parties, and the third copy to be filed at the agricultural cooperative society's centre of the district to which the village is attached; . . .

[27] [Source: The United Arab Republic, *op. cit.*, pp. 268–320.]

APPENDIX II

LAND REFORM RESULTS, TABLES

TABLE I

RESULTS OF REDISTRIBUTION OF PRIVATE LAND IN COLOMBIA 1962–1969

Unit of land: hectare

INCORA Activities	Number[a]	Area
Acquisition of Private Land by INCORA, Total	1,352	222,471
Purchase (direct negotiation)	1,217	155,299
Expropriation	·135	67,172
Redistribution of INCORA-Acquired Private Land, Total	7,594	125,051
Definitive titles	3,165	59,928
Preliminary assignments	4,429	65,123

[a] Refers to number of estates in the case of acquisition of private land, and to titles granted in the case of redistribution of private land.

SOURCE: INCORA, *La Reforma Agraria en Colombia* ([Bogota], 1970).

TABLE II

Results of Land Redistribution in India, 1951–1966

Unit of land: 1,000 acres

States	Number of Tenants that Received Land[a] (1,000)	Area Received[a]	Declared Surplus Area[b]
Andhra Pradesh (Telegana)	33	202	—
Assam	. . .	. . .	34.0
Gujarat	462	1,408	38.8
Jammu & Kashmir	. . .	. . .	450.0
Madhya Pradesh	358	. . .	67.1
Madras	. . .	. . .	20.2
Maharashtra	618	1,674	162.5
Punjab	22	147	368.5
Uttar Pradesh	1,500	2,000	222.7
West Bengal	. . .	800	776.6
Delhi	29	39	. . .
Himachal Pradesh	24	28	. . .
Tripura	10	12	. . .
Total	3,056	6,310	2,140.4

[a] Data relate to both *zamindari* and non-*zamindari* areas.

[b] Area of land in excess of the ceiling limits as declared, or possessed but not yet redistributed by the states.

Source: India, Planning Commission, *Implementation of Land Reforms: A Review by the Land Reforms Implementation Committee of the National Development Council* (New Delhi, August 1966), p. 278.

TABLE III

Results of Land Reform in Iran 1962-1967

First Phase	
Number of Villages Purchased or Expropriated:	
Public Domain, Crown Estates, and Private Land[a]	14,834
Number of Farm Families Receiving Land	587,566
Cost of Purchased Villages	8,878,595,462 rials
First Payment to Landowners in Cash	2,802,076,304 rials
Number of Rural Cooperatives in Reform Areas	7,520
Capital of Rural Cooperatives	890,805,200 rials
Second Phase	
Number of Villages Leased, Purchased by Farmers,	
or Divided between Farmers and Landowners:[a]	52,818
Farms	17,644
Number of Beneficiary Families	2,315,950

[a] Original data did not indicate if villages purchased or expropriated prior to 1962 were included. In any case, the number of these villages is not very large.

Source: Iran, Ministry of Agriculture, Land Reform Organization, *Land Reform in Iran* (Tehran 1967), p. 19.

TABLE IV

Results of Land Reform in Mexico, as of 1960

Unit of land: 1,000 hectares

Total Agricultural Land	169,084.2
Total Agricultural Land Redistributed[a]	44,497.1
Total Crop Land	23,816.9
Total Crop Land Redistributed[a]	10,329.2
Total Farm Holdings	2,870,238
Total Farm Holdings Benefited from Redistribution[b]	1,523,796

[a] *Ejido* land, including area developed for new settlements.
[b] Number of *ejidatarios*

Sources: Eduardo L. Venezian and William K. Gamble, *The Agricultural Development of Mexico: Its Structure and Growth since 1950* (New York: Frederick A. Praeger, Publishers, 1969), p. 49; and Hiroji Okabe, "Agrarian Reform in Mexico: an Interpretation," *The Developing Economies*, IV (June 1966), 189. Both sources were based on the 1960 agricultural census.

TABLE V

RESULTS OF LAND REDISTRIBUTION IN WEST PAKISTAN
1959–1965

Unit of land: acre

Landownership on the Eve of Redistribution	
Total number of owners	5,068,376
Total area of owned land	48,642,530
Expected Coverage of Redistribution	
Number of landowners	6,061
Area of land owned	7,490,933
Actual Impact of Redistribution[a]	
Number of owners actually affected by redistribution	910
Total area of land owned by affected owners	6,106,631
Total area of land transferred to heirs and female	
dependents of owners	505,695
Total area of land retained by owners	3,380,218
Total area of government acquired land	2,220,718
Types of Government Acquired Land, Total	2,220,718
Private land	1,903,788
Cultivated land	823,062
Uncultivated land	1,080,726
Uncultivable waste	643,593
Forest	59,670
Under bill	134,781
Under river	99,892
Other	142,790
Jagir land	316,930
Disposition of Government-Acquired Land[a]	
Area of land leased	36,643
Area of land sold to tenants	662,199
Area of land auctioned and sold to others	226,258
Area of land transferred to government	108,389
Total area disposed of	993,489
Balance	1,227,229
Number of farmers purchased land[b]	56,906
Compensation	
Total payable[a]	Rs. 96,866,879.84
Annual interest[c]	Rs. 3,346,699.05
Actual payment as of end of 1965,	
excluding interest[a]	Rs. 92,545,794.32

[a] Data relate to both private land and *jagir* land.

[b] As of June 30, 1962. The number of farmers purchasing land after this date was insignificant, if any.

[c] Data relate to private land only, not including *jagir* land.

SOURCES: West Pakistan, Land Reforms Commission, *Report of Land Reforms Commission for West Pakistan* (Lahore 1959), Appendix I; West Pakistan Land Commission, *Implementation of Land Reform Scheme in West Pakistan: Appraisal Paper for World Land Reforms Conference to Be Held in Rome (Italy) from June 20 to July 2, 1966* (Lahore 1966), *passim;* and Pakistan, Planning Commission, *Handbook of Agricultural Statistics, June 1964* (Karachi, 1964), p. 171.

TABLE VI

RESULTS OF LAND REFORM IN THE PHILIPPINES, 1954–1968

Unit of land: hectare

Period	Land Acquired for Redistribution	Number of Estates	Area
1954–1961	Public Land Developed for Resettlement of tenants	—	152,960
1954–1958	Land Acquired under the 1955 Reform law	—	50,000
	Results of 1963 Law		
1963–1966	Land Actually Expropriated	6	3,035
1967–1968	Land Actually Expropriated	6	704
1967–1968	Land of which Expropriation Has Been Approved	16	2,361
	Total	28	209,060

SOURCES: Isidro S. Macaspac, "Land Reform Aspects of the Agricultural Development Program," *Economic Research Journal*, VIII (December 1961), 152; Hugh L. Cook, "Land Reform and Development in the Philippines," in Walter Froehlich (ed.), *Land Tenure, Industrialization and Social Stability: Experience and Prospects in Asia* (Milwaukee, the Marquette University Press, 1961), p. 172; Ferdinand E. Marcos, *New Filipinism: the Turning Point, State of the Nation Message to the Congress of the Philippines, 27 January 1969* (Manila, 1969), p. 94; and "Report on Landed Estates Acquired by Land Bank," Memorandum of the National Land Reform Council, the Philippines, December 19, 1968.

TABLE VII

RESULTS OF LAND REDISTRIBUTION IN TAIWAN, 1951–1963

Unit of land: *chia*

Sale of Public Land, 1951–1963	
Total Area of public land before sale	181,490
Area of public land sold[a]	98,982
Area of public land sold as a percent of total	
public land	55
Number of tenants purchasing public land	165,443
Land-to-the-Tiller Program, 1953	
Total area of tenanted private land	253,957
Area of tenanted land redistributed	143,568
Area of tenanted land redistributed as a percent	
of total tenanted private land	56
Number of tenants purchasing private land	194,823
Tenants purchasing private land as a percent	
of total tenants	65
Number of landlords selling land	106,049
Area of land retained by landlords	103,437
Landlords selling land as a percent of total	
landowners[b]	17
Total Area of Public and Private Land Redistributed	242,550
Total Number of Tenants Purchasing Public and	
Private Land	360,266

[a] Over half of the area was sold prior to 1954.

[b] Including owner-farmers and landlords.

SOURCES: Hung-chao Tai, "Land Reform and National Development: Taiwan," The Michigan Academy of Science, Arts, and Letters, *Papers*, LI (1966), 310–313; JCRR, *JCRR Reports on Land Reform in the Republic of China, from October 1948 to June 1964* (Taipei, Taiwan, 1965), p. 75; and JCRR, *Abstracts of Land Statistics, Taiwan Province* (Taipei, Taiwan, 1953), p. 29.

TABLE VIII

CHANGES IN LAND TENURE IN TAIWAN, 1949–1961

Unit of land: *chia*

	1949 (A) Number or Area	1949 Percent	1961 (B) Number or Area	1961 Percent	Change in Percent $\frac{(B)-(A)}{(A)} \times 100$
Tenure Groups					
Owner-cultivators	198,542	35.06	500,268	64.47	+84
Part-owners	148,423	26.21	166,519	21.46	−18
Tenants	219,305	38.73	109,215	14.07	−64
Total	566,270	100.00	776,002	100.00	
Private Farm Area					
Owner-cultivated	372,964[a]	55.47	662,559[a]	89.80	+62
Tenanted	299,395	44.53	75,275	10.20	−75
Total	672,359	100.00	737,834	100.00	

[a] Including land owned by part-owners.

SOURCES: Taiwan, Provincial Government, Department of Agriculture and Forestry, *Taiwan Agricultural Yearbook 1951* (Taipei, 1951), pp. 20–21, 26–27; and Taiwan, *General Report on the 1961 Census of Agriculture, Taiwan, Republic of China* (Taichung, Taiwan: Taiwan Provincial Government Printing Press, 1963), pp. 13 and 54.

TABLE IX

RESULTS OF LAND REFORM IN THE U.A.R. 1952–1964

Unit of land: *feddan*

Area of Land Acquired for Redistribution	
Law No. 178 of 1952 (original land reform decree) and Law No. 598 (confiscation of royal land)	450,305
Law No. 152 of 1957 and Law No. 44 of 1962 (dealing with *Wakf* land)	148,787
Law No. 127 of 1961 (reduction of ceiling to 100 *feddans*)	214,132
Law No. 15 of 1963 (exclusion of foreigners from landownership)	61,910
Law No. 150 of 1964 (confiscation of land owned by persons put under sequestration)	43,516
Land purchased from Land Reclamation Companies and the Sequestration Administration	25,807
Total	944,457
Area of Land Actually Redistributed[a]	
1952–1961	371,510
1962	125,542
1963	185,937
1964	156,689
Total	839,678
Total Number of Farmers Receiving Land[a]	263,862

[a] Including various reclaimed and newly developed lands totalling 192,923 *feddans* as of 1964.

SOURCES: The U.A.R., Central Agency for Public Mobilisation and Statistics, *Statistical Handbook of the United Arab Republic, 1952–1964* (Cairo, 1965), *passim;* M. Riad El Ghonemy, "Economic and Institutional Organization of Egyptian Agriculture since 1952," in P. J. Vatikiotis (ed.), *Egypt Since the Revolution* (New York: Frederick A. Praeger, Publishers, 1968), p. 72; and Gabriel S. Saab, *The Egyptian Agrarian Reform, 1952–1962* (London: Oxford University Press, 1967), p. 188.

APPENDIX III

RURAL SURVEYS OF TAINAN, TAIWAN, AND LUZON, THE PHILIPPINES

With the support of The Ford Foundation, The Center for International Affairs of Harvard University, and the Social Science Research Council, the author conducted in 1968 and 1969 rural surveys in Taiwan and the Philippines as part of the work for a research project on Rural Political Participation in the Developing Countries: the Changing Provincial Elite. The surveys consisted of both oral and written interviews. Written interviews were administered on the basis of questionnaires which contained eighty-eight sets of multiple choice questions. An effort was made to include the same or similar questions in both the Taiwan and Philippines questionnaires. A portion of the two surveys specifically dealt with land reform and peasant political involvement; only the results of this portion were utilized in this book.

The Taiwan survey was confined to Tainan *hsien*, a predominantly rural community in south central Taiwan. With 900,000 residents, the community was fairly representative of Taiwan as a whole in terms of tenure conditions and pattern of political participation. In the fall of 1968, the author, leading a team of six researchers—social science graduate students from National Taiwan and National Chengchi Universities—visited sixteen of Tainan's thirty-one townships. Of the some 900 people interviewed, 550 were eventually selected as the sample of the study. In terms of tenure status the sample consisted of the following categories: landlords, 39; cultivating farmers (owner-farmers, part-owner-farmers, tenants, and landless farm workers), 280; non-farmers whose families owned or farmed some land, 120; non-farmers and those unrelated to farming, 43; and status unidentified, 68.

The Philippines survey was broader in scope, covering the entire nation. It was conducted in the spring and summer of 1969 by the author with the assistance of the Local Government Center of the University of the Philippines, the Philippine Presidential Arm on Community Development, and the Philippine Rural Reconstruction Movement. A total of 2155 respondents completed the written questionnaires.

Because land reform is at present a dominant concern in Luzon Island, only data relevant to this region were used in the present study. The Luzon survey covered twelve provinces with a heavy concentration in Central Luzon: Bataan, Batangas, Benguet, Cavite, Laguna, La Union, Mountain, Nueva Ecija, Quezon, Rizal, Tarlac, Zambles. The sample consisted of 407 respondents who were distributed into the following categories of tenure status: landlords, 47; cultivating farmers, 263; non-farmers whose families owned or farmed some land, 28; non-farmers and those unrelated to farming, 39; and status unidentified, 30.

APPENDIX IV

GLOSSARY

---

acasillados	Peons in Mexico
ampliación	Under the Mexican land redistribution program, the farm area of a beneficiary is enlarged by receiving an additional grant of land
ampro	Injunction in land redistribution proceedings in Mexico
babbe	Iranian word, one-twentieth of a *dang*
bargadars	Hindi word for sharecroppers or landless farm workers
Bhoodan Yagna	Land gift movement in India
bighas	A land unit in East Pakistan, about one seventh of a hectare
caciquism (*caciquimo*)	Land-based political owner in a locality
campesino	Spanish word for peasant
ceiling	The maximum amount of land a private landowner is allowed to retain under a land redistribution program
Central Luzon	Central region of Luzon Island in the Philippines, covering the following provinces: Bataan, Bulacan, Neuva Ecija, Pampanga, Pangasinan, Tarlac, and Zambales
chia	A Taiwanese unit of farm land, equivalent to 0.96992 hectare or 2.39680 acres
colono	Spanish word for colonizer. As used in the text of this book, it means a peasant who develops and cultivates a farm that may not belong to him
crore	An Indian word signifying 10,000,000
cultivator (cultivating farmer)	A person who applies his own labor to farming
dang	Iranian word, one-sixth of the area of a village, which is used as a measurement of farm area

Department (*Departamento*)	An administrative region in Colombia, comparable to a province
dotación	Grant of land under the Mexican land redistribution program
ejidatario	A holder of *ejido* land
ejido	A pre-Spain communal farm in Mexico, revived after the revolution of 1910 under the land-reform program
expropriation	Compulsory acquisition of land ownership with compensation
farm holding (farm)	An area of land farmed or owned as a unit by a family or an individual. It may consist of two or more parcels
farmer	A person who earns a living by working on land. A farmer may work manually, or through machines. In general, the term is interchangeable with cultivator. It covers the following categories of tenure status: owner-farmer, tenant, farm laborer, cooperative farmer, part-owner-farmer, sharecropper
feddan	An Egyptian unit of land, equivalent to 0.4201 hectare or 1.038 acres
fellah	Egyptian word for peasant; *fellahin* (plural)
gavband	Iranian word referring literally to an ox owner. In most cases it refers to an intermediary between a landowner and a tenant
hacendado	Spanish word for large landowner
hacienda	Spanish word for a large landholding
hsien	An administrative unit of a Chinese Province. Taiwan is divided into sixteen *hsien*, four municipalities and a special city, Taipei, the capital
Huks	Originally *Hukbo ng Bayan Laban sa Hapon* (People's Army Against The Japanese), now *Hukbong Magpalayang Bayan* or HMB (People's Liberation Army). Communist guerrilla army operating in Central Luzon, The Philippines
inafectabilidad	Land not subject to expropriation proceedings (Mexico)
Incumbent cultivator	The cultivator of a piece of land to which land reform applies

jagir	In India and Pakistan a person who, during the British rule, held an interest or ownership right in land as a result of public grant
jefe de operaciones	Local military commander, Mexico
juft (joft)	Iranian word for an area of farm land plowable by a pair of oxen
kadkhuda	Village head in Iran
Kasama	A Tagalog (Philippine) word for tenancy
khas	In India and Pakistan, the word refers to self-cultivated (land), self-cultivation, or self-utilized land
kisan	A Hindi word for peasant
kisan sabha	Peasant league (in India)
The Kuomintang	The Chinese Nationalist Party
lakh	Indian word signifying 100,000 (see *crore*)
land aristocracy	A land-based high class of the society, generally commanding national prestige and influence
land gentry	Politically and socially prestigious large land-holders, generally of local significance
landed class	A group of large landowners who generally do not apply their own labor to farming. The class consists of mainly landlords
landed interests	The interests (or members) of the landed class
landholder (landowner)	An owner of land who may or may not be a cultivator
landholding	An area of land owned as a unit by a family or individual. It may contain more than one parcel
landlord	Non-cultivating landowner who either rents his land to others or hires a manager to operate his land
latifundia	Spanish word for very large landholdings
Laurenista	A rightist faction of the Conservative Party of Colombia, taking its name from the late Laureano Gomez
la Violencia	Massive civil strife in Colombia, 1948–1958
lessee	A farmer who rents land by paying a rent fixed by a contract in accordance with law
Llanos Orientale	Eastern Plain, Colombia
Lok Sabha	The House of the People—the lower house of Parliament—of India

The Majlis	The lower house of Parliament of Iran
Malacañang	Presidential Palace of the Philippines
minifundia	Spanish word for fragmented small landholdings
municipio	A local government unit in Colombia and Mexico
Naxalites	A group of radical, violence-oriented Communists in India
nōkai	Agricultural association in Taiwan during the Japanese period, 1895–1945
owner-farmer	The farmer who owns the land he cultivates
panchayat	A village council in India, also a system of governments at local level
paracaidismo	Parachuting, used in Mexico to refer to land invasion
patwari	Indian village official who keeps land records and revenue rolls
peasant	Subsistence cultivator, generally including small owner-farmer, part-owner-farmer, tenant, and landless farm worker
pequeña propiedad	Small farm property (Mexico)
peso	Currency unit in Colombia, Mexico, and The Philippines
qanats	Iranian irrigation canals
raiyat	Indian or Pakistani word referring to (1) tenant under a landlord, or (2) tenant with permanent occupancy right subject to payment of land revenue (rent) to government
rent	A payment in cash or in kind or both by a cultivator to a landowner from whom he obtains a cultivating right to a piece of land
restitution (*restitución*)	Restoration of land to original landowner under the Mexican land redistribution program
Rial	Iranian currency unit
Rupee	Currency unit in India and Pakistan
satyagraha	Non-violent civil disobedience movement in India
Savak	The security force of Iran
surplus land	Area of land above the ceiling under a land redistribution program
Tangulans	A rurally based secret, violent organization

	operating in the Philippines in the late 1920s
tao	Philippine word for peasant
tenancy	An arrangement between a landowner and a cultivator by which the former leases agricultural land to the latter by receiving rent, in cash or in kind, or in both
tenant	A cultivator under tenancy
Tierra y Libertad	Land and Liberty, Mexican revolutionary slogan
Tung Min Hui	A predecessor organization of the Kuomintang
Under-raiyat	In India and Pakistan, a farmer who obtains cultivating rights to a piece of land from a *raiyat*
Villistas	Followers of Francisco Villa in the Mexican Civil War
Wakf (Waqf)	In Egypt, Iran, and Pakistan the word stands for property placed in trust for religious or charitable purposes
Yuan	Chinese word for a branch of the national government. Thus, Legislative Yuan refers to Parliament
Zamindar	Originally, a land revenue collector in British-ruled India. It has generally been accepted as a landlord
Zapatistas	Followers of Emiliano Zapata

INDEX